Social Intelligence
from Brain to Culture

Social Intelligence: from Brain to Culture

Edited by

NATHAN EMERY
NICOLA CLAYTON
AND
CHRIS FRITH

Originating from a Theme Issue first published in Philosophical
Transactions of the Royal Society B: Biological Sciences

http://publishing.royalsoc.ac.uk/philtransb

OXFORD

UNIVERSITY PRESS

Great Clarendon Street, Oxford ox2 6DP

Oxford University Press is a department of the University of Oxford.
It furthers the University's objective of excellence in research, scholarship,
and education by publishing worldwide in

Oxford New York

Auckland Cape Town Dar es Salaam Hong Kong Karachi
Kuala Lumpur Madrid Melbourne Mexico City Nairobi
New Delhi Shanghai Taipei Toronto

With offices in

Argentina Austria Brazil Chile Czech Republic France Greece
Guatemala Hungary Italy Japan Poland Portugal Singapore
South Korea Switzerland Thailand Turkey Ukraine Vietnam

Oxford is a registered trade mark of Oxford University Press
in the UK and in certain other countries

Published in the United States
by Oxford University Press Inc., New York

British Library Cataloguing in Publication Data

Data available

Library of Congress Cataloging-in-Publication Data

Social intelligence : from brain to culture / edited by Nathan Emery, Nicola Clayton, and Chris Frith.
p. cm.
"Originally published in Philosophical Transactions of the Royal Society, B: Biological Sciences."
ISBN 978-0-19-921654-3
1. Social intelligence. 2. Cognitive neuroscience. I. Emery, Nathan, 1971- II. Clayton, Nicola.
III. Frith, Christopher D.
BF323.S63S637 2008
302'.1--dc22
2007024927

Typeset by Cepha Imaging Private Ltd., Bangalore, India
Printed in Great Britain
on acid-free paper by
Biddles Ltd., King's Lynn, Norfolk

✓ ISBN 978–0–19–921654–3

1 3 5 7 9 10 8 6 4 2

Contents

List of Contributors

Louise Barrett Department of Psychology, Darwin Building, University of Central Lancashire, Preston PR1 2HE, UK; Behavioural Ecology Research Group, University of KwaZulu Natal, Durban 4041, South Africa; Behavioural Ecology Research Group, Department of Psychology, University of Lethbridge, Alberta AB T1K 3M4, Canada

Richard W. Byrne Centre for Social Learning and Cognitive Evolution and Scottish Primate Research Group, School of Psychology, University of St Andrews, Fife KY16 9JP, UK

Nicola S. Clayton Department of Experimental Psychology, University of Cambridge, Cambridge CB2 3EB, UK

Richard C. Connor Biology Department, University of Massachusetts at Dartmouth, North Dartmouth, MA 02747, USA

Joanna M. Dally Department of Experimental Psychology, University of Cambridge, Cambridge CB2 3EB, UK, Sub-department of Animal Behaviour, University of Cambridge, Cambridge CB3 8AA, UK

Kerstin Dautenhahn School of Computer Science, University of Hertfordshire, College Lane, Hatfield AL10 9AB, UK

R. I. M. Dunbar British Academy Centenary Research Project, School of Biological Sciences, University of Liverpool, Liverpool L69 7ZB, UK

Nathan J. Emery Sub-department of Animal Behaviour, University of Cambridge, Cambridge CB3 8AA, UK

Chris D. Frith Wellcome Department of Imaging Neuroscience, Institute of Neurology, University College London, 12 Queen Square, London WC1N 3BG, UK

Vittorio Gallese Department of Neuroscience, Section of Physiology, University of Parma, 43100 Parma, Italy

Peter Henzi Department of Psychology, Darwin Building, University of Central Lancashire, Preston PR1 2HE, UK; Behavioural Ecology Research Group, University of KwaZulu Natal, Durban 4041, South Africa; Behavioural Ecology Research Group, Department of Psychology, University of Lethbridge, Alberta AB T1K 3M4, Canada

Kay E. Holekamp Department of Zoology, Michigan State University Museum, Michigan State University, East Lansing, MI 48824, USA

Nicholas Humphrey Centre for Philosophy of Natural and Social Science, London School of Economics, Houghton Street, London WC2A 2AE, UK

Barbara L. Lundrigan Department of Zoology, Michigan State University Museum, Michigan State University, East Lansing, MI 48824, USA

Steven Mithen School of Human & Environmental Sciences, University of Reading, Whiteknights, PO Box 227, Reading RG6 6AB, UK

Henrike Moll Max Planck Institute for Evolutionary Anthropology, Deutscher Platz 6, 04103 Leipzig, Germany

Derek C. Penn Cognitive Evolution Group, University of Louisiana, Louisiana, Lafayette, LA 70504, USA

Daniel J. Povinelli Cognitive Evolution Group, University of Louisiana, Louisiana, Lafayette, LA 70504, USA

Vasudevi Reddy Department of Psychology, University of Portsmouth, King Henry Building, King Henry 1st Street, Portsmouth PO1 2DY, UK

Drew Rendall Behavioural Ecology Research Group, Department of Psychology, University of Lethbridge, Alberta AB T1K 3M4, Canada

Sharleen T. Sakai Department of Psychology, Michigan State University, East Lansing, MI 48824, USA

Carel P. van Schaik Anthropological Institute and Museum, University of Zürich, Winterthurerstrasse 190, 8057 Zürich, Switzerland

Amanda M. Seed Department of Experimental Psychology, University of Cambridge, Cambridge CB2 3EB, UK

Susanne Shultz British Academy Centenary Research Project, School of Biological Sciences, University of Liverpool, Liverpool L69 7ZB, UK

Joan B. Silk Department of Anthropology, University of California, Los Angeles, CA 90095, USA

Kim Sterelny Philosophy Program, Research School of the Social Sciences, Australian National University, 0200 Canberra, Australian Capital Territory, Australia and Philosophy Program, Victoria University of Wellington, PO Box 600, Wellington, New Zealand

Michael Tomasello Max Planck Institute for Evolutionary Anthropology, Deutscher Platz 6, 04103 Leipzig, Germany

Auguste M. P. von Bayern Sub-department of Animal Behaviour, University of Cambridge, Cambridge CB3 8AA, UK

Andrew Whiten Centre for Social Learning and Cognitive Evolution, School of Psychology, University of St Andrews, St Andrews KY16 9JP, UK

Introduction. Social intelligence: from brain to culture

Humans are perhaps the most social animals. Although some eusocial insects, herd mammals and seabirds live in colonies comprising millions of individuals, no other species lives in such a variety of social groups as *Homo sapiens*. We live in many different sized societies, from small, nomadic hunter-gatherer societies to cities consisting of millions of people living in close proximity; we form special social bonds with kin and many of us make lifelong commitments to one socio-sexual partner, represented in the shape of a marriage.

Although the fledgling concept of social intelligence was formulated over 50 years ago by Chance & Mead (1953), and more explicitly by Jolly 13 years later (1966), it was perhaps Nick Humphrey's (1976) seminal paper on the 'social function of intellect' that paved the way for the past 30 years of productive research in so many seemingly unrelated areas of the biological and social sciences. It is Nick's significant contributions, as evidenced by the number of quotations to his work in this special issue, and the anniversary of the birth of the 'social intelligence hypothesis' (SIH), that were celebrated at a Discussion Meeting of the Royal Society on 22 and 23 May 2006 and which form the basis of this special issue.

Humphrey (1976) argued that the physical problems which primates face in their day-to-day lives, such as finding and extracting food or hunting and evading predators, are not sufficient to explain the differences in intellectual capabilities of animals in laboratory tests. Indeed, many animals with very different levels of cognitive ability have to solve similar kinds of problems in their natural environment. So, why do primates, especially humans, have such large brains? Observations of social groups of gorillas in the field and macaques at the Sub-department of Animal Behaviour, Madingley, led Humphrey to suggest that recognizing, memorizing and processing 'technical' information was not the driving force behind the evolution of primate intelligence. He proposed that it was the intricate social interactions of these animals, their ability to recognize individuals, track their relationships and deceive one another, which occupied their time and substantial brainpower. In particular, it was Humphrey's emphasis on the importance of predicting and manipulating the behaviour and minds of conspecifics which led to the development of 'theory of mind' as a major research focus in both comparative and developmental psychology. The question of whether animals possess a 'theory of mind' occupies many researchers to this day, and forms a major focus in this special issue in the papers by Barrett *et al.* (2007), Clayton *et al.* (2007), Moll & Tomasello (2007) and Penn & Povinelli (2007).

The first series of papers in this special issue highlights comparative studies on a wider group of animals than have been previously described with respect to the intricacies of social life, including several species of birds as well as mammals. What is perhaps striking about all these papers is the renewed importance of the cognitive mechanisms of prosocial behaviour and social tolerance, particularly cooperation and coordination. Moll & Tomasello (2007) go as far as to propose a new form of social intelligence, the Vygotskian Intelligence Hypothesis, which states that sharing focus on the same events in the environment and directing such focus into mutual cooperation and collaboration is what separates us from other animals. Although not necessarily new, the role of intelligence in the positive side of sociality has tended to be the poor cousin of Machiavellianism, deception and competition as exemplified by Frans de Waal's 'Chimpanzee Politics' (de Waal 1982). It should be stressed that the key to surviving a complex social world is probably the delicate balance between cooperation and competition. Certainly, fostering successful affiliative relationships can lead to the procurement of resources ordinarily unavailable to singletons by joining forces and competing with others. Evidence for this can be found in the alliance formation of male dolphins (Connor 2007) and the pair bonds of rooks and jackdaws (Emery *et al.* 2007). Interestingly, both dolphins and corvids appear to maintain their relationships using mutual contact and behavioural synchrony, a clear case of convergent evolution between distantly related species living in very different environments.

This renewed focus on the nicer side of sociality does not mean that competition, deception and Machiavellianism are no longer seen as playing important roles in social interaction—far from it. The behaviour of western scrub-jays described by Clayton *et al.* (2007) suggests that these food-storing birds are very protective of their caches, particularly against the possibility of pilfering, either when the potential thief is still present, or in the future when the thief has left the scene. These birds implement a number of complex cache protection strategies such as hiding food behind barriers, in the shade or at a distance, move their caches around as a confusion tactic and even protect caches based on the identity of the observer or their knowledge state. Perhaps most interesting from the perspective of human 'theory of mind' is the fact that the jays need to have had experience of stealing another bird's caches before they can implement these strategies. As birds can play the roles of both cachers and stealers (often at the same time), Clayton *et al.* (2007) suggested that a 'cognitive arms race' can develop, in which cachers develop increasingly sophisticated strategies to protect their caches, therefore pilferers have to develop increasingly sophisticated counter-strategies in order to steal them. The implications of this research for the long-held assumption that big brains are required for developing cognitive strategies and counter-strategies are significant, as scrub-jays have small brains (even though the same relative size as apes). Similar deceptive behaviours are described in the papers by Moll & Tomasello (2007) for great apes, and Reddy (2007) for human children.

The early formulation of the SIH was, not surprisingly, very anthropocentric and primatocentric. Almost nothing was known about the cognitive abilities of non-primates from laboratory tests, and although many animals were studied in the field, including studies of their social behaviour, the focus of those studies was not to understand their intelligence. By contrast, monkeys and apes live in large social groups consisting of many individuals who recognize one another, and who appear to recognize who is affiliated to whom. Social intelligence, therefore, was originally formed to explain how a primate can keep track of multiple relationships, and use this information in a largely competitive framework, such as gaining access to resources. Thus, the quantity of relationships was deemed more important than the quality. A cursory glance to other distantly related taxa, such as birds, reveals that very few species form social groups of the same type as primates. Indeed, the most common social organization of birds is monogamy. Even though these birds form large aggregations during winter foraging before the breeding season, their core sociality is to form pair bonds, which in some species may last their whole lives. Although dolphins do not form pair bonds, their alliances can be very valuable and lead to increased fitness. By contrast, hyenas (Holekamp *et al.* 2007) and cercopithecine monkeys (Barrett *et al.* 2007; Silk 2007) form large, relatively stable matriline groups, which seem to be based on a balance between competition and cooperation. In these species, any bonds which form are either based on relatedness (kin) or are transient and unstable between unrelated individuals. Silk (2007) provides evidence from a number of mammals that fostering these relationships can lead to significant reproductive benefits, including an increased chance of offspring survival. Her paper is perhaps the first to describe in detail why being socially intelligent can be adaptive.

The formation of cohesive social groups also facilitates information transfer in the form of social learning. Although there is good evidence for social information transfer in many animals, and even suggestions of behavioural traditions in isolated populations, there is still little clear evidence for culture in non-human animals. Byrne (2007) suggests that the case for culture may have been overstated and the so-called evidence may be the result of a 'pattern of local ignorance based on environmental constraints on knowledge transmission'. For example, some populations of chimpanzees possess certain traditions, such as ant dipping, whereas a second population possesses a different tradition, such as termite fishing. These traditions are actually rather similar, differing in the type of prey item and therefore may be local stylistic differences rather than traditions *per se.* Byrne (2007) suggests that the focus should be on technically complex behaviour patterns, such as nettle stripping in gorillas, which may be learned by cultural transmission through a community, rather than these subtle behavioural differences which may be the result of environmental differences rather than differences in transmission. In their paper, Whiten & van Schaik (2007) differ in their approach to the question of culture in animals. They suggest that although there is a lot of evidence for social learning in animals, and even some rare cases of traditions which are sustained over generations, culture is very rare. They present evidence that different chimpanzee and orang-utan populations display different cultures, and argue that while social intelligence may lead to culture ('you need to be smart to sustain culture') it is also the case that 'culture makes you smart'.

The SIH has had a dramatic influence on other areas of the biological and social sciences aside from animal behaviour. The development of the SIH was instrumental in forming the concept of mental attribution (theory of mind), which has revealed much about human cognitive development and various psychopathological disorders of social cognition, such as autism (Moll & Tomasello 2007; Reddy 2007).

Most recently, cognitive neuroscientists have used the principles of social intelligence to investigate how the brain processes information about animate agents, including work on mirror neurons and the neural basis of imitation as discussed in the paper by Gallese (2007). Dunbar & Shultz (2007) extend their earlier work which proposed that the primate brain (especially the neocortex) coevolved with processing social information, recognizing individuals and their relationships, the so-called social brain hypothesis (Dunbar 1998). Using new statistical and comparative analysis techniques, they tested the relationship between brain size and group size in the context of ecology and life history. Their analysis shows that there is a clear relationship between neocortex size and sociality, but the oft rejected idea that diet does not influence brain size in primates is seen to be ill-founded. A large neocortex can only be supported by a large brain, which is costly to run in terms of energy. A diet rich in carbohydrates and protein can supply these energy requirements, and a life-history variable, such as long developmental period, allows the brain time to grow and provides increased opportunities for learning (social and non-social). Although the relationship between brains, sociality, diet and life history is clear at the level of complex statistical analyses, Barrett *et al.* (2007), 'at the coalface' in their long-term observations of monkey's behaviour in the wild, have reviewed the primate literature and found little convincing evidence that monkey sociality is cognitively complex.

Gallese (2007) reviews his studies of mirror neurons in monkeys and humans. Mirror neurons are a class of neurons (networks) in the premotor cortex which respond to the sight of particular actions and their associated motor patterns performed by the same individual who witnessed the actions. These neurons have been ascribed a multitude of functions, from imitation to empathy to language. Gallese (2007) expands his theory that mirror neurons are essential nodes of a 'theory of mind' network by suggesting that they play a role in linking mental states in the self with the same mental states in another (simulation). He goes further to suggest that mirror neurons allow the sharing of communicative intentions, and foster cooperation and collaboration with others (see also Moll & Tomasello 2007) through a process of empathy and embodied simulation. The notion of embodied and distributed cognition, in which we explicitly interact with our environment rather than just being passive viewers in it, is essential for how we process information (social and physical). These themes are also discussed in detail by Barrett *et al.* (2007).

By contrast, Frith (2007) discusses empirical studies investigating the neural correlates of social cognition, in particular 'theory of mind'. Although the field of social neuroscience is relatively new, it has struck a chord among neuroscientists. Frith (2007) reviews this work by focusing on three brain areas which have long been seen as integral components of the primate social brain network: the amygdala, the posterior superior temporal sulcus (STS) and the medial prefrontal cortex (PFC). Each of these regions plays a specific role in processing socially relevant information (amygdala—emotional valence; STS—perceiving biological motion and actions; medial PFC—thinking about mental states).

Empirical studies of how primates represent social agents are currently being used to develop robots with an artificial social intelligence, as discussed in the paper by Dautenhahn (2007). If such robots are to be integrated into society, either as tools or companions we are happy to interact with, then the design of future robots needs to accommodate thinking about how humans interact as a model (robot etiquette). This is particularly important when applying social robots in the treatment of children with autism.

Perhaps the most striking application of the SIH has been as a tool to describe how human intelligence may have evolved, how early human societies were structured and how the development of these societies leads to technological advances including farming, computers and communication between individuals living thousands of miles apart. Mithen (2007), an archaeologist, suggests a novel thesis derived from a quote by Humphrey that farming was derived from a 'misapplication' of the SIH. Mithen (2007) proposes that early humans demonstrated an enhanced cognitive fluidity which evolved from the flexibility required to process information about other social beings and their relationships. This cognitive fluidity was then co-opted for other tasks. He suggests that plants, such as squash, maize and beans in Mexico, were domesticated as an act of social prestige, to impress peers and to use in exchange for other commodities. As such, modern human cognition became more embodied due to artefacts located outside the body which represent and store information, such as books, computers and paintings, but also domesticated crops which provided an indication of social standing. Perhaps human-like sociable robots will be seen as the greatest example of embodied cognition.

Finally, the SIH provided philosophers with material to theorize about the evolution of the human mind. In some respects, Sterelny (2007) agrees with Mithen (2007) and Humphrey that the unique aspects of our *Homo sapiens* minds did not evolve to deal with problems in the physical world. Indeed, Sterelny (2007) argues that models of human cognitive evolution which rely on keeping track of changes in the external environment alone cannot explain these unique aspects, stressing that many animals face these same challenges. Sterelny (2007) states that both the 'ecological intelligence' hypothesis and the SIH are examples of niche construction, in which the 'world' is manipulated in some way. The way that early humans foraged had a profound effect on human sociality, but also led to the evolution of technology and our subsequent unique intellectual capabilities.

In ending this special issue, Humphrey (2007) updates his earlier suggestion that the dividing line between humans and other social animals is that humans are the only creatures that have a conscious self (Humphrey 1983, 1986). He suggests that humans are alone in their capacity to think about the contents of another individual's mind. Yet, surely given the existence of Darwinian evolution, consciousness and mind-reading cannot have arrived de novo in humans. Consequently, consciousness must have some precursors in non-human animals (even if these are only at the level of sophisticated behaviour-reading) and consciousness must have been adaptive (i.e. conferred some reproductive advantage). Humphrey (2007) goes one step further by suggesting that although humans are inherently social, they are also incredibly lonely, and it is this loneliness which allows us to step back and *really* appreciate one another as individual social beings.

We thank all the participants of the Discussion Meeting; Tony Dickinson, Bill McGrew, Uta Frith & Rob Boyd for skilfully chairing the sessions, but especially the speakers, who produced excellent talks and papers on their very best work and current thinking. We also thank the organizers at the Royal Society, particularly Chloe Sykes and her team, who made the experience so enjoyable and run so smoothly, and the student helpers; Auguste von Bayern, Chris Bird, Anne Helme and Amanda Seed for manning the microphones. Finally, we thank James Joseph at the *Phil. Trans. R. Soc. B* editorial office for his patience in putting this special issue together.

Nathan J. Emery[1,*]
Nicola S. Clayton[2]
Chris D. Frith[3]

December 2006

References

Barrett, L., Henzi, P. & Rendall, D. 2007 Social brains, simple minds: does social complexity really require cognitive complexity? *Phil. Trans. R. Soc. B* **362**, 561–575. (doi:10.1098/rstb.2006.1995)

Byrne, R. W. 2007 Culture in great apes: using intricate complexity in feeding skills to trace the evolutionary origin of human technical prowess. *Phil. Trans. R. Soc. B* **362**, 577–585. (doi:10.1098/rstb.2006.1996)

Chance, M. R. A. & Mead, A. P. 1953 Social behaviour and primate evolution. *Symp. Soc. Exp. Biol.* 7, 395–439.

Clayton, N. S., Dally, J. M. & Emery, N. J. 2007 Social cognition by food-caching corvids. The western scrub-jay as a natural psychologist. *Phil. Trans. R. Soc. B* **362**, 507–522. (doi:10.1098/rstb.2006.1992)

Connor, R. C. 2007 Dolphin social intelligence: complex alliance relationships in bottlenose dolphins and a consideration of selective environments for extreme brain size evolution in mammals. *Phil. Trans. R. Soc. B* **362**, 587–602. (doi:10.1098/rstb.2006.1997)

[1] Sub-department of Animal Behaviour, University of Cambridge, Madingley CB3 8AA, UK (nje23@cam.ac.uk)
[2] Department of Experimental Psychology, University of Cambridge, Cambridge CB2 3EB, UK
[3] Wellcome Department of Imaging Neuroscience, Institute of Neurology, University College London, London WC1N 3BG, UK

Dautenhahn, K. 2007 Socially intelligent robots: dimensions of human–robot interaction. *Phil. Trans. R. Soc. B* **362**, 679–704. (doi:10.1098/rstb.2006.2004)

de Waal, F. B. M. 1982 *Chimpanzee politics*. Baltimore, MD: John Hopkins University Press.

Dunbar, R. I. M. 1998 The social brain hypothesis. *Evol. Anthropol* **6**, 178–190.

Dunbar, R. I. M. & Shultz, S. 2007 Understanding primate brain evolution. *Phil. Trans. R. Soc. B* **362**, 649–658. (doi:10.1098/rstb.2006.2001)

Emery, N. J., Seed, A. M., von Bayern, A. M. P. & Clayton, N. S. 2007 Cognitive adaptations of social bonding in birds. *Phil. Trans. R. Soc. B* **362**, 489–505. (doi:10.1098/rstb.2006.1991)

Frith, C. D. 2007 The social brain? *Phil. Trans. R. Soc. B* **362**, 671–678. (doi:10.1098/rstb.2006.2003)

Gallese, V. 2007 Before and below 'theory of mind': embodied simulation and the neural correlates of social cognition. *Phil. Trans. R. Soc. B* **362**, 659–669. (doi:10.1098/rstb.2006.2002)

Holekamp, K. E., Sakai, S. T. & Lundrigan, B. L. 2007 Social intelligence in the spotted hyena (*Crocuta crocuta*). *Phil. Trans. R. Soc. B* **362**, 523–538. (doi:10.1098/rstb.2006.1993)

Humphrey, N. K. 1976 The social function of intellect. In *Growing points in ethology* (eds P. P. G. Bateson & R. A. Hinde), pp. 303–317. Cambridge, UK: Cambridge University Press.

Humphrey, N. K. 1983 *Consciousness regained: chapters in the development of mind*. Oxford, UK: Oxford University Press.

Humphrey, N. K. 1986 *The inner eye*. London, UK: Faber & Faber.

Humphrey, N. K. 2007 The society of selves. *Phil. Trans. R. Soc. B* **362**, 745–754. (doi:10.1098/rstb.2006.2007)

Jolly, A. 1966 Lemur social behavior and primate intelligence. *Science* **153**, 501–506. (doi:10.1126/science.153.3735.501)

Mithen, S. 2007 Did farming arise from a misapplication of social intelligence? *Phil. Trans. R. Soc. B* **362**, 705–718. (doi:10.1098/rstb.2006.2005)

Moll, H. & Tomasello, M. 2007 Cooperation and human cognition: the Vygotskian intelligence hypothesis. *Phil. Trans. R. Soc. B* **362**, 639–648. (doi:10.1098/rstb.2006.2000)

Penn, D. C. & Povinelli, D. J. 2007 On the lack of evidence that non-human animals possess anything remotely resembling a 'theory of mind'. *Phil. Trans. R. Soc. B* **362**, 731–744. (doi:10.1098/rstb.2006.2023)

Reddy, V. 2007 Getting back to the rough ground: deception and 'social living'. *Phil. Trans. R. Soc. B* **362**, 621–637. (doi:10.1098/rstb.2006.1999)

Silk, J. B. 2007 The adaptive value of sociality in mammalian groups. *Phil. Trans. R. Soc. B* **362**, 539–559. (doi:10.1098/ rstb.2006.1994)

Sterelny, K. 2007 Social intelligence, human intelligence and niche construction. *Phil. Trans. R. Soc. B* **362**, 719–730. (doi:10.1098/rstb.2006.2006)

Whiten, A. & van Schaik, C. P. 2007 The evolution of animal 'cultures' and social intelligence. *Phil. Trans. R. Soc. B* **362**, 603–620. (doi:10.1098/rstb.2006.1998)

Comparative Perspectives

1

Cognitive adaptations of social bonding in birds

Nathan J. Emery, Amanda M. Seed, Auguste M. P. von Bayern
and Nicola S. Clayton

The 'social intelligence hypothesis' was originally conceived to explain how primates may have evolved their superior intellect and large brains when compared with other animals. Although some birds such as corvids may be intellectually comparable to apes, the same relationship between sociality and brain size seen in primates has not been found for birds, possibly suggesting a role for other non-social factors. But bird sociality is different from primate sociality. Most monkeys and apes form stable groups, whereas most birds are monogamous, and only form large flocks outside of the breeding season. Some birds form lifelong pair bonds and these species tend to have the largest brains relative to body size. Some of these species are known for their intellectual abilities (e.g. corvids and parrots), while others are not (e.g. geese and albatrosses). Although socio-ecological factors may explain some of the differences in brain size and intelligence between corvids/parrots and geese/albatrosses, we predict that the type and quality of the bonded relationship is also critical. Indeed, we present empirical evidence that rook and jackdaw partnerships resemble primate and dolphin alliances. Although social interactions within a pair may seem simple on the surface, we argue that cognition may play an important role in the maintenance of long-term relationships, something we name as 'relationship intelligence'.

Keywords: avian brain; jackdaw; monogamy; pair bonding; rook; social intelligence

1.1 Introduction

Thirty years ago, Nicholas Humphrey (1976) suggested a radical proposal for how primates may have acquired their apparent superior intelligence when compared with other animals (see also Jolly 1966). From his observations of rhesus monkeys housed at the Sub-department of Animal Behaviour, Madingley, he was puzzled as to why these monkeys performed cognitive feats in the laboratory and yet seemed to have few, if any, problems to solve during their day-to-day existence. These laboratory housed monkeys did not have to search for food, they had no predators to evade and the enclosure in which they lived was relatively sparse. The monkeys in this environment, however, were housed in social groups. Humphrey therefore suggested that the physical environment did not present the kind of challenges which would lead to the evolution of a flexible, intelligent mind, but that the social environment did. This proposal has been named the 'Social Intelligence Hypothesis' (SIH). The social environment is ever changing and largely unpredictable, particularly in those societies in which individuals have a history of interactions with other individuals (e.g. comparing monkeys with social insects). This proposal has blossomed with the support of positive data, and mutated into the 'Machiavellian Intelligence Hypothesis' (Byrne & Whiten 1988; Whiten & Byrne 1997) or 'Social Brain Hypothesis' (SBH, Dunbar 1998), which focus on the manipulative and deceptive aspects of social life and the relationship between sociality and brain power respectively. However, from its inception, the SIH was discussed primarily with respect to the evolution of primate intelligence, and not other animals. It rapidly became clear that other social animals, such as dolphins, hyenas and elephants, also demonstrated many of the biological, ecological and behavioural preconditions for intelligence; sophisticated cognitive skills in the lab and field; and many of the complex social skills found in monkeys and apes (McComb 2001; de Waal & Tyack 2003; Connor 2007; Holekamp *et al.* 2007).

In 1996, Peter Marler attempted to widen the comparative nature of the SIH by asking whether birds also demonstrate similar aspects of social intelligence to primates, and if so, is their social intelligence of the same kind as primates? (Marler 1996). In reviewing data on cooperation, social learning and group defence in birds, Marler concluded that the social skills of primates did not appear to be more sophisticated than birds. Indeed, he suggested that most ornithologists were not as interested in the same questions of cognitive evolution as primatologists; however, if they started looking they would find many examples of social knowledge in a wide variety of birds.

When Marler wrote his paper over 10 years ago, there was little data available on avian social intelligence. Indeed, Marler based his review primarily on data collected by field ornithologists with no interest of the underlying cognitive processes involved in social interaction. Therefore, his analysis was necessarily, in general, including data from all available species. However, based on brain size and cognitive tests in the laboratory, it is not clear why there should be a simple relationship between sociality, intelligence and brain for the Class Aves, as this is not the case for the Class Mammalia. Although there appears to be a clear relationship between social group size and brain (i.e. neocortex) size within primates (Dunbar 1992), carnivores, insectivores (Dunbar & Bever 1998), bats (Barton & Dunbar 1997) and cetaceans (Marino 2002; Connor 2007), no such relationship exists within another mammalian order, ungulates (Shultz & Dunbar 2006). Although the brain size analyses presented later in the paper were performed at the class rather than family level, it should be kept in mind that such analyses have yet to be performed in mammals.

It is the aim of the current paper to evaluate Marler's claim that avian social intelligence is the same as primate social intelligence. First, we will review whether there is a relationship between flock (group) size and brain size in birds, as there is in primates, bats, cetaceans and carnivores. Unfortunately, these analyses are not directly comparable, as the majority of comparative brain size analyses in mammals have been performed on the neocortex, whereas data on the equivalent areas of the avian brain such as the nidopallium and mesopallium is not yet available for large numbers of birds. This is likely to be important, as other 'non-thinking' parts of the brain are relatively unspecialized, playing a role in many aspects of behaviour and cognition. Certainly, brain size is related to other biological and ecological variables, such as body size, long developmental period, diet and habitat. With this caveat in mind, we will assess the evidence for a relationship between sociality and brain size in birds. We report data from new analyses that those species which form lifelong pair bonds, including many corvids and parrots, tend to have the largest relative sized brains. However, there are also lifelong monogamous species, such as geese, with relatively small brains. We will make a suggestion as to why these differences may exist.

In the second part of this paper, we will consider whether the SIH still applies to birds, in accordance with the differences in sociality between the majority of birds and mammals. In particular, we will assess how lifelong monogamy, in combination with other socio-ecological factors, may have led to increased brain size. We will briefly review the socio-ecology of three lifelong monogamous species; greylag geese, jackdaws and rooks, to determine whether life-history traits and/or ecology may have influenced sociality in these species and subsequently the evolution of social intelligence. We will then present some data from behavioural observations of juvenile rooks suggesting that they form alliances, support one another in fights, exchange different behavioural commodities (e.g. food, social support and preening), recognize relationships between third parties and demonstrate third-party post-conflict affiliation. These behaviours have so far only been described for primates and dolphins. We conclude that rooks (and probably other large-brained, lifelong monogamous avian species, such as parrots) demonstrate a form of *relationship intelligence*, rather than a general social intelligence, allowing them to become 'in tune' with their partner, and so providing them with the competitive edge to out compete individuals who do not form similar partnerships.

1.2 The avian social brain?

In early discussions of the SIH, a number of biological, ecological and behavioural preconditions were proposed as essential to the presence of sophisticated social processing in primates. These were a large brain, long developmental period before maturation, individualized social groups and extended longevity (Humphrey 1976; Byrne & Whiten 1988; van Schaik & Deaner 2003). Indeed, in primate species with complex social systems, such as cerecopithecine monkeys and hominoid apes, these preconditions are fulfilled. In addition, primates with large brains (or more precisely, a large neocortex ratio against the rest of the brain) tended to form larger social groups than species with a smaller neocortex ratio (Dunbar 1992; Barton 1996).

We now know that these biological preconditions are not exclusive to primates and have been demonstrated in many social mammals, such as elephants (McComb 2001), hyenas (Holekamp *et al.* 2007) and cetaceans (Connor 2007). What about birds? Although birds do not possess absolute brain sizes anywhere in the region of most mammals (mean 3.38±0.11 g; range from 0.13 g (Cuban Emerald hummingbird) to 46.19 g (Emperor penguin; Iwaniuk & Nelson 2003) compared with the 7800 g brain of a sperm whale), some birds have brains that, relatively speaking, are the same size as those of chimpanzees (after removing the effects of body size; Emery & Clayton 2004).

Have avian brains evolved to solve the same or similar cognitive problems as mammalian brains? Emery (2006) reviewed evidence that some birds use and manufacture tools, possess episodic-like memory (i.e. remember what they cached, where they cached and when they cached it), predict the behaviour of conspecifics and possibly understand their mental states. These traits tended to be found in those birds with a large relatively sized brain, an omnivorous diet, a complex social system and which live in a harsh, changeable environment: traits which are shared with mammals that have been suggested to be the most intelligent. Indeed, Godfrey-Smith (1996), Sterelny (2003) and Potts (2004) have suggested that such environmental complexity presented numerous ecological problems for our hominid ancestors which could only be solved by the evolution of flexible forms of innovative behaviour.

The potential relationship between sociality and brain size in birds is complex. In three studies, no clear relationship was found between group size and brain size across various bird families (Beauchamp & Fernandez-Juricic 2004), cooperative breeding group size and brain size in corvids (Iwaniuk & Arnold 2004) or simple social structure and brain size across many bird families (Emery 2004).

Beauchamp & Fernandez-Juricic (2004) were the first to attempt to evaluate Dunbar's claims with respect to flock size in birds. As their measure of social complexity, Beauchamp & Fernandez-Juricic (2004) recorded the mean and maximum flock size outside the breeding season and flocking propensity; they also used three independent sources for brain volumes. They did not find any significant relationships. One reason for this lack of relationship may have been that group size is not a stable trait in many birds, which tend to form pair bonds during the breeding season and then foraging flocks of various sizes outside the breeding season. The size of these flocks is dependent largely on food availability and quality, rather than the underlying social interactions within the flock. Emery (2004) used a more conservative measure of sociality, categorizing species based on whether they tended to live territorially (solitary except during the breeding season), in pairs, in families, in small non-family groups (10–50), medium groups (greater than 50) or in large flocks (100 s and 1000 s). There was no significant difference in relative forebrain size across the various social categories, except when the different families and/or orders were analysed separately. At that level of evolutionary analysis, the corvids and parrots had much larger brains than other birds, but only those birds found in pairs, small flocks or medium flocks (Emery 2004).

Cooperative breeding birds tend to flock together throughout the year, and so may present a better reflection of the underlying social interactions. Iwaniuk & Arnold (2004) investigated any potential relationship between the brain size of cooperative and noncooperative corvids, or any correlation between cooperative group size and brain size in corvids. They failed to find any significant relationships at this family level.

As we have already suggested, any comparison between these studies and those on primates (or other mammals) has to be viewed with some caution as the analyses were performed at different neural levels (brain size in birds versus neocortex ratio in mammals). Although not directly comparable to the neocortex, the most extensive dataset in birds for a more specific brain area is the size of the telencephalon (forebrain). Burish et al. (2004) did find a strong relationship between social complexity and size of the avian telencephalon (forebrain); however, this analysis used a strange social category, 'transactional', that included those species which demonstrated 'complex' forms of behaviour (not necessarily social), such as ceremonial dancing, communal gatherings, fission–fusion societies, memory performance, food sharing, 'parliaments', 'weddings', aerial acrobatics, social play, milk-bottle opening and problem-solving. This category appears to be completely tautological—selecting complex behaviours likely to require a significant amount of brain power makes a significant relationship with brain size unsurprising. In addition, some of the species included in this category are solitary (e.g. woodpeckers; Winkler et al. 1995), and this does not align well with the SBH.

Perhaps avian sociality is too heterogeneous a concept to be used effectively in studies related to brain size? One problem in attempting to find a simple relationship between brain size and sociality across birds is that the social organization of most birds tends to be very flexible, both temporally and spatially. As such, species may vary in social system based on their geographical location and its different ecological pressures. A harsh environment in which food is scarce or difficult to locate could make raising healthy offspring more challenging. Long-term monogamy may be favoured in these conditions, as parents that cooperate in raising their offspring year-in-year-out may gain an advantage that would not apply in less harsh environments. Similarly, cooperative-breeding, in which the young remain with their parents to help raise the next brood, may be adopted because the environment is so harsh that it cannot provide for an additional family.

Carrion crows, for example, tend to be socially monogamous; however populations in Northern Spain, where conditions are harsh, are cooperative breeders (Baglione et al. 2002b). When crow eggs from Switzerland (non-cooperative breeders) were transferred to the nests of cooperative breeding crows in Spain, some of the chicks developed into helpers (Baglione et al. 2002a). Similarly, Florida scrub-jays are cooperative breeders (McGowan & Woolfenden 1989), whereas their close relatives, Western scrub-jays are typically semi-territorial (Carmen 2004) although they breed co-operatively in parts of Mexico (Curry *et al.* 2002). Although classified as two separate species, biologically they are almost identical, differing primarily in mating/ social system. Young Florida scrub-jays do not necessarily become helpers if the ecological conditions do not require additional aid in raising the brood or prevent them from finding a mate of their own (Woolfenden & Fitzpatrick 1984). Species may also demonstrate different social systems temporally, pair-bonding in the breeding season, and forming family groups once the young have fledged but remain with the parents, with the juveniles then leaving the colony to form larger foraging flocks. Many corvids and parrots appear to form such a variety of social systems within a species (Goodwin 1986; Juniper & Parr 1998).

1.3 Mating system, brains and social complexity

It is not clear from the previous section that there is any relationship between the avian brain and sociality. We have suggested that may be because avian social systems are flexible, depending on changing season or environmental conditions, and that the earlier analyses were based on factors that may not be good indicators of social complexity, such as group size. We therefore performed two new analyses, the first comparing species based on a simple measure of social network size (based on average group size) and the second comparing species based on mating system, as mating system may be a more robust measure of social complexity than group size (Bennett & Owens 2002).

We used an extensive dataset of avian brain volumes ($n=1482$ species; Iwaniuk & Nelson 2003). Information on social category was collated from the literature from as many avian species as possible (using the following categories: solitary/territorial, except for the breeding season; solitary/pair, typically solitary or in a pair year round; pair, breeding pair + offspring; small group, 5–30 individuals; medium group, 31–70 individuals; gregarious, 70–200 individuals; and very gregarious, greater than 200 individuals). Emery's earlier categorization of social system was based on maximum group size which may not be an accurate reflection of social complexity (Emery 2004). When it comes to interacting with the same individuals over a long time period, it may be quality rather than quantity which is important. For example, rooks live in colonies during the breeding season, forming long-term pair bonds and nesting in close proximity to other pairs, then they form small family groups once the offspring have fledged, and then join large winter foraging flocks and roost with up to 40 000 individuals. Rook pairs remain stable throughout the year (and across years). It is very unlikely that rooks will interact with every other bird in this size group or remember their interactions or their social relationships, in the same way that humans living in London do not interact with everyone they meet on the London Underground, only with a limited set of individuals they may see everyday. This does not mean that the capacity for interacting with a large number of individuals is absent.

Residuals from a regression of brain volume against body weight were used as the index of relative brain size. There was a significant effect of social system on relative brain size (ANOVA; $F_{6,473}= 23.05$, $p<0.00001$; figure 1.1), with birds in small groups having larger brains than birds with other social systems (Bonferroni correction, t-test, $p<0.008$ all comparisons). This was in direct contrast to results from mammals which report a relationship between increasing neocortex size and increasing social group size in mammals.

Given that almost 90% of birds are monogamous (Lack 1968), and that birds in small groups tend to have the largest brains, perhaps mating system may be a clearer indication of

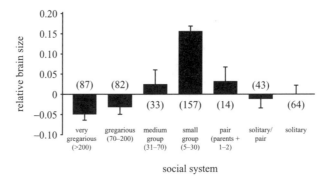

Fig. 1.1 Social system and relative brain size across 480 species of birds (raw brain volume data from Iwaniuk & Nelson (2003); social system data from various published sources).

social complexity, especially if we stress the importance of relationship quality rather than relationship quantity. Monogamy in birds takes different forms, from serially monogamous species which take new partners in every breeding season (e.g. most passerines) to pair-bonded species which mate for life (e.g. albatross). Serially monogamous species are often *socially monogamous*, which means they remain with the one partner during the breeding season, but often take part in extra-pair copulations (EPC). This compares to species (that are more often than not lifelong bonded species) which can be classified as *genetically monogamous*, which means they demonstrate mate fidelity with little or no evidence for EPCs (Henderson *et al.* 2000; Reichard 2003).

Although mating system can change, especially to reflect changes in climate or other environmental factors, it is perhaps a more stable representation of social structure in birds than social system, which can change quite dramatically across the space of a year for some species. For example, many birds form pairs during the autumn/winter, interacting primarily with their partner during the breeding season and then forming family groups when their offspring become independent, finally forming large roosting and foraging flocks later in the year. Such diversity within a species cannot easily be represented in an analysis of group size and brain size. Therefore, the relationship between brain size and mating system was investigated using the same brain volume dataset as above (Iwaniuk & Nelson 2003). Birds were classified according to whether they were monogamous, cooperative breeders, polygamous, polygynous or polyandrous. Monogamy often refers to the formation of a pair bond between a male and female which lasts throughout the breeding season, however in birds there are three alternative forms of monogamy. Birds which form pairs throughout the breeding season, but which are not exclusive (as determined by DNA paternity tests) and which do not re-form in the next season were classified as '1 year' monogamous. Birds which formed pairs for longer than 1 year were classified as '>1 year' monogamous, and birds which paired for life were classified as 'long-term' monogamous. Lifelong monogamy is extremely difficult to prove without the ability to track pairs across the seasons and across years, especially in very long-lived birds. In addition, there may be two forms of lifelong monogamy: those species such as rooks and jackdaws who remain together throughout the year, returning together to the same nest site (Cramp & Perrins 1994), and those species such as albatrosses, which pair during the breeding season and return to the same nesting site and partner every 2 years, but which travel separately from their partner outside of the breeding season (Perrins 2003).

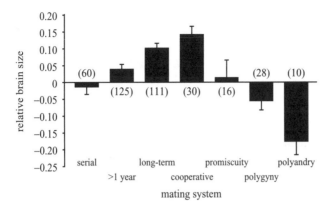

Fig. 1.2 Mating system and relative brain size across 480 species of birds (raw brain volume data from Iwaniuk & Nelson (2003); mating system data from various sources).

As with the earlier analysis, residuals from a regression of brain volume on body weight were used as an index of brain size. There was a significant relationship between mating system and brain size across birds (ANOVA; $F_{6,373}=9.73$, $p<0.00001$; figure 1.2) with those species forming long-term pair bonds or who are cooperative breeders (which also form long-term bonds) tending to have the largest relative brain size.

As brain size does not increase linearly with social group size, and the largest brains are found in long-term monogamous species rather than in species with a polygamous mating system, this suggests that the original formulation of the *social brain hypothesis* was primatocentric and should be reassessed for other animals (mammalian and non-mammalian). Even though the relationship between monogamy and brain size is significant, it seems counter-intuitive to suggest that cognitive complexity underlies the relationship between members of a long-term pair, rather than between many different individuals. Certainly, if competition was the only manifestation of social intelligence then this would be a fair conclusion. However, there is another aspect of social intelligence which is the polar opposite of deception and manipulation: cooperation. Cooperation is the key to establishing and maintaining a strong affiliative relationship of which the pair bond is the archetypal example; however competition still remains important for the interactions with conspecifics and the procurement of resources (see later).

According to the traditional formulation of the SBH, it is questionable whether primate brains increased in size in order to process and store information about social relationships. Indeed, the capacity to store and remember individuals, their current relationships to one another as well as previous ones has not been empirically tested. It seems unlikely that brains should function in such a one-to-one relationship, especially in those cases where the store only has a limited space available, such as in the bird brain. Hence, perhaps, the failure to find a linear relationship between group size and brain size in birds is not particularly surprising, especially when the absolute size of the avian brain is constrained by flight. As such, birds would not have the neural space available to put down large stores of social information (Nottebohm 1981). Even though corvids (crows, rooks, jackdaws, magpies) have almost twice the neural density in the forebrain than pigeons (Voronov *et al.* 1994), it remains unlikely that this could function as a *permanent* store of social memories of *large numbers of individuals*.

One speculative mechanism for how birds may circumvent this problem is neuronal plasticity. Bird brains are incredibly plastic, and some regions, such as the song control system and hippocampus, show marked changes in size and these changes correlate with use (e.g. song learning during the breeding season, Nottebohm (1981); or searching for nests during the breeding season in brood parasitic birds, Reboreda et al. 1996; Clayton et al. 1997; or caching food for the winter, Barnea & Nottebohm 1994; Clayton & Krebs 1994). In a similar manner, perhaps those regions of the avian brain which respond to social stimuli (such as the bed nucleus of the stria terminalis and amygdala, Bharati & Goodson 2006; Goodson & Wang 2006) also increase their size in response to seasonal changes in social complexity. These regions may decrease in size or decrease the rate of neurogenesis during the breeding season, when costs for maintaining a big brain are high (e.g. males constantly foraging and provisioning mate and offspring) and when social information processing is largely restricted to the mate when compared with increases in size and neurogenesis outside the breeding season when individuals form large social groups, when such social information may be important.

Some evidence in support of this hypothesis comes from studies of zebra finches raised in groups with different social complexity. Finches were raised in family groups and then either housed singly or transferred to groups of 40–45 strangers. Different sub-groups were then allowed to survive in these social conditions for various durations (40, 60 or 150 days) after the injection of [3H]-thymidine (a marker for neurogenesis). At the end of these time points, the birds were sacrificed and the number of new neurons counted in either the caudal nidopallium (NC) or the hippocampal complex (HC). There were a greater number of new neurons in the NC of communally housed birds than of singly housed birds, and the number of new neurons was highest after 40 days and lowest after 150 days (Barnea et al. 2006). By contrast, there were a higher number of new neurons in the HC in the communally housed birds than in the singly housed birds, but only at 40 days after [3H]-thymidine injection. In a corresponding study (Lipkind et al. 2002), an increase of new neurons was found in the NC, higher vocal centre (HVC) and Area X (both areas involved in song learning) 40 days after injection of [3H]-thymidine. This increase was specific to those birds housed in a more complex social environment (large heterosexual group rather than male–female pairs or singly housed).

Based on this data, we propose two neural systems in monogamous species which also form large groups outside the breeding season. The first would be a core neural system which may function as a permanent store of information about their bonded partner. Certainly, in lifelong pair-bonded species, the pair should be able to recognize their partner and ideally the subtleties of their relationship. The HC is a likely candidate for a core neural system as described in the study above (Barnea et al. 2006), in which new neurons did not appear to increase dramatically when housed in larger social groups for long periods. The second would be a more plastic secondary neural system which would function in processing and retaining information about transient social relationships, such as with individuals forming ephemeral flocks outside the breeding season. An example of this might be the NC described in the study above (Barnea et al. 2006), in which the number of new neurons increased significantly when housed in larger groups, across all time periods. This high turnover may reflect a high number of transient relationships with many individuals. As such, the social memories in the NC will be recent, and need to be updated frequently, whereas the social memories stored in the HC will be relatively older, representing both past events and declarative knowledge (e.g. a partner's typical responses in social situations, their preferences, their past history, etc.).

Although this suggestion is speculative these recent studies on the relationship between changes in sociality and neurogenesis provide a tantalizing glimpse of how such a system might be implemented in the avian brain. Indeed, the question of how mating system could affect the structure and function of avian brains is ready for comparative analysis along the same lines as studies on the distribution of receptors implicated in affiliation (e.g. oxytocin and vasopressin) in monogamous and promiscuous voles (Insel *et al.* 1994; Young *et al.* 2001). The avian brain may possess a similar 'social behaviour network' to the mammalian brain (Goodson 2005). Indeed, an analysis of arginine vasotocin (the non-mammalian equivalent to arginine vasopressin and oxytocin) distribution in the brains of various species of Estrildidae (grass finches and waxbills), which are all monogamous but which differ in species-typical group size, found patterns of receptor binding in the 'social behaviour network' which could be explained by social system (Goodson *et al.* 2006). It remains to be seen whether similar results would be found with corvids of different mating/social systems.

1.4 Can lifelong pair bonds be cognitively complex?

If the size of the avian brain is related to mating system, with especially large brains found in those species which form lifelong pair bonds or cooperative breeding groups, we need to address the following question, 'Which aspects of the pair bond may require this additional brain processing power?' Certainly, a problem arises, as this finding is counter intuitive to our thoughts about large brains and social complexity when they are formulated around the traditional primate view of the SBH. If we did not know something about the socio-cognitive abilities of birds (especially the cache protection strategies of corvids, see Clayton *et al.* 2007), we might be inclined to suggest that, perhaps, sociality was not an important factor for the evolution of the avian brain and intelligence.

It seems premature to discard the SIH with respect to birds without first thinking of alternative explanations for the relationship between brains and pair bonds. Hence, returning to the original question, 'why do lifelong pair-bonded avian species have the largest brains?', is there something special about retaining an exclusive partner over many years compared with mating with one individual during one breeding season and then taking a different partner the next or even mating with multiple partners during the same breeding season? Does lifelong monogamy require more than just reproductive collaboration? Are all lifelong pair-bonded species the same?

With respect to brain size, if we chose a random group of distantly related, lifelong monogamous species, and compared their brain sizes, would we expect any differences between them? We therefore chose five Procellariformes (white-capped albatross, grey-headed albatross, wandering albatross, black-browed albatross and black-footed albatross); five Anseriformes (snow goose, white-fronted goose, Brant goose, Bewick's swan & whooper swan); three Corvidae (jackdaw, rook and raven) and six Psittaciformes (white cockatoo, blue & yellow macaw, lorikeet, black-capped lorry, kea and African grey) from the Iwaniuk & Nelson (2003) dataset, and plotted brain volume against body mass. Interestingly, the data split into two grades; the swans, geese and albatrosses grouped around a low sloped regression line, whereas the corvids and parrots grouped around a steeper regression line (figure 1.3). Such a difference is unlikely to be due to ancestry as the groups are all distantly related; or to differences in diet, given that geese are herbivorous and albatrosses eat fish (higher protein value), yet have similar sized brains, and the corvids tend to be omnivorous, whereas the parrots eat fruit, nuts and seeds. The differences in brain size could be due to finding and processing food rather than the type of food *per se*, but again this does not explain the similarity in brain size for the geese and albatrosses (although the albatrosses brains are all above the regression line for that grade).

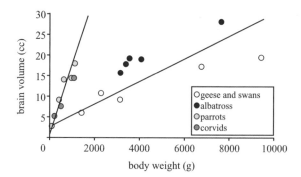

Fig. 1.3 Brain/body relationships in long-term, pair-bonded birds (geese, swans, albatrosses, corvids and parrots). Body size and brain volume data are from Iwaniuk & Nelson (2003). The lines represent two grade shifts between corvids and parrots, and geese, swans and albatrosses, but are do not represent actual regression statistics.

It also seems unlikely that these differences are due to processing information about home range, as geese migrate over long-distances, and albatrosses range for thousands of miles within a year; and hence perhaps, we would predict that they would have the largest brains if range size was the crucial factor. One difference may be amount of innovative behaviour, particularly with respect to novel foods and novel feeding techniques (Lefebvre *et al.* 1997) or extractive foraging and tool use (Lefebvre *et al.* 2002). However, we would like to suggest an alternative explanation for this neural difference (though not a mutually exclusive one), namely that the pair bond is more socially and cognitively complex in corvids and parrots than geese and albatrosses.

In an attempt to determine whether this is a plausible explanation, the remainder of this section will briefly review the social and mating system of three lifelong pair-bonded species: greylag geese, rooks and jackdaws. We appreciate that the choice of these species is rather arbitrary, indeed, many other species could have provided similar information (e.g. ravens; Heinrich 1990, 1999). However, these species were chosen because a lot is known about their reproductive and social behaviour from long-term field studies (see table 1.1), and owing to our own personal knowledge from working with the two corvid species.

All three species form lifelong partnerships; however there are striking similarities and differences in their socio-ecology. One clear difference is that infant geese are *precocial* (fully developed at hatching, and able to move unaided, finding food for themselves, imprinting on their mother and following her around), whereas infant corvids are *altricial* (hatch at a much earlier stage of development, where they are completely dependent on being fed by their parents, and cannot move out of the nest until they fledge). As such, altricial offspring are completely dependent on, at least, one parent (usually the mother), hence it becomes critical that the other parent takes the role of finding food for both his mate and his offspring, as all the mother's efforts are directed towards the needs of her offspring: feeding them when she receives food from the male and protecting them from predators. Therefore, it has been suggested that parents of altricial offspring have to cooperate in the raising of their brood (i.e. bi-parental care), at least until they become independent (Reichard 2003). Such close collaboration leads not only to joint care of the offspring, but also to extensive physical contact within the mated pair. Rook pairs collaborate in finding a nest site and build nests together (Coombs 1978), whereas

Table 1.1 Comparison between jackdaws, rooks and greylag geese of various socio-ecological variables which are relevant to lifelong monogamy.

	Jackdaws	Rooks	Greylag geese
pair for life?	✓[a]	✓[b]	✓[c]
pairs associate throughout the year?	✓[a,d,e]	✓[f,b]	✓[c]
extra pair copulations?	✗[g]	✓[b,h]	✓[?]
non-sexual relation ships?	✓	✓[i]	✓
social grouping	pairs in breeding season, large flocks throughout year	colonial in breeding season, large flocks thoughout year [j,k]	pairs whilst incubating, large flocks throughtout year [l–n]
retain smaller units (pairs, families) within larger groups?	(pairs only)	✓[f]	✓
social support	✓[o]	✓[i]	✓[p–r]
age at maturity	2 years[d,f]	2 years[s]	2–3 years[l]
paired affiliative behaviour	✓preening, food-sharing, displaying[a,d,e,t]	✓preening, food-sharing, displaying[u]	✗(except family triumph ceremony)[v]
altricial young?	✓[f]	✓[f]	✗(precocial) [l]
joint activities?	✓nest site establishment, territory defence, provisioning young,[a,e,w]	✓nest site establishment, territory defence, provisioning young,[x,y]	✓territory defence[c,l]
diet	omnivorous, largely insects[f]	omnivorous, largely cereals and earthworms[b]	herbivorous[l]

[a] Roell (1978). [b] Coombs (1978). [c] Lorenz (1991). [d] Lorenz (1970). [e] Goodwin (1986). [f] Cramp & Perrins(1994). [g] Henderson et al. (2000). [h] Røskaft (1983). [i] see current paper. [j] Røskaft (1980). Coombs(1960). [l] Cramp (1977). [m] Harrison (1967). [n] Lamprecht (1991). [o] A. von Bayern, unpublished observations. [p] Frigerio et al. (2001). [q] Frigerio et al. (2003). [r] Scheiber et al. (2005). [s] Patterson & Grace (1984). [t] Henderson & Hart (1993). [u] Richards (1976). [v] Fischer (1965). [w] Katzir (1983). [x] Marshall & Coombs (1957). [y] Røskaft (1981)

jackdaw pairs collaborate to acquire a nest hole, and then cooperate in defending this new nest site from other pairs and predators, as these are rare commodities (Roell 1978).

By comparison, the parents of precocial offspring do not need to cooperate in raising their offspring as they can provide for themselves. Food is abundant because geese are herbivorous, therefore goslings can find their own food and do not have to travel far to find it. Geese build simple nests on the ground, which are easily abandoned, but high risk from ground predators, therefore parents do cooperate in defending the goslings from predators.

It is clear that there are differences in both the ecology and life history of these species (table 1.1). What then is the role for lifelong monogamy in the evolution of intelligence? One possibility is that lifelong monogamy, once evolved, provides a platform for the partnership between mated pairs to become a synchronized, cooperative, year-round solution to the challenges of social and environmental complexity, for those species faced with such challenges.

Consistent with this notion is one further difference between geese, rooks and jackdaws: the quality of the relationship between the bonded male and female. In greylag geese, the pair will continue to associate throughout the year, even when forming large foraging flocks. There is no evidence of any prolonged physical contact between the male and female; there is no allofeeding, no allopreening, with the only real indication of a bond being the reduced proximity between the partners (when compared with other individuals), lack of aggression between them, behavioural synchrony, mate guarding and reciprocity in the triumph display (demonstrated primarily by the male after an aggressive encounter or used as a greeting when being re-introduced to the partner). Although geese provide social support to their partner, most examples are of passive social support, in which the mere presence of a partner has an effect on subsequent aggression. Active social support is less frequent, in which the partner actively interferes in a fight between their partner and a second individual (Scheiber *et al.* 2005).

It is the purpose of the next section to describe new data on rook partnerships and use this data to investigate the quality of their relationship. We suggest that pairs may become established through reciprocal acts of physical affiliative contact, such as food-sharing (allofeeding, possibly as a display of good parenting skills and the ability to provision the female when brooding chicks), bill twining and allopreening. Once pairs have become established, their behaviour resembles the alliances of many primates, with members of the pair aiding one another in fights (either ganging together against a common victim or passive social support or intervening in a current dispute), attacking the aggressor of their partner or their aggressor's partner, and directing affiliative behaviour towards their partner after they had been the victim or aggressor in a fight. Similar studies are being conducted on jackdaws (A. von Bayern 2004-2006, unpublished observations); however similar patterns are being reported, such as active food-sharing as an essential component for the development of the pair bond (von Bayern *et al.* 2007). Jackdaw pairs have been suggested to demonstrate similar forms of affiliative behaviour in other studies (e.g. Wechsler 1989).

1.5 Primate-like social complexity in rooks

Although relative brain size is a useful measure for predicting an animal's intellectual capacity (especially when comparing across a large number of species), it is also extremely limited. Only detailed behavioural observations and experiments can answer questions of social complexity in non-human animals. For individuals living within in a social group, it pays to develop selective relationships with others, to aid in the acquisition of resources and to receive protection against the threat of those who are intent on accessing your resources (Cords 1997). Monkeys, apes and dolphins either form temporary coalitions or occasionally more long-term alliances (Connor 2007); however it is not clear whether these relationships are more complex than in other animals, or only different (Harcourt 1992; Marler 1996). It is assumed that these relationships are fostered through reciprocal altruism and tactical manipulation (Seyfarth & Cheney 1984; de Waal & Lutrell 1988), mechanisms which may require sophisticated cognitive processes (Stevens & Hauser 2004). Although most previous studies of social complexity have focused on mammals, there is no reason to assume that the same processes are not important for birds, possibly occurring through a process of convergent evolution (Emery & Clayton 2004). Marler (1996) suggested that this lack of data was due to the research questions of field ornithologists rather than lack of data *per se*. As rooks have relatively large brains and form lifelong pair bonds, we chose them as a model corvid in which to investigate the formation of social relationships, and primate-like social knowledge. We therefore hand raised a group of rooks and followed their social development, including the development of affiliative relationships and pair bonds, until they were ten months old.

Twelve nestling rooks were taken from four different nests in Cambridgeshire and hand-raised in three separate groups until they fledged (approx. 32 days old). The birds' sex was determined through analysis of genetic material in their breast feathers. At fledging, the juveniles were released into an aviary. For the initial observations which occurred between July and October 2002, the rooks were observed once per day for approximately 1 h in the morning for five blocks (1 block = 1 week). During every trial, each rook was presented with small pieces of cheese in turn. The birds who begged first tended to receive the first pieces of cheese, but each bird received approximately similar amounts and in a semi-random order.

Observers made *ad lib* observations of the rooks' social behaviour (affiliative and aggressive), feeding, caching, recovery and vocalizations. Examples of aggressive behaviour included actual physical aggression (e.g. pecking and jabbing), displacements (i.e. one bird flies to the exact spot in which another bird is sitting and supplants that bird from its spot), chases and submissions. Examples of affiliative behaviour included food offering (e.g. active giving, begging, stealing and tolerated theft; de Kort *et al.* 2003, 2006), dual caching (i.e. two individuals cache the same piece of food together), bill-twining, play, allopreening and providing agonistic aid (i.e. two individuals either gang together against a third party or one individual intervenes in an ongoing fight).

Two additional blocks of trials (Blocks 6–7) were performed from December 2002 to January 2003 to determine whether the rooks' social behaviour had stabilized. A dominance index comparing number of wins minus number of losses over the total number of aggressive encounters was calculated for each individual for each block.

(a) The alliance as a valuable relationship

Valuable relationships come in different forms, from parent–offspring relationships to pair bonds and adult friendships. Such valuable relationships form owing to some mutual benefit for the two parties involved in the relationship. van Schaik & Aureli (2000) defined a valuable relationship by the presence of a number of properties. Individuals which spend more time in proximity, more friendly behaviours (e.g. grooming or preening) between two individuals, lower rates of agonistic conflict (e.g. aggression and submission) between two individuals and more agonistic support against a third party could be classified as forming a valuable relationship. This pattern of behaviours could be used to describe many forms of social bond, in which individuals are likely to derive considerable value from their relationship (Kummer 1978), such as parents and offspring, 'friends' and long-term mated pairs. To determine whether our group of juvenile rooks had formed valuable relationships, these properties will be examined in turn.

(i) Affiliative behaviour

The total frequency of affiliative behaviour in which one individual either directs their behaviour towards another (e.g. food sharing, allopreening, social support) or both individuals take part in a collaborative behaviour (e.g. dual caching, bill twining) was recorded for each potential dyad and the frequencies presented as sociograms. The thickness of the lines on the sociogram reflected the frequency of the behaviour and therefore the strength of the bond. In Blocks 1–5, the frequency of affiliative behaviour suggested that three pairs had formed based on the total amount of friendly behaviour directed towards a specific individual (pairs 41 & 42, 46 & 50 and 48 & 49; figure 1.4*a*). At this stage (i.e. six months old), these relationships were not exclusive, as there was evidence of some affiliative behaviour directed towards individuals outside the pair (figure 1.4*a*). These pairs did not appear to be based on sex, as 41 & 42 was a male–male pair, 46 & 50 was a female–female pair, and 48 & 49 was a male–female pair. Indeed, at six months old, the rooks would not have reached sexual maturity.

In the later observation period, when the rooks were nine months old (Blocks 6 & 7), the three pairs had stabilized, and two new pairs had formed (pairs 40 & 47 and 43 & 44; figure 1.4*b*). Both of the new pairs were male–female pairs, but still unlikely to have been sexually mature

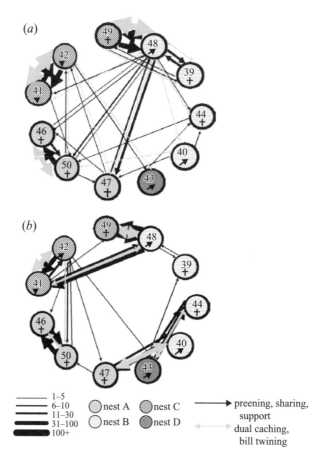

Fig. 1.4 Sociogram displaying the total frequency of affiliative behaviour between 11 hand-raised rooks (*a*) during Blocks 1–5, and (*b*) during Blocks 6–7. Numbers refer to individual birds (39, 40, 41, 42, 43, 44, 46, 47, 48, 49 & 50). The thickness of the lines represents the total frequency of affiliative behaviour across the time period represented. Black line represent unidirectional behaviours (food sharing, social support and allopreening), and the grey lines represent bidirectional behaviours (dual caching and bill-twining). The different patterned circles represent the nest from which the nestling was taken (A–D).

(Cramp & Perrins 1994). By this stage, the pairs appeared to be relatively exclusive, with little evidence of affiliation directed towards individuals outside the pair (figure 1.4*b*). There were exceptions to this, including a developing 'friendship' between 42 and 50, and between 41 and 48. This last affiliative relationship is particularly interesting, as 41 and 48 were two of the most dominant rooks (see a similar development for chimpanzees; de Waal 1982).

In the early stages of pair formation, food sharing appeared to be the most important affiliative behaviour, particularly the unsolicited transfer of highly valuable food from one individual to another (active giving; de Kort *et al.* 2003). The frequency of active giving appeared to be high at the initiation of the study when the rooks were approximately 3–4 months old (Block 1), but had significantly tailed off by the end of the first observation period (Block 5; figure 1.5).

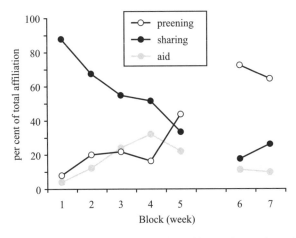

Fig. 1.5 Proportion of the total frequency of food sharing, allopreening and agonistic (social) support across Blocks 1–7 averaged across all 11 rooks.

During Blocks 6 and 7, active giving was vastly reduced and largely restricted to the two new pairs. A similar pattern of results was found during the development of jackdaw socialization using the same food provisioning and observational methods (von Bayern *et al.* 2007; de Kort *et al.* 2006). By comparison with food sharing, allopreening was relatively infrequent during Block 1, but steadily increased during Block 5, and began to level off during Blocks 6 and 7 (figure 1.5). Agonistic (social) support occurred at a relatively stable but low level across this whole period (figure 1.5). This suggests that active giving may be essential for the *formation* of the pair bond, but that allopreening takes over its affiliative role once the bond has become established, and so may be used to *maintain* the bond. We suggest that food sharing functions in this early role in bond formation owing to its similarity to parental feeding (the first individuals the young rooks and jackdaws bond with), and the fact that in hand-raised birds the parents are not around, and so the 'givers' may be taking on parental duties. However, this does not explain why some birds take on this role and why their food giving is so exclusive. Bond development in older birds is likely to be a consequence of reproduction, with the high frequency of food sharing as an example of courtship feeding (however in the young rooks described here, both partners give one another food).

(ii) Aggressive behaviour

Aggression in this particular group of rooks was extremely frequent during Blocks 1–5 (figure 1.6*a*), with various acts of aggression directed towards other individuals (from displacements to physical aggression to chases). Of course, this may have been exaggerated due to the nature of the observation sessions in which food was provisioned to the birds and an effect of being in captivity where space was somewhat restricted; however each bird was in the same situation and received the same amount of food. Of particular interest to the issue of valuable relationships was the fact that little or no acts of aggression were recorded between individuals in a pair (figure 1.6*a*). Aggression was less frequent in Blocks 6 and 7, but again little or no aggression was seen between partners (figure 1.6*b*).

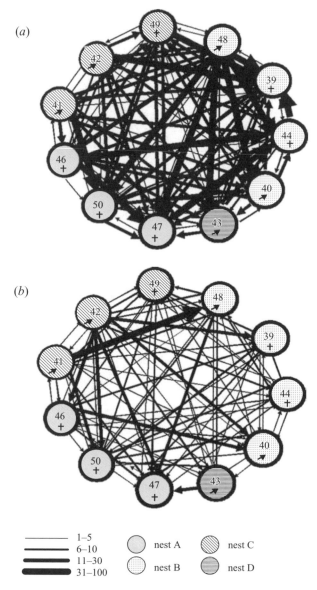

Fig. 1.6 Sociogram displaying the total frequency of aggressive behaviour between 11 hand-raised rooks (*a*) during Blocks 1–5, and (*b*) during Blocks 6–7. All symbols and lines are the same as figure 1.4.

(iii) Social support

Individuals within a pair should be more likely to provide social support (agonistic aid) to one another than non-partners, so that their partner has a better chance of winning a contest, and possibly gaining access to a resource which both individuals in the pair can benefit (Cords 1997). In this group of juvenile rooks, individuals were more likely to provide agonistic support to their partner than a non-partner, and to a member of their peer group (i.e. who shared their cat

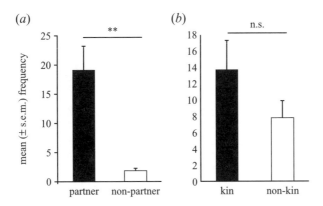

Fig. 1.7 Mean ± s.e.m. frequency with which (*a*) a social partner provided social support during an agonistic encounter with another individual when compared with a non-partner, (*b*) kin provided social support compared with non-kin. **p<0.01 (*t*-test).

box during hand-raising), but not to their kin (figure 1.7). Although two of the pairs were kin (41 & 42 and 46 & 50), choice was not significant. Interestingly, at sexual maturity these two pairs exchanged partners, so that 41 & 46 and 42 & 50 became male–female pairs who were not kin. This result suggests that the coalitions within a long-term alliance or partnership maybe akin to the pair bonds which develop at sexual maturity as they only choose non-kin as long-term partners.

(b) The benefits of being in a partnership

This data suggest that young hand-raised rooks form selective partnerships with a specific individual at a very early age, which is not due to sexual reproduction. What are the benefits of forming a partnership so early in life? Although rooks do not become sexually mature until the second year of life, they have to procure a nest site which is not occupied by an established pair, and which may be suitable for the life of the pair. This does not explain why same sex pairs form, especially when there are sufficient members of the opposite sex with whom to form a partnership. Perhaps, the benefits of being in a pair, such as gaining access to resources usually unavailable to a singleton, outweigh the importance of choice of partner, especially when a more appropriate partner may be chosen later on. This is not the case for jackdaws who become sexually mature earlier than rooks (in the first breeding season) and which have to locate a nest site, and guard it throughout most of the year. There is little evidence for divorce or EPC in jackdaws, even after multiple instances of reproductive failure; therefore, the choice of the right partner is a more crucial decision than in rooks. It is not clear why jackdaws have to make this decision so early on in life, and why their choice of partner is so permanent.

The most obvious benefit of being in a pair is to increase dominance, and the cascade of additional benefits this brings, which is the case for rooks. Figure 1.8 displays the mean rank of individual rooks in Blocks 1–5 based on whether they were in a pair or were singletons. Although the paired birds had a higher dominance than singletons throughout the observation period, the rank difference did increase over time suggesting the increase in status was a direct effect of becoming a pair.

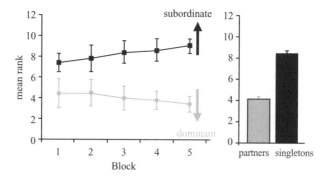

Fig. 1.8 Mean ± s.e.m. social rank of partners compared with singletons (i.e. those individuals without a partner) across Blocks 1–5, and the same data collapsed across blocks. Blocks 6–7 are not represented as only one bird remained a singleton during this period.

(c) Reciprocity, interchange and the maintenance of pair bonds

Once a non-sexual partnership has become established, even though there are direct benefits by remaining in the pair (see above), the relationship needs to be maintained if it is to survive till sexual maturity. This is particularly important for the types of social partnerships described here, as the requirements for being in a pair after sexual maturity are relatively transparent (e.g. sexual fidelity, paternal certainty, help with parental care, etc.). Breaking a partnership too prematurely causes a loss of social status, loss of nest site, but also the search for a new partner. Although we suggested earlier that allopreening may be important for the maintenance of a partnership, studies of primate behaviour have proposed that it is the 'trade' between different behavioural commodities (such as grooming, sharing, social support, etc.) which forms the basis for a solid partnership (Seyfarth & Cheney 1984; de Waal & Lutrell 1988). We therefore examined the frequency with which three different affiliative behaviours (allopreening, food sharing and provision of social support) were provided to others or received from others across the different blocks. This resulted in a number of actor-receiver matrices, which were then analysed using correlational methods. As these social behaviours may be influenced by dominance status of the two individuals or their time spent in proximity, we used permutation procedures (K_r-test) to remove the effect of social status (Hemelrijk 1990, 1994; Hemelrijk & Ek 1991). Proximity could not be controlled as it was not directly recorded in our data; however informal observations suggest that pairs spend almost all their time in proximity.

As seen in table 1.2, there were significant correlations between giving food and receiving food (reciprocity) and receiving preening (interchange), providing social support and receiving food or preening (interchange), and initiating preening and receiving food (interchange). There were also significant correlations between dual caching, bill twining and mutual social support (i.e. the direction of behaviour cannot be determined). Surprisingly, this pattern of results was not repeated during Blocks 6–7 (table 1.2). One interpretation of these results is that a complex suite of interrelated affiliative behaviours are used exclusively by both members of a partnership in order to solidify their social bond. The resultant correlations are therefore an inevitable outcome of being in close proximity to, and interacting exclusively with one other individual. This pattern was not repeated in Blocks 6–7 possibly because these behaviours are

Table 1.2 Correlations between various affiliative behaviours (unidirectional—give food, receive food, initiate allopreening, receive allopreening, provide social support; bidirectional—dual caching, bill-twining) during Blocks 1–5 & Blocks 6–7; $p<0.05$

	Blocks 1–5				Blocks 6–7			
	r^2	F	d.f.	p	r^2	F	d.f.	p
give food–receive food	0.45	7.48	1,9	**0.023**	0.03	0.3	1,9	0.6
initiate preen–receive preen	0.32	4.26	1,9	0.07	0.22	2.51	1,9	0.15
provide support–receive food	0.77	30.93	1,9	**0.0004**	0.2	2.20	1,9	0.17
give food–receive preen	0.45	7.5	1,9	**0.023**	0.004	0.03	1,9	0.86
preen–receive food	0.52	9.59	1,9	**0.01**	0.07	0.7	1,9	0.42
provide support–receive preen	0.68	18.75	1,9	**0.002**	0	0	1,9	1
dual caching–bill-twining	0.81	38.27	1,9	**0.0002**	0.1	0.98	1,9	0.35
dual caching–sharing	0.56	11.65	1,9	**0.008**	0.004	0.004	1,9	0.95
dual caching–support	0.76	28.49	1,9	**0.0005**	0.31	4.13	1,9	0.07

used in different frequencies (figure 1.5). An alternative explanation is that each individual keeps a score of each food transfer, assistance in a fight or bout of preening, and reciprocates to a same degree, even with different behaviours of 'equal value'. This mechanism would require some of the cognitive abilities discussed earlier (such as complex memory). We favour the first explanation, as being in an exclusive partnership is a mutual enterprise, in which the benefits cannot easily be quantified (such as increase in social status and therefore resources). This is not to say that reciprocity and interchange are outside of the repertoire of corvids, but that the social organization of rooks does not provide a stable platform for its evolution. We therefore need to collect similar kinds of data to this in other social corvids, which do not demonstrate a rook-like social organization.

(d) Understanding third-party relationships

Evidence that rooks may understand third party relationships was provided by an analysis of 'redirected aggression' (RA). This usually takes the form of selective aggression against the kin of a previously aggressive individual in monkeys and apes. In monkeys, this type of behaviour has been recorded up to 1 h after the initial aggressive act had taken place and may form the basis for a 'revenge' system (Aureli *et al.* 1992). We recorded all occurrences of aggression (inc. displacement) towards third parties not involved in the fight for the immediate period after the fight (less than 3 s), and also recorded all occurrences in the hour after the fight. We recorded three forms of RA; the aggressor (X_1) attacked the victim (Y_1), then either (i) the victim's partner (Y_2) attacked the aggressor (X_1), (ii) the victim (Y_1) attacked the aggressor's partner (X_2) or (iii) the victim's partner (Y_2) attacked the aggressor's partner (X_2). We recorded a total of 19 acts of RA in the immediate period after a fight across all the blocks. Four acts (21.05%) appeared to be random acts of 'frustration' which did not include the partners of those involved; however a significantly greater number of acts ($n = 15$; 78.95%) were partner-oriented (Binomial, $p < 0.01$). There were differences in the frequency of the different forms of RA. The majority of acts, 9 (60%), followed the $Y_2 \rightarrow X_1$ form, 4 acts (26.67%) followed the $Y_1 \rightarrow X_2$ form and 2 acts (13.33%) followed the $Y_2 \rightarrow X_2$ form.

The number of aggressive acts which occurred in the hour after a fight (where possible, due to the total length of each data collection session) was 106. We need to be cautious about the causal role of the targeted fight in the subsequent acts of RA, especially in such a long period after the fight. However, we need to use the same caution when discussing data from monkeys and apes. Across all the blocks, 29 acts (27.4%) were of the $Y_2 \rightarrow X_1$ form, 47 acts (44.3%) were of the $Y_1 \rightarrow X_2$ form and 30 acts (28.3%) were of the $Y_2 \rightarrow X_2$. This data tentatively suggests (with the above caveats) that rooks (i) remember past interactions (and the protagonists of those interactions), (ii) recognize the affiliative partners of others, and (iii) may use this information to act upon previous acts of aggression in which they were the victims, possibly as a form of 'revenge'.

(e) Managing valuable relationships

Post-conflict affiliation is unlikely to occur between individuals who do not have a valuable relationship (van Schaik & Aureli 2000; Aureli *et al.* 2002). Such a relationship does not necessarily have to be with only one individual; indeed, the only criteria should be that each individual benefits from maintaining the relationship (Silk 2002). As we have already seen, rooks form close partnerships with another individual, not necessarily of the same sex, which is categorized by the amount of time spent in close proximity, amount of affiliative behaviour directed exclusively towards their partner and level of support provided during agonistic encounters. Such partnerships may therefore be classified as the strongest form of valuable relationship (and particularly so when the individuals in the partnership become sexually mature). Frequency of aggression towards other non-affiliated members of the social group is relatively high (figure 1.6), but does not usually lead to sustained acts of physical aggression, rather taking the form of displacements and minor pecks. There is little or no aggression between affiliative partners (figure 1.6). Therefore, rooks in partnerships only form valuable relationships with one individual, their affiliative partner. The Valuable Relationship Hypothesis (van Schaik & Aureli 2000; Aureli *et al.* 2002) suggests that 'post-conflict reunions should occur more often when the opponents are mutually valued social partners, because disturbance of a more valuable relationship entails a larger loss of benefits for both opponents' (Aureli *et al.* 2002, p. 334). Therefore, if no aggression occurs between affiliative partners, then we would not expect to see reconciliation. As yet, we have not witnessed any occurrence of reconciliation within our colony of rooks (Seed *et al.* 2007).

By contrast, aggression does occur between non-affiliated members of the social group (figure 1.6). Consolation has been defined as 'contact between a recipient of aggression and an uninvolved bystander not long after the former was involved in a conflict' (de Waal & Aureli 1996, p. 93), however this is a rather anthropomorphic, functional term, which may not represent what is actually going on inside the animal's mind. Furthermore, there is evidence that affiliative contacts between actors and third-parties does not in fact serve to reduce stress levels in chimpanzees and long-tailed macaques (Koski & Sterck 2007; Das 2000). We therefore use the less loaded term 'third-party post-conflict affiliation'. We predicted that such affiliation should occur more frequently between affiliated partners post-conflict, either initiated by an individual involved in aggression or by an affiliated bystander, than in matched control conditions in which aggression did not occur. Indeed, in a study of rooks using the PC-MC method (post-conflict-matched control; de Waal & Yoshihara 1983), both initiators and targets of aggression engaged in third-party affiliation with a social partner at higher levels during the post-conflict period than in the matched control. Both former aggressors and uninvolved third-parties initiated affiliative contacts (Seed *et al.* 2007). The function of third-party affiliation remains to be explicitly tested, both for rooks and most primates, although dampening the stress response and strengthening or signalling alliances seem to be likely candidates. Rooks, like chimpanzees (de Waal & Aureli 1996), appear to use a specific affiliative behaviour during the post-conflict period, which may aid in reducing stress. Like the embracing and kissing of chimpanzees, rooks employ a special form of physical contact, bill twining, with their partner in the first minute after a fight, and almost exclusively within this period and this context (Seed *et al.* 2007).

Observations of the rooks' social interactions demonstrate a very rapid formation of selective long-term partnerships with individuals of either sex, normally a member of the same peer group, not kin. Membership of a partnership appeared to increase the social status of both partners. Food sharing was found within each partnership, and was both initiated and reciprocated. Sharing also increased the probability of receiving other affiliative behaviours, such as social support and preening. Partners also demonstrated RA towards the partners of those individuals that had aggressed against them or their partners in the immediate past and possibly up to 1 h after the fight.

These results suggest that rooks display many of the complex social traits so far only reported for hyenas, elephants, cetaceans, monkeys and apes (de Waal & Tyack 2003; Connor 2007; Holekamp *et al.* 2007; Silk 2007), but almost certainly dependent on different mechanisms. Certainly, the fact that rooks form strong bonds very early in development, which can be life-long, suggests a different scenario from mammals that do not form such strong, long-term pair-bonds.

1.6 Cooperation and coordination

One important factor for the formation, maintenance and longevity of the rooks' partnerships is their ability to cooperate. This most likely occurs through mutualism, rather than reciprocity. Mutualism is what Dugatkin (1997) has termed 'no cost cooperation', in which both individuals receive an equal gain from cooperating, with little potential for cheating because if they do not cooperate, both individuals will lose as there can never only be one benefactor. This makes sense for long-term partnerships in which the benefits, such as increased dominance and access to resources, are accrued by both members of the pair. During pair formation, both individuals demonstrate their willingness to cooperate by offering food to their chosen partner (de Kort *et al.* 2003; 2006; von Bayern *et al.* 2007), allopreening, and offering assistance during agonistic encounters (social support) or affiliating post-conflict.

Once a pair has become established, the partners provide one another with resources or 'commodities', thereby establishing a biological market which maintains the partnership and the resultant mutual benefits (Nöe & Hammerstein 1995). In such biological markets, commodities tend to be exchanged (same commodity) or interchanged (different commodity). For example, Rook X preens his partner Rook Y, and subsequently Rook Y aids her partner Rook X in a fight at a later time. In this form of cooperation, there is no need for mental score-keeping as both individuals (by the fact that they have formed a long-term affiliative relationship) will benefit from these actions equally. The primary benefit is the stability of the relationship, and the resultant effects on dominance status and resource acquisition.

Similarly to cooperation, individuals in long-term partnerships become coordinated in their behaviour, such as synchronizing their body movements, social displays and vocalizations. Individual vocalizations may contain a 'signature' which is unique to the caller. For example, interindividual variation in the peak frequency, maximum frequency, duration, energy, bandwidth and minimum frequency was found in the contact calls of spectacled parrotlets (Wanker & Fischer 2001). Importantly, individuals within a particular social class shared the same call structure and preferentially responded to calls made by individuals within the same social class (i.e. adults discriminated their mate's call, sub-adults responded to their sibling's call; Wanker et al. 1998). Spectacled parrotlets also discriminate between the contact calls of a family member versus a non-family member and use different contact calls for different social companions (e.g. mate, offspring; Wanker et al. 2005).

It has been suggested that this form of vocal categorization occurs through socialization, with individuals of a particular social class with convergence upon the same call structure with increasing socialization (Brown & Farabaugh 1997). By this process, individuals which are either strongly bonded, such as monogamous pairs, or siblings or parents to their offspring spend a long time in proximity and rapidly converge on the same call structure (vocal imitation). For example, in budgerigars, pair-bonded individuals converge on the same contact call within two weeks of their initial pairing (Hile et al. 2000). Similar examples of vocal sharing occur, with the warble vocalizations within groups of Australian magpies where magpies in the same group shared more warble syllables than magpies in different groups (Brown et al. 1988), the non-territorial song of American crows (Brown 1985) and the contact calls of budgerigars (Farabaugh et al. 1994).

Although we did not explicitly record whether the partners in our rook colony coordinated their actions, our casual observations of the pairs (now 4 + years old) have recorded many examples of motor imitation (figure 1.9). One striking example is the bowing and tail-fanning display in which one rook (usually the male) bows their head while loudly cawing (Coombs 1978). After bowing, their tail becomes raised and is then fanned out, with the wings kept close to the body. The rook then slowly raises its head and repeats this pattern, with renewed cawing vocalizations. Interestingly, paired individuals either alternate which element of the display they produce (usually if facing one another while greeting) or produce the elements in concert if directing the display towards a rival or a predator. It has been suggested that such a display may function in reinforcing the bond within the pair if they come together after being separated or it may function as a display of the bond for others in the social group (Armstrong 1965; Wickler 1976; Zahavi 1976; Wachtmeister 2001).

1.7 A reassessment of social complexity

What does this new data on rooks tell us about social complexity and its relationship to the evolution of the avian brain? Perhaps the concept of social complexity as proposed by the traditional SBH needs to be reassessed, at least for birds. Even Dunbar himself suggested that 'the SBH implies that constraints on group size arise from the information-processing capacity of the primate brain, and that the neocortex plays a role in this. However, even this proposal is open to several interpretations as to *how the relationship is mediated*'(Dunbar 1998, p. 184, our italics). Dunbar (1998) suggested that the constraint on group size could be mediated by the ability to recognize individuals and the unique pattern of their behaviour, the ability to remember who is in a relationship with whom, the ability to manipulate this information (e.g.

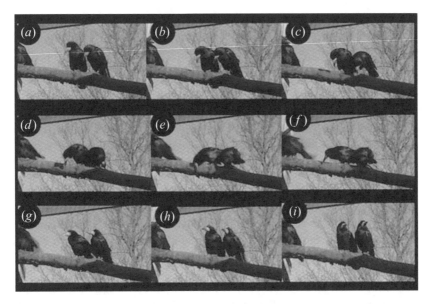

Fig. 1.9 Still frames (*a–i*) from a short film clip of one rook pair synchronizing or co-ordinating their behaviour. Frames (*a–c*), bowing; Frames (*d–f*), bill-wiping; and Frames (*g–i*), head-turning.

in managing relationships or using social information in a deceptive manner) or the ability to recognize and respond appropriately to others' emotional and mental states. In assessing the evidence for primates, Dunbar (1998) stated that the only ability which appeared to explain the relationship between brain and social complexity was the ability to manage social information. We would concur with this assessment, and expand the suggestion to include birds in long-term monogamous relationships.

In long-term monogamous birds, there may be little requirement to remember the individual characteristics of hundreds of individuals, even when forming large foraging flocks or roosts. Rather, keeping track of the accumulating, subtle behavioural characteristics of a bonded partner over the course of a relationship requires a different kind of processing: a form of relationship intelligence, which enables them to accurately read the social signals of their partner, respond appropriately to them, thereby predicting their behaviour and hence resulting in the stability of a successful partnership with mutual benefits for both parties. This suggestion does not eliminate processing social information altogether, as monogamous pairs do not live in a social vacuum (as suggested by the rook data presented earlier). On the contrary, it is likely that 'relationship intelligence' is a response to environmental complexity, and living in a social environment may provide additional challenges (such as competition over resources and nest sites) to which the maintenance of a strong pair bond throughout the year provides a cooperative solution. Similarly, ecological pressures may favour the evolution of this type of social intelligence in long-term monogamous birds.

This form of social intelligence has not been readily addressed in social primates, or other social mammals for that matter, largely because most adult primates do not form the same strong attachments to one individual (except monogamous mammals). Future studies need to address whether monogamous birds, such as rooks, really are 'in tune' with their partner when compared with other members of their social group as we suggest, and whether this requires cognitive abilities which are not found in polygamous species.

1.8 Conclusions

Although rooks (and possibly other large-brained birds) may have evolved similar socio-cognitive abilities to primates, such forms of social knowledge appear to be used primarily within the context of the pair bond, rather than applied to a larger social network, such as found in primates. Long-term monogamy depends on different forms of social information processing compared with polygyny (the most common mammalian mating system). For example, recognizing the subtle social signals produced by a partner and using such information to predict their future behaviour suggests different social skills than remembering who did what to whom. Indeed, long-term pair-bonded species, including those which form cooperative breeding groups, appear to have the largest brains within birds. There are differences between long-term monogamous species, in both brain size and the complexity of their partnerships, something which is highlighted by the social relationships of young rooks. The question of whether these partnerships are cognitively sophisticated, particularly whether pairs have an advantage in behaviour-reading (especially when their partner is the one providing the social cues), remains to be tested.

The importance of relationship intelligence in pair bonding is supported by the fact that the first and last authors are married, and were still together by the end of writing. The original research described in this paper was supported by grants from the BBSRC, Royal Society and University of Cambridge. Nathan Emery was supported by a Royal Society University Research Fellowship, Amanda Seed by a BBSRC studentship and an ASAB summer studentship, and Auguste von Bayern by a BBSRC studentship, the German Academic Exchange Service (DAAD), Cambridge European Trust and the Balfour Fund. Many thanks to Selvino de Kort for the help in hand raising and collecting some of the rook social behaviour data, and Richard Broughton for collecting data on avian social and mating systems. We also thank Kurt Kotrschal for useful discussion of geese sociality. All research conformed to UK Home Office and University of Cambridge regulations governing animal research.

References

Armstrong, E. A. 1965 *Bird display and behaviour*. New York: Dover Publications Inc.

Aureli, F., Cozzolino, R., Cordischi, C. & Scucchi, S. 1992 Kin-oriented redirection among Japanese macaques: an expression of a revenge system? *Anim. Behav.* **44**, 283–291. (doi:10.1016/0003-3472 (92)90034-7)

Aureli, F., Cords, M. & van Schaik, C. P. 2002 Conflict resolution following aggression in gregarious animals: a predictive framework. *Anim. Behav.* **64**, 325–343. (doi:10.006/anbe.2002.3071)

Baglione, V., Canestrari, D., Marcos, J. M., Greisser, M. & Ekman, J. 2002a History, environment and social behaviour: experimentally induced cooperative breeding in the carrion crow. *Proc. R. Soc. B* **296**, 1247–1251. (doi:10.1098/rspb.2002.2017)

Baglione, V., Marcos, J. M. & Canestrari, D. 2002b Cooperatively breeding groups of carrion crow, *Corvus corone corone* in northern Spain. *Auk* **119**, 790–799. (doi:10.1642/0004-8038(2002)119[0790: CBGOCC]2.0.CO;2)

Barnea, A. & Nottebohm, F. 1994 Seasonal recruitment of hippocampal neurons in adult free-ranging black-capped chickadee. *Proc. Natl Acad. Sci. USA* **91**, 11 217–11 221. (doi:10.1073/pnas.91.23. 11217)

Barnea, A., Mishal, A. & Nottebohm, F. 2006 Social and spatial regimes for new neurons in two regions of the adult brain: an anatomical representation of time? *Behav. Brain Res.* **167**, 63–74. (do:10.1016/j.bbr.2005.08.018)

Barton, R. A. 1996 Neocortex size and behavioural ecology in primates. *Proc. R. Soc. B* **263**, 173–177. (doi:10.1098/rspb.1996.0028)

Barton, R. A. & Dunbar, R. I. M. 1997 Evolution of the social brain. In *Machiavellian intelligence II* (eds A. Whiten & R. W. Byrne), pp. 240–263. Cambridge, UK: Cambridge University Press.

Beauchamp, G. & Fernandez-Juricic, E. 2004 Is there a relationship between forebrain size and group size in birds? *Evol. Ecol. Res.* **6**, 833–842.

Bennett, P. M. & Owens, I. P. F. 2002 *Evolutionary ecology of birds: life-history, mating system and extinction.* Oxford, UK: Oxford University Press.

Bharati, L. S. & Goodson, J. L. 2006 Fos responses of dopamine neurons to sociosexual stimuli in male zebra finches. *Neuroscience* **143**, 661–670. (doi:10.1016/j.neuro-science.2006.08.046)

Brown, E. D. 1985 Social relationship as a variable affecting responses to mobbing and alarm calls of common crows (*Corvus brachyrhynchos*). *Zeitschrift fur Tierpsychologie* **70**, 45–52.

Brown, E. D. & Farabaugh, S. M. 1997 What birds with complex social relationships can tell us about vocal learning: vocal sharing in avian groups. In *Social influences on vocal development* (eds C. T. Snowdon & M. Hausberger), pp. 98–127. Cambridge, UK: Cambridge University Press.

Brown, E. D., Farabaugh, S. M. & Veltman, C. J. 1988 Song sharing in a group-living songbird, the Australian magpie, *Gymnorhina tibcen*. I. Vocal sharing within and among groups. *Behaviour* **104**, 1–28.

Burish, M. J., Kueh, H. Y. & Wang, S. S.-H. 2004 Brain architecture and social complexity in modern and ancient birds. *Brain Behav. Evol.* **63**, 107–124. (doi:10.1159/000075674)

Byrne, R. W. & Whiten, A. (eds) 1988 *Machiavellian intelligence: social expertise and the evolution of intellect in monkeys, apes and humans.* Oxford, UK: Clarendon Press.

Carmen, W. J. 2004 Non-cooperative breeding in the California scrub-jay. *Stud. Avian Biol.*, 28.

Clayton, N. S. & Krebs, J. R. 1994 Hippocampal growth and attrition in birds affected by experience. *Proc. Natl Acad. Sci. USA* **91**, 7410–7414. (doi:10.1073/pnas.91.16.7410)

Clayton, N. S., Reboreda, J. C. & Kacelnik, A. 1997 Seasonal changes of hippocampal volume in parasitic cowbirds. *Behav. Process.* **41**, 237–243. (doi:10.1016/S0376-6357(97)00050-8)

Clayton, N. S., Dally, J. M. & Emery, N. J. 2007 Social cognition by food-caching corvids. The western scrub-jay as a natural psychologist. *Phil. Trans. R. Soc. B* **362**, 507–522. (doi:10.1098/rstb.2006.1992)

Connor, R. C. 2007 Dolphin social intelligence: complex alliance relationships in bottlenose dolphins and a consideration of selective environments for extreme brain size evolution in mammals. *Phil. Trans. R. Soc. B* **362**, 587–602. (doi:10.1098/rstb.2006.1997)

Coombs, C. F. G. 1960 Observations on the rook, *Corvus frugilegus*, in southwest Cornwall. *Ibis* **102**, 394–419.

Coombs, C. F. G. 1978 *The crows.* London, UK: Batsford.

Cords, M. 1997 Friendships, alliances, reciprocity and repair. In *Machiavellian Intelligence II: extensions and evaluations* (eds A. Whiten & R. W. Byrne), pp. 24–49. Cambridge, UK: Cambridge University Press.

Cramp, S. 1977 *Handbook of the birds of Europe, the Middle East and North Africa. The birds of the Western Palearctic. Ostrich to ducks,* vol. I. Oxford, UK: Oxford University Press.

Cramp, S. & Perrins, C. 1994 *Handbook of the birds of Europe, the Middle East and North Africa. The birds of the Western Palearctic. Crows to finches,* vol. VIII. Oxford, UK: Oxford University Press.

Curry, R. L., Towsend Peterson, A. & Langen, T. A. 2002 Western Scrub-Jay. In *The birds of North America, no. 712* (eds A. Poole & F. Gill), pp. 1–36. Philadelphia, PA: The Birds of North America, Inc.

de Kort, S. R., Emery, N. J. & Clayton, N. S. 2003 Food offering in jackdaws (*Corvus monedula*). *Naturwissenschaften* **90**, 238–240.

de Kort, S. R., Emery, N. J. & Clayton, N. J. 2006 Food sharing in jackdaws, *Corvus monedula*: what, why and with whom? *Anim. Behav.* **72**, 297–304. (doi:10.1016/j.anbe-hav.2005.10.016)

de Waal, F. B. M. 1982 *Chimpanzee politics.* Baltimore, MD: John Hopkins University Press.

de Waal, F. B. M. & Aureli, F. 1996 Consolation, reconcilation, and a possible cognitive difference between macaques and chimpanzees. In *Reaching into thought: the minds of the great apes* (eds A. E. Russon, K. A. Bard & S. T. Parker), pp. 80–110. Cambridge, UK: Cambrisge University Press.

de Waal, F. B. M. & Lutrell, L. M. 1988 Mechanisms of social reciprocity in three primate species: symmetrical relationship characteristics or cognition? *Ethol. Sociobiol.* **9**, 101–118. (doi:10.1016/0162-3095(88)90016-7)

de Waal, F. B. M. & Tyack, P. L. (eds) 2003 *Animal social complexity: intelligence, culture and individualised societies.* Cambridge, MA: Harvard University Press.

de Waal, F. B. M. & Yoshihara, D. 1983 Reconcilation and redirected affection in rhesus monkeys. *Behaviour* **85**, 224–241.

Das, M. 2000 Conflict management via third-Parties: post-conflict affiliation of the aggressor. In *Natural conflict resolution* (eds F. Aureli & F. B. M. de Waal). Berkeley, CA: University of California Press.

Dugatkin, L. A. 1997 *Cooperation among animals.* New York: Oxford University Press.

Dunbar, R. I. M. 1992 Neocortex size as a constraint on group size in primates. *J. Hum. Evol.* **20**, 469–493. (doi:10.1016/0047-2484(92)90081-J)

Dunbar, R. I. M. 1998 The social brain hypothesis. *Evol. Anthropol.* **6**, 178–190. (doi:10.1002/(SICI)1520-6505(1998)6:5<178::AID-EVAN5>3.0.CO;2-8)

Dunbar, R. I. M. & Bever, J. 1998 Neocortex size determines group size in insectivores and carnivores. *Ethology* **104**, 695–708.

Emery, N. J. 2004 Are corvids 'feathered apes'? Cognitive evolution in crows, jays, rooks and jackdaws. In *Comparative analysis of minds* (ed. S. Watanabe), pp. 181–213. Tokyo, Japan: Keio University Press.

Emery, N. J. 2006 Cognitive ornithology: the evolution of avian intelligence. *Phil. Trans. R. Soc. B* **361**, 23–43. (doi:10.1098/rstb.2005.1736)

Emery, N. J. & Clayton, N. S. 2004 The mentality of crows: convergent evolution of intelligence in corvids and apes. *Science* **306**, 1903–1907. (doi:10.1126/science.1098410)

Farabaugh, S. M., Linzenbold, A. & Dooling, R. J. 1994 Vocal plasticity in budgerigars *(Melopsittacus undulatus)*: evidence for social factors in the learning of contact calls. *J. Comp. Psychol.* **108**, 81–92. (doi:10.1037/0735-7036.108.1.81)

Fischer, H. 1965 Das Triumphgeschrei der Graugans *(Anser anser)*. *Zeitschrift fur Tierpsychologie* **22**, 247–304.

Frigerio, D., Weiss, B. M. & Kotrschal, K. 2001 Spatial proximity among adult siblings in greylag geese *(Anser anser)*: evidence for female bonding? *Acta Ethologica* **3**, 121–125. (doi:10.1007/s102110000028)

Frigerio, D., Weiss, B. M., Dittami, J. & Kotrschal, K. 2003 Social allies modulate corticosterone excretion and increase success in agonistic interactions in juvenile hand-raised greylag geese *(Anser anser)*. *Can. J. Zool.* **81**, 1746–1754. (doi:10.1139/z03-149)

Godfrey-Smith, P. 1996 *Complexity and the function of mind in nature.* Cambridge, UK: Cambridge University Press.

Goodson, J. L. 2005 The vertebrate social behavior network: evolutionary themes and variations. *Horm. Behav.* **48**, 11–22. (doi:10.1016/j.yhbeh.2005.02.003)

Goodson, J. L. & Wang, Y. 2006 Valence-sensitive neurons exhibit divergent functional profiles in gregarious and asocial species. *Proc. Natl Acad. Sci. USA* **103**, 17 013–17 017. (doi:10.1073/pnas.0606278103)

Goodson, J. L., Evans, A. K. & Wang, Y. 2006 Neuropeptide binding reflects convergent and divergent evolution in species-typical group sizes. *Horm. Behav.* **50**, 223–236. (doi:10.1016/j.yhbeh.2006.03.005)

Goodwin, D. 1986 *Crows of the world.* London, UK: British Museum (Natural History) Press.

Harcourt, A. H. 1992 Coalitions and alliances: are primates more complex than non-primates? In *Coalitions and alliances in humans and other animals* (eds A. H. Harcourt & F. B. M. de Waal), pp. 445–471. Oxford, UK: Oxford University Press.

Harrison, C. J. O. 1967 Allopreening as agonistic behaviour. *Behaviour* **24**, 161–209.

Heinrich, B. 1990 *Ravens in winter.* London, UK: Barrie & Jenkins.

Heinrich, B. 1999 *Mind of the raven*. New York, NY: Harper Collins.

Hemelrijk, C. 1990 Models of, and tests for, reciprocity, unidirectionality and other social interaction patterns at a group level. *Anim. Behav.* **39**, 1013–1029. (doi:10.1016/S0003-3472(05)80775-4)

Hemelrijk, C. 1994 Support for being groomed in long-tailed macaques, *Macaca fascicularis*. *Anim. Behav.* **48**, 479–481. (doi:10.1006/anbe.1994.1264)

Hemelrijk, C. & Ek, A. 1991 Reciprocity and interchange of grooming and' support' in captive chimpanzees. *Anim. Behav.* **41**,923–935. (doi:10.1016/S0003-3472(05) 80630-X)

Henderson, I. G. & Hart, P. J. B. 1993 Reproductive success in jackdaws, *Corvus monedula*, provisioning as a constraint on the mating system. *Ornis Scand.* **24**, 142–148.

Henderson, I. G., Hart, P. J. B. & Burke, T. 2000 Strict monogamy in a semi-colonial passerine: the jackdaw *Corvus monedula*. *J. Avian Biol.* **31**, 177–182. (doi:10.034/j.1600-048X.2000.310209.x)

Hile, A. G., Plummer, T. K. & Striedter, G. F. 2000 Male vocal imitation produces call convergence during pair bonding in budgerigars, *Melopsittacus undulatus*. *Anim. Behav.* **59**,1209–1218. (doi:10.1006/anbe.1999.1438)

Holekamp, K. E., Sakai, S. T. & Lundrigan, B. L. 2007 Social intelligence in the spotted hyena *(Crocuta crocuta)*. *Phil. Trans. R. Soc. B* **362**, 523–528.(doi:10.1098/rstb.2006.1993)

Humphrey, N. K. 1976 The social function of intellect. In *Growing points in ethology* (eds P. P. G. Bateson & R. A. Hinde), pp. 303–317. Cambridge, UK: Cambridge University Press.

Insel, T. R., Wang, Z. X. & Ferris, C. F. 1994 Patterns of brain vasopressin receptor distribution associated with social organization in microtine rodents. *J. Neurosci.* **14**, 5381–5392.

Iwaniuk, A. N. & Arnold, K. E. 2004 Is cooperative breeding associated with bigger brains? A comparative test in the corvida (Passeriformes). *Ethology* **110**, 203–220. (doi:10.1111/j.1439-0310.2003. 00957.x)

Iwaniuk, A. N. & Nelson, J. E. 2003 Developmental differences are correlated with relative brain size in birds: a comparative analysis. *Can. J. Zool.* **81**, 1913–1928. (doi:10.1139/z03-190)

Jolly, A. 1966 Lemur social behavior and primate intelligence. *Science* **153**, 501–507 (doi:10.1126/science.153.3735.501)

Juniper, T. & Parr, M. 1998 *Parrots: a guide to parrots of the world*. New Haven, CT: Yale University Press.

Katzir, G. 1983 Relationships between social structure and response to novelty in captive jackdaws, *Corvus monedula*. II. Response to novel palatable foods. *Behaviour* **83**, 183–208.

Koski, S. E. & Sterck, E. H. M. 2007 Triadic postconflict affiliation in captive chimpanzees: does consolation console? *Anim. Behav.* **73**, 133–142. (doi:10.1016/j.anbehav.2006.04.009)

Kummer, H. 1978 On the value of social relationships to nonhuman primates: a heuristic scheme. *Soc. Sci. Inf.* **17**, 687–705.

Lack, D. 1968 *Ecological adaptations for breeding in birds*. London, UK: Methuen.

Lamprecht, J. 1991 Factors influencing leadership: a study of goose families (*Anser indicus*). *Ethology* **89**, 265–274.

Lefebvre, L., Whittle, P., Lascaris, E. & Finkelstein, A. 1997 Feeding innovations and forebrain size in birds. *Anim. Behav.* **53**, 549–560. (doi:10.1006/anbe.1996.0330)

Lefebvre, L., Nicolakakis, N. & Boire, D. 2002 Tools and brains in birds. *Behaviour* **139**, 939–973. (doi:10,1163/156853902320387918)

Lipkind, D., Nottebohm, F., Rado, R. & Barnea, A. 2002 Social change affects the survival of new neurons in the forebrain of adult songbirds. *Behav. Brain Res.* **133**, 31–43. (doi:10.1016/S0166-4328(01) 00416-8)

Lorenz, K. 1970 Contributions to the study of the ethology of social *Corvidae* (1931). In *Studies in animal and human behaviour*, pp. 1–56. London, UK: Methuen & Co Ltd.

Lorenz, K. 1991 *Here I am—where are you? The behaviour of the greylag goose*. London, UK: Harper Collins.

Marino, L. 2002 Convergence of complex cognitive abilities in cetaceans and primates. *Brain Behav. Evol.* **59**, 21–32. (doi:10.1159/000063731)

Marler, P. 1996 Social cognition: are primates smarter than birds? In *Current ornithology* (eds V. Nolan & E. D. Ketterson), pp. 1–32. New York, NY: Plenum Press.

Marshall, A. J. & Coombs, C. F. J. 1957 The interaction of environmental, internal and behavioural factors in the rook, *Corvus frugilegus*. *Proc. Zool. Soc.* **128**, 545–589.

McComb, K. 2001 Matriarchs as repositories of social knowledge in African elephants. *Science* **292**, 491–494.

McGowan, K. J. & Woolfenden, G. E. 1989 A sentinel system in the Florida scrub jay. *Anim. Behav.* **37**, 1000–1006. (doi:10.1016/0003-3472(89)90144-9)

Noe, R. & Hammerstein, R. 1995 Biological markets. *Trends Ecol. Evol.* **10**, 336–339.

Nottebohm, F. 1981 A brain for all seasons: cyclical anatomical changes in song control nuclei of the canary brain. *Science* **214**, 1368–1370. (doi:10.1126/science.7313697)

Patterson, I. J. & Grace, E. S. 1984 Recruitment of young rooks, *Corvus frugilegus*, into breeding populations. *J. Appl. Ecol.* **53**, 559–572. Perrins, C. 2003 *The new encyclopedia of birds*. Oxford, UK: Oxford University Press.

Potts, R. 2004 Paleoenvironmental basis of cognitive evolution in great apes. *Am. J. Primatol.* **62**, 209–228. (doi:10.1002/ajp.20016)

Reboreda, J. C., Clayton, N. S. & Kacelnik, A. 1996 Species and sex differences in hippocampus size between parasitic and non-parasitic cowbirds. *NeuroReport* **7**, 505–508. (doi:10.1097/00001756-199601310-00031)

Reichard, U. H. 2003 Monogamy: past and present. In *Monogamy: mating strategies and partnerships in birds, humans and other mammals* (eds U. H. Reichard & C. Boesch), pp. 3–25. Cambridge, UK: Cambridge University Press.

Richards, P. R. 1976 Pair formation and pair bond in captive rooks. *Bird Study* **23**, 207–212.

Roell, A. 1978 Social behaviour of the jackdaw, *Corvus monedula*, in relation to its niche. *Behaviour* **64**, 1–124.

Røskaft, E. 1980 Reactions of rooks, *Corvus frugilegus*, during the breeding season to intrusions by other birds and mammals. *Fauna norv. Ser. C. Cinclus* **3**, 56–59.

Røskaft, E. 1981 The daily activity pattern of the rook, *Corvus frugilegus*, during the breeding season. *Fauna norv. Ser. C. Cinclus* **4**, 76–81.

Røskaft, E. 1983 Male promiscuity and female adultery by the rook *Corvus frugilegus*. *Ornis Scand.* **14**, 175–179.

Scheiber, I. B. R., Weiss, B. M., Frigerio, D. & Kotrschal, K. 2005 Active and passive social support in families of greylag geese (*Anser anser*). *Behaviour* **142**, 1535–1557. (doi:10.1163/156853905774831873)

Seed, A. M., Clayton, N. S. & Emery, N. J. 2007. Post-conflict third-party affiliation in rooks *Corvus frugilegus*. *Curr. Biol.* **17**, 152–158

Seyfarth, R. M. & Cheney, D. L. 1984 Grooming, alliances and reciprocal altruism in vervet monkeys. *Nature* **308**, 541–543. (doi:10.1038/308541a0)

Shultz, S. & Dunbar, R. I. M. 2006 Both social and ecological factors predict ungulate brain size. *Proc. R. Soc. B* **273**, 207–215. (doi:10.1098/rspb.2005.3283)

Silk, J. 2002 Using the 'F'-word in primatology. *Behaviour* **139**, 421–446. (doi:10.1163/156853902760102735)

Silk, J. B. 2007 The adaptive value of sociality in mammalian groups. *Phil. Trans. R. Soc. B* **362**, 539–559. (doi:10.1098/rstb.2006.1994)

Sterelny, K. 2003 *Thought in a hostile world*. New York, NY: Blackwell.

Stevens, J.R. & Hauser, M. D.2004 Why be nice? Psychological constraints on the evolution of coopera-tion. *Trends Cogn. Sci.* **8**, 60–65. (doi:10.1016/j.tics.2003.12.003)

van Schaik, C. P. & Aureli, F. 2000 The natural history of valuable relationships in primates. In *Natural conflict resolution* (eds F. Aureli & F. B. M. de Waal), pp. 307–333. Berkeley, CA: University of California Press.

van Schaik, C. P. & Deaner, R. O. 2003 Life history and cognitive evolution in primates. In *Animal social complexity* (eds F. B. M. de Waal & P. L. Tyack), pp. 5–25. Cambridge, MA: Harvard University Press.

von Bayern, A. M. P., de Kort, S. R., Clayton, N. S. & Emery, N. J. 2007 The role of food-and object-sharing in the development of social bonds in juvenile jackdaws (*Corvus monedula)*. *Behaviour* **144**, 711–733.

Voronov, L. N., Bogoslovskaya, L. G. & Markova, E. G. 1994 A comparative study of the morphology of forebrain in corvidae in view of their trophic specialization. *Zool. Z* **73**, 82–96.

Wachtmeister, C. A. 2001 Display in monogamous pairs: a review of empirical data and evolutionary explanations. *Anim. Behav.* **61**, 861–868. (doi:10.1006/anbe.2001.1684)

Wanker, R. & Fischer, J. 2001 Intra-and inter-individual variation in the contact calls of spectacled parrotlets (*Forpus conspicillatus*). *Behaviour* **138**, 709–726. (doi:10.1163/156853901752233361)

Wanker, R., Apcin, J., Jennerjahn, B. & Waibel, B. 1998 Discrimination of different social companions in spectacled parrotlets (*Forpus conspicillatus*): evidence for individual vocal recognition. *Behav. Ecol. Sociobiol.* **43**, 197–202. (doi:10.1007/s002650050481)

Wanker, R., Sugama, Y. & Prinage, S. 2005 Vocal labelling of family members in spectacled parrotlets, *Forpus conspicillatus*. *Anim. Behav.* **70**, 111–118. (doi:10.1016/j.anbe-hav.2004.09.022)

Wechsler, B. 1989 Measuring relationships in jackdaws. *Ethology* **80**, 307–317.

Whiten, A. & Byrne, R. W. 1997 *Machiavellian intelligence II: extensions and evaluations*. Cambridge, UK: Cambridge University Press.

Wickler, W. 1976 The ethological analysis of attachment: sociometric, motivational and sociophysiological aspects. *Zeitschrift für Tierpsycholgie* **42**, 12–28.

Winkler, H., Christie, D. A. & Nurney, D. 1995 *Woodpeckers: an identification guide to the woodpeckers of the world*. Boston, MA: Houghton Mifflin.

Woolfenden, G. E. & Fitzpatrick, J. W. 1984 *The Florida scrub jay*. Princeton, NJ: Princeton University Press.

Young, L. J., Lim, M. M., Gingrich, B. & Insel, T. R. 2001 Cellular mechanisms of social attachment. *Horm. Behav.* **40**, 133–138. (doi:10.1006/hbeh.2001.1691)

Zahavi, A. 1976 The testing of a bond. *Anim. Behav.* **25**, 246–247. (doi:10.1016/0003-3472(77)90089-6)

2

Social cognition by food-caching corvids.
The western scrub-jay as a natural psychologist

Nicola S. Clayton, Joanna M. Dally and Nathan J. Emery

Food-caching corvids hide food, but such caches are susceptible to pilfering by other individuals. Consequently, the birds use several counter strategies to protect their caches from theft, e.g. hiding most of them out of sight. When observed by potential pilferers at the time of caching, experienced jays that have been thieves themselves, take further protective action. Once the potential pilferers have left, they move caches those birds have seen, re-hiding them in new places. Naive birds that had no thieving experience do not do so. By focusing on the counter strategies of the cacher when previously observed by a potential pilferer, these results raise the intriguing possibility that re-caching is based on a form of mental attribution, namely the simulation of another bird's viewpoint. Furthermore, the jays also keep track of the observer which was watching when they cached and take protective action accordingly, thus suggesting that they may also be aware of others' knowledge states.

Keywords: experience projection; food caching birds; mental attribution; social intelligence; theory-of-mind; western scrub-jay

2.1 Introduction

A number of animals live in social groups, and indeed most primates do so. But according to the *social function of intellect* hypothesis (Humphrey 1976*a*), it is the ability to survive the political dynamics of a complex social world that has been the primary driving force shaping primate intelligence. Humphrey (1976*b*, p. 313) likened the dynamics of social life to a game of chess, but one in which the players are not purely selfish because 'the selfishness of social animals is tempered by sympathy...a tendency on the part of one's social partner to identify himself with the other and so make the other's goals to some extent his own'. This hypothesis about social intelligence was also described independently by Jolly (1966, p. 506), who pointed out that 'primate social life provided the evolutionary context of primate intelligence'.

Field observations of groups of lemurs (*Lemur catta*), gorillas (*Gorilla gorilla gorilla*) and macaques *(Macaca mulatta)* led both Humphrey and Jolly to suggest that the physical problems that primates encounter are not very different from those of other animals; what makes primates special is the complexity of their social lives. One critical aspect of this social complexity or 'primate politics' is the ability to keep track of who did what to you, where and when, and to use this information to predict the actions and intentions of other individuals in your social network (Humphrey 1980), as well as understanding how these relationships change over time (Barrett *et al.* 2003). Consequently, the need for effective competition and cooperation with conspecifics may have provided the main selective advantage for the evolution of primate intelligence (Byrne & Whiten 1988; Dunbar 1998). Indeed, Humphrey (1980) argued that self-consciousness evolved to enable primates to attribute mental states to other conspecifics and thereby anticipate the actions of those individuals, and that mental attribution is essential for coping with the trials and tribulations of complex social life. This in turn sets the stage for the development of Machiavellian intelligence, the ability to manipulate and deceive competitors (Byrne & Whiten 1988; Whiten & Byrne 1997).

In an extension of the social intelligence hypothesis, Dunbar (1992) suggested that the complexities of primate social life also led to a dramatic expansion of the neocortex to support this cognitive demand. Evidence in support of this *social brain* hypothesis comes from the finding that the 'neocortex ratio' (i.e. the volume of the neocortex divided by the volume of the rest of the brain) correlates positively with average group size in the primate genera. Dunbar (1992, 1998) argued that group size is a good indicator of social complexity in primates because the larger the group the more information conspecifics within that group have to remember in order to keep track of the dynamics of their social world.

Furthermore, there is an exponential increase in the amount of possible interactions and thus the information to be processed when individuals experience polyadic encounters than when individuals only interact with one other individual. Owing to the increased complexity of social networks in larger groups, Dunbar (1992) argued that the relative size of the neocortex served as a constraint on the evolution of group size. Subsequent work has established that relative neocortex size correlates with at least three other indices of sociality, namely the size of the grooming clique (Kudo & Dunbar 2001), the amount of social play (Lewis 2000) and the frequency of tactical deception (Byrne & Corp 2004).

Although this increase in intelligence in primates was thought to have evolved with the social domain, it is considered to have led to conceptual and inferential processes that transcend a purely social setting. Indeed, Humphrey (1976b, p. 316) has argued that 'styles of thinking which are primarily suited to social problem solving colour the behaviour of man and other primates even towards the inanimate world'. For example, many primates live in social groups that involve dominance hierarchies between group members and it is argued that primates are capable of observing dyadic relations and inferring complete dominance hierarchies from these observations.

To do so, the animals must be capable of making transitive inferences, using information about known dyadic relationships and applying the rule to novel pairs of relationships. For example, if A is known to be dominant over B and B is known to be dominant over C, then it follows that A must also be dominant over C. Primates can solve abstract transitive inference tests using symbols. Individuals are first trained on an ordered set of various pairwise comparisons (e.g. A+B–, B+C–, etc.). On test, they must transfer information about the dyadic relationships to novel pairs (e.g. B versus D) to solve the task (McGonigle & Chalmers 1977; Treichler & van Tilburg 1996). What is common to these various transfer tasks is the ability to abstract general rules or relationships that transcend the basic learning experience.

Although the social intelligence hypothesis was developed for primates, it is based on general evolutionary principles and consequently it should apply to other groups of large brained animals that face similar ecological challenges (Marino 2002; Emery & Clayton 2004a). Some support for this argument comes from the finding that relative neocortex size correlates with group size in other mammalian groups (e.g. Barton & Dunbar 1997). In principle, this relationship could also apply to more phylogenetically diverse groups of animals provided they possess a neural structure functionally analogous to the mammalian six-layered neocortex, such as the nidopallium of birds, the so-called avian prefrontal cortex (Avian Brain Consortium 2005; Emery & Clayton 2005).

As Emery *et al.* (2006) discuss, the relationship between brain size and social complexity is far from clear in birds (e.g. Burish *et al.* 2004, cf. Beauchamp & Fernández-Juricic 2004;

Iwaniuk & Arnold 2004), perhaps because not all species that live in large groups form complex social networks and some species that are semi-territorial, such as the western scrub-jay (*Aphelocoma californica*), are thought to have quite complex social cognition (e.g. Emery & Clayton 2001; Dally *et al.* 2006*b*). Furthermore, the size and composition of the social group often changes seasonally, and may differ between individuals within a species. In western scrub-jays, for example, the breeding adults form selective pairbonds, and these pairs are territorial, but there are also variable numbers of floaters and flocked non-breeders. As Curry *et al.* (2002, p. 18) point out 'frequent interactions with neighbouring territory holders and prolonged associations with some floaters may result in more complicated social networks than appears superficially'.

A further prediction arising from the social intelligence hypothesis is that animals which show high degrees of general intelligence, however phylogenetically diverse from primates, should also be socially astute. In this article, we shall focus on the cognitive capacities of corvids and argue that this family of food-caching birds provides a compelling case for studying social cognition owing to their high degree of general intelligence and their relatively large brains with expanded avian prefrontal cortex (nidopallium). In order to do so, we shall begin with a discussion of the general biology of corvids, and what features they share in common with primates.

2.2 Corvid biology and brain

The corvids are a family of songbirds that includes not only the black plumaged crows, ravens and rooks, but also the more brightly and variably coloured jays, magpies and nutcrackers. Like primates, many corvids have complex social lives and are among the most social groups of birds (Goodwin 1986). For example, in the cooperatively breeding Florida scrub-jay (*Aphelocoma coerulescens*), several closely related family members share the responsibility of raising the young with the parents (Woolfenden 1975; Woolfenden & Fitzpatrick 1984, 1996). A closely related species, the western scrub-jay, typically shows unassisted pair-breeding, although populations in southern Mexico breed cooperatively just as the Florida scrub-jays do (Burt & Peterson 1993; Curry *et al.* 2002). The breeding behaviour of carrion crows (*Corvus corone*) is also flexible, as a single population may comprise both unassisted pair-breeders and cooperatively breeding birds (Richner 1990; Baglione *et al.* 2002).

Rooks and jackdaws are probably the most social among the corvids, congregating in large colonies during the breeding season (Goodwin 1976). Emery (2004) has argued that the social societies in which these birds live share several features in common with chimpanzees. As Emery *et al.* (in press) discuss, they live in a fission–fusion society, form long-term alliances with other members of their group, and understand 'third-party' relationships (i.e. those among other individuals), an ability that is thought to be one of the pinnacles of primate cognition (Tomasello & Call 1997). Another similarity between primates and corvids is that the young experience a long developmental period in which the juveniles associate with many non-relatives as well as kin, and this provides increased opportunities for learning from many different group members (Joffe 1997).

Like primates, and in common with most other groups of birds, the corvids are also highly visual. Brothers (1990, p. 29) argued that, in primates, the evolutionary switch to a diurnal lifestyle 'was probably accompanied by two developments: (i) a greater reliance on visual social communication and (ii) more complex social structures. That these two developments should go together is not surprising, given that vision permits a high degree of temporal sequencing and brevity of signals compared to olfaction.' These principles also apply to corvids, given that they are highly visual and diurnal, as well as having complex social lives.

Another commonality between corvids and primates is the relative size of their brains. As Emery *et al.* (2006) discuss in considerable detail, corvids have the largest brains for their body size of any family of birds, and the same relative size as that of apes (Emery & Clayton 2004*b*). Corvids also have the largest nidopallium (avian prefrontal cortex), relative to overall brain size, of any group of birds (Emery & Clayton 2004*b*), and this large expansion of the crow nidopallium mirrors the increase in size of the frontal cortex in the apes (Semendeferi *et al.* 2002). With these similarities between primates and corvids in mind, notably in their social lives and enlarged brain size, let us now turn to the question of corvid intelligence.

2.3 Corvid general intelligence

Laboratory tests of cognition also support the notion that corvids are highly intelligent. Like primates, they are particularly good at solving laboratory tasks that rely on the ability to abstract a general rule to solve the task and then transfer the learned rule to new tasks (Wilson *et al.* 1985; Mackintosh 1988). Indeed, this ability to solve transfer problems by abstracting general rules is what distinguishes rule learners from rote learners. In learning sets, for example, the animals are presented with a series of different discriminations to learn. Like primates, corvids are able to solve these learning set tasks by extracting the general rule such as win–stay, lose–shift rather than having to learn each new discrimination afresh, whereas pigeons cannot solve the transfers. Indeed, pigeons appear to be rote learners, solving the task eventually by learning each of the discriminations individually (reviewed by Mackintosh 1988). Recent work by Paz-y-Miño *et al.* (2004) suggests that one member of the corvid family, the pinyon jay (*Gymnorhinus cyanocephalus*), can solve transitive inference tasks in a social setting and use transitive inference to predict dominance. So this may reflect another similarity between primates and corvids in their cognitive capacities.

Another classic feature of intelligence is the ability to devise novel solutions to problems, and one of the most dramatic examples of this is the manufacture of special tools to acquire otherwise unobtainable foods (Beck 1980). Chimpanzees (*Pan troglodytes*) have been observed to manufacture a range of different tools that are used for specific purposes (Beck 1980), and different geographical populations of chimpanzees use different tools for different uses, suggesting that there may be cultural variations in tool use (Whiten *et al.*1999). However, great apes are not the only animals to display diversity and flexibility in tool use and tool manufacture. New Caledonian crows (*Corvus moneduloides*) also manufacture different types of tool that have different functions (Hunt 1996). Furthermore, crows from different geographical areas have different designs of tool (Hunt & Gray 2003).

In the laboratory, when presented with a variety of sticks of different lengths and food positioned in a tube such that a stick was required in order to reach the food, New Caledonian crows correctly chose the appropriate length and diameter of stick to push out the piece of food (Chappell & Kacelnik 2002, 2004). Even more intriguingly, Weir *et al.* (2002) have shown that these crows can manipulate novel man-made objects to solve a problem. Two birds, Betty and Abel, were presented with the problem of reaching food in a bucket that was only accessible by using a hook to pull the bucket up. Unfortunately, Abel stole the bent wire and dropped it out of Betty's reach. Betty found a piece of straight wire that was lying on the floor, bent this wire into a hook and used it to lift up the bucket and reach the food. Betty proceeded to retrieve the food using the wire on 9 out of 10 test trials.

Evidence of tool use and manufacture suggests that animals can sometimes combine past experiences to produce novel solutions to problems. However, careful experimentation is required to establish whether the animal can flexibly exploit the tool in a way which suggests that they can understand and reason about the causal relations between the tool and the problem. One of the benchmark tests that has been used to test physical understanding is the trap-tube, which consists of a transparent horizontal tube with a trap along its length (Visalberghi & Trinca 1989). To solve the task, an animal must insert a tool into the tube and use it to push the piece of food out, without it falling into the trap from which it is no longer accessible. Both monkeys and apes can learn to solve this task, although typically only some of the individuals being tested do so, and they generally take somewhere between 60 and 100 trials to solve the task (capuchins, Visalberghi & Limongelli 1994; chimpanzees, Limongelli et al. 1995). However, this task can be solved in at least two ways: using a simple associative rule based on the position of the food in relation to the trap or by an understanding of how the task works. Previous studies have found no evidence that animals understand how the task works (Povinelli 2000). Indeed, Povinelli (2000, p. 7) concluded that 'chimpanzees do not represent abstract causal variables as explanations for why objects interact in the ways that they do'.

In a recent study by Seed et al. (2006), this classic design was modified to test a non-tool-using species of corvid, the rook (*Corvus frugilegus*). To do so, the experimenters inserted the tool into the tube, so it needed only to be pushed or pulled. A second trap-like structure was added to the tube, but one that would not trap the food, to test whether the birds could distinguish between a functional and non-functional trap. A variety of transfer tasks were used to determine what successful birds might have understood about the task's causal properties. For example, in one task, the non-functioning trap was bottomless, allowing food to fall through. In the visually distinct transfer test, the food could pass over the top. If the birds' solution was based simply on the arbitrary appearance of the task, they should have failed these transfers. Seven out of eight rooks rapidly solved the task and six of them the visually distinct transfer task. One bird transferred two additional transfer tasks that were impossible to solve using a simple associative rule based on the position of the food in relation to the traps, suggesting that this particular rook may have abstracted a general rule about the causally relevant features common to all four designs of the two-trap tube. Exactly what the rooks understand about physical cognition poses exciting questions for future research, including how other species, particularly primates, might perform on this modified version of the trap-tube.

In using tools to obtain otherwise inaccessible food, animals are clearly acting to fulfil a current need state. One feature of human intelligence is the ability to reminisce about the past (episodic memory) and plan for the future. In their *mental time travel* hypothesis, Suddendorf & Corballis (1997) have argued that mental time travel is unique to humans, and thus animals are incapable of mentally travelling backwards in time to recollect specific past events about what happened where and when or forwards to anticipate future needs. Tulving (2005, p. 47) has also endorsed this view: '… makes it possible for people to engage in a conscious activity, mental time travel, that is beyond the reach of living creatures who do not possess episodic memory. Mental time travel takes the form of remembering personally experienced and thought-about events, occasions, and situations that occurred in the past, together with imagining (pre-experiencing) personal happenings in the subjectively felt future'.

However, recent experiments on one species of corvid, the western scrub-jay, challenge the assumption that animals are incapable of episodic recall and planning for the long-term future.

Like most corvids, these birds cache food, i.e. they hide food items for future consumption, and rely on memory to recover their caches at a later date (see Shettleworth (1995) for a review). In a series of experiments, it has been shown that western scrub-jays recall specific past caching episodes by forming integrated memories of what they cached, and where and when they hid it (Clayton & Dickinson 1998; Clayton *et al.* 2003*c*), and who was watching when they did so (Dally *et al.* 2006*a*). As Clayton and colleagues have argued, this ability to remember the what-where-and-when of specific past caching episodes fulfils the behavioural criteria for episodic memory (Clayton *et al.* 2003*a*). Of course, in the absence of agreed behavioural markers of conscious experience in non-linguistic animals, the question of whether the jays travel back in their own mind's eye to reminisce about the past remains an open one (Clayton *et al.* 2003*b*; Suddendorf & Busby 2003). There is a similar difficulty with assessing whether or not animals can travel forward in the mind's eye to think about the future. However, the fact that the jays can adjust their caching behaviour in anticipation of future needs (Emery & Clayton 2001; Clayton *et al.* 2005; Dally *et al.* 2006*a*) and independently from current needs (Raby *et al* 2007; Correia *et al* 2007) suggests that they do possess some elements of future planning.

The ability to remember the 'what-where-and-when' of a particular episode has yet to be demonstrated in non-human primates. In a foraging paradigm, Hampton *et al.* (2005) found no evidence that Rhesus monkeys could remember the 'when' or previous past episodes, although they could remember which foods were hidden where. Although there is no evidence to suggest that monkeys have episodic memory, the past few years has seen increasing evidence that apes may do so. Studies on chimpanzees and gorillas suggest that they can recall 'what-where' and even 'what-where-and-who' memories of unique events (Menzel 1999; Schwartz & Evans 2001; Schwartz *et al.* 2002). To date, there is no evidence that apes can remember the temporal component that is central to episodic-like memory, but absence of evidence is not evidence of absence. Very recently, Mulcahy & Call (2006) have demonstrated that apes appear to select, transport and save tools for use in the future, ones they do not currently need, suggesting that they have some elements of future planning. In humans, episodic memory and future planning appear to go hand in hand; thus, patients who are unable to episodically encode and recall the past but whose semantic memories appear intact, are also unable to plan for the future (see review by Tulving 2005). If mental time travel is the cognitive feat that makes episodic memory special and distinct from other memory systems, as Tulving suggests, then based on the finding that apes do show elements of prospective mental time travel, it follows that they should also be capable of retrospective mental time travel.

Taken together, the results of studies of rule abstraction (e.g. learning sets and transitive inference), problem solving and physical causality, and mental time travel, present a compelling case for corvid cognition. Indeed, elsewhere we have argued that the general intelligence of corvids is comparable to that of chimpanzees and that these two very distantly related families face similar challenges (Emery & Clayton 2004*a*,*b*). But what of their social cognition?

2.4 Social cognition by corvids

Theory of mind, the ability to impute and reason about the mental states of other individuals, is thought to be the pinnacle of social cognition. The term was first introduced by Premack & Woodruff (1978) to describe the behaviour of their language-trained chimpanzee, Sarah, who appeared to impute intentions to a human experimenter. Sarah was shown video sequences of an experimenter in various predicaments. After each sequence, Sarah was presented with a number of photographs showing possible solutions to the problems. Sarah was highly accurate in her selection of the appropriate photographs, and it was argued that she therefore understood the actor's intentions ('he wanted to get out of the cage'). Sarah had more than 10 years of experience in laboratory tests of cognition, however, as well as extensive experience of watching human experimenters doing these everyday tasks, so the possibility that she selected the photograph that completed a familiar sequence cannot be ruled out.

Subsequent studies suggested that the evidence for theory of mind in primates was at best ambivalent. Indeed, the capacity for non-human animals to attribute others with mental states has been the subject of considerable debate (Heyes 1998; Povinelli *et al.* 2000; Karin-D'Arcy & Povinelli 2002; Povinelli & Vonk 2004). Traditional studies relied on the use of human trainers, and the chimpanzees were tested in a paradigm in which they were expected to cooperate with the trainers for food (e.g. Povinelli *et al.* 1990; Call & Tomasello 1998).

However, the most convincing studies of social cognition by chimpanzees have stemmed from the work by Hare *et al.* (2000, 2001), which exploited the competitive nature of chimpanzee social life and used conspecifics. Hare *et al.* (2000) placed a subordinate and a dominant individual in competition with one another for two food rewards, one of which was positioned such that it was visible only to the subordinate. Subordinates selectively retrieved those food items that only they could see, suggesting that they may understand the dominant's visual perspective. Subsequent experiments, in which the knowledgeable dominant who had witnessed the baiting of food was switched with a naive one who had not seen this event, suggested that the subordinate chimpanzees keep track of which dominant chimpanzee has seen which particular baiting of the cup. As a result of these experiments, Hare *et al.* (2001) argued and that chimpanzees are capable not only of understanding what others can and cannot see, but also of what conspecifics do and do not know.

The success of the food-competition paradigm in providing insight into the socio-cognitive abilities of chimpanzees can be credited both to the exploitation of a naturally occurring competitive behaviour, and to the use of conspecifics as protagonists (Hare 2001). Competition for resources is not an aspect of animal social life that is unique to primates, however. Indeed, as we shall go on to describe, it is possible to draw parallels between food competition by chimpanzees, and food caching by corvids such as the western scrub-jay.

(a) Caching and cache protection as a competitive foraging paradigm

Food-caching corvids compete not only for access to available food resources, as chimpanzees do, but also for access to hidden caches of food. Field observations suggest that cachers engage in a number of strategies to reduce this competition with other individuals at the time of caching (Clayton & Emery 2004). For example, they tend to cache in areas where the density of conspecifics is lowest and ideally zero (e.g. rooks, Kalländer 1978; magpies, *Pica pica*: Clarkson *et al.* 1986; ravens, Bugnyar & Kotrschal 2002). When other individuals are present, the cachers will wait until the potential pilferers are distracted or cannot see because a barrier obscures their view (e.g. ravens, *Corvus corax*: Heinrich & Pepper 1998; Heinrich 1999). Competition may also arise once the cache has been hidden. Indeed, returning to cache sites does not guarantee a cacher's recovery success: up to 30% of caches are lost each day to pilfering by competitors (Vander Wall & Jenkins 2003).

Cache theft is particularly problematic for scrub-jays and other members of the corvid family, where potentially pilfering conspecifics use observational spatial memory to accurately steal another's caches that they saw being made (Bednekoff & Balda 1996a,b; Heinrich & Pepper

1998; Clayton *et al.* 2001; Watanabe & Clayton 2007). Consequently, pilfering jays can wait until the cacher has left the scene and then steal its caches at will, whenever they are hungry, and without relying on successfully displacing a possibly more dominant cacher.

Bugnyar & Kotrschal (2002) suggested that the capacity for observational spatial memory in corvids represented the catalyst for an 'evolutionary arms race' between cachers and pilferers, such that pilferers should develop methods for observing cachers as unobtrusively as possible, and cachers develop strategies to counter the risk of cache pilferage. Critical to a cacher's use of tactics to counter the risk of cache theft, however, should be the risk that potential thieves pose to their caches, i.e. whether or not they witnessed the cacher caching and are therefore knowledgeable as to cache locations. Consequently, just as Hare *et al.*'s food-competition paradigm provided a competitive, and naturalistic, forum with which to probe the sociocognitive abilities of apes, experimental paradigms based on food-caching behaviour have the potential to do the same with respect to the cognitive abilities of corvids. Furthermore, Dally *et al.* (2006*b*) have argued that, because corvids such as the western scrub-jay act as both cacher and pilferer, this role-taking has led to a refinement of increasingly more sophisticated, cognitively based cache protection and pilfering strategies.

(b) Anticipating pilferage when observers are present

Jays use a number of cache protection strategies at the time of caching, all of which appear to reduce the amount of visual information available to the observer. In the first experiment, we tested whether scrub-jays, like chimpanzees, are sensitive to what competitors can and cannot see (Dally *et al.* 2005*a*). Rather than competing directly for access to food, some of which was in view and some of which was out of view, in our 'barrier' experiment, the cachers were given the opportunity to cache food in two different, visuospatially distinct trays that were placed in the bird's home cage. A second bird, the observer, was placed in a cage opposite to that of the cacher such that it could easily see the caching bird. One of the trays was placed behind a barrier such that it was out of view of the observer, but the other was in full view so that the observer could clearly see the location of caches hidden in the full-view tray. On some trials, the cacher consequently cached while being observed by an observer (observed condition), whereas on other trials the observer's view of the entire caching event was obscured by a screen so that the cache was able to hide its caches in privacy (in private condition). The design of this experiment is shown in figure 2.1.

Perhaps not surprisingly, in the observed caching condition, the jays cached preferentially in sites located behind barriers which observers could not see, whereas there was no preference to cache behind barriers when they cached in private. However, when an observer was present during caching, not all the caches were hidden behind the barrier. Indeed, figure 2.2 shows that the cacher placed approximately 25% of its caches in high-risk cache sites, namely in the full-view tray.

This pattern of results suggests that, like chimpanzees, scrub-jays prefer to take the food that is out of view of the competitor. One interpretation of these results is that the cachers are sensitive to what an observer can and cannot see, and that is why they place the majority of the caches in the tray behind the barrier. However, a simpler explanation is that the cachers are responding to what they themselves can see. When they cache behind the barrier, the observer is effectively out of sight, and consequently perhaps out of mind.

One way in which it might be possible to determine whether scrub-jays are sensitive to what others can and cannot see, as opposed to basing their cache protection strategies solely on their

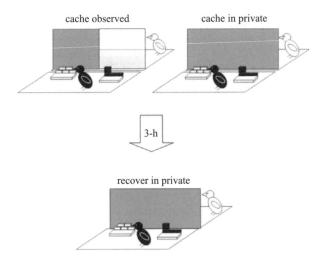

Fig. 2.1 The caching and recovery conditions for 'barrier' experiment. Storers cached in a single trial when 'observed' and when 'in private'. An opaque divider was attached to one side of the back of the storer's cage in the observed caching condition, such that the observer could only see one (full-view) tray, and to both sides of the cage during the in private caching condition preventing the observer from seeing either tray ⬛ full-view tray in the observed condition, ⬛ out of view tray in the observed condition. Recovery always took place in private.

own visual perspective, is to investigate whether they are able to exploit relative differences in the level of visual access that observers have to cache sites. By caching in sites that observers might find hard to see, cachers might reduce the quality and transfer of visual information to observers, thereby making the location of cache sites less certain. Critically, the 'out of sight, out of mind' hypothesis would be unable to explain a preference to cache in hard-to-see sites, as potential thieves would still be in view of the caching bird.

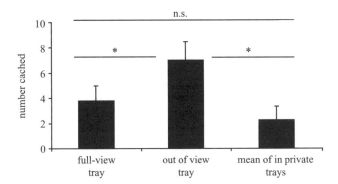

Fig. 2.2 The mean number of items (+ s.e.m.) cached in the full-view and out of view trays during the observed condition of the 'barrier' experiment, and the mean number of items cached in private (Friedman's ANOVA, $\chi_2^2 = 2.57$, $n = 8$, $p = 0.03$). As depicted on the figure, *post hoc* tests revealed that the birds cached significantly more items in the out of view tray compared to the full-view tray (Dunnett's test, $q = 2.9$, $n = 8$, $p<0.05$) and the mean of the private trays (Dunnett's test, $q = 4.1$, $n = 7$, $p<0.01$). No statistical difference was identified between the number of items cached in the full-view tray and the mean of the private trays (Dunnett's test, $q = 1.2$, $n = 7$, $p>0.05$). *, $p<0.05$.

To determine whether scrub-jays would exploit hard-to-see sites, we examined the effects of sun and shade on a scrub-jay's choice of where to cache (Dally *et al.* 2004). We hypothesized that scrub-jays might prefer to cache in shady sites, especially when another bird was watching them, because shady sites would reduce the visual information available to the potential pilferer and thus reduce the chance that the pilferer could accurately relocate the caches. Similarly, in the 'barrier' experiment, the birds were able to cache in two trays in each of two conditions, observed by a conspecific or in private. The critical difference, however, was that a lamp was placed close to each of the two caching trays. By switching one of the lamps on, and leaving the other switched off, we were able to create two sites that were identical except for the level to which they were lit such that ratio of luminance between the two sites was 4:1. The experimental design is shown in figure 2.3.

Figure 2.4 provides support for this hypothesis about where the birds should cache when observed by another jay. When another jay is present at the time of caching, the cachers do prefer to hide most of their items in shady areas compared to well-lit areas, whereas they are not selective about cache location when caching in private. Note, however, that not all the items were cached in the shady sites when an observer was watching: approximately 20% of the items were placed in the well-lit sites, a point we shall return to presently.

Subsequent experiments established that the jays also use distance as a cache protection strategy (Dally *et al.* 2005*a*). In the 'distance' experiment, the birds were given the opportunity to cache worms in each of two trays. The trays were positioned approximately 60 cm apart from one another, such that one tray was near to and one tray far from the observer's cage. As in the previous experiments, the birds cached either while observed or in private. The experimental design is shown in figure 2.5.

Figure 2.6 shows that the birds had a preference to hide most of their caches in the tray located far from the observer, as opposed to the other tray placed near to the observer. However, they

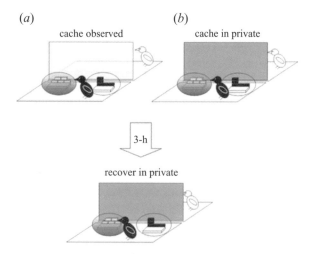

Fig. 2.3 The caching and recovery conditions of the 'sun/shade' experiment. ⬬ shady tray, ⬛ well-lit tray. Storers cached in a single trial in each of two conditions (*a*) separated from the observer by a transparent divider (observed condition) and (*b*) separated from the observer by an opaque divider which obscured the observer's view (in private condition). Cache recovery always occurred in private.

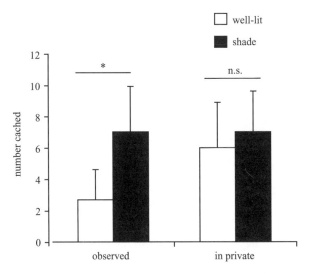

Fig. 2.4 The mean number of items (+ s.e.m.) cached in the well-lit and shady trays during the observed (Wilcoxon's paired test, $T = 21$, $n = 6$, $p = 0.016$) and in private caching conditions (Wilcoxon's paired test, $T = 21$, $n = 8$, $p = 0.38$). *, $p < 0.05$; ns, non-significant.

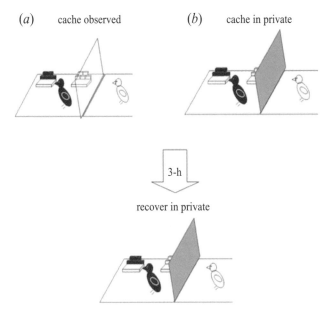

Fig. 2.5 The caching and recovery conditions of the 'distance' experiment. ![] far tray, ![] near tray, ![] storer, ![] observer. Storers were given four trials in each of two conditions (a) when a transparent divider separated the storer and the observer (observed condition), (b) when opaque dividers separated the storer and observer (in private condition). Irrespective of condition, recovery occurred in private.

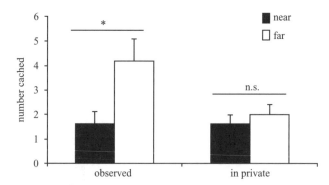

Fig. 2.6 The mean number of items (+ s.e.m.) cached in near and far trays during the observed and in private caching conditions of the 'distance' experiment. The number of items cached by the birds did not vary across trials in either the observed (Friedman's ANOVA, $\chi_2^2 = 6.0$, $p = 0.09$) or in private condition (Friedman's ANOVA, $\chi_2^2 = 6.0$, $p = 0.96$). Birds cached predominantly in the far tray when observed (Wilcoxon's paired test, $T = 4$, $n = 8$, $p = 0.027$), whereas no significant difference was identified between the number of items cache in the near and far trays during the private condition (Wilcoxon's paired test, $T = 16$, $n = 8$, $p = 0.67$). *, $p < 0.05$; ns, non-significant.

did not show a preference for distance when caching in private and instead cached equal amounts in both trays.

It therefore appears that the birds are able to exploit a range of environmental variables, such as the level of ambient light and the relative distance of cache sites to the observer, to reduce the transfer of visual information to potential pilferers. As in the previous two experiments, note that they did not cache exclusively in the far tray when observed, but that they cached approximately 25% of their caches in the near tray.

When competing with others for access to resources, an animal might not only adjust its behaviour as a result of the presence of a competitor, but also as a function of the competitor's social status. Consider Hare and colleagues' competitive paradigm. The finding that chimpanzees preferentially recovered food that competitors cannot see was specific to subordinate individuals, because their dominant competitors would be able to physically monopolize known food sources. The relative dominance of a competitor might also affect the use of cache protection tactics by foodcachers. Like Hare et al.'s chimps, the capacity for cachers to physically compete with other birds for access to cache sites is also specific to dominant scrub-jays (Dally et al. 2005b). Similarly, only dominant birds are able to physically defend cache sites against potential pilferers. We might therefore expect cachers to be most likely to engage in protective behaviours when caching in view of dominant birds, thereby reducing the need to actively defend cache sites and negating the need for aggressive interaction which carries a risk of injury or even death.

Field observations suggest that observer dominance might not be the only factor affecting the use of cache protection tactics by corvids. Instead, it appears that the social relationship between a cacher and an observe might affect the use of protective behaviours. For example, while ravens preferentially cache out of view of conspecifics (Bugnyar & Kotrschal 2002), there is evidence to suggest that this is not the case when the cacher's partner is the sole witness to a caching event (Heinrich & Pepper 1998). Moreover, caching jays commonly tolerate cache theft by their partner, but direct aggression towards other individuals that approach cache sites (Goodwin 1956; Dally et al. 2005b).

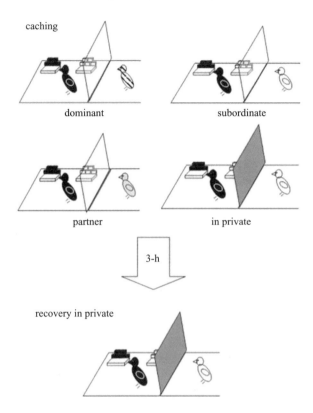

Fig. 2.7 The caching and recovery conditions of the 'distance' experiment in which storers (🦅) cached in a single trial in each of four conditions: observed by a dominant, (🦅) subordinate, (🦅) their partner (🦅) or in private. 🗄 far tray, 🗄 near tray. Transparent dividers separated the storer and the observer in the dominant, subordinate and partner conditions. Opaque dividers separated the storer and observer during the in private caching condition. Irrespective of condition, recovery occurred in private.

If corvids do not perceive their mate to represent a threat to cache safety, then the cachers should abstain from investing energy in the implementation of cache protection strategies when caching in their presence. To determine whether this is the case, we replicated the 'distance' experiment we described previously, such that jays were able to cache in sites that were either near to or far from a conspecific. As shown in figure 2.7, in this experiment the birds cached either observed by a dominant bird, a subordinate, their partner, or in private (Dally *et al.* 2006a). Based on the findings of our earlier experiments, we predicted that cachers should hide food preferentially in the distant sites in the presence of potential thieves, but cache in both trays in private. The question is whether, in the partner condition, cachers will cache preferentially in far sites just as they had done in the previous experiments when another bird was watching at the time of caching, or whether they differentiate between mates and other individuals and thus will refrain from engaging in protective behaviours in the presence of their mate.

As predicted, the jays cached equally in both the near and far trays when in private (figure 2.8). Intriguingly, however, although the birds cached chiefly in the far tray in the dominant and

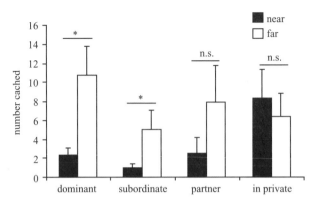

Fig. 2.8 The mean number of items (+ s.e.m.) cached in near and far trays during each caching condition: dominant, subordinate, partner, in private. Birds cached predominantly in the far tray in the dominant (Sign test; $S = 7/7$, $p = 0.02$) and subordinate conditions (Sign test; $S = 7/7$, $p = 0.02$), but not in the partner condition (Sign test; $S = 5/7$, $p = 0.13$) or in private (Sign test; $S = 3/7$, $p < 0.05$). *, $p < 0.05$; ns, non-significant.

subordinate conditions, they did not differentiate between the two trays when watched by their partner, suggesting that they did not perceive their mate as a competitor.

This finding suggests that, at least in some corvids, the specific risk that an observer poses, not just the presence or absence of an observer, governs whether or not cache protection strategies are employed.

(c) Multiple moves

In the wild, it may not be possible for cachers to cache in sites that afford hidden items a degree of visual protection. For example, if cache sites are equidistant to observers, then the cachers would be unable to use a distance strategy. Furthermore, if observers were not only present, but also non-stationary, it would be unlikely that any cache site would be consistently out of view of potential thieves. In this situation, a cacher's best chance of minimizing cache theft might be to reduce the accuracy with which competitors are able to relocate hidden items, perhaps by moving items around multiple times. In the wild, it is reported that Eurasian jays do just that (Goodwin 1956).

In a recent experiment (Dally *et al.* 2005*a*), western scrub-jays were given the opportunity to cache in two trays in each of two conditions (figure 2.9). In the 'constrained' condition, the position of observers relative to cache sites was reliable, such that one tray was constantly in view and one constantly out of view of a potential thief. By contrast, in the 'free' condition, whether or not a specific cache site was in view of a potential thief was dependant on the current position of that same observer. To elucidate, when an observer was on the left-hand side of its cage, the left-hand caching tray would be in view, whereas the right-hand tray would be hidden by an opaque barrier. If the observer moved to the right-hand side of its cage, however, the right-hand tray would be in view, and the barrier would block the observer's view of the left-hand tray.

As predicted by the results of the 'barrier' experiment we described previously, cachers predominantly cached out of view of the observer in both the constrained and free conditions. When caching in the free condition, however, cachers often recovered cached items and re-hid (*a*) free condition

(*b*) constrained condition

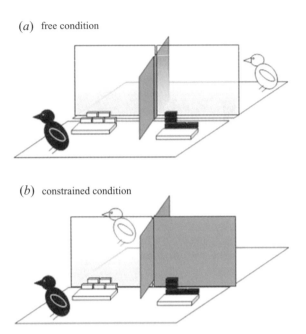

Fig. 2.9 The experimental set-up for (*a*) the free condition and (*b*) the constrained condition. In the free condition, the cages of both the storer and observer were partially divided with opaque dividers which restricted the visual access of both birds to one side of the opposite cage. In the constrained condition, the storer's cage was partially divided, and the observer's cage fully divided, with opaque screens. The observer therefore had visual access to only one side of the storer's cage. All storers received three caching trials in the free condition and two trials in the constrained condition. Irrespective of condition, recovery took place in private (solid dividers attached to both sides of the storer's cage).

them elsewhere. As shown in figure 2.10, the cachers moved items the observer had seen being cached up to six times, movements that occurred specifically in view of their competitor. By contrast, when cache sites were consistently in view or out of view of potential thieves (constrained condition), few items were moved. The repeated movement of caches in the free condition appears to be a response to the unpredictability of the observer's position, and consequently what they could and could not see.

(d) Cache protection at recovery when observers have left the scene

The use of tactics to reduce cache theft is not limited to the initial period of caching. In the wild, corvids have been observed to return alone to caches hidden in the presence of conspecifics, and to re-hide them in new places unbeknownst to potential thieves (Goodwin 1955; Heinrich 1999). To determine whether this 're-caching' behaviour could be attributed to the presence of potential thieves at the time of caching, we allowed our jays to cache either in private or while a conspecific was watching, and then recover their caches 3 h later (figure 2.11). Irrespective of caching condition, recovery always occurred in private, preventing the cacher's behaviour from being influenced by any cues provided by a prior observer. As a result, any differences in the birds' recovery behaviour after caching observed or in private must depend on

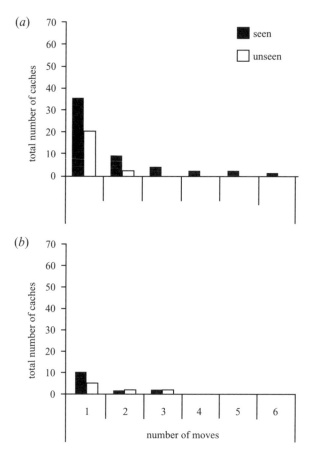

Fig. 2.10 The total number of times individual caches from seen and unseen sites were moved during the caching period of (a) the free condition and (b) the constrained condition. Caches were moved significantly more often during the free condition than in the constrained condition (Wilcoxon's paired test, $T = 2$, $n = 8$, $p = 0.01$). *, $p<0.05$; ns, non-significant.

a memory of the social context of a previous caching event (i.e. the absence or presence of an observer jay).

We predicted that the jays would be much more likely to re-cache if they had been observed by a conspecific while they were caching than after caching in private. Furthermore, these caches should be moved to new sites unbeknown to the observer, if this re-caching is indeed a cache protection strategy.

Figure 2.12 shows that, as predicted, the jays were much more likely to re-cache if they had been observed by a conspecific while they were caching than when they had cached in private. By re-caching items that the observer had seen them cache, the cachers significantly reduce the chance of cache theft, as observers would be unable to rely on memory to facilitate accurate cache theft.

At this juncture, it is perhaps worth describing how this re-caching behaviour differs from the multiple movement behaviour we described earlier. First, whereas re-caching occurs during recovery in private, the multiple movement of caches occurs at caching. Moreover, while re-cached items are moved once to new sites, items moved multiple times are commonly

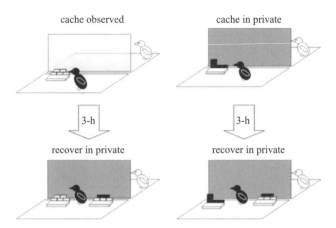

Fig. 2.11 The experimental set-up of the caching and recovery conditions. Storers cached either watched by a conspecific (observed) or when the observer's view was obscured by an opaque divider (in private). In each condition, storers cached in a single tray (⬭ observed tray, ⬛ in private tray). At recovery, which occurred in private, storers received the tray in which they had previously cached plus one 'new' tray(⬭).

moved to sites that have been used previously. Presumably, the principal benefit of re-caching at recovery is that items are moved from sites that the observer knows about to new sites of which the observer is ignorant. Repeatedly moving items around, however, might serve a very different function. By moving items the observer witnessed being cached multiple times, the observer's memory for each new cache site would suffer from interference from the memory

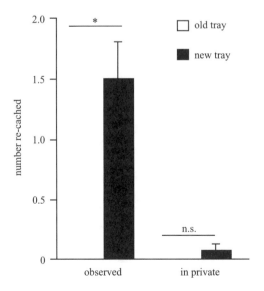

Fig. 2.12 The mean number of items (+ s.e.m.) re-cached in the new and old trays after the observed and in private caching conditions. Storers re-cached significantly more in new sites after being observed during caching (Wilcoxon's paired test, $Z = 2.4$, $n = 7$, $p < 0.05$), but did not discriminate between re-caching in old or new sites during the in private condition (no statistical comparison possible). *, $p < 0.05$; ns, non-significant.

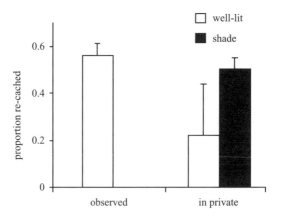

Fig. 2.13 The mean proportion of caches (+ s.e.m.) re-cached from the well-lit and shady trays after the observed and in private caching conditions. The data could not be analysed statistically as only three birds recovered their caches in the observed condition and two birds in the in private condition.

of old cache sites. Consequently, the accuracy with which potential thieves are able to steal hidden items may be reduced. Critically, however, cachers are able to recover moved and unmoved caches with equal precision.

While re-caching behaviour is a cache protection behaviour in its own right, the results of our experiments suggest that it is often used in conjunction with protective behaviours at the time of caching. Let us look again at the results of the sun and shade and distance experiment. As predicted by our first re-caching experiment, after being observed during caching, the birds engaged in re-caching behaviour during a private recovery period. By contrast, they engaged in much less re-caching when they had cached in private. Note, however, that it was the items that had been placed in the well-lit tray during the observed caching condition that were moved to new sites, even though the cacher had placed only approximately 20% of its caches in that tray (figure 2.13; Dally *et al.* 2004). The same pattern of results was identified for the distance and barrier experiments: re-caching occurred almost exclusively after the birds had cached in the observed condition, and was directed specifically at those caches that had been placed in risky sites (Dally *et al.* 2005*a*). This selectivity to re-cache items at the greatest risk of cache theft acts to confers them with a degree of cache protection, as prior observers would no longer be able to rely on memory to steal them.

The pattern of re-caching exhibited by cachers at recovery is clearly influenced by the location in which items were cached. A second point of interest, however, is whether a cacher's recovery behaviour is influenced by who was watching at the time of caching. Remember that at the time of caching, cachers engage in protective tactics only when observed by non-partners. It therefore follows that cachers might refrain from using cache protection tactics at recovery after caching in view of their partner, and this is indeed an accurate reflection of the cacher's behaviour. As shown in figure 2.14, after caching in view of a subordinate or a dominant bird, cachers re-cached hidden items specifically from the sites to which the observer had the best visual access (near tray). However, no such preference was exhibited if the cacher hid the caches in view of their partner. Cachers also appeared to differentiate between the relative risk the subordinate and dominant birds posed to their caches, as re-caching levels were highest after caching in view of a dominant bird (Dally *et al.* 2006*a*).

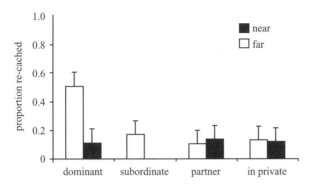

Fig. 2.14 The mean proportion of caches (+ s.e.m.) re-cached at recovery after each caching condition: dominant, subordinate, partner, in private. The data could not be analysed statistically as several birds only cached in one tray (two in the dominant condition, four in the partner condition, two in private).

(e) Keeping track of who was watching when

Until now, we have focused on the capacity for corvids to remember whether or not they were observed during a specific caching event, and, during a private recovery period, to adjust their cache recovery behaviour accordingly. In a naturalistic situation, however, cachers may not be able to recover their caches unobserved. It might be the case that observers do not leave the area in which the cacher has cached, or that while the same observers are not always present, there is always another bird in the immediate vicinity. This situation was mimicked in one of our most recent experiments (Dally *et al.* 2006*a*) in which, although observes were often present upon recovery, they different as to the specific caches they had witnessed the cacher hide. To elucidate, cachers were given the opportunity to cache in the presence of two different observers in two consecutive caching events, and then to recover their caches either when in private, watched by a prior observer (observed condition), or watched by a 'control' bird that had not witnessed either caching event. The experimental design is shown in figure 2.15.

In line with our previous findings, cachers re-cached hidden items in new sites when cache recovery occurred in private. By contrast, in the presence of a prior observer, cachers repeatedly moved caches the observer had seen them make. This propensity for birds to repeatedly move caches around in the presence of a prior observer is analogous to the multiple movement of caches we described previously, a behaviour that is apparent when cachers are unable to engage in a behaviour that affords their caches some form of visual protection (e.g. caching out of view). By moving caches repeatedly, cachers might reduce the accuracy with which the observer would be able to steal their caches. As shown in figure 2.16, while the cachers moved caches they had been observed to make multiple times, caches that the observer at recovery had not seen them hide were rarely moved. Similarly very few caches were moved during the control condition. In essence, moving these items would only have provided observers, who were currently ignorant to their existence, with observational information that might have been used to facilitate future cache theft.

Although the results of this experiment suggest that scrub-jays remember who was present when specific caches were being made, it is possible that the cacher was simply reacting to cues provided by the observer. For example, observers may spend more time attending to a tray they have seen a bird caching in. In order to determine whether the jays adjust their behaviour as a

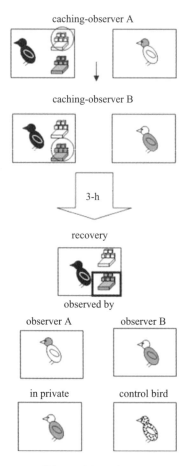

Fig. 2.15 The caching and recovery conditions of the 'who was watching' experiment. Storers received eight trials in which they (🐦) cached in one tray in the presence of observer A (🐦) and in a different tray in the presence of observer B (🐦). At recovery, storers were able to retrieve their caches in one of four conditions: in the presence of observer A, observer B, a control bird that had not been present when the storer cached (🐦) or in private (opaque dividers occluding a conspecifics view of the storer's recovery behaviour). Each bird received two trials in each recovery condition. ● Perspex strips, ⬚ 'observed' tray.

function of what the bird at recovery knows, or whether they rely on differences in the behaviour of the observers towards sites in which they have or have not watched caches being hidden, we ran a further experiment (Dally *et al.* 2006*a*). As shown in figure 2.17, we repeated the observed condition of our previous experiment, such that cachers cached successively in two trays, each in view of a different observer, and contrasted it with a second observer control condition. Critical to the observer control condition was that after the two caching periods, a control observer was given the opportunity to observe a control cacher caching in one of the two trays. In this way, both the original observers and the control observer witnessed a cacher hiding the food in one of the two trays. At recovery, both observer and control observer saw an original cacher recover its caches. Consequently, in the observed condition, the cacher was observed by the same observer at caching and recovery, whereas in the observer control condition, the cacher was observed by an observer at caching and the control observer at recovery.

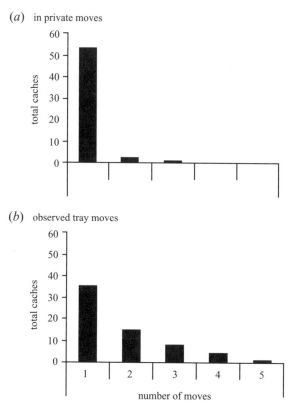

Fig. 2.16 The total number of times individual caches were moved from (*a*) the in private trays and (*b*) the observed tray. Caches in the observed tray were moved significantly more often than caches in the in private trays (Friedman's test, $\chi_1^2 = 8.0$, $p = 0.01$).

If the caching scrub-jay remembers who was present during caching, then its behaviour should differ between the observed and observer control conditions. Based on the previous experiment, cachers in the observed condition should re-cache items predominantly from the tray the observer at recovery had seen them cache in (observed tray) and not from the other tray. By contrast, cachers should re-cache few items from either tray in the observer control condition, because the control observer was not present when the cacher cached. If, however, the birds attend primarily. to trays in which they have observed caching, and cachers use this information to guide cache recovery, cachers should re-cache items from the observed tray in both conditions, as although the control observer was not present when the cacher cached, it would be attending the tray in which it had previously observed the control cacher cache.

As shown in figure 2.18, birds in the observed condition re-cached a significantly greater proportion of caches from the tray in which the observer at recovery had seen them cache. By contrast, in the observer control condition, items were re-cached from both trays without selectivity. Consequently, it seems rather unlikely that cacher's use of cache protection tactics is cued by the observers' behaviour. The results of these two experiments therefore support the hypothesis that the jays remember which individuals watched them cache during specific

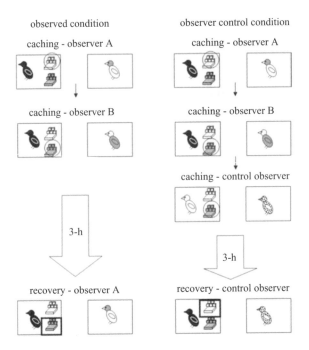

Fig. 2.17 The experimental set-up of the observed and observer control conditions. Storers (🐦) received two caching trials in each of the observed and observer control conditions. In each condition, storers cached in one tray in the presence of observer A (🐦) and in a different tray in the presence of observer B (🐦) In the observer control condition, an additional storer (🐦) also cached in one of the two trays in the presence of a control observer (🐦). At recovery, in the observed condition, storers recovered their caches in the presence of observer A or observer B. In the observer control condition, storers recovered their caches in the presence of the control observer. (●) Perspex strips, (⬚) observed tray.

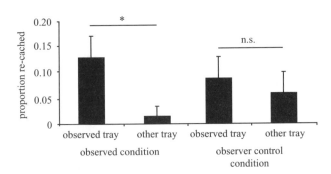

Fig. 2.18 Mean proportion (+ s.e.m.) of items re-cached from the observed and other trays in the observed (sign test; $S = 6/6$, $p = 0.03$) and observer control conditions (Sign test; $S = 4/6$, $p = 0.69$). *, $p < 0.05$; ns, non-significant.

events, and use this information to combat the future risk that particular observers pose to their caches.

Of course a more elaborate behaviour cueing account could be proposed given that in the observed condition, the observer saw the cacher hide food in tray A, whereas in the observer control condition the observer saw a different bird cache food in tray A. Consequently at recovery, the observer's behaviour may have differed between the two conditions, but to do so requires the observer to remember which particular cacher was present during the previous caching episode as well as which tray the cacher had stored the food in. Note that this more elaborate behavioural cueing account requires of the observer what we have claimed of the storer, namely an ability to recognize particular individuals and to remember which individuals were present and where they cached during specific past caching episodes. Consequently we argue that by either account, western scrub-jays keep track of who was watching when.

These findings raise questions about whether the scrub-jay has a 'theory of mind', given that the jays appear to be sensitive to what particular individuals have and have not seen when deciding which caches to protect. Furthermore, since the birds differentiate between dominant and subordinate observers, and between mate and other birds, even when these birds are not present at the time of recovery when they are re-caching the food items, they must recognize different individuals and use this social memory to take protective action accordingly. Finally, the fact that they can do so even when those observers are not present at the time of recovery means not only that the birds must have remembered who was present at the time of caching, but also that we can rule out a behaviour-reading account of re-caching behaviour.

Of course, as we have pointed out in the original paper (Dally *et al.* 2006*a*), we caution that these abilities do not necessarily require a human-like theory of mind. For one thing, it is hard to imagine how a nonlinguistic subject could theorize about the minds of other individuals. Clearly, it would be informative to develop a model of how the jays might achieve this seemingly complex behaviour (see Emery & Clayton (in press) for our attempt to construct a cognitive architecture of mind-reading in scrub-jays). However, the selectivity of the cache protection behaviours does appear to depend on a sensitivity to what others have and have not seen, and who is and is not a threat. In short, these studies show that scrub-jays keep an eye on the competition and protect their caches accordingly. Such behaviour would appear to meet the behavioural criteria for one form of theory of mind, namely knowledge attribution, if by the term we mean the ability to attribute different informational states to particular individuals.

(f) The role of experience

There is one particularly striking finding about the re-caching behaviour of these birds, i.e. not all western scrub-jays engage in it. Emery & Clayton (2001) found that re-caching behaviour depends not only on whether or not the cacher was observed by another jay during caching, but that it also depends upon experience of being a pilferer. Whereas experienced thieves engaged in high levels of re-caching at recovery when they were observed during the previous caching episode, control birds, who had not been thieves in the past and therefore had no prior experience of stealing other birds' caches, showed hardly any re-caching at all, as shown in figure 2.19.

The fact that only experienced birds re-cache has a number of important implications. The first is that this behaviour cannot be innate, otherwise all scrub-jays should re-cache. Importantly, we can also rule out a simple conditioning explanation because the birds never received any positive reinforcement or any punishment for re-caching, given that they never had the

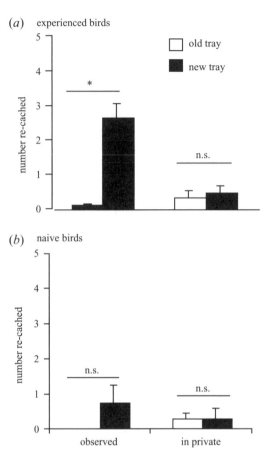

Fig. 2.19 The mean number (+ s.e.m.) of items re-cached in new and old sites at recovery after the observed and in private caching conditions for (*a*) birds that had previously stolen the caches of others (experienced birds; Wilcoxon's paired test, $Z = 2.2$, $n = 7$, $p < 0.05$), and (*b*) birds that had not experienced stealing other's caches (native birds; Wilcoxon's paired test, $Z = 1.6$, $n = 7$, $p > 0.05$).*, $p < 0.05$; ns, non-significant.

opportunity to learn about the fate of the caches that they had re-cached. As a consequence, we can make the inference that the jay used information gained during the previous caching event to anticipate whether or not its caches were likely to be stolen, and thus engaged in the appropriate cache protection strategy at recovery, namely whether or not to re-cache and, if so, to re-cache those that had previously been placed in high-risk sites. The fact that they appear to anticipate cache risk in the future lends further credence to the idea that they can plan for the future, as discussed in §3. Emery & Clayton (2004*b*) have argued that the fact that experienced birds differ so dramatically from control birds who lack the experience of being a thief suggests that the experienced jays are not only capable of future planning, but also experience projection. Experience projection refers to a second form of theory of mind, namely the ability to use one's own experiences, in this case of having been a thief, to predict how another individual might think or behave, in this case what the potential pilferer might do. Experience projection has yet to be demonstrated in any of the great apes, other than humans.

Consequently, most people have assumed that experience projection is a uniquely human trait. The jay studies challenge this assumption, though it should be reiterated that we do not suppose that their abilities need to be akin to human theory of mind, and of course simply using such terminology offers no mechanistic explanation of how the jays might express these abilities.

2.5 Conclusions

According to the social function of intellect hypothesis (Humphrey 1976*a,b*), it is the need to survive the trials and tribulations of social life that has selected for increased socio-cognitive skills. Indeed, Humphrey (1980, p. 59) argued that 'If a social animal is to become—as it must become—one of "Nature's psychologists" it must somehow come up with the appropriate ideology for doing psychology' and that they do so by introspection, modelling the behaviour of other individuals by reasoning by analogy of their own experiences.

Although this hypothesis was formulated with primates in mind, in principle it could be applied to other organisms. In this paper, we have argued that at least one member of the corvid family fulfils these criteria. Consequently, we conclude that the western scrub-jay is by Humphrey's definition one of 'nature's psychologists'.

There are two important implications that arise from this conclusion. The first is that elements of complex social cognition appear to have evolved independently in at least two very disparate groups of animals, namely the apes and corvids (Emery & Clayton 2004*a*). The second is that since birds do not have the typical six-layered cortex found in humans and other mammals, this divergence in structural organization of the brain raises the question of whether these cognitive abilities are achieved by similar or different neurocognitive mechanisms in the avian and mammalian brain (Emery & Clayton 2005).

References

Avian Brain Nomenclature Consortium 2005 Avian brains and a new understanding of vertebrate brain evolution. *Nat. Rev. Neurosci.* **6**, 151–159.

Baglione, V., Marcos, J. M. & Canestrari, D. 2002 Cooperatively breeding groups of carrion crow (*Corvus corone corone*) in Northern Spain. *Auk* **119**, 790–799. (doi:10.1642/0004-8038(2002)119[0790: CBGOCC]2.0. CO;2)

Barrett, L., Henzi, P. & Dunbar, R. 2003 Primate cognition: from 'what now?' to 'what if?' *Trends Cogn. Sci.* **7**, 494–497. (doi:10.1016/j.tics.2003.09.005)

Barton, R. A. & Dunbar, R. I. M 1997 Evolution of the social brain. In *Machiavellian intelligence II: extensions and evaluations* (eds A. Whiten & R. W. Byrne), pp. 240–263. Cambridge, UK: Cambridge University Press.

Beauchamp, G. & Fernández-Juricic, E. 2004 Is there a relationship between forebrain size and group size in birds? *Evol. Ecol. Res.* **6**, 833–842.

Beck, B. 1980 *Animal tool behavior: the use and manufacture of tools by animals.* New York, NY: Garland Press.

Bednekoff, P. & Balda, R. 1996*a* Social caching and observational spatial memory in pinyon jays. *Behaviour* **133**, 807–826.

Bednekoff, P. & Balda, R. 1996*b* Observational spatial memory in Clark's nutcrackers and Mexican jays. *Anim. Behav.* **52**, 833–839.

Brothers, L. 1990 The social brain: a project for integrating primate behavior and neurophysiology in a new domain. *Concepts Neurosci.* **1**, 27–51.

Bugnyar, T. & Kotrschal, K. 2002 Observational spatial learning and the raiding of food caches in ravens, *Corvus corax*: is it tactical deception? *Anim. Behav.* **64**, 185–195. (doi:10.1006/anbe.2002. 3056)

Burish, M. J., Kueh, H. Y. & Wang, S. S. 2004 Brain architecture and social complexity in modern and ancient birds. *Brain Behav. Evol.* **63**, 107–124. (doi:10.1159/000075674)

Burt, D. B. & Peterson, A. T. 1993 Biology of cooperative-breeding scrub jays (*Aphelocoma coerulescens*) of Oaxaca, Mexico. *Auk* **110**, 207–214.

Byrne, R. W. & Corp, N. 2004 Neocortex size predicts deception rate in primates. *Proc. R. Soc. B* **271**, 1693–1699. (doi:10.1098/rspb.2004.2780)

Byrne, R. W. & Whiten, A. 1988 *Machiavellian intelligence: social expertise and the evolution of intellect in monkeys, apes and humans*. Oxford, UK: Clarendon Press.

Call, J. & Tomasello, M. 1998 Distinguishing intentional from accidental actions in orangutans (*Pongo pygmaeus*), chimpanzees (*Pan troglodytes*) and human children (*Homo sapiens*). *J. Comp. Psychol.* **112**, 192–206. (doi:10.1037/ 0735-7036.112.2.192)

Chappell, J. & Kacelnik, A. 2002 Tool selectivity in a non-primate, the New Caledonian crow (*Corvus moneduloides*). *Anim. Cogn.* **5**, 71–76. (doi:10.1007/s10071-002-0130-2)

Chappell, J. & Kacelnik, A. 2004 Selection of tool diameter by New Caledonian crows *Corvus moneduloides*. *Anim. Cogn.* **7**, 121–127. (doi:10.1007/s10071-003-0202-y)

Clarkson, K., Eden, S. F., Sutherland, W. J. & Houston, A. I. 1986 Density dependence and magpie food hoarding. *J. Anim. Ecol.* **55**, 111–121.

Clayton, N. S. & Dickinson, A. 1998 Episodic-like memory during cache recovery by scrub-jays. *Nature* **395**, 272–274. (doi:10.1038/26216)

Clayton, N.S. & Emery, N. J. 2004 Cache robbing. In *Encyclopedia of animal behaviour* (eds M. Bekoff & J. Goodall), pp. 251–252. Westport, CT: Greenwood Publishing Group.

Clayton, N. S., Griffiths, D. P., Emery, N. J. & Dickinson, A. 2001 Elements of episodic-like memory in animals. *Phil. Trans. R. Soc. B* **356**, 1483–1491. (doi:10.1098/rstb.2001. 0947)

Clayton, N. S., Bussey, T. J. & Dickinson, A. 2003a Can animals recall the past and plan for the future? *Nat. Rev. Neurosci.* **4**, 685–691. (doi:10.1038/nrn1180)

Clayton, N. S., Bussey, T. J., Emery, N. J. & Dickinson, A. 2003b Prometheus to Proust: the case for behavioural criteria for 'mental time travel'. *Trends Cogn. Sci.* **7**, 436–437. (doi:10.1016/j.tics.2003. 08.003)

Clayton, N. S., Yu, K. S. & Dickinson, A. 2003c Interacting cache memories: evidence of flexible memory use by scrub jays. *J. Exp. Psychol. Anim. Behav. Proc.* **29**, 14–22.

Clayton, N. S., Dally, J. M., Gilbert, J. D. J. & Dickinson, A. 2005 Food caching by western scrub-jays (*Aphelocoma californica*) is sensitive to conditions at recovery. *J. Exp. Psychol. Anim. Behav. Proc.* **31**, 115–124.

Correia, S. P. C., Dickinson, A. & Clayton, N. S. 2007 Western scrub-jays (Aphelocoma californica) anticipate future needs independently of their current motivational state. *Current Biology* **17**, 856–861.

Curry, R. L., Towsend Peterson, A. & Langen, T. A. 2002 Western scrub-jay. In *The birds of North America*, vol. 712 (eds A. Poole & F. Gill), pp. 1–36. Philadelphia, PA; Washington, DC: Academy of Natural Sciences, American Ornithologists Union.

Dally, J. M., Emery, N. J. & Clayton, N. S. 2004 Cache protection strategies by western scrub-jays (*Aphelocoma californica*): hiding food in the shade. *Proc. R. Soc. B* **271**(Suppl.6), S387–S390. (doi:10.1098/rsbl.2004.0190)

Dally, J. M., Emery, N. J. & Clayton, N. S. 2005a Cache protection strategies by western scrub-jays: implications for social cognition. *Anim. Behav.* **70**, 1251–1263. (doi:10.1016/j.anbehav.2005.02.009)

Dally, J. M., Emery, N. J. & Clayton, N. S. 2005b The social suppression of caching in western scrub-jays (*Aphelocoma calfornica*). *Behaviour* **142**, 961–977. (doi:10.1163/1568539055010084)

Dally, J. M., Emery, N. J. & Clayton, N. S. 2006a Food-caching western scrub-jays keep track of who was watching when. *Science* **312**, 1662–1665. (doi:10.1126/science.1126539)

Dally, J. M., Clayton, N. S. & Emery, N. J. 2006b The behaviour and evolution of cache protection and pilferage. *Anim. Behav.* **72**, 13–23. (doi:10.1016/j.anbehav.2005.08.020)

Dunbar, R. I. M. 1992 Neocortex size as a constraint on group size in primates. *J. Human Evol.* **20**, 469–493. (doi:10.1016/0047-2484(92)90081-J)

Dunbar, R. I. M. 1998 The social brain hypothesis. *Evol. Anthropol.* **6**,178–190. (doi:10.1002/(SICI) 1520-6505(1998)6:5<178::AID-EVAN5>3.0.CO;2-8)

Emery, N. J. 2004 Are corvids 'feathered apes'? Cognitive evolution in crows, jays, rooks and jackdaws. In *Comparative analysis of minds* (ed. S. Watanabe), pp. 181–213. Tokyo, Japan: Keio University Press.

Emery, N. J. & Clayton, N. S. 2001 Effects of experience and social context on prospective caching strategies in scrub jays. *Nature* **414**, 443–446.

Emery, N. J. & Clayton, N. S. 2004*a* The mentality of crows. Convergent evolution of intelligence in corvids and apes. *Science* **306**, 1903–1907. (doi:10.1126/science.1098410)

Emery, N. J. & Clayton, N. S. 2004*b* Comparing the complex cognition of birds and primates. In *Comparative vertebrate cognition* (eds L. J. Rogers & G. S. Kaplan), ch. 1, pp. 3–55. The Hague, The Netherlands: Kluwer Academic Press.

Emery, N. J. & Clayton, N. S. 2005 Evolution of avian brain and intelligence. *Curr. Biol.* **15**, R1–R5. (doi:10.1016/j.cub.2005.11.029)

Emery, N. J. & Clayton, N. S. In press. How to build a scrub-jay that reads minds. In: *Origins of the social mind: evolutionary and developmental perspectives* (eds S. Itakura & K. Fujita). Tokyo, Japan: Springer.

Emery, N. J., Seed, A. M. & von Bayern, A. M. P. 2006 Cognitive adaptations of social bonding in birds. *Phil. Trans. R. Soc. B* **362**, 489–505. (doi:10.1098/rstb.2006.1991)

Goodwin, D. 1955 Jays and crows recovering hidden food. *Br. Birds* **48**, 181–183.

Goodwin, D. 1956 Further observations on the behaviour of the jay (*Garrulus glandarius*). Ibis **98**, 186–219.

Goodwin, D. 1976 *Crows of the world*. Bury St Edmunds, UK: British Museum (Natural History).

Goodwin, D. 1986 *Crows of the world*, 2nd edn. London, UK: British Museum (Natural History).

Hampton, R. R., Hampstead, B. M. & Murray, E. A. 2005 Rhesus monkeys (*Macaca mulatta*) demonstrate robust memory for what and where, but not when, in an open-field test of memory. *Learn. Motiv.* **36**, 245–259. (doi:10.1016/j.lmot.2005.02.004)

Hare, B. 2001 Can competitive paradigms increase the validity of experiments on primate social cognition? *Anim. Cogn.* **4**, 269–280. (doi:10.1007/s100710100084)

Hare, B., Call, J., Agnetta, M. & Tomasello, M. 2000 Chimpanzees know what conspecifics do and do not see. *Anim. Behav.* **59**, 771–785. (doi:10.1006/anbe.1999.1377)

Hare, B., Call, J. & Tomasello, M. 2001 Do chimpanzees know what conspecifics know? *Anim. Behav.* **61**, 139–151. (doi:10.1006/anbe.2000.1518)

Heinrich, B. 1999 *Mind of the raven*. New York, NY: Harper Collins.

Heinrich, B. & Pepper, J. 1998 Influence of competitors on caching behaviour in the common raven (*Corvus corax*). *Anim. Behav.* **56**,1083–1090. (doi:10.1006/anbe.1998. 0906)

Heyes, C. 1998 Theory of mind in non-human primates. *Behav. Brain Sci.* **21**, 101–148. (doi:10.1017/S0140525X98000703)

Humphrey, N. K. 1976*a* The social function of intellect. In *Machiavellian intelligence: social expertise and the evolution of intellect in monkeys, apes and humans* (eds R. W. Byrne & A. Whiten), pp. 285–305. Oxford, UK: Clarendon Press.

Humphrey, N. K. 1976*b* The social function of intellect. In *Growing points in ethology* (eds P. P. G. Bateson & R. A. Hinde), pp. 303–317. Cambridge, UK: Cambridge University Press.

Humphrey, N.K. 1980 Nature's psychologists. In *Consciousness and the physical world* (eds B. D. Josephson & V. S. Ramachandran), pp. 57–80. Oxford, UK: Pergamon Press.

Hunt, G. R. 1996 Manufacture and use of hook-tools by New Caledonian crows. *Nature* **379**, 249–251. (doi:10.1038/379249a0)

Hunt, G. R. & Gray, R. D. 2003 Diversification and cumulative evolution in New Caledonian crow tool manufacture. *Proc. R. Soc. B* **270**, 867–874. (doi:10.1098/rsbl.2003.0009)

Iwaniuk, A. N. & Arnold, K. 2004 Is cooperative breeding associated with bigger brains? A comparative test in the Corvids (*Passeriformes*). *Ethology* **10**, 203–220. (doi:10.1111/j.1439-0310.2003.00957.x)

Joffe, T. H. 1997 Social pressures have selected for an extended juvenile period in primates. *J. Human Evol.* **32**, 593–605. (doi:10.1006/jhev.1997.0140)

Jolly, A. 1966 Lemur social behaviour and intelligence. *Science* **153**, 501–506. (doi:10.1126/science. 153.3735.501)

Kalländer, H. 1978 Hoarding in the rook (*Corvus frugilegus*). *Anser Suppl.* **3**, 124–128.

Karin-D'Arcy, R. & Povinelli, D. 2002 Do chimpanzees know what others see? A closer look. *Int. J. Comp. Psychol.* **15**, 21–54.

Kudo, H. & Dunbar, R. I. M. 2001 Neocortex size and social network in primates. *Anim. Behav.* **62**, 711–722. (doi:10.1006/anbe.2001.1808)

Lewis, K. P. 2000 A comparative study of primate play behaviour: implications for the study of cognition. *Folia Primatol.* **71**, 417–421.

Limongelli, L., Boysen, S. T. & Visalberghi, E. 1995 Comprehension of cause–effect relations in a tool-using task by chimpanzees (*Pan troglodytes*). *J. Comp. Psychol.* **109**, 18–26. (doi:10.1037/0735-7036. 109.1.18)

Mackintosh, N. J. 1988 Approaches to the study of animal intelligence. *Br. J. Psychol.* **79**, 509–525.

Marino, L. 2002 Convergence in complex cognitive abilities in cetaceans and primates. *Brain Behav. Evol.* **59**, 21–32.

McGonigle, B. O. & Chalmers, M. 1977 Are monkeys logical? *Nature* **267**, 694–696.

Menzel, C. R. 1999 Unprompted recall and reporting of hidden objects by a chimpanzee (*Pan troglodytes*) after extended delays. *J. Comp. Psychol.* **113**, 426–434. (doi:10.1037/0735-7036.113.4.426)

Mulcahy, N. & Call, J. 2006 Apes save tools for future use. *Science* **312**, 1038–1040. (doi:10.1126/science.1125456)

Paz-y-Miño, G. C., Bond, A. B., Kamil, A. C. & Balda, R. P. 2004 Pinyon jays use transitive inference to predict social dominance. *Nature* **430**, 778–781.

Povinelli, D. 2000 *Folk physics for apes. The chimpanzee's theory of how the word works.* Oxford, UK: Oxford University Press.

Povinelli, D. J. & Vonk, J. 2004 We don't need a microscope to explore the chimpanzee's mind. *Mind Lang.* **19**, 1–28.

Povinelli, D. J., Nelson, K. E. & Boysen, S. T. 1990 Inferences about guessing and knowing by chimpanzees (*Pan troglodytes*). *J. Comp. Psychol.* **104**, 203–210. (doi:10.1037/0735-7036.104.3.203)

Povinelli, D. J., Bering, J. M. & Giambrone, S. 2000 Towards a science of other minds: escaping the argument by analogy. *Cogn. Sci.* **24**, 509–541. (doi:10.1016/S0364-0213(00)00023-9)

Premack, D. & Woodruff, G. 1978 Does the chimpanzee have a theory of mind? *Behav. Brain Sci.* **1**, 515–526.

Raby, C. R., Alexis, D. M., Dickinson, A. & Clayton, N. S. 2007 Planning for the furture by western scrub-jays. *Nature* **445**, 919–921.

Richner, H. 1990 Helpers at the nest in carrion crows (*Corvus corone corone*). *J. Anim. Ecol.* **58**, 427–440.

Schwartz, B. L.& Evans, S. 2001 Episodic memory in primates. *Am. J. Primatol.* **55**,71–85.(doi:10.1002/ajp.1041)

Schwartz, B. L., Colon, M. R., Sanchez, I. C., Rodriguez, I. A. & Evans, S. 2002 Single-trial learning of "what" and "who" information in a gorilla (*Gorilla gorilla gorilla*): implications for episodic memory. *Anim. Cogn.* **5**, 85–90. (doi:10.1007/s10071-002-0132-0)

Seed, A. M., Tebbich, S., Emery, N. J. & Clayton, N. S. 2006 Investigating physical cognition in rooks (*Corvus frugilegus*). *Curr. Biol.* **16**, 697–701. (doi:10.1016/j.cub.2006.02.066)

Semendeferi, K., Lu, A., Schenker, N. & Damasio, H. 2002 Humans and great apes share a large frontal cortex. *Nat. Neurosci.* **5**, 272–276. (doi:10.1038/nn814)

Shettleworth, S. J. 1995 Comparative studies of memory in food storing birds: from the field to the Skinner box. In *Behavioural brain research in naturalistic and semi-naturalistic settings* (eds E. Alleva, A. Fasolo, H.-P. Lipp, L. Nadel & L. Ricceri), pp. 159–194. Dordrecht, The Netherlands: Academic Press.

Suddendorf, T. & Busby, J. 2003 Mental time travel in animals? *Trends Cogn. Sci.* **7**, 391–396. (doi:10.1016/S1364-6613(03)00187-6)

Suddendorf, T. & Corballis, M. C. 1997 Mental time travel and the evolution of the human mind. *Genet. Soc. Gen. Psychol. Monogr.* **123**, 133–167.

Treichler, F. R. & Van Tilburg, D. 1996 Concurrent conditional discrimination tests of transitive inference by macaque monkeys: list linking. *J. Exp. Psychol. Anim. Behav. Proc.* **22**, 105–117.

Tomasello, M. & Call, J. 1997 *Primate cognition.* New York, NY: Oxford University Press.

Tulving, E. 2005 Episodic memory and autonoesis: uniquely human? In *The missing link in cognition: evolution of self-knowing consciousness* (eds H. Terrace & J. Metcalfe), pp. 3–56. Oxford, UK: Oxford University Press.

Vander Wall, S. B. & Jenkins, S. H. 2003 Reciprocal pilferage and the evolution of food-hoarding behaviour. *Behav. Ecol.* **14**, 656–667. (doi:10.1093/beheco/arg064)

Visalberghi, E. & Limongelli, L. 1994 Lack of comprehension of cause–effect relations in tool-using capuchin monkeys *(Cebus apella)*. *J. Comp. Psychol.* **108**, 15–22. (doi:10.1037/ 0735-7036.108.1.15)

Visalberghi, E. & Trinca, L. 1989 Tool use in capuchin monkeys: distinguishing between performing and understanding. *Primates* **30**, 511–521. (doi:10.1007/BF02380877)

Watanabe, S. & Clayton, N. S. 2007 Observational visuospatial encoding of the cache locations of others by western scrub-jays *(Aphelocoma californica)*. *J. Ethol.* (doi:10.1007/s10164-006-0023-y)

Weir, A. A. S., Chappell, J. & Kacelnik, A. 2002 Shaping of hooks in New Caledonian crows. *Science* **297**, 981. (doi:10.1126/science.1073433)

Whiten, A. & Byrne, R. W. 1997 *Machiavellian intelligence II.* Cambridge, UK: Cambridge University Press.

Whiten, A., Goodall, J., McGrew, W. C., Nishida, T., Reynolds, V., Sugiyama, Y., Tutin, C. E. G., Wrangham R. W. & Boesch, C. 1999 Cultures in chimpanzees. *Nature* **399**, 682–685. (doi:10.1038/ 21415)

Wilson, B. J., Mackintosh, N. J. & Boakes, R. A. 1985 Transfer of relational rules in matching and oddity learning by pigeons and corvids. *Q. J. Exp. Psychol.* **37B**, 313–332.

Woolfenden, G. E. 1975 Florida scrub jay helpers at the nest. *Auk* **92**, 1–15.

Woolfenden, G. E. & Fitzpatrick, J. W. 1984 The Florida scrub-jay; demography of a cooperative breeding bird. *Monographs of population biology*, vol. 20. Princeton, NJ: Princeton University Press.

Woolfenden, G. E. & Fitzpatrick, J. W. 1996 Florida scrub-jay *(Aphelocoma coerulescens)*. In *The birds of North America*, vol. 228 (eds A. Poole & F. Gill). Philadelphia, PA; Washington, DC: The Academy of Natural Sciences, American Ornithologists' Union.

3

Social intelligence in the spotted hyena (*Crocuta crocuta*)

Kay E. Holekamp, Sharleen T. Sakai and Barbara L. Lundrigan

If the large brains and great intelligence characteristic of primates were favoured by selection pressures associated with life in complex societies, then cognitive abilities and nervous systems with primate-like attributes should have evolved convergently in non-primate mammals living in large, elaborate societies in which social dexterity enhances individual fitness. The societies of spotted hyenas are remarkably like those of cercopithecine primates with respect to size, structure and patterns of competition and cooperation. These similarities set an ideal stage for comparative analysis of social intelligence and nervous system organization. As in cercopithecine primates, spotted hyenas use multiple sensory modalities to recognize their kin and other conspecifics as individuals, they recognize third-party kin and rank relationships among their clan mates, and they use this knowledge adaptively during social decision making. However, hyenas appear to rely more intensively than primates on social facilitation and simple rules of thumb in social decision making. No evidence to date suggests that hyenas are capable of true imitation. Finally, it appears that the gross anatomy of the brain in spotted hyenas might resemble that in primates with respect to expansion of frontal cortex, presumed to be involved in the mediation of social behaviour.

Keywords: hyena; hyaena; intelligence; social cognition; brain morphology

3.1. Introduction

Primates appear to be endowed with cognitive abilities that are superior to, and qualitatively different from, those observed in most other mammals (reviewed in Byrne & Whiten 1988; Harcourt & de Waal 1992; Tomasello & Call 1997). The social complexity hypothesis suggests that the key selection pressures shaping the evolution of these cognitive abilities have been imposed by complexity associated with the labile social behaviour of conspecific group members (reviewed in Byrne & Whiten 1988). Predictions of this hypothesis have now been confirmed in a number of primate species, suggesting that the evolution of intelligence has been more strongly influenced by social pressures than by non-social aspects of the environment (reviewed in Byrne 1994; Tomasello & Call 1997). Unfortunately, the generality of this hypothesis is severely limited by the current dearth of information about social cognition in animals other than primates (Harcourt & de Waal 1992). The social complexity hypothesis predicts that, if indeed the large brains and great intelligence found in primates evolved in response to selection pressures associated with life in complex societies, then cognitive abilities and nervous systems with primate-like attributes should have evolved convergently in non-primate mammals living in large, elaborate societies in which individual fitness is strongly influenced by social dexterity.

Mammalian carnivores represent an excellent group, outside of the primates, within which to evaluate the relationship between cognitive abilities and social complexity. Carnivores often form social groups that are comparable in size and complexity to those of primates;

many species live in large, permanent social units that contain both males and females from multiple, overlapping generations. Recent studies of phylogenetic relationships among the orders of eutherian mammals suggest that Carnivora and Primates are not sister taxa, but rather are members of distinct clades (Laurasiatheria and Euarchontoglires, respectively) that last shared a common ancestor between 90 and 100 Myr ago (Springer *et al.* 2003, 2005). Therefore, mammalian carnivores offer the opportunity for an independent test of the hypothesis that demands imposed by social living have driven the evolution of both intelligence and nervous systems in mammals. Here, we adopt Kamil's (1987) broad definition of intelligence, and therefore define social intelligence as 'those processes by which animals obtain and retain information about their social environments, and use that information to make behavioural decisions'.

Gregarious carnivores engage in a variety of behaviours, such as cooperative hunts of large vertebrate prey, that have prompted many observers to infer that these predators must possess extraordinary intellectual powers (e.g. Guggisberg 1962). However, the cognitive abilities of carnivores have seldom been the subject of systematic study, and they are currently poorly understood (e.g. Byrne 1994). In our research, we are examining the perceptual, cognitive and neural mechanisms underlying complex social behaviour in one gregarious carnivore, the spotted hyena (*Crocuta crocuta*). One of our primary objectives is to determine whether or not these hyenas exhibit some of the same specific cognitive abilities as those found in primates. Evidence for the existence of shared cognitive abilities would suggest convergent evolution in these two distantly related taxa and would strongly support the social complexity hypothesis. Another major objective is to evaluate the possibility that there has been convergent evolution in the gross anatomy of the brain in hyenas and primates, favoured in both groups by the need to predict and interpret the labile social behaviour of conspecifics. After briefly reviewing the relevant aspects of *Crocuta*'s biology below, we summarize our progress to date towards achieving each of these objectives.

3.2. Relevant biology of spotted hyenas

Spotted hyenas are large terrestrial predators occurring throughout sub-Saharan Africa. Although they occupy a different trophic niche than primates and have various sensory capabilities not shared with primates, hyenas nevertheless exhibit many remarkable similarities to cercopithecine primates with respect to their life histories and to the size and complexity of their social groups. Like macaques and baboons, spotted hyenas are large-bodied mammals with slow life histories. Although *Crocuta*'s diet matches that of other large African carnivores (Kruuk 1972; Schaller 1972; Mills 1990; Caro 1994), the foods of both hyenas and cercopithecine primates generally occur in rich scattered patches appearing unpredictably in space and time. Female hyenas bear litters containing only one or two cubs, and they nurse each litter for up to 24 months. Thus, hyenas, like primates, produce small litters at long intervals, and their offspring require an unusually long period of nutritional dependence on the mother. Both hyenas and primates experience a long juvenile period during which every individual must learn a great deal about its physical and social environments. Males reach reproductive maturity at 24 months of age, and most females start bearing young in their third or fourth year. Like many primates, hyenas have a long lifespan: they are known to live up to 19 years in the wild (Drea & Frank 2003) and up to 41 years in captivity (Jones 1982).

(a) Group size and structure

The complexity of spotted hyena societies is comparable in most respects to that found in societies of cercopithecine primates, and far exceeds that found in the social lives of any other terrestrial carnivore (e.g. Gittleman 1989, 1996; Holekamp *et al.* 2000). *Crocuta* live in permanent complex social groups, called clans, that range in size from 6 to 90 individuals. All members of a clan recognize each other, cooperatively defend a common territory and rear their cubs together at a communal den (Kruuk 1972; Henschel & Skinner 1991). Like cercopithecine primates, *Crocuta* establish enduring relationships with clan mates that often last many years. Clan size and territory size vary with prey abundance across the species' range, but the clans inhabiting the prey-rich plains of eastern Africa are as large as sympatric baboon troops (e.g. Sapolsky 1993), and often contain more than 70 individuals (Kruuk 1972). Like baboon troops, hyena clans contain multiple adult males and multiple matrilines of adult female kin with offspring, including individuals from several overlapping generations. Relatedness is high within matrilines but, on average, clan members are only very distantly related due to high levels of male-mediated gene flow among clans, and mean relatedness declines only slightly across clan borders (Van Horn *et al.* 2004).

Like many primates, hyenas within each clan can be ranked in a linear dominance hierarchy based on outcomes of agonistic interactions, and priority of resource access varies with social rank (Tilson & Hamilton 1984; Andelman 1985; Frank 1986). As in many cercopithecine primates, dominance ranks in hyena society are not correlated with size or fighting ability; instead, power in hyena society resides with the individuals having the best network of allies. In both hyenas and cercopithecine primates, members of the same matriline occupy adjacent rank positions in the group's hierarchy, and female dominance relations are extremely stable across a variety of contexts and over periods of many years. One interesting difference between hyenas and cercopithecines in regard to rank is that adult female hyenas dominate adult males, whereas male cercopithecines dominate females. However, as in virtually all cercopithecine species, male hyenas disperse voluntarily from their natal groups after puberty, whereas females are usually philopatric (Cheney & Seyfarth 1983; Henschel & Skinner 1987; Mills 1990; Smale *et al.* 1997; Boydston *et al.* 2005). Although adult natal male hyenas dominate adult females ranked lower than their own mothers in the clan's dominance hierarchy so long as they remain in the natal clan, when males disperse they behave submissively to all new hyenas encountered outside the natal area. This is the point during ontogenetic development at which females come to dominate males (Smale *et al.* 1993, 1997). When a male joins a new clan, he assumes the lowest rank in that clan's dominance hierarchy (Smale *et al.* 1997). Immigrant males rarely fight among themselves; instead, they form a queue in which the immigrant that arrived first in the clan holds the highest rank in the male hierarchy and the most recently arrived male the lowest (Smale *et al.* 1997; East & Hofer 2001).

(b) Competition and cooperation

In contrast to the social groups of most cercopithecine primates, which tend to be extremely cohesive, *Crocuta* clans are fission–fusion societies in which individual hyenas spend much of their time alone or in small groups, particularly when foraging (Holekamp *et al.* 1997*a,b*). Ungulate carcasses represent extremely rich but ephemeral food resources: a group of hungry hyenas can reduce a large antelope to a few scattered bones in less than half an hour. Competition when feeding at carcasses is therefore extremely intense, and dominant hyenas, which can most effectively displace conspecifics from food, gain access to the choicest bits and largest quantities of food. *Crocuta* often need kin and other allies to defend a carcass from other clan mates. In addition, *Crocuta* need allies during cooperative defence of the clan's territory against alien hyenas (e.g. Henschel & Skinner 1991; Boydston *et al.* 2001). Members of multiple hyena matrilines frequently cooperate to defend their kills against lions or hyenas from other clans, and by doing so risk serious injury or death (Kruuk 1972; Mills 1990; Henschel & Skinner 1991; Hofer & East 1993; Boydston *et al.* 2001). Help from clan mates is also often required while hunting ungulate prey; the probability of successfully making a kill increases by approximately 20% with the presence of each additional hunter (Holekamp *et al.* 1997*b*). Thus, as in cercopithecine primates, the enduring cooperative relationships found among these long-lived carnivores affect survival and reproduction of individual group members.

The many aspects of their social lives and life histories that hyenas share with cercopithecine primates set an ideal stage for comparative analysis of social cognition and nervous system organization. Here, we first review what is known about hyena communication signals, perception of those signals and demonstrated abilities in the domain of social cognition. We then describe work we have recently initiated comparing gross anatomy of the brain in spotted hyenas with that in less gregarious carnivores.

3.3. Communication signals, perceptual abilities and social cognition

Cercopithecine primates possess well-developed cognitive abilities, making them unusually adept at predicting outcomes of behavioural interactions among their conspecifics (e.g. Kamil 1987; Byrne & Whiten 1988; Cheney & Seyfarth 1990, 2003; Harcourt & deWaal 1992; Byrne 1994). They recognize individual conspecifics based on information acquired via multiple sensory modalities, they remember outcomes of earlier encounters with particular conspecifics, and they modify their social behaviour on the basis of interaction histories. Furthermore, cercopithecines clearly possess knowledge about the social relationships among other group members, and adaptively base their decision-making in social situations upon this knowledge (e.g. Cheney & Seyfarth 1990). Here, we review what spotted hyenas know about their social companions, and how they use that knowledge.

(a) Individual recognition

Social complexity is often reflected in the variety of communication signals emitted by a species and in the ability of receivers to perceive and process that information (Blumstein & Armitage 1997). Furthermore, perceptual mechanisms influence and constrain cognitive abilities (Barrett & Henzi 2005). Spotted hyenas emit a rich repertoire of visual, acoustic and olfactory signals. They use these signals to discriminate clan members from alien hyenas (Kruuk 1972; Mills 1990; Henschel & Skinner 1991), to recognize the other members of their social units as individuals and to obtain information about signallers' affect and current circumstances.

Hans Kruuk (1972) was the first observer to become convinced, based on watching spotted hyenas interact in nature, that they can recognize all their group mates using visual, acoustic or olfactory cues. No systematic analysis has been done of visual recognition. However, den-dwelling cubs in our study populations respond appropriately when their mothers, approaching the den silently from downwind, are still hundreds of metres away, suggesting good visual acuity and its application in individual recognition. In the presence of conspecifics, hyenas attend closely to body postures and visual displays of other animals, and especially while feeding at a carcass, they attend to the relative positions of conspecifics; young hyenas, in particular, attempt to gain access to carcasses by entering each feeding melee next to one or more potential allies.

Recognition of conspecifics using vocal and olfactory cues has been systematically studied in *Crocuta*. Spotted hyenas emit a rich repertoire of sounds that includes groans, growls, lows, yells, screams, rumbles and giggles (Kruuk 1972). However, the only hyena call that has been analysed to date is the long-distance 'whoop' vocalization. A whoop bout, which lasts several seconds, is a loud vocalization containing several brief calls separated by pauses. Whoops are emitted by hyenas of both sexes and all ages, starting a few hours after birth (East & Hofer 1991*a,b*). A whoop travels up to 5 km, and clearly has a number of different functions depending on which individuals whoop, and the circumstances under which these calls are emitted. Whereas the acoustic structure of whoop vocalizations varies markedly among individual hyenas, the whoops produced by any single hyena are highly consistent, even over periods of up to several years (East & Hofer 1991*a*). Thus, an acoustic basis exists for individual recognition in *Crocuta*.

We used playback experiments, modelled after those conducted earlier with vervet monkeys by Cheney & Seyfarth (1980), to determine whether hyenas are capable of identifying individual conspecifics on the basis of their whoop vocalizations (Holekamp *et al.* 1999). Hyena mothers frequently respond to the whoops of their own cubs by rushing to help them, much like vervet females respond to the distress cries of their offspring (Cheney & Seyfarth 1980). In fact, one of the most important functions of whoops by cubs is to request assistance when they are threatened or frightened (East & Hofer 1991*b*). Our experiments revealed that a cub's whoops were far more likely to elicit approach and intervention behaviour by its mother than by other listeners (Holekamp *et al.* 1999).

In addition to coding information about the individual identity of callers, whoops also convey information about the caller's age and sex (East & Hofer 1991*a*; Holekamp *et al.* 1999). Whoops by cubs typically contain fewer harmonics, wider spacing between harmonics, shorter durations of low-frequency sections of calls and higher fundamental frequencies than do whoops emitted by adults (East & Hofer 1991*a*). In addition, Theis *et al.* (2007) have recently found that hyenas encode information about their current emotional state by altering the rate at which they produce individual whoops within a whoop bout and by adjusting the length of intervals between these calls. When callers are frightened or upset, they produce calls within bouts at higher rates and reduce inter-whoop interval length. Listeners are significantly more likely to respond to calls with shorter inter-whoop intervals, and from this we infer that listening hyenas monitor the urgency signalled in such calls.

Olfaction plays a similarly important role in the social lives of spotted hyenas. These animals have a keen olfactory sense, and they engage in frequent scent-marking behaviour. Each clan appears to have a unique scent signature (Hofer *et al.* 2001), and wild hyenas mark the boundaries of their group territories with secretions from their scent glands (Kruuk 1972; Henschel & Skinner 1991; Boydston *et al.* 2001). Drea *et al.* (2002*a,b*) found that captive female hyenas spent more time investigating the scents of male than female conspecifics, and that adult subjects of both sexes investigated scents of familiar conspecifics for shorter amounts of time than they spent investigating scents of unfamiliar individuals. These studies demonstrated clearly that *Crocuta* can use olfactory cues to discriminate sex and familiarity of conspecifics (Drea *et al.* 2002*a*,*b*).

Recent field experiments by Theis *et al.* (in press) have shown that wild hyenas can use olfactory cues to acquire additional information as well, and that adults perform differently from cubs in these experiments. Both cubs and older hyenas can distinguish scents of their clan mates from those of hyenas from other clans. Furthermore, cubs express equal interest in scents from males and females, and they also express equal interest in scents from pregnant and lactating females. By contrast, adult females in the wild show clear preferences for scents from females over those from males (the opposite of what was found among captives) and for scents from pregnant over lactating females. The differences in performance between cubs and adults in these olfactory discrimination experiments suggest that these scents and their meanings are learned.

(b) Recognition of kin

As in most primates (e.g. Seyfarth 1980; Seyfarth & Cheney 1984), nepotism is common among *Crocuta*, kin spend more time together than do non-kin (Holekamp *et al*.1997*a*), and individuals direct affiliative behaviour towards kin more frequently than towards non-kin (Walters 1980; East *et al.* 1993; Wahaj *et al.* 2004). Hyenas can distinguish vocalizations of kin from those of non-kin, and in fact the intensity of their responses to whoop vocalizations increases with degree of relatedness between vocalizing and listening animals (Holekamp *et al.* 1999). Results of our playback experiments suggest that kin recognition may occur among hyenas as distantly related as great-aunts and cousins. Although male hyenas do not participate at all in parental care, Van Horn *et al.* (2004) found that sires identified by molecular genetic analysis associated more closely with their daughters than with unrelated control females. In addition, these workers found that cubs favoured their fathers by directing less intense aggression at them than at unrelated adult males. Cubs of both sexes associate more closely with their fathers than with control males after cubs become independent of the communal den. All these results indicate that fathers can recognize their offspring as is the case in baboons (Buchan *et al.* 2003) and that offspring can also recognize their sires.

In an analysis of nepotism between siblings, Wahaj *et al.* (2004) found that full siblings from twin litters associate more closely, and direct more affiliative behaviour towards each other, than do half-sibling littermates. This, like the ability of offspring to recognize their sires, indicates that spotted hyenas use phenotype matching (Holmes & Sherman 1982) to recognize kin. However, Wahaj *et al.* (2004) also found that young hyenas associate more closely with maternal half-siblings than with paternal half-siblings, which suggests the operation of an association-based mechanism along with phenotype matching in *Crocuta*'s kin recognition.

(c) Imitation and coordination of behaviour among multiple animals

Understanding how, when and why animals coordinate their behaviour can shed light on the underlying cognitive and neurobiological processes (Barrett & Henzi 2005). Like cercopithecine primates, spotted hyenas often appear to modify their behaviour after observing the goal-directed behaviour of their group mates. However, although we have made no experimental inquiries about this, we have found no evidence to date that hyenas engage in true imitation, defined as emulating a novel act from the repertoire of a conspecific (Byrne 1995). Instead, spotted hyenas appear to engage on a daily basis in simpler forms of social learning that make fewer cognitive demands than true imitation, including observational conditioning (Emery & Clayton 2005) and response facilitation (Byrne 1994). For example, in response to the played-back sound of a cub whooping in distress, hyenas related to that cub orient to the sound, but only start searching for it when the mother does so first (Holekamp *et al.* 1999). This suggests that response facilitation in this species might be an important proximate mechanism mediating decisions regarding whether or not to aid others. In general, this and other forms of social facilitation appear to play much larger roles in the social lives of spotted hyenas than they do in the lives of cercopithecine primates (e.g. Woodmansee *et al.* 1991; Yoerg 1991; Glickman *et al.* 1997; Holekamp *et al.* 2000). In addition to mediating aiding behaviour, response facilitation strongly affects the behaviour of spotted hyenas engaged in feeding, scent-marking, coalition formation, greeting ceremonies and group hunts (reviewed in Glickman *et al.* 1997).

Cooperative hunting permits hyenas to capture prey animals many times larger than any individual hunter. Group hunts by spotted hyenas, lions and other gregarious carnivores often appear to involve intelligent coordination and division of labour among hunters (e.g. Guggisberg 1962; Peters & Mech 1973). Group hunts by mammalian carnivores certainly represent more complexly organized phenomena than mere opportunistic grabs at prey (e.g. Stander 1992*a,b*). However, although myriad observers have claimed that the group hunting activity of large carnivores requires the operation of human-like mental processes, coordinated hunting behaviour by hyenas can in fact most parsimoniously be explained by the operation of a few simple mental rules of thumb, such as 'Move wherever you need to in order to keep the selected prey animal between you and another hunter' (Holekamp *et al.* 2000). Currently, there is no evidence that hyenas use mental algorithms more complex than simple rules of thumb to capture prey during group hunts. Falsification of the simple 'rules of thumb' hypothesis will require experimental evidence, not only that individual hyenas monitor both their prey and their fellow hunters (e.g. Stander 1992*b*), but also that they accurately anticipate the behaviour of the latter based on knowledge of their goals.

(d) Rank acquisition and social memory

Spotted hyenas appear to enter the world prepared (*sensu* Bolles 1973) to learn their positions in the clan's dominance hierarchy and to remember their histories of interactions with individual conspecifics. During an early period of intensive learning, each hyena comes to understand its own position in a dominance hierarchy that may contain dozens of other individuals (Holekamp & Smale 1993). During the first 2 years of life, juvenile hyenas of both sexes acquire ranks immediately below those of their mothers (Holekamp & Smale 1991, 1993; Smale *et al.* 1993). This occurs through an elaborate process of associative learning called 'maternal rank inheritance' in which the mediating mechanisms are virtually identical to those operating during the period of rank acquisition in many cercopithecine primates (Horrocks & Hunte 1983; Jenks *et al.* 1995; Engh *et al.* 2000). In particular, coalitionary aggression plays an important role in acquisition and maintenance of social rank in *Crocuta* (Mills 1990; Zabel *et al.* 1992; Holekamp & Smale 1993; Smale *et al.*1993), as it does in these primates (e.g. Cheney 1977; Walters 1980; Datta 1986; Chapais 1992).

When hyena cubs first arrive at the clan's communal den, at approximately one month of age, they are just as likely to attack cubs from higher-ranking matrilines as they are to attack offspring of lower-ranking females (Holekamp & Smale 1991, 1993). However, through maternal interventions and coalitionary support from maternal kin and unrelated clan mates, juvenile hyenas learn during early life that they can dominate individuals ranked lower than their mothers (Horrocks & Hunte 1983; Holekamp & Smale 1993; Smale *et al.* 1993; Engh *et al.* 2000). By the time they are eight to nine months of age, their attack behaviour directed at higher-born peers has been completely extinguished, and they now restrict their attacks to lower-born individuals. The process of rank acquisition relative to non-peer clan mates appears to be complete by around 18 months of age (Smale *et al.* 1993). Furthermore, non-littermate hyena siblings assume relative ranks that are inversely related to age in a pattern of 'youngest ascendancy' exactly like that seen in cercopithecine primates (Horrocks & Hunte 1983; Holekamp & Smale 1993). Here too, the mechanisms involved appear to be identical to those in primates (Kurland 1977; Chapais & Schulman 1980); mothers assist their youngest cubs during resource competition, even when this forces mothers to behave aggressively towards their older offspring (Holekamp & Smale 1993).

Spotted hyenas appear to remember the identities and ranks of their clan mates throughout their lives. Although we have conducted no formal studies of social memory in this species, anecdotes provide some basic information about it. For example, we have observed hyenas behave as though they remember individuals from whom they have been separated for one to several years. In one case, two females that had been absent from the clan for an entire year were allowed to rejoin it, albeit at the lowest possible rank positions in the female hierarchy, whereas all other females intruding into the clan's territory were inevitably expelled (Holekamp *et al.* 1993). On another occasion during a border skirmish between members of neighbouring hyena clans, a male that had dispersed from one of these clans several years earlier came racing onto the scene with tail bristled, clearly excited to engage in battle, as were the other immigrant males present at the scene. However, upon orienting towards and recognizing some of its female kin from afar among the opposing combatants, the male immediately desisted, lowering its tail and exhibiting other signs of loss of enthusiasm for battle. From cases like these, we deduce that hyenas can long remember their histories of past interactions with particular conspecifics, and modify their behaviour accordingly.

(e) Application of knowledge about social rank

To see that spotted hyenas adaptively use their knowledge of the social ranks of their clan mates, one needs only spend a few minutes watching them fight over a fresh carcass. Despite the fact that all the hyenas present at a kill are often covered in blood from the prey animal, individual *Crocuta* are astoundingly good at knowing which conspecifics are safe to attack and displace from the carcass, and which ones are better left alone. Adult hyenas only attack animals lower-ranking than themselves in the clan's dominance hierarchy, and they never attack higher-ranking individuals as to do so would most probably result in counterattack by the target animal and its allies, as well as potentially serious injury. The only 'mistakes' we have ever seen under these circumstances have involved young hyenas at kills: here a youngster that had recently become independent of the communal den would inappropriately attack a high-ranking hyena with which the attacker had most probably had very little or no prior experience.

Aside from competing over carcasses, another situation in which it would be adaptive for *Crocuta* to be able to discriminate among clan mates of different ranks occurs during courtship interactions between adult males and females. Szykman *et al.* (2001) found that male–female interactions and associations in this species are almost exclusively initiated and maintained by males. These authors also found that the social ranks of both male and female hyenas influenced intersexual patterns of association. Both high-and middle-ranking males associated most closely with the highest-ranking females. Since female reproductive success varies enormously with social rank in *Crocuta* (Frank *et al.* 1995; Holekamp *et al.* 1996; Hofer & East 2003), males should attempt to associate and mate with the highest-ranking females possible if males are able to discriminate among females based on status. Indeed, when female reproductive condition is controlled, high-and middle-ranking males preferentially seek out high-ranking females, suggesting that males can discern relative rank relationships among their prospective mates (Szykman *et al.* 2001). Interestingly, low-ranking immigrant males, which had only recently arrived in the study clan, failed to exhibit a preference for high-ranking females. One interpretation of this is that these low-ranking males were disadvantaged by their lack of experience in the social group such that they were less adept than males with longer tenure at assessing rank (hence reproductive value) among clan females, and indicating that it may take immigrant males some time to learn the relative ranks of resident females (Szykman *et al.* 2001).

(f) Partner choice and recognition of relationship value

The value of a relationship reflects the magnitude of social or ecological benefits likely to accrue from it, with highly valuable relationships most worthy of maintenance and protection (Cords 1988). Owing to the strict linear dominance hierarchy that structures every *Crocuta* clan, an individual's social rank should reflect its value as a social partner, and thus potential social partners should vary greatly in their value to conspecifics in this species. When conspecifics vary in their relative value as social partners, individuals should possess the ability to assess the value of each potential partner, and compete for partners of the highest relative value based on those assessments (Noë & Hammerstein 1994). Primatologists have long known that cercopithecine primates associate most closely with unrelated dominants ranking immediately above them in the social hierarchy (see Cheney *et al.* 1986; Schino 2001 for reviews), and even assign higher value to information they receive about high-than low-ranking social partners (e.g. Deaner *et al.* 2005).

Hyenas associate most often with their kin (Holekamp *et al.* 1997*a*). Since kin are most often involved in group hunts, coalition formation and cooperative defence of carcasses, kin are highly valuable as social partners. However, as in cercopithecine primates (e.g. Seyfarth 1980), hyenas strongly prefer high-ranking non-kin over lower-ranking non-kin as social companions (Holekamp *et al.* 1997*a*). Furthermore, patterns of greeting behaviour in *Crocuta* follow primate patterns of social grooming (East *et al.* 1993), in which individuals prefer to spend time with, and direct affiliative behaviour towards, high-ranking non-kin (Seyfarth & Cheney 1984). This indicates that hyenas, like many primates, recognize that some group members are more valuable social partners than others. Smith *et al.* (2007) recently found that adult *Crocuta* of both sexes associate most often with non-kin holding ranks similar to their own, and that high-ranking animals are more gregarious than low-ranking individuals. Unrelated female hyenas associate most often with dominant and adjacent-ranking females, as occurs in cercopithecines. Females join subgroups based on the presence of particular conspecifics such that subordinates join focal females at higher rates than do dominants.

Dominant hyenas benefit from association with unrelated subordinates by enjoying priority of access to resources obtained and defended by multiple group members, whereas subordinates benefit because dominants direct less aggression against unrelated females with whom they associate more closely, and they also permit them better access to food at kills (Smith *et al.* 2007). Thus, there is some evidence that reciprocal exchange of goods and services occurs among hyenas as it does among primates. Our results resemble the positive relationship found between proximity and tolerance at drinking and feeding sites among unrelated adult female rhesus monkeys (de Waal 1986, 1991). Although *Crocuta* resemble most cercopithecine primates in that kinship fails to protect them from aggression (Wahaj *et al.* 2004), close association was found by Smith *et al.* (2007) to reduce rates of aggression received from non-kin. These findings suggest that social relationships among adult females are valued commodities within the biological marketplace of a *Crocuta* clan; social rank determines the value of social partners, and *Crocuta* possess the ability to assess relative partner value.

(g) Repair of damaged relationships

Affiliative gestures functioning to repair social relationships damaged during a fight are called reconciliation behaviours (de Waal 1993). Reconciliation is an important behavioural mechanism regulating social relationships and reducing social tension in hierarchical primate societies (Aureli & de Waal 2000). Reconciliation occurs in many primates during friendly reunions between former opponents shortly after aggressive conflicts (reviewed by Aureli & de Waal 2000). Similarly, spotted hyenas use unsolicited appeasement and greeting behaviours to reconcile approximately 15% of their fights (East *et al.* 1993; Hofer & East 2000; Wahaj *et al.* 2001). As is also true in many primates (Aureli & van Schaik 1991*a,b*; Aureli 1992; Kappeler 1993), victims in hyena fights are significantly more likely to reconcile than are aggressors, and male hyenas are more likely to reconcile than females. The latter finding is not surprising in a female-dominated society as males may benefit from information about the state of their relationships with higher-ranking females (Wahaj *et al.* 2001).

The vast majority of conflicts we observe among wild hyenas occur between unrelated opponents, suggesting that kin are more tolerant of each other than non-kin in *Crocuta* and that kin may require conciliatory behaviours to repair their relationships less often than do non-kin. Unrelated hyenas exhibit significantly higher rates of reconciliation and are more likely to reconcile their conflicts than are kin. Since related spotted hyenas associate more closely and interact at higher rates than do non-kin (East *et al.* 1993; Holekamp *et al.* 1997*a*), they might be expected to be most 'forgiving' of aggressive displays from relatives or to minimize the potential costs of conflicts with relatives (Aureli *et al.* 1989).

Species differences in reconciliation may reflect the amount of social cohesion necessary to survive in the wild (de Waal & Ren 1988). The conciliatory tendency of 12% found by Wahaj *et al.* (2001) in spotted hyenas falls relatively low on the conciliatory tendency scale observed in primates, and may reflect the fission–fusion nature of hyena society. Although hyenas depend on cooperation from other clan members for survival and reproduction, they appear to rely more heavily than primates on dispersive rather than non-dispersive mechanisms of conflict resolution.

(h) Quotidian expedience

Barrett & Henzi (2005) recently suggested that, rather than surpassing other mammals with respect to Machiavellian mind-reading or strategic planning abilities, monkeys are more complex than other animals in terms of the number and variety of ways in which they achieve their short-term goals. They referred to this broadly as 'quotidian expedience'. They argued that monkeys can achieve the same goal in a number of different ways. For example, a monkey might avoid aggression by hiding from the aggressor, using 'protected threats', or alarm calling as a distraction. They also suggested that a monkey can achieve a number of different goals in the same way, as when using grooming to achieve access to meat, tolerance, mates, infants or the product of a skilled individual's labour. Barrett & Henzi (2005) further suggested that perhaps monkeys and apes are better than other mammals with respect to their ability to select whatever tactic is necessary to solve an immediate problem, regardless of the possible long-term consequences of such an action. However, it is not clear to us that spotted hyenas differ appreciably from monkeys with respect to the number or variety of ways in which they accomplish their short-term social goals. For example, a hyena can avoid aggression by leaving the aggressor's subgroup, exhibiting appeasement behaviour or distracting the aggressor (Engh *et al.* 2000; Wahaj *et al.* 2001). A hyena can potentially use greeting ceremonies to reconcile fights, reintroduce itself to conspecifics from which it has been separated, or increase conspecifics' arousal levels in preparation for a border patrol or group hunt (Holekamp *et al.* 2000). Whereas the ability to solve the same problem in multiple ways or use one behaviour to solve multiple problems may be a characteristic of complex mammalian societies, *Crocuta*'s social behaviour suggests these traits are not unique to monkeys and apes.

(i) Recognition of third-party relationships

One aspect of social intelligence in which, until recently, primates appeared to differ qualitatively from other gregarious animals was their ability to recognize tertiary, or third-party, relationships among conspecific group members (de Waal 1982; Tomasello & Call 1997). These involve interactions and relationships in which the observer is not directly involved. For example, female vervet monkeys (*Cercopithecus aethiops*) respond to the distress call of an infant by orienting towards the infant's mother, indicating that they perceive an association between the mother and infant regardless of whether or not they are related to that mother–infant pair (Cheney & Seyfarth 1980). Several primate species have been shown to use information about the social relationships among conspecifics in activities, such as recruiting useful allies, challenging competitors, redirecting aggression and reconciling after fights (Bachmann & Kummer 1980; Cheney & Seyfarth 1989; Silk 1999). Laboratory tests have suggested that macaques can use mental representations to categorize tertiary kin relationships (Dasser 1988), and recent field experiments have shown that baboons (*Papio ursinus*) categorize information hierarchically about tertiary rank and kin relationships among other group members (Bergman *et al.* 2003). Tomasello & Call (1997) hypothesized that the ability to recognize third-party relationships is unique to primates and that this distinguishes their mental abilities from those of all other animals, but now this hypothesis has been falsified in both corvids (Paz-y-Miño *et al.* 2004) and spotted hyenas (Engh *et al.* 2005).

As in many cercopithecine primates, the ranks of very young hyenas are dependent on the presence or absence of their mothers (Smale *et al.* 1993; Engh *et al.* 2000). When the mother is absent, animals lower-ranking than the mother sometimes behave aggressively towards the cub, but when the mother is nearby, lower-ranking animals rarely direct aggression towards its cub. Since hyenas treat these youngsters differently in the presence of their mothers than in the presence of other higher-ranking adults, it appears that they might recognize the association represented by the mother–cub pair. On the other hand, it may be that the hyenas are simply learning to use the mother's presence as a discriminative stimulus. If they distress the cub when its mother is nearby, they are likely to be attacked, whereas bothering the cub in the absence of its mother results in no punishment.

Studies of reconciliation and triadic agonistic interactions in cercopithecine primates have indicated that recognition of third-party relationships occurs in many different species (e.g. Cheney & Seyfarth 1986, 1989; Judge 1991; Sinha 1998; Judge & Mullen 2005). Cercopithecines are known to reconcile after fights, not only with their former opponents, but also with the kin of former opponents (e.g. Cheney & Seyfarth 1989), indicating that the conciliatory monkeys recognize those tertiary relationships. In contrast, we rarely observe hyenas reconciling with any animals but their former opponents (Wahaj *et al*. 2001). This suggests either that the ability to recognize tertiary relationships under these circumstances does not significantly enhance their fitness or that hyenas lack this ability.

We have conducted two different studies in which we specifically sought to determine whether spotted hyenas exhibit a primate-like ability to recognize tertiary relationships. In our first study, an experiment designed after Cheney & Seyfarth (1980), we played recordings of cub whoops to groups of female hyenas and monitored reactions of the mother and other adult (control) females (Holekamp *et al*. 1999). In contrast to control monkeys, control hyenas were no more likely to look towards the mother of the whooping cub after the playback than before. At this point, it was unclear whether our results meant that hyenas truly lacked the ability to recognize third-party relationships or that hyenas simply failed to demonstrate this ability in our playback test situation. Therefore, we focused attention in our second study on the behaviour of hyenas during and after fights (Engh *et al*. 2005).

We expected that, if indeed hyenas can recognize third-party relationships based on the social ranks and kin relationships of other hyenas, then they would be able to use this knowledge adaptively in two ways during and after agonistic interactions. First, we predicted that hyenas would be able to discriminate between the ranks of two individuals engaged in a fight and that they would aid the higher-ranking combatant, regardless of their own social ranks in relation to those of the fighters. Second, we predicted that hyenas would be able to recognize the relatives of their former opponents and that they would increase their rates of aggression towards relatives of their opponents after a fight, as occurs in cercopithecine primates (e.g. Cheney & Seyfarth 1986, 1989).

When aggression between two hyenas escalates, one or more others may join the skirmish by forming a coalition with the attacker against the target individual. Typically, animals joining to form coalitions are all dominant to the victim. Thus, a hyena considering an attack might benefit, for example, when attempting to displace a larger subordinate animal from food, by delaying its attack until the arrival of a potential coalitionary ally that is higher-ranking than the target animal. If hyenas increase their rates of aggression only after higher-ranking hyenas arrive on the scene, then they may be following a simple rule of thumb, such as 'only attack a larger subordinate when another individual is present who is higher-ranking than yourself'. Alternatively, if the attack rate also increases following the arrival of an individual that is dominant to the victim but subordinate to the attacker, then the attacking hyena must recognize the relative ranks of the other two individuals. In the latter case, the hyenas would be demonstrating that they can indeed recognize tertiary relationships. This assumes the behaviour of the subordinate animal does not change in ways perceived by the dominant when a new hyena arrives on the scene. Although we looked for behavioural changes in the subordinate under these circumstances, we could not see any.

Our results strongly indicated that hyenas can and do recognize third-party relationships (Engh *et al*. 2005). We found evidence that hyenas which join ongoing disputes do so in a manner consistent with recognition of relative rank relationships. When hyenas joined fights in progress, they almost always joined on the side of the dominant animal, even when that animal was lower-ranking than they were. Zabel *et al.* (1992) suggested that hyenas have a strong tendency to do what other hyenas are doing and therefore that hyenas often join coalitions as a result of social facilitation (Zajonc 1965) rather than based on an assessment of relative ranks. Since most aggression in hyena society is directed towards lower-ranking individuals, simply joining an aggressor is likely to result in the pattern observed by Engh *et al.* (2005), in which the dominant animal is aided far more frequently than the subordinate animal. However, when we looked at rare instances of rank reversals, situations in which the initiator of aggression was lower-ranking than the target, animals that intervened in these fights overwhelmingly came to the aid of the dominant animal. Assuming that the winning subordinate behaves like a dominant animal when it wins a fight, this suggests that hyenas recognize third-party rank relationships, and that they are not just following simple rules, such as 'join in support of aggressors' or 'join whichever animal is winning'. Clearly, hyenas will aid the dominant animal even when that individual is losing the fight. Our post-conflict aggression data also strongly supported the notion that hyenas recognize tertiary kin relationships. Aggressors were more likely to attack the relatives of their opponents after a fight than during a matched control period, and after a fight they were more likely to attack relatives of their opponents than to attack other lower-ranking animals unrelated to their opponents (Engh *et al.* 2005).

(j) Tactical deception, gaze-following and theory of mind

In an effort to replicate with spotted hyenas, Menzel's (1974) classic study of spatial knowledge and non-vocal communication in chimpanzees, Yoerg (in an unpublished study described in Drea & Frank 2003) found that captive hyenas appeared to be deceptive about their knowledge of the environment and that the hyenas' behaviour varied with their immediate social circumstances. When a dominant hyena was informed about the location of food hidden among various potential caches, it approached the baited cache directly, whether alone or accompanied by naive group members. By contrast, a subordinate hyena tested under identical conditions initially led naive group members astray, and later surreptitiously returned to the baited site to claim the prize (Drea & Frank 2003, p 137).

Similarly, we have made anecdotal observations of seemingly deceptive behaviour by wild hyenas. For example, we once observed a low-ranking male, which was travelling with several higher-ranking hyenas, spy a leopard with a young wildebeest it had killed only moments before. The leopard had not yet had time to move its kill to a safe place and was crouching in a creek bed beside the carcass. The group of hyenas crossed the creek bed just upwind of the kill, and none of the other hyenas appeared to note the leopard or its prey. However, four different human observers saw the low-ranking male hyena look directly at the kill as he crossed the creek, but continue past it with the rest of the group until he was well over 100 m beyond the creek. At that point, he turned and loped directly back to the kill and wrangled it away from the leopard without having to compete for it with any higher-ranking hyenas. On other occasions, we have seen low-ranking individuals emit alarm vocalizations in what appeared to be deceptive attempts to gain access to food. Ordinarily, an alarm rumble (Kruuk 1972) emitted by any hyena around an ungulate carcass causes all hyenas present to race off a short distance, then scan for danger (e.g. lions or humans). On each of these particular occasions, however, the low-ranking individual giving the alarm raced directly to the carcass and fed alone until its clan mates realized that there was in fact no danger. On other occasions, we have seen mothers emit alarm rumbles in what appeared to be deceptive efforts to interrupt attacks on their cubs by conspecifics. Although these anecdotes suggest that individual hyenas may sometimes exhibit tactical deception, more systematic work like that of Yoerg (in Drea & Frank 2003) must be done before alternative explanations can be ruled out.

Although gaze-following has never been systematically studied in *Crocuta*, our observations of wild hyenas suggest that, like canids (Hare & Tomasello 1999), hyenas often follow the gaze cues of conspecifics to locate food or danger. However, we have no evidence that hyenas know anything at all about the current mental state or future intentions of conspecifics unless they directly perceive sensory cues that provide them with such information. Thus, like monkeys (e.g. Cheney & Seyfarth 1990; Povinelli & Preuss 1995), spotted hyenas appear to show no understanding of the thoughts or beliefs of others.

(k) Cultural traditions

Rather than intelligence evolving by natural selection favouring animals that can anticipate and manipulate the behaviour of their social companions, van Schaik (2006) recently suggested that intelligence evolves by selection favouring culture in animal societies. He argued that intelligence is likely to evolve in species in which individual animals generate behavioural innovations and conspecifics are tolerated in close enough proximity sufficiently frequently to permit social learning of these innovations by others, as well as the transmission of these innovations between members of consecutive generations. Although we know that *Crocuta* engage in extensive social learning early in life, the topic of culture in hyenas is totally unexplored. However, studies have now been conducted on spotted hyenas in many different parts of sub-Saharan Africa and on multiple clans in some locales, without reports of behavioural variants among clans, other than strong preferences for particular prey species, that might be construed as cultural transmission. On the other hand, cultural variants have never been specifically sought in these study populations, researchers seldom work with hyena clans separated by large distances or other significant barriers to dispersal, and no laboratory experiments have yet been conducted on this with captive *Crocuta*. Thus, it would be premature to rule out the possibility that socially learned behavioural innovations occur in hyenas.

(l) Future directions in the study of hyena cognition

We need to follow up our field studies of cognition in free-living spotted hyenas with more carefully controlled experiments in the laboratory with captive hyenas. For example, although the study by Engh *et al*. (2005) strongly suggested *Crocuta* can recognize third-party relationships based on rank and relatedness, we were forced to make certain assumptions in the field that can only be confirmed in laboratory experiments. However, given that birds living in far simpler societies than those of spotted hyenas have been shown in controlled experiments to be able to recognize tertiary relationships among conspecifics (Bond *et al*. 2003; Paz-y-Miño *et al*. 2004), it would certainly surprise us if spotted hyenas could not also perform this cognitive feat when the ability to do so could so strongly affect their fitness.

An ideal test of the social complexity hypothesis would include data documenting the cognitive abilities of hyenas other than the spotted hyena. In particular, evidence that less gregarious hyaenids (e.g. brown hyenas, *Hyaena brunnea* and striped hyenas, *Hyaena hyaena*) lack some of the cognitive abilities previously documented in *Crocuta* would provide further support for the notion that social complexity favours enhancement of intelligence. We are currently initiating a field study of striped hyenas, which are known to be solitary (Wagner in press). We plan to administer simple standardized 'intelligence tests' to individuals in our study populations of both spotted and striped hyenas. Although these two species are very closely related and confront many of the same ecological problems, the social complexity hypothesis predicts spotted hyenas should perform far better on such standardized tests than striped hyenas, because *Crocuta* have been challenged for many thousands of generations by the labile behaviour of conspecifics.

3.4. Brain organization

Cognitive processes are, of course, mediated by nervous systems; thus the social complexity hypothesis predicts that non-primates living in complex societies should possess brain structures mediating social behaviour that are similar to those in primates. The social complexity hypothesis considered specifically in relation to nervous systems has been dubbed 'the social brain hypothesis' (Brothers 1990; Barton & Dunbar 1997). Considered in relation to body size, the brains of primates are relatively large and complex compared with those of other animals, including most non-primate mammals (Jerison 1973; Macphail 1982; Harvey & Krebs 1990). The relatively large brain size noted among primates is due primarily to the unusually large expanse of neocortex, the laminated, almost uniformly thick grey matter covering much of the outer surface of the brain (Dunbar 2003). Such variables as social group size (Dunbar 1992, 1995), number of social partners, grooming clique size (Kudo & Dunbar 2001) and frequency of social play (Lewis 2001) all correlate strongly with neocortical volume in primates.

The mammalian brain comprises a number of functionally distinct systems, and natural selection acting on particular behavioural capacities causes size changes selectively in the systems mediating those capacities (Barton & Harvey 2000). Frontal cortex is known to mediate complex social behaviour in humans and other mammals (Adolphs 2001; Amodio & Frith 2006); therefore, the social brain hypothesis predicts that we should find larger frontal cortex volumes in gregarious species than in closely related solitary species. Among primates, neocortex disproportionately covers the frontal area whereas a similar relationship does not appear to exist among other mammalian species. Dunbar (2003) suggested that the relatively large frontal neocortex in primates is specifically associated with the demands imposed by life in complex social groups. Thus, social complexity in primates appears to be related generally to greater brain volume and specifically to the expansion of frontal cortex (Dunbar & Bever 1998). If the social brain hypothesis is correct, we should find these same patterns in the brains of non-primate mammals that, although closely related to each other, vary with respect to the complexity of their social lives.

Radinsky (1969) noted a moderate expansion of the frontal cortex of dogs that, like hyenas, are gregarious carnivores. Furthermore, Dunbar & Bever (1998) found that neocortex size in carnivores is correlated with group size and lies on the same grade as does neocortex size in primates. However, Bush & Allman (2004) recently evaluated scaling of frontal cortex across a wide array of mammals, and concluded that frontal cortex in non-primate species does not undergo the same expansion as that observed among primates. These authors examined volume of the frontal cortex, neocortical volume and subcortical brain volume in 55 mammalian species and noted significant differences between primates and carnivores in the scaling of frontal cortex. These differences support the hypothesis that frontal cortex in primates is functionally distinct from that in carnivores and suggest that frontal cortex in each taxon may have been shaped by different selection pressures (Preuss 1995; Bush & Allman 2004).

The conflicts between the results obtained by Dunbar & Bever (1998) and those of Bush & Allman (2004) may derive from problems associated with making meaningful comparisons between brains of primates and carnivores. In particular, Bush & Allman (2004) defined frontal cortex as consisting of all cortex anterior to and including motor cortex. Motor cortex is involved in mediating the planning and execution of movement. Electrophysiological mapping studies of motor cortex have demonstrated that the representation of the hand and face is expanded in primate motor cortex relative to the representation of the remainder of the body (Penfield & Rasmussen 1950; Woolsey 1958). In contrast, similar studies in carnivores including cats and dogs have shown no comparable expansion of forelimb representation in motor cortex (Woolsey 1958; Górska 1974). When motor cortex is included in frontal cortical volume, it is likely to inflate the relative volume of frontal cortex in primates while possibly diminishing the relative frontal cortical volume among carnivores. Moreover, the surface of the brain in most primates has a prominent central sulcus, a deep infolding of tissue that separates somatosensory cortex caudally from motor and frontal cortex rostrally. Unfortunately, this important landmark is not present in carnivore brains. The post-cruciate dimple in carnivores (figure 3.1) is hypothesized to be homologous to the central sulcus in primates in that it demarcates the boundary between motor and somatosensory cortex (Hardin *et al.* 1968; Górska 1974). However, the post-cruciate dimple is not visible on the brain surface in many carnivore species, so it is not a reliable landmark.

Accurate comparisons of frontal cortical volumes between primates and other mammalian orders are extremely difficult, particularly when the large sulcus that demarcates primate

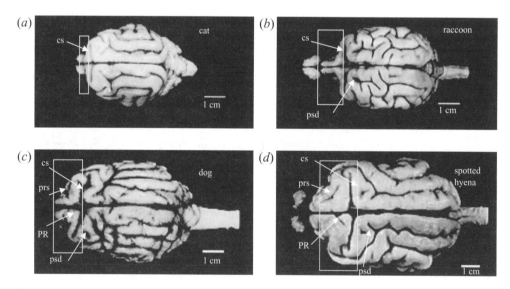

Fig. 3.1 Dorsal views of the cerebral hemispheres of four carnivore species. The box indicates the approximate area of the frontal cortex, defined as the cortex rostral to the cruciate sulcus (cs). Note the relative volume differences among the species. The relative amount of frontal cortex appears greatest in dog and spotted hyena. Other abbreviations: PR, proreal gyrus; prs, presylvian sulcus; psd, post-cruciate dimple. Whole brain images from the University of Wisconsin Comparative Mammalian Brain Collections (supported by the National Science Foundation) at http:// www.brainmuseum.org.

frontal cortex is absent in many taxa of interest. Although different cell types and their distribution can be used to determine the boundary between the rostrally located agranular motor cortex and the caudal granular somatosensory cortex, this determination must be based on microscopic cytoarchitectonic analysis of serial brain sections. Since hyenas lack a central sulcus to delimit the border between motor and somatosensory cortex, we are using cytoarchitectonic analysis in *Crocuta* to determine the volume of frontal cortex both including and excluding motor cortex. For purposes of comparison with primates, the latter measurement may prove to be the best indicator of frontal cortex volume in carnivores, since this will eliminate the exaggerated representation of certain body parts (e.g. forelimb) within the motor cortex as a variable. Ultimately, we hope to undertake a large-scale comparison of primates and carnivores to determine whether we obtain results more closely resembling those of Bush & Allman (2004) or those of Dunbar & Bever (1998).

Our second goal here is to conduct accurate volumetric assessments of frontal cortex in relation to total brain volume in spotted hyenas, and compare these measurements with those obtained from *Crocuta*'s closest living relatives and other carnivore species that vary with respect to social complexity. The spotted hyena is one of only four extant species in the family Hyaenidae. These four species span a wide spectrum of social complexity. In contrast to the highly social *Crocuta*, the striped hyena is solitary (Wagner in press), the aardwolf (*Proteles cristatus*) lives in monogamous pairs (Richardson 1988) and the brown hyena lives in small family groups of up to nine individuals (Mills 1990). *Crocuta* occur sympatrically with all three of these other species in Africa. The four hyena species last shared a common ancestor approximately 11 Myr ago (Koepfli *et al.* 2006). Using skeletal material from the four extant hyaenids, we have recently started using computed tomography (CT) to image hyena brains to examine the relationship between frontal cortex volume and social complexity.

The use of CT technology for addressing comparative questions is a relatively recent phenomenon. The CT scanner makes X-ray slices through an object. These slices display differences in X-ray absorption arising mainly through differences in density within an object. When the slices are put back together, the object can literally be seen, inside and out, in three dimensions. The object itself is untouched. Therefore, high-resolution CT can produce three-dimensional images that permit analyses of deep structures without tissue destruction. Since the CT method can produce detailed images of the interior of a skull, including surface impressions left by the sulcal pattern on the brain's surface, it is a useful technique for generating virtual endocasts of the brain (figure 3.2). We are using CT imagery to determine whether volume of frontal cortex varies with social complexity among hyena species as it does among primates.

In contrast to primate brains, carnivore brains exhibit a large cruciate sulcus (figure 3.1). Based on both anatomical and physiological studies, this prominent sulcus is coincident with much of the rostral extent of motor cortex in cat (Hassler & MühsClement 1964), dog (Górska 1974; Stanton *et al.* 1986; Tanaka 1987; Sakai *et al.* 1993) and raccoon (Sakai 1982, 1990). Our current cytoarchitectonic analysis of *Crocuta* brains will determine whether this is also true in hyenas. If so, then the cruciate sulcus is likely to offer the most reliable landmark for demarcating the boundary between frontal and motor cortex in carnivores. Our preliminary work suggests that the relative amount of cortex rostral to the cruciate sulcus is greater in the spotted hyena than in the other carnivore species we have examined to date (figure 3.1). Our new CT analysis of virtual brains reconstructed from multiple skulls from each hyena species, combined with our on-going cytoarchitectonic analysis, should offer a strong test of

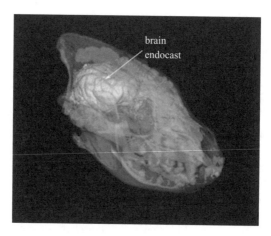

Fig. 3.2 Rendering of CT images from an adult female spotted hyena skull showing both the skull and virtual brain endocast (arrow).

the social brain hypothesis. Specifically, the hypothesis predicts that size of frontal cortex should increase relative to total cortical volume and brain volume in the following order within the family Hyaenidae, as we move from solitary to highly gregarious: striped hyenas; aard-wolves; brown hyenas; and spotted hyenas. We anticipate that our current work with the hyena family will set the stage for a larger-scale analysis of the relationship between social complexity and brain structure in other carnivores to determine whether the same relationship between frontal cortex and social complexity found in primates holds within this second large order of mammals.

3.5 Conclusions

The social complexity hypothesis posits that big brains and great intelligence have been favoured by selection pressures associated with life in challenging social environments (Jolly 1966; Humphrey 1976; Byrne & Whiten 1988). de Waal & Tyack (2003) suggest that the most challenging societies are those in which animals live in stable multi-generational units, group members recognize each other individually, individuals cooperate as well as compete for resource access and a substantial amount of learning occurs during social development. Although some primatologists argue there is already ample evidence that primate societies are more complex than those of other mammals (e.g. Dunbar 2003), we are not entirely convinced this is true. Work to date on spotted hyenas has shown that they live in social groups just as large and complex as those of cercopithecine primates, that they experience an extended early period of intensive learning about their social worlds like primates, that the demand for social dexterity during competitive and cooperative interactions is no less intense than it is in pri-mates, and that hyenas appear to be capable of many of the same feats of social recognition and cognition as are primates.

Much remains to be learned about social cognition in hyenas. For example, we do not yet know whether *Crocuta* use hierarchical classification of rank and kinship as occurs in baboons (Bergman *et al.* 2003). Nor do we know to what extent hyenas might be able to 'keep score', as tamarins do (Hauser *et al.* 2003), of earlier altruistic and selfish acts directed at them by conspecifics. Whether hyenas are capable of tactical deception or cultural transmission of behaviour will not be fully revealed until the appropriate controlled experiments can be conducted. However, based on existing information, it appears that *Crocuta* differ from 'more intelligent' species in that they give us no indication that they are capable of true imitation and in that they rely more intensively on simple rules of thumb in social decision-making. In any case, along with odontocete cetaceans and elephants, hyenas continue to offer a useful model system in which to test hypotheses suggesting cognitive abilities that distinguish primates from other mammals. Furthermore, a comparison between the cognitive abilities and brains of spotted hyenas and those of other hyena species with less complex social systems should allow us to determine whether convergent evolution of brain and behaviour has occurred in non-primate mammals in response to social complexity.

This work was supported by grant 05IRGP358 from Michigan State University and NSF grants 0343381 and IOB0618022. We thank L. Smale for insightful comments on an earlier draft of this paper, and J. E. Smith and S. Benson-Amram for helpful discussions. Finally, thanks to Andrea Kaiser, Colleen Hammond, Dr Kevin Berger and the Department of Radiology, Michigan State University.

References

Adolphs, R. 2001 The neurobiology of social cognition. *Curr. Opin. Neurobiol.* **11**, 231–239. (doi:10.1016/S0959-4388 (00)00202-6)

Amodio, D. M. & Frith, C. D. 2006 Meeting of the minds: the medial frontal cortex and social cognition. *Nat. Rev. Neurosci.* **7**, 268–277. (doi:10.1038/nrn1884)

Andelman, S. J. 1985 Ecology and reproductive strategies of vervet monkeys (*Cercopithecus aethiops*) in Amboseli National Park, Kenya. Unpublished Ph.D. dissertation, University of Washington, Seattle, WA.

Aureli, F. 1992 Post-conflict behaviour among wild long-tailed macaques. *Behav. Ecol. Sociobiol.* **31**, 329–337. (doi:10.1007/BF00177773)

Aureli, F. & de Waal, F. B. M. 2000 *Natural conflict resolution*. Berkeley, CA: University of California Press.

Aureli, F. & van Schaik, C. P. 1991*a* Post-conflict behaviour in long-tailed macaques (*Macaca fascicularis*): I. The social events. *Ethology* **89**, 89–100.

Aureli, F. & van Schaik, C. P. 1991*b* Post-conflict behaviour in long-tailed macaques (*Macaca fascicularis*): II. Coping with uncertainty. *Ethology* **89**, 101–114.

Aureli, F., van Schaik, C. P. & van Hooff, J. A. R. A. M. 1989 Functional aspects of reconciliation among captive long-tailed macaques (*Macaca fascicularis*). *Am. J. Primatol.* **19**, 39–51. (doi:10.1002/ajp.1350190105)

Bachman, C. & Kummer, H. 1980 Male assessment of female choice in hamadryas baboons. *Behav. Ecol. Sociobiol.* **6**, 315–321. (doi:10.1007/BF00292774)

Barrett, L. & Henzi, P. 2005 The social nature of primate cognition. *Proc. R. Soc. B* **272**, 1865–1875. (doi:10.1098/rspb.2005.3200)

Barton, R. A. & Dunbar, R. I. M. 1997 Evolution of the social brain. In *Machiavellian intelligence II: extensions and evaluations* (eds A. Whiten & R. W. Byrne), pp. 240–263. Cambridge, UK: Cambridge University Press.

Barton, R. A. & Harvey, P. H. 2000 Mosaic evolution of brain structure in mammals. *Nature* **405**, 1055–1058. (doi:10.1038/35016580)

Bergman, T. J., Beehner, J. C., Cheney, D. L. & Seyfarth, R. M. 2003 Hierarchical classification by rank & kinship in baboons. *Science* **302**, 1234–1236. (doi:10.1126/science. 1087513)

Blumstein, D. T. & Armitage, K. B. 1997 Does sociality drive the evolution of communicative complexity? A comparative test with ground-dwelling sciurid alarm calls. *Am. Nat.* **150**, 179–200. (doi:10.1086/286062)

Bolles, R. C. 1973 The comparative psychology of learning: the selective association principle and some problems with 'general' laws of learning. In *Perspectives in animal behaviour* (eds G. Bermant & I. L. Glenview). New York, NY: Scott, Foreman & Co.

Bond, A. B., Kamil, A. C. & Balda, R. P. 2003 Social complexity and transitive inference in corvids. *Anim. Behav.* **65**, 479–497. (doi:10.1006/anbe.2003.2101)

Boydston, E. E., Morelli, T. L. & Holekamp, K. E. 2001 Sex differences in territorial behaviour exhibited by the spotted hyena (*Crocuta crocuta*). *Ethology* **107**, 369–385. (doi:10.1046/j.1439-0310.2001.00672.x)

Boydston, E. E., Kapheim, K. M., Van Horn, R. C., Smale, L. & Holekamp, K. E. 2005 Sexually dimorphic patterns of space use throughout ontogeny in the spotted hyaena (*Crocuta crocuta*). *J. Zool.* **267**, 271–281. (doi:10.1017/S0952836905007478)

Brothers, L. 1990 The social brain: a project for integrating primate behaviour and neurophysiology in a new domain. *Concept. Neurosci.* **1**, 27–251.

Buchan, J. C., Alberts, S. C., Silk, J. B. & Altmann, J. 2003 True paternal care in a multi-male primate society. *Nature* **425**, 179–181. (doi:10.1038/nature01866)

Bush, E. C. & Allman, J. M. 2004 The scaling of frontal cortex in primates and carnivores. *Proc. Natl Acad. Sci. USA* **101**, 3962–3966. (doi:10.1073/pnas.0305760101)

Byrne, R. W. 1994 The evolution of intelligence. In *Behaviour and evolution* (eds P. J. B. Slater & T. R. Halliday), pp. 223–265. Cambridge, UK: Cambridge University Press.

Byrne, R. W. 1995 *The thinking ape.* Oxford, UK: Oxford University Press.

Byrne, R. W. & Whiten, A. (eds) 1988 *Machiavellian intelligence.* Oxford, UK: Clarendon Press.

Caro, T. 1994 *Cheetahs of the Serengeti plains.* Chicago, IL: University of Chicago Press.

Chapais, B. 1992 The role of alliances in the social inheritance of rank among female primates. In *Coalitions and alliances in humans and other animals* (eds A. H. Harcourt & F. B. M. de Waal), pp. 29–60. Oxford, UK: Oxford Science.

Chapais, B. & Schulman, S. 1980 An evolutionary model of female dominance relations in primates. *J. Theor. Biol.* **82**, 47–89. (doi:10.1016/0022-5193(80)90090-9)

Cheney, D. L. 1977 The acquisition of rank and the development of reciprocal alliances among free-ranging immature baboons. *Behav. Ecol. Sociobiol.* **2**, 303–318. (doi:10.1007/BF00299742)

Cheney, D. L. & Seyfarth, R. M. 1980 Vocal recognition in free-ranging vervet monkeys. *Anim. Behav.* **28**, 362–367. (doi:10.1016/S0003-3472(80)80044-3)

Cheney, D. L. & Seyfarth, R. M. 1983 Non-random dispersal in free-ranging vervet monkeys: social and genetic consequences. *Am. Nat.* **122**, 392–412. (doi:10.1086/284142)

Cheney, D. L. & Seyfarth, R. M. 1986 The recognition of social alliances by vervet monkeys. *Anim. Behav.* **34**, 1722–1731. (doi:10.1016/S0003-3472(86)80259-7)

Cheney, D. L. & Seyfarth, R. M. 1989 Redirected aggression and reconciliation among vervet monkeys, *Cercopithecus aethiops. Behaviour* **110**, 258–275.

Cheney, D. L. & Seyfarth, R. M. 1990 *How monkeys see the world.* Chicago, IL: University of Chicago Press.

Cheney, D. L. & Seyfarth, R. M. 2003 The structure of social knowledge in monkeys. In *Animal social complexity* (eds F. B. M. de Waal & P. L. Tyack), pp. 207–229. Cambridge, MA: Harvard University Press.

Cheney, D. L., Seyfarth, R. M. & Smuts, B. 1986 Social relationships and social cognition in nonhuman primates. *Science* **234**, 1361–1366. (doi:10.1126/science.3538419)

Cords, M. 1988 Resolution of aggressive conflicts by immature long-tailed macaques *Macaca fascicularis. Anim. Behav.* **36**, 1124–1135. (doi:10.1016/S0003-3472(88)80072-1)

Dasser, V. 1988 A social concept in Java monkeys. *Anim. Behav.* **36**, 225–230. (doi:10.1016/S0003-3472(88)80265-3)

Datta, S. B. 1986 The role of alliances in the acquisition of rank. In *Primate ontogeny, cognition and social behaviour* (eds J. G. Else & P. C. Lee), pp. 219–225. Cambridge, UK: Cambridge University Press.

Deaner, R. O., Khera, A. V. & Platt, M. L. 2005 Monkeys pay per view: adaptive value of social images by rhesus macaques. *Curr. Biol.* **15**, 543–548. (doi:10.1016/j.cub. 2005.01.044) de Waal, F. B. M. 1982 *Chimpanzee politics*. New York, NY: Harper and Row Publishers.

de Waal, F. B. M. 1986 Class structure in a rhesus monkey group: the interplay between dominance and tolerance. *Anim. Behav.* **34**, 1033–1040. (doi:10.1016/S0003-3472(86)80162-2)

de Waal, F. B. M. 1991 Rank distance as a central feature of rhesus monkey social organization: a sociometric analysis. *Anim. Behav.* **41**, 383–395. (doi:10.1016/S0003-3472(05)80839-5)

de Waal, F. B. M. 1993 Reconciliation among primates: a review of empirical evidence and unresolved issues. In *Primate social conflict* (eds W. A. Mason & S. P. Mendoza), pp. 111–144. New York, NY: State University of New York Press.

de Waal, F. B. M. & Ren, R. M. 1988 Comparison of the reconciliation behaviour of stumptail and rhesus macaques. *Ethology* **78**, 129–142.

de Waal, F. B. M. & Tyack, P. (eds) 2003 *Animal social complexity*. Chicago, IL: University of Chicago Press.

Drea, C. M. & Frank, L. G. 2003 The social complexity of spotted hyenas. In *Animal social complexity* (eds F. B. M. de Waal & P. L. Tyack), pp. 121–148. Cambridge, MA: Harvard University Press.

Drea, C. M., Vignieri, S. N., Cunningham, S. B. & Glickman, S. E. 2002*a* Responses to olfactory stimuli in spotted hyenas (*Crocuta crocuta*): Investigation of environmental odors and the function of rolling. *J. Comp. Psychol.* **116**, 331–341. (doi:10.1037/0735-7036.116.4.331)

Drea, C. M., Vignieri, S. N., Kim, H. S., Weldele, M. L. & Glickman, S. E. 2002*b* Responses to olfactory stimuli in spotted hyenas (*Crocuta crocuta*): II. Discrimination of conspecific scent. *J. Comp. Psychol.* **116**, 342–349. (doi:10.1037/0735-7036.116.4.342)

Dunbar, R. I. M. 1992 Neocortex size as a constraint on group size in primates. *J. Hum. Evol.* **20**, 469–493. (doi:10.1016/0047-2484(92)90081-J)

Dunbar, R. I. M. 1995 Neocortex size and group size in primates: a test of the hypothesis. *J. Hum. Evol.* **28**, 287–296. (doi:10.1006/jhev.1995.1021)

Dunbar, R. I. M. 2003 The social brain: mind, language and society in evolutionary perspective. *Annu. Rev. Anthropol.* **325**, 163–181. (doi:10.1146/annurev.anthro.32.061002. 093158)

Dunbar, R. I. M. & Bever, J. 1998 Neocortex size predicts group size in carnivores and some insectivores. *Ethology* **104**, 695–708.

East, M. L. & Hofer, H. 1991*a* Loud-calling in a female-dominated mammalian society: I. Structure and composition of whooping bouts of spotted hyaenas, *Crocuta crocuta*. *Anim. Behav.* **42**, 637–649. (doi:10.1016/S0003-3472(05)80246-5)

East, M. L. & Hofer, H. 1991*b* Loud-calling in a female-dominated mammalian society: II. Behavioural contexts and functions of whooping of spotted hyaenas, *Crocuta crocuta*. *Anim. Behav.* **42**, 651–669. (doi:10.1016/S0003-3472(05)80247-7)

East, M. L. & Hofer, H. 2001 Male spotted hyenas (*Crocuta crocuta*) queue for status in social groups dominated by females. *Behav. Ecol.* **12**, 558–568. (doi:10.1093/beheco/12.5.558)

East, M. L., Hofer, H. & Wickler, W. 1993 The erect 'penis' as a flag of submission in a female-dominated society: greetings in Serengeti spotted hyenas. *Behav. Ecol. Sociobiol.* **33**, 355–370. (doi:10.1007/BF00170251)

Emery, N. J. & Clayton, N. S. 2005 Animal cognition. In *The behaviour of animals: mechanisms, function and evolution* (eds J. J. Bolhuis & L. A. Giraldeau), pp. 170–196. Malden, MA: Blackwell Publishing.

Engh, A. L., Esch, K. & Smale, L. 2000 Mechanisms of maternal rank 'inheritance' in the spotted hyaena, *Crocuta crocuta*. *Anim. Behav.* **60**, 323–332. (doi:10.1006/anbe. 2000.1502)

Engh, A. L., Siebert, E. R., Greenberg, D. A. & Holekamp, K. E. 2005 Patterns of alliance formation and post-conflict aggression indicate spotted hyenas recognize third party relationships. *Anim. Behav.* **69**, 209–217. (doi:10.1016/j.anbehav.2004.04.013)

Frank, L. G. 1986 Social organization of the spotted hyaena (*Crocuta crocuta*): II. Dominance and reproduction. *Anim. Behav.* **35**, 1510–1527. (doi:10.1016/S0003-3472(86)80221-4)

Frank, L. G., Holekamp, K. E. & Smale, L. 1995 Dominance, demography, and reproductive success of female spotted hyenas. In *Serengeti II: conservation, research, and management* (eds A. R. E. Sinclair & P. Arcese), pp. 364–384. Chicago, IL: University of Chicago Press.

Gittleman, J. L. 1989 *Carnivore behaviour, ecology and evolution*. Ithaca, NY: Cornell University Press.

Gittleman, J. L. 1996 *Carnivore behaviour, ecology and evolution II*. Ithaca, NY: Cornell University Press.

Glickman, S. E., Zabel, C. J., Yoerg, S. I., Weldele, M. L., Drea, C. M. & Frank, L. G. 1997 Social facilitation, affiliation, and dominance in the social life of spotted hyenas. *Ann. N. Y. Acad. Sci.* **807**, 175–184. (doi:10.1111/j.1749-6632.1997.tb51919.x)

Górska, T. 1974 Functional organization of cortical motor areas in adult dogs and puppies. *Acta Neurobiol. Exp.* **34**, 171–203.

Guggisberg, C. A. W. 1962 *Simba*. London, UK: Bailey Brothers and Swinfen.

Harcourt, A. H. & de Waal, F. B. M. 1992 Coalitions and alliances in humans and other animals. In *Coalitions and alliances in humans and other animals* (eds A. H. Harcourt & F. B. M. de Waal), pp. 445–471. Oxford, UK: Oxford Science.

Hardin Jr, W. B., Arumugasamy, N. & Jameson, H. D. 1968 Pattern of localization in 'precentral' motor cortex of raccoon. *Brain Res.* **11**, 611–617. (doi:10.1016/0006-8993(68)90149-2)

Hare, D. & Tomasello, M. 1999 Domestic dogs (*Canis familiaris*) use human and conspecific social cues to locate hidden food. *J. Comp. Psychol.* **113**, 173–177. (doi:10.1037/0735-7036.113.2.173)

Harvey, P. H. & Krebs, J. R. 1990 Comparing brains. *Science* **249**, 140–146. (doi:10.1126/science.2196673)

Hassler, R. & MühsClement, K. 1964 Architektonischer Aufbau des sensorimotorischen und parietalen Cortex der Katze. *J. Hirnforsch.* **6**, 377–420.

Hauser, M. D., Chen, M. K., Chen, F. & Chuang, E. 2003 Give unto others: genetically unrelated cotton-top tamarin monkeys preferentially give food to those who altruistically give food back. *Proc. R. Soc. B* **270**, 2363–2370. (doi:10.1098/rspb.2003.2509)

Henschel, J. R. & Skinner, J. D. 1987 Social relationships and dispersal patterns in a clan of spotted hyaenas *Crocuta crocuta* in the Kruger National Park. *S. Afr. J. Zool.* **22**, 18–24.

Henschel, J. R. & Skinner, J. D. 1991 Territorial behaviour by a clan of spotted hyenas (*Crocuta crocuta*). *Ethology* **88**, 223–235.

Hofer, H. & East, M. L. 1993 The commuting system of Serengeti spotted hyaenas: how a predator copes with migratory prey. II. Intrusion pressure and commuter's space use. *Anim. Behav.* **46**, 559–574. (doi:10.1006/anbe.1993.1223)

Hofer, H. & East, M. L. 2000 Conflict management in female-dominated spotted hyenas. In *Natural conflict resolution* (eds F. Aureli & F. B. M. de Waal), pp. 232–234. Berkeley, CA: University of California Press.

Hofer, H. & East, M. L. 2003 Behavioural processes and costs of co-existence in female spotted hyenas: a life-history perspective. *Evol. Ecol.* **17**, 315–331. (doi:10.1023/A:1027352517231)

Hofer, H., East, M. L., Sammang, I. & Dehnhard, M. 2001 Analysis of volatile compounds in scent-marks of spotted hyenas (*Crocuta crocuta*) and their possible function in olfactory communication. In *Chemical signals in vertebrates*, vol. 9 (eds A. Marchlewska-Koj, J. J. Lepri & D. Muller-Schwarze), pp. 141–148. New York, NY: Kluwer Academic/Plenum.

Holekamp, K. E. & Smale, L. 1991 Rank acquisition during mammalian social development: the 'inheritance' of maternal rank. *Am. Zool.* **31**, 306–317.

Holekamp, K. E. & Smale, L. 1993 Ontogeny of dominance in free-living spotted hyaenas: juvenile rank relations with other immature individuals. *Anim Behav.* **46**, 451–466. (doi:10.1006/anbe.1993.1214)

Holekamp, K. E., Ogutu, J., Frank, L. G., Dublin, H. T. & Smale, L. 1993 Fission of a spotted hyena clan: consequences of female absenteeism and causes of female emigration. *Ethology* **93**, 285–299.

Holekamp, K. E., Smale, L. & Szykman, M. 1996 Rank and reproduction in the female spotted hyaena. *J. Reprod. Fertil.* **108**, 229–237.

Holekamp, K. E., Cooper, S. M., Katona, C. I., Berry, N. A., Frank, L. G. & Smale, L. 1997*a* Patterns of association among female spotted hyenas (*Crocuta crocuta*). *J. Mammal.* **78**, 55–64. (doi:10.2307/1382638)

Holekamp, K. E., Smale, L., Berg, R. & Cooper, S. M. 1997*b* Hunting rates and hunting success in the spotted hyaena. *J. Zool.* **242**, 1–15.

Holekamp, K. E., Boydston, E. E., Szykman, M., Graham, I., Nutt, K. J., Birch, S., Piskiel, A. & Singh, M. 1999 Vocal recognition in the spotted hyaena and its possible implications regarding the evolution of intelligence. *Anim. Behav.* **58**, 383–395. (doi:10.1006/anbe.1999.1157)

Holekamp, K. E., Boydston, E. E. & Smale, L. 2000 Group travel in social carnivores. In *On the move: how and why animals travel in groups* (eds S. Boinksi & P. Garber), pp. 587–627. Chicago, IL: University of Chicago Press.

Holmes, W. G. & Sherman, P. W. 1982 The ontogeny of kin recognition in two species of ground squirrels. *Am. Zool.* **22**, 491–517.

Horrocks, J. & Hunte, W. 1983 Maternal rank and offspring rank in vervet monkeys: an appraisal of the mechanisms of rank acquisition. *Anim. Behav.* **31**, 772–782. (doi:10.1016/S0003-3472(83)80234-6)

Humphrey, N. K. 1976 The social function of intellect. In *Growing points in ethology* (eds P. P. G. Bateson & R. A. Hinde), pp. 303–317. Cambridge, UK: Cambridge University Press.

Jenks, S. M., Weldele, M. L., Frank, L. G. & Glickman, S. E. 1995 Acquisition of matrilineal rank in captive spotted hyaenas emergence of a natural social system in peer-reared animals and their off-spring. *Anim. Behav.* **50**, 893–904. (doi:10.1016/0003-3472(95)80092-1)

Jerison, H. J. 1973 *Evolution of the brain and intelligence*. New York, NY: Academic Press.

Jolly, A. 1966 Lemur social behaviour and primate intelligence. *Science* **152**, 501–506. (doi:10.1126/science.153.3735.501)

Jones, M. L. 1982 Longevity of captive mammals. *Zool. Gart.* **52**, 113–128.

Judge, P. G. 1991 Dyadic and triadic reconciliation in pigtail macaques (*Macaca nemistrina*). *Am. J. Primatol.* **23**, 225–237. (doi:10.1002/ajp.1350230403)

Judge, P. G. & Mullen, S. H. 2005 Quadratic post-conflict affiliation among bystanders in a hamadryas baboon group. *Anim. Behav.* **69**, 1345–1355. (doi:10.1016/j.anbehav.2004.08.016)

Kamil, A. C. 1987 A synthetic approach to the study of animal intelligence. *Nebr. Symp. Motiv.* **7**, 257–308.

Kappeler, P. M. 1993 Reconciliation and post-conflict behaviour in ringtailed lemurs, *Lemur catta* and redfronted lemurs, *Eulemur fulvus rufus*. *Anim. Behav.* **45**, 901–915. (doi:10.1006/anbe.1993.1110)

Koepfli, K. P., Jenks, S. M., Eizirik, E., Zahirpour, T., Can Valkenburgh, B. & Wayne, R. K. 2006 Molecular systematics of the Hyaenidae: relationships of a relictual lineage resolved by a molecular supermatrix. *Mol. Phylogenet. Evol.* **38**, 603–620. (doi:10.1016/j.ympev.2005.10.017)

Kruuk, H. 1972 *The spotted hyena: a study of predation and social behaviour.* Chicago, IL: University of Chicago Press.

Kudo, H. & Dunbar, R. I. M. 2001 Neocortex size and social network size in primates. *Anim. Behav.* **62**, 711–722. (doi:10.1006/anbe.2001.1808)

Kurland, J. A. 1977 *Kin selection in the Japanese monkey. Contributions to primatology,* vol. 12. Basel, Germany: S. Karger.

Lewis, K. 2001 A comparative study of primate play behaviour: implications for the study of cognition. *Folia Primatol.* **71**, 417–421. (doi:10.1159/000052740)

Macphail, E. M. 1982 *Brain and intelligence in vertebrates*. Oxford, UK: Clarendon Press.

Menzel, E. W. 1974 A group of chimpanzees in a 1-acre field: leadership and communication. In *Behaviour of nonhuman primates* (eds A. M. Schrier & F. Stollnitz), pp. 83–153. New York, NY: Academic Press.

Mills, M. G. L. 1990 *Kalahari hyaenas: the behavioural ecology of two species*. London, UK: Unwin Hyman.

Noë, R. & Hammerstein, P. 1994 Biological markets: supply and demand determine the effect of partner choice in cooperation, mutualism, and mating. *Behav. Ecol. Sociobiol.* **35**, 111.

Paz-y-Miño, G. C., Bond, A. B., Kamil, A. C. & Balda, R. P. 2004 Pinyon jays use transitive inference to predict social dominance. *Nature* **430**, 778–781. (doi:10.1038/nature02723)

Penfield, W. & Rasmussen, T. 1950 *The cerebral cortex of man. A clinical study of localization function.* New York, NY: Macmillan.

Peters, R. & Mech, L. D. 1973 Behavioural and intellectual adaptations of selected mammalian predators to the problem of hunting large animals. In *Socioecology and psychobiology of primates* (ed. R. H. Tuttle), pp. 279–300. The Hague, The Netherlands: Mouten Publishing.

Povinelli, D. J. & Preuss, T. M. 1995 Theory of mind: evolutionary history of a cognitive specialization. *Trends Neurosci.* **18**, 418–424. (doi:10.1016/0166-2236(95)93939-U)

Preuss, T. M. 1995 Do rats have a prefrontal cortex? The Rose–Woolsey–Akert program reconsidered. *J. Cogn. Neurosci.* **7**, 1–24.

Radinsky, L. B. 1969 Outlines of canid and felid brain evolution. *Ann. N. Y. Acad. Sci.* **167**, 277–288. (doi:10.1111/j.1749-6632.1969.tb20450.x)

Richardson, P. R. K. 1988 Mate desertion in response to female promiscuity in the socially monogamous aardwolf, *Proteles cristatus. S. Afr. Tydskr. Dierk.* **23**, 306–308.

Sakai, S. T. 1982 The thalamic connectivity of the primary motor cortex (MI) in the raccoon. *J. Comp. Neurol.* **204**, 238–252. (doi:10.1002/cne.902040304)

Sakai, S. T. 1990 Corticospinal projections from area 6 in the raccoon. *Exp. Brain Res.* **79**, 240–248. (doi:10.1007/BF00608232)

Sakai, S. T., Stanton, G. B. & Isaacson, L. 1993 Thalamic afferents of areas 4 and 6 in the dog: a multiple retrograde fluorescent dye study. *Anat. Embryol.* **188**, 551–559. (doi:10.1007/BF00187010)

Sapolsky, R. M. 1993 Endocrinology alfresco: psychoendocrine studies of wild baboons. *Rec. Prog. Horm. Res.* **48**, 437–468.

Schaller, G. 1972 *The Serengeti lion*. Chicago, IL: University of Chicago Press.

Schino, G. 2001 Grooming, competition, and social rank among female primates: a metaanalysis. *Anim. Behav.* **62**, 265–271. (doi:10.1006/anbe.2001.1750)

Seyfarth, R. M. 1980 The distribution of grooming and related behaviours among adult female vervet monkeys. *Anim. Behav.* **28**, 798–813. (doi:10.1016/S0003-3472(80)80140-0)

Seyfarth, R. M. & Cheney, D. L. 1984 Grooming, alliances, and reciprocal altruism in vervet monkeys. *Nature* **308**, 541–543. (doi:10.1038/308541a0)

Silk, J. B. 1999 Male bonnet macaques use information about third-party rank relationships to recruit allies. *Anim. Behav.* **58**, 45–51. (doi:10.1006/anbe.1999.1129)

Sinha, A. 1998 Knowledge acquired and decisions made: triadic interactions during allogrooming in wild bonnet macaques, *Macaca radiata. Phil. Trans. R. Soc. B* **353**, 619–631. (doi:10.1098/rstb.1998.0230)

Smale, L., Frank, L. G. & Holekamp, K. E. 1993 Ontogeny of dominance in free-living spotted hyenas: juvenile rank relations with adults. *Anim. Behav.* **46**, 467–477. (doi:10.1006/anbe.1993.1215)

Smale, L., Nunes, S. & Holekamp, K. E. 1997 Sexually dimorphic dispersal in mammals: patterns, causes and consequences. *Adv. Stud. Behav.* **26**, 181–250.

Smith, J. E., Memenis, S. K. & Holekamp, K. E. 2007 Rank-related partner choice in the fission–fusion society of the spotted hyena (*Crocuta crocuta*). *Behav. Ecol. Sociobiol.* **61**, 753–765. (doi:10.1007/s00265-006-0305-y)

Springer, M. S., Murphy, W. J., Eizirik, E. & O'Brien, S. 2003 Placental mammal diversification and the Cretaceous-Tertiary boundary. *Proc. Natl Acad. Sci. USA* **100**, 1056–1061. (doi:10.1073/pnas.0334222100)

Springer, M. S., Murphy, W. J., Eizirik, E. & O'Brien, S. 2005 Molecular evidence for major placental clades. In *The rise of placental mammals* (eds K. D. Rose & J. D. Archibald), pp. 37–49. Baltimore, MD: The Johns Hopkins University Press.

Stander, P. E. 1992a Foraging dynamics of lions in a semiarid environment. *Can. J. Zool.* **70**, 8–21.

Stander, P. E. 1992b Cooperative hunting in lions: the role of the individual. *Behav. Ecol. Sociobiol.* **29**, 445–454. (doi:10.1007/BF00170175)

Stanton, G. B., Tanaka, D., Sakai, S. T. & Weeks, O. I. 1986 The thalamic and subcortical afferents of area 6 subdivisions on the anterior sigmoid gyrus in the dog. *J. Comp. Neurol.* **252**, 446–467. (doi:10.1002/cne.902520403)

Szykman, M., Engh, A. L., Van Horn, R. C., Funk, S., Scribner, K. T. & Holekamp, K. E. 2001 Association patterns between male and female spotted hyenas reflect male mate choice. *Behav. Ecol. Sociobiol.* **50**, 231–238. (doi:10.1007/s002650100356)

Tanaka, D. 1987 Neostriatal projections from cytoarchitecturally defined gyri in the prefrontal cortex of the dog. *J. Comp. Neurol.* **261**, 48–73. (doi:10.1002/cne.902610105)

Theis, K. R., Heckla, A. L., Verge, J. R. & Holekamp, K. E. In press. The ontogeny of pasting behaviour in free-living spotted hyenas (*Crocuta crocuta*). In *Chemical signals in vertebrates*, vol. 11 (eds J. Hurst & R. Beynon). New York, NY: Springer.

Theis, K. R., Greene, K., Benson-Amram, S. R. & Holekamp, K. E. 2007 Sources of variation in the long-distance vocalizations of spotted hyenas. *Behaviour* **144**, 557–584.

Tilson, R. T. & Hamilton, W. J. 1984 Social dominance and feeding patterns of spotted hyaenas. *Anim. Behav.* **32**, 715–724. (doi:10.1016/S0003-3472(84)80147-5)

Tomasello, M. & Call, J. 1997 *Primate cognition*. Oxford, UK: Oxford University Press.

Van Horn, R. C., Wahaj, S. A. & Holekamp, K. E. 2004 Role-reversed nepotistic interactions between sires and offspring in the spotted hyena. *Ethology* **110**, 1–14. (doi:10.1111/j.1439-0310.2004.00984.x)

van Schaik, C. 2006 Why are some animals so smart? *Sci. Am.* **294**, 64–71.

Wagner A. P. In press. *Hyaena hyaena* (Linnaeus). In *The mammals of Africa* (eds J. Kingdon, D. Happold & T. Butynski). London, UK: Elsevier Science.

Wahaj, S., Guze, K. & Holekamp, K. E. 2001 Reconciliation in the spotted hyena (*Crocuta crocuta*). *Ethology* **107**, 1057–1074. (doi:10.1046/j.1439-0310.2001.00717.x)

Wahaj, S. A., Van Horn, R. C., Van Horn, T., Dreyer, R., Hilgris, R., Schwarz, J. & Holekamp, K. E. 2004 Kin discrimination in the spotted hyena (*Crocuta crocuta*): nepotism among siblings. *Behav. Ecol. Sociobiol.* **56**, 237–247.

Walters, J. 1980 Interventions and the development of dominance relationships in female baboons. *Folia Primatol.* **34**, 61–89.

Woodmansee, K. B., Zabel, C. J., Glickman, S. E., Frank, L. G. & Keppel, G. 1991 Scent marking (pasting) in a colony of immature spotted hyenas (*Crocuta crocuta*): a developmental study. *J. Comp. Psychol.* **105**, 1014. (doi:10.1037/0735-7036.105.1.10)

Woolsey, C. N. 1958 Organization of somatic sensory and motor areas of the cerebral cortex. In *Biological and biochemical bases of behaviour* (eds H. F. Harlow & C. N. Woolsey), pp. 63–81. Madison, WI: University of Wisconsin Press.

Yoerg, S. I. 1991 Social feeding reverses learned flavour aversions in spotted hyenas (*Crocuta crocuta*). *J. Comp. Psychol.* **105**, 185–189. (doi:10.1037/0735-7036.105.2.185)

Zabel, C. J., Glickman, S. E. & Frank, L. G. 1992 Coalition formation in a colony of prebubertal spotted hyaenas. In *Coalitions and alliances in humans and other animals* (eds A. H. Harcourt & F. B. M. de Waal), pp. 113–135. Oxford, UK: Oxford Science.

Zajonc, R. B. 1965 Social facilitation. *Science* **149**, 269–274. (doi:10.1126/science.149.3681.269)

4

The adaptive value of sociality in mammalian groups

Joan B. Silk

According to behavioural ecology theory, sociality evolves when the net benefits of close association with conspecifics exceed the costs. The nature and relative magnitude of the benefits and costs of sociality are expected to vary across species and habitats. When sociality is favoured, animals may form groups that range from small pair-bonded units to huge aggregations. The size and composition of social groups have diverse effects on morphology and behaviour, ranging from the extent of sexual dimorphism to brain size, and the structure of social relationships. This general argument implies that sociality has fitness consequences for individuals. However, for most mammalian species, especially long-lived animals like primates, there are sizable gaps in the chain of evidence that links sociality and social bonds to fitness outcomes. These gaps reflect the difficulty of quantifying the cumulative effects of behavioural interactions on fitness and the lack of information about the nature of social relationships among individuals in most taxa. Here, I review what is known about the reproductive consequences of sociality for mammals.

Keywords: sociality; fitness; reproductive success; social organization; social bonds; reproductive strategies

4.1 Introduction

Although many studies of insects, birds, and mammals have documented the functional significance of single interactions such as fights, the reproductive benefits of long-term social bonds are less immediately obvious.

(Cheney *et al.* 1986)

It has been 20 years since this observation was made. During the interim, we have documented some of the characteristics that contribute to individual variation in reproductive performance. For example, in ungulates, female reproductive success is influenced by their age, maternal experience and longevity (Clutton-Brock *et al.* 1988; Gaillard *et al.* 2000; Weladji *et al.* 2006). For animals that live in social groups, reproductive success is also influenced by the outcome of certain types of social interactions. Thus, there are positive correlations between dominance rank and reproductive performance in many taxa (Pusey & Packer 1997). In some species, social conditions influence the physiological responses of individuals. For example, the presence of familiar conspecifics buffers the effects of experimentally-induced stress in rats, mice, goats and monkeys (House *et al.* 1988; Seeman & McEwen 1996). Social integration is linked to reduced levels of basal cortisol levels in male baboons (Sapolsky *et al.* 1997), and the existence of close bonds between adult male baboons and lactating females mitigates females' stress responses in the presence of potentially infanticidal males (Beehner *et al.* 2005; Engh *et al.* 2006a). Although it seems plausible that the quality and stability of social bonds may have long-term reproductive consequences for individuals, the links between sociality, social relationships and fitness remain quite tenuous.

This represents a critical gap in our knowledge because we have built a body of theory about the functional consequences of sociality. The forms of social cognition that are described in this volume have presumably been favoured by natural selection because they enhance the ability of group-living individuals to reproduce successfully. These capacities are deployed as animals develop relationships, form alliances, court mates and compete for resources with conspecifics. The capacity to form and maintain social bonds plays an integral role in functional interpretations of many aspects of behaviour, such as reconciliation in monkeys (Aureli & de Waal 2000), coalitions in cetaceans (Connor et al. 1998; Connor 2007) and pair bonding in microtine rodents (Young & Wang 2004). To critically evaluate these hypotheses, we must be able to document the reproductive consequences of sociality for individuals.

According to behavioural ecology theory, sociality evolves when the net benefits of close association with conspecifics exceed the costs (Krause & Ruxton 2002). In mammals, sociality can be beneficial for individuals because it provides greater protection from predators, enhances success in locating or maintaining access to resources, creates mating opportunities or reduces vulnerability to infanticide. At the same time, sociality can be costly for individuals because it increases competition over access to resources and mating opportunities, exposes them to infection and may increase their conspicuousness to predators. The nature and relative magnitude of the benefits and costs of sociality are expected to vary across species and habitats. For primates and many other mammals, it is generally thought that the main benefit of sociality is protection against predators and the main cost of sociality is increased competition for resources with other group members (e.g. Sterck et al. 1997; Isbell & Young 2002).

When sociality is favoured, animals may form groups that range from small pair-bonded units to huge aggregations. The size and composition of social groups have diverse effects on morphology and behaviour, ranging from the extent of sexual dimorphism (primates: Clutton-Brock et al. 1977; Plavcan 2003; ungulates: Clutton-Brock et al. 1980; Pérez-Barbería et al. 2002) to relative brain size (primates: Sawaguchi & Kudo 1990; Dunbar 1992, 1995; Barton & Dunbar 1997; cetaceans: Connor et al. 1998; carnivores and insectivores: Dunbar & Bever 1998; ungulates: Shultz & Dunbar 2006), and the prevalence of infanticide (Hausfater & Hrdy 1984; van Schaik & Janson 2000).

This general argument implies that sociality has fitness consequences for individuals. However, for most mammalian species, especially long-lived animals like primates, there are sizable gaps in the chain of evidence that links sociality and social bonds to fitness outcomes. These gaps reflect the difficulty of quantifying the cumulative effects of behavioural interactions on fitness. This problem is common to almost all studies of the adaptive function of social behaviour in animals. Instead, we generally rely on what Grafen (1991) called the 'phenotypic gambit', the assumption that the short-term benefits that individuals derive from social interactions are ultimately translated into long-term differences in fitness. For example, if group size reduces vigilance time, then individuals will be able to forage more efficiently, and enhanced foraging efficiency will be ultimately transformed into fitness gains. Similarly, we assume that animals which are regularly supported in agonistic confrontations or groomed frequently gain short-term benefits that enhance their lifetime fitness. Social relationships that provide these kinds of short-term benefits are therefore assumed to have selective value for individuals. This logic is sometimes extended one step further. It is hypothesized that the magnitude of the investment that animals make in their social relationships provides a measure of their adaptive value (Kummer 1978). This hypothesis cannot be tested without information about the adaptive consequences of social bonds.

The goal of this paper is to venture beyond the phenotypic gambit and to review what we know about the adaptive consequences of sociality in mammalian groups. I focus on females for both theoretical and practical reasons. Males disperse more regularly and over longer distances than females do in most mammalian taxa (Greenwood 1980; Waser & Jones 1983), including primates (Pusey & Packer 1986). Female philopatry enhances the potential for cooperative relationships to arise through kin selection, and may thus facilitate the development of social bonds and the formation of social groups. Practical considerations also favour an emphasis on females because it is considerably easier to assess female reproductive performance than male reproductive performance in most species.

If living in social groups confers fitness benefits on females, then it should be possible to demonstrate that *intraspecific* variation in sociality influences female reproductive success. Group size is the dimension of sociality that is most commonly evaluated in this context, partly because it is straightforward to measure. However, groups can also differ in various aspects of their composition, such as the ratio of adult males to females, the age structure or the degree of relatedness among group members. Variations in any or all of these aspects of group composition might influence the reproductive performance of individuals. Finally, there may be fitness consequences associated with variation in the number, quality and stability of social bonds that females form.

Here, I review published information about the effects of intraspecific variation in group size, group composition and the nature of social bonds on the reproductive performance of females in mammalian species. Although much of the work on social cognition has focused on primates, I have expanded the taxonomic scope of this review beyond primates for several reasons. First, there is no particular reason to think that the evolutionary consequences of sociality in primate females are different from the evolutionary consequences of sociality in other mammalian taxa. Primate females share basic features of their reproductive biology with females in other mammalian taxa, and face many of the same tradeoffs between the costs and the benefits of living in social groups. Second, some valuable information about the proximate and ultimate consequences of sociality come from experimental studies that would be impractical to conduct on primates. Third, there is a vast literature on mammals which provides a rich source of evidence about the adaptive consequences of variation in sociality.

4.2 Effects of group size

The size of animal groups reflects the combined effects of the benefits and costs of grouping. For any particular species in any particular habitat, there will be some group size which maximizes the fitness of individuals. This means that females which live in groups that are smaller or larger than the optimal size will reproduce less successfully than females living in intermediate-sized groups. Considerable theoretical and empirical research on optimum group size indicates that the size of groups that animals actually live in often exceeds the optimal group size. The discrepancy between the optimal and the actual size of groups is related to mechanisms that regulate group size. Animals living in groups that are larger than the optimal group might try to oust other residents or disperse themselves. They might also attempt to exclude immigrants. All of these courses of action will be costly to individuals who undertake them. Moreover, animals that make efforts to regulate group size provide benefits to other group members, thus providing a form of altruistic public service. As a result, animals will often find themselves living in groups that exceed the optimal size.

If the individual costs of regulating group size tend to lead groups to exceed the optimal size, then we might expect to find negative relationships between group size and female reproductive performance under some circumstances. For example, according to the ecological constraints model (Chapman & Chapman 2000), an increase in group size produces an increase in the distance that members of groups must travel each day because larger groups deplete food patches more rapidly or require larger search fields. Animals that travel further expend more energy and reproduce less efficiently. Day range and group size are positively associated in a variety of primate and carnivore species (Wrangham *et al.* 1993). These kinds of ecological pressures may have broad impacts in mammalian species. Clutton-Brock and his colleagues (2001) have observed that: 'In social mammals whose young are reared principally by their parents and are rarely (or never) fed directly by other group members, competition for resources commonly increases in large groups and breeding success either declines with increasing group size or shows no consistent relation to it'.

Competition for resources may not be the only factor producing a negative relationship between group size and female reproductive performance. For example, in some species, such as langurs and lions, large groups of females are attractive targets for takeover attempts by males. If male takeovers are associated with infanticide, as is the case in a number of mammalian species (van Schaik & Janson 2000), then rates of infant mortality may be higher in large groups than in small ones.

There may also be circumstances in which positive correlations between group size and reproductive performance are expected to occur. For example, Clutton-Brock and his colleagues (2001) noted that '. . . positive relations between breeding success and group size are common in social mammals whose young are reared by helpers'. Similarly, for species that do not rely on foods which occur in discrete depletable patches, including some folivores, there may be little cost associated with living in large groups (Chapman & Chapman 2000).

Here, I review evidence about the effects of group size on reproductive performance in a range of mammalian taxa. Following the observation of Clutton-Brock *et al.* (2001) that the relationship between group size and female fitness tends to be negative or neutral when females rear their young alone, but positive when young are reared by helpers, species are loosely ordered by the extent of reproductive skew and the amount of assistance that females receive from other group members. At one end of the continuum are plural breeding species in which all females regularly reproduce and parents, particularly mothers, provide nearly all of their own infants' care. At the other end of the continuum are species in which reproduction is monopolized by a single breeding female, and females are unable to reproduce without non-breeding helpers. In the middle are plural breeding species with communal care of offspring. The relationship between group size and female fitness is expected to become increasingly positive as we move across this continuum.

(a) Plural breeding species without communal care of young

Long-term studies of yellow-bellied marmots (*Marmota flaviventris*) in Colorado conducted by Armitage and his colleagues provide detailed information about the effects of sociality on female reproductive performance. Yellow-bellied marmots live in montane meadows in western North America, and they typically form groups composed of several breeding females and their offspring (Blumstein & Armitage 1999). Females cooperatively defend their home ranges against intruders (Allainé 2000). They hibernate alone at low altitudes and together at higher elevations (Blumstein & Armitage 1999). Offspring remain in their natal areas through the first year of life. Then, nearly all yearling males disperse, while about half of all yearling females remain in their natal territories. The recruitment of daughters leads to high degrees of relatedness among females within yellow-bellied marmot groups (Allainé 2000). Females reproduce more successfully in groups that contain multiple females than in groups that contain only one female. However, females that live in exceptionally large groups reproduce less successfully than females that live in intermediate-sized groups (Armitage & Schwartz 2000). Very large groups do not occur often and are unlikely to persist from one year to the next. When group size is reduced through natural causes, females' reproductive success improves. Female reproductive success in very large groups is apparently depressed by competition among females.

Further analyses of the same dataset indicate that the effects of group size have the most pronounced effects on young females. Females who begin to reproduce as 2-year-olds have greater individual fitness than females who delay reproduction (Oli & Armitage 2003), but less than half of the females who survive to age 2 begin to reproduce at this age. Two-year-old females are substantially more likely to reproduce if there are no older females in the group, but after females have begun to reproduce the number of females present has no subsequent effect on their reproductive performance. Thus, the number of females that are present in the group when females begin to reproduce has a significant negative effect on their lifetime fitness. Although young females are reproductively suppressed in large groups, they may be even worse off if they attempt to disperse. Dispersing animals suffer high rates of mortality and few suitable territories are available. Moreover, if females do find a vacant territory, they will constitute a matriline of one and are unlikely to reproduce successfully (Armitage & Schwartz 2000).

Tuco-tucos (*Ctenomys sociabilis*) are small subterranean rodents from southwestern Argentina (Lacey 2004). They form groups that contain one adult male, one to six breeding females and their offspring. All females reproduce and rear their young in a single nest in an underground burrow, and all group members participate in burrow maintenance and predator detection. Dispersal is uncommon and is limited to a short period at the end of females' first year. Females who do not disperse at this stage remain in their natal groups throughout their lives. Females who disperse and survive to reproduce, breed alone as yearlings, but may be joined by philopatric daughters in subsequent breeding seasons. There is a strong negative effect of group living on females' reproductive performance. Females living in groups produce fewer surviving offspring per capita than lone females. Moreover, for females that live in groups, there is a negative relationship between the number of adult females and the per capita number of pups reared to weaning. There is evidence that group size has a direct effect on female reproductive performance because decreases in group size from year to year are associated with increases in female reproductive success across years. Even though lone females produce significantly more surviving offspring than group living females, there are no detectable differences in the lifetime reproductive success of dispersing and philopatric females, perhaps because group living females are more likely to survive from one year to the next.

On the island of Rhum, female red deer (*Cervus elaphus*) occupy home ranges of approximately 2 km^2 and make intensive use of smaller core areas within their ranges (Clutton-Brock *et al.* 1982, 1988). Maternal kin share a common home range and females' core areas often overlap or adjoin the core areas of their mothers and sisters. Matrifocal groups range in size from 2 to 12 breeding females. Females that belong to very small and very large matrilines reproduce less successfully than females that live in matrifocal groups of intermediate size. Competition with related females for preferred resources within their core areas seems to reduce the reproductive success of females in large matrifocal groups.

Bottle-nose dolphins (*Tursiop* spp.) live in fission–fusion groups. While males form stable associations with other males and cooperate in mating efforts, females form less stable associations (Connor *et al.* 1998, 2001). Some females are consistently sighted in larger parties than other females, although the range of variation in female party size is relatively small (Mann *et al.* 2000). It is not entirely clear how females might benefit from associating with other females, but calves may be safer from predation when females are in parties. This is consistent with the observation that party size is largest when calves are youngest. However, mean party size is unrelated to female reproductive success, measured as the number of calves raised over a 10-year period.

Comparisons of the lifetime reproductive success of females living in large and small groups of long-tailed macaques (*Macaca fasicularis*) suggest that living in large groups depresses female fitness (van Noodwijk & van Schaik 1999). However, it is not entirely clear why the fitness of females living in large groups is reduced. There may be higher levels of resource competition in large groups. This is supported by the fact that females in large groups spend more time travelling and less time resting than females in smaller groups do (van Schaik *et al.*1983). Resource competition may influence females' fertility in several different ways. It may limit the amount of food that females obtain and thus impair their nutritional status or increase the amount of harassment they receive and elevate stress levels that females experience. Both of these factors could contribute to differences of the reproductive performance of females in large and small groups.

A recent analysis of cortisol levels in free ranging ring-tailed lemurs (*Lemur catta*) living in groups of different sizes provides evidence that females' stress levels are elevated in groups that deviate from the optimal size (Pride 2005). Lemurs live in groups that range in size from approximately 5 to 25 individuals. Price found that females' cortisol levels were higher in small and large groups than in intermediate-sized groups. Cortisol levels were lowest in groups that were close to the mean group sizes that characterize ring-tailed lemurs in the population.

Comparative analyses conducted on a number of primate taxa suggest that the females which live in large groups suffer reproductive costs. van Schaik (1983) compiled data from a number of primate populations representing about a dozen primate genera. For each population, he evaluated the relationship between the number of females in groups and their fertility, measured as the number of infants per female. The slopes of the regressions were predominantly negative, indicating that females' fertility is depressed in the largest groups. Very similar findings have been obtained for lion-tailed macaques (Kumar 1995) in Tamil Nadu, langurs (Treves & Chapman 1996) and howler monkeys (Treves 2001) using larger datasets and somewhat different analytic methods. These data suggest that females often find themselves living in groups that exceed the optimum group size.

(b) Plural breeding species with communal care of young

Prairie voles (*Microtus ochrogaster*) live in extended family groups (Solomon 1991, 1994; Marfori *et al.* 1997; Hayes 2000; McGuire *et al.* 2002; Hayes & Solomon 2004). Prairie vole groups are typically composed of several adults and offspring from previous and current litters (McGuire *et al.* 2002). In some cases, more than one female produces offspring (Hayes & Solomon 2004). However, the majority of male and female offspring remain in their natal groups as non-breeding helpers. Adult males share nests with females and help care for pups (Gruder-Adams & Getz 1985; McGuire & Novak 1984; Oliveras & Novak 1986). All group members help to brood, groom and retrieve pups (Solomon 1991). Prairie vole pups benefit from the presence of non-breeding helpers. Pups that are reared in groups with helpers live longer than pups reared by a single female (Getz *et al.* 1997; McGuire *et al.* 2002). Pups that are reared with helpers also spend less time alone in the nest, develop faster and weigh more at weaning than pups reared by a breeding pair alone (Solomon 1991). These differences in body weight may have important effects on lifetime reproductive success because higher body weight at weaning is associated with higher probabilities of reproducing in the following year, being chosen as a mate by a member of the opposite sex, and winning competitive encounters over mates with members of the same sex (Hayes & Solomon 2004).

Giant gerbils (*Rhombomys opimus*) are desert-adapted rodents which live in groups that consist of one male and one to six related females (Randall *et al.* 2005). They occupy interconnected burrows and cooperatively defend their territories, harvest food and contribute to predator detection. Pups from different litters interact freely after they emerge from their burrows and females with and without pups provide some care for pups. Females are more philopatric than males and the likelihood that females will disperse is linked to local population densities. When population densities are high, dispersal opportunities are limited, hence females tend to remain in their natal territories and group size increases. Group size has no consistent effect on females' reproductive performance. The number of emergent pups per female and pup survivorship do not differ among females who live alone, with just one male, and in larger groups.

Banded mongoose (*Mungos mungo*) live in mixed sex groups that contain multiple adult males, multiple breeding females and their offspring (Cant 2000; de Luca & Ginsberg 2001; Gilchrist *et al.* 2004). Nearly all females become pregnant during each highly synchronized breeding event and then all give birth at the same time in the same den. Pups remain in the den for approximately 30 days, and while they are in the den, all group members help to babysit them. Mothers seem to nurse pups indiscriminately (Cant 2000). As the number of breeding females increases, the per capita number of pups emerging from the den increases (Cant 2000). Litters produced by one or two females routinely fail completely, while litters produced by larger number of females are progressively more likely to survive to emergence.

When the pups emerge, all group members provide care for them (Cant 2000; Gilchrist 2004; Hodge 2005). Most pups form stable associations with a single helper, or 'escort', who provisions and protects them from predators. Most escorts are yearlings. There is considerable variation in the amount of time that pups spend with escorts. Pups that spend more time in association with escorts grow faster and weigh more at independence than pups from the same litter that spend less time with escorts (Hodge 2005). Pups that spend more time with escorts are also more likely to survive to 1 year of age, probably because pups are less vulnerable to predation when they are with escorts (Gilchrist 2004; Hodge 2005). Differences in growth rates are likely to have important effects on lifetime fitness because weight at independence is correlated with weight at 1 year, and females that weigh more at independence conceive their first litters significantly earlier than lighter females (Hodge 2005). Hodge's analyses are particularly powerful because she was able to establish that variation in the extent of association with escorts affects pups from the same litter.

Female lions (*Panthera leo*) form prides composed of closely related females (Packer *et al.* 1988; Packer & Pusey 1995). Prides must contain at least three adult females to be viable; smaller prides are unable to maintain their territories. Members of prides hunt together and vigorously defend their territories against intruders (Packer *et al.* 1990). Mothers of cubs also defend their cubs from attacks by infanticidal males (Packer *et al.* 2001). There are no dominance hierarchies in lion prides and all females reproduce equitably (Packer *et al.* 2001). Females give birth alone and are extremely secretive during the first few weeks after parturition. When cubs are five or six weeks old, they join other cubs in a 'crèche' and remain part of the crèche until they are approximately 18 months old (Packer & Pusey 1995). Cubs continue to nurse primarily from their own mothers, but are sometimes nursed by the mothers of other cubs in the crèche (Pusey & Packer 1994; Packer & Pusey 1995). The extent of allonursing increases as the degree of relatedness within crèches increases, and females who do not have cubs in the crèche do not participate in their care.

Female lions' reproductive success is positively related to the number of other mothers who have cubs in the crèche. In the Serengeti, where the availability of food varies seasonally, solitary females cannot raise large litters as successfully as females living in prides can (Packer & Pusey 1995). Moreover, cubs are more likely to survive when there are more mothers who have given birth at about the same time and when cubs are raised in crèches with many cubs of the same age (Packer & Pusey 1995; Packer *et al.* 2001). Cubs reared in crèches do not receive more milk than cubs reared alone, hence these effects are likely to reflect the benefits derived from communal defence against infanticide (Pusey & Packer 1994), which is a major cause of cub mortality (Pusey & Packer 1994).

In most of their range, Eurasian badgers (*Meles meles*) are solitary (da Silva *et al.* 1994; Johnson *et al.* 2000; Carpenter *et al.* 2005). But in some locations in the United Kingdom, badgers live in groups composed of one or more males, one to six closely related females and their offspring (da Silva *et al.* 1994; Woodroffe & Macdonald 2000; Carpenter *et al.* 2005). Group members share a den, but forage alone. For badgers in the United Kingdom, which feed mainly on earthworms, sociality may be a response to a patchy distribution of shareable resources (Johnson *et al.* 2000). Plural breeding occurs in badger groups, but not all females give birth each year. Older females reproduce more successfully than younger females, but there is no evidence of systematic reproductive suppression of individual females. When females live in groups, births are loosely synchronized and females who do not have cubs of their own provide care for the offspring of other females.

The size of social groups has no significant effect on the average reproductive success of females, but the rates of female reproductive failure seem to be higher in group-living populations than in solitary populations of badgers (da Silva *et al.* 1994). It is not clear whether these differences reflect the costs of living in social groups or differences in environmental conditions across populations. Woodroffe & Macdonald (2000) found that the number of cubs that survive to 1 year of age is positively related to the number of available helpers, but this effect seems to be an artefact of variation in territory quality. Groups that occupy high-quality territories contain more non-breeding females, more yearlings and more surviving cubs than groups that occupy lower quality territories. When the effects of territory quality are controlled statistically, the number of available helpers has no effect on the number or proportion of cubs that survive their first year of age. Woodroffe and Macdonald argue that females in large groups suffer more competition for resources than females in smaller groups, and this competition depresses their fat reserves and induces reproductive failure. This process creates more non-breeding females in larger groups. This interpretation is supported by the observation that the body condition of mothers is markedly worse when they live in groups with non-breeding females than when they live in groups without non-breeding females.

Black-tailed prairie dogs (*Cynomys ludovicianus*) live in extensive burrow systems ('towns') which are subdivided in wards and coteries (Hoogland 1981, 1983; Hoogland *et al.* 1989). Coteries typically include one adult male, three or four closely related adult females and their offspring. Mothers give birth in isolated nests and rear their pups alone for several weeks. Females respond aggressively when intruders attempt to approach their nests during this period. Maternal protectiveness is probably a response to infanticide, which is common in prairie dogs. The main perpetrators of infanticide are other lactating females, often close kin

(Hoogland 1985). Pups emerge from their mothers' burrows when they are approximately four to six-weeks-old, and then begin to mix with pups from other coteries. Females may sleep with and sometimes nurse other females' pups during this phase (Hoogland *et al.* 1989). The annual reproductive success of adult females is negatively related to the size of the coterie in which they live (Hoogland 1981, 1983). If females are better off in smaller coteries than large ones, then they might be expected to emigrate to smaller coteries or establish new ones. However, females' dispersal options may be constrained because suitable unoccupied burrows are scarce in prairie dog towns and the costs of establishing new burrow systems for individuals is prohibitive.

(c) Singular breeding with cooperative care of young

In singularly breeding species with cooperative care of young, there is a considerable amount of reproductive skew. This complicates efforts to assess the effects of group size on reproductive success because group members may derive disparate benefits from group living. When non-breeding group members are closely related to the breeding pair, they may accrue inclusive fitness benefits from helping, but help is not limited to relatives in all cooperatively breeding mammals (Clutton-Brock 2002). Most analyses focus on the effects of group size on the number of offspring produced or offspring survival, emphasizing the fitness consequences for the breeding pair rather than non-breeding group members.

Although red fox (*Vulpes vulpes*) are primarily solitary, they sometimes form pairs or larger groups (Macdonald 1979; Zabel & Taggart 1989; Baker *et al.* 1998, 2004). In high-density populations in the United Kingdom, red fox typically form groups consisting of one dominant male, one dominant female, several subordinate adults and immature offspring (Baker *et al.* 1998). Most groups include some closely related adults, but the degree of relatedness within groups is relatively low because both males and females frequently mate with partners from outside the group (Baker *et al.* 2004). Dominant females monopolize reproduction, but subordinate females sometimes become pregnant and produce litters. However, dominant females live longer and have more offspring than subordinate females. Non-breeding adults guard, retrieve, provision, groom and play with pups (Macdonald 1979). In a sample of seven litters, pup survival was unrelated to the size of the group or the number of adult females in the group (Baker *et al.* 1998).

Dwarf mongoose (*Helogale parvula*) live in stable groups that typically consist of a single breeding pair, several offspring from previous litters and a few unrelated immigrants (Rood 1990; Creel & Waser 1991, 1994). The group forages and travels together, and shares a den. Subordinate females sometimes become pregnant, but rarely rear their litters successfully. Breeding females produce several litters of one to six pups over the course of the six-month birth season. Group members, including unrelated immigrants, take turns guarding pups in the den, bringing them insects and transporting them from one den to another. After pups emerge from the den, older pack members dig up insects for them and protect them from predators. Subordinate females, who have produced litters or experienced a pseudopregnancy, may lactate and nurse pups of the dominant female. There seem to be several advantages associated with living in larger packs. Adult mortality is lower in large groups than in small groups. Breeding females who have more helpers are also able to spend more time feeding (Creel & Creel 1991). Moreover, pups grow faster and are more likely to survive in large packs than small ones (Creel & Creel 1991). Packs above the median size produce on average 3.8 surviving pups, while packs below the median size produce on average 1.8 surviving pups.

This relationship could be an artefact of variation in environmental conditions that influence both pack size and pup survival. However, analyses based on annual changes in group size and reproductive success within packs indicated that pack size has a direct effect on offspring survival (Creel & Waser 1994).

Meerkats (*Suricata suricatta*) in the Kalahari desert live in groups that are typically composed of a dominant breeding pair and 3–20 non-breeding helpers (Clutton-Brock *et al.* 2001; Russell *et al.* 2002, 2003). The dominant pair produces approximately 80% of all offspring born in the group; when subordinate females do breed, their offspring suffer high levels of mortality, probably due to infanticide. Females produce litters of three to six pups and may give birth to several litters per year. Helpers guard pups in the den, and then help feed them from the time they emerge from the den until they begin to forage independently at approximately three months of age.

There is no simple relationship between the size of social groups and offspring survival in meerkat groups. Clutton-Brock and his colleagues (1999) compared the effects of group size on pup survival to six months at two sites in the Kalahari. One site was located within the Kalahari Gemsbok National Park and the other was located on a fenced ranch. The density and diversity of predators was substantially higher in the park than on the ranch, but the sites were otherwise very similar. Rates of mortality between birth and weaning when pups are inside the den were similar at the two sites, but rates of juvenile and adult mortality were considerably higher in the park than on the ranch. The effect of group size on juvenile mortality also differed at the two sites. Juvenile mortality declined with increasing group size in the park, but showed the opposite pattern on the ranch. Clutton-Brock *et al.* suggested that the most likely explanation of the negative relationship between group size and mortality in the park was that helpers provided less effective defence of juveniles when the ratio of helpers to pups was low. If this argument is correct, then the ratio of pups to helpers may be more important than the absolute number of helpers. Subsequent studies of meerkats in the Kalahari confirm the importance of the ratio of pups to helpers in meerkats.

The presence of helpers has no effect on female litter size or on the survival of infants between birth and weaning among Kalahari meerkats (Clutton-Brock *et al.* 1999; Russell *et al.* 2002, 2003). However, after pups emerge from the den, the effects of helpers become apparent. The ratio of pups to helpers is significantly related to the rate of daily food intake for pups and their daily weight gain (Russell *et al.* 2002, 2003). Experimental manipulations of the ratio of pups to helpers confirm the causal link between help and pup growth rates. Thus, when experimenters temporarily removed pups from their packs, and decreased the ratio of pups to helpers by 75%, daily weight gains increased. Similarly, when experiments temporarily added pups to packs and increased the ratio of pups to helpers by 75%, pup weight gains declined. The effects of helpers on daily weight have important downstream effects: daily weight gains are related to juvenile weights, juvenile survivorship, the chance of breeding as subordinates and acquiring dominant status (Clutton-Brock 2002; Clutton-Brock *et al.* 2001).

The number of helpers in the group also has direct effects on females' reproductive success (Russell *et al.* 2002, 2003). Approximately 43% of all litters fail completely; none of the offspring survive to weaning. Litter failure is mainly a function of maternal status: 16% of the litters produced by dominant females failed completely, while 77% of the litters produced by subordinate females failed completely (Russell *et al.* 2003). For litters in which at least one pup survived to weaning, litter size at weaning was significantly related to maternal weight and the number of helpers. Heavier mothers with more helpers raised more offspring to the age of weaning than lighter mothers with fewer helpers (Russell *et al*. 2003). However, pup survival showed a 'bell-shaped distribution with group size' (Russell *et al*. 2002), as pups in the smallest and largest groups were less likely to survive than pups in intermediate-sized groups. Helpers also reduce the costs of maternal investment. The number of helpers present is negatively related to the length of subsequent interbirth intervals, and positively related to females' weight at the next conception. Female weight at conception is, in turn, positively related to litter size. Thus, helpers make it possible for females to increase their reproductive output without jeopardizing their condition.

Black-backed jackals (*Canis mesomelas*) are omnivores that live in brush land habitats (Moehlman 1979). They form stable pair bonds and cooperatively defend their territories, hunt and share food. Groups are usually composed of a single breeding pair, their offspring and several adult helpers who are believed to be offspring from previous litters. Helpers regurgitate food for lactating females and guard, play, groom and feed pups. Pups spend less time alone at the den in groups with larger number of helpers. Although some pairs are able to raise offspring without helpers, the number of surviving pups is closely related to the number of helpers. The incremental effect of each helper is equivalent to 1.5 pups.

Wolves (*Canis lupus*) in northern Minnesota live in packs that are composed of one breeding pair and their descendants (Harrinton *et al*. 1983). Non-breeding group members help care for pups, providing them with food and protection. Starvation is the main natural cause of mortality for wolf pups, hence the presence of helpers could have a substantial impact on pup survival. Harrington *et al*. (1983) monitored a number of packs at two different sites. At one site, prey density was high and population size was increasing. There, the number of non-breeding adults in packs was positively correlated with the number of surviving pups. In the other population, there had been a major decline in prey availability and the population size was declining. In the packs at this site, there was a non-significant negative relationship between the pack size and the number of surviving pups.

African wild dogs (*Lycaon pyctus*) live in groups that typically include one breeding pair, a number of non-breeding adults and offspring from several litters (Malcolm & Marten 1982; Creel & Creel 2002). Packs sometimes include adults that are unrelated to the breeding pair (McNutt 1996). Males are philopatric and females disperse with other females from the same litter (Malcolm & Marten 1982). Females produce one litter per year of about eight pups (Creel & Creel 2002). All group members, including those who are unrelated to other group members, help care for pups. Helpers regurgitate meat for pups that are too small to travel to kills and protect pups from predators. In times of food shortages, yearlings may not regurgitate for pups and sometimes appropriate food that is brought back to the den for pups. In contrast, adult dogs continue to regurgitate for pups even when food is scarce. Using data from three different sites, Creel & Creel (2002) demonstrated that the number of surviving pups is positively related to the number of adults in packs. However, pup survivorship is reduced in both exceptionally small and exceptionally large packs.

Cooperative breeding occurs in several genera of the primate family, Callitrichidae (*Callithrix, Leontopithecus* and *Saguinus*). These animals live in small, territorial groups of 4–15 individuals (French 1997; Tardif 1997; Bales *et al*. 2000, 2001; Dietz 2004). Unlike other anthropoid primates, callitrichid females typically give birth to twins and can produce two litters per year. The cost of reproduction in callitrichids, measured in terms of litter weight and standardized for allometry, is considerably higher than in solitary, pair-bonded or plural breeding primate species (Harvey *et al*. 1986). Females would be unable to sustain these costs without substantial help from other group members.

Breeding is monopolized by the dominant female in the group (French 1997; Tardiff 1997; Dietz 2004). This reproductive monopoly is sometimes the product of social suppression of reproductive physiology and sometimes the result of inbreeding avoidance (Saltzman *et al.* 2004*a,b*). In common marmosets, subordinate females were only able to rear litters if they gave birth when the dominant female did not have dependent infants (Digby 1995). In several cases, dominant females have killed infants produced by subordinate females (Digby 2001). In golden lion tamarin groups (*Leontopithecus rosalia*) approximately 10% of females share reproduction with subordinate females temporarily. Females are most likely to share breeding with their own daughters, less commonly with sisters and rarely with unrelated females. Only mothers and daughters were both successful in rearing infants in the same season (Dietz 2004). Although the number of surviving infants per female is lower in groups in which two females breed than in groups in which only one female reproduces (Dietz & Baker 1993), demographic models suggest that the cost of allowing daughters to breed is relatively low when unrelated mates are available and daughters do not pose a threat to mothers' social status within their groups.

Genetic analyses of group composition are now available for a small number of wild callitrichid groups. Some groups represent a single nuclear family, while others include adults that are unrelated to the dominant breeding pair (Nievergelt *et al.* 2000; Faulkes *et al.* 2003; Huck *et al.* 2005). In most groups that have been observed, helpers provide care for all group infants and do not seem to discriminate on the basis of relatedness (Dietz 2004; Fite *et al.* 2005).

In free-ranging populations of callitrichids, the presence of helpers, particularly adult males, is positively related to females' reproductive success. In moustached tamarins (*Saguinus mystax*) and common marmosets (*Callithrix jacchus*), the number of adult males, but not overall group size, is positively associated with the number of surviving infants (Garber *et al.* 1984, Koenig 1995), but not overall group size. In golden lion tamarins, groups with two adult males raise more surviving infants than groups with just one adult male. The fact that infant survival is more closely tied to the number of adult males than to overall group size suggests that the effects on infant survival are not an artefact of variation in territory quality. However, it is not entirely clear why infant survivorship is more closely related to the number of adult males than to overall group size. It is possible that adult males play a more important role in rearing offspring than adult females or juveniles members do. Bales *et al.* (2000) suggest that differences in the experience of helpers may contribute to these findings. They found that the number of adult males had a more consistent effect on infant survival in newly established groups than in long-established groups of golden lion tamarins, which had more experienced helpers. If the populations that Garber *et al.* and Koenig surveyed happened to include a substantial number of recently established groups, their results may be influenced by the experience of potential helpers.

Studies of cooperatively breeding rodent and primate species suggest that the benefits of helpers are greatly attenuated under captive conditions. In the wild, Mongolian gerbils (*Meriones unguiculatus*) form groups that include one breeding pair and a number of subordinates (Ågren *et al.* 1989, cited in French 1994). French (1994) reared pairs of experienced Mongolian gerbils in small indoor cages with and without juvenile helpers. When juveniles were present, they helped their parents make nests and tend pups. However, the presence of juvenile helpers has no consistent effect on litter size, offspring survival, pup group rates or the length of interbirth intervals. Pine voles (*M. pinetorum*), which are found throughout eastern North America, also form extended family groups with a single breeding pair (Solomon *et al.* 1998). Powell & Fried (1992) examined the effects of juveniles on the growth and development of younger siblings in small outdoor enclosures. One pair of adults was placed in each enclosure and allowed to rear one litter. When the next litter was born, juveniles were removed to create families with zero to three juvenile 'helpers'. The number of juveniles present did not significantly affect pup growth rates or pup survival to 21 days of age, but interbirth intervals were significantly shorter in groups with three juveniles than in groups with smaller numbers of juveniles. Pups spent significantly more time alone in groups that had no juveniles than in groups in which juveniles were present. Similarly, although helpers reduce the costs of rearing offspring for callitrichid parents, especially fathers, housed in the laboratory (Price 1992; Santos *et al*. 1997; Fite *et al*. 2005), the number of juvenile helpers available does not seem to affect infant survival (Jaquish *et al*. 1997).

4.3 Effects of group composition on females' reproductive performance

The benefits that females derive from living in social groups may be influenced by the characteristics of the other members of their groups. Strong biases in favour of female philopatry among mammalian species are generally attributed to the inclusive benefits derived from living with relatives. If so, the kin composition of social groups is expected to be related to females' reproductive performance.

A considerable amount of information about the effects of group composition on reproductive performance in rodents is derived from studies that were designed to evaluate mechanisms underlying the 3–5 year cycles in population density that characterize many microtine rodent populations. Charnov & Finerty (1980) hypothesized that cycling population dynamics might be the product of kin selection. They reasoned that kin selection will favour greater tolerance towards kin than non-kin, and this would therefore encourage association among kin. If animals settle near their relatives, clusters of closely related animals will develop. Tolerance among closely related animals will enhance the reproductive success of individuals and produce higher rates of population growth. However, as population density increases and suitable territories become scarce, animals will be forced to disperse over greater distances. Long-distance dispersal will lower the average degree of relatedness among animals that occupy neighbouring territories. This will lead to higher levels of aggression between individuals, suppress reproduction and reduce population density.

Three empirical predictions derived from the model are of particular interest here: (i) animals will associate preferentially with relatives, (ii) the presence of kin will reduce levels of competition, and (iii) association with relatives will enhance female reproductive performance. A number of studies of voles were designed to test these predictions. Researchers focused on the effects of kinship on the behaviour of females because male voles typically disperse over greater distances than females (Ims 1989; Ylönnen *et al*. 1990; Lambin & Krebs 1993; Lambin & Yaccoz 1998; Dalton 2000). The model is usually tested by establishing enclosed populations composed of kin or non-kin and appropriate numbers of adult males, and monitoring patterns of population growth, infant survivorship and females' reproductive performance. In most of these experimental studies, movement into the study populations is prevented and predators are excluded.

A number of vole species, including meadow voles (*M. pennsylvanicus*), grey-tailed voles (*M. canicaudus*), Townsend's voles (*M. townsendiia*), field voles (*M. agrestis*), red-backed voles (*Clethrionomys rofocanus*) and bank voles (*C. glareolus*), have very similar social organizations (Wolff 1994). In these species, females sometimes form huddling groups during the winter to reduce thermoregulatory costs. But as temperatures rise in the spring, females generally establish individual home ranges and rear their young alone. Females usually settle near their natal territories, while males disperse further (Boonstra *et al.* 1987). In these species, males' ranges overlap the territories of multiple females. Males do not help females build or maintain nests and do not tend offspring, and females may mate with multiple males (Gruder-Adams & Getz 1985; McGuire & Novak 1986; Oliveras & Novak 1986; Boonstra *et al.* 1993; Spitzer *et al.* 2005). Females defend their home ranges against intruders (Mappes *et al.* 1995) and may not begin to breed until they have established individual home ranges (Kawata 1986).

One of the first studies designed to test the Charnov–Finnerty hypothesis was conducted on meadow voles (*M. pennsylvanicus*). Boonstra & Hogg (1988) monitored the rate of population growth in one enclosure stocked with three sisters and their daughters and a second enclosure that was stocked with an equal number of unrelated females. Females in the kin enclosure were 16% more likely to carry pregnancies to term than females in the unrelated enclosure. Some litters were located by tracking females back to their nests from the trapping sites. Litters of females in the kin enclosures were approximately 13% larger than the litters of females in the non-kin enclosure. In addition, a significantly larger proportion of infants from the litters located in the kin enclosure survived and were subsequently trapped than in the non-kin enclosure. However, the number of surviving offspring per litter was about the same in the two treatments. By the end of the six-month experiment, both enclosures had reached extremely high densities and population sizes were roughly equal, leading Boonstra and Hogg to conclude that 'relatedness among females had no effect on demography', and to dismiss the differences in reproductive parameters in the two enclosures as statistical anomalies.

Dalton (2000) also found that relatedness among female grey-tailed voles had no consistent effect on females' reproductive performance. Dalton seeded each of eight enclosures with six unrelated adult females and six unrelated adult males. Four enclosures were not manipulated further and relatedness was allowed to build-up through recruitment. In the other four enclosures, juveniles were removed from their natal enclosures and replaced with juveniles of the same age and weight from other enclosures. This procedure maintained population size, but prevented levels of relatedness from building up. Over the course of the six-month study period, there were no significant differences in the reproductive performance of females in the two groups.

Other studies of voles suggest that the presence of kin may increase female tolerance and enhance reproductive performance. In experimental enclosures, females tend to settle closer to their relatives than to non-relatives (Kawata 1986; Lambin & Krebs 1993; Pusenius *et al.* 1998), and their home ranges overlap more with their relatives than with non-relatives (Wolff *et al.* 1994; Mappes *et al.* 1995). In some cases, settlement near kin facilitates the establishment of individual home ranges (Kawata 1986) and earlier initiation of reproductive activity (Pusenius *et al.* 1998). In several experimental studies, females who settled near kin reared higher numbers of surviving offspring than females with no close kin nearby (Kawata 1990; Ylönnen *et al.* 1990; Mappes *et al.* 1995; Lambin & Yaccoz 1998; Pusenius *et al.* 1998; Wolff *et al.* 2002). In one study, which was allowed to continue across years, females who settled near close kin were more likely to survive from one year to the next (Lambin & Krebs 1993).

The mechanisms underlying observed differences in reproductive performance between females living near kin and females living near unrelated females are not well established. However, living near kin seems to reduce the intensity of competition with conspecifics. In enclosures that are seeded with unrelated females, females' reproductive success increases as their distance from their nearest neighbours increases. In contrast, when kin are present, the distance to nearest neighbours has no effect on females' reproductive success (Mappes *et al.* 1995;

Pusenius *et al.* 1998). Analyses of trapping patterns suggest that subordinates may be less intimidated by the presence of dominant individuals when enclosures are seeded with groups of relatives than when they are seeded with non-kin (Ylönnen *et al.* 1990). In these vole species, living near kin may lower levels of aggression, reduce the extent of competition for resources or lower the risk of infanticide (Dalton 2000). Such competition may have important effects on females' ability to rear young successfully. Juvenile survivorship generally declines as female density increases (Rodd & Boonstra 1988). In one study, juveniles were reared in groups that differed in the ratio of mature males to mature females. The survival of juvenile females was lower and age to maturation was later in groups with a female-biased sex ratio than in groups with an even sex ratio or a male-biased sex ratio (Wolff *et al.* 2002).

In wild populations of cooperatively breeding prairie voles, group composition influences females' reproductive performance. Females that lived in groups composed of three adults reared more surviving pups than females who lived in smaller or larger groups (McGuire *et al.* 2002), but females reproduced most successfully when they lived in groups with two other adult males and no other adult females. Information about the relatedness of females in groups that contained more than one adult female was not available in this study, but captive studies suggest that the costs of reproduction may be reduced when related females are present. Sera & Gaines (1994) compared female prairie voles housed in enclosures with familiar littermate sisters or with unrelated females. When females were housed with kin, their homes ranges were larger and overlapped more with the home ranges of neighbouring females. Females who were housed with kin were significantly more likely to have multiple pregnancies each season than females housed with unrelated females. However, these differences were not reflected in differences in the number of surviving offspring produced per female. Hayes & Solomon (2004) compared the breeding success of females in groups composed of two adult littermate sisters and one unrelated adult male with the breeding success of females housed with a single adult male under conditions of high and low food availability. In this experiment, litter size was adjusted so that all litters were composed of three pups. In some of the groups that contained sisters, both females produced litters and pooled their litters. Litters from plurally breeding groups weighed significantly more at the end of the lactation period than litters from groups that contained only one adult female; litters from groups composed of one breeding and one non-breeding female fell between the two extremes. Mothers in plurally breeding groups spent less time nursing pups than mothers in groups that included just one female. In addition, mothers in plurally breeding groups were able to maintain their body weight over the course of lactation when food was limited, while mothers in groups that included just one female lost weight. Mothers in groups in which only one of the two females reproduced experienced intermediate weight losses and nursing levels.

White-footed mice (*Peromyscus leucopus*) and deer mice (*P. maniculatus*) are sympatric in the southern Appalachian Mountains of Virginia. In both species, mothers typically nest alone and rear one litter at a time at low densities, but when densities increase female dispersal is delayed and extended family groups are formed (Wolff 1994). Male deer mice are more fully involved in offspring care than male white-footed mice (Wolff & Cicirello 1991). Wolff (1994) monitored the reproductive performance of female deer mice and white-footed mice that nested in artificial nest boxes and evaluated the effects of group composition on their reproductive performance. Some females nested alone (solitary), with juveniles from previous litters (extended family), with other breeding females (communal) or with other breeding females plus juveniles from previous litters (communal-extended). When communal breeding groups were formed, they typically consisted of mothers and daughters or sisters. There was no effect of the type of social group on the number of weanlings raised or the number of off-spring that survived to six weeks, the median age of dispersal for juveniles. Solitary female white-footed mice had shorter residence in nest boxes than females that lived in communal-extended groups, but there was no consistent effect of group size on residence times in deer mice. Thus, living in extended family groups and nesting communally had no positive or nega-tive effects on females' reproductive performance. Wolff (1994) suggests that extended families and communal nesting represent 'alternative breeding tactics in response to limited breeding space (usually in response to high density conditions) . . . Social tolerance of relatives may be an adaptation that provides offspring with extended parental care during times of environmental or social uncertainty'.

Commensal house mice (*Mus musculus, M. domesticus*) typically form groups composed of one male, one or more breeding females and their litters. Females nearly always pool their litters if they are born about the same time and nurse them communally (König 1994*a*,*b*; Hayes 2000). Several lines of evidence suggest that females preferentially nest with close kin. In wild populations, females are more closely related to other females in their own groups than to females in other groups (Saltzman *et al*. 2004*b*). Females prefer to nest with females that have similar major histocompatibility complex (MHC) alleles, and MHC similarity is a reli-able correlate of genetic relatedness (Manning *et al*. 1992). Females are more likely to form associations and nest communally in semi-natural enclosures seeded with groups of sisters than in enclosures seeded with unrelated, unfamiliar females (Dobson *et al*. 2000; Rusu & Krackow 2004).

Associations with familiar partners also confer reproductive benefits on females. König (1994*a*,*b*) compared the reproductive performance of females over a standardized lifespan of 120 days when they were housed alone, housed with littermate sisters and housed with unrelated, unfamiliar females. The lifetime reproductive success of females housed with sisters was on average 25% higher than the lifetime reproductive success of females housed with unrelated females and 30% higher than the lifetime reproductive success of females housed alone. There is also evidence that reproduction is more egalitarian when females form associations with kin than when they form associations with non-kin. Dobson *et al*. (2000) compared groups composed of two or three littermate sisters with groups composed of two or three unrelated, unfamiliar females. When females were housed with sisters, all females produced offspring. However, when females were housed with unrelated females, one female in each group failed to reproduce. There was no difference in litter size among breeding females housed with sisters and unrelated females, but the level of mortality during the interval between birth and weaning was significantly lower when females were housed with sisters than when females were housed with unrelated females. Mortality between birth and weaning was mainly due to infanticide, although it is not known if pups were killed by nesting females or adult males.

The dynamics of population outbreaks among feral house mice in Australia also suggest that associations with kin enhance females' reproductive performance (Sutherland *et al*. 2005). Early in the cycle, population size is low and females maintain separate home ranges. Related females tend to be found in neighbouring home ranges. As the size of the population increases, the extent of kin clustering becomes more pronounced and related females share home ranges. Females selectively interact with their relatives. At the peak of the population outbreak, kin structuring breaks down, but females continue to interact preferentially with close kin. Sutherland and colleagues suggest that association with kin reduces vulnerability to infanti-cide, thus increasing rates of recruitment and population size.

Bushy-tailed wood rats (*Neotoma cinerea*) live on discrete rocky outcrops in mountainous areas of North America (Moses & Millar 1994). There are a limited number of suitable nest sites and this may create considerable competition among females. Females tend to remain on their natal outcrop throughout their lives. Mothers and daughters are frequently found in the same locations within the outcrop and are more likely to be found together than unrelated females are. For mothers, there were no apparent effects of having daughters nearby. Mothers reared as many offspring when daughters were present as they did when there were no daughters present. But females whose mothers are present have larger litters and fewer litter failures than females whose mothers are not present. Moreover, females are more likely to survive their first winter when their mothers are present than when their mothers are absent. Differences in daughters' survival disappear when population density is experimentally reduced, which suggests that mothers enhance their daughters' survival by reducing the intensity of competition for resources.

Wood mice (*Apodemus sylvaticus*) reproduce alone or in communal groups of two related or unrelated females (Gerlach & Bartmann 2002). Gerlach and Bartmann compared the reproductive performance of females housed in small indoor enclosures under four different conditions: (i) one female alone, (ii) mother–daughter pairs, (iii) two familiar sisters, and (iv) two unrelated, unfamiliar females. When females were housed in pairs, one of the females generally produced about twice as many offspring as the other female. The more successful of the two females in communally breeding groups produced as many offspring as females that bred alone, while the less successful of the two females produced significantly fewer offspring than females that bred alone. However, females do gain some advantages from breeding communally. Females that were housed in pairs spent significantly less time nursing than females who bred alone. This might enable communally breeding females to conserve energy for future reproductive attempts. It is not clear whether the energetic benefits of reproducing in communally breeding groups outweigh the costs of reduced fertility for all females in more natural circumstances.

Alpine marmots (*M. marmota*) live at high elevations in areas with short growing seasons and long, harsh winters. They form extended family groups that are typically composed of a dominant breeding pair, offspring from several litters and some unrelated individuals (Arnold 1990; Allainé 2000). Juveniles delay dispersal for several years after reaching maturity (Allainé 2000). The dominant female produces all offspring born in the group, although all mature females come into oestrus. Most, but not all offspring, are sired by the dominant male in the group (Hackländer *et al.* 2003). Infants are particularly vulnerable to thermoregulatory stress during their first winter because they have accumulated relatively little fat by the time the winter begins, and their small body size and high surface to volume ratio increases the rate of heat loss. Thermoregulatory stress is reduced by huddling together during hibernation (Hayes 2000). Infants are more likely to survive their first winter in groups in which most individuals are closely related than in groups in which most individuals are not closely related (Arnold 1990). Moreover, mortality is lower in groups that contain a breeding pair and other adults than in groups that contain a breeding pair and yearlings or a breeding pair alone. There is some evidence that living with unrelated females can be costly for breeding females. Thus, the reproductive success of dominant females is negatively related to the number of unrelated subordinate females in the group, but is not affected by the number of daughters present (Hackländer *et al.* 2003).

Grey seals (*Helichoerus grypus*) forage at sea and come ashore to mate, give birth and nurse their young. Females tend to return to the same sites each year and some females return to their natal sites to breed (Pomeroy *et al.* 2000, 2001). Genetic analyses indicated that females that occupied certain breeding locations were more closely related to the colony as a whole than females that occupied other breeding locations (Pomeroy *et al.* 2001). Females that occupied these areas of higher than average relatedness produced larger and faster growing pups than females that occupied other locations. Since larger pups are more likely to survive than smaller pups, females that bred in these favoured locations may achieve higher reproductive success and contribute more to the genetic composition of the colony than other females. The combination of high site fidelity and site-specific variation in reproductive performance could create the observed genetic structuring of the population, even if associations among females were entirely passive. This does not seem to be the case. Although females showed considerable site fidelity, some did shift their pupping locations from one year to the next. Using a model based on random patterns of association, Pomeroy *et al.* (2005) demonstrated that the likelihood of association among mothers that shifted their pupping locations substantially is much greater than expected by chance. These data indicate that particular pairs of females actively coordinate their movements. Pomeroy *et al.* (2005, p. 533) speculate that 'Familiarity may then lead to behavioural modifications between the individuals concerned, which ultimately produce some measurable fitness benefit, either in reduced costs to the mother or increased performance in raising offspring. Likely possibilities include reduction of aggression between familiar associates, or preferential access to limited resources'.

Female African elephants (*Loxodonta africana*) live in complex fission–fusion societies. Females form stable core groups which consist of 1–20 adult females and their offspring. Females typically remain in their natal core groups when they mature, while males disperse. These core groups may temporarily fragment into smaller parties and multiple core groups may join to form large aggregations. Some pairs or trios of core groups consistently associate together and are said to form a 'bond group' (Moss & Poole 1983; Moss 1988). Recent analyses indicate that the average level of genetic relatedness among females within core groups is approximately 0.15, just higher than expected for aunts and nieces (Archie *et al.* 2006). Analyses of the patterns of association among females indicate that kinship also predicts the patterns of association among females within bond groups. Females who spend most of their time together are generally first-order relatives. Members of bond groups are related through the matriarchs of the core groups. The long-term stability of core groups may have important reproductive consequences for females. Females who belong to core groups led by old matriarchs have significantly higher reproductive success than females who belong to core groups led by younger matriarchs (McComb *et al.* 2001).

Studies of howler monkeys (*Alouatta* spp.) also demonstrate that the composition of social groups influences female reproductive performance. In red howler (*A. seniculus*) groups, the number of adult females in groups is confined within relatively narrow limits. Most groups contain two to four adult females (Treves 2001). Groups with too few females cannot defend their territories, while groups with too many females face more competition for access to resources and become more attractive targets for male takeovers (Pope 2000*a*). This means that female dispersal strategies are tightly linked to the number of adult females present: in mantled howler (*A. palliata*) groups with two adult females, 50% of all natal females disperse; in groups with three adult females, 90% disperse; and in groups with four adult females, 100% disperse (Crockett & Pope 1993; Pope 1998). Recruitment into the natal group is advantageous because females that mature and breed in their natal groups have higher quality diets and give birth at earlier ages than ones which emigrate (Crockett & Pope 1993). This creates competition for the limited number of breeding positions within established groups. Adult females actively harass maturing females in an effort to force them to emigrate, and recruitment opportunities are concentrated among the descendants of a single female (Pope 2000*b*).

Non-random recruitment of daughters of high-ranking females would generate an increase in the average degree of relatedness among breeding females over time. In fact, in long-established groups, females represent a single matriline and the average degree of relatedness approaches that of first degree relatives (Pope 1998, 2000*a,b*). In newly established groups, which are composed of migrants from a number of different social groups, relatedness is approximately zero. The genetic composition of groups is associated with their reproductive performance. Females in newly established groups have fewer surviving infants per year than females in well-established groups do (Pope 2000*a*). These differences suggest that females benefit from living in groups of close kin, but it is also possible that differences in reproductive performance are linked to other factors, such as differences in territory quality.

In matrilineal primate species, females interact preferentially with close kin and selectively support close kin in agonistic encounters (Silk 2002, 2006; Kapsalis 2004). Although the presence of kin seems to have an important effect on females' everyday lives, the impact of the presence of kin on females' reproductive performance is harder to evaluate. In captive vervet monkeys (*Chlorocebus aethiops*), young females whose mothers are present are less likely to be harassed and more likely to be defended than females whose mothers have died. Females' firstborn infants are more likely to survive when the grandmother is present (Fairbanks & McGuire 1986). These effects are not confounded by differences in the dominance rank of females whose mothers are present and absent. Semi-free-ranging Japanese macaques, *M. fuscata*, produce their first infant at significantly younger ages and tend to have shorter interbirth intervals when their mothers are present in the group than when their mothers are dead (Pavelka *et al.* 2002). For wild baboons, the effects of mothers' presence on the reproductive success of their daughters seem to be less consistent. Thus, at Gombe in Tanzania, mothers' presence has no consistent effect on their daughters' age at menarche or the length of their interbirth intervals, or on their grandchildren's survival (Packer *et al.* 1998). In the Okavango Delta of Botswana, the daughters of high- and mid-ranking females produced their first infant at significantly younger ages when they had mothers or adult sisters in the group. For low-ranking females, however, the pattern was reversed (Cheney *et al.* 2004). The presence of mothers or adult sisters tended to reduce females' interbirth intervals, but did not influence infant survival, perhaps because infanticide is the main source of mortality for infants at this site.

4.4 Effects of social bonds on females' reproductive performance

Very little is known about the relationship between the nature of social bonds and the females' lifetime fitness. One reason for this is that there is a taxonomic mismatch between the availability of information about social behaviour and fitness. The most complete information about female reproductive performance comes from studies of small, short-lived animals, like voles and house mice. Many of these studies are based on trapping data, which tell us little about the nature of interactions among females. We know much more about the social relationships among females in other taxa, including hyenas, elephants, sperm whales, lions and various species of primates (de Waal & Tyack 2003). Unfortunately, all of these animals are relatively large and long-lived, making it difficult to document the lifetime reproductive performance of sizable numbers of individuals. This creates a mismatch between the availability of information about social behaviour and the reproductive performance. However, we are beginning to make some progress in efforts to evaluate the adaptive value of social relationships for females in some primate taxa.

In their 1986 paper, Cheney and her colleagues focused on three kinds of relationships to provide examples of the 'possible function' of long-term social bonds in primate groups: relationships with close kin; close associations, or 'friendships', between adult male and females; and male–male alliances. Over the last 20 years, we have gained a considerably more complete understanding of the structure and function of these kinds of relationships. Much of this information comes from studies of baboons, which have been intensively studied over extended periods at multiple sites across Africa (Henzi & Barrett 2003; Swedell & Leigh 2006). These long-term studies provide a valuable database for testing adaptive hypotheses and an important source of information about the proximate and distal consequences of variation in sociality.

The first clue about the link between social bonds and female fitness came from analyses of the relationship between female dominance rank and reproductive success in primate groups. Like a number of other Old World monkeys (Chapais 1992) and spotted hyenas (*Crocuta crocuta*; Engh & Holekamp 2003; Engh *et al.* 2000), baboons form matrilineal dominance hierarchies in which maternal kin occupy adjacent ranks (Silk *et al.* 2003). In baboons, coalitionary support from relatives plays an important role in the acquisition of female dominance rank (Johnson 1987) and may also contribute to the extraordinary stability of female dominance hierarchies, even though coalitions among adult females are not common at all sites (Silk *et al.* 2003). High rank confers some short-term advantages on females. Thus, dominant females sometimes gain priority of access to food (Barton 1993) and high-ranking matrilines are more cohesive than low-ranking matrilines (Silk *et al.* 1999, 2004).

There may also be long-term benefits associated with high rank. High-ranking females' infants grow faster than lower ranking females' offspring do (Johnson 2003; Altmann & Alberts 2005) and their daughters reach menarche at earlier ages (Altmann *et al.* 1988; Wasser *et al.* 2004). High-ranking females also have shorter interbirth intervals (Bulger & Hamilton 1987; Rhine *et al.* 1988; Smuts & Nicholson 1989; Barton & Whiten 1993) and their infants are more likely to survive their first year of life (Bulger & Hamilton 1987; Rhine *et al.*1988; Silk *et al.* 2003; Wasser *et al.* 2004). In Mikumi, the lifetime reproductive success of females in the highest ranking quartile is about four times higher than the lifetime reproductive success of females in the lowest ranking quartile (Wasser *et al.* 2004). However, significant effects of female dominance rank on all of the components of female reproductive success are not observed in all baboon populations (e.g. Packer *et al.* 1995; Cheney *et al.* 2004) or during all periods (Altmann & Alberts 2005).

The biological significance of the moderate and seemingly inconsistent effects of dominance rank may be interpreted in several different ways. Packer *et al.* (1995) suggested that stabilizing selection on the kinds of traits that confer high rank on females, such as aggressiveness, might lower the fitness of the highest ranking females. It is also possible that most analyses are based on samples that are too small to detect the effects of dominance rank. A 5% selective differential can have powerful effects on the evolution of a trait, but very large samples would be required to detect a statistically significant effect of this magnitude. We also must consider the possibility that the effects of dominance rank may be swamped by other factors that are largely independent of dominance rank, such as predation or infanticide (Cheney *et al.* 2004). The effects of dominance rank may only be expressed under certain kinds of environmental conditions. In Amboseli, the effects of dominance rank on female reproductive performance were considerably more pronounced under harsh environmental conditions than under more benign conditions (Alberts & Altmann 2003; Altmann & Alberts 2003). In Mikumi, rank-related differences in reproductive performance disappeared during a period of drastic population decline (Wasser *et al.* 2004). Finally, it is possible that females adopt social strategies to compensate for rank-related disparities in reproductive success. For example, Henzi and his colleagues have shown that female baboons tend to direct more of their grooming towards higher ranking females during periods of food scarcity than when food is more abundant (Henzi *et al.* 2003). Females might also develop social strategies that insulate them from some of the costs of being low ranking.

Several lines of evidence suggest that social bonds among females play an important role in females' lives and may influence their reproductive performance. First, comparative analyses of baboon time budgets indicate that females preserve time for socializing (Dunbar & Sharman 1984). When food is scarce, females devote more time to foraging and moving between feeding sites. However, they do not reduce the amount of time that they spend interacting peacefully with other group members. Instead, they cut back on resting time. One interpretation of these findings is that females continue to groom group members when environmental conditions deteriorate because these relationships have enough value to females that they maintain them even under difficult conditions.

Second, the social lives of female baboons revolve around a tight core of close associates (Silk *et al.* 1999; Silk *et al.* 2006a,b). In Amboseli, females show pronounced preferences for close kin, including mothers, daughters and sisters. Females also prefer to groom and associate with unrelated age mates and those who are close to their own rank. But even in the absence of close maternal kin, most females form strong social bonds with at least one partner. Although demographic factors impose important constraints on the availability of preferred types of partners, some of the close social bonds that females form last for a number of years. Females tend to form the most enduring bonds with close kin and age mates. The quality of social bonds has a direct effect on their strength and stability. Females who groom most equitably have the strongest and most enduring social bonds, and these effects are independent of the degree of relatedness and age proximity among females.

Third, females respond strongly to the sudden loss of favoured companions. Engh and her colleagues analysed hormone levels in faeces collected from known female baboons in Moremi, Botswana (Engh *et al.* 2006b). They found that the levels of glucocorticoids rise sharply after the disappearance of close relatives. Nearly all of the disappearances were attributed to predators, hence Engh *et al.* considered the possibility that females' reactions reflect the stress of the predator attacks, not the loss of close companions. If that is the case, then all group members who survive attacks ought to react in the same way. However, only females who lose close kin show elevated glucocorticoid levels.

Fourth, females compensate for the loss of preferred partners by strengthening their relationships with others. Engh and her colleagues found that females increase the frequency and diversity of their grooming relationships after they lose close companions, suggesting that they attempt to compensate for their losses by forging new relationships. Similarly, females in Amboseli form stronger bonds with their maternal and paternal sisters when their mothers are not present than when their mothers are available (Silk *et al.* 2006a).

Female baboons may also gain important benefits from the relationships that they form with adult males. These kinds of relationships, sometimes labelled 'friendships', are a conspicuous feature of social life in baboon groups. After females give birth to infants, they often form close associations with one or sometimes two adult males (see Smuts 1985). Females are principally responsible for maintaining proximity to their male associates and groom males much more than they are groomed in return (Smuts 1985; Palombit *et al*. 1997). Males sometimes protect their female associates from harassment (Smuts 1985). Moreover, field playback experiments conducted in the Okavango Delta of Botswana indicate that males are more responsive to their female associates' distress calls than are unaffiliated males, and males respond more strongly to their female associates' distress calls than to the distress calls of other females (Palombit *et al*. 1997). If males' responses can be taken as evidence that they are prepared to intervene on behalf of their female associates or their infants, then the results of these experiments suggest that females gain protection for themselves and their infants from their male associates.

The value and scope of such protection may vary across sites. In Amboseli, where the risk of infanticide is apparently low, males preferentially support their juvenile offspring when they are involved in agonistic disputes (Buchan *et al*. 2003). Males' ability to recognize their offspring may be at least partly influenced by their previous associations with mothers and their infants. In southern Africa, where males often kill unweaned infants when they join new groups and acquire top-ranking positions, females' associations with males may protect their infants from infanticidal attacks (Palombit *et al*. 1997; Weingrill 2000; Palombit 2003).

This interpretation is supported by several lines of evidence from Moremi. First, lactating females typically respond fearfully to new males and attempt to avoid them. Males who have seemed indifferent to infants may abruptly change their behaviour towards infants sired during their tenure after they are deposed, carrying them on their ventrum when new males are in the vicinity. Second, lactating females' glucocorticoid levels rise substantially when new males join the group and acquire high-ranking positions (Beehner *et al*. 2005; Engh *et al*. 2006a). The fact that these effects are confined to lactating females suggests that females respond to the threats to their infants, not just to the presence of unfamiliar males. Moreover, lactating females' responses to the presence of potentially infanticidal males were influenced by their associations with adult males. Females who had established associations with adult males were much less distressed than females who had not established such associations.

The short-term benefits that females gain from their associations with other females and with adult males are reflected in females' reproductive performance. In Amboseli, females that are more fully socially integrated into their groups reproduce more successfully than other females (Silk *et al*. 2003). In this study, female social integration was measured in terms of the proportion of time that females spend in close association with other group members and grooming. Female reproductive success was measured as the proportion of infants that survive to 1 year, which is a major component of variation in lifetime fitness among baboon females in this population (Alberts & Altmann 2003; Altmann & Alberts 2003). A positive relationship between the extent of social integration and the reproductive success might also occur because some females lived in more favourable habitats or during more favourable time periods than others. These females might have been more social and reproduced more successfully than other females. However, the results remained unchanged when the measure of social integration was corrected to account for group membership and changes in environmental conditions over time.

The positive relationship between the extent of social integration and reproductive success observed in Amboseli might arise because high-ranking females have higher reproductive success and belong to larger matrilines than lower ranking females do. However, the relationship between social integration and reproductive success remains significant when dominance rank and lineage size are controlled statistically. In fact, when the sample is partitioned by dominance rank and the sociality index score, we find that the most social low-ranking females reproduce as successfully as the most social high-ranking females. Thus, sociality seems to insulate females from some of the costs of low rank.

4.5 Summary and conclusions

Sociality influences female fitness in diverse ways. In general, there seems to be support for the observation of Clutton-Brock *et al.* (2001) that negative correlations between group size and fitness characterize species in which females rear their infants on their own and in species that rear their offspring communally. In cooperatively breeding species, with high reproductive skew, group size has clear positive effects on offspring survival and the reproductive success of breeders, but the effects on non-breeding helpers have not been assessed. This makes it impossible to draw firm conclusions about the effects of breeding systems on female fitness.

As expected from kin selection theory, the presence of kin generally enhances females' reproductive performance, although kinship does not provide blanket immunity from fitness-reducing behaviour. Prairie dogs sometimes nurse the pups of closely related females and sometimes kill them. Data from long-term studies of baboons suggest that social bonds may have a direct and positive effect on female fitness, but the causal mechanisms creating these effects and the generality of these findings are still unclear.

One of the most obvious lessons that readers will draw from this review is that there is a lot more work to be done. Our knowledge about the effects of the relationship between group size, group composition and social relationships on the fitness of females is incomplete for even the best-studied mammal species. It would be useful to be able to replicate the analyses of the relationship between group size and group composition in a larger number of species and a much wider range of taxa. If we were able to describe the shape of the function which describes the relationship between fitness and group size, we might be able to develop broader insight about the nature of forces that influence females' reproductive performance in different mammalian taxa.

The second lesson to draw from this review is that long-term studies of free-ranging populations provide an enormously valuable source of information about the adaptive consequences of sociality. It is no accident that the most valuable insights about the functional consequences of sociality come from studies of free-ranging populations, including red deer, Kalahari meerkats, yellow-bellied marmots, lions and savannah baboons, that span decades.

One lesson that I hope primatologists draw from this review is that there are valuable payoffs for venturing beyond the primate literature. Comparative analyses that extend beyond the primates provide more powerful tests of adaptive hypotheses. For example, the fact that various measures of brain size and group size are consistently related in primates, cetaceans, ungulates, carnivores and insectivores (references above) gives much greater weight to the finding. The mammal literature is also useful if we want to understand the function of traits that are uncommon in primates, but occur in other taxa, such as cooperative breeding, fission–fusion social organization or pair-bonding.

A lesson that mammalogists might take from this review is that there is a sizable gap in the state of knowledge about social relationships in primates and other mammals. Primatologists have compiled detailed information about the social behaviour of individuals in a broad range of species. Comparable data are largely unavailable for other mammalian taxa, even those that have been studied carefully for long periods. In the absence of such data, we cannot make meaningful comparisons between primates and other animals in a number of important dimensions. This is important for our understanding of the evolution of social cognition. The social brain hypothesis posits that social complexity has created selection pressures for larger and more complex brains. This hypothesis is consistent with evidence that brain and group size are associated in various taxa. However, group size may be a poor proxy for social complexity (Blumstein & Armitage 1998). Valid assessments of social complexity require more detailed information about the nature of social interactions among individuals than is available for most taxa.

The absence of such information makes it very difficult to make any systematic comparisons of the consequences of sociality, the extent of social complexity or the nature of social cognition in primates and other taxa. For example, we generally take it for granted that primates are more socially complex than other animals. However, it is not clear that we have a firm basis for this conclusion. Spotted hyenas establish matrilineal dominance hierarchies, form coalitions, reconcile after conflicts, recognize paternal kin, hunt cooperatively and recognize third party relationships (Holekamp & Smale 1991; Engh *et al.* 2000, 2005; Wahaj *et al.* 2001, 2004). African elephants can recognize the vocalizations of at least 100 other individuals (McComb *et al.* 2001) and bottlenosed dolphins form stable, multi-level alliances (Connor *et al.* 2001). Corvids may share many of the elements of the cognitive toolkit that underlies complex cognition (Emery & Clayton 2004).

While the long lives of some of our study animals and the short term of most research grants make it difficult to assess effects of sociality on the fitness of females, the data reviewed here suggest that it is possible to move beyond the phenotypic gambit. These studies give us some idea about how to approach this task in the field and in more controlled conditions in the laboratory. It is hoped that the body of work described here provides a foundation for further analyses of these questions.

This paper was written while I was a visitor in the Large Animal Research Group in the Department of Zoology at the University of Cambridge. While my resolve to venture out of the safe shallows of primatology into the depths of the mammalian literature is a direct result of many congenial lunchtime conversations with the members of LARG, they bear no responsibility for any errors that have found their way into this manuscript.

References

Ågren, G., Zhou, Q. & Zhong, W. 1989 Ecology and social behavior of Mongolian gerbils, *Meriones unguiculatus*, at Xilinhot, Inner Mongolia, China. *Anim. Behav.* **37**, 11–27. (doi:10.1016/0003-3472(89)90002-x)

Alberts, S. C. & Altmann, J. 2003 Variability in reproductive success viewed from a life-history perspective in baboons. *Am. J. Hum. Biol.* **15**, 401–409. (doi:10.1002/ajhb.10157)

Allainé, D. 2000 Sociality, mating system and reproductive skew in marmots: evidence and hypotheses. *Behav. Process.* **51**, 21–34.

Altmann, J. & Alberts, S. C. 2003 Intraspecific variability in fertility and offspring survival in a nonhuman primate: behavioural control of ecological and social sources. In *Offspring: the biodemography of fertility and family behaviour* (eds K. W. Wachter & R. A. Bulatao), pp. 140–169. Washington, DC: National Academy Press.

Altmann, J. & Alberts, S. C. 2005 Growth rates in a wild primate population: ecological influences and maternal effects. *Behav. Ecol. Sociobiol.* **57**, 490–501. (doi:10.1007/s00265-004-0870-x)

Altmann, J., Hausfater, G. & Altmann, S. A. 1988 Determinants of reproductive success in savannah baboons *Papio cynocephalus*. In *Reproductive success* (ed. T. H. Clutton-Brock), pp. 403–418. Chicago, IL: University of Chicago Press.

Archie, E. A., Moss, C. J. & Alberts, S. C. 2006 The ties that bind: genetic relatedness predicts the fission and fusion of social groups in wild African elephants. *Proc. R. Soc. B* **273**, 513–522. (doi:10.1098/rspb.2005.3361)

Armitage, K. B. & Schwartz, O. A. 2000 Social enhancement of fitness in yellow-bellied marmots. *Proc. Natl Acad. Sci. USA* **97**, 12 149–12 152. (doi:10.1073/pnas.200196097)

Arnold, W. 1990 The evolution of marmot sociality: II. Costs and benefits of joint hibernation. *Behav. Ecol. Sociobiol.* **27**, 239–246.

Aureli, F. & de Waal, F. B. M. 2000 Why natural conflict resolution? In *Natural conflict resolution* (eds F. Aureli & F. B. M. de Waal), pp. 3–10. Berkeley, CA: University of California Press.

Baker, P. J., Robertson, C. P. J., Funk, S. M. & Harris, S. 1998 Potential fitness benefits of group living in the red fox, *Vulpes vulpes. Anim. Behav.* **56**, 1411–1424. (doi:10. 1006/anbe.1998.0950)

Baker, P. J., Funk, S. M., Bruford, M. W. & Harris, S. 2004 Polygynandry in a red fox population: implications for the evolution of group living in canids. *Behav. Ecol.* **15**, 766–778. (doi:10.1093/beheco/arh077)

Bales, K., Dietz, J., Baker, A., Miller, K. & Tardif, S. D. 2000 Effects of allocare-givers on fitness of infants and parents in callitrichid primates. *Folia Primatol.* **71**, 27–38. (doi:10.1159/000021728)

Bales, K., O'Herron, M., Baker, A. J. & Dietz, J. M. 2001 Sources of variability in live births in wild golden lion tamarins (*Leontopithecus rosalia*). *Am. J. Primatol.* **54**, 211–221. (doi:10.1002/ajp.1031)

Barton, R. A. 1993 Sociospatial mechanisms of feeding competition in female olive baboons, *Papio anubis. Anim. Behav.* **46**, 791–802. (doi:10.1006/anbe.1993.1256)

Barton, R. A. & Dunbar, R. I. M. 1997 Evolution of the social brain. In *Machiavellian intelligence. II. Extensions and evaluations* (eds A. Whiten & R. W. Byrne), pp. 240–263. Cambridge, UK: Cambridge University Press.

Barton, R. A. & Whiten, A. 1993 Feeding competition among female olive baboons, *Papio anubis. Behav. Ecol. Sociobiol.* **38**, 321–329. (doi:10.1007/s002650050248)

Beehner, J. C., Bergman, T. J., Cheney, D. L., Seyfarth, R. M. & Whitten, P. L. 2005 The effect of new alpha males on female stress in free-ranging baboons. *Anim. Behav.* **69**, 1211–1221. (doi:10.1016/j.anbehav.2004.08.014)

Blumstein, D. T. & Armitage, K. B. 1998 Life history consequences of social complexity: a comparative study of ground-dwelling sciurids. *Behav. Ecol.* **9**, 8–19.

Blumstein, D. T. & Armitage, K. B. 1999 Cooperative breeding in marmots. *Oikos* **84**, 369–382.

Boonstra, R. & Hogg, I. 1988 Friends and strangers: a test of the Charnov-Finerty hypothesis. *Oecologia* **77**, 95–100. (doi:10.1007/BF00380931)

Boonstra, R., Krebs, C. J., Gaines, M. S., Johnson, M. L. & Craine, I. T. M. 1987 Natal philopatry and breeding systems in voles (*Microtus* spp.). *J. Anim. Ecol.* **56**, 655–673. (doi:10.2307/5075)

Boonstra, R., Xia, X. & Pavone, L. 1993 Mating system of the meadow vole, *Microtus pennsylvanicus. Behav. Ecol.* **4**, 83–89.

Buchan, J. C., Alberts, S. C., Silk, J. B. & Altmann, J. 2003 True paternal care in a multi-male primate society. *Nature* **425**, 179–181. (doi:10.1038/nature01866)

Bulger, J. & Hamilton, W. J. 1987 Rank and density correlates of inclusive fitness measures in a natural chacma baboon (*Papio ursinus*) population. *Int. J. Primatol.* **8**, 635–650.

Cant, M. A. 2000 Social control of reproduction in banded mongooses. *Anim. Behav.* **59**, 147–158. (doi:10.1006/anbe.1999.1279)

Carpenter, P. J., Pope, L. C., Greig, C. & Dawson, D. A. 2005 Mating system of the European badger, *Meles meles*, in a high density population. *Mol. Ecol.* **14**, 273–284. (doi:10.1111/j.1365-294X.2004.02401.x)

Chapais, B. 1992 The role of alliances in social inheritance of rank among female primates. In *Coalitions and alliances in humans and other animals* (eds A. H. Harcourt & F. B. M. de Waal), pp. 29–59. Oxford, UK: Oxford Science Publications.

Chapman, C. A. & Chapman, L. J. 2000 Constraints on group size in red colobus and red-tailed guenons: examining the generality of the ecological constraints model. *Int. J. Primatol.* **21**, 565–585. (doi:10.1023/A:1005557002854)

Charnov, E. & Finerty, J. P. 1980 Vole population cycles: a case for kin-selection? *Oecologia* **45**, 1–2. (d oi:10.1007/ BF00346698)

Cheney, D., Seyfarth, R. & Smuts, B. 1986 Social relationships and social cognition in nonhuman primates. *Science* **234**, 1361–1366. (doi:10.1126/science.3538419)

Cheney, D. L., Seyfarth, R. M., Fischer, J., Beehner, J., Bergman, T., Johnson, S. E., Kitchen, D. M., Palombit, R. A. & Silk, J. B. 2004 Factors affecting reproduction and mortality among baboons in the Okavango Delta, Botswana. *Int. J. Primatol.* **25**, 401–428. (doi:10.1023/B:IJOP.0000019159.75573.13)

Clutton-Brock, T. H. 2002 Behavioral ecology—breeding together: kin selection and mutualism in cooperative vertebrates. *Science* **296**, 69–72. (doi:10.1126/science.296.5565.69)

Clutton-Brock, T. H., Harvey, P. H. & Rudder, B. 1977 Sexual dimorphism, socionomic sex ratio and body weight in primates. *Nature* **269**, 797–800. (doi:10.1038/269797a0)

Clutton-Brock, T. H., Albon, S. D. & Harvey, P. H. 1980 Antlers, body size and breeding group size in the Cervidae. *Nature* **285**, 565–566. (doi:10.1038/285565a0)

Clutton-Brock, T. H., Albon, S. D. & Guiness, F. E. 1982 Competition between female relatives in a matrilocal mammal. *Nature* **300**, 178–180. (doi:10.1038/300178a0)

Clutton-Brock, T. H., Albon, S. D. & Guiness, F. E. 1988 Reproductive success in male and female red deer. In *Reproductive success* (ed. T. H. Clutton-Brock), pp. 325–343. Chicago, IL: University of Chicago Press.

Clutton-Brock, T. H., Gaynor, D., McIlrath, G. M., Maccoll, A. D. C., Kansky, R., Chadwick, P., Manser, M., Skinner, J. D. & Brotherton, P. N. M. 1999 Predation, group size and mortality in a cooperative mongoose, *Suricata suricatta*. *J. Anim. Ecol.* **68**, 672–683. (doi:10.1046/j.1365-2656.1999.00317.x)

Clutton-Brock, T. H., Russell, A. F., Sharpe, L. L., Brotherton, P. N. M., McIlrath, G. M., White, S. & Cameron, E. Z. 2001 Effects of helpers on juvenile development and survival in meerkats. *Science* **293**, 2446–2449. (doi:10.1126/science.1061274)

Connor, R. C., Mann, J., Tyack, P. L. & Whitehead, H. 1998 Social evolution in toothed whales. *Trends Ecol. Evol.* **13**, 228–232. (doi:10.1016/S0169-5347(98)01326-3)

Connor, R. C., Heithaus, M. R. & Barre, L. M. 2001 Complex social structure, alliance stability and mating access in a bottlenose dolphin 'super-alliance'. *Proc. R. Soc. B* **268**, 263–267. (doi:10.1098/rspb.2000.1357)

Connor, R. C. 2007 Dolphin social intelligence: complex alliance relationships in bottlenose dolphins and a consideration of selective environments for extreme brain size evolution in mammals. *Phil. Trans. R. Soc. B* **362**, 587–602. (d oi:10.1098.rstb.2006.1997)

Creel, S. R. & Creel, N. M. 1991 Energetics, reproductive suppression and obligate communal breeding in carnivores. *Behav. Ecol. Sociobiol.* **28**, 263–270. (doi:10.1007/BF00175099)

Creel, S. & Creel, N. M. 2002 *The African wild dog: behavior, ecology, and conservation*. Princeton, NJ: Princeton University Press.

Creel, S. R. & Waser, P. M. 1991 Failures of reproductive suppression in dwarf mongooses (*Helogale parvula*): accident or adaptation? *Behav. Ecol.* **2**, 7–15.

Creel, S. R. & Waser, P. M. 1994 Inclusive fitness and reproductive strategies in dwarf mongooses. *Behav. Ecol.* **5**, 339–348.

Crockett, C. M. & Pope, T. R. 1993 Consequences for sex difference in dispersal for juvenile red howler monkeys. In *Juvenile primates: life history, development, and behavior* (eds M. E. Pereira & L. A. Fairbanks), pp. 104–118. Oxford, UK: Oxford University Press.

Dalton, C. L. 2000 Effects of female kin groups on reproduction and demography in the gray-tailed vole, *Microtus canicaudus*. *Oikos* **90**, 153–159. (doi:10.1034/j.1600-0706.2000.900115.x)

da Silva, J., Macdonald, D. W. & Evans, P. G. 1994 Net costs of group living in a solitary foragers, the Eurasian badger (*Meles meles*). *Behav. Ecol.* **5**, 151–158.

de Luca, D. W. & Ginsberg, J. R. 2001 Dominance, reproduction and survival in banded mongooses: toward an egalitarian social system. *Anim. Behav.* **61**, 17–30. (doi:10.1006/anbe.2000.1559)

de Waal, F. B. M. & Tyack, P. L. (eds) 2003 *Animal social complexity*. Cambridge, MA: Harvard University Press.

Dietz, J. M. 2004 Kinship structure and reproductive skew in cooperatively breeding primates. In *Kinship and behavior in primates* (eds B. Chapais & C. Berman), pp. 223–241. Oxford, UK: Oxford University Press.

Dietz, J. M. & Baker, A. J. 1993 Polygyny and female reproductive success in golden lion tamarins, *Leontopithecus rosalia*. *Anim. Behav.* **46**, 1067–1078. (doi:10.1006/anbe.1993.1297)

Digby, L. 1995 Infant care, infanticide, and female reproductive strategies in polygynous groups of common marmosets (*Callithrix jacchus*). *Behav. Ecol. Sociobiol.* **37**, 51–61. (doi:10.1007/s002650050173)

Digby, L. 2001 Infanticide by female mammals: implications for the evolution of social systems. In *Infanticide by males and its implications* (eds C. P. van Schaik & C. H. Janson), pp.423–446. Cambridge, UK: Cambridge University Press.

Dobson, F. S., Jacquot, J. & Baudoin, C. 2000 An experimental test of kin association in the house mouse. *Can. J. Zool.* **78**, 1806–1812. (doi:10.1139/cjz-78-10-1806)

Dunbar, R. I. M. 1992 Neocortex size as a constraint on group size in primates. *J. Hum. Evol.* **20**, 469–493. (doi:10.1016/0047-2484(92)90081-J)

Dunbar, R. I. M. 1995 Neocortex size and group size in primates: a test of the hypothesis. *J. Hum. Evol.* **28**, 287–296. (doi:10.1006/jhev.1995.1021)

Dunbar, R. I. M. & Bever, J. 1998 Neocortext size predicts group size in carnivores and some insectivores. *Ethology* **104**, 695–708.

Dunbar, R. I. M. & Sharman, M. 1984 Is social grooming altruistic? *Zeitschrift fur Tierpsychologie* **64**, 163–173.

Emery, N. J. & Clayton, N. S. 2004 The mentality of crows: convergent evolution of intelligence in corvids and apes. *Science* **306**, 1903–1907. (doi:10.1126/science.1098410)

Engh, A. L. & Holekamp, K. E. 2003 Maternal rank 'inheritance' in the spotted hyena. In *Social complexity* (eds F. B. M. De Waal & P. L. Tyack), pp. 149–152. Cambridge, MA: Harvard University Press.

Engh, A. L., Esch, K., Smale, L. & Holekamp, K. E. 2000 Mechanisms of maternal rank 'inheritance' in the spotted hyaena (*Crocuta crocuta*). *Anim. Behav.* **60**, 323–332. (doi:10.1006/anbe.2000.1502)

Engh, A. L., Siebert, E. R., Greenberg, D. A. & Holekamp, K. E. 2005 Patterns of alliance formation and post-conflict aggression indicate spotted hyaenas recognize third party relationships. *Anim. Behav.* **69**, 209–217. (doi:10.1016/j.anbehav.2004.04.013)

Engh, A. L., Beehner, J. C., Bergman, T. J., Whitten, P. L., Hoffmeier, R. R., Seyfarth, R. M. & Cheney, D. L. 2006a Female hierarchy instability, male immigration, and infanticide increase glucocorticoid levels in female chacma baboons. *Anim. Behav.* **71**, 1227–1237. (doi:10.1016/j.anbehav.2005.11.000)

Engh, A. L., Beehner, J. C., Bergman, T. J., Whitten, P. L., Hoffmeier, R. R., Seyfarth, R. M. & Cheney, D. L. 2006b Behavioural and hormonal responses to predation in female chacma baboons. *Proc. R. Soc. B* **273**, 707–712. (doi:10.1098/rspb.2005.3378)

Fairbanks, L. A. & McGuire, M. T. 1986 Age, reproductive value, and dominance-related behaviour in vervet monkey females: cross-generational influences on social relationships and reproduction. *Anim. Behav.* **34**, 1710–1721. (doi:10.1016/S0003-3472(86)80258-5)

Faulkes, C. G., Arruda, M. F. & Monteiro da Cruz, A. O. 2003 Matrilineal genetic structure within and among populations of the cooperatively breeding common marmoset, *Callithrix jacchus*. *Mol. Ecol.* **12**, 1101–1118. (doi:10.1046/j.1365-294X.2003.01809.x)

Fite, J. R., Patera, K. J., French, J. A., Rukstalis, M., Hopkins, E. C. & Ross, C. 2005 Opportunistic mothers: female marmosets (*Callithrix kuhlii*) reduce their investment in offspring when they have to, and when they can. *J. Hum. Evol.* **49**, 122–142. (doi:10.1016/j.jhevol.2005.04.003)

French, J. A. 1994 Alloparents in the Mongolian gerbil: impact on long-term reproductive performance of breeders and opportunities for independent reproduction. *Behav. Ecol.* **5**, 273–279.

French, J. A. 1997 Proximate regulation of singular breeding in callitrichid primates. In *Cooperative breeding in mammal* (eds N. G. Solomon & J. A. French), pp. 34–75. Cambridge, UK: Cambridge University Press.

Gaillard, J. M., Festa-Bianchet, M., Yoccoz, N. G., Loison, A. & Toïgo, C. 2000 Temporal variation in fitness components and population dynamics of large herbivores. *Annu. Rev. Ecol. Syst.* **31**, 367–393. (doi:10.1146/annurev.ecolsys.31.1.367)

Garber, P. A., Moya, L. & Malaga, C. 1984 A preliminary field study of the moustached tamarin monkeys (*Saguinus mystax*) in Northeastern Peru: questions concerned with the evolution of a communal breeding system. *Folia Primatol.* **42**, 17–32.

Gerlach, G. & Bartmann, S. 2002 Reproductive skew, costs, and benefits of cooperative breeding in female wood mice (*Apodemus sylvanticus*). *Behav. Ecol.* **13**, 408–418. (doi:10.1093/beheco/13.3.408)

Getz, L., Simms, L., McGuire, B. & Snarski, M. 1997 Factors affecting life expectancy of the prairie vole, *Microtus ochrogaster*. *Oikos* **80**, 362–370. (doi:10.2307/3546604)

Gilchrist, J. S. 2004 Pup escorting in the communal breeding banded mongoose: behavior, benefits, and maintenance. *Behav. Ecol.* **15**, 952–960. (doi:10.1093/beheco/arh071)

Gilchrist, J. S., Otali, E. & Mwanguhya, F. 2004 Why breed communally? Factors affecting fecundity in a communally breeding mammal: the banded mongoose (*Mungos mungo*). *Behav. Ecol. Sociobiol.* **57**, 119–131. (doi:10.1007/s00265-004-0837-y)

Grafen, A. 1991 Modelling in behavioural ecology. In *Behavioural ecology* (eds J. R. Krebs & N. B. Davies), pp. 5–31. Oxford, UK: Blackwell.

Greenwood, P. J. 1980 Mating systems, philopatry, and dispersal in birds and mammals. *Anim. Behav.* **28**, 1140–1162. (doi:10.1016/S0003-3472(80)80103-5)

Gruder-Adams, S. & Getz, L. L. 1985 Comparison of the mating system and paternal behavior in *Microtus ochrogaster* and *M. pennsylvanicus*. *J. Mammal.* **66**, 165–167. (doi:10.2307/1380976)

Hackländer, K., Möstl, E. & Arnold, W. 2003 Reproductive suppression in female Alpine marmots, *Marmota marmota*. *Anim. Behav.* **65**, 1133–1140. (doi:10.1006/anbe.2003.2159)

Harrington, F. H., Mech, D. L. & Fritts, S. H. 1983 Pack size and wolf pup survival: their relationship under varying ecological conditions. *Behav. Ecol. Sociobiol.* **13**, 19–26. (doi:10.1007/BF00295072)

Harvey, P. H., Martin, R. D. & Clutton-Brock, T. H. 1986 Life histories in comparative perspective. In *Primate societies* (eds B. B. Smuts, D. L. Cheney, R. M. Seyfarth, R. W. Wrangham & T. T. Struhsaker), pp. 181–196. Chicago, IL: University of Chicago Press.

Hausfater, G. & Hrdy, S. B. (eds) 1984 *Infanticide: comparative and evolutionary perspectives.* New York, NY: Aldine.

Hayes, L. D. 2000 To nest communally or not to nest communally: a review of rodent communal nesting and nursing. *Anim. Behav.* **59**, 677–688. (doi:10.1006/anbe.1999.1390)

Hayes, L. D. & Solomon, N. G. 2004 Costs and benefits of communal rearing for female prairie voles (*Microtus ochrogaster*). *Behav. Ecol. Sociobiol.* **56**, 585–593. (doi:10.1007/s00265-004-0815-4)

Henzi, S. P. & Barrett, L. 2003 Evolutionary ecology, sexual conflict and behavioral differentiation among baboon populations. *Evol. Anthropol.* **12**, 217–230. (doi:10.1002/evan.10121)

Henzi, S. P., Barrett, L., Gaynor, D., Greef, J., Weingrill, T. & Hill, R. A. 2003 Effect of resource competition on the long-term allocation of grooming by female baboons: evaluating Seyfarth's model. *Anim. Behav.* **66**, 931–938. (doi:10.1006/anbe.2003.2244)

Hodge, S. J. 2005 Helpers benefit offspring in both the short and long-term in the cooperatively breeding banded mongoose. *Proc. R. Soc. B* **272**, 2479–2484. (doi:10.1098/rspb.2005.3255)

Holekamp, K. E. & Smale, L. 1991 Dominance acquisition during mammalian social development: the 'inheritance' of maternal rank. *Am. Zool.* **31**, 306–317.

Hoogland, J. L. 1981 The evolution of coloniality in white-tailed and black-tailed prairie dogs (Sciuridae: *Cynomys leucurus* and *C. ludovicianus*). *Ecology* **62**, 252–272. (doi:10.2307/1936685)

Hoogland, J. L. 1983 Black-tailed prairie dog coteries are cooperatively breeding unit. *Am. Nat.* **121**, 275–280. (doi:10.1086/284057)

Hoogland, J. L. 1985 Infanticide in prairie dogs: lactating females kill offspring of close kin. *Science* **230**, 1037–1040. (doi:10.1126/science.230.4729.1037)

Hoogland, J. L., Tamarin, R. H. & Levy, C. K. 1989 Communal nursing in prairie dogs. *Behav. Ecol. Sociobiol.* **24**, 91–95. (doi:10.1007/BF00299640)

House, J. S., Umberson, D. & Landis, K. R. 1988 Structure and processes of social support. *Annu. Rev. Sociol.* **14**, 293–318. (doi:10.1146/annurev.so.14.080188.001453)

Huck, M., Löttker, P., Böhle, U.-R. & Heymann, E. W. 2005 Paternity and kinship patterns in polyandrous moustached tamarins (*Saguinus mystax*). *Am. J. Primatol.* **127**, 449–464.

Ims, R. A. 1989 Kinship and origin effects on dispersal and space sharing in *Clethrionomys rufocanus*. *Ecology* **70**, 607–616. (doi:10.2307/1940212)

Isbell, L. A. & Young, T. P. 2002 Ecological models of female social relationships in primates: similarities, disparities, and some directions for future clarity. *Behaviour* **139**, 177–202. (doi:10.1163/156853902760102645)

Jaquish, C. E., Tardif, S. D. & Cheverud, J. M. 1997 Interactions between infant growth and survival: evidence for selection on age-specific body weight in captive common marmosets (*Callithrix jacchus*). *Am. J. Primatol.* **42**, 269–280. (doi:10.1002/(SICI)1098-2345(1997)42:4%3C269::AID-AJP2%3E3.0.CO;2-V)

Johnson, J. A. 1987 Dominance rank in juvenile olive baboons, *Papio anubis*—the influence of gender, size, maternal rank and orphaning. *Anim. Behav.* **35**, 1694–1708. (doi:10.1016/S0003-3472(87)80062-3)

Johnson, S. E. 2003 Life history and the competitive environment: trajectories of growth, maturation, and reproductive output among chacma baboons. *Am. J. Phys. Anthropol.* **120**, 83–98. (doi:10.1002/ajpa.10139)

Johnson, D. D. P., Macdonald, D. W. & Dickman, A. J. 2000 An analysis and review of models of the sociobiology of the Mustelidae. *Mamm. Rev.* **30**, 171–196. (doi:10.1046/j.1365-2907.2000.00066.x)

Kapsalis, E. 2004 Matrilineal kinship and primate behavior. In *Kinship and behavior in primates* (eds B. Chapais & C. Berman), pp. 153–176. Oxford, UK: Oxford University Press.

Kawata, M. 1986 The effect of kinship on spacing among female red-backed voles, *Clethrionomys rufocanus bedfordiae*. *Oecologia* **72**, 115–122. (doi:10.1007/BF00385054)

Kawata, M. 1990 Fluctuating populations and kin interaction in mammals. *Trends Ecol. Evol.* **5**, 17–20. (doi:10.1016/0169-5347(90)90007-Z)

Koenig, A. 1995 Group size, composition, and reproductive success in wild common marmosets (*Callithrix jacchus*). *Am. J. Primatol.* **35**, 311–317. (doi:10.1002/ajp.1350350407)

König, B. 1994a Fitness effects of communal rearing in house mice: the role of relatedness versus familiarity. *Anim. Behav.* **48**, 1449–1457. (doi:10.1006/anbe.1994.1381)

König, B. 1994b Components of lifetime reproductive success in communally and solitarily nursing house mice—a laboratory study. *Behav. Ecol. Sociobiol.* **34**, 275–283. (doi:10.1007/s002650050043)

Krause, J. & Ruxton, G. D. 2002 *Living in groups*. Oxford, UK: Oxford University Press.

Kumar, A. 1995 Birth rate and survival in relation to group size in the lion-tailed macaque, *Macaca silenus*. *Primates* **30**, 1–9. (doi:10.1007/BF02381911)

Kummer, H. 1978 On the value of social relationships to nonhuman primates: a heuristic scheme. *Soc. Sci. Inf.* **17**, 687–705.

Lacey, E. A. 2004 Sociality reduces individual direct fitness in a communally breeding rodent, the colonial tuco-tuco (*Ctenomys sociabilis*). *Behav. Ecol. Sociobiol.* **56**, 449–457. (doi:10.1007/s00265-004-0805-6)

Lambin, X. & Krebs, C. J. 1993 Influence of female relatedness on the demography of Townsend's vole populations in spring. *J. Anim. Ecol.* **62**, 536–550. (doi:10.2307/5203)

Lambin, X. & Yaccoz, N. G. 1998 The impact of population kin-structure on nestling survival in Townsend's voles, *Microtus townsendii*. *J. Anim. Ecol.* **67**, 1–16. (doi:10.1046/j.1365-2656.1998.00181.x)

Macdonald, D. W. 1979 'Helpers' in fox society. *Nature* **282**, 69–71. (doi:10.1038/282069a0)

Malcolm, J. R. & Marten, K. 1982 Natural selection and the communal rearing of pups in African wild dogs (*Lycaon pictus*). *Behav. Ecol. Sociobiol.* **10**, 1–13. (doi:10.1007/BF00296390)

Mann, J., Connor, R. C., Barre, L. M. & Heithaus, M. R. 2000 Female reproductive success in bottlenose dolphins (*Tursiops* sp.): life history, habitat, provisioning, and group-size effects. *Behav. Ecol.* **11**, 210–219. (doi:10.1093/beheco/11.2.210)

Manning, C. J., Wakeland, E. K. & Potts, W. K. 1992 Communal nesting patterns in mice implicate MHC genes in kin recognition. *Nature* **360**, 581–583. (doi:10.1038/360581a0)

Mappes, T., Ylonen, H. & Viitala, J. 1995 Higher reproductive success among kin groups of bank voles (*Clethrionomys glareolus*). *Ecology* **76**, 1276–1282. (doi:10.2307/1940934)

Marfori, M. M., Parker, P. G., Gregg, T. G., Vandenbergh, J. G. & Solomon, N. G. 1997 Using DNA fingerprinting to estimate relatedness within social groups of pine voles. *J. Mammal.* **78**, 715–724. (doi:10.2307/1382930)

McComb, K., Moss, C., Durant, S. M., Baker, L. & Sayialel, S. 2001 Matriarchs as repositories of social knowledge in African elephants. *Science* **292**, 491–494.

McGuire, B. & Novak, M. 1984 A comparison of maternal behaviour in the meadow vole (*Microtus pennsylvanicus*), prairie vole (*M. ochrogaster*), and pine vole (*M. pinetorum*). *Anim. Behav.* **32**, 1132–1141. (doi:10.1016/S0003-3472(84)80229-8)

McGuire, B., Getz, L. L. & Oli, M. K. 2002 Fitness consequences of sociality in prairie voles, *Microtus ochrogaster*: influence of group size and composition. *Anim. Behav.* **64**, 645–654. (doi:10.1006/anbe.2002.3094)

McNutt, J. W. 1996 Adoption in African wild dogs, *Lycaon pictus*. *J. Zool.* **240**, 163–173.

Moehlman, P. D. 1979 Jackal helpers and pup survival. *Nature* **277**, 382–383. (doi:10.1038/277382a0)

Moses, R. A. & Millar, J. S. 1994 Philopatry and mother–daughter associations in bushy-tailed wood-rats: space use and reproductive success. *Behav. Ecol. Sociobiol.* **35**, 131–140. (doi:10.1007/s002650050079)

Moss, C. J. 1988 *Elephant memories*. Chicago, IL: University of Chicago Press.

Moss, C. J. & Poole, J. H. 1983 Relationships and social structure of African elephants. In *Primate social relationships* (ed. R. A. Hinde), pp. 315–325. Sunderland, MA: Sinauer.

Nievergelt, C. M., Digby, L. J., Ramakrishnan, U. & Woodruff, D. 2000 Genetic analysis of group composition and breeding system in a wild common marmoset (*Callithrix jacchus*) population. *Int. J. Primatol.* **21**, 1–20. (doi:10.1023/A:1005411227810)

Oli, M. K. & Armitage, K. B. 2003 Sociality and individual fitness in yellow-bellied marmots: insights from a long-term study (1962–2001). *Oecologia* **136**, 543–550. (doi:10.1007/s00442-003-1291-7)

Oliveras, D. & Novak, M. 1986 A comparison of paternal behaviour in the meadow vole *Microtus pennsylvanicus*, the pine vole *M. pinetorum* and the prairie vole *M. orchrogaster*. *Anim. Behav.* **34**, 519–526. (doi:10.1016/S0003-3472(86)80120-8)

Packer, C. & Pusey, A. E. 1995 The Lack clutch in a communal breeder: lion litter size is a mixed evolutionarily stable strategy. *Am. Nat.* **145**, 833–841. (doi:10.1086/285771)

Packer, C., Herbst, L., Pusey, A. E., Bygott, J. D., Hanby, J. P., Cairns, S. J. & Borgerhoff Mulder, M. 1988 Reproductive success of lions. In *Reproductive success: studies of individual variation in contrasting breeding systems* (ed. T. H. Clutton-Brock), pp. 363–383. Chicago, IL: University of Chicago Press.

Packer, C., Scheel, D. & Pusey, A. E. 1990 Why lions form groups: food is not enough. *Am. Nat.* **136**, 1–19. (doi:10.1086/285079)

Packer, C., Collins, D. A., Sindimwo, A. & Goodall, J. 1995 Reproductive constraints on aggressive competition in female baboons. *Nature* **373**, 60–63. (doi:10.1038/373060a0)

Packer, C., Tatar, M. & Collins, A. 1998 Reproductive cessation in female mammals. *Nature* **392**, 807–811. (doi:10.1038/33910)

Packer, C., Pusey, A. E. & Eberly, L. E. 2001 Egalitarianism in female African lions. *Science* **293**, 690–693. (doi:10.1126/science.1062320)

Palombit, R. A. 2003 Male infanticide in savanna baboons: adaptive significance and intraspecific variation. In *Sexual selection and reproductive competition in primates: new perspectives and directions* (ed. C. B. Jones), pp. 367–412. Noman, OK: American Society of Primatologists.

Palombit, R. A., Seyfarth, R. M. & Cheney, D. L. 1997 The adaptive value of 'friendship' to female baboons: experimental and observational evidence. *Anim. Behav.* **54**, 599–614. (doi:10.1006/anbe.1996.0457)

Pavelka, M. S. M., Fedigan, L. M. & Zohar, S. 2002 Availability and adaptive value of reproductive and postreproducive Japanese macaque mothers and grandmothers. *Anim. Behav.* **64**, 407–414. (doi:10.1006/anbe.2002.3085)

Pérez-Barbería, F. J., Gordon, I. J. & Pagel, M. 2002 The origins of sexual dimorphism in body size in ungulates. *Evolution* **56**, 1276–1285.

Plavcan, J. M. 2003 Mating system, intrasexual competition and sexual dimorphism in primates. In *Comparative primate socioecology* (ed. P. C. Lee), pp. 241–269. Cambridge, UK: Cambridge University Press.

Pomeroy, P. P., Twiss, S. D. & Redman, P. 2000 Philopatry, side fidelity and local kin associations within grey seal breeding colonies. *Ethology* **106**, 899–919. (doi:10.1046/j.1439-0310.2000.00610.x)

Pomeroy, P. P., Wilmer, J. W., Amos, W. & Twiss, S. D. 2001 Reproductive performance links to fine-scale spatial patterns of female grey seal relatedness. *Proc. R. Soc. B* **268**, 711–717. (doi:10.1098/rspb.2000.1422)

Pomeroy, P. P., Redman, P. R., Ruddell, S. J. S., Duck, C. D. & Twiss, S. D. 2005 Breeding site choice fails to explain interannual associations of female grey seals. *Behav. Ecol. Sociobiol.* **57**, 546–556. (doi:10.1007/s00265-004-0882-6)

Pope, T. R. 1998 Effects of demographic change on group kin structure and gene dynamics of populations of red howling monkeys. *J. Mammal.* **79**, 692–712. (doi:10.2307/1383081)

Pope, T. R. 2000a Reproductive success increases with degree of kinship in cooperative coalitions of female red howler monkeys (*Alouatta seniculus*). *Behav. Ecol. Sociobiol.* **48**, 253–267. (doi:10. 1007/s002650000236)

Pope, T. R. 2000b The evolution of male philopatry in neotropical monkeys. In *Primate males* (ed. P. M. Kappeler), pp. 219–235. Cambridge, UK: Cambridge University Press.

Powell, R. A. & Fried, J. J. 1992 Helping by juvenile pine voles (*Microtus pinetorum*), growth and survival of younger siblings, and the evolution of pine vole sociality. *Behav. Ecol.* **3**, 325–333.

Price, E. C. 1992 The benefits of helpers: effects of group size and litter size on infant care in tamarins (*Saguinus oedipus*). *Am. J. Primatol.* **26**, 179–190. (doi:10.1002/ajp.1350260304)

Pride, E. R. 2005 Optimal group size and seasonal stress in ring-tailed lemurs (*Lemur catta*). *Behav. Ecol.* **16**, 550–560. (doi:10.1093/beheco/ari025)

Pusenius, J., Viitala, J., Marienberg, T. & Rivanen, S. 1998 Matrilineal kin clusters and their effect on reproductive success in the field vole *Microtus agrestis*. *Behav. Ecol.* **9**, 85–92.

Pusey, A. E. & Packer, C. 1986 Dispersal and philopatry. In *Primate societies* (eds B. B. Smuts, D. L. Cheney, R. M. Seyfarth, R. W. Wrangham & T. T. Struhsaker), pp. 150–166. Chicago, IL: University of Chicago Press.

Pusey, A. E. & Packer, C. 1994 Infanticide in lions: consequences and counterstrategies. In *Infanticide and parental care* (eds S. Parmigiani & F. vom Saal), pp. 277–299. Chur, Switzerland: Harwood Academic Publishing.

Pusey, A. E. & Packer, C. 1997 The ecology of relationships. In *Behavioural ecology* (eds J. Krebs & N. B. Davies), pp. 254–283. 4th edn. Oxford, UK: Blackwell.

Randall, J. A., Rogovin, K., Parker, P. G. & Eimes, J. A. 2005 Flexible social structure of a desert rodent, *Rhombys opimus*: philopatry, kinship, and ecological constraints. *Behav. Ecol.* **16**, 961–973. (doi:10. 1093/beheco/ari078)

Rhine, R. J., Wasser, S. K. & Norton, G. W. 1988 Eight-year study of social and ecological correlates of mortality among immature baboons of Mikumi National Park, Tanzania. *Am. J. Primatol.* **16**, 199–212. (doi:10.1002/ajp.1350160303)

Rood, J. 1990 Group size, survival, reproduction, and routes to breeding in dwarf mongooses. *Anim. Behav.* **39**, 566–572. (doi:10.1016/S0003-3472(05)80423-3)

Rodd, F. H. & Boonstra, R. 1988 Effects of adult meadow voles, *Microtus pennsylvanicus*, on young conspecifics in field populations. *J. Anim. Ecol.* **57**, 755–770. (doi:10.2307/5091)

Russell, A. F., Clutton-Brock, T. H., Brotherton, P. N. M., Sharpe, L. L., McIlrath, G. M., Dalerum, F. D., Cameron, E. Z. & Barnard, J. A. 2002 Factors affecting pup growth and survival in co-operatively breeding meerkats, *Suricata suricatta*. *J. Anim. Ecol.* **71**, 700–709. (doi:10.1046/j.1365-2656. 2002.00636.x)

Russell, A. F., Brotherton, P. N. M., Ilrath, G. M., Sharpe, L. L. & Clutton-Brock, T. H. 2003 Breeding success in cooperative meerkats: effects of helper number and maternal state. *Behav. Ecol.* **14**, 486–492. (doi:10.1093/beheco/arg022)

Rusu, A. S. & Krackow, S. 2004 Kin-preferential cooperation, dominance-dependent reproductive skew and competition for mates in communally nesting female house mice. *Behav. Ecol. Sociobiol.* **56**, 298–305. (doi:10.1007/s00265-004-0787-4)

Saltzman, W., Pick, R. R., Salper, O. J., Liedl, K. J. & Abbott, D. H. 2004a Onset of plural cooperative breeding in common marmoset families following replacement of the breeding male. *Anim. Behav.* **68**, 59–73. (doi:10.1016/j.anbehav.2003.07.020)

Saltzman, W., Prudom, S. L., Schultz-Darken, N. J., Wittwer, D. J. & Abbott, D. H. 2004b Social suppression of cortisol in female marmoset monkeys: role of circulating ACTH levels and glucocorticoid negative feedback. *Psychoneuroendocrinology* **29**, 141–161. (doi:10.1016/S0306-4530(02)00159-2)

Santos, C. V., French, J. A. & Otta, E. 1997 Infant carrying behavior in callitrichid primates: *Callithrix* and *Leontopithecus*. *Int. J. Primatol.* **18**, 889–907. (doi:10.1023/A:1026340028851)

Sapolsky, R. M., Alberts, S. C. & Altmann, J. 1997 Hypercortisolism associated with social subordinance or social isolation among wild baboons. *Arch. Gen. Psychiatry* **54**, 1137–1143.

Sawaguchi, T. & Kudo, H. 1990 Neocortical development and social-structure in primates. *Primates* **31**, 283–289. (doi:10.1007/BF02380949)

Shultz, S. & Dunbar, R. I. M. 2006 Both social and ecological factors predict ungulate brain size. *Proc. R. Soc. B* **273**, 207–215. (doi:10.1098/rspb.2005.3283)

Seeman, T. E. & McEwen, B. 1996 Impact of social environment characteristics on neuroendocrine regulation. *Psychosom. Med.* **58**, 459–471.

Sera, W. E. & Gaines, M. S. 1994 The effect of relatedness on spacing behavior and fitness of female prairie voles. *Ecology* **75**, 1560–1566. (doi:10.2307/1939617)

Silk, J. B. 2002 Kin selection in primate groups. *Int. J. Primatol.* **23**, 849–875. (doi:10.1023/A:1015581016205)

Silk, J. B. 2006 Practicing Hamilton's rule: Kin selection in primate groups. In *Cooperation in primates and humans: mechanisms and evolution* (eds P. M. Kappeler & C. P. van Schaik), pp. 25–46. Berlin, Germany: Springer.

Silk, J. B., Cheney, D. L. & Seyfarth, R. M. 1999 The structure of social relationships among female savannah baboons in Moremi Reserve, Botswana. *Behaviour* **136**, 679–703. (doi:10.1163/156853999501522)

Silk, J. B., Alberts, S. C. & Altmann, J. 2003 Social bonds of female baboons enhance infant survival. *Science* **302**, 1331–1334. (doi:10.1126/science.1088580)

Silk, J. B., Alberts, S. C. & Altmann, J. 2004 Patterns of coalition formation by adult female baboons in Amboseli, Kenya. *Anim. Behav.* **67**, 573–582. (doi:10.1016/j.anbe-hav.2003.07.001)

Silk, J. B., Altmann, J. & Alberts, S. C. 2006a Social relationships among adult female baboons (*Papio cynocephalus*) I. Variation in the strength of social bonds. *Behav. Ecol. Sociobiol.* **61**, 183–195. (doi:10.1007/s00265-006-0249-2)

Silk, J. B., Alberts, S. C. & Altmann, J. 2006b Social relationships among adult female baboons (*Papio cynocephalus*) II. Variation in the quality and stability of social bonds. *Behav. Ecol. Sociobiol.* **61**, 197–204. (doi:10.1007/s00265-006-0250-9)

Smuts, B. B. 1985 *Sex and friendship in baboons*. New York, NY: Aldine.

Smuts, B. & Nicolson, N. 1989 Reproduction in wild female olive baboons. *Am. J. Primatol.* **19**, 229–246. (doi:10.1002/ajp.1350190405)

Solomon, N. G. 1991 Current indirect fitness benefits associated with philopatry in juvenile prairie voles. *Behav. Ecol. Sociobiol.* **29**, 277–282. (doi:10.1007/BF00163985)

Solomon, N. G. 1994 Effect of the pre-weaning environment on subsequent reproduction in prairie voles, *Mictrotus ochrogaster*. *Anim. Behav.* **48**, 331–341. (doi:10.1006/anbe.1994.1246)

Solomon, N. G., Vandenbergh, J. G. & Sullivan, W. T. 1998 Social influences on intergroup transfer by pine voles (*Microtus pinetorum*). *Can. J. Zool.* **76**, 2131–2136. (doi:10.1139/cjz-76-12-2131)

Spitzer, M. D., Meikle, D. G. & Solomon, N. G. 2005 Female choice based on male spatial ability and aggressiveness among meadow voles. *Anim. Behav.* **69**, 1121–1130. (doi:10.1016/j.anbehav.2004.06.033)

Sterck, E. H. M., Watts, D. P. & van Schaik, C. P. 1997 The evolution of female social relationships in nonhuman primates. *Behav. Ecol. Sociobiol.* **41**, 291–309. (doi:10.1007/s002650050390)

Sutherland, D. R., Spencer, P. B. S., Singleton, G. R. & Taylor, A. C. 2005 Kin interactions and changing social structure during a population outbreak of feral house mice. *Mol. Ecol.* **14**, 2803–2814. (doi:10.1111/j.1365-294X.2005.02623.x)

Swedell, L. & Leigh, S. (eds) 2006 *Reproduction and fitness in baboons: behavioral, ecological, and life history perspectives*. New York, NY: Springer.

Tardiff, S. 1997 The bioenergetics of parental behavior and the evolution of alloparental care in marmosets and tamarins. In *Cooperative breeding in mammals* (eds N. G. Solomon & J. A. French), pp. 11–33. Cambridge, UK: Cambridge University Press.

Treves, A. 2001 Reproductive consequences of variation in the composition of howler monkey (*Alouatta* spp.) groups. *Behav. Ecol. Sociobiol.* **50**, 61–71. (doi:10.1007/s002650100328)

Treves, A. & Chapman, C. A. 1996 Conspecific threat, predation avoidance, and resource defense: implications for grouping in langurs. *Behav. Ecol. Sociobiol.* **39**, 43–53. (doi:10.1007/s002650050265) van Noordwijk, M. A. & van Schaik, C. P. 1999 The effects of dominance rank and group size on female lifetime reproductive success in wild long-tailed macaques, *Macaca fasicularis*. *Primates* **40**, 105–130.

van Schaik, C. P. 1983 Why are diurnal primates living in groups? *Behaviour* **87**, 120–144.

van Schaik, C. P. & Janson, C. H. (eds) 2000 *Male infanticide and its implications*. Cambridge, UK: Cambridge University Press.

van Schaik, C. P., van Noordwijk, M. A., de Boer, R. J. & den Tonkelaar, I. 1983 The effect of group size on time budgets and social behaviour in wild long-tailed macaques (*Macaca fasicularis*). *Behav. Ecol. Sociobiol.* **13**, 173–181. (doi:10.1007/BF00299920)

Wahaj, S. A., Guse, K. & Holekamp, K. E. 2001 Reconciliation in the spotted hyena (*Crocuta crocuta*). *Ethology* **107**, 1057–1074. (doi:10.1046/j.1439-0310.2001.00717.x)

Wahaj, S. A., Van Horn, R. C., Van Horn, T., Dreyer, R., Hilgris, R., Schwarz, J. & Holekamp, K. E. 2004 Kin discrimination in the spotted hyena (*Crocuta crocuta*): nepotism among siblings. *Behav. Ecol. Sociobiol.* **56**, 237–247. (doi:10.1007/s00265-004-0783-8)

Waser, P. M. & Jones, W. T. 1983 Natal philopatry among solitary mammals. *Q. Rev. Biol.* **58**, 355–390. (doi:10.1086/413385)

Wasser, S. K., Norton, G. W., Kleindorfer, S. & Rhine, R. J. 2004 Population trend alters the effects of maternal dominance rank on lifetime reproductive success in yellow baboons. *Behav. Ecol. Sociobiol.* **56**, 338–345. (doi:10.1007/s00265-004-0797-2)

Weingrill, T. 2000 Infanticide and the value of male-female relationships in mountain chacma baboons (*Papio cynocephalus ursinus*). *Behaviour* **137**, 337–359. (doi:10.1163/156853900502114)

Weladji, R. B., Gaillard, J.-M., Yoccoz, N. G., Holand, Ø., Mysterud, A., Loison, A., Nieminen, M. & Stenseth, N. C. 2006 Good reindeer mothers live longer and become better in raising offspring. *Proc. R. Soc. B* **273**, 1239–1244. (doi:10.1098/rspb.2005.3393)

Wolff, J. O. 1994 Reproductive success of solitarily and communally nesting white-footed mice and deer mice. *Behav. Ecol.* **5**, 206–209.

Wolff, J. O. & Cicerello, D. M. 1991 Comparative paternal and infanticidal behavior of white-footed mice and deermice. *Behav. Ecol.* **2**, 38–45.

Wolff, J. O., Edge, W. D. & Bentley, R. 1994 Reproductive and behavioral biology of the gray-tailed vole. *J. Mammal.* **75**, 873–879. (doi:10.2307/1382469)

Wolff, J. O., Edge, W. D. & Wang, G. 2002 Effects of adult sex ratios on recruitment of juvenile gray-tailed voles, *Microtus canicaudus*. *J. Mammal.* **83**, 947–956. (doi:10.1644/1545-1542(2002)083<0947:EOASRO>2.0.CO;2)

Woodroffe, R. & Macdonald, D. W. 2000 Helpers provide no detectable benefits in the European badger (*Meles meles*). *J. Zool.* **250**, 113–119. (doi:10.1111/j.1469-7998.2000.tb00582.x)

Wrangham, R. W., Gittleman, J. L. & Chapman, C. A. 1993 Constraints on group size in primates and carnivores: population density and day range as assays of exploitation competition. *Behav. Ecol. Sociobiol.* **32**, 199–209. (doi:10.1007/BF00173778)

Ylönnen, H., Mappes, T. & Viitala, J. 1990 Different demography of friends and strangers: an experiment on the impact of kinship and familiarity in *Clethrionomys glareolus*. *Oecologia* **83**, 333–337.

Young, L. J. & Wang, Z. 2004 The neurobiology of pair bonding. *Nat. Neurosci.* **7**, 1048–1054. (doi:10.1038/nn1327)

Zabel, C. J. & Taggart, S. J. 1989 Shift in red fox, *Vulpes vulpes*, mating system associated with El Niño in the Bering Sea. *Anim. Behav.* **38**, 830–838. (doi:10.1016/S0003-3472(89)80114-9)

5

Social brains, simple minds: does social complexity really require cognitive complexity?

Louise Barrett, Peter Henzi and Drew Rendall

The social brain hypothesis is a well-accepted and well-supported evolutionary theory of enlarged brain size in the non-human primates. Nevertheless, it tends to emphasize an anthropocentric view of social life and cognition. This often leads to confusion between ultimate and proximate mechanisms, and an over-reliance on a Cartesian, narratively structured view of the mind and social life, which in turn lead to views of social complexity that are congenial to our views of ourselves, rather than necessarily representative of primate social worlds. In this paper, we argue for greater attention to embodied and distributed theories of cognition, which get us away from current fixations on 'theory of mind' and other high-level anthropocentric constructions, and allow for the generation of testable hypotheses that combine neurobiology, psychology and behaviour in a mutually reinforcing manner.

Keywords: social complexity; primates; anthropocentrism; social brain; distributed cognition; embodied cognition

5.1 Introduction

The social intelligence (social brain) hypothesis states that the demands of social life selected for large brains within the primate order (Humphrey 1976; Byrne & Whiten 1988; Dunbar 1998). This rests, necessarily, on the assumption that social life is complex, where this complexity makes demands that can only be solved with the use of flexible, cognitive strategies in real-time, rather than evolved 'rules-of-thumb' (Byrne & Whiten 1988; Dunbar 1998). The evidence in favour of the social brain hypothesis is persuasive, but based largely on proxy measures for both intelligence and social complexity, such as brain size and group size (e.g. Dunbar 1992a, 1995, 1998; Joffe 1997; Byrne & Corp 2004).

While the social intelligence hypothesis is not solely directed at primates—it hypothesizes that all socially living species should show enlarged brain sizes relative to more solitary congeners—it nonetheless implies that primate social groups will, in some way, be more complex than those of other socially living animals: since primates have disproportionately large brains, the selection pressures coming from the social environment must therefore have been stronger.

There are a number of hypotheses and explanations as to what might increase the complexity of primate groups. All of these have hinged, in one way or another, on the view that primates are more 'political' than other animals—more Machiavellian—such that their interactions occur at a number of different levels, within individualized societies, and involve more complex, polyadic forms of social engagement (de Waal 1982, 1986; Byrne & Whiten 1988; Cords 1997; Dunbar 1998). Here, we argue that evidence in support of this assumption reflects our own unspoken, and often unrecognized, anthropocentric commitments. These commitments lead us to confuse proximate and ultimate explanations and to endorse a Cartesian and propositional view of the mind generally, and of social cognition in particular. We believe that there is merit in considering primates, not as hermetically sealed cogitators, but as agents whose social cognition is determined, at least in part, by their being both 'embodied' and socially 'situated' (Clark 1997; Anderson 2003).

5.2 Social life and social complexity

It is undoubtedly true that the diurnal anthropoid primates, monkeys in particular, are intensely social. They form permanent groups in which one sex or another generally spends its entire life, with the result that groups are composed of extended networks of both matrilineal and patrilineal kin (Dunbar 1988; Strier 1990). Group living is thought to represent an evolutionary response to predation risk (and infanticide; van Schaik & Kappeler 1997), while the internal structure of groups—the degree to which the sexes are related, the nature of dominance hierarchies, the patterning of grooming interactions between individuals, particularly females—is argued to be a response to ecological constraints, specifically to the level of competition for food within and between groups (van Schaik 1983; Dunbar 1988). Group size and structure therefore represent a balance between the centripetal force of predation risk and the centrifugal force of competition. This is assumed to have created a selection pressure on individuals to evolve strategies and tactics that alleviate the negative effects of competition on reproductive success. The social brain hypothesis dovetails neatly with this, since the proposed strategies involve the formation of 'coalitions and alliances' (Harcourt & de Waal 1992) that enable individual animals to combine forces and prevent other individuals from monopolizing resources.

Socio-ecological models are generally silent on whether such strategies represent some form of conscious cognitive processing (although see Dunbar 1984) or if they represent evolved strategies, where action derives from some rule-of-thumb that does not require overt, conscious calculation of goals and consequences. Nevertheless, the incorporation of the social brain hypothesis into socio-ecological explanations does weight them in favour of the former: the complexity of social life in primate groups must require some more complex form of cognitive assessment if the links between social life and behaviour are to underpin brain size.

This comes about, at least partly, because our reasoning runs from brains to behaviour, rather than the reverse: since we know that primates have big brains, it follows that they should be doing more with them than other animals. This being so, the social behaviours that we see are assumed to be built on high-level, flexible cognitive assessment, where driving selection has ratcheted up the capacity to meet strategy with counter-strategy, thereby establishing the relative complexity of primate groups. These more complex mechanisms are therefore assumed to require more brain tissue.

Coalition formation is commonly invoked to explain complexity of this kind because it decouples rank and power (de Waal 1982; Datta 1983). Although rank might derive initially from intrinsic resource holding potential, it can be augmented, and the decline of intrinsic ability compensated for, by the 'extrinsic' power acquired through coalitionary relationships (Datta 1983; Chapais 1992). This makes life inherently more complex because strategizing individuals must then base their decisions not only on observables, such as the body size or the current whereabouts of others, but also on details of the differentiated relationships between individuals within the group.

Coalitions are thought to be cultivated and maintained through allogrooming (Dunbar 1998). Grooming represents an investment of time and effort by one individual in another that establishes a special relationship among associating animals and increases the probability of coalitionary support at some indeterminable point in the future. Strong grooming bonds are signals of the likelihood of 'unstinting mutual support' (Dunbar 1988, 1998, see also Kummer 1968). As this is 'the core process that gives primate social groups their internal structure and coherence' (Dunbar 1998, p. 186), and because both grooming clique size and group size correlate with neocortex ratio (Dunbar 1998; Kudo & Dunbar 2001), it follows that cognitive complexity has been selected by the need to monitor and sustain one's own grooming relationships, while simultaneously monitoring those of others across time in order to keep a running tally of their levels of extrinsic power (Dunbar 1988, 1998; Kudo & Dunbar 2001). This is a compelling proposition, supported by the apparently superior ability of higher primates to detect and identify third-party relationships (Dasser 1988; Cheney & Seyfarth 1990; Tomasello & Call 1997; Bergman et al. 2003).

5.3 Coalitions and relationships

However, as we have argued elsewhere (Henzi & Barrett 1999; Barrett & Henzi 2002; Barrett & Henzi 2005, 2006), there is only equivocal evidence, at best, to support any causal link between grooming and coalition formation, while the formation of coalitions by adults against other adults is also rare in wild populations (Henzi & Barrett 1999; Silk et al. 2004). This is unexpected, given that such coalitions define the complexity of primate groups (Henzi & Barrett 1999). However, while the counterargument—that the rarity of coalitions belies their central importance (Silk et al. 2004)—works for other rare events, like predation or infanticide, it does not hold here. The risks of infanticide and predation form the selection pressures to which primates are thought to have evolved specific countermeasures, such as group-living itself (van Schaik 1983) and female promiscuity (Hrdy 1977). Female promiscuity and group-living are therefore common, which is why infanticide and predation are rare (Dunbar 1988). Coalitions, however, are not the selection pressure, but the evolved response to the selection pressure generated by resource competition. Coalitions should therefore be common and competition rare, whereas the reverse is actually the case: there are many studies demonstrating the existence and extent of competition (see Strier 2002 for review), but very few establish a reliable, causal link between grooming and coalition formation in either the wild or captivity (see Cords 1997; Henzi & Barrett 1999). A recent study that explicitly set out to do so found no evidence of a direct link between the two (Silk et al. 2004), while grooming persists in the absence of coalitions (Barrett & Henzi 2006). This rarity of coalition formation, and the lack of a well-established link between coalitions and grooming, suggests that this behaviour is unlikely to represent a general explanation for the social complexity of primates and their groups.

It remains possible, of course, that monkeys sustain and monitor relationships for other valuable reasons besides coalition formation (see Silk et al. 2003a). Even so, the implicit assumption on which the argument rests—that monkeys can track their own and other relationships through time—has not been tested adequately (Cords 1997; Barrett & Henzi 2002). The point about tracking time is central to this argument because it is assumed that the obligate sociality imposed by predation risk entails, for each participant, a future in which competition is certain but its precise timing is unknown. Selection then favours a prospective cognition that can prepare for this uncertainty.

Of course, this ability is not necessary for relationships to be adaptive, as individuals could, in principle, achieve the same result with evolved rules-of-thumb that do not involve cognitive assessment. However, the social brain hypothesis needs more than this, since non-cognitive, evolved rules-of-thumb do not require particularly large brains. The problem with assuming cognitive solutions that rely on some form of temporal projection is that monkeys, at least, despite large brains, seem to live very much in the here and now, and have yet to provide evidence that they can plan for future contingencies (Roberts 2002), inhibit inappropriate pre-potent responses (Chapais 1992) or remember when an event happened, in addition to what happened and where (Hampton *et al.* 2005).

There is also a lack of evidence to show that they can reason in a truly analogical, conceptual fashion (i.e. understand relations between relations), which would limit their ability to understand the equivalence between their own bonds and those of others (Thompson & Oden 2000). Dasser's (1988) classic study, indicating that female macaques can understand bonds conceptually, does not rule out some form of perceptual matching between individuals, nor are the simple discrimination testing and match-to-sample designs sufficient to show relational matching (Thompson 1995; Thompson & Oden 2000). The two successful monkeys in Dasser's (1988) study were not asked to match mother–offspring pairs with other mother–offspring pairs (i.e. to judge relations between relations by first identifying identity versus non-identity pairs and then matching appropriately on the basis of these relations), but only to match a picture of a mother with one of the two potential offspring, or to discriminate between a picture of a mother–offspring pair and a non-mother–offspring pair. The finding that chimpanzees can accurately match unfamiliar mothers with their offspring suggests that perceptual matching is a possible explanation for Dasser's results (Vokey *et al.* 2004), while subsequent studies of monkeys using the appropriate relational tasks have not found evidence of analogical reasoning, although they used only physical matching tasks (geometric shapes) and not social ones (Thompson & Oden 2000). These findings contrast with observational and field experimental evidence, indicating that monkeys behave as though they do recognize third-party relationships (Tomasello & Call 1997), but whether this amounts to true conceptual, abstract understanding has not specifically been addressed. At least one study demonstrates that simple, associative rules-of-thumb can underpin this ability (Range & Noë 2005).

When Humphrey (1976, p. 309) originally proposed the evolution of a specifically social intelligence, he suggested that primates inhabit a world 'where the evidence on which their calculations are based is ephemeral, ambiguous and liable to change, not least as a consequence of their own actions'. Here, as Carrithers (1991) notes, use of words like 'ephemeral' serve to emphasize the close temporal horizons over which monkeys must perceive and act on events, and does not argue specifically for foresight and intentional planning. There is little doubt that selection has produced cognitive abilities that allow individuals to perceive and respond appropriately to fast-acting dynamic changes in others' behaviour (Barrett & Henzi 2005), but there is no a *priori* reason why selection should have acted to extend these abilities in time. The ability to respond flexibly and expediently to others' behaviour does not demand the ability to plot and plan in any meta-representational fashion.

This all raises an obvious question: given the lack of clear empirical support, why do we persist with this particular view of primate complexity and the social brain? It seems to us that there is something unusually beguiling about the structure and form of the social brain hypothesis that has led us all to take a good deal of it on trust. One reason for this, of course, is that it possesses a very coherent internal logic that binds together two empirically undisputed endpoints (forced sociality; large brains) by means of some direct and intuitively appealing links between behavioural complexity and cognition. There is a clear, if implicit, equation of functional behavioural complexity with underlying mechanistic cognitive complexity, without demonstration (or even argument) of what kinds of mechanistic complexity are actually needed to produce behavioural complexity (or that they are needed at all). If so, it might be useful to ask why these links are so appealing.

Our answer to this question is that the reassuring congeniality of the social brain hypothesis is a direct consequence of the manner in which our own social cognition is built, i.e. we somehow see our former selves very clearly in this picture of primate social life. Indeed, it is our attempt to explain the evolution of human brains that drives, in part at least, the whole social brain project. Crucially, as is often pointed out (*inter alia* Wittgenstein 1968), although we ostensibly look on dispassionately, we can actually do so only through our own socio-cognitive spectacles. There is abundant evidence that we are heavily prone to perceiving and interpreting other components of the world, besides ourselves, in anthropocentric terms. As a result, we may impose complexity on a system that lacks it (or at least lacks the kind of complexity we usually attribute to it). In the case of the social brain hypothesis, we may inadvertently have used primates as a kind of tautological instrument: we have told them what we want them to be in order to validate our own view of who we think we are.

So what facets of human social cognition are important and into what assumptions are we consequently tempted? Answers to these questions may both reveal the commitments that certain arguments and hypotheses entail with respect to social complexity and illustrate how they might mislead us if they remain subliminal and unacknowledged. There are three particular facets of human cognition that we should consider: our inevitably anthropocentric attitude to the world; the way in which this leads us to view other species anthropomorphically; and the manner in which we structure our world as narrative. The first two lead us to view the worlds of other primates, and other species in general, in ways that resonate for us, while we artificially impose an extra layer of order on their worlds by means of the latter.

5.4 Anthropocentrism and anthropomorphism

An anthropocentric stance is something from which, to a large degree, we cannot retreat: by definition, neither can we see the world in anything other than human terms nor can we describe or discuss it in anything other than ordinary human language. It also means that we have a natural consequent tendency to anthropomorphize and attribute human characteristics to other animals (Guthrie 1993). It is clear, moreover, that we are prone to do so on the basis of the quite simple perception–action mechanisms that form the foundations of our folk psychology and which are cognitively impenetrable. We perceive, tellingly, animacy and goal-directedness in a single white dot as it moves across a background, despite the fact that this is induced by nothing more than the way in which it changes speed and direction (Scholl & Tremoulet 2000; Tremoulet & Feldman 2000). We also attribute motives and personality traits to simple geometric shapes on the basis only of the way they move in relation to each other (Heider & Simmel 1944) and, as a by-product of selection for such pattern recognition, we have an overwhelming and automatic urge to see human faces and forms in the most unlikely objects (Guthrie 1993). These basic, apparently evolved mechanisms, on which our sophisticated and culturally constructed understanding of ourselves and other human beings is based (Tomasello 1999), mean that we need to take care to avoid being led astray by our folk psychological understanding of ourselves and other people: the more something resembles us, or the more familiar it is, the more likely its behaviour will trigger these mechanisms, leading us to interpret it as human-like (Eddy *et al.* 1993; Povinelli *et al.* 2000).

The debate regarding the appropriateness of anthropomorphism as a scientific research strategy waxes and wanes regularly. There is, however, an overall sense that it is always a mistaken approach for scientists to take (e.g. Wynne 2004). As Tyler (2003, p. 270) notes, 'the very suggestion that a theory or approach is anthropomorphic is, implicitly, always an objection or an accusation'. Those who employ such a strategy are inevitably required to defend a deeply suspect position. By the same token, however, there is also an argument to the effect that anti-anthropomorphism is equally suspect, since it assumes implicitly that there are unique human traits, identifiable *a priori*, and that these should not be attributed to creatures to which they do not 'belong' (Sheets-Johnstone 1992; Sober 1998; de Waal 2001; Tyler 2003; Keeley 2004).

Whether any 'anti-anthropomorphites' actually hold such a philosophical position is moot and a more realistic characterization of this stance might be that we simply do not know whether other animals have human-like traits (and, if one's outlook is particularly bleak, is something that we can never know; e.g. Nagel 1974). Attributing human-like traits to other animals is inappropriate because it has the effect of sealing the matter before it has been properly studied. Even worse, it is likely that we have mischaracterized the nature of at least some of those human traits in the first place (Tyler 2003; Fernàndez-Armesto 2004; Rendall *et al.* 2007), so applying human traits to other animals merely results in a layering of confusion: we are confused about ourselves and if we then apply that confused view to other animals, we compound the error (Andrews 2005; Rendall *et al.* 2007).

This bias can work both ways. In addition to ascribing human attributes to other animals inappropriately, we can also deny them certain cognitive capacities in an equally inappropriate manner, because we confuse what is necessarily required with the specific form these capacities happen to take in humans. The objections raised with respect to episodic memory in non-human animals are a case in point (Suddendorf & Busby 2003). Here, aspects of episodic memory, such as autonoesis, which can only ever be demonstrated empirically in humans, were made an integral and essential part of its definition. To criticize any claims for avian episodic memory (Clayton *et al.* 2003a) by arguing that episodic memory is partly defined by elements that 'belong' to humans necessarily prescribes the investigation. The real issue, of course, is whether episodic memory is a cognitive mechanism available to other species, not whether other animals have a specifically *human* episodic memory. It should be obvious that they do not, since they are not human and, as Clayton *et al.* (2003a, p. 437) point out, it is inappropriate to insist that episodic memory should be defined by 'the phenomenology of the modern human mind, rather than in terms of core cognitive capacities': to do so is just anthropocentric narrow-mindedness.

The argument that anthropocentrism obscures the social lives of primates is not, therefore, a simple criticism of an 'anthropomorphic' approach *per se*: there is no reason why, taking an evolutionarily grounded view of cognition, other species should not also manifest some of the same cognitive capacities as humans, either by descent or convergence. This being so, we need to avoid an approach to animal sociality that places humans at the comparative centre. We should, instead, ask questions about what it means to be a living being of any kind, rather than immediately restricting ourselves to some comparison with humans. The proposition is, then, that anthropocentrism, whether positively or negatively anthropomorphic, needs to be acknowledged and contained because it denies animals their own voices.

In the case of social cognition, anthropocentrism leads us to ask questions about other primates' social cognition from an unduly distorted perspective. This is one that privileges conscious, 'higher' forms of cognition, based on language and meta-representational 'theory of mind' (ToM) skills, because we think of these as essential and fundamental to the understanding of the behaviour of other humans, even though this is not generally the case (Liberman *et al.* 2002; Hutto 2004; Andrews 2005; Gallagher 2005). We consequently gear our research efforts explicitly to detecting these abilities or, more commonly, their precursors, in monkeys and apes, either as a check on our own uniqueness and/or as a means of identifying how our own skills in these domains have been derived from evolutionarily simpler mechanisms (e.g. Dunbar 1996; Bergman *et al.* 2003; Povinelli & Vonk 2003; Tomasello *et al.*2003; Zuberbuhler 2003; Cheney & Seyfarth 2005).

A research strategy of this kind requires commitments that, on reflection, might be problematic. Looking explicitly for precursors of human sociocognitive attributes, for one, judges primate capacities against a human standard and therefore necessarily sees in them some fraction of this standard at best, where these might better be regarded as adaptations in their own right (Tyler 2003). Adopting a 'folk-theoretic' stance that places unobservable mental states to the fore, for another, creates all kinds of problems about how to define such states and justify their inference on the basis of observable behaviour (Johnson & Oswald 2001, p. 454; Povinelli & Vonk 2003; Andrews 2005). Finally, an emphasis on higher cognition leads to a neglect of the perception–action mechanisms by which animals actually engage with the world, on which selection has acted for a much longer period, and from which these higher-level processes emerge (Brooks 1999). This is the most relevant problem from our point of view because, by placing social cognition firmly 'in the head' as an abstract, logical, disembodied process, we ignore differences in active, bodily engagement with the world. So, when de Waal (2005) argues that Georgia, the chimpanzee, should be regarded as possessing a 'complex and familiar inner life' because her behaviour looks so very similar to our own, it disregards the fact that her body interacts with the world very differently from the ways that ours do. How might our own physical grounding of concepts differ if we could use our feet as effectively as our hands (or if we had flippers or a wholly carnivorous diet)?

5.5 Narrative intelligence

We distort our view of other animals further by virtue of a particular anthropocentric tendency to construct meaning through narrative. Humans are a literary and story-telling species (Turner 1996). Like those of all other animals, human brains are, generally speaking, machines for distilling pattern from the world. Chaotic randomness does not appeal to us, and our particular means of extracting meaning and purpose from the events in our lives is to form them into narratives that, owing to the strictures of language, are linearly conceived and structured. To do so, we rely on abstraction, the specific form of which depends on what we are trying to convey: stories told to entertain involve elaboration and sometimes exaggeration, while stories told to inform omit unnecessary detail and follow more direct linear trajectories (Tversky 2004). In addition, and importantly, 'stories have an extended temporal horizon, they relate to past and future, and they are created depending on the social context' (Dautenhahn 2002, p. 111). Stories are formed by events that, in turn, can only be understood in relation to the story as a whole (Carrithers 1991). This natural story-telling ability, like our tendency to anthropomorphize, is indiscriminate and promiscuous: we are obliged to tell stories about everything we see and we structure narratives around both ourselves and other living creatures.

Understanding narrativity is argued to be crucial to understanding human cognition, generally (Bruner 1990, 1991; Carrithers 1991; Turner 1996), and the evolution of human social cognition in particular (Read & Miller 1995; Dautenhahn 2001, 2002). Dautenhahn's (2001) Narrative Intelligence hypothesis, for example, argues that the evolutionary origin of communicating using stories reflects the increasingly complex social dynamics that evolved among our early human ancestors. The point here is that, even when we are not explicitly assuming that other animals have minds like our own, our natural tendency to understand the world through narrative means that we may nevertheless observe, experiment on and interpret their behaviour in narrative forms that rely on an essential anthropocentrism.

5.6 Whose complexity is it?

With respect to primate sociality, our narrative tendencies are most clearly revealed by the fact that anybody who has worked on primates will have found themselves, at one time or another, describing the life of a primate group as a 'soap opera'—an on-going open-ended narrative involving a familiar set of characters (e.g. Dunbar 1996, p. 28). The question, of course, is: do other animals see themselves in this way? It is our view that narrative structuring is not part of the world of at least one primate group—the monkeys—and that when we impose a narrative structure on their social interactions, we make their worlds more complex than is warranted.

Hinde (1976, 1983) identified three levels of social structure: *interactions* (between particular individuals), *relationships* (the frequency, quality and patterning of these interactions over time) and *social structure* (the overall patterning of relationships within the group). Although he saw relationships as emergent, irreducible phenomena, Hinde also emphasized their fluidity, regarding them as dynamic equilibria in which an impression of stability can be created by the contingent shifts and adjustments in interactions. As Silk (2002) suggests, however, we have largely assumed that such irreducible social relationships exist, rather than providing well-defined, rigorous means of identifying them (see also Cords 1997). Despite this, they have come increasingly to be seen as evermore stable entities that, as we know, can be subdivided into such forms as 'friendships' (Silk 2002), 'coalitions' (Dunbar 1984, 1988) or 'alliances' (Harcourt & de Waal 1992) that animals sustain consistently and cooperatively. Consequently, whereas grooming and proximity maintenance (two measures of affiliation) might once have been viewed as constituting the relationship in and of themselves, they are now more often regarded as an index of some underlying bond that exceeds the sum of its parts. This, in turn, may reflect the fact that, to identify relationships, we abstract many interactions over time, therefore adding a temporal component, and temporal consistency, to our analyses of monkey life (which actually reflects an arbitrary, human-relative time frame, rather than one relevant to the animals themselves). In this way, the grooming we record between animals now can token 'unstinting mutual support' in the future (Harcourt 1992; Dunbar 1998). This, however, amounts to the reification of a relationship concept that we still need to show has more than human significance (Barrett & Henzi 2002; Silk 2002).

The well-documented demonstration that social animals can reconcile after aggression (de Waal & van Roosmalen 1979; de Waal 1989) has helped bed down this supposition that individuals service and repair their relationships in order to sustain them (Aureli & de Waal 2000). The recent finding that the lifetime reproductive success of female baboons increases with their sociability links all these elements together evolutionarily, and further suggests that selection could act on the psychological mechanisms that support these differing forms of association (Silk *et al.* 2003a). This, as already mentioned, is argued to drive complexity: the cultivation of relationships, while simultaneously monitoring those of others, places a significant cognitive burden on participants who track their status through time, and who pick up social knowledge and information that is not vital at the time, but can be used adaptively later on (Harcourt 1988, 1989, 1992; Whiten 2000).

If this is so, how might this social knowledge be constructed? Cheney & Seyfarth (2005, p. 152), for example, have used a suite of rigorous playback experiments to argue that wild female baboons' ' . . . knowledge is propositional'. By this, apparently they mean that it is a declarative, explicit form of knowledge (i.e. 'knowing that' an individual A has a relationship with B), rather than an implicit, procedural knowledge of others (i.e. 'knowing how' to engage with others, without any explicit understanding of their relationships). The empirical data comprise the time an animal spends looking towards a hidden speaker. Longer looking times are said to indicate that 'listeners responded as if they parsed a call sequence as a dramatic narrative: *Hannah is threatening Sylvia and Sylvia is screaming. But Sylvia belongs to the alpha-matriline and Hannah belongs to the beta. This can only mean that the beta-family is attempting to depose the alpha'* (p. 152). This is a rich interpretation, given the nature of the data, and is really only possible because the 'parsing of narratives' is already built into the experimental design and the baboons cannot do otherwise. The questions concern whether monkey narratives are hierarchically organized by kin and rank, but beg the question of whether such narratives exist at all, which seems crucial. More importantly, the actual cognitive mechanism underlying this looking time response remains opaque. The design of the experiment, which uses an introspective consideration of our own folk psychological mechanisms to rationalize the behaviour of the animals, probably tells us more about how we think our own minds work, as opposed to revealing anything significant about the mind of the baboon.

There is further reason to suspect that monkeys may not view their interactions as relationships with an inherently temporal, narrative format. Long-term data from baboons reveal that there is a good deal of variability in partner choice over time, with changes in preference associated strongly with reproductive events (Barrett & Henzi 2002). This, in itself, can explain why more sociable females are more reproductively successful: females with young infants attract significantly more social attention than non-lactating females (Altmann 1980; Henzi & Barrett 2002; Silk *et al.* 2003b), with the result that those females who give birth more often experience increased levels of social interaction. Here, therefore, causality may run in the direction opposite to that which is assumed (Silk *et al.* 2003a). In addition, it is probable that individuals groom and maintain proximity to others owing to short-term concerns, such as access to infants or to 'skilled' individuals, tolerance around resources and avoidance of aggression (Silk 1982; Stammbach 1988; Muroyama 1994; Barrett & Henzi 2001; Henzi & Barrett 2002; Chapais 2006; Noë 2006).

Data from samango monkeys also show that when the opportunity exists for increased social investment, females allocate the time to resting instead (Payne *et al.* 2003, Pazol & Cords 2005). Similarly, while Dunbar & Dunbar (1988) suggested that weaning behaviour in gelada was prompted by the stresses placed on female social relationships (due to an increase in feeding time to fuel lactation), and the need to ensure relationship integrity could be maintained over time, analyses of two *Papio* baboon populations have found that, when possible, females actively reduce social time as part of an energy-sparing strategy, but show no changes in the diversity of their grooming partners as a consequence (Kenyatta 1995; Barrett *et al.* 2006).

Finally, recent analyses of baboon social networks show that these do not have the temporal durability that is usually assumed. When food is abundant, females from two markedly different environments forego 'companionships' (*sensu* Whitehead 1995) and like herding antelope are perhaps better regarded as merely gregarious. Only when food is scarce do the 'constant companionships' indicative of strong, differentiated relationships emerge. For part of each year, then, adult female baboons downgrade the qualitative status of their associations from what we would see as relationships to what network analysis reveals as 'casual acquaintances' (Henzi *et al*, Submitted). There is no suggestion that the phases without companionships trigger either temporary or permanent fission. This being so, models of social life that are predicated on the value of grooming effort as a bonding agent may benefit from reconsideration (Dunbar 1992*b*). If relationships can regularly dissolve without affecting group integrity, it is hard to see why imposed reductions in social time should inevitably lead to group fission as these models predict, and why group size should necessarily be limited by cognitive constraints on relationship tracking.

Overall, then, these findings suggest that the need for individuals to service, protect and repair relationships through time may have been overestimated, for wild populations at least. This is reinforced by the fact that most data in support of grooming bonds come from Old World monkeys; studies of New World primates have shown that grooming is much less common, despite group and brain sizes similar to those found in Old World species (Strier 2002). In captivity, from where much of the data on relationship value come (e.g.Cords 1997; de Waal 2003 for reviews), individuals may well need to ensure that they sustain contact with others owing to an absence of alternative responses to aggression. At the same time, of course, they have more time to engage in social interaction and little else to occupy them. This, in itself, is interesting and shows that primates have the flexibility to adopt a variety of social solutions to their quotidian problems. We argue, in fact, that this kind of behavioural flexibility is the key to understanding primate social adaptation (Barrett & Henzi 2005). The construal of primate social engagement in terms of narrative relationships, on the other hand, seems comparatively less secure. At the very least, these concerns suggest that we should be sceptical about assuming that monkeys see their relationships as we see them.

5.7 The interpretative gap

If we cannot avoid our own socio-cognitive biases, and acknowledge that they might lead us astray, we are obliged to find a way to proceed. The most sensible approach is probably to acknowledge the gravitational pull of an anthropocentric narrative and to ask explicitly how something might be achieved if it is not being achieved in a human-like way. What we have to do, in other words, is to deal with Dennett's 'interpretative gap'.

As Dennett (1989) has made clear, we adopt a stance when we predict or explain a system. Whereas we might accurately predict the behaviour of a baboon by ascribing reason to its actions (the 'intentional stance'), which natural selection licenses us to do, this does not naturally entitle us to use reason as an explanation of the action (see also Kennedy 1992). Or to put it more simply, it is not necessarily the case that an animal which behaves 'as if' it is thinking, actually is. Or if it is, there is no need for it to be doing so in the way that we do (Povinelli *et al.* 2000). Although the intentional stance is unavoidable (Dennett 1989), it necessarily opens up an interpretative gap—between prediction and explanation, and between function and mechanism—that must be closed. Our argument, then, is that the current conception of the social intelligence/social brain hypothesis inevitably opens up the interpretative gap because it is a hypothesis that elides evolutionary response with proximate mechanism, and allows evidence for the former to be taken as support for the latter.

The original social intelligence hypothesis, as put forward by Jolly (1966) and Humphrey (1976), was a strongly evolutionary hypothesis, which aimed to explain why primates were more brainy than other animals, despite the fact that the environmental challenges facing them were no more taxing, and sometimes considerably less so, than those that faced other species. The hypothesis put forward was that the social environment provided the cognitive challenges, so that improvement in cognitive ability in one part of the population would over time ratchet up the level in the rest of the population due to the interactive and dynamic nature of social engagement, with the smartest animals enjoying increased survival and reproductive success. As we have shown, the behaviours assumed to have been selected were those associated with relationship formation, maintenance and protection (which were also seen as characteristic of primates), and these in turn were assumed to require certain sophisticated cognitive capacities, based largely on a folk psychological projection of our own abilities in these domains (see also Silk (2002) for a similar argument with respect to the evolution of reconciliation).

Consequently, evidence in support of the evolutionary argument, such as the correlation between group size and brain size across the primate order (Dunbar 1995), has also been taken as implicit support for the postulated proximate behavioural and cognitive mechanisms by which individual animals increase survival and reproductive success. But such evidence does not, and cannot, tell us anything directly about proximate mechanisms. Moreover, the same is true even if we move down a level and show that the behaviours themselves are deployed by females in a way that is directly fitness enhancing (e.g. Silk *et al.* 2003*a*). This is because females that act as if they know their relationships are valuable and worth protecting may well be doing so in an evolutionary sense, but not necessarily at a more proximate level: the selection pressures acting on the actual cognitive mechanisms by which females engage with each other may be very different from the evolutionary forces that have shaped fitness-enhancing sociality in general. The successful application of our own folk psychological understanding of primates to generate functional hypotheses and explanations of behaviour cannot, therefore, be taken to indicate that we understand anything about the psychological mechanisms that primates might use to understand each other.

One way that researchers have used to get around the problem of the interpretative gap is by appealing to phylogenetic similarity and, in essence, closing the gap by fiat. Consequently, de Waal (2001, p. 70), for one of many examples, argues that the 'mere five to six million years' which separate chimpanzees and humans shift the burden of proof (concerning behavioural or cognitive similarities) to those who deny the relevance of this fact: 'But doesn't . . . parsimony argue against assuming a huge cognitive gap when the evolutionary distance between humans and apes is so small?' (de Waal 1997, p. 53). Interestingly, in this regard, baboons emerged as a species only some 2.5 Myr ago. Nevertheless, they have subsequently differentiated into a number of forms that are distinctively different in behaviour. Here, an assumption of interpretative continuity can—and has—lead to misinterpretation (Henzi & Barrett 2003). In truth, as Dennett has indicated, the interpretative gap is only narrowed by adopting the intentional stance and then setting out specifically to test its starting assumptions. The burden of proof, therefore, falls squarely on all of us, all of the time.

If we begin by acknowledging explicitly our anthropocentric perspective, our objective must be an examination of the mechanisms by which we and other animals do the things that we do. In other words, our questions must become explicitly proximate mechanistic, and not evolutionary functional. We cannot use the 'as if' reasoning of functional hypotheses when asking questions about cognition because it blurs the distinction between proximate and ultimate explanation and makes it possible to slide between evolutionary and cognitive causes of action (Kennedy 1992). Arguing that baboons act 'as if' they are parsing calls into narratives or that Diana monkeys act '. . . as if they recognized that chimpanzee alarm screams signalled the presence of a leopard' (Zuberbuhler 2003, p. 283), actively avoids considering mechanism.

This is fine if our concerns are the assessment of functional (fitness-based) outcomes, but clearly problematic for an elaboration of cognitive evolution, which is the ostensible intention of many of these studies. Merely arguing that monkeys act 'as if' they understand the chimpanzee calls, for example, does not really get us anywhere because the 'meaning' of the vocalization, in this instance, is neither its function nor the proximate mechanism giving rise to it. It sits uneasily somewhere in between as an intentional heuristic that, sooner or later, has to get cashed out for a concrete explanation in terms of mechanism, as well as function.

It is important to stress that this pursuit of mechanism is not in any way a caricatured, radical behaviourist denial of higher-order cognition. Analytically, since it is the comparison of plausible competing hypotheses concerning the nature of underlying mechanisms, it would have, in fact, the welcome and opposite effect of ending the use of statistical null models as the benchmark against which ideas or propositions are assessed (see also Gigerenzer 2004). At present, highly cognitive hypotheses are tested against null models, which is the equivalent of saying: 'we are testing whether *something* is happening in these animals' heads, rather than *nothing*'. Rejecting the null hypothesis, then, does not mean that the postulated cognitive mechanism has been shown to exist, only that a cognitive mechanism of some kind is operating, rather than a simple stimulus–response link. Identifying and pitting alternative cognitive mechanisms against each other is the only way to establish what kind of cognitive mechanism is actually being used, as studies of memory development in children (Russell & Thompson 2003) and prospective cognition in jays (Clayton & Dickinson 1999) illustrate to great effect.

Given this, the question then arises as to where these alternative kinds of plausible mechanisms might come from. Our approach in what follows is to suggest that apparent cognitive complexity may emerge from the interaction of brain, body and world, and is not merely due to the level of internal complexity the animal itself possesses.

5.8 Complex social space

With respect to monkeys, and their social interactions, this means recognizing, first of all, that the shifting and varied encounters which we view anthropocentrically as the evolutionary precursors to human relationships, and which we have assumed to possess a significant temporal component, may, from the monkey's perspective, be better conceptualized as a form of spatial pattern recognition. In other words, monkeys may engage each other in a highly action-centred, continuous, spatial jockeying for position and influence within the confines of the group, using social contact and proximity as a means to achieving immediate goals, and monitoring the concurrent actions of others, but without any conceptual, representational knowledge of what they are doing, or any projection of this through time.

If this is the case, then fission may not be the result of weakening and fragmentation of relationships, followed by fracturing along lines of least resistance (Dunbar 1992b), but may simply reflect the inability to maintain ongoing contact with all other group members as groups become larger and more spatially dispersed. Where animals are frequently separated by the need to find food, fission can emerge as a gradual mechanical process in which subgroups become increasingly spatially disjunct. The formation of new groups is likely to be hastened where sleeping sites are readily available and where perceived predation risk does not set a high lower limit on the size of foraging group an individual feels comfortable in.

Similarly, we can view coalitions as only one component of a suite of tactics that monkeys use when they offer immediate benefits for both parties, i.e. as short-term mutualism (e.g. Silk *et al.* 2004) and not as prospective investment governed by reciprocal altruism (e.g. Seyfarth & Cheney 1984). Reconfigured in this way, they can be seen as the presentation of a spatially integrated 'united front' by two or more animals, where current need drives conjoint action and reduces the social stress experienced by the participants. Maintenance of spatial proximity may, by the same token, function as a more 'passive' form of coalitionary support reducing the likelihood of displacement or aggression and reflecting an immediate, dynamic response to changes in spatial positioning. The tendency of many female-bonded species to groom up the dominance hierarchy may involve a similar tendency to seek tolerance around higher-ranked animals both for the benefits this may offer directly and to reduce the likelihood of interference by third parties while in a dominant's zone of tolerance (e.g. Silk 1982).

Under these conditions, individuals do not need to hold abstract conceptual notions of 'bonds' or track others' relationships because they can gauge circumstances directly by looking at what is happening around them: the spatial structuring of the animals in their environment may obviate the need for certain kinds of high-level processing in the animals themselves, and they can 'use the world as its own best model' as Brooks (1999) suggests (see also Gibson 1979). This kind of 'just in time' learning is both less costly and time consuming than the 'just in case' learning proposed by Whiten (2000), which requires much more complex internal models of the world for efficient functioning. It fits, too, with Silk's (1996) proposal that reconciliation acts fundamentally as a short-term signal of benign intent. In all cases, such manoeuvring is performed in the 'here and now' and we do not need to infer any form of planning or anticipation of the future.

Rejection of a narrative component to primate relationships is not a rejection of the possibility of complex social engagement *per se,* but an expectation that any complexity will be dynamic and result from on-going spatial engagement in real-time. It need not be a consequence of the integration of information across many social events and many actors. New World primates, incidentally, are among the beneficiaries of this conception since the absence of a strong relationship between group size and grooming time in the platyrrhines (Dunbar 1991) has led to suggestions that they may lack the strategic capabilities of the catarrhines. Thinking in terms of space, from a highly action-centred perspective, rather than about time and representations, may give us new insights into the social engagement of all primates, while also shedding light on the differences between monkey and ape cognition (Barrett *et al.* 2003).

5.9. Being in the world

The second means of dealing with the interpretative gap is to reject the Cartesian viewpoint that places an intentional (anthropomorphic) stance to the fore. If we assume that relationships are temporally constructed narratives in the heads of the animals, and use the intentional stance to make predictions about behaviour, we are immediately drawn into a view of animals as 'thinking subjects' and so privilege questions that deal with how subjects gain knowledge of the world, how they relate to it and how they acquire an understanding of the social worlds of others. If instead we adopt a more embodied approach to cognition generally (Anderson 2003) and to primatesocial cognition in particular (Gallese 2001, 2005, 2006, 2007; Barrett & Henzi 2005), we move from thinking of ourselves and other animals as detached observers of the world, but as beings situated in the world, and inseparable from it (Heidigger 1927/1978). This immediately gives us greater purchase on the mechanisms by which animals actively cope with the world, because many of these will be visible to us in the form of perception–action loops, and not as invisible mental constructs.

This fits with findings from various areas of cognitive science, including computer science, artificial intelligence and robotics, which argue that we should think of brains and cognition as behaviour control systems, designed to help humans and other animals engage actively with the world, rather than reflect on it (Clark 1997; Brooks 1999). Representations of the world, therefore, will be grounded in an animal's physical skills and bodily experiences (Anderson 2003). Such a perspective has a much stronger evolutionary flavour (Damasio 1994) and, by focusing on the physical means by which an animal engages with the world, it immediately reduces our anthropocentric tendencies. It allows us to discount the association of cognition with high-level thought processes alone and to study perception, action and cognition as a functionally integrated system (Barrett & Henzi 2005; Barton 2006, 2007). In so doing, it returns us to Leslie Brothers' (1990) original concept of the social brain, where neural activity and bodily responses to social stimuli form the basic building blocks for participation in social acts, and therefore gets us away from the 'neuroist' approach that places all the important stuff solely in the brain itself (Brothers 2001).

As a consequence, embodied cognition (EC) places a different emphasis on evolutionary continuity. It proposes that we investigate the way in which perception–action mechanisms, and bodily engagement with the world, can exploit the structure of the environment (Gibson 1979) and so limit the need for expensive (often slow), high-level internal processing, as a cost-effective evolutionary process should (Humphrey 1976). More importantly, it turns an anthropocentric research strategy on its head by proposing that, instead of looking for the cognitive precursors of sophisticated human cognition, we should investigate the ways in which perception–action mechanisms constrain (in the sense of canalize) the evolution of high-level processes (Brooks 1999; Anderson 2003; see also Panksepp 1998).

An embodied perspective, therefore, moves us away from an anthropocentric, mentalistic view of cognition and extends it beyond 'skin and skull' to the body and the world (Clark 1997), with the aim of understanding how cognitive processes are rooted in bodily experience and interwoven with bodily action and interaction with other individuals (Merleau-Ponty 1962/2002; Varela et al. 1991; Damasio 1994; Clark 1997; Lakoff & Johnson 1999; Anderson 2003; Garbarini & Adenzato 2004; Barrett & Henzi 2005). It is therefore an approach that has much in common with the research strategy that Shettleworth (1998) characterizes as ecological; here the assumption is that evolution has selected for the behaviours and mechanisms that enable animals to cope with life in particular ecological niches. It acknowledges that animals may show skilled and sophisticated performance in specific domains, where they may be superior to humans, but that this need not manifest itself in other domains, indicate some general form of anthropocentrically defined 'intelligence' or reflect phylogenetic proximity to humans (as implicitly assumed by anthropocentric imperatives such as Morgan's canon). The striking social and cognitive skills of corvids, for example (Clayton et al. 2003b; Emery & Clayton 2004), expressed in the context of food caching, can therefore be seen in this light. Similarly, the inability of Old World monkeys to match the cooperative behaviour and tool-use capacities of capuchin moneys (e.g. Mendres & de Waal 2000; Moura et al. 2004) are a puzzle only if we adopt an anthropocentric, phylogenetic perspective.

There is strong neurobiological support for an embodied primate cognition (Perrett *et al.* 1990; Barton 1996, 1998; Rizzolatti *et al.* 1996; Gallese 2005, 2006, 2007; Gallese *et al.* 2004). This provides the necessary springboard from which to test the 'physical grounding hypothesis' (Brooks 1999), which is the central project of EC (Anderson 2003). Gallese (2001, 2003, 2005, 2006, 2007; Gallese *et al.* 2004), in particular, has presented an extremely compelling argument for mirror mechanisms (systems of motor and pre-motor neurons, activated by one's own performance of action and the observations of others' actions) as the basis of an implicit, automatic and unconscious understanding of others as goal-directed agents.

The fundamental ability of the motor system to resonate when viewing action (and that extends to emotions and sensations; see Gallese 2006, 2007, for a review) suggests that primates can establish a meaningful understanding of others, and of themselves, without any need for mental state understanding or overt conscious simulation. This is therefore a basic form of inter-subjectivity or empathy (Preston & de Waal 2002; Gallese 2005). As a result, individuals automatically generate affordances—possibilities for action—for the animals that observe them; affordances that are built directly into an animal's perceptual representations. Social engagement may not therefore require the 'propositional' knowledge that is often assumed (Zuberbuhler 2003; Cheney & Seyfarth 2005). Social understanding may, instead, be a form of pattern recognition involving 'active' perception (Noë 2004). It will then be better modelled and understood as embodied in the patterns of activation of neuronal units, linked in distributed networks, than as some form of logical, syntactically organized computation (Clark 1993).

Mechanistic explanations of this type can explain why kin recognition in primates appears to be based on familiarity and not on more specialized mechanisms like phenotype matching (Rendall 2004). Since neural networks require experience, they have the flexibility to cope with changes in cue features over time (as naturally happens as individuals develop and age) lacked by the other more deterministic processes. Indeed, neural networks are the 'cellular instantiation' of familiarity: what the network 'knows' is that with which it is most familiar. The experiential plasticity of neural networks also allows a continuous updating of social signals, which can account for the proficiency with which animals can perceptually track changing social cues (Rendall 2004). This makes such mechanisms potentially more powerful than highly specialized mechanisms, because they are robust to deviations in cues or context. By contrast, the narrowly tuned, specialized mechanisms used by, e.g. ants and digger wasps, work extremely well in the correct context, but can be perturbed by the smallest deviation from normal triggering conditions, revealing themselves as robotic and 'stupid'. Generalized mechanisms, as they are more flexible, allow for more flexible, contingent behaviour.

For long-lived social primates, for whom both physical and social environments are inherently unstable, such mechanisms are arguably more adaptive than specialized cognitive routines, such that we should expect flexible, experientially informed pattern-recognition to form the basis for much of primate cognition. The potential downside of such mechanisms is that they are tissue intensive: large-scale pattern recognizers require a lot of connectivity to implement (Clark 1993). In this case, however, it adds strength to our argument, since it is precisely this extra requirement for neural tissue that the social brain hypothesis must explain. While evolution is cost-effective, as Humphrey (1976) originally argued, this does not mean that it must also be an efficient engineer, as we tend to assume. Convoluted, messy solutions may be both necessary due to inherent, physical constraints on neuronal functioning, and made possible by the fact that evolution is liberated by having the time in which to come up with non-obvious, but effective solutions (Clark 2000).

Our take-home message, therefore, is that primate groups are not more socially complex than those of other animals *per se*, and it is not social complexity alone that has selected for greater brain size. Rather, these long-lived, group-living animals face significant changes in both social and ecological environments over the course of their lifespan, and synergistic effects between the two (Sterelny 2007). Consequently, they require high levels of behavioural flexibility ('quotidian cognition'; Barrett & Henzi 2005), instantiated in generalized pattern-recognition networks, in order to survive.

The generation of hypotheses and predictions linked to pattern recognition argues for an increased focus on naturalistic, observational studies of primate social interaction—the manner in which individuals respond to the social cues of others, the cues they themselves display and how this leads to forms of behavioural coordination—rather than observations and experiments designed to tap into abstract, conceptual knowledge. The classic demonstration that monkeys understand rank relations, for example, does so by showing how the lower ranking of two individuals retreats at the approach of a third, higher-ranking female (Cheney & Seyfarth 1990). This is usually interpreted as an indication that individuals compute the rank relationships of others and do not rely on a purely egocentric assessment. It could equally, however, be achieved by a simpler embodied mechanism, more related to 'intentional attunement' (Gallese 2006, 2007) than to 'propositional knowledge' (Cheney & Seyfarth 2005). Individuals may attend to the salient features of the responses of others to particular events, generating distributed networks that can match these patterns when they recur. If the approaching female provides physical cues and directs her gaze more towards one female, the approached animals can respond in different ways, depending on whether they are the focus of attention and for how long this lasts. The lower-ranking female may show greater muscle tension, stiffen her posture, show facial expressions or make preparatory movements all of which enable the other female to infer an intention to leave and respond accordingly by remaining.

While this is crude conjecture, it is, in principle, plausible and can be tested. Monitoring the attention structure of such triads may tell us more about how individuals manage social engagement than does interpreting social responses in terms of abstract rank structure alone (e.g. Johnson & Oswald 2001). The study by Paukner *et al.* (2004) showing how pigtailed macaques preferred to watch a mimicking experimenter, despite no overt recognition of the mimicry, is therefore very interesting in this regard, since it flags up, quite literally, the salience of close behavioural coordination among partners. The findings of Chartrand & Bargh (1999) that similar non-conscious mimicry can facilitate intimacy in humans, perhaps forming the true 'social glue' which bonds groups (Lakin *et al.* 2003), therefore generate a testable prediction with regard to the behavioural coordination shown by monkey affiliates. Placing a stronger, more ethological focus on how individuals coordinate their behaviour under various conditions, we can begin to hypothesize and test how the mechanisms that govern how they perceive, act and move in such an environment are linked to the internal representations they generate: as Anderson (2003) states, representations are more likely to be governed by these practical criteria than by abstract or logical ones. Gallese (2007) is already making great strides in specifying how embodiment scaffolds representational schema and influences higher-order cognition (see also Gallese & Goldman 1998; Gallese *et al.* 2004). If behavioural studies also begin to pay more attention to the details of how animals perceive and act in the world, rather than what we think they think about it, then we can begin to consider seriously how 'lower' faculties might relate to 'higher' ones. Alternatively, as we argued above, they may reveal how the interleaving of perception and action in response to environmental structures eliminates the need for certain high-level forms of processing altogether (Brooks 1999), or at least greatly reduces the complexity of internal mechanisms.

Again, it is important to stress that this emphasis on embodied behaviour is not a return to *behaviourism*. This is because perception and action form 'loopy structures', where action generates perceptual feedback that, in turn, generates further action, so that outward behaviour becomes an important co-contributor to the processes, including neural processes, which generate further behavioural response (Keijzer 2005). As Hurley (1998) notes, by contrast, behaviourism assumes a linear, one-way process where perception causes action (i.e. input to output), but there is no further feedback from action to perception (i.e. output to input).

An embodied perspective, then, is one that allows us to consider social cognition as an observable, distributed event (Hutchins 1985; Brothers 2001; Johnson 2001), rather than as purely invisible, private ones. This view owes much to Heidigger (1927/1978), and the rejection of a 'Cartesian homunculus peering out at the world and seeing what's there' (Dourish 2001, p. 108) in favour of a world that is already structured meaningfully through a process of common, social practice. By the same token, when monkeys are born into their groups, they encounter a world of common social practice and what they learn, over the course of development, is how to participate. This is something that is learned through participation itself (Dourish 2001; Anderson 2003).

For psychologists, this view goes back at least to Vygotsky (1978) and the idea that cognition initially begins by being social and visible and is only later internalized and invisible. Models of mental representation are not rejected by such a view, as some might suspect, but rather can 'inform models of mental representation by charting ontogeny through embodied interactions in the infant and its caretaker, the juvenile and its cohorts and the adult and its society' (Johnson 2002, p. 628). A distributed view, therefore, emphasizes that behaviour—or more accurately interaction— is the source and cause of what must ultimately end up inside the head (Johnson 2002). Moreover, despite reservations that a socially distributed view is only of any real relevance to humans (Tomasello & Call 1997), Strum *et al.* (1997), Johnson (2001) and Johnson & Oswald (2001) illustrate how this can be applied to other primate species.

In addition to other individuals, the surrounding physical environment provides cognitive resources. Objects in the environment present animals with certain 'possibilities for action' (Gibson 1979) and afford certain responses (e.g. for humans, a chair affords the possibility of sitting down on it). These affordances and their relation to ongoing activity can help us to understand how and why certain behaviours are played out in certain ways at certain times. Strum *et al.* (1997), for example, show how consort takeovers among male baboons are structured by the properties of the sleeping cliffs where these take place: the limits they place on movement can be used to a male's advantage and lead to an unfolding of events quite different to those on the plains (see also Johnson & Oswald 2001 on 'social tool use' in bonobos). In this way, Machiavellian intelligence need not be Machiavellian in the sense that currently holds sway, because the flexibility, unpredictability and ingenuity shown by animals is due to processes that are distributed across brain, body and world.

The basic tenet of a distributed approach, therefore, is that dynamic social interactions do not merely point to internal cognitive acts but *are* cognitive acts in themselves (Kirsh 1996; Johnson 2001). Kirsh (1996) in particular distinguishes between 'pragmatic acts' that move an individual closer to a better state in the external environment, and 'epistemic acts' that move an individual to a better state in its cognitive environment. Epistemic acts, therefore, change the world in order to have useful cognitive effects on the actor; they create cognitive affordances that help improve the speed, accuracy or robustness of cognitive processes, rather than enable the agent to make literal progress in a task (Kirsh 1996). In humans, for example, moving Scrabble tiles around makes it easier to see the potential words that can be formed, and can therefore be considered an epistemic act. This close interleaving of physical and mental actions to reduce the complexity of a task means that it becomes important to pay attention to the means by which an individual tackles a particular task, because the task is carried out partly in the individual's head and partly in its environment. The degree to which primates and other species engage in any kind of epistemic action is an empirical issue at present, largely because we have not looked for these kinds of behaviours in order to understand cognitive processes.

It should be readily apparent how this kind of behaviourally oriented approach can also be used to test and develop the theories of intentional attunement and embodied simulation that emanate from neurobiology (Gallese 2006, 2007). Mirror systems, in particular, show us how, at the most fundamental neuronal level, our understanding of others is a distributed process that requires action in the world. Hopefully, a better understanding of the embodied and distributed nature of social cognition in our fellow primates will enable us to understand them on their own terms. Tying this to work demonstrating the embodied and distributed nature of cognition in humans (e.g. Varela *et al.* 1991; Vygotsky 1978; Fogel 1993; Gallagher 2005) may then enable us to identify true commonalities across species, rather than anthropocentric chimera.

We would like to thank the organisers of the discussion meeting, Chris Frith, Nicky Clayton and Nathan Emery, for inviting us to participate. We are also grateful to John Vokey for many enlightening discussions of the issues presented here, and an anonymous reviewer for helpful comments on a previous draft.

References

Altmann, J. 1980 *Baboon mothers and infants*. Cambridge, MA: Harvard University Press.

Anderson, M. L. 2003 Embodied cognition: a field guide. *Artif. Intell.* **149,** 91–130. (doi:10.1016/S0004-3702(03)00054-7)

Andrews, K. 2005 Chimpanzee theory of mind: looking in all the wrong places? *Mind Lang.* **20,** 521–536.

Aureli, F. & de Waal, F. B.M 2000 *Natural conflict resolution*. Berkeley, CA: University of California Press.

Barrett, L. & Henzi, S. P. 2001 The utility of grooming in baboon troops. In *Economics in nature: social dilemmas, mate choice and biological markets* (eds R. Noe¨, J. A. R. A. M. van Hooff & P Hammerstein), pp. 119–145. Cambridge, MA: Cambridge University Press.

Barrett, L. & Henzi, S. P. 2002 Constraints on relationship formation among female primates. *Behaviour* **139,** 263–289. (doi:10.1163/156853902760102672)

Barrett, L. & Henzi, S. P. 2005 The social nature of primate cognition. *Proc. R. Soc. B* **272,** 1865–1875. (doi:10.1098/rspb.2005.3200)

Barrett, L & Henzi, S. P. 2006 Monkeys, markets and minds: biological markets and primate sociality. In *Cooperation in primates and humans: mechanisms and evolution* (eds P. M. Kappeler & C. P. van Schaik), pp. 209–232. New York, NY: Springer.

Barrett, L., Henzi, S. P. & Dunbar, R. I. M. 2003 Primate cognition: from what now to what if? *Trends Cogn. Sci.* **7,** 494–497. (doi:10.1016/j.tics.2003.09.005)

Barrett, L., Halliday, J. & Henzi, S. P. 2006 The ecology of motherhood: structuring lactation costs in chacma baboons. *J. Anim. Ecol.* **75,** 875–886. (doi:10.1111/ j.1365-2656.2006.01105.x)

Barton, R. A. 1996 Neocortex size and behavioural ecology in primates. *Proc. R. Soc. B* **263,** 173–177. (doi:10.1098/rspb.1996.0028)

Barton, R. A. 1998 Visual specialisation and brain evolution in primates. *Proc. R. Soc. B* **265,** 1933–1937. (doi:10.1098/rspb.1998.0523)

Barton, R. A. 2006 Primate brain evolution: integrating comparative, neurophysiological and ethological data. *Evol. Anthropol.* **15,** 224–236.

Barton, R. A. 2007 Evolution of the social brain as a distributed neural system. In *The Oxford handbook of evolutionary psychology* (eds R. I. M. Dunbar & L. Barrett), pp. 129–144. Oxford, UK: Oxford University.

Bergman, T. J., Beehner, J. C., Cheney, D. L. & Seyfarth, R. M. 2003 Hierarchical classification by rank and kinship in baboons. *Science* **302**, 1234–1236. (doi:10.1126/science.1087513)

Brooks, R. A. 1999 *Cambrian intelligence: the early history of the new A.I.* Cambridge, MA: MIT Press.

Brothers, L. 1990 The social brain: a project for integrating primate behaviour and neurophysiology in a new domain. *Concepts Neurosci.* **4**, 107–118.

Brothers, L. 2001 *Mistaken identity: the mind-brain problem reconsidered.* New York, NY: State University of New York Press.

Bruner, J. 1990 *Acts of meaning.* Cambridge, MA: Harvard University Press.

Bruner, J. 1991 The narrative construction of reality. *Crit. Inq.* **18**, 1–21. (doi:10.1086/448619)

Byrne, R. W. & Corp, N. 2004 Neocortex size predicts deception rate in primates. *Proc. R. Soc. B* **271**, 1693–1699. (doi:10.1098/rspb.2004.2780)

Byrne, R. W. & Whiten, A. 1988 *Machiavellian intelligence: social expertise and the evolution of intellect in monkeys, apes and humans.* Oxford, UK: Clarendon Press.

Carrithers, M. 1991 Narrativity: mind reading and making societies. In *Natural theories of mind: evolution, development and simulation* (ed. A. Whiten), pp. 317–331. Oxford, UK: Basil Blackwell.

Chapais, B. 1992 The role of alliances in social inheritance of rank among female primates. In *The role of alliances in social inheritance of rank among female primates* (eds A. H. Harcourt & F. B. M. de Waal), pp. 29–59. Oxford, UK: Oxford University Press.

Chapais, B. 2006 Kinship, competence and cooperation in primates. In *Cooperation in primates and humans: mechanisms and evolution* (eds P. Kappeler & C. P. van Schaik), pp. 47–66. Berlin: Springer.

Chartrand, T. L. & Bargh, J. A. 1999 The chameleon effect: the perception-behaviour link and social interaction. *J. Per. Soc. Psychol.* **76**, 893–910. (doi:10.1037/0022-3514.76.6.893)

Cheney, D. L. & Seyfarth, R. M. 1990 *How monkeys see the world: inside the mind of another species.* Chicago, IL: University of Chicago Press.

Cheney, D. L. & Seyfarth, R. M. 2005 Constraints and preadaptations in the earliest stages of language evolution. *Linguistic Rev.* **22**, 135–159. (doi:10.1515/tlir.2005.22.2-4.135)

Clark, A. 1993 *Associative engines: connectionism, concepts, and representational change.* Cambridge, MA: MIT Press.

Clark, A. 1997 *Being there: bringing brain, body and world together again.* Cambridge, MA: MIT Press.

Clark, A. 2000 *Mindware: an introduction to the philosophy of cognitive science.* Oxford, UK: Oxford University Press.

Clayton, N. S. & Dickinson, A. 1999 Memory for contents of caches by scrub jays. *J. Exp. Psychol. Anim. Behav. Process* **25**, 82–91. (doi:10.1037/0097-7403.25.1.82)

Clayton, N. S., Bussey, T. J., Emery, N. J. & Dickinson, A. 2003*a* Prometheus to Proust: the case for behavioural criteria for mental time-travel. *Trends Cogn. Sci.* **7**, 436–437. (doi:10.1016/j.tics.2003.08.003)

Clayton, N. S., Bussey, T. J. & Dickinson, A. 2003*b* Can animals recall the past and plan for the future? *Nat. Rev. Neurosci.* **4**, 685–691. (doi:10.1038/nrn1180)

Cords, M. 1997 Friendships, alliances, reciprocity and repair. In *Machiavellian intelligence. II. extensions and evaluations* (eds A. Whiten & R. W. Byrne), pp. 24–49. Cambridge, MA: Cambridge University Press.

Damasio, A. R. 1994 *Descartes' error.* Putnam.

Dasser, V. 1988 A social concept in java monkeys. *Anim. Behav.* **36**, 225–230. (doi:10.1016/S0003-3472(88)80265-3)

Datta, S. 1983 Relative power and the acquisition of rank. In *Primate social relationships* (ed. R. Hinde), pp. 91–103. Oxford, UK: Blackwell Scientific Publications.

Dautenhahn, K. 2001 The narrative intelligence hypothesis: in search of the transactional formats of narratives in humans and other animals. In *Proc. Fourth Int. Cogn. Tech. Conference CT2001: instruments of mind* (eds M. Beynon, C. L. Nehaniv & K. Dautenhahn), pp. 248–266. New York, NY: Springer.

Dautenhahn, K. 2002 The origins of narrative: in search of the transactional formats of narratives in humans and other social animals. *Int. J. Cogn. Technol.* **1**, 97–123.

de Waal, F. B. M. 1982 *Chimpanzee politics: power and sex among primates*. Baltimore, MD: Johns Hopkins University Press.

de Waal, F. B. M. 1989 *Peace-making among primates*. Cambridge, MA: Harvard University Press.

de Waal, F. B. M. 1997 Are we in anthropodenial? *Discover* **18**, 50–53.

de Waal, F. B. M. 2001 *The ape and the sushi master*. New York, NY: Basic Books.

de Waal, F. B. M. 2003 Social syntax: the 'if-then' structure of social problem solving. In *Animal social complexity: intelligence, culture and individualised societies* (eds F. B. M. de Waal & P. L. Tyack), pp. 230–248. Cambridge, MA: Harvard University Press.

de Waal, F. B. M. 2005 Animals and us: suspicious minds. *New Sci.* **186**, 48.

de Waal, F. B. M. & van Roosmalen, A. 1979 Reconciliation and consolation among chimpanzees. *Behav. Ecol. Sociobiol.* **5**, 55–66. (doi:10.1007/BF00302695)

Dennett, D. 1989 *The intentional stance*. Cambridge, MA: MIT press.

Dourish, P. 2001 *Where the action is: the foundations of embodied interaction*. Cambridge, MA: MIT Press.

Dunbar, R. I. M. 1984 *Reproductive decisions*. Princeton, NJ: Princeton University Press.

Dunbar, R. I. M. 1988 *Primate social systems*. London, UK: Chapman & Hall.

Dunbar, R. I. M. 1991 Functional significance of social grooming in primates. *Folia Primatol.* **57**, 121–131.

Dunbar, R. I. M. 1992*a* Neocortex size as a constraint on group size in primates. *J. Hum. Evol.* **20**, 469–493. (doi:10.1016/0047-2484(92)90081-J)

Dunbar, R. I. M. 1992*b* Time: a hidden constraint on the behavioural ecology of baboons. *Behav. Ecol. Sociobiol.* **31**, 35–49. (doi:10.1007/BF00167814)

Dunbar, R. I. M. 1995 Neocortex size and group size in primates: a test of the hypothesis. *J. Hum. Evol.* **28**, 287–296. (doi:10.1006/jhev.1995.1021)

Dunbar, R. I. M. 1996 *Grooming, gossip and the evolution of language*. London, UK: Faber & Faber.

Dunbar, R. I. M. 1998 The social brain hypothesis. *Evol. Anthropol.* **6**, 178–190. (doi:10.1002/(SICI)1520-6505(1998)6:5<178::AID-EVAN5>3.0.CO;2-8)

Dunbar, R. I. M. & Dunbar, P. 1988 Maternal time budgets of gelada baboons. *Anim. Behav.* **36**, 970–980. (doi:10.1016/S0003-3472(88)80055-1)

Eddy, T. J., Gallup, G. G. & Povinelli, D. J. 1993 Attribution of cognitive states to animals: anthropomorphism in comparative perspective. *J. Soc. Issues* **49**, 87–101.

Emery, N. J. & Clayton, N. S. 2004 The mentality of crows: convergent evolution of intelligence in corvids and apes. *Science* **306**, 1903–1907. (doi:10.1126/science.1098410)

Fernàndez-Armesto, F. 2004 *So you think you're human?* Oxford, UK: Oxford University Press.

Fogel, A. 1993 *Developing through relationships: origins of self, communication and culture*. Chicago, IL: University of Chicago Press.

Gallagher, S. 2005 *How the body shapes the mind*. Oxford, UK: Oxford University Press.

Gallese, V. 2001 The 'shared manifold' hypothesis: from mirror neurons to empathy. *J. Conscious Stud.* **8**, 33–50.

Gallese, V. 2003 The roots of empathy: the shared manifold hypothesis and the neural basis of intersubjectivity. *Psychopathology* **36**, 171–180. (doi:10.1159/000072786)

Gallese, V. 2005 Embodied simulation: from neurons to phenomenal experience. *Phenomenol. Cogn. Sci.* **4**, 22–48.

Gallese, V. 2006 Intentional attunement: a neurophysiological perspective on social cognition and its disruption in autism. *Brain Res.* **1079**, 15–24.

Gallese, V. 2007 Before and below 'theory of mind': embodied simulation and the neural correlates of social cognition. *Phil. Trans. R. Soc. B* **362**, 659–669. (doi:10.1098/rstb.2006.2002)

Gallese, V. & Goldman, A. 1998 Mirror neurons and the simulation theory of mind-reading. *Trends Cogn. Sci.* **12**, 593–609.

Gallese, V., Keysers, C. & Rizzolatti, G. 2004 A unifying view of the basis of social cognition. *Trends Cogn. Sci.* **8**, 396–403. (doi:10.1016/j.tics.2004.07.002)

Garbarini, F. & Adenzato, M. 2004 At the root of embodied cognition: cognitive science meets neurophysiology. *Brain Cogn.* **56**, 100–106. (doi:10.1016/j.bandc.2004.06.003)

Gibson, J. J. 1979 *The ecological approach to visual perception*. Boston, MA: Houghton-Miller.

Gigerenzer, G. 2004 Mindless statistics. *J. Soc. Econ.* **33**, 587–606. (doi:10.1016/j.socec.2004.09.033)

Guthrie, S. E. 1993 *Faces in the clouds: a new theory of religion*. Oxford, UK: Oxford University Press.

Hampton, R. R., Hampstead, B. M. & Murray, E. A. 2005 Rhesus monkeys (*Macaca mulatta*) demonstrate robust memory for what and where, but not when, in an open-field test. *Learn. Motiv.* **36**, 245–259. (doi:10.1016/j.lmot. 2005.02.004)

Harcourt, A. H. 1988 Alliances in contests and social intelligence. In *Machiavellian intelligence: social expertise and the evolution of intellect in monkeys, apes and humans* (eds R. W. Byrne & A. Whiten), pp. 132–152. Oxford, UK: Clarendon Press.

Harcourt, A. H. 1989 Social influences on competitive ability: alliances and their consequences. In *Comparative socioecology* (eds V. Standen & R. Foley), pp. 223–242. Oxford, UK: Blackwell Scientific Publications.

Harcourt, A. H. 1992 Coalitions and alliances: are primates more complex than non-primates? In *Coalitions and alliances in humans and other animals* (eds A. H. Harcourt & F. B. M. de Waal), pp. 445–471. Oxford, UK: Oxford University Press.

Harcourt, A. H. & de Waal, F. B. M. 1992. *Coalitions and alliances in humans and other animals*. Oxford, UK: Oxford University Press.

Heider, F. & Simmel, M. 1944 An experimental study of apparent behaviour. *Am. J. Psychol.* **57**, 243–259. (doi:10.2307/1416950)

Heidigger, M. 1927/1978. *Being and time*. Oxford, UK: Blackwell.

Henzi, S. P. & Barrett, L. 1999 The value of grooming to female primates. *Primates* **40**, 47–59.

Henzi, S. P. & Barrett, L. 2002 Infants as a commodity in a baboon market. *Anim. Behav.* **63**, 915–921. (doi:10.1006/ anbe.2001.1986)

Henzi, S. P. & Barrett, L. 2003 Evolutionary ecology, sexual conflict and behavioral differentiation among baboon populations. *Evol. Anthropol.* **12**, 217–230. (doi:10.1002/evan.10121)

Henzi, S. P., Lusseau, D., Weingrill, T., van Schaik, C. P. & Barrett, L. Submitted. Qualitative variation in social networks and social bond strength among female baboons.

Hinde, R. A. 1976 Interactions, relationships and social structure. *Man* **11**, 1–17. (doi:10.2307/2800384)

Hinde, R. A. 1983 A conceptual framework. In *Primate social relationships: an integrated approach* (ed. R. A. Hinde), pp. 1–7. Oxford, UK: Blackwell Scientific Publications.

Hrdy, S. B. 1977 *The langurs of Abu*. Cambridge, MA: Harvard University Press.

Humphrey, N. 1976 The social function of intellect. In *Growing points in ethology* (eds P. P. G. Bateson & R. A. Hinde), pp. 303–317. Cambridge, MA: Cambridge University Press.

Hurley, S. 1998 *Consciousness in action*. Cambridge, MA: Harvard University Press.

Hutchins, E. 1985 *Cognition in the wild*. Cambridge, MA: MIT Press.

Hutto, D. H. 2004 The limits of spectatorial folk psychology. *Mind Lang.* **19**, 548–573.

Joffe, T. H. 1997 Social pressures have selected for an extended juvenile period in primates. *J. Hum. Evol.* **32**, 593–605. (doi:10.1006/jhev.1997.0140)

Johnson, C. M. 2001 Distributed primate cognition: a review. *Anim. Cogn.* **4**, 167–183. (doi:10.1007/ s100710100077)

Johnson, C. M. 2002 The Vygotskian advantage in cognitive modelling: participation precedes and thus prefigures understanding. *Behav. Brain Sci.* **25**, 628–629. (doi:10.1017/S0140525X02300116)

Johnson, C. M. & Oswald, T. M. 2001 Distributed cognition in apes. In *Proc. 23rd Annual Conf. of the Cognitive Science Society* (eds J. D. Moore & K. Stenning), pp. 453–458. Edinburgh, UK: Human Communication Research Centre.

Jolly, A. 1966 Lemur social behaviour and primate intelligence. *Science* **153**, 501–506.

Keeley, B. L. 2004 Anthropomorphism, primatomorphism, mammalomorphism: understanding cross-species comparisons. *Biol. Philos.* 19, 521–540. (doi:10.1007/sBIPH-004-0540-4)

Keijzer, F. 2005 Theoretical behaviourism meets embodied cognition: two theoretical analyses of behaviour. *Philos. Psychol.* **18**, 123–143.

Kennedy, J. S. 1992 *The new anthropomorphism*. Cambridge, MA: Cambridge University Press.

Kenyatta, C. G. 1995 Ecological and social constraints on maternal investment strategies. Ph.D. thesis, University of London, London.

Kirsh, D. 1996 Adapting the environment instead of oneself. *Adapt. Behav.* **4**, 415–452.

Kudo, N. & Dunbar, R. I. M. 2001 Neocortex size and social network size in primates. *Anim. Behav.* **62**, 711–722. (doi:10.1006/anbe.2001.1808)

Kummer, H. 1968 *Primate social organisation*. Chicago, IL: University of Chicago Press.

Lakin, J. L., Jefferis, V. E., Cheng, C. M. & Chartrand, T. L. 2003 The chameleon effect as social glue: evidence for the evolutionary significance of non-conscious imitation. *J. Non-Verbal Behav.* **23**, 145–162.

Lakoff, G. & Johnson, M. 1999 *Philosophy in the flesh: the embodied mind and its challenge to western thought*. New York, NY: Basic Books.

Liberman, M. D., Gaunt, R., Gilbert, D. T. & Trope, Y. 2002 Reflection and reflexion: a social cognitive neuroscience approach to attributional inference. *Adv. Exp. Psychol.* **34**, 199–249. (doi:10.1016/S0065-2601(02)80006-5)

Mendres, K. A. & de Waal, F. B. M. 2000 Capuchins do cooperate: the advantage of an intuitive task. *Anim. Behav.* **60**, 523–529. (doi:10.1006/anbe.2000.1512)

Merleau-Ponty, M. 1962/2002 *Phenomenology of perception*. London, UK: Routledge Classics.

Moura, A. C., de, A. & Lee, P. C. 2004 Capuchin stone tool use in Caatinga dry forest. *Science* **306**, 1909. (doi:10.1126/science.1102558)

Muroyama, Y. 1994 Exchange of grooming for allomothering in female patas monkeys. *Behaviour* **128**, 103–129.

Nagel, T. 1974 What is it like to be a bat? *Philos. Rev.* **83**, 435–450. (doi:10.2307/2183914)

Noë, A. 2004 *Action in perception*. Cambridge, MA: MIT Press.

Noë, R. 2006 Digging for the roots of trade. In *Cooperation in primates and humans: mechanisms and evolution* (eds P. Kappeler & C. P. van Schaik), pp. 233–262. New York, NY: Springer.

Panksepp, J. 1998 *Affective neuroscience: the foundations of human and animal emotions*. Oxford, UK: Oxford University Press.

Paukner, A., Anderson, J. R., Borelli, E., Visalberghi, E. & Ferrari, P. F. 2004 Macaques (*Macaca nemestrina*) recognise when they are being imitated. *Biol. Lett.* **1**, 219–222. (doi:10.1098/rsbl.2004.0291)

Payne, H. F. P., Lawes, M. J. & Henzi, S. P. 2003 Competition and the exchange of grooming in female samango monkeys (*Cercopithecus mitis erytharcus*). Behaviour **140**, 453–471. (doi:10.1163/156853903322127931)

Pazol, K. & Cords, M. 2005 Seasonal variation in feeding behaviour, competition and female social relationships in a forest-dwelling guenon, the blue monkey (*Cercopithecus mitis stuhlmanni*) in the Kakamega Forest, Kenya. *Behav. Ecol. Sociobiol.* **58**, 566–577. (doi:10.1007/s00265-005- 0953-3)

Perrett, D. *et al.* 1990 Social signals analyzed at the single cell level: someone is looking at me, something touched me, something moved! *Int. J. Comp. Psychol.* **4**, 25–55.

Povinelli, D.J.& Vonk, J. 2003 Chimpanzee minds: suspiciously human? *Trends Cogn. Sci.* **7**, 157–160. (doi:10.1016/S1364-6613(03)00053-6)

Povinelli, D., Bering, J. & Giambrone, S. 2000 Toward a science of other minds: escaping the argument by analogy. *Cogn. Sci.* **24**, 509–541. (doi:10.1016/S0364-0213(00)00023-9)

Preston, S. D. & de Waal, F. B. M. 2002 Empathy: its ultimate and proximate bases. *Behav. Brain Sci.* **25**, 1–72. (doi:10.1017/S0140525X02000018)

Range, F. & Noë, R. 2005 Simple rules account for the pattern of triadic relations in juvenile and adult sooty mangabeys. *Anim. Behav.* **69**, 445–452. (doi:10.1016/j.anbehav.2004.02.025)

Read, S. J. & Miller, L. C. 1995 Stories are fundamental to meaning and memory: for social creatures could it be otherwise? In *Knowledge and memory: the real story* (ed. R. S. Wyer), pp. 139–152. Mahwah, NJ: Lawrence Erlbaum Associates.

Rendall, D. 2004 "Recognizing" kin: mechanisms, media, minds, modules and muddles. In *Kinship and behaviour in primates* (eds B. Chapais & C. Berman). Oxford, UK: Oxford University Press.

Rendall, D., Notman, H. & Vokey, J. R. 2007 Homologizing the mind. In *The Oxford handbook of evolutionary psychology* (eds R. I. M. Dunbar & L. Barrett), pp. 59–70. Oxford, UK: Oxford University.

Rizzolatti, G., Fadiga, L., Gallese, V. & Fogassi, L. 1996 Premotor cortex and recognition of motor actions. *Cogn. Brain Res.* **3**, 131–141. (doi:10.1016/0926-6410(95)00038-0)

Roberts, W. A. 2002 Are animals stuck in time? *Psychol. Bull.* **128**, 473–489. (doi:10.1037/0033-2909.128.3.473)

Russell, J. & Thompson, D. 2003 Memory development in the second year: for events or locations? *Cognition* **87,** B97–B105. (doi:10.1016/S0010-0277(02)00238-X)

Scholl, B. J. & Tremoulet, P. D. 2000 Perceptual causality and animacy. *Trends Cogn. Sci.* **4,** 299–309. (doi:10.1016/S1364-6613(00)01506-0)

Seyfarth, R. M. & Cheney, D. L. 1984 Grooming, alliances and reciprocal altruism in vervet monkeys. *Nature* **308,** 541–543. (doi:10.1038/308541a0)

Sheets-Johnstone, M. 1992 Taking evolution seriously. *Am. Philos. Q.* **29,** 343–352.

Shettleworth, S. 1998 *Cognition, evolution and behaviour.* Oxford, UK: Oxford University Press.

Silk, J. 1982 Altruism among female *Macaca radiata*: explanations and analysis of patterns of grooming and coalition formation. *Behaviour* **79,** 162–168.

Silk, J. B. 1996 Why do primates reconcile? *Evol. Anthropol.* **5,** 39–42. (doi:10.1002/(SICI)1520-6505 (1996)5:2<39:: AID-EVAN2>3.0.CO;2-R)

Silk, J. B. 2002 Using the F-word in primatology. *Behaviour* **139,** 421–446. (doi:10.1163/ 156853902760102735)

Silk, J. B., Alberts, S. C. & Altmann, J. 2003*a* Social bonds of female baboons enhance infant survival. *Science* **302,** 1231–1234. (doi:10.1126/science.1088580)

Silk, J. B., Rendall, D., Cheney, D. L. & Seyfarth, R. M. 2003*b* Natal attraction in adult female baboons (*Papio cycnocephalus ursinus*) in the Moremi Reserve, Botswana. Ethology **109,** 627–644. (doi:10.1046/ j.1439-0310.2003.00907.x)

Silk, J. B., Alberts, S. C. & Altmann, J. 2004 Patterns of coalition formation by adult female baboons in Amboseli, Kenya. *Anim. Behav.* **67,** 573–582. (doi:10.1016/j.anbe-hav.2003.07.001)

Sober, E. 1998 Morgan's canon. In *The evolution of mind* (eds C. Allen & D. Cummins), pp. 224–242. Oxford, UK: Oxford University Press.

Stammbach, E. 1988 Group responses to specially skilled individuals in a *Macaca fascicularis* group. *Behaviour* **107,** 241–266.

Sterelny, K. 2007 Social intelligence, human intelligence and niche construction. *Phil. Trans. R. Soc. B* **362,** 719–730. (doi:10.1098/rstb.2006.2006)

Strier, K. B. 1990 New world primates, new frontiers: insights from the woolly spider monkeys, or muriqui (*Brachyteles arachnoids*). *Int. J. Primatol.* **11,** 7–19. (doi:10.1007/BF02193693)

Strier, K. B. 2002 *Primate behavioural ecology,* 2nd edition Boston, MA: Allyn & Bacon.

Strum, S. C., Forster, D. & Hutchins, E. 1997 Why Machiavellian intelligence may not be Machiavellian. In *Machiavellian intelligence. II. extensions and evaluations* (eds A. Whiten & R. W. Byrne), pp. 50–87. Cambridge, MA: Cambridge University Press.

Suddendorf, T. & Busby, J. 2003 Mental time travel in animals? *Trends Cogn. Sci.* **7,** 391–396. (doi:10.1016/S1364-6613(03)00187-6)

Thompson, R. K. R. 1995 Natural and relational concepts in animals. In *Comparative approaches to cognitive science* (eds H. L. Roitblat & J.-A. Meyer), pp. 175–224. Cambridge, MA: MIT Press.

Thompson, R. K. R. & Oden, D. L. 2000 Categorical perception and conceptual judgments by non-human primates: the paleological monkey and the analogical ape. *Cogn. Sci.* **24,** 363–396. (doi:10.1016/S0364-0213(00)00029-X)

Tomasello, M. 1999 *The cultural origins of human cognition.* Cambridge, MA: Harvard University Press.

Tomasello, M. & Call, J. 1997 *Primate cognition.* Oxford, UK: Oxford University Press.

Tomasello, M., Call, J. & Hare, B. 2003 Chimpanzees understand psychological states—the questions is which ones and to what extent. *Trends Cogn. Sci.* **7,** 153–156. (doi:10.1016/S1364-6613(03)00035-4)

Tremoulet, P. D. & Feldman, J. 2000 Perception of animacy from the motion of a single object. *Perception* **29,** 943–951. (doi:10.1068/p3101)

Turner, M. 1996 *The literary mind: the origins of thought and language.* Oxford, UK: Oxford University Press.

Tversky, B. 2004 Narratives of space, time and life. *Mind Lang.* **19,** 380–392.

Tyler, T. 2003 If horses had hands. *Soc. Anim.* **11,** 267–281. (doi:10.1163/156853003322773069)

van Schaik, C. P. 1983 Why are diurnal primates living in groups? *Behaviour* **87,** 120–144.

van Schaik, C. P. & Kappeler, P. 1997 Infanticide risk and the evolution of permanent male–female association in nonhuman primates: a new hypothesis and comparative test. *Proc. R. Soc. B* **264,** 1687–1694. (doi:10.1098/rspb.1997. 0234)

Varela, F. J., Thompson, E. & Rosch, E. 1991 *The embodied mind: cognitive science and human experience*. Cambridge, MA: MIT Press.

Vokey, J. R., Rendall, D., Tangen, J. M., Parr, L. A. & de Waal, F. B. M. 2004 On visual kin recognition and family resemblance in chimpanzees. *J. Comp. Psychol.* **118**, 194–199. (doi:10.1037/0735-7036. 118.2.194)

Vygotsky, L. 1978 *Mind in society*. Cambridge, MA: Harvard University Press.

Whitehead, H. 1995 Investigating structure and temporal scale in social organisations using identified individuals. *Behav. Ecol.* **6**, 199–208.

Whiten, A. 2000 Social complexity and social intelligence. In *The nature of intelligence*. pp. 185–201, New York, NY: Wiley (Novartis Foundation Symposium 233).

Wittgenstein, L. 1968/1999 *Philosophical investigations*, 3rd edn. Englewood Cliffs, NJ: Prentice Hall.

Wynne, C. 2004 The perils of anthropomorphism. *Nature* **428**, 606. (doi:10.1038/428606a)

Zuberbuhler, K. 2003 Referential signalling in non-human primates: cognitive precursors and limitations for the evolution of language. *Adv. Study Behav.* **33**, 265–308

6

Culture in great apes: using intricate complexity in feeding skills to trace the evolutionary origin of human technical prowess

Richard W. Byrne

Geographical cataloguing of traits, as used in human ethnography, has led to the description of 'culture' in some non-human great apes. Culture, in these terms, is detected as a pattern of local ignorance resulting from environmental constraints on knowledge transmission. However, in many cases, the geographical variations may alternatively be explained by ecology. Social transmission of information can reliably be identified in many other animal species, by experiment or distinctive patterns in distribution; but the excitement of detecting culture in great apes derives from the possibility of understanding the evolution of cumulative technological culture in humans. Given this interest, I argue that great ape research should concentrate on technically complex behaviour patterns that are ubiquitous within a local population; in these cases, a wholly non-social ontogeny is highly unlikely. From this perspective, cultural transmission has an important role in the elaborate feeding skills of all species of great ape, in conveying the 'gist' or organization of skills. In contrast, social learning is unlikely to be responsible for local stylistic differences, which are apt to reflect sensitive adaptations to ecology.

Keywords: animal cultures; social learning; cognition; behavioural complexity; technical intelligence

6.1 Introduction

Biologists usually become interested in animal culture for one of two rather different reasons. On the one hand, their concern may be directly with the 'second inheritance system' (Whiten 2005) that social learning potentially offers: what information is transmitted; how fast it spreads; what environmental features slow or block transmission; how this information interacts with genetically coded information; and so forth. For these purposes, the starting point is to identify clear cases of social transmission, either by experimental interventions (e.g. removal or translocation of knowledgeable individuals) or by a pattern of spread that is distinctive of social transmission (e.g. a historical record of the relatively rapid, monotonic spread of a habit, checked by major environmental barriers). Ideal species to use are ones that are common, widely distributed and easily manipulated, such as garden birds or reef fishes. Ideal traits for study are those that are relatively unrelated to the local features of the environment, such as habits of social behaviour or display.

On the other hand, biological interest in animal culture may derive from culture's privileged status as (putatively) uniquely human and from its role in human technological superiority over other species. As with all claims of uniqueness, human technology holds out a challenge to the biologist to find the evolutionary origins of the unique human pattern. In this case, we might expect interest to have focused chiefly on behaviours that clearly involve technological skills but are found in non-human species, in particular the closely related great apes.

This article will make the case that, in fact, these two different approaches have become mixed together in their methods and that this risks impeding a biological understanding of the origins of human technological culture.

6.2 Culture in great apes: patterns of local ignorance

Begun nearly 50 years ago, the systematic observational field study of the chimpanzee soon revealed striking behavioural variations from one site to another: in diet; in manual feeding skills including tool-use; and in social signals (Goodall 1963, 1973; Nishida 1973, 1980; Sugiyama & Koman 1979). More recently, some of these differences have been described as constituting *culture* in the chimpanzee (McGrew 1992; Whiten *et al.* 1999), with a similar argument made for the orangutan (van Schaik, *et al.* 2003) and the bonobo (Hohmann & Fruth 2003). These claims, based as they were on very extensive fieldwork, generated considerable interest and excitement: not surprisingly, when for so long culture has been considered a hallmark of our own species, unique and inaccessible to analysis by the comparative method.

The identification of great ape culture has been based on patterns of behaviour, 'transmitted repeatedly through social or observational learning to become a population-level characteristic' (Whiten *et al.* 1999), forming 'a system of socially transmitted behaviour' (van Schaik *et al.* 2003). However, because apes are long lived, and because even the most intensive field study is insufficient to trace ontogeny in detail, social learning was diagnosed retrospectively, by excluding alternative explanations. Field experiments involving translocation or removal are simply not feasible with endangered and rather large animals in remote locations of Africa. The approach taken in the recent 'ape culture' papers has been to focus only on traits that showed a pattern of site-to-site behavioural variation, on the grounds that universal behaviours could be more parsimoniously explained without reliance on social learning. The idea is that any behavioural differences between sites that can be satisfactorily explained by genetic variations or by ecological difference should be set aside, and then those traits that remain can be safely considered to be cultural traditions. This procedure is a conservative one, and clearly risks excluding behaviours that are in fact socially transmitted but have already spread to universal coverage, or whose patchy distribution correlates with ecology because their function is ecological (Perry & Manson 2003).

In the case of the chimpanzee, 42 behavioural traits were considered to be customary or at least habitual (i.e. 'has occurred repeatedly in several individuals') in one or more communities but absent in one or more others (Whiten *et al.* 1999, 2001). These candidate cultural variants were then pared down by exclusion. If a trait differed systematically between two genetically separate populations, such as the subspecies *Pan troglodytes verus* and *Pan troglodytes schweinfurthii*, but was found universally within each population, it would be ascribed to a genetic difference. In fact, none of the behavioural variants examined in chimpanzees were set aside on such a basis (although, in fact, evidence of nut-cracking is found entirely within the two western subspecies of chimpanzee, *P. t. verus* and *P. t. vellerosus*, and variation across Africa in chimpanzee nut-cracking might thus have been attributed to genetic causation). Conversely, if the distribution of a behavioural trait correlated closely with some relevant ecological variable, it would be ascribed to ecological determination. Three of the behavioural variants were considered 'explicable by local conditions': scooping algae with a stick; making night nests on the ground; and using a rock to level an anvil. The 39 remaining patterns were identified as cultural variants for the chimpanzee: for the orang-utan, the corresponding figure was 24 (van Schaik *et al.* (2003); however, in five of these, the variation was noted to be potentially explicable on ecological grounds.

The logic of this process is that the remaining behavioural variations must result from limitations on knowledge transmission. Invention is a rare event (or else all apes would be able individually to acquire the skills), but social learning allows knowledge to spread within the social network, within and sometimes between social communities; spread is limited by breaks in the social network caused by natural barriers. Outside the network of privileged knowledge, apes will remain in ignorance, or may acquire a characteristically different behavioural variant by virtue of membership of another social network in which a different technique has been invented. In short, by means of cultural transmission, apes are able to acquire beneficial abilities that they would otherwise lack, but imperfections in social transmission impose a distinctive variation from optimality. Evidence that large rivers *can* sometimes constitute barriers to knowledge flow comes from chimpanzee nut-cracking (Boesch *et al.* 1994; McGrew *et al.* 1997) and orang-utan *Neesia* eating with tools (van Schaik & Knott 2001); across the rivers, the same potential foods are present, but remain unexploited.

Most strikingly, a single important chimpanzee foraging technique, ant-dipping, was found to vary in behavioural *style* rather than merely presence, with resulting effects on efficiency. The two-handed method used at Gombe, East Africa, was estimated to be four times as efficient, in ants/minute, than the one-handed Taï, West African equivalent (McGrew 1974; Boesch & Boesch 1990). The cultural explanation is that ant-dipping must have been invented at least twice, but different ways of achieving the purpose became stable in different knowledge networks. Despite the dramatic difference in efficiency, behaviour did not converge on the optimal form, but continued to conform to the socially learnt original: 'Taï chimpanzees restrict themselves to the suboptimal solution that must be maintained by a social norm' (Boesch 1996). Researchers concluded that 'it is difficult to see how such behaviour patterns could be perpetuated by social learning processes simpler than imitation' (Whiten *et al.* 1999); and they postulated that the more complex technique derived culturally from the simpler method by 'differentiation in concert with diffusion, a process more deserving of the term "cultural evolution"' (Whiten *et al.* 2001).

Detection of ape culture, then, has been based on identification of local ignorance (Byrne *et al.* 2004). The biggest difficulty in ascribing ignorance is of that of conclusively ruling out all alternative ecological explanations (Tomasello 1990, 1994; Galef 1992), and this is a significant weakness in the approach. Whiten *et al.* (2001), for instance, consider invulnerable to ecological explanation those variations in plant-based behaviours that 'depend on leaves or other simple configurations of vegetation, of which many different kinds appear suitable for the task'. Yet, until the properties of the key plant materials have been compared between sites where they are or are not used, such claims will always be open to sceptical reappraisal. Slight differences in material that correlate with—and potentially explain—the behavioural variation may be missing simply owing to lack of detail on the identity and properties of plant material in the primary accounts. This is not hypothetical concern: major behavioural differences in the method used by West and East African chimpanzees to feed on *Dorylus* ants were overlooked for many years, despite the level of scientific interest in ape tool use. Ecological influences form a complex web of interconnections, many of which may currently be unknown, particularly in a species like the chimpanzee with its immensely varied diet and behavioural repertoire (Nishida & Uehara 1983; Nishida *et al.* 1999).

Of the 'cultural variants' in chimpanzees, 18 involve feeding on specific plants or animals, 21 employ specific plant material as the means and 2 involve removal of specific noxious insects. Taking these together, some ecological explanation for variation could be made in 32 of 39 cases, in addition to the three cases actually rejected as potentially explicable by ecology.

This concern is not merely theoretical: ecological differences in chimpanzee foods can be subtle. Mound-building termites are found at three study sites on the eastern shores of Lake Tanganyika, yet chimpanzees at one of them (Kasoje) do not use stems to fish for them. Collins & McGrew (1987) carried out detailed study of the termites and found that three different termite species of two genera were involved, concluding that the chimpanzees' behaviour matched the termite species available rather than reflecting cultural differences. More generally, the foraging ecology of the chimpanzee is little understood at any one site, and the site-by-site differences even less so. This has already become evident in the celebrated case of variations in ant-dipping style, initially discussed as a rock-solid case of cultural transmission, which are now known to depend significantly on ecological differences. Species of *Doryulus* ants vary from site to site, and at one location both methods have been found to be used by the *same* individual chimpanzees, for different species of ant and at different phases of the ant foraging cycle (Humle & Matsuzawa 2002). Rather than a pattern of patchy ignorance, it now seems that behavioural variation in ant-dipping, like that of termite-fishing, shows exquisite sensitivity to local task demands.

Of course, any innovative, large-scale research programme is likely to include occasional mistakes that need later correction, but there are reasons to think that the problems of separating ecological from cultural determination may go deeper in this case. The chimpanzee and the orang-utan are unusual in the richness of their known diet sets and behavioural repertoires, even among primates living in tropical forests. Yet neither has been subject to phytochemical and nutritional examination in the kind of detail needed to reveal subtle interactions among alternative diet items, nor study of the mechanical properties of material that may potentially be employed in tool use. This level of ignorance is unsettling in the context of a study method that depends on exclusion of ecological factors. Geographical comparisons can be telling where a particularly distinctive pattern is found: that of universal spread checked by a barrier, as for orangutan *Neesia* eating. However, this distinctive pattern is the exception rather than the norm; for instance, in the chimpanzee only nut-cracking with hammer and anvil (West Africa) and intense grooming of leaves (East Africa) were found to be so (Whiten *et al.* 2001). Most locally varying habits are patchily found right across the chimpanzee range. It would seem that the traits identified as cultural are not difficult for chimpanzees to invent, and that invention has occurred independently at many sites. Still less, has any sign been found in nonhuman great apes of the pattern more typical of human culture, where a whole suite of differences co-occur between one group of people and another: people who build pagodas are likely to use chopsticks to eat rice, people who build water turbines to grind barley are likely to show fraternal polyandry, and so on. In chimpanzees, there are no such 'packages' of correlated behavioural traits, and the level of behavioural difference is often as high between nearby study sites as distant ones.

With no opportunity for translocation/relocation experiments, no historical evidence of habits spreading across geographical areas and few patterns clearly implicating past spread by social transmission, the case for great ape culture rests on much weaker foundations even than that for culture in birds or fishes (Laland & Hoppit 2003). In the absence of these stronger types of evidence, patchiness of distribution does not necessarily signify culture. If a habit can be invented multiple times, perhaps it can be invented by every individual that has real need of it? This is evidenced by the fact that a number of 'chimpanzee cultural variants' have also been identified in the bonobo (Hohmann & Fruth 2003), not only a different species but also one separated from the chimpanzee by Africa's largest river; these include the grooming handclasp (see McGrew & Tutin 1978), leaf-clipping as a social signal, aimed throwing and fly-whisking with vegetation. The two ape species must both possess a propensity to invent and re-invent the same actions under similar circumstances. Given such a propensity, tracing which patterns of variation are in fact due to cultural transmission becomes difficult.

Finally, if most or all of the 'cultural variation' of chimpanzees is indeed a result of imperfect social transmission, the continued existence of the differences logically presents a puzzle (Byrne *et al.* 2004). Female chimpanzees regularly transfer between communities when they reach adolescence (Nishida & Kawanaka 1972), an age at which they should already possess the cultural knowledge of their natal community, thus making this knowledge available to at least the younger members of the new community. (In orang-utans, major barriers, including mountain ranges and seas, make isolation of knowledge more likely; in this case, the corresponding likelihood of isolated gene pools is more of a challenge to the identification of definitely cultural variation.) Over time, regular female transfer between chimpanzee communities means that very large areas of Africa have been until recently part of the same potential knowledge network. Yet the site-to-site variation in behaviour patterns charted by Whiten *et al.* (1999, 2001) does not, in general, follow natural boundaries to chimpanzee movement. Nor is there any sign that this situation is temporary; the differences are apparently stable and long lasting, over decades of study at several sites, in contrast to the rapidly changing cultural traits of capuchin monkeys (Perry & Manson 2003; Perry *et al.* 2003).

If a socially acquired trait is beneficial, or there is an optimally efficient way of carrying it out, this knowledge *should* spread between communities; local ignorance should only be temporary. If the behaviours concerned relatively trivial fads, not conferring any real advantage to their possessors, then their spread might be haphazard and it could be argued that a tendency to conformity (Whiten *et al.* 2005) could prevent knowledge invading a geographical area of relative ignorance. This might be the case for some of the odder and less obviously functional variants, but if the ape cultural traits were found in general to be no more than fads, their interest to anthropology and zoology would decline. Thus, the stable but patchy distribution of apparently useful traits in the chimpanzee is itself something of a challenge to the idea that the variations result from cultural transmission.

6.3 An alternative approach: intricate complexity and local ubiquity

The use of geographical patterning to identify culture in great apes is liable to lead to a trap. In human cultures, distinctive patterns of variation persist in non-Western societies owing to the relative slowness of change by human invention compared to the rapidity of cultural diffusion and owing to xenophobic social mechanisms. In non-human great apes, distinctive patterns are always more likely to derive from ecological fit; stable patterns of local ignorance seem improbable in a species that regularly transfers individuals between groups. This challenge forces attention onto traits with site-to-site variations that have no possible ecological correlates (or invites criticism from sceptics). Often, these are just the traits which are the least likely to give insights into the evolutionary origins of human technological cultures, because they are very simple actions or because their ecological impact is trivial. In the process, many real cases of socially learnt skills are potentially discarded, because they do not vary sufficiently or because they correlate with ecological factors. At best, the result is liable to be a heterogeneous collection of traits for which geographical variation is socially caused, but few of which have any relevance to the cumulative skills of human culture. To get out of this trap, and make a serious attempt at using great ape data to explain the evolution of human technological culture, a different method may be needed than ape ethnography.

Recall that the original reason for picking on traits that showed geographical variation, and then retrospectively ruling out ecological and genetical causes for some of them, was to identify which traits originated from social learning (given the non-feasibility of establishing this experimentally). The need for this process is indisputable for simple habits, easily picked up individually, as indeed are many of those discussed as potential great ape cultural variants. However, as the complexity of a skill increases, the likelihood of wholly individual learning decreases. Compare, for instance, the human traits of 'eat pistachio nuts' and 'raise water by making a shadoof'. Individual exploration and trial-and-error learning is just not likely to be the sole origin of an individual person's tendency to make a shadoof, and it would not be sensible to require the same degree of evidence for shadoof-making as a social tradition as for an easily learnt dietary choice. Of course, great apes make nothing as complex as a shadoof. But where the biological interest is to begin to understand human technological supremacy—resulting from the cultural accumulation of knowledge that underwrites a wealth of skilful abilities—it would seem to make sense to focus first on just those activities that manifestly require some skill. For this reason, it should not be surprising that, even though there is very much better evidence in both rodents and fishes for local differences in behaviour that are firmly established to be a result of knowledge transfer by social learning (Helfman & Schultz 1984; Warner 1988; Galef 1990, 2003; Laland & Hoppit 2003), this work has nevertheless not led to comparable claims of 'rat culture' or 'fish culture'. None of these undoubtedly socially transmitted habits is closely relevant to the cumulative culture of human technology.

As van Schaik et al. (2003) note, culture—as they define it, local variation not obviously explained by ecology or genetics—may contain a number of very different sorts of information. At the most basic, this may simply concern whether something is edible or where females tend to be when spawning: such 'labels' are culturally acquired in a wide range of taxa. Going beyond mere labels, song dialects in oscine passerines also furnish clear evidence of culturally mediated patterning. These birds reliably acquire their species song by social learning, and what is learnt can then be termed a 'signal'. In contrast to these widely distributed kinds of culture, van Schaik et al. (2003) assert that the cultural transmission of *skills* is unique to orang-utans, chimpanzees and humans. If ape culture is worthy of special attention—beyond that accorded to cultural transmission processes in more easily studied species such as birds and fishes—then it is because great ape feeding ecology is reliant on complex skills that may need to be acquired culturally.

Many species of animal occasionally use a tool, and a diverse range of species are known regularly to use a single type of tool for a particular purpose (Beck 1980). But in many populations of chimpanzee, and one of orang-utans, the intricate series of actions involved in selecting, constructing and employing tools goes well beyond these minimal cases; one example from each will suffice to illustrate. Chimpanzee termite-fishing is not a logical response to the perception of edible insects. Indeed, the insects are hidden deep within termite mounds which have no visible entrances. The ape must know that at a certain season it becomes possible to pick open a hole in certain places. In fact, this is only possible above what will later become the nocturnal emergence tunnel for the sexual forms of the termites, so the chimpanzee must also know how to recognize a sealed exit. Only when a suitably long, thin and flexible plant stem is inserted slowly through this entrance (and sometimes the plant stems are picked, stripped of leaves and bitten to a standard length, in advance of arrival at the mound) can it be with-drawn with termites attached (Goodall 1986). Comparable skills are shown by orang-utans at Suaq, Sumatra, which make small tools by biting off a twig and stripping it of bark, then use it to scrape out the irritating hairs from a ripe, part-open *Neesia* fruit. When the hairs are cleaned away, the same tool is used to dislodge the seeds to eat (van Schaik *et al.* 1996).

These two examples are also, as it happens, geographically patchy, but in general local patchiness of distribution does not single out traits of manifest difficulty. Few of the dozens of reportedly cultural traits of great apes involve any real skill, in terms of subtlety, complexity and likely difficulty of acquisition without a skilful model. Only hole-probing with tools in the orang-utan, and ant-dipping, nut-cracking and hole-chiselling in chimpanzees, in addition to the two examples already noted, require manifest skill. Conversely, geographical *uniformity* does not exclude social learning as critical for acquisition. Indeed, ecologically important skills that depend on social learning would be expected to spread steadily through the population until checked by a major natural barrier. Within in the ranges of the African great apes, natural barriers chiefly consist of great rivers, and the patchy distribution of behaviour traits does not map onto the distribution of rivers. Another criterion is needed to direct research attention to the most informative behaviour.

I propose that the combination of *intricate complexity* of behaviour, and *near-ubiquity* among a contiguous population, can be used as an alternative hallmark of culture in great apes. This criterion has the advantage of focusing attention on great ape behaviour that is in principle relevant to better understanding the origins of human culture—where it is the intricate patterns of complex action that have long impressed anthropologists. Intricately complex behaviour patterns are highly unlikely to be invented multiple times, making cultural transmission an essential feature of their widespread dissemination, and near-uniformity within a population points to the skills' importance for survival.

Removing the need for 'local variations without ecological correlate' opens the gate to a much wider range of great ape skills potentially acquired culturally. As noted above, ant-dipping by chimpanzees varies in style in ways that make good ecological sense as ecological adaptations to different ant species (Humle & Matsuzawa 2002), but this need not disqualify the behaviour itself as cultural. The elaborate series of skilled actions involved in ant-dipping is highly unlikely to be learnt by a solitary chimpanzee. Of course, many of the important details of how the job is done are likely discovered individually, as with any complex skill; it is most probably only the *idea* or *gist* of ant-dipping with a stick that is socially learnt. The same may apply to several other chimpanzee tool-using skills (e.g. nest construction, algae-scooping, leaf-sponging), not considered as part of chimpanzee culture, and to plant-preparation skills not involving tool-using, such as opening and eating *Saba* fruit (Corp & Byrne 2002). Almost all orang-utan populations lack elaborated tool use, but most show intricate, complex skills for dealing with plants, in particular to enable pith consumption from spiny palms and rattans (Russon 1998).

Using the alternative definition of 'intricate complexity and local ubiquity' allows great ape culture to be studied in other species where patchy geographical distribution would be unde-tectable with current data. Gorillas do not make tools in the wild, and only one population has been studied at the level of detail needed to detect complex skills in plant-processing. But sev-eral of their food-processing skills consist of highly structured, multi-stage sequences of bimanual action, hierarchically organized and flexibly adjusted to plants of highly specific local distribution (Byrne & Byrne 1993; Byrne *et al.* 2001*a,b*); and these abilities are near-ubiquitous among the local population. In terms of intricate complexity, gorilla plant-processing actually *exceeds* anything yet described in chimpanzees, unless tool-use *per se* is taken to be intrinsically more complex than non-tool-use. *Gorilla*, like *Pan* and *Pongo*, apparently sometimes relies for its survival on elaborate, deft and intricate feeding skills that are highly unlikely ever to be discovered by a solitary individual (Byrne 1997, 2004). Since nothing of the kind has been reported in any monkey species, the underlying cognitive ability is likely to have a relatively recent (i.e. ancestral great ape) origin and relate directly to the origins of human technological superiority.

6.4 Possible concerns

It could be argued that shifting the focus of ape culture research firmly towards behaviour of intricate complexity, rather than requiring geographical patchiness, opens the possibility of confusion with genetically determined traits or with behaviour that can be acquired without social learning at all. How serious are these concerns for great ape research? Many species of animal show intricate complexity of behaviour, most obviously in construction of nests, bowers and dams (Hansell 2005); and many animal displays are is also complex and highly patterned. However, such traits are far less evident for primates, species whose flexibility of repertoire and reliance on learning have always impressed researchers. Some of the most intricate great ape skills make no sense at all when viewed as genetical products. For instance, the plant-processing of mountain gorillas (*Gorilla beringei*) is so specific to plants of limited altitudinal range as to be valueless a few miles away from where they were recorded, yet the distribution of this species of gorilla extends for hundreds of miles.

Alternatively, it has been suggested that even the most elaborate skills of wild great apes could in fact be discovered by each individual separately, and would then be channelled towards near-uniformity in the population by the affordances of the hands and the natural materials involved (Tomasello & Call 1997). Whether or not this proposal is considered plausible, no evidence has yet been offered that it is correct; and several pieces of circumstantial evidence are against the idea. These include: (i) as discussed above, the complex skills of apes are occasionally distributed in a way that implies spread effectively blocked by natural barriers, (ii) apes that have suffered maiming from snare wounds to the hands in infancy nevertheless acquire the same techniques of skill as their able-bodied peers, rather than discovering different methods consistent with the very different affordances of their maimed hands (Stokes & Byrne 2001; Byrne & Stokes 2002), and (iii) while great ape skills show extensive individual variation at a detailed level and in handedness, as would be expected from individual accommodation to task demands, the overall structural organization seems to be universal in the local population (Byrne & Byrne 1993).

Working with natural data, no perfect method exists for the identification and study of cultural phenomena. Defining ape culture on the basis of intricately complex skills that are near-uniform in a contiguous population has several advantages, however, over the use of geographical patchiness. Research focus is brought firmly to bear upon behaviours of ecological importance to the species concerned, which are in important ways 'like' those that underpin human cultural uniqueness. In particular, they are elaborately complex activities, exquisitely adjusted to solving practical problems, relatively obvious in broad outline 'once you see it', but unlikely to be discovered by an individual restricted to lone experimentation. Interpopulation variations in behaviour may sometimes result from breaks in a knowledge network, and these cases are fascinating to study; more often, variation is likely to result from hidden ecological differences, especially in species whose ecology is not fully understood. Population uniformity of complex, apparently skilful behaviour may occasionally result from tight genetical channelling ('an innate trait'), and any cases discovered would be worthy of study; but none is particularly likely in a simian primate species. In general, intricate complexity, in a trait that is near-uniform in the population, signals culturally guided acquisition of an important survival skill.

6.5 Postscript: measuring complexity of behaviour

To apply this criterion, some way of measuring and comparing complexity across tasks is needed, as a way of estimating the likelihood of individual invention (thus 'complexity' is here used to include all aspects of the task that make learning more difficult). There are a number of possibilities. Mathematically, complexity can be measured as information (Shannon & Weaver 1949), and a simple way of estimating information content—by counting repertoire sizes—has been advocated for estimating the complexity of animal behaviour (Sambrook & Whiten 1997). Since any complex task will be composed of simpler building blocks, on this approach one would count the number of elemental 'building blocks' of behaviour involved in any task—and if the species carries out several complex activities, as in the case of some chimpanzee, gorilla and orang-utan populations, these actions can be summed to estimate the total 'skill relevant repertoire'. The feasibility of this approach was investigated for mountain gorilla plant-processing skills, defining as different actions those that differed in their visible form and movement patterns (e.g. precision holding with fingers 1/3 versus fingers 1/2). Significantly more elements were found to be used when gorillas process leaves of thistle *Carduus* than those of bedstraw *Galium* or nettle *Laportea*, for a given amount of data (Byrne *et al.* 2001*b*). For this one thistle species, in processing both stem and leaves a total repertoire of 222 elements was recorded. However, the estimated repertoire of individuals correlated closely with the number of processed handfuls of food analysed for each task, showing no sign of reaching asymptote. If massive samples of behaviour need to be analysed in detail even to count repertoire size, then the practical usefulness of this method is limited; but the problem seemed to stem from relatively trivial variations in how a function was accomplished. This suggested an alternative approach of defining actions as different only if they had different effects on the plant material, regardless of the hand, fingers or precise action used. When such 'functionally equivalent' actions were used, much greater commonality between individuals was found, implying that estimates of repertoire were more reliable; in this case, 46 functionally distinct elements were found for thistle compared to 13 for nettle-and bedstraw-processing treated together.

Although repertoire-counting can evidently be used for broad comparisons, this method risks missing the most interesting aspects of task complexity. As an analogy, the English language has a very much larger lexicon of words than either French or Spanish, but few linguists would claim that English was therefore a more complex language. Similarly, a large repertoire of actions does not automatically equate to a complex task; the structural organization of behaviour is also critical. A rough and ready estimate of organizational complexity is given by the overall length of goal-directed sequences of action. Of course, an unstructured sequence of more or less randomly chosen actions may also be long, so it is necessary to focus only on strings of actions whose sequence is *repeated* on different occasions to achieve the same goal. Equally, as with repertoire-counting, care needs to be taken in delineating an action: to achieve a single effect, many unsuccessful attempts, or repeated identical actions with cumulative effect may be used. Here again, length does not equal complexity; one way to avoid inflated estimates is to split a process into *stages*, defined again by the effect upon the physical substrate.

This approach was also evaluated against the plant-processing tasks of mountain gorillas. For each task, individuals were found to have a small number of preferred techniques; among adults and juveniles, the number of techniques was found not to vary significantly with age (Byrne *et al.* 2001*b*). Qualitative differences among preferred techniques were themselves quite minor, and mainly a matter of which mirror form was preferred and slight variations associated with different plant material. Thus, for the local population of gorillas, a *modal technique* could be used to describe the skill common to all able-bodied individuals (Byrne & Byrne 1991, 1993; Byrne *et al.* 2001*b*). Flow charts give a convenient representation of modal techniques (see figure 6.1 for an example from the chimpanzee; Corp & Byrne 2002). While great ape feeding techniques show flexibility in response to variations in the problem presented by particular individual plants, the modal technique's organization is highly structured, so its length should give some indication of complexity.

In order to compare different feeding skills by calculating the length of the programme of actions needed to perform them, the start point was arbitrarily taken to be when the animal was in a position to reach the material (which might itself have required considerable effort and planning; see Russon 1998), and the end point was taken to be the ingestion of a mouthful of processed material ready to chew (although in many cases the individual then began work on processing the next mouthful, and might continue for some time). Only feeding techniques signalled by regularly occurring, goal-directed activities were examined. Stages in the process were defined as composed of activity directed at a single effect on the world—in this case, on the plant material—in order to avoid inflating estimations by counting actions repeated for cumulative effect or owing to initial failures. When a stage occurred reliably when needed but was omitted whenever it was unnecessary, it was considered part of the modal process. Conversely, if several stages were repeated as a whole 'subroutine' more than once, in order to achieve a cumulatively greater effect, only a single sequence was considered. By these criteria, mountain gorilla consumption of nettles *Laportea* and thistle *Carduus* were both found to be five-stage processes, whereas bedstraw *Galium* processing is a four-stage one (Byrne *et al.* 2001*b*; note that the precise way that the processed food was put into the mouth varied across these three cases, but ingestion was not counted as a separate stage, so the lengths may have been slightly underestimated). As can be seen from figure 6.1, chimpanzee consumption of *Saba* fruits is also a five-stage process by these criteria.

Comparable analysis has yet to be done for tool-based skills of the chimpanzee, but published accounts suggest similar or greater lengths in some cases (e.g. termite-fishing: pick stem, strip off leaves, bite end, pick open termite hole, probe in, gently retract). In contrast, most monkey feeding is carried out by a one-stage process (see Panger *et al.* (2002) and O'Malley & Fedigan (2005) for some of the most elaborate processes yet described in monkeys).

While estimating the overall length of organized repeated processes is a more appropriate method of comparison than repertoire-counting, it is still by no means ideal. No account is taken of the potential complexity of hierarchical embedding of subroutines—if this indeed contributes to task complexity, which presumably would depend on the cognitive architecture of the animal, currently an unknown. No differentiation is made between stages which are more or less obligatory at a certain point in the process, or optionally omitted, or a matter of choice among several different options. And simply measuring length in stages does not take account of variations in the degree to which 'what to do next' at each stage is influenced

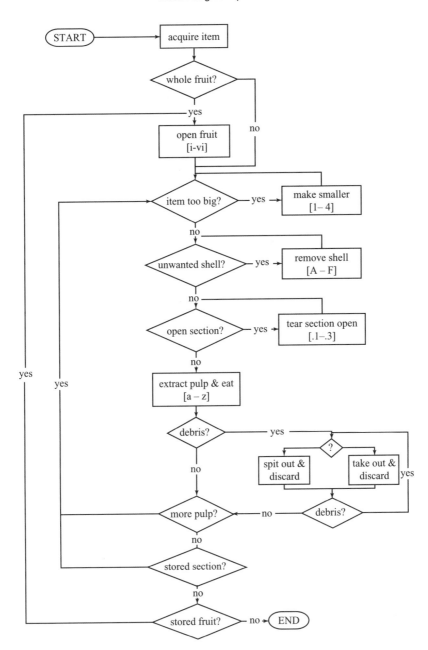

Fig. 6.1 Flow diagram showing the overall organization of behaviour and the apparent decision processes used in *Saba florida* fruit-processing (Corp & Byrne 2002). Actions are represented by boxes and decision processes by diamonds; when the underlying factor dictating a decision is unknown, this is denoted by a question mark. Square brackets enclose a series of options that each serves to achieve certain actions; choice between them is presumably a function of local stimulus conditions, rather than contributing to the overall complexity of the task organization.

by constraints in the local environment and the affordances of the animals' effector organs. At present, little research effort has gone into refining methods of estimating complexity, and these weaknesses may yet be circumvented. However, it may also be worth examining possible *correlates* of complexity—such as degree of individual or population-level laterality, or age of acquisition of techniques not limited by physical strength—to see whether these factors covary with sequence length.

I would like to thank Nathan Emery, Nicky Clayton and Chris Frith for organizing the stimulating Royal Society discussion meeting, 'Social Intelligence: from brain to culture', at which the ideas in this paper were first presented; to the Royal Society for inviting me to take part; and to all participants whose generous discussion clarified my ideas. Bill McGrew read an earlier draft of this paper and his careful scholarship has greatly reduced the number of mistakes, but for those that remain the responsibility is mine.

References

Beck, B. B. 1980 *Animal tool behaviour*. New York, NY: Garland Press.

Boesch, C. 1996 The emergence of cultures among wild chimpanzees. In *Evolution of social behaviour patterns in monkeys and man* (eds W. G. Runciman, J. Maynard-Smith & R. I. M. Dunbar), pp. 251–268. London, UK: British Academy.

Boesch, C. & Boesch, H. 1990 Tool use and tool making in wild chimpanzees. *Folia Primatol.* **54**, 86–99.

Boesch, C., Marchesi, P., Marchesi, N., Fruth, B. & Joulian, F. 1994 Is nut cracking in wild chimpanzees a cultural behaviour? *J. Hum. Evol.* **26**, 325–338. (doi:10.1006/jhev.1994.1020)

Byrne, R. W. 1997 The technical intelligence hypothesis: an additional evolutionary stimulus to intelligence? In *Machiavellian intelligence II: extensions and evaluations* (eds A. Whiten & R. W. Byrne), pp. 289–311. Cambridge, UK: Cambridge University Press.

Byrne, R. W. 2004 The manual skills and cognition that lie behind hominid tool use. In *Evolutionary origins of great ape intelligence* (eds A. E. Russon & D. R. Begun), pp. 31–44. Cambridge, UK: Cambridge University Press.

Byrne, R. W. & Byrne, J. M. E. 1991 Hand preferences in the skilled gathering tasks of mountain gorillas (*Gorilla g. beringei*). *Cortex* **27**, 521–546.

Byrne, R. W. & Byrne, J. M. E. 1993 Complex leaf-gathering skills of mountain gorillas (*Gorilla g. beringei*): variability and standardization. *Am. J. Primatol.* **31**, 241–261. (doi:10.1002/ajp.1350310402)

Byrne, R. W. & Stokes, E. J. 2002 Effects of manual disability on feeding skills in gorillas and chimpanzees: a cognitive analysis. *Int. J. Primatol.* **23**, 539–554. (doi:10.1023/A:1014917600198)

Byrne, R. W., Corp, N. & Byrne, J. M. 2001a Manual dexterity in the gorilla: bimanual and digit role differentiation in a natural task. *Anim. Cogn.* **4**, 347–361. (doi:10.1007/s100710100083)

Byrne, R. W., Corp, N. & Byrne, J. M. E. 2001b Estimating the complexity of animal behaviour: how mountain gorillas eat thistles. *Behaviour* **138**, 525–557. (doi:10.1163/156853901750382142)

Byrne, R. W., Barnard, P. J., Davidson, I., Janik, V. M., McGrew, W. C., Miklósi, Á. & Wiessner, P. 2004 Understanding culture across species. *Trends Cogn. Sci.* **8**, 341–346. (doi:10.1016/j.tics.2004.06.002)

Collins, D. A. & McGrew, W. C. 1987 Termite fauna related to differences in tool-use between groups of chimpanzees *(Pan troglodytes)*. *Primates* **28**, 457–471. (doi:10.1007/BF02380861)

Corp, N. & Byrne, R. W. 2002 The ontogeny of manual skill in wild chimpanzees: evidence from feeding on the fruit of *Saba florida*. *Behaviour* **139**, 137–168. (doi:10.1163/15685390252902328)

Galef, B. G. 1990 Tradition in animals: field observations and laboratory analyses. In *Interpretations and explanations in the study of behaviour: comparative perspectives* (eds M. Bekoff & D. Jamieson), pp. 74–95. Boulder, CO: Westview Press.

Galef, B. G. 1992 The question of animal culture. *Hum. Nat.* **3**, 157–178.

Galef, B. G. 2003 "Traditional" foraging behaviours of brown and black rats (*Rattus norwegicus* and *Rattus rattus*). In *The biology of traditions: models and evidence* (eds D. M. Fragaszy & S. Perry), pp. 159–186. Cambridge, UK: Cambridge University Press.

Goodall, J. 1963 Feeding behaviour of wild chimpanzees: a preliminary report. *Symp. Zool. Soc. Lond.* **10**, 39–48.

Goodall, J. v. L. 1973 Cultural elements in a chimpanzee community. In *Precultural primate behaviour* (ed. E. W. Menzel), pp. 144–184. Basel, Switzerland: Karger.

Goodall, J. 1986 *The chimpanzees of Gombe: patterns of behavior*. Cambridge, MA: Harvard University Press.

Hansell, M. 2005 *Animal architecture*. Oxford, UK: Oxford University Press.

Helfman, G. S. & Schultz, E. T. 1984 Social transmission of behavioural traditions in a coral reef fish. *Anim. Behav.* **32**, 379–384. (doi:10.1016/S0003-3472(84)80272-9)

Hohmann, G. & Fruth, B. 2003 Culture in bonobos? Between-species and within-species variation in behavior. *Curr. Anthropol.* **44**, 563–571. (doi:10.1086/377649)

Humle, T. & Matsuzawa, T. 2002 Ant dipping among the chimpanzees of Bossou, Guinea, and some comparisons with other sites. *Am. J. Phys. Anthropol.* **58**, 133–148.

Laland, K. N. & Hoppit, W. 2003 Do animals have culture? *Evol. Anthropol.* **12**, 150–159. (doi:10.1002/evan.10111)

McGrew, W. C. 1974 Tool use by wild chimpanzees feeding on driver ants. *J. Hum. Evol.* **3**, 501–508. (doi:10.1016/0047-2484(74)90010-4)

McGrew, W. C. 1992 *Chimpanzee material culture: implications for human evolution*. Cambridge, UK: Cambridge University Press.

McGrew, W. C. & Tutin, C. E. G. 1978 Evidence for a social custom in wild chimpanzees? *Man* **13**, 234–251. (doi:10.2307/2800247)

McGrew, W. C., Ham, R. M., White, L., Tutin, C. G. & Fernandez, M. 1997 Why don't chimpanzees in Gabon crack nuts? *Int. J. Primatol.* **18**, 353–374. (doi:10.1023/A:1026382316131)

Nishida, T. 1973 The ant-gathering behaviour by the use of tools among wild chimpanzees of the Mahali Mountains. *J. Hum. Evol.* **2**, 357–370. (doi:10.1016/0047-2484(73)90016-X)

Nishida, T. 1980 The leaf-clipping display: a newly discovered expressive gesture in wild chimpanzees. *J. Hum. Evol.* **9**, 117–128. (doi:10.1016/0047-2484(80)90068-8)

Nishida, T. & Kawanaka, K. 1972 Inter-unit-group relationships among wild chimpanzees of the Mahali Mountains. *Kyoto Univ. Afr. Stud.* **7**, 131–169.

Nishida, T. & Uehara, S. 1983 Natural diet of chimpanzees (*Pan troglodytes schweinfurthii*): long-term record for the Mahale Mountains, Tanzania. *Afr. Stud. Monogr.* **3**, 109–130.

Nishida, T., Kano, T., Goodall, J., McGrew, W. C. & Nakamura, M. 1999 Ethogram and ethnography of Mahale chimpanzees. *Anthropol. Sci.* **107**, 141–188.

O'Malley, R. C. & Fedigan, L. 2005 Variability in food-processing behavior among white-faced capuchins (*Cebus capucinus*) in Santa Rosa National Park, Costa Rica. *Am. J. Phys. Anthropol.* **128**, 63–73. (doi:10.1002/ajpa.20186)

Panger, M. A., Perry, S., Rose, L., Gros-Louis, J., Vogel, E., Mackinnon, K. C. & Baker, M. 2002 Cross-site differences in foraging behavior of white-faced capuchins (*Cebus capucinus*). *Am. J. Phys. Anthropol.* **119**, 52–66. (doi:10.1002/ajpa.10103)

Perry, S. & Manson, J. H. 2003 Traditions in monkeys. *Evol. Anthropol.* **12**, 71–81. (doi:10.1002/evan.10105)

Perry, S. *et al.* 2003 Social conventions in wild white-faced capuchin monkeys—evidence for traditions in a neotropical primate. *Curr. Anthropol.* **44**, 241–268.(doi:10.1086/345825)

Russon, A. E. 1998 The nature and evolution of intelligence in orangutans (*Pongo pygmaeus*). *Primates* **39**, 485–503.

Sambrook, T. & Whiten, A. 1997 On the nature of complexity in cognitive and behavioural science. *Theory Psychol.* **7**, 191–213.

Shannon, C. E. & Weaver, W. 1949 *The mathematical theory of communication*. Urbana, IL: University of Illinois Press.

Stokes, E. J. & Byrne, R. W. 2001 Cognitive capacities for behavioural flexibility in wild chimpanzees (*Pan troglodytes*): the effect of snare injury on complex manual food processing. *Anim. Cogn.* **4**, 11–28. (doi:10.1007/s100710100082)

Sugiyama, Y. & Koman, J. 1979 Tool-using and tool-making behaviour in wild chimpanzees at Bossou, Guinea. *Primates* **20**, 513–524. (doi:10.1007/BF02373433)

Tomasello, M. 1990 Cultural transmission in the tool use and communicatory signaling of chimpanzees? In *"Language" and intelligence in monkeys and apes* (eds S. T. Parker & K. R. Gibson), pp. 274–311. Cambridge, UK: Cambridge University Press.

Tomasello, M. 1994 The question of chimpanzee culture. In *Chimpanzee cultures* (eds R. W. Wrangham, W. C. McGrew, F. B. M. de Waal & P. G. Heltne), pp. 301–317. London, UK: Harvard University Press.

Tomasello, M. & Call, J. 1997 *Primate cognition*. New York, NY: Oxford University Press.

van Schaik, C. P. & Knott, C. D. 2001 Geographic variation in tool use on *Neesia* fruits in orangutans. *Am. J. Phys. Anthropol.* **114**, 331–342. (doi:10.1002/ajpa.1045)

van Schaik, C. P., Fox, E. A. & Sitompul, A. F. 1996 Manufacture and use of tools in wild Sumatran orangutans. Implications for human evolution. *Naturwissenschaften* **83**, 186–188.

van Schaik, C. P., Ancrenaz, M., Borgen, G., Galdikas, B., Knott, C. D., Singleton, I., Suzuki, A., Utami, S. S. & Merrill, M. 2003 Orangutan cultures and the evolution of material multure. *Science* **299**, 102–105. (doi:10.1126/science.1078004)

Warner, R. R. 1988 Traditionality of mating-site preferences in a coral reef fish. *Nature* **335**, 719–721. (doi:10.1038/335719a0)

Whiten, A. 2005 The second inheritance system of chimpanzees and humans. *Nature* **437**, 52–55. (doi:10.1038/nature04023)

Whiten, A., Goodall, J., McGrew, W. C., Nishida, T., Reynolds, V., Sugiyama, Y., Tutin, C. E. G., Wrangham, R. W. & Boesch, C. 1999 Cultures in chimpanzees. *Nature* **399**, 682–685. (doi:10.1038/21415)

Whiten, A., Goodall, J., McGrew, W. C., Nishida, T., Reynolds, V., Sugiyama, Y., Tutin, C. E. G., Wrangham, R. W. & Boesch, C. 2001 Charting cultural variation in chimpanzees. *Behaviour* **138**, 1481–1516. (doi:10.1163/156853901317367717)

Whiten, A., Horner, V. & de Waal, F. B. M. 2005 Conformity to cultural norms of tool use in chimpanzees. *Nature* **437**, 737–740. (doi:10.1038/nature04047)

7

Dolphin social intelligence: complex alliance relationships in bottlenose dolphins and a consideration of selective environments for extreme brain size evolution in mammals

Richard C. Connor

Bottlenose dolphins in Shark Bay, Australia, live in a large, unbounded society with a fission–fusion grouping pattern. Potential cognitive demands include the need to develop social strategies involving the recognition of a large number of individuals and their relationships with others. Patterns of alliance affiliation among males may be more complex than are currently known for any non-human, with individuals participating in 2–3 levels of shifting alliances. Males mediate alliance relationships with gentle contact behaviours such as petting, but synchrony also plays an important role in affiliative interactions. In general, selection for social intelligence in the context of shifting alliances will depend on the extent to which there are strategic options and risk. Extreme brain size evolution may have occurred more than once in the toothed whales, reaching peaks in the dolphin family and the sperm whale. All three 'peaks' of large brain size evolution in mammals (odontocetes, humans and elephants) shared a common selective environment: extreme mutual dependence based on external threats from predators or conspecific groups. In this context, social competition, and consequently selection for greater cognitive abilities and large brain size, was intense.

Keywords: dolphins; brain size; alliances; social complexity

The open sea is an environment where technical knowledge can bring little benefit and thus complex societies—and high intelligence—are contraindicated (dolphins and whales provide, maybe, a remarkable and unexplained exception).

(Humphrey 1976)

7.1 Introduction

In his famous essay on 'The social function of intellect', Humphrey linked social complexity to environments where improvements in 'technical knowledge' paid large dividends. Dolphins were left as an unexplained puzzle. Many would agree now that Humphrey's essay deserves praise for getting it right as to *what* we use our big brains for (social competition) but not necessarily *why* the environment humans lived in was one where social success paid big dividends (although technical knowledge may have played two very important roles in human brain evolution, as I describe below).

The most complex social relationships described so far in cetaceans are found in bottlenose dolphins (*Tursiops aduncus*, family Delphinidae) that live in Shark Bay, Australia. Males affiliate in nested alliances that vary in stability, size and relatedness. Synchrony may play an important role in mediating alliance relationships, suggesting an interesting convergence with humans based on imitative abilities, motion perception or relationship *uncertainty*. A consideration of the ecology of alliance formation reveals that the interaction between ecology, alliance relationships and degree of social competition is a complex arena in dolphins just as it is in primates.

The evolution of a large brain probably played a key role in the impressive delphinid radiation. One of the reasons the delphinids have large brains is that they can afford them. A high quality diet supports a high metabolic rate that renders large brains less costly. The small-brained dolphins also consume a high quality diet, but it remains unclear whether they have a high metabolic rate. I offer a novel cost-saving hypothesis for delphinid brain evolution, based on the evolution of a high energy budget for group-feeding on schooling fish.

Increasingly, it seems that the social competition hypothesis may be the best explanation for all three 'peaks' in mammalian brain size: humans (and apes), elephants and odontocetes (primarily delphinids and sperm whales). It seems a good time, therefore, to revisit the question of environment to see if we can find common selective pressures that favoured extreme brain size evolution in these groups. This presents an interesting challenge, as one would be hard pressed to find three more different types of mammals in appearance and lifestyle.

In §17, I argue that extreme brain size evolution in elephants, toothed whales and humans was driven by a shared feature of their environment: a threat from conspecifics and/or predators leading to an extreme degree of mutual dependence. The relative importance of inter-group conflict seems secure for humans, and protection from predators is clearly important for odontocetes and elephants. An important role for inter-group competition is indicated by the nested alliance structure in dolphins and can be plausibly suggested for elephants and sperm whales, given their pattern of affiliation between stable groups.

7.2 The Shark Bay dolphins: general features

(a) Relationship uncertainty

The social cognition hypothesis for primates was captured succinctly by Seyfarth & Cheney (2002), 'Primates . . . live in large groups where an individual's survival and reproductive success depends on its ability to manipulate others within a complex web of kinship and dominance relations'. Knowledge of the kin and dominance relationships between others has been touted by some as a characteristic that distinguishes primates from other mammals (Harcourt 1988, 1992), but this claim is undermined by the recent finding that hyenas recognize third party relationships (Engh *et al.* 2005). I suspect that recognition of third party relations does not represent a pinnacle of social intelligence but instead provides a necessary foundation that allows individuals to 'manipulate others'.

Recognition of third party relations has not been demonstrated in dolphins. However, our research in Shark Bay implies that if dolphins have this ability, their knowledge of third party relations must be incomplete and this *uncertainty* presents special perceptual and cognitive challenges. Relationship uncertainty is imposed by the sheer size and 'open' nature of the Shark Bay society as well as their fission–fusion grouping pattern.

(b) Size

The Shark Bay dolphin society is large and apparently unbounded. We have currently identified over 600 dolphins in our approximately 200 km² study area. The dolphins inhabit a mosaic

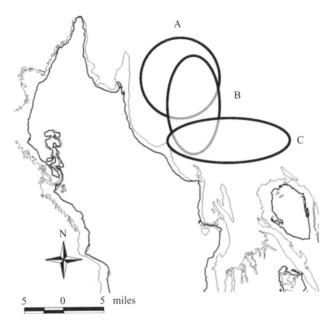

Fig. 7.1 *Relationship uncertainty* in Shark Bay occurs because of the fission–fusion grouping pattern and is exacerbated by the mosaic of overlapping ranges. Individual B might know A and C well, but minimal range overlap will prevent A and C from knowing each other well.

of overlapping ranges where A might know B and B might know C but A and C do not know each other because their ranges do not overlap (figure 7.1; Connor & Mann 2006). Estimating the number of associates is not an easy matter for a large open society with a fission–fusion grouping pattern. Combining 4 years of survey data, we found that individuals typically had around 60–70 associates (Connor *et al.* in preparation), similar to the largest primate societies (Dunbar 1992; Barton 1996). Given the small percentage of time we actually observe the dolphins, this number is likely an underestimate. In addition to knowing some individuals and not others, the dolphins' distribution suggests that they might know some individuals well and some not at all well. Whereas in closed primate societies, individuals might be able to develop a fairly complete picture of third party relations (kin and rank), even if dolphins have such an ability, considerable uncertainty in their knowledge of third party relations may be unavoidable.

(c) Fission–fusion

The Shark Bay dolphins live in a classic fission–fusion society where individuals associate in small groups that change composition frequently (Smolker *et al.* 1992; Connor *et al.* 2000). A fission–fusion grouping pattern presents two types of cognitive challenge. First, social relationships occur in a constantly changing social milieu 'placing a premium on the evolution of cognitive abilities' (Smolker *et al.* 1992; see also Barrett *et al.* 2003). This is especially true when the fission–fusion is of the 'atomistic' type (Rodseth *et al.* 1991). Second, fission–fusion also introduces uncertainty into an individual's knowledge of third party relations. Changes in relationships between others, even well-known individuals, may occur in other groups or 'off camera', posing significant cognitive challenges (Connor & Mann 2006).

7.3 The duration of relationships: life history and philopatry

(a) Philopatry

Natal philopatry by both sexes may be common in cetaceans (Connor *et al.* 2000). At the two longest running bottlenose dolphin field sites, Sarasota and Shark Bay, it is clear that at least some individuals of both sexes continue to use their natal range as adults (Wells 1991, 2003; Connor *et al.* 2000; Connor & Mann 2006). This may allow individuals to begin very early in life to shape relationships strategically that will have reproductive consequences when they mature. Möller & Beheregaray (2004) maintain that genetic evidence from Port Stephens, Australia, contradicts the 'bisexual philopatry' hypothesis (Connor *et al.* 2000) in favour of 'females being the more philopatric and males being the more dispersing sex'. It is worth avoiding a sterile debate by pointing out here that both Wells (1991, 2003) and Connor *et al.* (2000) have stated that (i) males may have larger ranges than females and (ii) philopatry by some males does not preclude complete dispersal by others (some males and females disappear). We are not surprised to see this produce differences in local relatedness, as it has in Shark Bay (Krützen *et al.* 2004). That some male and female offspring continue to use their natal ranges as adults in both locations is not a hypothesis but a fact, and one that raises interesting possibilities in the arena of social cognition.

7.4 The structure of male dolphin alliances in Shark Bay

Males in Shark Bay form two, and possibly three, distinct levels of alliance *within* their social network (Connor *et al.* 1992*a*,*b*; Connor & Mann 2006). The first level of alliance is associated with the formation and maintenance of consortships with females that may last for minutes to weeks (Connor *et al.* 1992*a*,*b*, 1996). These associations almost invariably involve two or three males consorting a single female.

The second level of alliance is associated with cooperation between first-order alliances to take females from other alliances or to defend against such theft attempts (Connor *et al.* 1992*a*,*b*). In spite of thefts being relatively uncommon (we are lucky if we observe 2–3 in a field season lasting several months and including several hundred hours of observation) males in second-order alliances exhibit high levels of association (Smolker *et al.* 1992; Connor *et al.* 1992*a*, 1999; Connor & Mann 2006). This likely reflects the importance of defence in these formations: during the peak of the mating season it is not unusual to find most or all members of a second-order alliance together or near each other, even though the group is 'saturated', or nearly so, with female consorts.

The size of second-order alliances varies considerably, from 4 to 14 or more males. A possible correlate of the second-order alliance size is first-order alliance stability (Connor & Krützen 2003). At one extreme, we find bonds between particular males that are highly stable for up to 20 years (Connor *et al.* 2000; Connor & Krützen 2003; Connor & Mann 2006). Such stable pairs or trios are usually found alone or in small second-order alliances. At the other extreme, members of one large 14 member second-order alliance (the 'super-alliance') shifted partners often between consortships but with distinct partner preferences and avoidances (Connor *et al.* 2001). Another possible correlate of alliance size and stability is relatedness. Krützen *et al.* (2003) found that males in stable first-order alliances that formed small second-order alliances were more related to their allies than expected by chance. However, relatedness in the super-alliance, even among preferred partners, was not above chance expectations (Krützen *et al.* 2003).

In recent years (2001–2005), as we expanded our study area to monitor alliance affiliations of over 100 adult males, it became evident that some second-order alliances associated regularly and amicably with other groups, suggesting a third level of alliance formation (Connor & Mann 2006). Our discovery in 1987 of two levels of alliance formation was preceded by similar observations of consistent associations between particular first-order alliances. The alternative to three levels of alliance is two levels with varying degrees of association between first-order alliances (Connor & Mann 2006). Association and network analysis will resolve this issue. In 2001, we observed two conflicts involving the same three second-order alliances (Connor & Mann 2006). In each case, one second-order alliance attacked another, but the engagements were, unfortunately, too chaotic for either us or our video-cameras to discern if the third second-order alliance present supported one of the other two groups.

7.5 Maintaining alliance relationships: affiliative interactions

The obvious dolphin equivalent to primate grooming is petting or 'gentle rubbing' where dolphins touch and stroke each other with their pectoral fins (Tavolga & Essapian 1957; Connor *et al.* 2000). Adult males pet with first- and second-order alliance partners and occasionally other males. Although commonly observed, petting typically occurs underwater where it is visible but individual identification is spotty. A behaviour that is more easily quantified and potentially interesting from the 'social cognition' perspective is synchrony. Commonly two, and sometimes three, dolphins will surface side-by-side synchronously, usually less than a metre apart (Connor *et al.* 2006). Frame-by-frame video analysis reveals that in cases judged to be synchronous by observers in real time, the males broke the surface within 80–120 ms of each other (Connor *et al.* 2006). The synchronous surfacing of male dolphins may be a by-product of proximity, for example, if synchrony reduces the overall drag on the pair or at least prevents one from having a drafting advantage (e.g. Weihs 2004). However, Connor *et al.* (2006) argued that synchrony is most likely an adaptive signal because normal synchronous surfacing is a common component of the astonishingly variable synchronous displays males perform around females (Connor *et al.* 1992b, 2000). These displays, which may include a variety of underwater and aerial leaps and turns, are not explicable as by-products of proximity.

Connor *et al.* (2006) examined patterns of synchrony among males that formed stable first-order alliances and small second-order alliances. Unsurprisingly, we found that when two first-order alliances were together, synchrony was more common between first-order alliance partners. Of more interest were the patterns that emerged when synchrony was examined in relation to activity. Inter-alliance synchrony, when a male from one first-order alliance surfaces side-by-side synchronously with a male from another first-order alliance, was much more common when the males were socializing, especially when they were engaging in excited socializing (chasing, mounting and splashing) with a female consort. Connor *et al.* (2006) suggested that inter-alliance synchrony in such a potentially competitive context might reduce tension between the males.

A comparison of several male trios revealed significant variation in several measures of synchrony including rates of synchrony and the proportion of synchronous surfacing that included all three males (measured as the ratio of triple synchs pair + triple synchs for the alliance). These measures may reflect alliance 'unity' more accurately than coefficients of association, and synchrony may be more common in males that are mature and engage in frequent consortships (Connor *et al.* 2006).

7.6 Synchrony and dolphin cognition

The degree to which synchrony is observed in the alliance behaviour of male dolphins appears unique among mammals, with the exception of our own species (McNeill 1995; Hagen & Bryant 2003). If synchronous movement is prominent in human and dolphin alliance behaviour, why is synchrony not found more often in non-human primates that form alliances? Descriptions of synchrony are rare in non-human primates and we are not aware of any quantitative studies linking synchrony to social bonds. The fact that allied baboon males, *Papio anubis*, do employ synchronous manoeuvres on occasion (e.g. Ransom 1981) simply begs the question of why such visually oriented mammals do not employ such a powerful signal consistently. Here, we consider several adaptive hypotheses to explain this apparent dolphin–human convergence.

(a) Motion perception

Several authors have suggested that the dolphins' visual system may be well adapted for motion detection (Dawson 1980; Madsen & Herman 1980). These suggestions are based mostly on peripheral anatomy: a horizontally elliptical eye that should cause images to sweep rapidly across the retina and a class of giant cells in the ganglion layer that subserve large regions of the visual field (Walls 1942; Dawson 1980; Madsen & Herman 1980). An enhanced ability to perceive motion could select for motion-based signals. At any rate, it seems likely that the social cues (e.g. spacing, posture and glance) that effectively signal alliance behaviour in primates might be less effective in lower light levels underwater and in animals where selection for streamlined form disfavours the ability to exhibit subtle facial contortions.

Intriguingly, recent magnetic resonance imaging studies indicate that humans have a region of the brain, the intraparietal sulcus, where motion detection is much more prominent than in the macaque homologue (Orban *et al.* 2003). Thus, humans and bottlenose dolphins may have converged on the use of synchrony as a social signal owing to a convergent enhancement of motion perception. In other words, the puzzle of why non-human primates do not use synchrony is one of our own (perceptual) making—it is not a powerful visual stimulus to them.

However, the likely functional reasons for a convergence between humans and dolphins in motion perception are different. Orban *et al.* (2003) suggest that the use of tools and hunting with primitive weapons may have favoured a greater investment in motion detection in humans. Of course, conflict between humans using hand-held or distance weapons may have been an even stronger selective factor. In contrast, a dolphin motion adaptation would likely be associated with the detection, pursuit and avoidance of prey and predators. Further research is needed on motion perception in other non-human primates such as chimpanzees. Unless humans have a motion perception adaptation that is unique among alliance forming primates, this hypothesis fails.

(b) Imitation

A provocative possibility is that the convergent use of synchrony in alliance behaviour by humans and dolphins reflects a broader convergence related to having large brains and impressive cognitive abilities. Motor synchrony is under sophisticated cognitive control in bottlenose dolphins.

Herman (2002, 2006) trained bottlenose dolphins to perform novel synchronous behaviours on command. Specifically, when dolphins were given two commands, 'tandem' (perform a behaviour together) and 'create' (perform any behaviour), the dolphins would self-select a behaviour and perform it synchronously. Of 79 different behaviours elicited with the 'tandem+create' commands, 23 were novel in the sense that they were not under the control of established gestures (Herman 2002, 2006). Imitation of one dolphin by the other is the most likely explanation for this ability (Herman 2002). In contrast, considerable research effort has failed to produce comparable skills in most non-human primates (Call & Carpenter 2002; Visalberghi & Fragaszy 2002), but the debate on whether apes ape is far from over (e.g. Whiten *et al.* 2004). The relative lack of imitation in non-human primates is puzzling, given the discovery of mirror neurons in monkeys and the finding that macaques recognize when they are being imitated by humans (Paukner *et al.* 2004). Byrne (2005) suggests that monkeys fail to learn by imitation because imitation is actually two different processes, 'social mirroring' or the more complex 'learning by copying', which involves 'hierarchical construction of a behavioural program' (Byrne & Russon 1998). Byrne (2005) suggests that monkeys are limited to social mirroring. Unfortunately, this distinction does not help us understand why allied monkeys fail to employ motor synchrony as an alliance signal. Dolphin synchrony may be parsimoniously interpreted as social mirroring and monkeys do not do it, at least not systematically.

While Herman's work shows that synchrony in dolphins is under cognitive control of some kind, it is no more necessary to invoke complex cognitive processes for the simple repetitive movements of dolphins surfacing synchronously than for synchronous claw waving by fiddler crabs (Backwell *et al.* 1999). Indeed, dolphins may have been pre-disposed to incorporate synchrony into their social signals if motor synchrony was already an important part of their behavioural repertoire. Synchronous movements in schooling dolphins may have been favoured originally because they induced confusion in predators, much like the schooling behaviour of fish (Norris & Schilt 1988). An obvious objection to this line of argument is the same as given for the 'proximity by-product' hypothesis for synchronous surfacing. If synchronous displays are under cognitive control and synchronous surfacing is a common component of such displays, then it follows that synchronous surfacing must be under cognitive control as well. I am not particularly concerned with the outcome of this argument, however, because I think that a more inviting 'cognitive constraints' hypothesis can be developed if we focus on the *social* context of synchrony. While imitation may not be necessary to explain synchronous surfacing in dolphins, their ability to imitate may have rendered synchrony more useful as a signal in the richly varying social contexts of within-group hierarchical alliances. For example, the relationship between inter-alliance synchrony and behaviour reveals that dolphin synchrony depends on context and not merely the strength or duration of an association. Facility with imitation may make it easier for a dolphin to surface synchronously with the right individual at the right time.

(c) Signalling benefits

Another possibility is that humans and dolphins are distinguished from non-human primates by the benefits they accrue from having a clear alliance signal such as synchrony. Lack of knowledge about alliance relationships could be very costly to individuals attempting to take resources from others (as well as to those they attack). Thus, factors that increase uncertainty about who is allied with whom should favour a strong alliance signal like synchrony. A male dolphin may learn who is allied by observing synchrony in others and may use synchrony to 'test the bond' (Zahavi 1977) with his putative allies. We identify three factors, shared by humans and Shark Bay bottlenose dolphins, which increase uncertainty about alliance relationships relative to most non-human primates. As noted earlier, changes in alliance affiliation may be unobserved in a fission–fusion society (Connor & Mann 2006); second, unobserved changes are more likely to occur in larger, open social networks; and third, unobserved changes are also more likely (other factors being equal) with additional alliance levels. Most primates, living in smaller bounded social groups, may simply not need such a signal.

7.7 Alliance relationships and social complexity

Alliances and coalitions are, at a minimum, an important category of relationship, usefully illustrative of how social interactions can become complex, and at most, may be the kind of relationship that drove large brain evolution generally (Alexander 1989; Cords 1997; Harcourt 1992; Connor 1992*b*).

7.8 Levels of alliance

As pointed out by Kummer (1967), within-group alliances are complex because they involve *triadic* interactions. Consider the trio of individuals labelled A, B and C (figure 7.2*a*). Any of these three individuals might try, using a variety of affiliative interactions, to form an alliance with another against the third; possibly giving rise to competition for alliance partners (see also Harcourt 1988, 1992). In contrast, interactions between non-human primate groups are not complex because they are not triadic (Connor *et al.* 1992*a*, figure 7.2*b*), but they may complicate within-group interactions by increasing mutual dependence within groups (see §15).

Having nested alliances *within* their social network allows dolphins to engage in triadic interactions between individuals *and* alliances (Connor *et al.*1992*b*; Connor & Krützen 2003; Connor & Mann 2006, figure 7.2*c*). Such nested alliances are a hallmark of human social structure but are rare in other primates. The best primate examples come from female cercopithecines where matrilines may cooperate to overthrow higher ranking matrilines (see discussion in Connor & Krützen 2003; Connor & Mann 2006). The decisions individuals make at one level of triadic interaction may be further complicated by possible impacts at the other level(s). Consider the trio ABC (figure 7.2*c*). A decision by individual A to recruit B against C could injure C and render ABC less attractive as an ally to DEF who might instead ally with GHI (Connor *et al.* 2006). It is not difficult to imagine the potential for this sort of problem to intensify demands on social intelligence. At this point, the word *potential* must be emphasized, for two factors must be in play for selection to put a premium on strategic alliance formation requiring enhanced social cognition: *options* and *risk.*

(a) Options

Imagine that alliances are formed only between close relatives, and members of alliance ABC are related to DEF but not GHI. In this case, a sibling spat between A and C will not impact the choice of alliance DEF because the simple 'kinship rule' eliminates strategic options. Thus, even though they have multilevel within-group alliances, the social world of cercopithecine females may be simplified significantly by the kinship rule (Connor & Mann 2006).

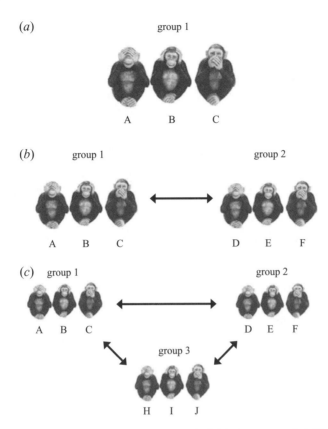

Fig. 7.2 (*a*) Within group alliances may be complex when individuals compete for allies, e.g. if A and B compete for C. (*b*) Alliances against other groups are not usually complex because they are exclusively hostile. They may impact within group alliances by increasing mutual dependence within groups. (*c*) Humans and dolphins are exceptional to the degree to which they form 'alliances of alliances'. Here alliance ABC could side with DEF or GHI against the other. Triadic interactions complicate within and between group interactions.

Options that might increase selection for greater social intelligence range from which potential ally to choose or compete for, to how much reproduction to yield to a partner, to how much to groom or stroke an ally. The number of potential partners will impact the difficulty of the decisions of how to behave towards a partner. This follows because there will often be a correlation between the number of options for an individual and that individual's potential partners: if A can choose B and C for alliance partners then B may choose A or C and so on. Asymmetries in resource holding power may render A the obvious ally for the other two (e.g. Noë 1990) but that does not make A's decisions necessarily simpler. B might have to be clever to win A's allegiance, but A might need to be clever about extracting the maximum benefit from B and C.

Connor & Mann (2006) reviewed the evidence for options at both levels of male alliance in Shark Bay. The greatest restriction on options appears to be among males that form stable pairs and trios, sometimes with close relatives (Krützen *et al.* 2003). However, strategic alliance shifts do occur among these males, who are not always close relatives (see Connor & Mann 2006). We have also documented males moving between second-order alliances.

(b) Risk

If alliance partners are interchangeable, so that the choice of B or C makes no difference to the fitness of A, or the choice of ABC or GHI makes no difference to the success of DEF, then decisions will be unimportant and alliance relations will not pose great demands on social cognition. In this case, individuals might employ a simple equivalence rule (Schusterman *et al.* 2003). The frequent partner changes in the 14 member super-alliance invite such an interpretation, but permutation tests revealed strong preferences and avoidances within the group (Connor *et al.* 2001).

A high risk decision is one where the difference between a good and bad decision has a high probability of a significant fitness gain or loss (the sum of many 'smaller' decisions could have the same impact). Note that decisions could be the difference between maintaining a fitness 'status quo' versus toppling off a fitness cliff (if you are ostracized or killed) or enjoying a huge fitness bonanza (choosing the right ally that allows you to assume top rank). In two cases where we observed Shark Bay males discontinue their second-order alliance affiliations (in one case the male appeared to have been ostracized; Connor & Mann 2006), they began associating with juveniles and ceased participating in consortships. In both cases, they began participating in consortships again several years later when those juveniles matured.

My studies have focused on adult males that are already members of alliances. Studies of what happens prior to maturation will be essential to answering the question of how and how many potential alliance partners are evaluated during the juvenile period.

7.9 The ecology of alliance formation

(a) First-order alliance size

Given that most consortships involve three males, but a minority two, it was commonly speculated among our research group that the optimal size of first-order alliances was a bit less than three males. For example, of the 58 consortships by non-provisioned males documented by Connor *et al.*(1992*a,b*), 26 were by pairs and 32 by trios for an average of 2.6 males. Of 100 consortships by males in the 14 member super-alliance, 95 were performed by trios and five by pairs, for an average of 2.95 males per consortship. During 2001–2002, we observed 103 males participate in 135 consortships with an average of 2.9 males. This latter sample affirms that the average across the whole study area is likely closer to 3.0 than 2.5.

Whitehead & Connor (2005) examined the question of alliance size using individual-based models in which alliances of greater net competitive ability out-compete those with less, and where males could switch alliances based on expected success. The most critical variable was the average number of males (m) competing for each receptive female. For example, the average alliance size ranged from 2.6 to 2.8 when $m = 4$–5, with a clumped alliance distribution (versus Poisson) and assuming that males can leave alliances in pairs with no cost but suffer a cost when leaving alone. These assumptions are reasonable. Males probably do not move randomly among receptive females, likely avoiding those strongly defended by large second-order alliances. Further, a pair of males can leave as an alliance capable of consorting females, but we do not see consortships by single males. Thus, leaving alone would be more costly than leaving an alliance with another male. The value of m may well be less than five in Shark Bay. The adult sex ratio is not highly biased (Mann & Sargeant 2003, report that 46% of sexed non-calves are males). The operational sex ratio will be male-biased, given the typical 3.5 year interval between cycling periods for females that become pregnant and successfully wean calves (Connor *et al.* 1996). The average interval will likely be less than this, given the 44% calf mortality, two-thirds of which occurs in the first year (Mann *et al.* 2000).

In Sarasota Bay, Florida, adult males form stable pairs, but trios and second-order alliances are not in evidence (Wells *et al.* 1987; Connor *et al.* 2000; Wells 2003). Greater sexual size dimorphism, a less male-biased operational sex ratio or fewer sharks could explain the lack of trios (Connor *et al.* 2000), but the population density and thus overall encounter rates between males may be much higher in Shark Bay, favouring larger and more levels of alliances (Connor *et al.* 2000; Connor & Whitehead 2005).

(b) Second-order alliance size and stability

While first order alliance size is constrained within a narrow range of 2–3 males, the size of second-order alliances is much more labile, ranging from 4 to 14 or more males. In primates, larger groups suffer more feeding competition as revealed by higher daily travel costs (Janson & Goldsmith 1995). Two factors might mitigate this problem for dolphins. First, dolphin travel costs are very low compared with terrestrial mammals (Williams 1999), so the costs of grouping should be substantially less (Connor *et al.* 1998; Connor 2000). More subtly, slight increases in grouping costs might be offset by a slight increase in some benefit of grouping, producing a benefit/cost ratio that is similar across a range of group sizes (Connor & Krützen 2003). Second, individual differences in foraging strategies are common in Shark Bay and these may impose different grouping costs on individuals. The 'sponge-carriers' (Smolker *et al.* 1997) are suggested to be relatively solitary owing to higher grouping costs, specifically the time it takes to forage successfully in this manner and the distribution and size of prey patches (Connor *et al.* 2000). If males differ in the average patch size they exploit (e.g. solitary benthic prey versus schooling fish) then they will experience different costs of grouping that might be reflected in the size of second-order alliances.

7.10 Ecological influences on social cognition

The differences we find between the Sarasota and Shark Bay bottlenose dolphin populations are likely ecological (but possibly owe to morphology or even phylogeny; see Connor *et al.* 2000). Perhaps, owing to their habitat and/or size, Sarasota males may have a less challenging social environment than males in Shark Bay. Sarasota males do not appear to have to negotiate second-order alliances, they do not experience the complications of trios, and once they choose their alliance partner the association may last a lifetime (Wells 2003). Further, the large size range of second-order alliances in Shark Bay may effectively create an 'imbalance of power' problem, putting smaller groups at risk (Manson & Wrangham 1991).

Should we expect the Sarasota dolphins to have relatively smaller brains and less advanced cognitive skills? Perhaps, but primatologists will recognize the 'orangutan problem' here, where one of the great apes appears to live in a less challenging social environment than the other two, especially the chimpanzee, but nonetheless has a large brain and in captivity seems quite clever. In the orangutan case, detailed observations in a new habitat revealed a more complex society than was known previously, as well as more complex, learned foraging cultures (van Schaik *et al.* 2003; van Schaik 2004). Compared with the great apes, the radiation of large-brained

Table 7.1 Three brain size comparisons for small odontocetes of approximately the same body size. (*Sotalia, Dephinus* and *Tursiops* belong to the family Delphinidae. Each of the others belongs to a different family with only 1–2 species in each (Adapted from Connor *et al*. 1992*b*; Connor & Mann 2006).)

species	N	body length (cm)	body mass (kg)	brain mass (g) or volume (cm³)	brain size ratio
Pontoporia	9	153	39	227	
Sotalia	1	158	42	688	3.0
Platanista	4	197	60	295	
Delphinus	10	193	68	836	2.8
Lipotes	2	252	167	570	
Tursiops	19	246	231	1588	2.8

delphinids is huge and likely includes a range of social systems. Until a wider range of species are studied, we cannot begin to speculate as to what sort of ancestral society or pattern of alliance relationships was involved with the expansion of the delphinid brain. The bottlenose dolphins studied in Sarasota Bay and Shark Bay are in many ways ecological outliers of the family, as most genera live father offshore in more open and deeper water habitats. What we can say is that the Shark Bay population reveals the level of social complexity that becomes possible in dolphins under the right ecological conditions. And we should not imagine that we have stumbled, so early in the game, on the most complex society in the entire family.

7.11 Extreme brain size evolution in primates, proboscidians and odontocetes

There are three 'peaks' in brain size evolution in mammals: in the primates, elephants and odontocetes. Outside of humans, the highest degrees of encephalization are found in the delphinid odontocetes (Jerison 1978; Connor *et al*. 1992*b*; Marino 1998).

Comparisons of species similar in body size demonstrate clearly extreme differences in brain size among odontocetes (Connor *et al*. 1992*b*; Connor & Mann 2006). The large-brained delphinids, ranging from 1.5 to 2.5 m in length, have brains in the 650–1600 g range. The smallest brained (non-monophyletic) group includes four single species families (*Pontoporia, Platanista, Lipotes, Inia*) that live in rivers, with the exception of *Pontoporia* which is marine. These animals range in size from 1.5 to 2.5 m and have brains in the 225–625 g range. Table 7.1 shows three size-specific comparisons revealing 2.8–3.0 fold differences in brain size, a figure similar to the difference between apes and humans. Members of the porpoise family Phocoenidae, appear to have brains of intermediate size (Marino 1998; Connor *et al*. 1992*b*; Connor & Mann 2006). Recent phylogenies confirm that the sperm whale is an ancient sister group to other odontocetes (Cassens *et al*. 2000; Nikaido *et al*. 2001; Hamilton *et al*. 2001; Arnason *et al*. 2004). Thus, the large sperm whale brain was most likely derived independently and will be considered separately. This distinction is also interesting given the remarkable convergence between sperm whales and elephants (Weilgart *et al*. 1996).

The 'encephalization quotient' or EQ is a popular way to compare species of different body sizes. The EQ is the ratio of actual brain size to the brain size 'expected' for a similar sized mammal, usually calculated from the slope for all or a large sample of mammals (Jerison 1973). Given that brain–body slopes change with taxonomic level (Martin & Harvey 1985;

Pagel & Harvey 1989), the interpretation of EQs of different sized animals is problematic. Brain–body slopes differ between orders and, in some orders, with taxonomic level. Thus, evaluating the encephalization of cetaceans with the overall mammalian slope (usually close to 0.75) might disguise what Martin (1980) called 'grade' differences. A grade difference is implied when regression lines for two groups at a given taxonomic level are found to have similar slopes but differ in their vertical displacement. The vertical displacement is taken to represent an adaptive shift in relative brain size (Martin 1980). For example, Manger (2006) argues that large brain evolution in odontocetes was driven by selection for increased thermogenesis in cold water, a feat he contends is accomplished by increasing the number of glial cells. Manger considers the encephalization of the bottlenose dolphin (*Tursiops truncatus*) to be similar to the much smaller harbour porpoise (*Phocoena phocoena*) based on similar EQs calculated from the general slope for mammals (note that Marino 1998, calculated lower EQs for *Phocoena phocoena*). However, comparison of similar sized delphinids and phocoenids removes the scaling problem and suggests that the delphinids may be more encephalized (tables in Connor *et al.* 1992a; Connor & Mann 2006), a conclusion that is problematic for Manger's 'thermogenesis' hypothesis as porpoises are generally distributed in cooler water than similar sized delphinids. More generally, if the odontocete brain size increase was driven by thermogenesis, we would expect a tight correlation between water temperature and brain size given that the 'ratchet effect' often postulated for the brain size evolution (see Humphrey 1976) holds only for information processing capacity. Selection should, for example, strongly favour a smaller brain in delphinids that live in warm water habitats. The warm water riverine but highly encephalized delphinid, *Sotalia* shows this not to be a necessary outcome.

7.12 Paying the costs

(a) Brains, food and metabolic rates in dolphins

Some hypotheses to explain primate brain size differences focused exclusively on costs (e.g. Martin 1981, 1982, 1983; Armstrong 1982, 1983) and were rejected convincingly (McNab & Eisenberg 1988). However, relative brain size differences among mammals must be determined *partly* by differences in available energy. Delphinids are fortunate, in this regard, to enjoy a high-energy diet that can be characterized as 'fish, squid and the occasional invertebrate'.

It is worth noting that the metabolic costs of a large brain for dolphins may be even less than indicated by their basal metabolic rate (BMR). What really matters, of course, is the proportion of the total energy budget used by the brain. The BMR was established as a standard by which different species could be compared. BMR comparisons will reflect relative brain costs only if BMR correlates closely with the total energy budget. Many terrestrial mammals, ourselves included, spend a large proportion of a 24 h day in a state that closely approximates standard metabolic conditions (e.g. during sleep). Evidence suggests, however, that many dolphins do not remain at rest for such extended periods and may continue to travel for nearly the entire day (see Connor 2000). The Ganges River platanistid, the susu, swims continuously in captivity, a habit Pilleri *et al.* (1976) attributed to the ever-present currents in the susu's river habitat. Therefore, to the extent that the total energy budget/BMR ratio of dolphins is relatively greater than that for terrestrial mammals, their brains will be relatively cheaper to maintain than is indicated by their BMR alone.

In primates, brain size differences are sometimes associated with categorical differences in the energy yield of the diet, e.g. folivores versus fruigivores (Clutton-Brock & Harvey 1980; but see Oftedal 1991; Dunbar 1992). This is not the case in odontocetes as the 'fish, squid and occasional invertebrate' characterization fits both the small- and large-brained dolphins. *Pontoporia* is an especially interesting case because, unlike the slower swimming river dolphins, they live in the marine habitat and have a scapular morphology indicating that they are stronger, more manoeuvrable swimmers than the small-brained riverine species (Strickler 1978). An extensive recent study of diet in this species could have been taken from the delphinid play-book, revealing *Pontoporia* to be an opportunistic feeder eating a variety of schooling and solitary fish and squid (Bassoi 2005). One has to look outside of the cetaceans, to the herbivorous sirenians, to find categorical differences in diet quality (see Connor & Mann 2006).

A measure of energetic requirements, the amount of food required to maintain body weight, indicates that *Inia* may have a lower metabolic rate than delphinids (Best & da Silva 1989) but data from a single captive *Lipotes* were in the same range as delphinids (Peixun 1989). A phocoenid, *Phocoenoides dalli*, whose brain size falls between the delphinids and 'river' dolphins, consumed much more fish than two delphinid species, likely owing to the importance of maintaining a high BMR for thermoregulation in this cold water deep-diving species (Ridgway & Johnston 1966).

(b) Brain size differences in small odontocetes: the schooling fish hypothesis

At this juncture, the data do not suggest a strong correlation between brain size and available energy in odontocetes. The data on metabolic rate in *Phocoenoides* clearly contradict the energy availability hypothesis, but it cannot be refuted for the smallest brained dolphins, *Inia, Platanista, Lipotes* and *Pontoporia*. To encourage further work in this area, I construct a diet-related hypothesis that takes into account the lack of obvious categorical differences in food type among small- and large-brained dolphins. Schooling fish offer a possibility. Fish schools represent a large patch of high quality but also highly mobile food. Dolphins digest quickly and with a high efficiency of assimilation (Shapunov 1973) using a longer than expected small intestine (Williams *et al*. 2001). Williams *et al*. argue that the additional investment in metabolically expensive gastrointestinal tissue is required to maintain the dolphins' high BMR. The metabolic rate/intestine relationship described by Williams *et al*. (2001) is just the sort of adaptation that would allow dolphins to take maximal advantage of feeding on fish schools. It allows dolphins to eat a lot quickly and move rapidly over long distances between schools. Operating on a higher energy budget would render a larger brain more affordable. An obvious weakness of this hypothesis is that even the small-brained *Pontoporia* feeds on schooling fish (Bassoi 2005). However, if the early delphinids specialized more on schooling fish than other groups, and this specialization was associated with coordinated group feeding to corral or trap fish schools (as occurs in a wide variety of delphinids, e.g. spinner dolphins, *Stenella longirostris*, Benoit-Bird & Au 2003; killer whales, *Orcinus orca*, Simila & Ugarte 1993; the dusky dolphin, *Lagenorhynhcus obscurus*, Wursig 1980; bottlenose dolphins, Gazda *et al*. 2005), then the hypothesis is feasible. I also note that a prominent function of the delphinid whistle is to maintain contact over distances (Smolker *et al*. 1993; Janik & Slater 1998), an important ability for coordinated group hunting (Herman & Tavolga 1980). Delphinid whistles are so different from those of other species that Podos *et al*. (2002) argued that they were a derived character for the group. The delphinid whistle may be adapted to provide information to others about orientation as well as distance. Lammers & Au (2003) suggest that the relatively high frequency of spinner dolphin whistles may provide useful information on whistler orientation to school members.

While delphinids are racing around digesting all those schooling fish, they are generating a lot of metabolic heat. Thus, the same adaptations that might have allowed dolphins to take full advantage of this rich resource generated additional body heat that allowed them to inhabit colder water. Can we distinguish these ideas conceptually? Consider an ancestral, sluggish, warm water dolphin. Selection acted to increase the energy budget, allowing investment in the musculature and digestive tissue needed to travel further and faster to capture and digest, quickly and efficiently, schooling fish. The benefit of this investment had to be greater reproductive success. Assume that the reproductive returns were associated with additional energy intake (as opposed to, for example, reduced predation risk) so the dolphins were essentially paying 5 to get 10. If the benefit of consuming additional energy was entirely heat production then the reproductive advantages might be associated with being able to live in new habitats and exploit new prey (or, yes, avoid predators). The schooling fish hypothesis is independent of the thermoregulation hypothesis only to the extent that the additional energy from feeding on schooling fish was associated with increasing fat stores and the ability to invest in offspring. Investment in brain tissue would have increased adult and offspring fitness in a challenging 'k'-selected environment. Most likely, given that heat production from increased digestion was inevitable, the two selective factors often operated in tandem. Differences in encephalization between delphinids and phocoenids suggest that the distinction may be useful.

It should be possible to test the 'schooling fish' hypothesis with comparative tests of small odontocetes' habitat and feeding modes to estimate the 'ancestral feeding type' and comparative studies of larger and smaller brained dolphins' feeding efficiency, basal and field metabolic rates, heat balance, gut anatomy and feeding behaviour.

(c) The sperm whale and the elephant

A major early increase in odontocetes' brain size took place roughly 35 Myr ago (Marino *et al.* 2004). The more recent expansion of the brain in delphinids occurred about 15 Myr ago (Marino *et al.* 2004), long after sperm whales split from other toothed whales (Heyning 1997). The large sperm whale brain may have evolved independently, eased as well by a squid and fish diet, and additionally, a *large body size*. As noted by Whitehead (2003), the fraction of metabolism devoted to the brain depends on relative brain size which declines with increasing body size. Simply, other things being equal, big brains are cheaper for larger animals such as elephants and sperm whales. Elephants do not consume the high quality food of sperm whales, but may compensate by processing a lot of food at a high rate (Clauss *et al.* 2003).

(d) Humans

One possible role 'technical abilities' played during human evolution (Humphrey 1976) was in the realm of food processing. Several authors (Milton & Demmet 1988; Wrangham *et al.* 1999) have argued that early humans used tools (including fire) to make foods more digestible. This improved food quality could have paved the way for a reduced gut size and large energetic savings that could be redirected to the brain (Aiello & Wheeler 1995).

7.13 Reaping the benefits

(a) The non-social cognitive challenges: food

Although the focus here is on social cognition, I would be remiss not to discuss, at least briefly, how resource acquisition may have favoured enhanced cognitive abilities in dolphins and sperm whales. Cetaceans have enormous day and home ranges relative to terrestrial mammals and often feed on food that is distributed in patches (Connor 2000). I emphasize that the 'patchiness' of cetacean resources varies to an extreme degree across spatial and temporal scales (see Whitehead 2003). A bottlenose dolphin in Shark Bay may seek mobile patches of schooling prey or feed on benthic prey that occur only on patchily distributed shallow water banks. A sperm whale may move between patches separated by hundreds of kilometres and given areas may change productivity over periods of months or longer (Whitehead 1996, 2003). Greater memory and spatial knowledge may be favoured to the extent to which patch availability fluctuates predictably in space and time. To some extent, the mobility of dolphin prey will render 'mapping' difficult (Whitehead 2003). Ridgway (1990, 2000), has argued that the large delphinid brain was driven by the demand for more neural tissue to map acoustically the dolphins' environment in real time. However, it is not clear why delphinids would need to map a larger area in real time than, for example, the wide ranging, pelagic and deep diving but smaller brained beaked whales of the family Ziphiidae.

As Nicholas Humphrey was writing his 1976 essay, he would have been pleasantly surprised to learn what we know today: the sea is indeed a place where 'technical knowledge' may bring benefits and innovation is highly rewarded (see Rendell & Whitehead 2001; Reader & Laland 2002). Bottlenose dolphins exhibit a remarkable range of feeding behaviours that they employ throughout the water column and even into the air, onto the beach and into the substrate (reviewed in Connor *et al.* 2000) which likely require considerable learning (e.g. Mann & Sargeant 2003). Moreover, compared with terrestrial environments, the marine habitat also seems to be the one that favours learned individual foraging specializations. Connor (2001) suggested that any or all of the following four factors might explain why individual foraging specializations are more prominent in the marine environment: a greater density of high quality foods; a greater variety of high quality foods; reduced seasonality; and greater improvements in feeding efficiency with practice. Whitehead (1999, 2003) suggests that significant differences in reproductive success between groups of matrilineal whales may result from innovations developed in one group and transmitted vertically.

7.14 The social competition hypothesis

In many primates, individuals compete for high-ranking alliance partners and solicit help in contests from those that outrank themselves and their opponent (see Harcourt 1992). This behaviour implies that individuals know the rank relations of others in the group, a challenging task when group size is large.

The claims of Harcourt and others for the uniqueness of primate strategic alliances were challenged with the finding that hyenas can also recognize third party relations in the context of coalition formation (Engh *et al.* 2005). In hindsight, as usual, the findings of Engh *et al.* are not surprising. After all, the brains of hyenas and the mid-sized old world monkeys that exhibit an understanding of third party relations are not vastly different, and the hyenas live in large complex societies (Drea & Frank 2003; Engh & Holekamp 2003; Wahaj & Holekamp 2003).

Further, most of the 'complex web of kinship and dominance relations' perhaps is not so complex if the monkeys follow a few simple rules, such as ally with close kin (female cercopithecines) and compete for the highest ranking ally available (Connor & Krützen 2003; Connor & Mann 2006). *Greater* social cognition would be required if individual rank or kinship were less of a deciding factor so that other strategies, such as cultivating friends based on more than simple rank, were employed to maximize reproductive success (see Cords 1997; Silk 2003).

What of the very largest mammalian brains? Among mammals that usually includes humans, with brains three times larger than similar sized apes, many delphinids, who place second behind humans in relative brain size and which boast brains 2–3 times larger than similar sized non-delphinid odontocetes (table 1, Jerison 1978; Connor *et al.* 1992*a*; Marino 1998; Connor & Mann 2006), and perhaps elephants and sperm whales, animals so large they are hard to compare with anything else and whose social lives and life history have converged to a remarkable degree (Weilgart *et al.* 1996).

Alexander (1979, 1989, reviewed in Flynn *et al.* 2005) emphasized the importance of mental simulations of social situations or 'scenario building'—a much more cognitively challenging skill than simply recognizing the relations between any two other individuals. This is the social equivalent of Jerison's original (1973) argument that brains provided a model of the external world. Mental simulations might permit an individual to preview alternative future social outcomes based on choosing different options (e.g. A or B as an ally). A socially skilled brain must not only model the complexities of the current world but mentally play out the longer-term consequences of alternative scenarios (smack this individual, embrace that one). Recognizing third party relationships might be the basic foundation upon which increasingly sophisticated abilities to model social scenarios are based. And as I suggested earlier, it may not be the ability to learn third party relations that matters for big-brained mammals, but trying to keep track of many third party relations when the size of the social network and pattern of grouping constantly introduce varying degrees of uncertainty in that knowledge.

Why did humans get shunted down this path? Alexander (1989) argues that it was not predators but other human groups that drove the extraordinary evolution of the human brain. Ecologically removed from the risk of predation, inter-group conflict became the greatest threat to humans. As mutual dependence increased exponentially, so did the importance of *coalition cognition*. This is the second area where 'technical benefits' played an important role in humans; improvements of weapons would have given some groups a great advantage over others (see also Flynn *et al.* 2005).

7.15 Convergent brain and life history evolution in humans, toothed whales and elephants

van Schaik & Deaner (2003) and Deaner *et al.* (2003) revisit the correlation between slow life history and large brain size (see Sacher 1959; Sacher & Staffeldt 1974; Pagel & Harvey 1988, 1989). Their new analysis, based on mammalian orders, revealed a weak relationship between EQs (observed brain size/expected based on body size) and longevity quotients (observed maximum lifespan/expected maximum lifespan based on body size) that became highly significant once the outlier Chiroptera were removed.

Low mortality is essential for slow life history to be favoured (Sterns 1992); this may derive from larger body size (Read & Harvey 1989) or an escape from terrestrial predators by flying or climbing (van Schaik & Deaner 2003). In primates, there is a weak relationship between arboreality and life history but not arboreality and brain size.

Although, as van Schaik & Deaner (2003) suggest, arboreality may have induced the initial evolution of slow life history favouring larger brains in early primates, it seems clear that the three peaks in brain evolution (or four if you count sperm whales as an independent case) occurred in open, exposed habitat on the ground or in the sea. Humans, dolphins, sperm whales and elephants all depend on group living, and in some cases large size, to reduce mortality risk necessary for the evolution of long lives and large brains. The key is the vulnerability of offspring for animals that invest a lot in each one (Connor & Norris 1982). Alexander (1979, 1989) made a persuasive case for extreme mutual dependence based on inter-group conflict during human evolution. In elephants, sperm whales and dolphins, offspring vulnerability is extreme; elephant infants can neither run nor hide effectively and infant dolphins and sperm whales live in an open three-dimensional habitat without refuge (Connor & Norris 1982; Whitehead 2003 Connor & Mann 2006). A positive feedback loop may develop between sociality, group defence, reduced adult mortality and slow life-history processes for those species with a high investment in vulnerable offspring (see Whitehead 2003).

The extraordinary mutual dependence among individuals in these groups creates exactly the situation that leads to high risk social strategies. Individuals are in social competition with the same individuals their lives depend on: 'individual reproductive success would depend increasingly on making the right decisions in complex social interactions involving selves, relatives, friends and enemies' (Alexander 1979, p. 214). The key is that as group living, and in some cases large size, reduced adult mortality, smaller infants remained extremely vulnerable.

As longer-lived adults invest proportionally more in fewer offspring, mutual dependence increases in two ways. First, each offspring represents a higher proportion of lifetime reproduction. Second, as the period of parental dependency increases, so does the total number of predation attempts that have to be prevented (or, more exactly, the larger dependent offspring of larger, longer-lived mothers will be less vulnerable to the smaller, more abundant, predators and so will be attacked less often. However, this decrease in attack *rate* should not be in proportion to the increased duration of parental dependency, i.e. an infant dependent on its mother for 4 years will experience more threats than one weaned after 4 months).

The importance of group living and mutual dependence can explain why bats are an outlier in the relationship between longevity and brain size (see van Shaik & Deaner 2003) and why the relationship between life history and arboreality in primates is not matched by a similar relationship between arboreality and brain size.

We can consider also whether the source of the mutual dependence experienced by humans, toothed whales and elephants have elements in common. We have assigned the extreme mutual dependence in humans to other human groups and the elephants and toothed whales to predators. However, the nested alliances of male dolphins in Shark Bay and patterns of affiliation between female elephant and sperm whale groups hint at a role for inter-alliance conflict (see also Connor & Krützen 2003).

7.16 Life history and social cognition: additional considerations

van Schaik & Deaner (2003) also argue that the longer inter-birth intervals associated with slow life histories will bias the operational sex ratio more towards males because fewer females will be receptive at any point in time. This greater potential for inter-sexual conflict, including infanticide, may favour more complex social strategies by both males and females (van Schaik & Deaner 2003). A male-biased operational sex ratio may impact directly the formation of alliances. Whitehead & Connor (2005) found that the expected size of roving male alliances was impacted primarily by the number of males competing for a female.

Another impact of slow life histories is less direct but no less important. By investing more in fewer offspring, long-lived animals reduce the options for forming same-sex alliances with close kin. If kin are favoured, and females produce litters with several males, then ready-made alliances of kin may be the preferred option. This eliminates the need for choosing partnerships strategically with the development of friendships and constant testing of bonds (Zahavi 1977). Longer inter-birth intervals also reduce the chance that a single born male will have close male relatives available as potential allies. Dolphins are at one extreme, where a female gives birth to one calf at a time several years apart. Consistent adherence to a simple rule such as ally with close kin will be less viable compared with offspring that are part of litters, or even better, synchronized litters of related females, e.g. lions (Packer & Pusey 1987). As it is clear that some male dolphins form alliances with close kin, but many and probably most do not, it is likely that kinship is the only one factor influencing their partner choice (although it may be a highly preferred characteristic when similar age relatives are available).

7.17 Communication

It is appropriate to end this discussion of peaks in mammalian brain evolution with communication, because humans have the largest brain relative to body size and only humans have the facility of language. Language opened possibilities for social manoeuvring and manipulation that were not possible before. It is easy to imagine how just one of the abilities bestowed by language, communication about others in their absence, might have been put to advantage by those skilled in using and dispensing such information (and misinformation) to enhance their social position (e.g. Dunbar 2003). It follows that language may have become more than a tool necessary to maintain a large number of relationships (Dunbar 2003); by opening new frontiers in social manoeuvring, language itself may have generated selection for greater social intelligence.

It is easy to argue that our language facility is what really separates humans from other large-brained mammals such as elephants and dolphins, but if history teaches us anything, it would be to proceed cautiously with this conjecture. A lack of language does not preclude a priori complex communication about relationships, even relationships of those not present. It will be useful to illustrate how such a system might work, given what we know of dolphin vocalizations.

Consider our current understanding of social communication in dolphins (which means the bottlenose dolphin, *Tursiops*). Dolphins produce a bewildering range of vocalizations that are easily divided into two types: whistles, which are relatively long duration (mean duration 0.1–2.3 s; Matthews *et al.* 1999) often frequency-modulated tonal sounds; and pulsed sounds, which have a short duration and are relatively broad band. The communication functions of pulsed sounds have been studied hardly at all, primarily because they are difficult; they often *appear* to be graded and they are certainly difficult to quantify. Whistles come in discrete research-friendly packages which can be recorded and played back to dolphins with relative ease. In short, we have learned that a prominent type of whistle produced by bottlenose dolphins is their 'signature' whistle (Caldwell & Caldwell 1965; Caldwell *et al.* 1990), a learned vocalization (Tyack 1997; Miksis *et al.* 2002) that yields information about identity

(Sayigh *et al.* 1999) based not on voicing but frequency contour (Janik *et al.* 2006), and that whistles are used as a contact call when animals are out of visual range (Smolker *et al.* 1993, Janik & Slater 1998).

The possibilities get very interesting when the dolphins' imitative abilities are juxtaposed with the recent finding that it is the contour of the signature whistle that conveys identity (Janik *et al.* 2006). These two ingredients could form the basis of a system that allows dolphins to communicate about others in their absence, especially when combined with other whistle attributes or pulsed sounds that communicate affect (that pulsed sounds play an important role in communicating affect seems clear; beyond that our understanding of this rich vocal output is minimal, but see Connor & Smolker 1996; Herman & Tavolga 1980, pp. 164–166).

What is the current evidence for signature whistle imitation by dolphins—that dolphins can address each other 'by name'? Dolphins certainly can imitate whistles, and a variety of other artificial sounds, with astonishing speed (Richards *et al.* 1984). Reiss & McCowan (1993) linked four distinct artificial whistles to the presentation of four different objects given to captive dolphins that later produced imitations of these sounds when interacting with the objects.

There are several reports of 'sharing' or 'matching' of signature whistles. Tyack (1986) recorded two captive dolphins producing whistles of two types in roughly inverse proportions (78 and 22% versus 31 and 69%). Obviously, similar data from a larger number of individuals would be more convincing. Janik & Slater (1998) and Burdin *et al.* (1975) found a few examples of whistle matching in captivity. Smolker & Pepper (1999) demonstrated convergence in the use of one whistle type by three male Indian Ocean bottlenose dolphins as their alliance developed. Similar whistle sharing was reported for allied males in Sarasota Bay, Florida (Watwood *et al.* 2004). The existence of such a learned alliance 'badge' has very interesting implications for communication about alliance status, but may result from a slower learning process and does not imply context-dependent imitation of others' whistles.

Using a hydrophone array to localize underwater sounds, Janik (2000) reported whistle matching by unidentified individuals in the Moray Firth, Scotland. He recorded 176 whistle 'interactions' where whistles occurred in close temporal proximity but too far apart spatially for one individual to have swum rapidly between locations to produce both. Of these, 39 (22%) were matching interactions, where the same whistle type was produced. In one case three individuals produced the same whistle. The distance between individuals producing matching whistles was significantly less than for non-matching whistle interactions.

While Janik's (2000) results might be explained by imitation of signature whistles where individuals are specifically 'addressed' by others, there is a more mundane possibility. Sayigh *et al.* (1995) report that in Sarasota Bay, Florida 9 of 21 (43%) male calves and 2 of 21 (10%) female calves developed signature whistles that were 'very similar' to their mothers. Given the long duration of parental care and the continued use of their natal range by males and females, the matching exchanges in the Moray Firth might be between mothers and offspring that have very similar signature whistles or allied males that have converged on a whistle type. In sum, the evidence for context-dependent signature whistle imitation in bottlenose dolphins, i.e. calling others 'by name', is suggestive but remains inconclusive. Evidence confirming spontaneous and context-specific whistle matching should not surprise us; rather, it would be surprising if the complexity of social relationships we find in Shark Bay is *not* matched by complexity in social communication.

I thank Richard Wrangham for, as always, encouraging me to think more about cost-saving adaptations. Lori Marino and Louis M. Herman provided numerous helpful suggestions to improve the manuscript.

The Male Alliance Project in Shark Bay has been supported almost continuously by the National Geographic Society (1987–2004), and also by grants from The Eppley Foundation, The Seaworld Research Foundation an NSF pre-doctoral grant, an NIH postdoctoral fellowship, a National Science Foundation LTRG, and a grant from the Australian Research Council. The Monkey Mia Dolphin Resort has provided 15 years of financial and logistic support. CALM has also provided assistance.

References

Aiello, L. C. & Wheeler, P. 1995 The expensive-tissue hypothesis: the brain and the digestive system in human and primate evolution. *Curr. Anthropol.* **36**, 199–121. (doi:10.1086/204350)

Alexander, R. D. 1979. *Darwinism & human affairs*. Seattle, WA: University of Washington Press.

Alexander, R. D. 1989 Evolution of the human psyche. In *The human revolution: behavioural and biological perspectives on the origins of modern humans* (eds P. Mellars & C. Stringer), pp. 455–513. Princeton, NJ: Princeton University Press.

Armstrong, E. 1982 A look at relative brain size in mammals. *Neurosci. Lett.* **34**, 101–104. (doi:10.1016/0304-3940(82)90159-8)

Armstrong, E. 1983 Relative brain size and metabolism in mammals. *Science* **220**, 1302–1304. (doi:10.1126/science.6407108)

Arnason, U., Gullberg, A. & Janke, A. 2004 Mitogenomic analysis provides new insights into cetacean origin and evolution. *Gene* **333**, 27–34. (doi:10.1016/j.gene.2004.02.010)

Backwell, P. R. Y., Jennions, M. D., Christy, J. H. & Passmore, N. I. 1999 Female choice in the synchronously waving fiddler crab *Uca annulipes*. *Ethology* **105**, 415–421. (doi:10.1046/j.1439-0310.1999.00387.x)

Barrett, L., Henzi, P. & Dunbar, R. I. M. 2003 Primate cognition: from 'what now?' to 'what if?' *Trends Cogn. Sci.* **7**, 494–497. (doi:10.1016/j.tics.2003.09.005)

Barton, R. A. 1996 Neocortex size and behavioural ecology in primates. *Proc. R. Soc. B* **263**, 173–177. (doi:10.1098/rspb.1996.0028)

Bassoi, M. 2005. Feeding ecology of franciscana dolphin, *Pontoporia blainvillei* (Cetacea: Pontoporiidae), and oceanographic processes on the southern Brazilian coast. Ph.D. thesis, p. 190. University of Southampton, Faculty of Engineering Science and Mathematics, School of Ocean and Earth Science.

Benoit-Bird, K. J. & Au, W. W. L. 2003 Prey dynamics affect foraging by a pelagic predator (*Stenella longirostris*) over a range of spatial and temporal scales. *Behav. Ecol. Sociobiol.* **53**, 364–373.

Best, R. C. & da Silva, V. M. F. 1989 Amazon river dolphin, boto, *Inia geoffrensis* (de Blainville, 1817). In *Handbook of marine mammals*, vol. 4 (eds S. H. Ridgway & R. Harrison). *River dolphins and the larger toothed whales*, pp. 1–23. New York, NY: Academic Press.

Burdin, V. I., Reznik, A. M., Skornyakov, V. M. & Chupakov, A. G. 1975 Communication signals of the Black Sea bottlenose dolphin. *Sov. Phys. Acoust.* **20**, 314–318.

Byrne, R. W. 2005 Social cognition: imitation, imitation, imitation. *Curr. Biol.* **15**, R496–R500.

Byrne, R. W. & Russon, A. E. 1998 Learning by imitation: a hierarchical approach. *Behav. Brain Sci.* **21**, 667–721. (doi:10.1017/S0140525X98001745)

Caldwell, M. C. & Caldwell, D. K. 1965 Individual whistle contours in bottlenose dolphins (*Tursiops truncatus*). *Nature* **207**, 434–435. (doi:10.1038/207434a0)

Caldwell, M. C., Caldwell, D. K. & Tyack, P. L. 1990 Review of the signature–whistle hypothesis for the Atlantic bottlenose dolphin. In *The bottlenosed dolphin* (eds S. Leatherwood & R. R. Reeves), pp. 199–234. San Diego, CA: Academic Press.

Call, J. & Carpenter, M. 2002 Three sources of information in social learning. In *Imitation in animals and artifacts* (eds K. Dautenhahn & C. L. Nehaniv), pp. 211–228. Cambridge, MA: MIT Press.

Cassens, I. *et al.* 2000 Independent adaptation to riverine habitats allowed survival of ancient cetacean lineages. *Proc. Natl Acad. Sci. USA* **97**, 11 343–11 347. (doi:10.1073/pnas.97.21.11343)

Clauss, M., Loehlein, W., Kienzle, E. & Weisner, H. 2003 Studies on feed digestibilities in captive Asian elephants (*Elephas maximus*). *J. Anim. Physiol. Anim. Nutr.* **87**, 160–173.

Clutton-Brock, T. H. & Harvey, P. H. 1980 Primates, brains and ecology. *J. Zool.* **190**, 309–323.

Connor, R. C. 2000 Group living in whales and dolphins. In *Cetacean societies: field studies of whales and dolphins* (eds J. Mann, R. Connor, P. Tyack & H. Whitehead), pp. 199–218. Chicago, IL: University of Chicago Press.

Connor, R. C. 2001 Individual foraging specializations in marine mammals: culture and ecology. *Behav. Brain Sci.* **24**, 329–330. (doi:10.1017/S0140525X01283964)

Connor, R. C. & Krützen, M. 2003 Levels and patterns in dolphin alliance formation. In *Animal social complexity: intelligence, culture, and individualized societies* (eds F. B. M. de Waal & P. L. Tyack), pp. 115–120. Cambridge, MA: Harvard University Press.

Connor, R. C. & Mann, J. 2006 Social cognition in the wild: Machiavellian dolphins? In *Rational animals?* (eds S. Hurley & M. Nudds), pp. 329–367. Oxford, UK: Oxford University Press.

Connor, R. C. & Norris, K. S. 1982 Are dolphins reciprocal altruists? *Am. Nat.* **119**, 358–374. (doi:10.1086/283915)

Connor, R. C. & Smolker, R. A. 1996 "Pop" goes the dolphin: a vocalization male bottlenose dolphins produce during consortships. *Behaviour* **133**, 643–662.

Connor, R. C. & Whitehead, H. 2005 Alliances II: rates of encounter during resource utilization: a general model of intrasexual alliance formation in fission–fusion societies. *Anim. Behav.* **69**, 127–132. (doi:10.1016/j.anbehav.2004.02.022)

Connor, R. C., Smolker, R. A. & Richards, A. F. 1992*a* Dolphin alliances and coalitions. In *Coalitions and alliances in animals and humans* (eds A. H. Harcourt & F. B. M. de Waal), pp. 415–443. Oxford, UK: Oxford University Press.

Connor, R. C., Smolker, R. A. & Richards, A. F. 1992*b* Two levels of alliance formation among male bottlenose dolphins (*Tursiops* sp.). *Proc. Natl Acad. Sci. USA* **89**, 987–990. (doi:10.1073/pnas.89.3.987)

Connor, R. C., Richards, A. F., Smolker, R. A. & Mann, J. 1996 Patterns of female attractiveness in Indian Ocean bottlenose dolphins. *Behaviour* **133**, 37–69.

Connor, R. C., Mann, J., Tyack, P. L. & Whitehead, H. 1998 Social evolution in toothed whales. *Trends Ecol. Evol.* **13**, 228–232. (doi:10.1016/S0169-5347(98)01326-3)

Connor, R. C., Heithaus, M. R. & Barre, L. M. 1999 Super-alliance of bottlenose dolphins. *Nature* **371**, 571–572. (doi:10.1038/17501)

Connor, R. C., Wells, R., Mann, J. & Read, A. 2000 The bottlenose dolphin: social relationships in a fission–fusion society. In *Cetacean societies: field studies of whales and dolphins* (eds J. Mann, R. Connor, P. Tyack & H. Whitehead), pp. 91–126. Chicago, IL: University of Chicago Press.

Connor, R. C., Heithaus, M. R. & Barre, L. M. 2001 Complex social structure, alliance stability and mating access in a bottlenose dolphin 'super-alliance'. *Proc. R. Soc. B* **268**, 263–267. (doi:10.1098/rspb.2000.1357)

Connor, R. C., Smolker, R. A. & Bejder, L. 2006 Synchrony, social behaviour & alliance affiliation in Indian Ocean bottlenose dolphins (*Tursiops aduncus*). *Anim. Behav.* **72**, 1371–1378. (doi:10.1016/j.anbehav.2006.03.014)

Connor, R.C., Bejder, L., Randic, S., *et al.* In preparation. The number of social relationships in an open fission–fusion society.

Cords, M. 1997 Friendships, alliances, reciprocity and repair. In *Machiavellian intelligence II: extensions and evaluations* (eds A. Whiten & R. W. Byrne), pp. 24–49. Cambridge, UK: Cambridge University Press.

Dawson, W. W. 1980 The cetacean eye. In *Cetacean behavior: mechanisms and functions* (ed. L. Herman), pp. 53–100. New York, NY: Wiley.

Deaner, R. O., Barton, R. A. & van Schaik, C. P. 2003 Primate brains and life histories: renewing the connection. In *Primate life histories and socioecology* (eds P. M. Kappeler & M. E. Periera), pp. 233–265. Chicago, IL: University of Chicago Press.

Drea, C. M. & Frank, L. G. 2003 The social complexity of spotted hyenas. In *Animal social complexity: intelligence, culture, and individualized societies* (eds F. B. M. de Waal & P. L. Tyack), pp. 121–148. Cambridge, MA: Harvard University Press.

Dunbar, R. I. M. 1992 Neocortex size as a constraint on group size in primates. *J. Hum. Evol.* **22**, 469–493. (doi:10.1016/0047-2484(92)90081-J)

Dunbar, R. I. M. 2003 The social brain: mind, language, and society in evolutionary perspective. *Ann. Rev. Anthropol.* **32**, 163–181. (doi:10.1146/annurev.anthro.32.061002.093158)

Engh, A. L. & Holekamp, K. E. 2003 Maternal rank inheritance in the spotted hyena. In *Social complexity* (eds F. B. M. de Wall & P. L. Tyack), pp. 149–152. Cambridge, MA: Harvard University Press.

Engh, A. L., Siebert, E. R., Greenberg, D. A. & Holekamp, K. E. 2005 Patterns of alliance formation and post-conflict aggression indicate spotted hyenas recognize third party relationships. *Anim. Behav.* **69**, 209–217. (doi:10.1016/j.anbehav.2004.04.013)

Flynn, M. V., Geary, D. C. & Ward, C. V. 2005 Ecological dominance, social competition, and coalition-ary arms races: why humans evolved extraordinary intelligence. *Evol. Hum. Behav.* **26**, 10–46. (doi:10.1016/j.evolhumbehav.2004.08.005)

Gazda, S., Connor, R. C., Edgar, R. & Cox, F. 2005 A division of labor with role specialization in group-hunting bottlenose dolphins (*Tursiops truncatus*) off Cedar Key, Florida. *Proc. R. Soc. B* **272**, 135–140. (doi:10.1098/rspb.2004.2937)

Hagen, E. H. & Bryant, G. A. 2003 Music and dance as a coalition signaling system. *Hum. Nat.* **14**, 21–51.

Hamilton, H., Caballero, S., Collins, A. G. & Brownell Jr, R. L. 2001 Evolution of river dolphins. *Proc. R. Soc. B* **268**, 549–558. (doi:10.1098/rspb.2000.1385)

Harcourt, A. H. 1988 Alliances in contests and social intelligence. In *Machiavellian intelligence* (eds R. W. Byrne & A. Whiten), pp. 132–152. Oxford, UK: Clarendon Press.

Harcourt, A. H. 1992 Coalitions and alliances: are primates more complex than non-primates? In *Coalitions and alliances in humans and other animals* (eds A. H. Harcourt & F. B. M. deWaal), pp. 445–471. Oxford, UK: Oxford University Press.

Herman, L. H. 2002 Vocal, social, and self-imitation by bottlenosed dolphins. In *Imitation in animals and artifacts* (eds K. Dautenhahn & C. L. Nehaniv), pp. 63–108. Cambridge, MA: MIT Press.

Herman, L. H. 2006 Intelligence and rational behaviour in the bottlenosed dolphin. In *Rational animals?* (eds S. Hurley & M. Nudds), pp. 439–468. Oxford, UK: Oxford University Press.

Herman, L. M. & Tavolga, W. N. 1980 The communication systems of cetaceans. In *Cetacean behavior: mechanisms and functions* (ed. L. M. Herman), pp. 149–209. New York, NY: Wiley.

Heyning, J. E. 1997 Sperm whale phologeny revisited: analysis of the morphological evidence. *Mar. Mammal Sci.* **13**, 596–613. (doi:10.1111/j.1748-7692.1997.tb00086.x)

Humphrey, N. K. 1976 The social function of intellect. In *Growing points in ethology* (eds P. P. G. Bateson & R. A. Hinde), pp. 303–317. Cambridge, UK: Cambridge University Press.

Janik, V. M. 2000 Whistle matching in wild bottlenose dolphins (*Tursiops truncatus*). *Science* **289**, 1355–1357. (doi:10.1126/science.289.5483.1355)

Janik, V. M. & Slater, P. J. B. 1998 Context-specific use suggests that bottlenose dolphin signature whistles are cohesion calls. *Anim. Behav.* **56**, 829–838. (doi:10.1006/anbe.1998.0881)

Janik, V. M., Sayigh, L. S. & Wells, R. S. 2006 Signature whistle shape conveys identity information to bottlenose dolphins. *Proc. Natl Acad. Sci. USA* **103**, 8293–8297. (doi:10.1073/pnas.0509918103)

Janson, C. H. & Goldsmith, M. 1995 Predicting group size in primates: foraging costs and predation risks. *Behav. Ecol.* **6**, 326–336.

Jerison, H. J. 1973. *Evolution of the brain and intelligence.* New York, NY: Academic Press.

Jerison, H. J. 1978 In *Brain and intelligence in whales*, vol. 2 (ed. S. Frost). *Whales and whaling*, pp. 159–197. Canberra, Australia: Australian Government Publication Service.

Krützen, M., Sherwin, W. B., Connor, R. C., Barré, L. M., Van de Casteele, T., Mann, J. & Brooks, R. 2003 Contrasting relatedness patterns in bottlenose dolphins (*Tursiops* sp.) with different alliance strategies. *Proc. R. Soc. B* **270**, 497–502. (doi:10.1098/rspb.2002.2229)

Krützen, M., Sherwin, W. B., Berggren, P. & Gales, N. J. 2004 Population structure in an inshore ceta-cean revealed by microsatellite and mtDNA analysis: bottlenose dolphins (*Tursiops* sp.) in Shark Bay, Western Australia. *Mar. Mammal Sci.* **20**, 28–47. (doi:10.1111/j.1748-7692.2004.tb01139.x)

Kummer, H. 1967 Tripartite relations in hamadryas baboons. In *Social communication among primates* (ed. S. A. Altman), pp. 63–71. Chicago, IL: University of Chicago Press.

Lammers, M. O. & Au, W. W. L. 2003 Directionality in the whistles of Hawaiian spinner dolphins (*Stenella longirostris*): a signal feature to cue direction of movement? *Mar. Mammal Sci.* **19**, 249–264. (doi:10.1111/j.1748-7692.2003.tb01107.x)

Madsen, C. J. & Herman, L. M. 1980 Social and ecological correlates of vision and visual appearance. In *Cetacean behaviour: mechanisms and functions* (ed. L. M. Herman), pp. 101–147. New York, NY: Wiley.

Manger, P. R. 2006 An examination of cetacean brain structure with a novel hypothesis correlating thermogenesis to the evolution of a big brain. *Biol. Rev.* **81**, 293–338. (doi:10.1017/S1464793106007019)

Mann, J. & Sargeant, B. 2003 Like mother, like calf: the ontogeny of foraging traditions in wild Indian Ocean bottlenose dolphins (*Tursiops* sp.). In *The biology of traditions: models and evidence* (eds D. Fragaszy & S. Perry), pp. 236–266. Cambridge, UK: Cambridge University Press.

Mann, J., Connor, R. C., Barre, L. M. & Heithaus, M. R. 2000 Female reproductive success in bottlenose dolphins (*Tursiops* sp.): life history, habitat, provisioning, and group size effects. *Behav. Ecol.* **11**, 210–219. (doi:10.1093/beheco/11.2.210)

Manson, J. & Wrangham, R. W. 1991 Intergroup aggression in chimpanzees and humans. *Curr. Anthropol.* **32**, 369–390. (doi:10.1086/203974)

Marino, L. 1998 A comparison of encephalization between odontocete cetaceans and anthropoid primates. *Brain Behav. Evol.* **51**, 230–238. (doi:10.1159/000006540)

Marino, L., McShea, D. W. & Uhen, M. D. 2004 Origin and evolution of large brains in toothed whales. *Anat. Rec.* **281A**, 1247–1255. (doi:10.1002/ar.a.20128)

Martin, R. D. 1980 Adaptation and body size in primates. *Z. Morph. Anthrop.* **71**, 115–124.

Martin, R. D. 1981 Relative brain size and basal metabolic rate in terrestrial vertebrates. *Nature* **293**, 57–60. (doi:10.1038/293057a0)

Martin, R. D. 1982 Allometric approaches to the evolution of the primate nervous system. In *Primate brain evolution: methods and concepts* (eds E. Armstrong & D. Falk), pp. 39–56. New York, NY: Plenum Press.

Martin, R. D. 1983 *Human brain evolution in an ecological context. 52nd James Arthur lecture on the evolution of the human brain, 1982.* New York, NY: American Museum of Natural History.

Martin, R. D. & Harvey, P. H. 1985 Brain size allometry: ontogeny and phylogeny. In *Size and scaling in primate biology* (ed. W. L. Jungers), pp. 147–173. New York, NY: Plenum Press.

Matthews, J. N., Rendell, L. E., Gordon, J. C. D. & Macdonald, D. W. 1999 A review of frequency and time parameters of cetacean tonal calls. *Bioacoustics* **10**, 47–71.

McNab, B. K. & Eisenberg, J. F. 1989 Brain size and its relation to the rate of metabolism in mammals. *Am. Nat.* **133**, 157–167. (doi:10.1086/284907)

McNeill, W. M. 1995. *Keeping together in time: dance and drill in human history.* Cambridge, MA: Harvard University Press.

Miksis, J. L., Tyack, P. L. & Buck, J. R. 2002 Captive dolphins, *Tursiops truncatus*, develop signature whistles that match acoustic features of human-made model sounds. *J. Acoust. Soc. Am.* **112**, 728–739. (doi:10.1121/1.1496079)

Milton, K. & Demment, M. 1988 Digestive and passage kinetics of chimpanzees fed high-and low-fiber diets and comparison with human data. *J. Nutr.* **118**, 1–7.

Möller, L. M. & Beheregaray, L. B. 2004 Genetic evidence of sex-biased dispersal in resident bottlenose dolphins (*Tursiops aduncus*). *Mol. Ecol.* **13**, 1607–1612. (doi:10.1111/j.1365-294X.2004.02137.x)

Nikaido, M. *et al.* 2001 Retroposon analysis of major cetacean lineages: the monophyly of toothed whales and the paraphyly of river dolphins. *Proc. Natl Acad. Sci. USA* **98**, 7384–7389. (doi:10.1073/pnas.121139198)

Noë, R. 1990 A veto game played by baboons: a challenge to the use of the prisoner's dilemma as a paradigm for reciprocity and cooperation. *Anim. Behav.* **39**, 78–90. (doi:10.1016/S0003-3472(05)80728-6)

Norris, K. S. & Schilt, C. R. 1988 Cooperative societies in three-dimensional space: on the origin of aggregations, flocks, and schools, with special reference to dolphins and fish. *Ethol. Sociobiol.* **9**, 149–179. (doi:10.1016/0162-3095(88)90019-2)

Oftedal, O. T. 1991 The nutritional consequences of foraging in primates: the relationship of nutrient intakes to nutrient requirements. *Phil. Trans. R. Soc. B* **334**, 161–170. (doi:10.1098/rstb.1991.0105)

Orban, G. A., Fize, D., Peuskens, H., Denys, K., Nelissen, K., Sunaert, S., Todd, J. & Vanduffel, V. 2003 Similarities and differences in motion processing between the human and macaque brain: evidence from fMRI. *Neuropsychologia* **41**, 1757–1768. (doi:10.1016/S0028-3932(03)00177-5)

Packer, C. & Pusey, A. 1987 Intrasexual cooperation and the sex ratio in African lions. *Am. Nat.* **130**, 636–642. (doi:10.1086/284735)

Pagel, M. D. & Harvey, P. H. 1988 How mammals produce large-brained offspring. *Evolution* **42**, 948–957. (doi:10.2307/2408910)

Pagel, M. D. & Harvey, P. H. 1989 Taxonomic differences in the scaling of brain on body weight among mammals. *Science* **24**, 1589–1593.

Paukner, A., Anderson, J. R., Borelli, E., Visalberghi, E. & Ferrari, P. F. 2005 Macaques (*Macaca nemestrina*) recognize when they are being imitated. *Biol. Lett.* **1**, 219–222. (doi:10.1098/rsbl.2004.0291)

Peixun, C. 1918 In *Bajii–Lipotes vexillifer Miller, 1918*, vol. 4 (eds S. H. Ridgway & R. Harrison). *Handbook of marine mammals*, pp. 25–43. London, UK: Academic Press.

Pilleri, G., Gihr, M., Purves, P. E., Zbinden, K. & Kraus, C. 1976 On the behaviour, bioacoustics and functional morphology of the Indus river dolphin (*Platanista indi* Blyth, 1859). *Investig. Cetacea* **6**, 13–141.

Podos, J., da Silva, V. M. F. & Rossi-Santos, M. R. 2002 Vocalization of Amazon river dolphins, *Inia geoffrensis*: insights into the evolutionary origins of delphinid whistles. *Ethology* **108**, 601–612. (doi:10.1046/j.1439-0310.2002.00800.x)

Ransom, T. 1981. *Beach troop of the Gombe*. East Brunswick, NJ: Associated University Presses.

Read, A. F. & Harvey, P. H. 1989 Life history differences among the eutherian radiations. *J. Zool. (London)* **214**, 199–219.

Reader, S. K. & Laland, K. 2002 Social intelligence, innovation and enhanced brain size in primates. *Proc. Natl Acad. Sci. USA* **99**, 4436–4441. (doi:10.1073/pnas.062041299)

Reiss, D. & McCowan, B. 1993 Spontaneous vocal mimicry and production by bottlenose dolphins (*Tursiops truncatus*): evidence for vocal learning. *J. Comp. Psychol.* **3**, 301–312. (doi:10.1037/0735-7036.107.3.301)

Rendell, L. & Whitehead, H. 2001 Culture in whales and dolphins. *Behav. Brain Sci.* **24**, 309–382. (doi:10.1017/ S0140525X0100396X)

Richards, D. G., Wolz, J. P. & Herman, L. M. 1984 Vocal mimicry of computer generated sounds and vocal labeling of objects by a bottlenose dolphin, *Tursiops truncatus*. *J. Comp. Psychol.* **98**, 10–28. (doi:10.1037/0735-7036.98.1.10)

Ridgway, S. H. 1990 The central nervous system of the bottlenose dolphin. In *The bottlenose dolphin, Tursiops spp.* (eds S. Leatherwood & R. Reeves), pp. 69–97. New York, NY: Academic Press.

Ridgway, S. H. 2000 The auditory central nervous system of dolphins. In *Hearing in whales and dolphins* (eds W. W. L. Au, A. N. Popper & R. R. Fay), pp. 273–293. New York, NY: Springer.

Ridgway, S. H. & Johnston, D. G. 1966 Blood oxygen and ecology of porpoises of three genera. *Science* **151**, 456–458. (doi:10.1126/science.151.3709.456)

Rodseth, L., Wrangham, R. W., Harrigan, A. M. & Smuts, B. B. 1991 The human community as a primate society. *Curr. Anthropol.* **32**, 221–254. (doi:10.1086/203952)

Sacher, G. A. 1959 Relation of lifespan to brain weight and body weight in mammals. In *The lifespan of animals*, vol. 5 (eds G. E. W. Wolstenholme & M. O'Connor). *CIBA Foundation Colloquia on Ageing*, pp. 115–133. Boston, MA: Little, Brown.

Sacher, G. A. & Staffeldt, E. F. 1974 Relation of gestation time to brain weight for placental mammals: implications for the theory of vertebrate growth. *Am. Nat.* **108**, 593–615. (doi:10.1086/282938)

Sayigh, L. S., Tyack, P. L., Wells, R. S., Scott, M. D. & Irvine, A. B. 1995 Sex difference in whistle production in free-ranging bottlenose dolphins, *Tursiops truncatus*. *Behav. Ecol. Sociobiol.* **36**,171–177.(doi:10.1007/s002650050137)

Sayigh, L. S., Tyack, P. L., Wells, R. S., Solow, A., Scott, M. & Irvine, A. B. 1999 Individual recognition in wild bottlenose dolphins: a field test using playback experiments. *Anim. Behav.* **57**, 41–50. (doi:10.1006/anbe.1998.0961)

Schusterman, R. J., Reichmuth-Kastak, C. & Kastak, D. 2003 Equivalence classification as an approach to social knowledge: from sea lions to simians. In *Animal social complexity: intelligence, culture, and individualized societies* (eds F. B. M. deWaal & P. L. Tyack), pp. 179–206. Cambridge, MA: Harvard University Press.

Seyfarth, R. M. & Cheney, D. L. 1999 What are big brains for? *Proc. Natl Acad. Sci. USA* **99**, 4141–4142. (doi:10.1073/pnas.082105099)

Shapunov, V. M. 1973 Food requirements and energy balance in the Black Sea bottlenose dolphin (*Tursiops truncatus ponticus* Barabasch). In *Morphology & ecology of marine mammals* (eds K. K. Chapskii & V. E. Solokov), pp. 207–212. New York, NY: Wiley.

Silk, J. B. 2003 Genetic and cultural evolution of cooperation. In *Genetic and cultural evolution of cooperation* (ed. P. Hammerstein). Cambridge, MA: MIT Press.

Simila, T. & Ugarte, F. 1993 Surface and underwater observations of cooperatively feeding killer whales in northern Norway. *Can. J. Zool.* **71**, 494–499.

Smolker, R. A. & Pepper, J. 1999 Whistle convergence among allied male bottlenose dolphins (Delphinidae, *Tursiops* sp.). *Ethology* **105**, 595–617. (doi:10.1046/j.1439-0310.1999.00441.x)

Smolker, R. A., Richards, A. F., Connor, R. C. & Pepper, J. 1992 Association patterns among bottlenose dolphins in Shark Bay, Western Australia. *Behaviour* **123**, 38–69.

Smolker, R. A., Mann, J. & Smuts, B. B. 1993 The use of signature whistles during separations and reunions among wild bottlenose dolphin mothers and calves. *Behav. Ecol. Sociobiol.* **33**, 393–402. (doi:10.1007/BF00170254)

Smolker, R. A., Richards, A. F., Connor, R. C. & Mann, J. 1997 Sponge carrying by dolphins (Delphinidae *Tursiops* sp.): a foraging specialization involving tool use? *Ethology* **103**, 454–465.

Sterns, S. 1992 *The evolution of life histories*. Oxford, UK: Oxford University Press.

Strickler, T. L. 1978 Myology of the shoulder of *Pontoporia blainvillei*, including a review of the literature on shoulder morphology in the cetacea. *Am. J. Anat.* **152**, 419–432. (doi:10.1002/aja.1001520310)

Tavolga, M. C. & Essapian, F. S. 1957 The behavior of the bottle-nosed dolphin (*Tursiops truncatus*): mating, pregnancy, parturition and mother–infant behaviour. *Zoologica* **42**, 11–31.

Tyack, P. 1986 Whistle repertoires of two bottlenose dolphins, *Tursiops truncatus:* mimicry of signature whistles? *Behav. Ecol. Sociobiol.* **18**, 251–257. (doi:10.1007/BF00300001)

Tyack, P. 1997 Development and social functions of signature whistles in bottlenose dolphins *Tursiops truncatus*. *Bioacoustics* **8**, 21–46.

van Schaik, C. P. 2004 *Among orangutans: red apes and the rise of human culture*. Cambridge, MA: Belknap/Harvard University Press.

van Schaik, C. P. & Deaner, R. O. 2003 Life history and brain evolution. In *Animal social complexity: intelligence, culture, and individualized societies* (eds F. B. M. de Waal & P. L. Tyack), pp. 1–25. Cambridge, MA: Harvard University Press.

van Schaik, C. P., Ancrenaz, M., Borgen, G., Galdikas, B., Knott, C. D., Singleton, I., Suzuki, A., Utami, S. S. & Merrill, M. Y. 2003 Orangutan cultures and the evolution of material culture. *Science* **299**, 102–105. (doi:10.1126/science.1078004)

Visalberghi, E. & Fragaszy, D. 2002 "Do monkeys ape"—ten years after. In *Imitation in animals and artifacts* (eds K. Dautenhahn & C. L. Nehaniv), pp. 471–499. Cambridge, MA: MIT Press.

Wahaj, S. A. & Holekamp, K. E. 2003 Conflict resolution in the spotted hyena. In *Animal social complexity* (eds F. B. M. de Waal & P. L. Tyack), pp. 249–253. Cambridge, MA: Harvard University Press.

Walls, G. 1942 *Vertebrate eye and its adaptive radiation*. New York, NY: McGraw-Hill.

Watwood, S. L., Tyack, P. L. & Wells, R. S. 2004 Whistle sharing in paired male bottlenose dolphins, *Tursiops truncatus*. *Behav. Ecol. Sociobiol.* **55**, 531–543. (doi:10.1007/s00265-003-0724-y)

Weihs, D. 2004 The hydrodynamics of dolphin drafting. *J. Biol.* **3**, 1–16. (doi:10.1186/jbiol2)

Weilgart, L., Whitehead, H. & Payne, K. 1996 A colossal convergence. *Am. Sci.* **84**, 278–287.

Wells, R. S. 1991 The role of long-term study in understanding the social structure of a bottlenose dolphin community. In *Dolphin societies: discoveries and puzzles* (eds K. Pryor & K. S. Norris), pp. 199–225. Berkeley, CA: University of California Press.

Wells, R. S. 2003 Dolphin social complexity: lessons from long-term study and life history. In *Dolphin social complexity: lessons from long-term study and life history* (eds F. B. M. de Waal & P. L Tyack) *Animal social complexity*, pp. 32–56. Cambridge, MA: Harvard University Press.

Wells, R. S., Scott, M. D. & Irvine, A. B. 1987 The social structure of free-ranging bottlenose dolphins. In *Current mammalogy*, vol. 1 (ed. H. Genoways), pp. 247–305. New York, NY: Plenum Press.

Whitehead, H. 1996 Variation in the feeding success of sperm whales: temporal scale spatial scale and relationship to migrations. *J. Anim. Ecol.* **65**, 429–438. (doi:10.2307/5778)

Whitehead, H. 1999 Culture and genetic evolution in whales. *Science* **284**, 2055. (doi:10.1126/science.284.5423.2055a)

Whitehead, H. 2003 *Sperm whales: social evolution in the ocean.* Chicago, IL: University of Chicago Press.

Whitehead, H. & Connor, R. C. 2005 Alliances I: how large should alliances be? *Anim. Behav.* **69**, 117–126. (doi:10.1016/j.anbehav.2004.02.021)

Whiten, A., Horner, V., Litchfield, C. & Marshall-Pescini, S. 2004 How do apes ape? *Learn. Behav.* **32**, 36–52.

Williams, T. M. 1999 The evolution of cost efficient swimming in marine mammals: limits to energetic optimization. *Phil. Trans. R. Soc. B* **354**, 193–201. (doi:10.1098/rstb.1999.0371)

Williams, T. M., Haun, J., Davis, R. W., Fuiman, L. & Kohin, S. 2001 A killer appetite: metabolic consequences of carnivory in marine mammals. G. L. Kooyman Symposium. *Comp. Biochem. Physiol. A* **129**, 785–796. (doi:10.1016/S1095-6433(01)00347-6)

Wrangham, R. W., Jones, J. H., Laden, G., Pilbeam, D. & Conklin-Brittain, N. 1999 The raw and the stolen: cooking and the ecology of human origins. *Curr. Anthropol.* **40**, 567–594. (doi:10.1086/300083)

Wursig, B. 1980 The behavior and ecology of the dusky dolphin, *Lagenorhynchus obscurus*, in the South Atlantic. *Fish. Bull.* **77**, 781–790.

Zahavi, A. 1977 The testing of a bond. *Anim. Behav.* **25**, 246–247. (doi:10.1016/0003-3472(77)90089-6)

8

The evolution of animal 'cultures' and social intelligence

Andrew Whiten and Carel P. van Schaik

Decades-long field research has flowered into integrative studies that, together with experimental evidence for the requisite social learning capacities, have indicated a reliance on multiple traditions ('cultures') in a small number of species. It is increasingly evident that there is great variation in manifestations of social learning, tradition and culture among species, offering much scope for evolutionary analysis. Social learning has been identified in a range of vertebrate and invertebrate species, yet sustained traditions appear rarer, and the multiple traditions we call cultures are rarer still. Here, we examine relationships between this variation and both social intelligence—sophisticated information processing adapted to the social domain—and encephalization. First, we consider whether culture offers one particular confirmation of the social ('Machiavellian') intelligence hypothesis that certain kinds of social life (here, culture) select for intelligence: 'you need to be smart to sustain culture'. Phylogenetic comparisons, particularly focusing on our own study animals, the great apes, support this, but we also highlight some paradoxes in a broader taxonomic survey. Second, we use intraspecific variation to address the converse hypothesis that 'culture makes you smart', concluding that recent evidence for both chimpanzees and orang-utans support this proposition.

Keywords: social intelligence; social learning; tradition; culture; brain size

8.1 Introduction

The study of animal social intelligence has a pedigree of several decades (Whiten & Byrne 1988*a*, 1997, 2004), but has flourished in recent years through an exciting expansion of discoveries discussed throughout this issue. The topics of the present paper, spanning social learning, traditions and culture, have an arguably more ancient pedigree of over a century (Whiten & Ham 1992; Avital & Jablonka 2000 for reviews), yet recent years have likewise seen an enormous flowering of new knowledge in these areas. A diverse range of developments has been responsible for this, ranging from the coming-to-fruition of numerous long-term studies of specific species at different geographical locations, through the development of more refined experimental techniques, to advances in brain science and robotics. Up-to-date surveys of the resulting broad-ranging field can be found in Fragaszy & Perry (2003); *Evolutionary Anthropology* vol. 12, whole issues 2 & 3 (2003); Galef & Heyes (2004); Hurley & Chater (2005); Mesoudi *et al.* (2006*b*).

How does research in these domains relate to the topic of social intelligence? To a first approximation, the answer is that if social intelligence is taken to refer broadly to adaptive social information processing then the kinds of social learning implicated in the transmission of tradition and culture answer to this requirement. However, both of these terms, 'social intelligence' and 'social learning', cover an enormous range and diversity of phenomena. Accordingly, we begin by briefly examining the scope of each in turn and anticipating some possible links between them.

(a) What is the scope of 'social intelligence'?

If we can define intelligence then the rest is relatively easy, for social intelligence is essentially the intelligence applied to the social world. If, for example, we define intelligence as problem-solving ability, then social intelligence refers to a capacity to solve novel problems in one's social life. However, 'intelligence' is itself a term applied in highly varied ways in the psychology literature, from speed of associative learning to reasoning and innovation (Passingham 1981; Weiskrantz 1985). We suggest this history means that intelligence is nowadays best treated as a relatively broadly defined umbrella term that connotes relatively sophisticated forms of information processing, each of which requires more specific definition and more focussed investigation to generate real scientific progress. According to this logic, 'social intelligence' connotes relatively complex forms of information processing applied to the social world, a concept that thus has inherently fuzzy edges.

An influential reason for interest in animal social intelligence lies in the notion first explicitly elaborated by Nicholas Humphrey, and before him in more tentative forms by Michael Chance and Alison Jolly (Whiten & Byrne 1988*a*), that has become known as the 'Machiavellian Intelligence Hypothesis' (MIH; Byrne & Whiten 1988) or the 'Social Intellect Hypothesis' (SIH; Kummer *et al.* 1997). In broad terms, the MIH was originally developed to explain the special intelligence attributed to monkeys and apes (Humphrey 1976) as adaptations for dealing with the distinctive complexities of their social lives, such as volatile social alliances. The term 'Machiavellian' was used by Byrne & Whiten (1988) to capture the central concept of adaptive social manoeuvring within groups made up of companions subject to similar pressures to be socially smart, and the spiralling selection pressures this implies. With time, these central ideas have been applied to a variety of different species thought to display the relevant kinds of social complexity, as is evident in the present issue.

Although these hypotheses are frequently referred to as *the* SIH or *the* MIH, each can be expressed in terms that have significantly different implications, which are perhaps too often forgotten or unappreciated. Whiten & Byrne (1988*b*) distinguished three different, increasingly specific hypotheses:

   (i) 'Intelligence is manifested in social life'. Historically, animal intelligence was investigated primarily in isolated individuals interacting with problems in the physical world, often in a laboratory setting. The mildest version of the MIH was simply that in reality, intelligence was to be observed operating also in certain animals' natural social worlds.
  (ii) 'Complex society selects for enhanced intelligence'. This hypothesis proposes that there is something particularly challenging about the complexities of social life that select for greater intelligence. Here, 'intelligence' is regarded as a domain-general capacity (as in 'g'; Jensen 2000), contrasting with the third hypothesis.
 (iii) 'Complex society shapes the forms intelligence takes'. This version of the hypothesis suggests that social interactions may have special properties that select not for generalized intelligence, but for particular forms of intelligence. Social intelligence might thus incorporate several dimensions or modules, each adapted to deal with a special social problem domain. An example well researched since 1988 is 'theory of mind' or 'mentalizing', the capacity to discriminate states of mind in other social beings, the underlying brain mechanisms for which are now being charted (Frith & Frith 2003).

Nowadays, Hypothesis 1 can be considered to be accepted, perhaps to the point of being thought obvious (with hindsight!). Hypotheses 2 and 3 remain more interesting and actively controversial. The primary way in which the MIH has been empirically tested is by examining interspecific relationships between encephalization and (i) social variables such as group size (predicted by the MIH) and (ii) ecological variables such as home range size (predicted by the competing hypothesis that foraging constitutes a more important selection pressure for intelligence) (Barton & Dunbar 1997; Dunbar & Shultz 2007). In such analyses, brain size is assumed to offer a summary index of cognitive capacity. Variations on this approach that examine particular parts of the brain, such as the neocortex ratio (neocortex relative to the remainder; Dunbar 1998) are often attempts to focus on the most 'intelligent' components of the brain, rather than dissect subcomponents implicated in more specific functions that might become more apt for testing Hypothesis 3. Such neuro-anatomical approaches are relevant to our studies of culture, because parallel techniques have been applied to test relationships between encephalization and social learning, reviewed in §2a below.

In the case of culture, hypotheses of type 3 will most obviously address the question of whether in species for which acquiring (and perhaps transmitting) culture becomes important or takes particular forms, there will be selection pressures honing the nature and functional significance of the relevant social learning processes. In addition, social structure may interact with these, generating complex mutual selection pressures between (i) the forms of social living, (ii) culture, and (iii) social learning mechanisms.

(b) What is the scope of culture and how does it relate to social intelligence?

Many authors equate culture and tradition, using the terms interchangeably. Others make distinctions between them of various kinds, usually requiring additional criteria to classify a phenomenon as cultural. Accordingly, there appears to be more agreement on what counts as a tradition than there is in the case of culture. A recent volume on 'The Biology of Traditions' defined tradition as 'a distinctive behaviour pattern shared by two or more individuals in a social unit, which persists over time and that new practitioners acquire in part through socially aided learning' (Fragaszy & Perry 2003, p. xiii). This definition would probably be accepted by most researchers and we follow it here. Note that as indicated above, for many biologists, this definition of traditions will also be sufficient to define culture (Laland & Hoppitt 2003).

By contrast, authors for whom the existence of a tradition does not in itself warrant the ascription of culture typically require some additional characteristic(s) assumed to be associated with the complexity of traditions that constitute human culture. For example, Galef (1992), perhaps the most influential researcher in animal social learning, proposed that 'culture' be reserved for traditions transmitted by imitation or teaching, assumed to be high-level social learning processes that would imply homology with the human case. Others adopt different criteria such as that culture must accumulate complexity over time, as it has done so impressively in the human case; non-human species thus 'do not make the grade' (Levinson 2006, p. 10).[1]

Whether either imitation or teaching is crucial to support traditions, as Galef (1992) assumes, is an empirical issue not yet resolved (Whiten *et al.* 2003). Here, we focus on another distinction (although it may turn out to overlap much with Galef's in practice) that arises from the accumulating data on traditions in the animal kingdom, including the species we ourselves have studied (chimpanzees and orang-utans). This leads us to define culture as the possession of *multiple traditions, spanning different domains of behaviour*, such as for-aging techniques and social customs (Whiten 2005). We think that a distinction between the existence of a tradition *per se*, and culture defined by a certain *complexity* in traditions, may prove an instructive one for evolutionary studies because (i) it makes reference to perhaps the most fundamental features of any two contrasting human cultures—that each is differentiated from the other by a multitude of different and varied types of tradition and (ii) as Galef himself argued, a higher criterion is set for culture than for tradition *per se*, giving us two levels in relation to which we can pursue detailed comparative analyses. We discuss this in more depth in §2*b* below.

Whether one treats tradition and culture as synonyms or not, an essential component in each is that transmission of behaviour between individuals occurs through social learning, which provides the obvious focus point for examining culture in relation to the general topic of social intelligence. At first sight, this aspect of culture might not be thought to fit well the perspective on social intelligence connoted by the 'Machiavellian' tag earlier promoted by one of us. However, in analysing the scope of Machiavellian Intelligence, both Whiten & Byrne (1988*b*) and Byrne & Whiten (1997) argued for the productivity of taking a wide, permissive perspective on the variety of socio-cognitive adaptations through which an individual may exploit the potential benefits of its social world, as well as deal with the hostile aspects of it. Whiten & Byrne (1988*b*) and Whiten (2000) accordingly recognized numerous potential facets to Machiavellian Intelligence: social knowledge; discovery techniques; social curiosity; social problem solving; innovation; flexibility; social expertise; social play; mind-reading; and self-awareness. Imitation and culture were also explicitly included. In the same volume, Hauser (1988, p. 326) suggested that 'social learning allows many individuals to 'become intelligent'. The title of Russon's (1997) chapter 'Exploiting the expertise of others' in *Machiavellian Intelligence II* indicates pithily how social learning relates to the larger concept. Jolly's (1966) and Humphrey's (1976)foundational papers also frequently addressed the topics of imitation and culture, and it is notable that the largest section in the most recent compilation of 'animal social complexity' research (de Waal & Tyack 2003) is headed 'cultural transmission'.

(c) Exploring links between the evolution of culture and intelligence[2]

Social learning, tradition and culture can each be investigated in relation to the three different versions of the MIH outlined in §1a. In relation to Hypothesis 2, we may accordingly ask whether there is evidence consistent with the hypothesis that a certain complexity of social life—in this case, the scale and diversity of traditions and/or culture—selects for intelligence. In §2*a* below, we first describe recent research that tackles this question by testing for correlations between encephalization and the prevalence of social learning in different animal taxa, echoing earlier tests of the MIH. In §2*b*, we extend this focus to review the distribution of cultural complexity among animals, finding evidence for this in only a small set of species, all of which are relatively highly encephalized.

In relation to Hypothesis 3, we can take a further step of asking whether there is evidence that complexity of culture selects for more sophisticated forms of social learning. We do this in §2*c*, focusing particularly on great apes, for which a suite of experimental studies has now been completed.

In addition to these hypotheses framed in relation to evolutionary selection processes, the phenomenon of culture raises the prospect of an ontogenetic version of the MIH, namely that being raised within a rich, accumulated culture can make an individual's ways of dealing with the world more intelligent: that 'culture can make you smart'. We are all familiar with this idea in human culture, for it is the basis of our educational systems. The idea becomes graphic when one compares a contemporary educated person with a person born with equivalent brain power just, say, 20 millennia in the past. Our present-day understanding of the world and the techniques available to us, for example, knowing the concept of the wheel and of horticulture (Mithen 2007), makes us truly smarter. In §3, we discuss evidence that in simpler ways, the same may be true in some non-human species. We attempt to complete the circle by discussing the evolutionary consequences of these ontogenetic effects on intelligence, suggesting that cultural species should more easily be able to reap the selective benefits of intelligence. This then links with the predictions of interspecific associations between culture and intelligence.

8.2 Is the evolution of social intelligence coupled with the evolution of traditions and culture?

(a) Encephalization and social learning in primates

The predictions of the MIH have mainly been tested against competing hypotheses by examining relationships between predictor variables such as social group size and indices of encephalization, with the outcomes increasingly supporting the MIH (Barton & Dunbar 1997; Dunbar 1998; but see Deaner *et al.* 2000). Early studies used social group size as a relatively crude proxy for social complexity (Dunbar 1995). More recent studies explored more refined measures. Thus, Kudo & Dunbar (2001) showed that the size of social cliques in a primate species was a good predictor of neocortex ratio (the ratio of the neocortex, generally implicated in higher mental processes, to the rest of the brain). Similarly, Byrne & Corp (2004) used the frequency of tactical deception (Whiten & Byrne 1988*c*), corrected for research effort, and found a strong relationship with neocortex ratio.

Reader & Laland (2002) have now extended this approach to include social learning and other related variables among primates, with interesting results. Reader and Laland scanned the primate literature, including approximately 1000 primate journal articles and other sources, extracting 445 reports of social learning, 533 reports of innovation and 607 reports of tool use, concerning 116 species of primate. They then examined relationships between the frequency of such reports, corrected for research effort, and three measures of encephalization, such as the executive brain ratio, which computes the ratio of the 'executive brain' (neocortex and striatum) to the brainstem. The use of several alternative brain indices, together with analysis through both correlation of raw data for all species, and more refined independent contrast methods that counter the risk of pseudo-replication arising from phylogenetic relatedness between species, added robustness to the conclusions of the study.

Of most relevance to the focus of the present paper, Reader and Laland found highly significant relationships between the prevalence of reports of social learning and executive brain ratio (figure 8.1). Similar correlations were also found for the frequency of innovation and tool use. In each case, the variance explained was remarkably high, with the highest $r^2 = 0.48$ for social learning, and $r^2 = 0.34$ and $r^2 = 0.40$ for innovation and tool use, respectively. Reader & Laland (2002, p. 4440) conclude these results 'suggest an alternative social intelligence hypothesis to those stressing the Machiavellian characteristics of mind-reading, manipulation, and deception', especially since they found no correlation between social group size (as mentioned above, a commonly used proxy for social complexity) and social learning

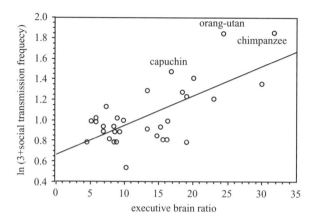

Fig. 8.1 Social learning and encephalization in primates. Frequency of social learning in the survey of Reader & Laland (2002) is plotted against executive brain ratio (see text for further explanation). Labels added here refer to three species with complex cultures discussed extensively in the text.

frequency; instead, 'individuals capable of inventing new solutions to ecological challenges, or exploiting the discoveries and inventions of others, may have had a selective advantage over less able conspecifics, which generated selection for those brain regions that facilitate complex technical and social behaviour'. These conclusions thus do not support the proposition that social factors were more powerful than non-social in brain evolution; rather, they implicate a cognitive complex involving both innovation and social learning in the emergence of large brains among primates. This is an important finding in relation to the topic of this paper, for it is in the nature of culture to require both innovations and social learning processes, the latter being powerful enough to turn innovations into traditions. We will return to this in §3.

A recent Bayesian analysis of numerous studies of primate cognition found that species could be ranked on a single dimension of cognitive ability (Johnson *et al.* 2002). Deaner *et al.* (in press) found that this general cognitive ability was best predicted by absolute brain size, with the frequently used neocortex ratio a close second, indicating that these measures are reasonably good interspecific predictors of 'intelligence'. Together with Reader & Laland's (2002) finding that both innovation and social learning are correlated with an expansion of the executive brain in primates (and innovation also predicted neocortex ratio), these results suggest that innovation (as a form of intelligence), social learning (as a form of social intelligence) and encephalization evolved in concert. These are important results, although the indirect estimation of innovation and social learning tendencies, much of which relies on observers' judgements rather than experimental evidence, means that additional ways should be sought to further test these tentative conclusions.

Some remarkably convergent results have been reported for birds by Lefebvre *et al.* (2004). Using a very similar approach, they assembled an even larger database of 1796 records of avian innovation and found that the best predictor of innovation was the relative size of the hyperstriatum ventrale and neostriatum, structures described as analogous to the mammalian neocortex (Rehkamper & Zilles 1991; but see Avian Brain Nomenclature Consortium 2005; Emery & Clayton 2005 for revised neuroanatomical nomenclatures). In large-brained birds, these regions show the largest increases in size, like the neocortex in mammals (Rehkamper *et al.* 1991).

Accordingly, in both mammals and birds, there is now evidence supporting a relationship between innovation and brain size.

Innovation, however, is but one half of what is required for traditions and culture: the other half is social learning. Lefebvre and colleagues did not investigate the relationship between social learning and encephalization, but the reason for this is itself of interest; the relevant data were relatively few. While there were 1796 observations of innovation, only 72 cases of social learning were recorded. This contrasts with the ratio of 558 cases of innovation and 451 of social learning in the primate study of Reader & Laland (2002). Lefebvre & Bouchard (2003, p. 110) conclude that 'what these relative numbers seem to suggest is that a feeding innovation does not as readily spread to others in birds at it does in primates', and that this appears to represent a paradox when contrasted with the fact that all 76 avian experimental studies they review successfully evoked social learning. We return to this puzzle in the concluding discussion.

(b) The evolution of cultural complexity

Reader & Laland's (2002) analysis did not explicitly examine traditions, but only social learning; nor did it examine the nature of the social learning. However, the picture of traditions and culture now emerging from decades of field research shows some interesting consistencies with their findings reviewed above.

Natural variations in behaviour in different communities of chimpanzees were increasingly recognized as likely traditions as field data accumulated, and began to be tabulated on the basis of published records (Goodall 1986; McGrew 1992; Boesch 1996; Boesch & Tomasello 1998). However, as Whiten et al. (1999) noted, reliance on published records generates an inevitably patchy and incomplete account. Instead, for the first time, Whiten and colleagues systematically pooled all the published and the unpublished information available from the most long-term study sites to identify as many as 39 traditions, defined as behaviour patterns common in at least one community, yet absent in at least one other, with no simple environmental explanation (such as that nut-cracking is absent because no suitable nuts are available). Identifying traditions in this way depends largely on integrating three sources of evidence: (i) exclusion of environmental or genetic explanations, which attribute the geographical variation to convergent individual learning or predispositions (clearest for many cases that involve differences between geographically close communities), (ii) relevant records of close, direct observation of adult expertise by novices, typically juveniles (Goodall 1973), and (iii) reliable background knowledge of the social learning propensities of chimpanzees, gained through controlled experiments (Tomasello & Call 1997).

Precisely the same approach was applied to orang-utans by van Schaik et al. (2003a), yielding a picture remarkably similar to that in the chimpanzee study in three important respects. First, traditions are numerous (19 clear cases plus a further 5 where ecological explanations could not be entirely excluded). Second, each community displays its own unique profile of traditions. Third, the traditions are of many different kinds, including tool use, foraging techniques, locomotory skills and social signals. Observational and experimental studies have also demonstrated a capacity for imitation and other forms of observational learning in orang-utans (Russon & Galdikas 1993; Stoinski & Whiten 2003; Whiten et al. 2004).

This threefold pattern of complexity in both chimpanzees and orang-utans goes beyond the mere existence of tradition and it is how we here mark off the more elaborate phenomenon of 'culture'. Looking towards humans, it is precisely this pattern of multiple and varied traditions that define each culture and differentiates it from others (e.g. Scottish versus English culture). Looking towards other non-human animals, this richness distinguishes what has been observed in great apes from most of the studies reporting animal traditions, that each typically cites only a single tradition. Lefebvre & Bouchard (2003), for example, tabulate 157 records of social learning in birds, in field and captivity, but none appear to correspond to multiple different behaviour patterns being transmitted. Similarly, birds with extensive geographical variation in song dialects do not stand out as having traditions in other domains (Catchpole & Slater 1995).

At the most pedantic level, our criterion for culture will mean that any species displaying at least two different traditions becomes eligible to be described as cultural. The more interesting implication is that as the total number of traditions rises and as the profile and diversity of traditions in each community increases, social inheritance becomes more all pervading, with potentially evolutionary effects on the sophistication of social learning, as well as other characteristics like life-history variables. On this perspective, it is likely that the complexity of culture will be manifested in many different evolutionary grades, rather than in an all-or-none fashion.

Apes are not the only non-human animals to meet our criteria, as several recent reports attest. Perhaps the most thorough and persuasive evidence concerns capuchin monkeys (*Cebus spp.*). Perry *et al.* (2003*a,b*) have described several social conventions that differ between populations of white-faced capuchins (*Cebus capucinus*; table 8.1) and meet our cultural criteria. Ascription of social transmission in this case is particularly strong, because in the case of such purely social conventions, it is difficult to envisage alternative ecological explanations.

Table 8.1 Social traditions among capuchins (*C. capucinus*). Differential distribution of five social conventions across five study sites (after Perry *et al.* 2003*a,b*). Since finger game and hair game share the same distribution and share several behavioural characteristics, they may be regarded as a single tradition; thus, there are four traditions, differentiated by their distributions. Note that the profile for each community is unique.

	Lambas Barbadul, Abby group	Lambas Barbadul, Rambo group	Santa Rosa, Cerco	Santa Rosa, Nancite	Curú, Bette's group
hand-sniff: place another's hand or foot over own face and with eyes closed, inhale deeply and repeatedly over more than 1 min.	++	(+)	++	—	—
suck: suck lengthily on another's fingers, toes, ears or tails.	++	++	—	—	(+)
finger game: put finger(s) in mouth of another, who clamps down firmly, so lengthy effort required to withdraw finger(s).	++	—	—	—	—
hair game: monkey A bites tuft of hair from B, B extracts hair from A's mouth, A reciprocates, followed by more turn-taking.	++	—	—	—	—
toy game: turn-taking game extracting non-food objects (stick, leaf, bark, inedible fruit, etc.) from each other's mouths repeatedly.	++	—	—	—	++

Table 8.2 Examples of putative foraging traditions among capuchins (*C. capucinus*). Eight examples of differential distribution of foraging patterns across three study sites, drawn from the larger chart of Panger *et al.* (2002). Two examples for each of 'pound' and 'rub' are differentiated only by the way the techniques are applied to specific targets: the patterns of pound and rub are universal, shown at all study sites. (C, customary (performed by most individuals); H, habitual (performed repeatedly by several individuals, consistent with social diffusion); —, absent without ecological explanation.)

	Lomas Barbudal	Palo Verde	Santa Rosa
army ant following: several monkeys follow foraging ant column and catch prey flushed by ants.	—	—	H
fulcrum use: using force on an object against a substrate acting as fulcrum, as in breaking fruit to obtain beetles inside.	—	H	H
leaf wrap: wrap object in leaf then rub leaf against substrate, protecting hands—applied to *Autmeris* spp. caterpillars.	H	—	H
tap: tap against object using fingertips—probably checking fruit ripeness, presence of insects in wood—applied to *Stemandia*.	—	—	C
pound: hit object against fixed substrate—applied to *Randia* fruits.	H	H	—
pound: hit object against fixed substrate—applied to *Cecropia* fruits.	—	—	C
rub: slide an object against a surface—applied to *Tabebuia*.	C	H	—
rub: slide an object against a surface—applied to *Pithecellobium*.	—	—	C

Moreover, the observed rise and later attenuation of these behaviour patterns over a period of years argues against their being transmitted genetically. However, this ephemeral character appears to distinguish them from most cultural variants described for great apes, many of which have been recorded for decades. Foraging behaviour also differs between sites in ways that suggest social transmission (Panger *et al.* 2002); examples are shown in table 8.2 The complete set of published comparisons includes over 20 such variations. However, this tally cannot be directly used to compare cultural complexity with the apes, because the capuchin records concern just six main techniques (the level at which the 39 chimpanzees records are described, for example; table 8.3 for comparison), differentiated at the study sites in terms of how they are applied to specific foodstuffs (e.g. 'Rub *Sterculia* fruit' is habitual at Lomas Barbadul (LB) yet absent at Palo Verde (PV), whereas 'Rub *Sterculia* husks' is habitual only at PV; and 'Rub *Acacia* thorns' is habitual only at Santa Rosa (SR)). Finally, Rose *et al.* (2003) offer additional data indicating traditions concerning interactions with other species. For example, LB monkeys catch and kill squirrels with a bite to the neck, whereas SR monkeys start to eat them before killing.

Although it is not appropriate to attempt direct numerical comparisons between the complexity of ape and capuchin cultures,[3] capuchins do fit our criteria for culture, assuming these comparisons are confirmed by detailed future observations. The reason for this convergence between capuchins and great apes is not entirely clear, for although capuchins have unusually large brains for their body size, they neither have large brains in absolute terms nor high neocortex ratios (Rumbaugh *et al.* 1996; Deaner *et al.* in press). Perhaps the greatest convergences with great apes are their slow development and remarkably high social tolerance, creating extensive opportunities for social learning.

The other group of mammals that has been claimed to exhibit cultural complexity is cetaceans (Rendell & Whitehead 2001), although it is generally acknowledged that constraints on

Table 8.3 Examples of traditions among orang-utans. Six examples illustrate the differential distributions that define different traditions; the diversity of types of behaviour patterns involved (cf. universal patterns of pound and rub in table 8.2); and the unique profiles that define local cultures. These examples are drawn from the full list of 19–24 (van Schaik *et al.* 2003a). (C, customary (performed by most individuals); H, habitual (performed repeatedly by several individuals, consistent with social diffusion); —, absent without ecological explanation; r, rare; e, absent for ecological reasons.)

	Gunung Palung (Borneo)	Tanjung Puting (Borneo)	Kutai (Borneo)	Lower Kinaba-tangan (Borneo)	Leuser Ketambe (Sumatra)	Leuser Suaq Balimbing (Sumatra)
snag-riding: ride on pushed-over snag it falls, then grab onto vegetation before it crashes on ground.	—	C	—	—	—	—
kiss-squeak with leaves: using leaves on mouth to amplify sound, then drop leaf.	C	—	H	—	—	—
sun cover: building cover on nest during bright sunshine (rather than rain).	—	?	C	C	H	—
leaf gloves: using leaf gloves to handle spiny leaves or spiny branch, or as seat cushions in trees with spines.	—	r	—	—	H	e
tree-hole tool use: using tool to poke into tree holes to obtain social insects or their products.	—	—	—	—	—	C
branch scoop: drinking water from deep tree hole using leafy branch (water dripping from leaves).	—	—	—	—	—	H

observation limit the inferences that can reliably be made so far. Dolphins present perhaps the most comprehensive information to date, although to our knowledge, systematic collaborative studies like those reported above for primates remain to be completed. Nevertheless, Mann & Sargeant (2003) note that evidence of population-specific foraging techniques includes sponge-carrying, thought to be used to ferret fish from the sea bed (Smolker *et al.* 1997; Krützen *et al.* 2005), tail-whacking the surface to scare up fish (Connor *et al.* 2000), belly up chasing of fish at the surface (Mann & Smuts 1999) and several others. In addition, Mann & Sargeant (2003) identify correlation between mothers and daughters for many of 11 different foraging techniques, as well as in the overall size of their repertoire, within a single population of dolphins. The authors conclude that adding to existing evidence of acoustic traditions in cetaceans (Janik & Slater 1997, 2000), 'our data suggest that elaborate motor skills can also be socially learned and maintained across generations' (p. 262). They do not discuss the possibility of a role for genetic inheritance in the mother–calf concordances in behaviour, presumably seeing this as implausible given the range and diversity of techniques involved (but see Krützen *et al.* 2005). If the putative traditions of dolphins and other cetaceans are indeed socially transmitted, then once again cultural complexity is manifest, and here we are dealing with species with the highest encephalization among non-human animals. Mammals meeting the criteria for complex culture are thus, so far, those that can be described as relatively highly encephalized on one or more indices.

Among birds, the most likely candidate for multiple tradition culture is the New Caledonian crow (*Corvus moneduloides*), which uses at least two different tools (twigs, and strips cut from the edges of *Pandanus* leaves, the barbed edges of which make the tool particularly effective) to extract invertebrates like caterpillars from crevices (Hunt 1996, 2000). On various parts of New Caledonia, crows cut leaves to different designs ranging from a simple step shape to ones with several steps, the latter providing a thicker 'handle' at one end and a tapering tip at the other, both apparently making the tool more effective. These variations form a graded series with a distribution across New Caledonia that is consistent with cumulative evolution of step-complexity as the habit diffused through the population (Hunt & Gray 2003). This raises the prospect not only of multiple traditions, consistent with our notion of culture, but of cumulative cultural evolution, for which there is only the weakest evidence in primates other than humans (Whiten *et al.* 2003). However, some doubt over the role of social learning has arisen because naive captive crows of this species have been shown to spontaneously cut and use *Pandanus* tools on first contact with leaves of the plant (Kenward *et al.* 2005), echoing the finding that woodpecker finches, the other bird species to use stick tools, do not depend on social learning in acquiring tool use (Tebbich *et al.* 2001). This contrasts with experimental evidence for social learning of tool use in captive apes. In a recent study, Whiten *et al.* (2005) trained one individual from each of two groups of chimpanzees to use a tool in just one of two alternative ways to free trapped food items, and showed that each technique spread preferentially in the group it was seeded in, creating traditions. Similar experimental evidence now extends to non-tool actions (Horner *et al.* 2006; Bonnie *et al.* 2007; Whiten *et al.* 2007). Until similar studies are done with corvids, the findings of Kenward *et al.* suggest caution is needed in concluding that the two kinds of tool use shown by these animals represent multiple traditions. Since crows in the experiment did not make stepped tools, it remains a possibility that a predisposition exists to strip leaf tools, but that social learning is required to refine this into one of the forms of stepped tool making. Further experiments are needed to test this.

We end this section with a note of caution. In most cases, the evidence for animal cultures in the wild is still incomplete, in that the major alternatives, individual learning due to ecological conditions or genetic predispositions, have not been refuted to the satisfaction of all (e.g. Galef 2003; Laland & Janik 2006). Thus, the conclusion that these taxa possess rich cultures is preliminary; it has become parsimonious for the great apes and capuchins, but remains controversial for other taxa. Further studies are needed to confirm these emerging patterns.

(c) Does culture call for (social) intelligence?

A 'cultural' version of the MIH would translate as: 'cultural complexity selects for intelligence', where cultural complexity refers to the scale, diversity of function and cognitive sophistication of the traditions concerned. This would correspond to MIH type 2 (p. 2), referring to general, and generalizable intelligence. Alternatively, one might predict, as in MIH type 3 (p. 2), that intelligence would in this case be shaped to particular forms, presumably involving social learning, the aspect of cognition most obviously necessary for a cultural animal.

Social learning of the simplest kinds has increasingly been identified among vertebrates and also invertebrates (Coolen *et al.* 2006; Worden & Papaj 2005). However, such social learning can serve a variety of purposes such as gaining useful information about local foraging hotspots, and other eavesdropping functions useful in the very short term, yet not necessarily the basis for traditions (Danchin *et al.* 2004). Perhaps the social learning associated with culturally complex species is more sophisticated? We address this question further below.

However, culture also requires innovation. This complicates the picture, predicting that culturally complex species will also be stronger innovators; and this in turn might seem to make it difficult in practice to differentiate enhanced general intelligence under MIH 2 (which might be applied to both social and non-social worlds) from the existence of cognitive capacities specialized for social learning and intelligent innovation, respectively, as predicted by MIH 3.

One reason to think the latter is at least plausible comes from research on autism in humans. Autistic spectrum disorders have become well known for providing some of the clearest evidence for modularity in social intelligence, for individuals with Asperger's syndrome in particular are often high in general intelligence, yet show deficits and delays in their mentalizing, or theory of mind (Frith & Frith 1999). More recently, it has become appreciated that autism is also associated with difficulties in imitation in childhood (Whiten 1996; Williams *et al.* 2004). Thus, there can indeed be independence between the cognitive machinery for this form of social learning and nonsocial aspects of intelligence in a primate.

Turning to comparative studies of primates, data appear to fit the prediction of MIH 3 insofar as the apes with the most complex cultures show evidence of imitation, whereas such evidence has been remarkably lacking for monkeys (Visalberghi & Fragaszy 1990, 2002; but see Voelkl & Huber 2000). However, widening the perspective, a series of carefully controlled 'two-action' studies has recently demonstrated imitation in birds, including pigeons, quails, starlings and budgerigars (Zentall 2004), which are not relatively encephalized and for which culture has not been claimed in the sense we define it. In their comprehensive avian review, Lefebvre & Bouchard (2003) noted the paradox that their database recorded few episodes of spontaneous social learning in birds when compared with those available for primates, whereas experimental laboratory studies typically returned positive evidence of social learning more often in birds than in monkeys and other mammals. We discuss these puzzles in §4 of this paper. In the present section, we focus instead on chimpanzees and orang-utans, where the scale of cultural complexity still appears considerably greater than in any other non-human species, and we ask whether there is evidence that their social learning displays the greater sophistication this predicts. A more comprehensive analysis than can be offered here is in Whiten *et al.* (2004).

(i) *Dimensions of encoding*

Two-action studies with birds have tended to demonstrate imitation that is close to two-dimensional (e.g. push manipulandum to left versus right; Klein & Zentall 2003; push bung down versus pull it out: Heyes & Saggerson 2002) or binary (depress treadle with beak versus foot; Zentall *et al.* 1996). By contrast, in studies in which chimpanzees and orang-utans have been trained to 'Do-as-I-do' (Custance *et al.* 1995; Call 2001), an elaborate three-dimensional mapping has been confirmed that extends to matching acts directed at many different points of the body, and coordinating manual and other configurations at detailed levels. Examples in the category 'asymmetric use of hands' are 'clap one hand on back of other' versus 'clap two digits on other palm' and 'grab thumb of other hand'. This suggests that apes may be able to encode complex dimensions of action that bear some correspondence to the enormous diversity of actions possible with a pair of primate hands. Unfortunately, comparative studies are constrained because other species have failed to grasp the concept of 'Do-as-I-do' (§2*c*(iv) below).

(ii) *Rationality in copying*

Another way to address the issue of intelligence in social learning is to ask whether when apes ape, they do so blindly or selectively. Horner & Whiten (2005) presented young chimpanzees with either of two boxes with top and front holes, protected by various defences. A familiar human model tackled each box in the same way, first ramming a stick tool into the top hole several times, then withdrawing it and inserting it into the front hole to extract a food reward. Although the food was hidden in a central tunnel in both boxes, one box was otherwise transparent, so that the initial ramming action could be seen to be ineffectual, beating on a false ceiling, which was not apparent with the alternative, opaque box. Chimpanzees tended to repeat all actions in the latter case, but to omit probing in the top hole after witnessing the model do this ineffectually with the transparent version, indicating their copying was rationally selective. In this experiment, it was in fact young children who were the indiscriminate copiers, probing in the top hole with either box. This intriguing result implies that rationality may not be crucial for significant cultural learning to occur. However, this is not necessarily inconsistent with the view that rationality has been important in making human culture as a whole as sophisticated as it is.

(iii) *Copying sequential structure*

Whiten (1998) presented chimpanzees with a human model performing a series of acts required to open an 'artificial fruit' in different, sequential orders. By the third demonstration and attempt, subjects almost perfectly matched the sequence witnessed. The study of Horner & Whiten (2005) described above offers complementary evidence that chimpanzees do not merely 'replay' the chain of events witnessed, but can instead parse it (Byrne 2000) before assembling their own version, because in the opaque box condition, they repeated both acts in the correct order (probe top, then bottom) whereas in the transparent condition, they tended to perform only the second of these. These studies suggest that chimpanzees may have at least some capacity to grasp the higher-level structure of complex actions and copy them, going some way towards the more elaborate concept of hierarchically sensitive 'program-level imitation' hypothesized by Byrne & Russon (1998). Nguyen *et al.* (2005) have since provided evidence that pigeons will imitate a chain of two events, such as stepping on a treadle and then pushing a screen, but did not test whether they would copy alternative sequential organizations of the elements involved (treadle–screen versus screen–treadle).

(iv) *Recognizing the imitative process*

The fact that chimpanzees and orang-utans have been able to learn the 'do-as-I-do' routine implies that they can grasp, or learn, a concept of what counts as imitation. Interestingly, attempts to train this in monkeys have failed (capuchins, Fragaszy *et al.* unpublished, cited in Visalberghi & Fragaszy 2002; macaques, Mitchell & Anderson 1993). Dolphins have grasped the concept (Herman 2002), raising the prospect that there is a link with the ability to recognize oneself in a mirror, which is also known only for the great apes (including humans of course; Tomasello & Call 1997) and dolphins (Reiss & Marino 2001), an otherwise remarkable coincidence. Just what the significance of this is for everyday social learning remains something of a mystery but it does appear to put the social cognition underlying ape imitation onto some qualitatively higher plane.

The scope of culture in great apes may also be predicted to have effects on other related aspects of social cognition. One is conformity to cultural norms. The chimpanzees in the

Whiten (1998) study described above discovered some alternative sequences that worked, but nevertheless converged on the sequence used by the model, suggested an element of conformity akin to that identified in humans (Asch 1956), but has remained unconfirmed in the literature. More recently, in a two-action diffusion study, some chimpanzees likewise discovered for themselves the alternative technique seeded in a different group but rare in their own, yet later re-converged on the norm for their group, demonstrating conformity in the face of discovering a functional alternative themselves (Whiten et al. 2005). In one sense, this is the opposite of intelligent—it could even be re-described as 'mindlessly following the herd'. However, it is a marked characteristic of human cultural behaviour and requires a capacity to recognize the local norm and react to it. Yet, conformity of the basic 'follow the majority' kind has been demonstrated in a variety of species including fish (Day et al. 2001). What may be distinctive about the chimpanzee and human cases is that conformity overrides the discovery of valid alternative means. It is therefore better thought of as a particularly strong motivation to copy others rather than use one's own knowledge. This may become the more adaptive when cultural transmission is pervasive in reasonably stable environments (Henrich & Boyd 1998).

8.3 Does culture make you smart?

The phenotypic expression of all traits depends on the interplay between genetic factors and the effects of environmental conditions, both internal and external to the organism, during development (West-Eberhard 2003). The extent to which environmental influences can affect the adult phenotype varies across traits and species, and at least some of this variability may reflect adaptations. Developmental plasticity is greater for many behavioural features than for morphological ones, especially for behaviours that rely on cognitive processes emanating in the cortical brain regions (Rosa & Tweedale 2005). Thus, although a species' intelligence is often considered an innate given, we should rather expect it to be affected by the interaction between innate components and environmental inputs during development. This expectation is, of course, amply met in humans, where numerous studies have examined the interaction between genetic endowment and developmental inputs in determining intelligence (Jensen 2000). Environmental shaping of intelligence might be expected more generally in primates owing to their relatively large adult brains (Passingham 1981), very slow development (Case 1978) and extensive postnatal brain growth and differentiation, the extent of which is an excellent predictor of the duration of immaturity (Barrickman et al. in review), and therefore of the time available for learning.

In species where immature individuals are in close association with parents, caretakers or other tolerant adults, social learning may be additionally facilitated. Social learning can improve the signal:noise ratio in available information relative to independent individual exploration, and the frequency of opportunities for social learning may therefore enhance adult cognitive performance more than an equal number of opportunities for individual exploration and learning. Such a positive impact of social learning on realized intelligence might occur merely through selective attention to those stimuli and contexts where the acquisition of valuable skills is most likely. If more specialized social learning mechanisms are available, such as those discussed in §2c above, then cognitively richer, more rarely invented innovations may be more reliably acquired by maturing individuals and their fitness enhanced accordingly.

To van Schaik (2006), these *a priori* arguments suggest not only a dependence of adult cognitive abilities on the quality and quantity of environmental inputs during development, in primates and probably other animals with long development periods, but more importantly, a special role for social learning in this process. To test these conjectures, we can turn first to experiments that artificially reduce or increase environmental inputs during primate development. Social deprivation is well known to lead to major cognitive deficits in rhesus monkeys, as demonstrated by numerous classical studies (e.g. Sackett *et al.* 1999). The opposite of deprivation, enrichment, may produce increases in cognitive performance. Indeed, in captivity, where animals have access to enriched material conditions and no need for frequent vigilance, a far greater number of primate species is capable of using and even making tools, in the absence of obvious conditioning, than is documented from the wild (van Schaik *et al.* 1999). The enculturation effect, observed when great ape infants are raised like human children, similarly suggests that increases in socially guided exploration opportunities bring about enhanced cognitive performance (Gardner & Gardner 1989; Tomasello & Call 2004). Perhaps the most striking effect of enculturation has been in producing unusually elaborate comprehension of human language in great apes that do not use such symbolic signalling in the wild (Savage-Rumbaugh & Levin 1994). Thus, the intelligence of adult primates is clearly impacted by experimentally induced variation in environmental conditions during development, some of them socially mediated.

Is there enough variation in nature to expect similar effects of developmentally differentiated social inputs on adult cognitive performance? The fact that great ape populations vary widely in the degree to which animals spend time together in tolerant proximity could affect the frequency of opportunities for social learning in this way, and thus perhaps later cognitive performance. East African chimpanzee females may spend over half of their time alone (Wrangham *et al.* 1996), especially when they have dependent infants, whereas West African females tend to be gregarious, even if they have infants (Boesch & Boesch-Achermann 2000). Among orang-utans, on average less gregarious than chimpanzees, Bornean females are much less gregarious than Sumatran females (van Schaik *et al.* 1999). Only Sumatran orang-utans share food outside the mother–infant context, and among Sumatrans this food sharing is most pronounced at Suaq Balimbing, where close proximity (less than 2 m) is by far the most common (van Schaik 2004). Similarly, the more gregarious West-African chimpanzees also show greater social tolerance, with food sharing being a more orderly process, under control of the original owner of the food (Boesch & Boesch-Achermann 2000), whereas in the less gregarious East-African chimpanzees, food sharing appears better characterized as sharing under pressure (Gilby 2006).

The field data for both chimpanzees and orang-utans show that inter-population variation in tolerant proximity is positively correlated with the number of cultural variants classed as cognitively complex in each population, whereas the relationship is not significant for variants that appear more cognitively simple (figure 8.2).[4] Cultural variants, by definition, are innovations that have become common in a population through social learning. The relationship in figure 8.2 suggests that cognitively complex cultural variants are more likely to be invented or maintained in populations with more opportunities for close-range social interactions. Figure 8.2 also suggests that chimpanzees have greater repertoire sizes than orang-utans. This species difference is consistent with the same principles, because overall, chimpanzees are more gregarious than orang-utans.[5]

The relationships illustrated in figure 8.2 are correlations and must therefore be interpreted with appropriate care. However, it is unlikely that variation in cultural repertoires causes

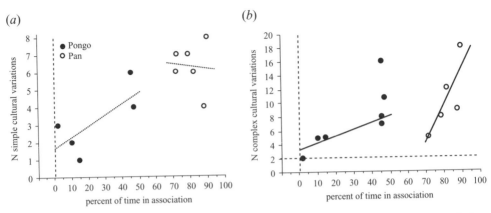

Fig. 8.2 Relationship between association time and number of cultural variants across populations of orang-utans or chimpanzees, for (*a*) cognitively simple and (*b*) cognitively complex variants. For (*a*), analysis of covariance reveals no significant effects of association or species, nor of their interaction; for (*b*) all these effects are significant (association, *p* = 0.003; species, *p* = 0.01; interaction, *p* = 0.02). Data on cultural variants are from Whiten *et al.* (1999) for chimpanzees, and van Schaik *et al.* (2003*a*) for orang-utans; see text and endnote 4 for assignment of cognitive complexity of variants. Animals were 'in association' when they had one or more independent conspecifics at less than 40 or 50 m (variable between studies); data from Boesch (1996) for chimpanzees and van Schaik *et al.* (2003*a*) for orang-utans.

differences in gregariousness, because gregariousness does not depend on particular contexts in which especially valuable cultural variants are performed. Indeed, gregariousness in orang-utans is better explained by local ecological productivity (van Schaik 2004). Hence, we infer that the causal arrow is most likely to run from tolerant gregariousness to the size of the cultural repertoire.

Several alternative mechanisms might explain this. One possibility is that animals in more gregarious populations have higher developmentally enhanced general intelligence and are thus more likely to invent cognitively complex innovations. An alternative hypothesis is that these animals encounter more innovations, including those that can form the point of origin for more complex versions. Data currently available are insufficient to properly distinguish these propositions. In either case, however, the outcome is that individuals in populations with more tolerant gregariousness end up performing more cognitively complex behaviours, and can therefore be considered more intelligent in this respect as adults.

What happens across populations is also to some extent seen within populations. Among the orang-utans at Suaq Balimbing, for instance, tree-hole tool use, while customary (van Schaik *et al.* 2003*a*), does show remarkable variation in its rate (van Schaik *et al.* 2003*b*). The females can be divided into clusters, based on range use and association (Singleton & van Schaik 2002). The northern females at the site are far less gregarious than the central and southern females—a difference that is stable over time and also includes maturing females, who tend to settle in or near their natal range. However, their home ranges show large overlap, and in the overlap zone they are equally likely to forage for insects and hence have equal opportunity to engage in tree-hole tool use, yet the northern females do so far less (figure 8.3). Since they occasionally do so, we assume that they know in principle how to solve the task if they encounter it. This suggests that they have more difficulty recognizing when the opportunity presents itself.

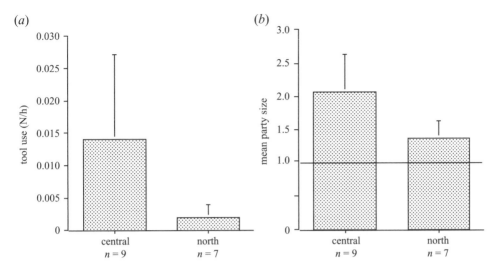

Fig. 8.3. The propensity to use tree-hole tools in two clusters of (sub)adult orang-utan females at Suaq Balimbing that vary in mean party size (including only independent individuals in association with focal females; hence, minimum party size is 1). Numbers in parentheses indicate the number of females; vertical bars are standard deviations. Results of t-tests for tool use rate: $p < 0.05$; for party size: $p < 0.01$. Party size differences among females remained constant over time, including following maturation. Data from van Schaik *et al.* (2003*b*).

The difference, then, is probably primarily one of experience in recognizing tree holes that are good for tool use. This experience is probably built up during the formative years, and may depend dramatically on the frequency of opportunities to engage in the task from start to finish during this period. The central and southern females are far more gregarious, therefore much more likely to accompany experienced foragers, and to develop a sharp search image for opportunities for tool-supported extractive use of tree holes.

Overall, then, there is circumstantial evidence for the impact of developmental inputs on adult cognitive performance in wild great apes. There is no evidence for intraspecific variation in other primates as yet, but the above-mentioned deprivation experiments suggest that we should expect similar variation in monkeys, and perhaps other organisms as well. Variation in the frequency of opportunities for close-range social learning may also partially determine differences in cognitive performance across species. This may be particularly relevant to understanding the prevalence of traditions among capuchins, for as noted above, these monkeys develop slowly and form unusually tolerant societies.

8.4 Concluding discussion

The emerging picture of social learning, traditions and culture appears to have the form of a pyramid, the base of which represents the occurrence of social information transfer of many different kinds in many taxa of the animal kingdom (figure 8.4; see also van Schaik *et al.* 1999; van Schaik 2004; for related evolutionary models). Social learning, at least in its simpler forms, is well established in mammals, birds and fish (Laland & Hoppitt 2003) and recent

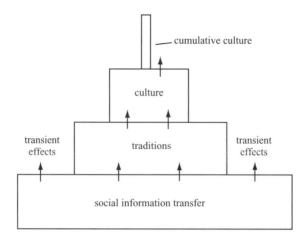

Fig. 8.4 Culture pyramid. Social information transfer (foundation layer) is widespread in vertebrates and occurs also in invertebrates (see text for references). However, only a subset of such transfer eventuates in sustained traditions (layer two), because effects of social learning are often transitory only (e.g. using public information to judge profitable foraging patches). The occurrence of traditions may also be more restricted taxonomically than use of social information *per se*. More rarely still, cultures exist that are defined by the existence in the same species of multiple traditions forming unique local complexes (layer three). Cumulative culture (layer 4) occurs when more complex traditions arise by elaboration on earlier ones, generating the richness of human cultures yet minimally evidenced in other species. Relative sizes of each layer are notional. Arrows indicate the reliance of each layer on pre-existing lower layers.

reports extend to invertebrates (Worden & Papaj 2005). Much of this learning exploits public information that is functional in the shorter term, such as learning about temporarily productive foraging patches or avoiding the current location of a predator (Danchin *et al.* 2004), rather than the consistent habits we call traditions. Sustained traditions thus constitute the second, smaller layer of the pyramid, built upon the existence of social information transfer. How much social learning eventuates in traditions and how much serves shorter-term functions, whether in terms of learning events, or representation in different animal taxa, is at present difficult to estimate. The answer will probably be different for different levels of social learning and in any case presents formidable problems of appropriate measurement in practice.

The existence of a tradition does not yet constitute culture as we define it. It is the third layer of the pyramid that thus represents the occurrence of the multiple and diverse sets of traditions we call cultures. The evidence for such cultures that we have reviewed in this paper indicates that in contrast to the occurrence of traditions in a wide range of vertebrates including fish, only an as-yet small set of relative highly encephalized, socially living mammalian taxa show significant cultural complexity. The fourth level of the pyramid represents cumulative cultural evolution, in which more sophisticated traditions are progressively built through elaboration on earlier ones. It is this process that has evidently been responsible for the current complexity of human culture, from our languages to our diverse and burgeoning technologies. Evidence for cumulative culture in non-human species is minimal at best (Whiten *et al.* 2003; but see McGrew 2005; Byrne 2007), which appears to explain the major gulf between the content of human versus non-human culture (Boyd & Richerson 1996; Tomasello 1999).

Taken together, the inter- and intraspecific correlations we identified between cultural complexity, social learning capacities, social learning opportunities and encephalization suggest an evolutionarily spiralling process in which social learning may engender traditions, the emergence of multiple traditions selects for enhanced social learning, multiple traditions generate smarter individuals, smarter individuals innovate and learn better, and there is associated selection for encephalization; moreover, positive feedback is expected between many of these effects. Other characteristics may additionally be associated with this 'adaptive complex' that we have insufficient space to discuss in matching detail, prime candidates being life-history variables such as the length of the juvenile period of dependency on parents (van Schaik *et al.* 1999). For example, there is evidence in birds that relative brain size is well predicted by how long young birds stay with their parents after fledging, a period of potential apprenticeship (Iwaniuk & Nelson 2003). It may be that the encephalization involved here reflects not only neural tissue devoted to social learning mechanisms, but also the storage needs for all that is acquired and remembered in this apprenticeship. In apes, this cultural knowledge-base—of 'know-how' and 'knowing-that' must be very demanding of neural storage provision; more particularly, the demands of storing all that is learned culturally by humans (language, technology and the rest) may explain more of our extraordinary encephalization than has been appreciated.

The central links we have proposed here between complex culture and intelligence constitute a 'Cultural Intelligence Hypothesis' (CIH) that can be seen as complementing the MIH. A CIH can be regarded as a particular instance of the 'behavioural drive' and 'cultural drive' hypotheses described by Wyles *et al.* (1983) and Wilson (1985), respectively, which proposed that a combination of innovation and social learning allowed some taxa to more effectively invade new niche space through behavioural means, in turn driving biological evolution at higher rates. Wilson and his colleagues argued that these effects are notable in mammals and birds particularly, their hypothesis being supported by an almost perfect correlation ($r = 0.97$) between relative brain size and rate of anatomical evolution across major groups of reptiles, amphibians, mammals and birds (the arbitrariness of some of the specific taxonomic contrasts used urges caution in taking this correlation at face value; but see Sol *et al.* (2005) for avian analyses consistent with Wilson *et al.*'s hypothesis).

The hypothesis of Wyles *et al.* has interesting precursors, not cited by these authors, such as that now referred to as the Baldwin effect (see Bateson 1988; Baldwin 1902), which posits that behavioural innovation may permit certain species to invade new niches, thus modifying selection pressures that in turn cause corresponding, genetically based changes. Other theoretical affinities that merit exploration are with more recent hypotheses described as cultural niche construction (Laland *et al.* 2000), in which the traditions that animals themselves create become part of the selective landscape affecting other characteristics, such as encephalization and life-history strategy. In similar vein, Tomasello (1999) has offered a detailed case for the evolutionary shaping of human cognitive capabilities by the special characteristics of culture that arose in our species.

Of particular interest, for the present issue, is that the CIH joins a growing family of selection hypotheses whose distinctive feature is positive feedback, creating the potential for spiralling, or runaway, evolution (Bateson 2004). Thus, as in the MIH itself, as well as in sexual selection and behavioural drive, evolutionary change is predicted to be racked up without any necessary pressure from the external environment, but instead through spiralling interactions between conspecifics. In the case of the MIH, CIH and behavioural drive hypotheses, 'socially intelligent conspecifics' are key. The central idea in all of these proposals is that whatever the cause of an initial rise in social intelligence, the fact that this is manifested in social interactions means that an increase in intelligence in any one individual selects for increases in others, and so on in spiralling, positive-feedback fashion. As in the case of sexual selection, this is potentially a runaway process. Of course some additional factor must eventually apply a brake, where the costs (for example, of manufacturing and maintaining expensive brain tissue) outweigh benefits in the current ecological niche. Conversely, additional factors must be identified to explain the release of such a brake in a particular case, as happened in the exceptional escalation in encephalization, social intelligence and cultural complexity that occurred in hominin evolution (Whiten 1999, 2006; and see Mithen 2007; Sterelny 2007).

If the CIH is suggested by what we know of chimpanzees and orang-utans, are its predictions supported by data from the other taxa we discussed? The evidence from cetaceans is supportive, insofar as there is evidence for multiple and diverse traditions, particularly in some specific cases including dolphins and killer whales, and these species are among the most highly encephalized mammals. Dolphins have demonstrated perhaps the most impressive imitative capacity of any non-human animals, great apes included, in precisely copying the actions of both conspecifics and humans (Herman 2002). However, an important note of caution here is that this capacity has principally been demonstrated in terms of the dolphins' existing repertoire of bodily movements. Social learning of relatively novel techniques of food-handling, for example, has yet to be demonstrated. A priority is thus to perform experiments of the kinds completed for apes and reviewed above, particularly to test the capacity to acquire and sustain alternative traditions in different groups (Whiten *et al.* 2005; Bonnie *et al.* 2007; Horner *et al.* 2006; Whiten *et al.* 2007).

Whether the capuchin findings are consistent with our CIH is less clear. Although they display multiple traditions and are encephalized in terms of EQ (brain size relative to body size), they do not have absolutely large brains or high neocortex ratios and their social learning has for some time been characterized as minimal, rather than common and sophisticated (Visalberghi & Fragaszy 1990, 2002). However, more recent studies have indicated that monkeys may have more imitative capacity than earlier thought (Voelkl & Huber 2000), and studies with capuchins specifically have identified social learning (Custance *et al.* 1999), some including the sophistication of discriminating the value of specific outcomes of others' actions (Brosnan & de Waal 2004). An ongoing study by Fragaszy and colleagues (Fragaszy *et al.* 2004*a,b*, p. 255) provides preliminary experimental evidence of diffusion of alternative foraging techniques. Thus, capuchins may be better social learners than earlier research suggested. At the same time, the traditions so far described for them appear less elaborate than those of chimpanzees and orang-utans. While most of the dozens of traditions described for the latter can be described as behavioural techniques, many of the differences for white-faced capuchins listed by Panger *et al.* (2002) involve applying universally occurring techniques like *rub* and *pound* differentially to various food types at different sites. Descriptions of a number of more elaborate foraging techniques including tool use are emerging for brown capuchins (*Cebus apella*; Ottoni & Mannu 2001; Fragaszy *et al.* 2004*a,b*; Moura & Lee 2004), but these remain to be systematically compared across sites, as done for their white-faced cousins. In sum, the capuchin data cause some doubt about the generality and scope of the CIH, but much remains to be confirmed about the nature of their traditions and social learning to permit comprehensive comparisons of *Cebus* and the great apes.

Finally, we noted that although there is much evidence for social learning and traditions in birds, there is so far little evidence of complex culture as we defined it. Perhaps this is simply because nobody has seriously attended to the distribution of traditions in this manner yet (West *et al.* 2003). In addition, the specific question of how much Caledonian crow tool use depends on social learning really needs to be answered. In the meantime, we can refer only to

Lefebvre & Bouchard's (2003) finding that the ratio of social learning to innovation was remarkably low in their bird database compared to what has been reported for primates. This is perhaps surprising given the several parallels that have been identified between manifestations of intelligence in apes and in some birds such as corvids (Emery & Clayton 2004). Lefebvre & Bouchard (2003) consider several potential explanations for the bird/primate contrast they identify, dismissing observer biases and other factors in favour of the fundamental difference in 'food-handling organs': beaks versus a pair of hands with multiple digits. Still, some birds have been shown to be good at social learning, extending to imitation; New Caledonian crows are skilled in the use of more than one tool-type; and corvids in general have displayed various forms of social cognition: these together suggest we ought to remain surprised if they do not exhibit multiple-tradition cultures. Is a higher absolute brain mass important to achieve this? Or might other aspects of avian sociality provide the key (Emery *et al.* 2007)? We hope further experiments and observations in nature will clarify how avian and other taxa relate to the larger patterns we have identified in this paper.

In conclusion, the emerging patterns in the recent research we have reviewed have led us to formulate an embryonic Cultural Inheritance Hypothesis, linking social intelligence and complexities of animal culture. This is not presented as a direct competitor to the MIH. Rather, we see the CIH as one manifestation of the MIH in its original, broadly framed sense. A graphic example of this is that the marked encephalization of the orang-utan has always been an anomaly in relation to the MIH when the hypothesis was tested using group size as the proxy for social complexity (van Schaik 2004), for these apes are typically associated with some of the most minimal social groupings among primates. By contrast, they are a perfect fit with the CIH, as illustrated in figure 8.1 and discussed in relation to several sections of this paper. Barrett & Henzi (2005) have recently advocated an expansion of our theories of animal social intelligence to encompass a broader range of cooperative phenomena than are connoted by the narrow sense of 'Machiavellianism', and the present issue continues to expand our theories and knowledge of social intellect in new directions. Exploration of the diverse manifestations of culturally related phenomena among animals likewise extends our understanding of the special implications of social intelligence in new and productive dimensions. The fact that so much of the material we have drawn on has been collated only in the last few years highlights not only the exciting large-scale patterns in nature we can now begin to discern, but also emphasizes how large are the gaps in our knowledge that beg to be filled for so many animal taxa, besides the small set we have been able to discuss in depth.

A.W. was supported by a Leverhulme Trust Major Research Fellowship during the writing of this paper. We are grateful for comments on an earlier draft of the paper by Nathan Emery, Lydia Hopper and especially Simon Reader.

Endnotes

1. Recognizing that for some, the gap is so great that culture should be ascribed only to humans, we put culture in quotation marks in our title.
2. Space limits force the omission of any detailed consideration of other kinds of links between social intelligence and culture. Notable among these are (i) evidence that, consistent with the MIH, social information such as gossip achieves higher fidelity social transmission (Mesoudi *et al.* 2006a) and (ii) there is increasing evidence in primates for cultural transmission of sociality, as in the example of an unusual 'pacific culture' among baboons (Sapolsky & Share 2004; de Waal & Bonnie in press).

3. There has been much controversy over the potential utility of recognizing 'memes' as units of cultural transmission (Dawkins 1976; Aunger 2000). This has most preoccupied students of human evolution, but the specific set of traditions tabulated for apes (Whiten *et al.* 1999, 2001; van Schaik *et al.* 2003*a*) suggests that the notion of memes might gain better purchase in these simpler cases. However, animal culture research has only begun to wrestle with the 'demarcation issue' of how traditions should properly be circumscribed. If one community of chimpanzees uses hammer-stones to crack two different nuts and another does neither, is that a difference in two memes or one? The examples of 'pound' and 'rub' in table 2 further illustrate this difficulty. In general, we suggest the answer must be, by analogy with the gene, that a meme is whatever cluster of behaviour patterns is transmitted as a package, but comparisons surmounting this problem in animal culture research are in their infancy.

4. Cognitively simple innovations are those that could arise by individual discovery, and where the animals must merely repeat such an act in the same particular context. For instance, an orang-utan producing a kiss-squeak vocalization could accidentally have had its hand or a leafy branch right in front of its lips, have noted the change in sound quality this produces, and subsequently deliberately reproduce these contexts in order to bring about the new sound. Cognitively complex innovations are defined as those that appear to require some causal inference and require some deliberate action, not likely to arise by accident. Tool-use techniques fall in this category. Cognitively complex innovations tend to require practice before individuals adopting them can use them productively. We list the variants and their categorization in the electronic supplementary material.

5. Some of this difference is due to the high-average gregariousness of chimpanzee males (Boesch & Boesch-Achermann 2000) and the low-average gregariousness of flanged orang-utan males (van Schaik 1999). If the focus were on mothers, for whom no separate published numbers exist, the species curves would be closer together and the chimpanzee curve less steep. A focus on mothers would be warranted if it is assumed that most cultural variants are learned as mature individuals, although extensive social learning is possible in adolescence and adulthood, as confirmed in recent experiments (Whiten *et al.* 2005).

References

Asch, S. E. 1956 Studies of independence and conformity: 1. A minority of one against a unanimous majority. *Psychol. Monogr.* **70**, 1–70.

Aunger, R. 2000 *Darwinizing culture.* Oxford, UK: Oxford University Press.

Avian Brain Nomenclature Consortium 2005 Avian brains and a new understanding of vertebrate brain evolution. *Nat. Rev. Neurosci.* **6**, 151–159.

Avital, E. & Jablonka, E. 2000 *Animal traditions: behavioural inheritance in evolution.* Cambridge, UK: Cambridge University Press.

Baldwin, J. M. 1902 *Development and evolution.* New York, NY: Macmillan.

Barrett, L. & Henzi, P. 2005 The social nature of primate cognition. *Proc. R. Soc. B* **272**, 1865–1875. (doi:10.1098/ rspb.2005.3200)

Barrickman, N. L., Bastian, M. L., Isler, K. & van Schaik, C. P. In review. Life history costs and benefits of increased brain size: a comparative test using primates.

Barton, R. A. & Dunbar, R. I. M. 1997 Evolution of the social brain. In *Machiavellian intelligence II: extensions and evaluations* (eds A. Whiten & R. W. Byrne), pp. 240–263. Cambridge, UK: Cambridge University Press.

Bateson, P. P. G. 1988 The active role of behaviour in evolution. In *Process and metaphors in evolution* (eds M.-W. Ho & S. Fox), pp. 191–207. Chichester, UK: Wiley.

Bateson, P. P. G. 2004 The active role of behaviour in evolution. *Biol. Philos.* **19**, 283–298. (doi:10.1023/ B:BIPH.0000024468.12161.83)

Boesch, C. 1996 The emergence of cultures among wild chimpanzees. In *Evolution of social behaviour patterns in primates and man* (eds W.G.Runciman, J.Maynard-Smith & R. I. M. Dunbar), pp. 251–268. Oxford, UK: Oxford University Press.

Boesch, C. & Boesch-Achermann, H. 2000 *The chimpanzees of the Taï forest: behavioural ecology and evolution.* Oxford, UK: Oxford University Press.

Boesch, C. & Tomasello, M. 1998 Chimpanzee and human cultures. *Curr. Anthropol.* **39**, 591–614. (doi:10.1086/204785)

Bonnie, K. E., Horner, V., Whiten, A. & de Waal, F. B. M. 2007 Spread of arbitrary customs among chimpanzees: a controlled experiment. *Proc. R. Soc. B* **274**, 367–372. (doi:10.1098/rspb.2006.3733)

Boyd, R. & Richerson, P. 1996 Why culture is common but cultural evolution is rare. *Proc. Br. Acad.* **88**, 73–93.

Brosnan, S. F. & de Waal, F. B. M. 2004 Socially learned preferences for differentially rewarded tokens in the brown capuchin monkey *(Cebus apella). J. Comp. Psychol.* **118**, 133–139. (doi:10.1037/0735-7036.118.2.133)

Byrne, R. W. 2000 Imitation without intentionality: using string-parsing to copy the organization of behaviour. *Anim. Cogn.* **2**, 63–72. (doi:10.1007/s100710050025)

Byrne, R. W. 2007 Culture in great apes: using intricate complexity in feeding skills to trace the evolutionary origin of human technical prowess. *Phil. Trans. R. Soc. B* **362**, 577–585. (doi:10.1098/rstb.2006.1996)

Byrne, R. W. & Corp, N. 2004 Neocortex size predicts deception rate in primates. *Proc. R. Soc. B* **271**, 1693–1699. (doi:10.1098/rspb.2004.2780)

Byrne, R. W. & Russon, A. E. 1998 Learning by imitation: a hierarchical approach. *Behav. Brain Sci.* **21**, 667–721. (doi:10.1017/S0140525X98001745)

Byrne, R. W. & Whiten, A. 1988 *Machiavellian intelligence: social complexity and the evolution of intellect in monkeys, apes and humans.* Oxford, UK: Oxford University Press.

Byrne, R. W. & Whiten, A. 1997 Machiavellian intelligence. In *Machiavellian intelligence II: extensions and evaluations* (eds A. Whiten & R. W. Byrne), pp. 1–23. Cambridge, UK: Cambridge University Press.

Call, J. 2001 Body imitation in an enculturated orangutan *(Pongo pygmaeus). Cybern. Syst.* **32**, 97–119. (doi:10.1080/ 019697201300001821)

Case, T. J. 1978 On the evolution and adaptive significance of post-natal growth rates in terrestrial vertebrates. *Q. Rev. Biol.* **53**, 243–282. (doi:10.1086/410622)

Catchpole, C. K. & Slater, P. J. B. 1995 *Bird song: biological themes and variations.* Cambridge, UK: Cambridge University Press.

Connor, R. C., Heithaus, M. R., Bergrenn, P. & Miksis, J. L. 2000 "Kerplunking"; surface fluke-splashes during shallow-water bottom foraging by bottlenose dolphins. *Mar. Mamm. Sci.* **16**, 646–653. (doi:10.1111/j.1748-7692. 2000.tb00959.x)

Coolen, I., Dangles, O. & Casas, J. 2006 Social learning in noncolonial insects? *Curr. Biol.* **15**, 1931–1935. (doi:10. 1016/j.cub.2005.09.015)

Custance, D. M., Whiten, A. & Bard, K. A. 1995 Can young chimpanzees *(Pan troglodytes)* imitate arbitrary actions? Hayes and Hayes (1952) revisited. *Behaviour* **132**, 837–859.

Custance, D. M., Whiten, A. & Fredman, T. 1999 Social learning of artificial fruit processing in capuchin monkeys *(Cebus apella). J. Comp. Psychol.* **113**, 13–23. (doi:10.1037/0735-7036.113.1.13)

Danchin, E., Giraldeau, L.-A., Valone, T. J. & Wagner, R. H. 2004 Public information: from nosy neighbours to cultural evolution. *Science* **305**, 487–491. (doi:10.1126/science.1098254)

Dawkins, R. 1976 *The selfish gene.* Oxford: Oxford University Press.

Day, R., Macdonald, T., Brown, C., Laland, K. N. & Reader, S. M. 2001 Interactions between shoal size and conformity in guppy social foraging. *Anim. Behav.* **62**, 917–925. (doi:10.1006/anbe.2001.1820)

Deaner, R. O., Nunn, C. L. & van Schaik, C. P. 2000. Comparative tests of primate cognition: different scaling methods produce different results. *Brain Behav. Evol.* **55**, 44–52. (doi:10.1159/000006641)

Deaner, R. O., Burkart, J., Isler, K. & van Schaik, C. P. 2007. Overall brain size, not encephalization quotient, best predicts cognitive ability across non-human primates. *Brain Behav. Evol.* **70**, 115–124.

de Waal, F. B. M. & Bonnie, K. E. In press. In tune with others: the social side of primate culture. In *The question of animal culture* (eds K. N. Laland & B. G. Galef Jr) Cambridge, MA: Harvard University Press.

de Waal, F. B. M. & Tyack, P. L. 2003 *Animal social complexity: intelligence, culture and individualized societies.* Cambridge, MA: Harvard University Press.

Dunbar, R. I. M. 1995 Neocortex size and group size in primates: a test of the hypothesis. *J. Hum. Evol.* **28**, 287–296. (doi:10.1006/jhev.1995.1021)

Dunbar, R. I. M. 1998 The social brain hypothesis. *Evol. Anthropol.* **6**, 178–190. (doi:10.1002/(SICI) 1520-6505 (1998)6:5<178::AID-EVAN5>3.0.CO;2-8)

Dunbar, R. I. M. & Shultz, S. 2007 Understanding primate brain evolution. *Phil. Trans. R. Soc. B* **362**, 649–658. (doi:10.1098/rstb.2006.2001)

Emery, N. J. & Clayton, N. S. 2004 The mentality of crows: convergent evolution of intelligence in corvids and apes. *Science* **306**, 1903–1907. (doi:10.1126/science.1098410)

Emery, N. J. & Clayton, N. S. 2005 Evolution of the avian brain and intelligence. *Curr. Biol.* **15**, R946–R950. (doi:10.1016/j.cub.2005.11.029)

Emery, N. J., Seed, A. M., von Bayern, A. M. P. & Clayton, N. S. 2007 Cognitive adaptations of social bonding in birds. *Phil. Trans. R. Soc. B* **362**, 489–505. (doi:10.1098/ rstb.2006.1991)

Fragaszy, D. M. & Perry, S. (eds) 2003 *The biology of traditions: models and evidence.* Cambridge, UK: Cambridge University Press.

Fragaszy, D. M., Izar, P., Visalberghi, E., Ottoni, E. B. & de Oliveria, M. G. 2004a Wild capuchin monkeys *(Cebus libidinosus)* use anvils and stone pounding tools. *Am. J. Primatol.* **64**, 359–366. (doi:10.1002/ajp.20085)

Fragaszy, D. M., Visalberghi, E. & Fedigan, L. M. (eds) 2004b *The complete capuchin: the biology of the genus Cebus.* Cambridge, UK: Cambridge University Press.

Frith, C. D. & Frith, U. 1999 Interacting minds—a biological basis. *Science* **286**, 1692–1695. (doi:10.1126/ science.286.5445.1692)

Frith, U. & Frith, C. 2003 Development and neurophysiology of mentalizing. *Phil. Trans. R. Soc. B* **358**, 459–473. (doi:10.1098/rstb.2002.1218)

Galef, B. G. 1992 The question of animal culture. *Hum. Nat.* **3**, 157–178.

Galef Jr, B. G. 2003 "Traditional" foraging behaviors of brown and black rats *(Rattus norvegicus and Rattus rattus). In The biology of traditions: models and evidence* (eds D. M. Fragaszy & S. Perry), pp. 159–186. Cambridge, UK: Cambridge University Press.

Galef Jr, B. G. & Heyes, C. M. (eds) 2004 Social learning and imitation. Whole issue *Learn. Behav.* **32**.

Gardner, B. T. & Gardner, R. A. 1989 Prelinguistic development of children and chimpanzees. *Hum. Evol.* **4**, 433–460. (doi:10.1007/BF02436294)

Gilby, I. C. 2006 Meat sharing among the Gombe chimpanzees: harassment and reciprocal exchange. *Anim. Behav.* **71**, 953–963. (doi:10.1016/j.anbehav.2005.09.009)

Goodall, J. 1986 *The chimpanzees of Gombe: patterns of behaviour.* Boston, MA: Harvard University Press.

Goodall, J. van Lawick 1973 Cultural elements in a chimpanzee community. In *Precultural primate behaviour* (ed. E. W. Menzel), pp. 144–1841. Basel, Germany: Karger.

Hauser, M. D. 1988 Invention and social transmission: new data from wild vervet monkeys. In *Machiavellian intelligence* (eds R. W. Byrne & A. Whiten), pp. 327–343. Oxford, UK: Clarendon Press.

Henrich, J. & Boyd, R. 1998 The evolution of conformist transmission and the emergence of between-group differences. *Evol. Hum. Behav.* **19**, 215–241. (doi:10.1016/S1090-5138(98)00018-X)

Herman, L. M. 2002 Vocal, social and self-imitation by bottlenosed dolphins. In *Imitation in animals and artifacts* (eds K. Dautenhahn & C. L. Nehaniv), pp. 63–108. Cambridge, MA: MIT Press.

Heyes, C. M. & Saggerson, A. 2002 Testing for imitative and non-imitative social learning in the budgerigar using a two-object/two-action test. *Anim. Behav.* **64**, 851–859. (doi:10.1006/ anbe.2003.2002)

Horner, V. & Whiten, A. 2005 Causal knowledge and imitation/emulation switching in chimpanzees *(Pan troglodytes)* and children. *Anim. Cogn.* **8**, 164–181. (doi:10.1007/s10071-004-0239-6)

Horner, V., Whiten, A., Flynn, E. & de Waal, F. B. M. 2006 Faithful replication of foraging techniques along cultural transmission chains by chimpanzees and children. *Proc. Natl Acad. Sci. USA* **103**, 13 878–13 883. (doi:10.1073/pnas.0606015103)

Humphrey, N. K. 1976 The social function of intellect. In *Growing points in ethology* (eds P. P. G. Bateson & R. A. Hinde), pp. 303–317. Cambridge, UK: Cambridge University Press.

Hunt, G. R. 1996 Manufacture and use of hook-tools by New Caledonian crows. *Nature* **379**, 249–251. (doi:10.1038/ 379249a0)

Hunt, G. R. 2000 Tool use by the New Caledonian crow, *Corvus moneduloides,* to obtain *Cerambycidae* from dead wood. *Emu* **100**, 109–114. (doi:10.1071/MU9852)

Hunt, G. R. & Gray, R. D. 2003 Diversification and cumulative evolution in New Caledonian crow tool manufacture. *Proc. R. Soc. B* **270**, 867–874. (doi:10.1098/rsbl.2003.0009)

Hurley, S. & Chater, N. (eds) 2005 *Perspectives on imitation: from mirror neurons to memes.* Boston, MA: MIT Press.

Iwaniuk, A. N. & Nelson, J. E. 2003 Developmental differences are correlated with relative brian size in birds: a comparative analysis. *Can. J. Zool.* **81**, 1913–1928. (doi:10.1139/z03-190)

Janik, V. & Slater, P. J. B. 1997 Vocal learning in mammals. *Adv. Stud. Behav.* **26**, 59–99.

Janik, V. & Slater, P. J. B. 2000 The different roles of social learning in vocal communication. *Anim. Behav.* **60**, 1–11. (doi:10.1006/anbe.2000.1410)

Jensen, A. R. 2000 The g factor: psychometrics and biology. In *The nature of intelligence,* vol. 233 (eds G. R. Bock, J. A. Goode & K. Webb) *Novartis foundation symposium,* pp. 37–47. Chichester, UK: Wiley.

Johnson, V. E., Deaner, R. O. & van Schaik, C. P. 2002 Bayesian analysis of multi-study rank data with application to primate intelligence ratings. *J. Am. Stat. Soc.* **97**, 8–17.

Jolly, A. 1966 Lemur social behavior and primate intelligence. *Science* **153**, 501–506. (doi:10.1126/ science.153.3735.501)

Kenward, B., Weir, A. A. S., Rutz, C. & Kacelnik, A. 2005 Tool manufacture by naïve juvenile crows. *Nature* **433**, 121. (doi:10.1038/433121a)

Klein, E. D. & Zentall, T. R. 2003 Imitation and affordance learning by pigeons (*Columbia livia). J. Comp. Psychol.* **117**, 414–419. (doi:10.1037/0735-7036.117.4.414)

Krützen, M., Mann, J., Heithaus, M. R., Connor, R. C., Bejder, L. & Sherwin, W. B. 2005 Cultural transmission of tool use in bottlenose dolphins. *Proc. Natl Acad. Sci.* **102**, 8939–8943. (doi:10.1073/ pnas.0500232102)

Kudo, H. & Dunbar, R. I. M. 2001 Neocortex size and social network size in primates. *Anim. Behav.* **62**, 711–722. (doi:10.1006/anbe.2001.1808)

Kummer, H., Daston, L., Gigerenzer, G. & Silk, J. 1997 The social intelligence hypothesis. In *Human by nature: between biology and the social sciences* (eds P. Weingart, P. Richerson, S. D. Mitchell & S. Maasen), pp. 157–179. Hillsdale, NJ: Lawrence Erlbaum.

Laland, K. N. & Hoppitt, W. 2003 Do animals have culture? *Evol. Anthropol.* **12**, 150–159. (doi:10.1002/evan.10111)

Laland, K. N. & Janik, V. 2006 The animal cultures debate. *Trends Ecol. Evol.* **21**, 542–547.

Laland, K. N., Odling-Smee, J. & Feldman, M. W. 2000 Niche construction, biological evolution and cultural change. *Behav. Brain Sci.* **23**, 131–175. (doi:10.1017/S0140525X00002417)

Lefebvre, L. & Bouchard, J. 2003 Social learning about food in birds. In *The biology of traditions: models and evidence* (eds D. M. Fragaszy & S. Perry), pp. 94–126. Cambridge, UK: Cambridge University Press.

Lefebvre, L., Reader, S. M. & Sol, D. 2004 Brains, innovations and evolution in birds and primates. *Brain Behav. Evol.* **63**, 233–246. (doi:10.1159/000076784)

Levinson, S. C. 2006 Introduction: the evolution of culture in a microcosm. In *Evolution and culture* (eds S. C. Levinson & P. Jaisson), pp. 1–41. Cambridge, MA: MIT Press.

McGrew, W. C. 1992 *Chimpanzee material culture: implications for human evolution.* Cambridge, UK: Cambridge University Press.

McGrew, W. C. 2005 *The cultured chimpanzee: reflections on cultural primatology.* Cambridge, UK: Cambridge University Press.

Mann, J. & Sargeant, B. 2003 Like mother, like calf: the ontogeny of foraging traditions in wild Indian ocean bottlenose dolphins (*Tursiops sp.*). In *The biology of traditions: models and evidence* (eds D. M. Fragaszy & S. Perry), pp.237–266.Cambridge, UK: Cambridge University Press.

Mann, J. & Smuts, B. B. 1999 Behavioral development in wild bottlenose dolphins *(Tursiops sp.). Behaviour* **136**, 529–566. (doi:10.1163/156853999501469)

Mesoudi, A., Whiten, A. & Dunbar, R. I. M. 2006a A bias for social information in human cultural transmission. *Br. J. Psychol.* **97**, 405–423. (doi:10.1348/000712605X85871)

Mesoudi, A., Whiten, A. & Laland, K. 2006b Towards a unified science of culture. *Behav. Brain Sci.* **29**, 329–383. (doi:10.1017/S0140525X06009083)

Mitchell, R. W. & Anderson, J. R. 1993 Discrimination learning of scratching, but failure to obtain imitation and self-recognition in a long-tailed macaque. *Primates* **34**, 301–309. (doi:10.1007/BF02382625)

Mithen, S. 2007 Did farming arise from a misapplication of social intelligence? *Phil. Trans. R. Soc. B* **362**, 705–718. (doi:10.1098/rstb.2006.2005)

Moura, A. C. D. & Lee, P. C. 2004 Capuchin stone tool use in Caatinga dry forest. *Science* **306**, 1909. (doi:10.1126/ science.1102558)

Nguyen, N. H., Klein, E. D. & Zentall, T. R. 2005 Imitation of a two-action sequence by pigeons. *Psychol. Bull. Rev.* **12**, 514–518.

Ottoni, E. B. & Mannu, M. 2001 Semifree-ranging tufted capuchins (*Cebus apella*) spontaneously use tools to crack open nuts. *Int. J. Primatol.* **22**, 347–358. (doi:10.1023/A:1010747426841)

Panger, M. A., Perry, S., Rose, L., Gros-Luis, J., Vogel, E., Mackinnon, K. C. & Baker, M. 2002 Cross-site differences in foraging behavior of white-faced capuchins *(Cebus capuchinus). Am. J. Phys. Anthropol.* **119**, 52–56. (doi:10.1002/ajpa.10103)

Passingham, R. E. 1981 *The human primate.* New York, NY: W. H. Freeman.

Perry, S. *et al.* 2003a Social conventions in white-face capuchins monkeys: evidence for behavioral traditions in a neotropical primate. *Curr. Anthropol.* **44**, 241–268. (doi:10.1086/345825)

Perry, S. *et al.* 2003b Traditions in wild white-faced capuchin monkeys. In *The biology of traditions: models and evidence* (eds D. M. Fragaszy & S. Perry), pp. 391–425. Cambridge, UK: Cambridge University Press.

Reader, S. & Laland, K. 2002 Social intelligence, innovation, and enhanced brain size in primates. *Proc. Natl Acad. Sci. USA* **99**, 4436–4441. (doi:10.1073/pnas.062041299)

Rehkamper, G. K. & Zilles, K. 1991 Parallel evolution in mammalian and avian brains: comparative cytoarchitectonic and cytochemical analysis. *Cell Tissue Res.* **263**, 23–28. (doi:10.1007/BF00318396)

Rehkamper, G. K., Frahm, H. D. & Zilles, K. 1991 Quantitative development of brain structures in birds (Galliformes and Passeriformes) compared with that in mammals (Insectivores and primates). *Brain Behav. Evol.* **37**, 125–143.

Reiss, D. & Marino, L. 2001 Mirror self-recognition in the bottlenose dolphin: a case of cognitive convergence. *Proc. Natl Acad. Sci. USA* **98**, 5937–5942. (doi:10.1073/pnas.101086398)

Rendell, L. & Whitehead, H. 2001 Cultures in whales and dolphins. *Behav. Brain Sci.* **24**, 309–382. (doi:10.1017/ S0140525X0100396X)

Rosa, M. G. P. & Tweedale, R. 2005 Brain maps, great and small: lessons from comparative studies of primate visual cortical organization. *Phil. Trans. R. Soc. B* **360**, 665–691. (doi:10.1098/rstb.2005.1626)

Rose, L. M., Perry, S., Panger, M., Jack, K., Manson, J., Gros-Luis, J., Mackinnon, K. C. & Vogel, E. 2003 Interspecific interactions between *Cebus capuchinus* and other species in Costa Rican sites. *Int. J. Primatol.* **24**, 759–796. (doi:10.1023/A:1024624721363)

Rumbaugh, D. S., Savage-Rumbaugh, E. S. & Washburn, D. A. 1996 Toward a new outlook on primate learning and behavior: complex learning and emergent processes in comparative perspective. *Jpn. Psychol. Res.* **38**, 113–125.

Russon, A. E. 1997 Exploiting the expertise of others. In *Machiavellian intelligence II: extensions and evaluations* (eds A. Whiten & R. W. Byrne), pp. 174–206. Cambridge, UK: Cambridge University Press.

Russon, A. E. & Galdikas, B. M. F. 1993 Imitation in free-ranging rehabilitant orangutans *(Pongo pygmaeus). J. Comp. Psychol.* **107**, 147–161. (doi:10.1037/0735-7036.107.2.147)

Sackett, G. P., Novak, M. F. S. X. & Kroeker, R. 1999 Early experience effects on adaptive behavior: theory revisited. *Ment. Retard. Dev. Disabil. Res. Rev.* **5**, 30–40. (doi:10.1002/(SICI)1098-2779 (1999)5:1<30::AID-MRDD4>3.0.CO;2-J)

Sapolsky, R. M. & Share, L. J. 2004 A pacific culture among wild baboons: its emergence and transmission. *Public Libr. Sci. Biol.* **2**, 534–541.

Savage-Rumbaugh, E. S. & Levin, R. 1994 *Kanzi: the ape at the brink of the human mind.* New York, NY: Wiley.

Singleton, I. S. & van Schaik, C. P. 2002 The social organisation of a population of Sumatran orang-utans. *Folia Primatol.* **73**, 1–20. (doi:10.1159/000060415)

Smolker, R. A., Richards, A. F., Connor, R. C., Mann, J. & Bergson, P. 1997 Sponge-carrying by Indian Ocean bottlenose dolphins: possible tool-use by a delphinid. *Ethology* **103**, 454–465.

Sol, D., Stirling, D. G. & Lefebvre, L. 2005 Behavioral drive or behavioral inhibition in evolution: sub-specific diversification in Holocene passerines. *Evolution* **59**, 2669–2677.

Sterelny, K. 2007 Social intelligence, human intelligence and niche construction. *Phil. Trans. R. Soc. B* **362**, 719–730. (doi:10.1098/rstb.2006.2006)

Stoinski, T. & Whiten, A. 2003 Social learning by orangutans (*Pongo abelii and Pongo pygmaeus*) in a simulated food processing task. *J. Comp. Psychol.* **117**, 272–282. (doi:10.1037/0735-7036.117.3.272)

Tebbich, S., Taborsky, M., Fessl, B. & Blomqvist, D. 2001 Do woodpecker finches acquire tool use by social learning. *Proc. R. Soc. B* **268**, 2189–2193. (doi:10.1098/rspb.2001.1738)

Tomasello, M. 1999 *The cultural origins of human cognition.* Cambridge, MA: Harvard University Press.

Tomasello, M. & Call, J. 1997 *Primate cognition.* Oxford, UK: Oxford University Press.

Tomasello, M. & Call, J. 2004 The role of humans in the cognitive development of apes revisited. *Anim. Cogn.* **7**, 213–215. (doi:10.1007/s10071-004-0227-x)

van Schaik, C. P. 1999 The socioecology of fission–fusion sociality in orangutans. *Primates* **40**, 73–90.

van Schaik, C. P. 2004 *Among orangutans: red apes and the rise of human culture.* Cambridge, MA: Harvard University Press (Belknap).

van Schaik, C. P. 2006 Why are some animals so smart? *Sci. Am.* **294**, 64–71.

van Schaik, C. P., Deaner, R. O. & Merrill, M. Y. 1999 The conditions for tool use in primates: implications for the evolution of material culture. *J. Hum. Evol.* **36**, 719–741. (doi:10.1006/jhev.1999.0304)

van Schaik, C. P., Ancrenaz, M., Borgen, G., Galdikas, B., Knott, C. D., Singleton, I., Suzuki, A., Utami, S. S. & Merrill, M. 2003*a* Orangutan cultures and the evolution of material culture. *Science* **299**, 102–105. (doi:10.1126/ science.1078004)

van Schaik, C. P., Fox, E. A. & Fechtman, L. T. 2003*b* Individual variation in the rate of use of tree-hole tools among wild orang-utans: implications for hominin evolution. *J. Hum. Evol.* **44**, 11–23. (doi:10.1016/S0047- 2484(02)00164-1)

Visalberghi, E. & Fragaszy, D. 1990 Do monkeys ape? In *Language and intelligence in monkeys and apes: comparative developmental perspectives* (eds S. Parker & K. Gibson), pp.247–273. Cambridge, UK: Cambridge University Press.

Visalberghi, E. & Fragaszy, D. M. 2002 Do monkeys ape?— Ten years after. In *Imitation in animals and artifacts* (eds K. Dautenhahn & C. L. Nehaniv), pp. 471–499. Cambridge, MA: MIT Press.

Voelkl, B. & Huber, L. 2000 True imitation in marmosets. *Anim. Behav.* **60**, 195–202.(doi:10.1006/ anbe.2000.1457)

Weiskrantz, L. (ed.) 1985 *Animal intelligence.* Oxford, UK: Oxford University Press.

West, M. J., King, A. P. & White, D. J. 2003 Discovering culture in birds: the role of learning and development. In *Animal social complexity: intelligence, culture and individualized societies* (eds F. B. M. de Waal & P. L. Tyack), pp. 470–492. Cambridge, MA: Harvard University Press.

West-Eberhard, M. J. 2003 *Developmental plasticity and evolution.* New York, NY: Oxford University Press.

Whiten, A. 1996 Mindreading, pretence and imitation: secondary representation in comparative prima-tology and developmental psychology? In *Reaching into thought: the minds of the great apes* (eds A. E. Russon, K. A. Bard & S. T. Boysen), pp. 300–324. Cambridge, UK: Cambridge University Press.

Whiten, A. 1998 Imitation of the sequential structure of actions by chimpanzees *(Pan troglodytes).* *J. Comp. Psychol.* **112**, 270–281. (doi:10.1037/0735-7036.112.3.270)

Whiten, A. 1999 The evolution of deep social mind in humans. In *The descent of mind: psychological perspectives on hominid evolution* (eds M. C. Corballis & S. E. G. Lea), pp. 173–193. Oxford, UK: Oxford University Press.

Whiten, A. 2000 Social complexity and social intelligence. In *The nature of intelligence*, vol. 233 (eds G. R. Bock, J. A. Goode & K. Webb), *Novartis foundation symposium*, pp. 185–196. Chichester, UK: Wiley.

Whiten, A. 2005 The second inheritance system of chimpanzees and humans. *Nature* **437**, 52–55. (doi:10.1038/nature04023)

Whiten, A. 2006 The place of 'deep social mind' in human evolution. In *Human nature* (ed. M. A. Jeeves), pp. 207–222. Edinburgh, UK: Royal Society of Edinburgh.

Whiten, A. & Byrne, R. W. 1988*a* The Machiavellian intelligence hypotheses. In *Machiavellian intelligence: social complexity and the evolution of intellect in monkeys, apes and humans* (eds R. W. Byrne & A. Whiten), pp. 1–9. Oxford, UK: Oxford University Press.

Whiten, A. & Byrne, R. W. 1988*b* Taking Machiavellian intelligence apart. In *Machiavellian intelligence: social complexity and the evolution of intellect in monkeys, apes and humans* (eds R. W. Byrne & A. Whiten), pp. 50–65. Oxford, UK: Oxford University Press.

Whiten, A. & Byrne, R. W. 1988c Tactical deception in primates. *Behav. Brain Sci.* **11**, 233–273.

Whiten, A. & Byrne, R. W. (eds) 1997 *Machiavellian intelligence II: extensions and evaluations.* Cambridge, UK: Cambridge University Press.

Whiten, A. & Byrne, R. W. 2004 Machiavellian intelligence: a concise eight-year update. In *Machiavellian intelligence II* (transl. by M. Tomonaga, R. Oda, S. Hirata, K. Fujita), pp. 381–389. Kyoto, Japan: Nakanishiya Suppan. (in Japanese: English translation available from authors).

Whiten, A. & Ham, R. 1992 On the nature and evolution of imitation in the animal kingdom: reappraisal of a century of research. *Adv. Stud. Behav.* **11**, 239–283.

Whiten, A., Goodall, J., McGrew, W. C., Nishida, T., Reynolds, V., Sugiyama, Y., Tutin, C. E. G., Wrangham, R. W. & Boesch, C. 1999 Cultures in chimpanzees. *Nature* **399**, 682–685. (doi:10.1038/21415)

Whiten, A., Goodall, J., McGrew, W. C., Nishida, T., Reynolds, V., Sugiyama, Y., Tutin, C. E. G., Wrangham, R. W. & Boesch, C. 2001 Charting cultural variation in chimpanzees. *Behaviour* **138**, 1481–1516. (doi:10.1163/ 156853901317367717)

Whiten, A., Horner, V. & Marshall-Pescini, S. R. J. 2003 Cultural panthropology. *Evol. Anthropol.* **12**, 92–105. (doi:10.1002/evan.10107)

Whiten, A., Horner, V., Litchfield, C. A. & Marshall-Pescini, S. 2004 How do apes ape? *Learn. Behav.* **32**, 36–52.

Whiten, A., Horner, V. & de Waal, F. B. M. 2005 Conformity to cultural norms of tool use in chimpanzees. *Nature* **437**, 737–740. (doi:10.1038/nature04047)

Whiten, A., Spiteri, A., Horner, V., Bounie, K. E., Lambeth, S. P., Schapiro, S. J. & de Waal, F. B. M. 2007 Transmission of multiple traditions within and between chimpanzee groups. *Current Biology*, **17**, 1038–1043.

Williams, J. H. G., Whiten, A. & Singh, T. 2004 A systematic review of action imitation in autistic spectrum disorder. *J. Autism Dev. Disord.* **34**, 285–299. (doi:10.1023/B: JADD.0000029551.56735.3a)

Wilson, A. C. 1985 The molecular basis of evolution. *Sci. Am.* **253**, 148–157.

Worden, B. D. & Papaj, D. R. 2005 Flower choice copying in bumble bees. *Biol. Lett.* **1**, 504–507. (doi:10.1098/rsbl.2005.0368)

Wrangham, R. W., Chapman, C. A., Clark-Arcadi, A. P. & Isabirye-Basuta, G. 1996 Social ecology of Kanyawara chimpanzees: implications for understanding the costs of great ape groups. In *Great ape societies* (eds W. C. McGrew, L. F. Marchant & T. Nishida), pp. 45–57. Cambridge, UK: Cambridge University Press.

Wyles, J. S., Kunkel, J. G. & Wilson, A. C. 1983 Birds, behavior and anatomical evolution. *Proc. Natl Acad. of Sci. USA* **80**, 4394–4397. (doi:10.1073/pnas.80.14.4394)

Zentall, T. R. 2004 Action imitation in birds. *Learn. Behav.* **32**, 15–23.

Zentall, T. R., Sutton, J. E. & Sherburne, L. M. 1996 True imitative learning in pigeons. *Psychon. Sci.* **7**, 343–346. (doi:10.1111/j.1467-9280.1996.tb00386.x)

Developmental & Neural Perspectives

9

Getting back to the rough ground: deception and 'social living'

Vasudevi Reddy

At the heart of the social intelligence hypothesis is the central role of 'social living'. But living is messy and psychologists generally seek to avoid this mess in the interests of getting clean data and cleaner logical explanations. The study of deception as intelligent action is a good example of the dangers of such avoidance. We still do not have a full picture of the development of deceptive actions in human infants and toddlers or an explanation of why it emerges. This paper applies Byrne & Whiten's functional taxonomy of tactical deception to the social behaviour of human infants and toddlers using data from three previous studies. The data include a variety of acts, such as teasing, pretending, distracting and concealing, which are not typically considered in relation to human deception. This functional analysis shows the onset of non-verbal deceptive acts to be surprisingly early. Infants and toddlers seem to be able to communicate false information (about themselves, about shared meanings and about events) as early as true information. It is argued that the development of deception must be a fundamentally social and communicative process and that if we are to understand why deception emerges at all, the scientist needs to get 'back to the rough ground' as Wittgenstein called it and explore the messy social lives in which it develops.

Keywords: communication; deception; human infants; pretence; social intelligence; tactical deception

I have often thought that all philosophical debates are ultimately between the partisans of structure and the partisans of 'goo'.... We must be aware that today, the particular academic and scientific fashion leans heavily in the direction of structure and nominalism.

Alan W. Watts 1965. The Individual as Man/World.

The more narrowly we examine the actual language, the sharper becomes the conflict between it and our requirement. (For the crystalline purity of logic was, of course, not a result of investigation: it was a requirement.) The conflict becomes intolerable; the requirement is now in danger of becoming empty. We have got on to slippery ice where there is no friction and so in a certain sense the conditions are ideal, but also, just owing to that, we are unable to walk. We want to walk: so we need friction. Back to the rough ground!

(Ludwig Wittgenstein 1953),
Philosophical investigations, S 107.

9.1 Rough ground, goo and social living

Social living is as rough and 'gooey' as you can get. By virtue of its infinite variety (because it is indeed 'living' and creative), it defies logical reduction, mocks at frequency counts in its celebration of the unique and the unusual, and is inherently relational even in the question of its visibility to others. Its importance was highlighted explicitly in Humphrey's (1976/1988) argument that the 'complexities of social living' must be an 'adaptive force in the development of intelligence'. But even a century ago, Dewey (1910), Baldwin (1909), Mead (1934) and others put social 'action' at the heart of the matter, arguing that from a Darwinian perspective, psychology had to be a 'social' psychology. Sound biological reasons support these calls to focus on social living: if intelligence *matters* it can only really matter in the 'wild' as it were. If we are to take social intelligence on board, then, knowing and understanding the goo of social living *must* be our prime task.

There are two senses in which the complexity that surrounds social living is important for us as scientists. In one sense, the gooeyness and impurities of everyday life are often seen as impediments to the scientist trying to study his/her phenomena. They are the 'noise' in the *recording* of the data that stops us from seeing the phenomena clearly, or the uncontrollable *contextual* variations and influences that stop us from ascertaining the 'essence' of the phenomena with certainty, or the *rare* occurrences that defy our insistence on replicability and inferential statistics. In another sense, however, and much more importantly, goo is what makes the phenomena *happen*, and trying to circumvent it in our theories by looking for the essence or the pure forms of phenomena stops us from understanding them at all. The mess of social life, I am arguing, is precisely what is needed not only for social intelligence to show itself, but also to develop at all. Wittgenstein's call to arms on attempts to find the pure forms and essences of language (or in this case of social intelligence) argued that when we refine and purify the logic and requirements for phenomena and find them only unsatisfactorily met on the ground in action, we end up with a problem. The 'requirements' as he calls them, which are a result of *logic* rather than empirical *investigation*, become 'empty'. We would have purified the conditions for the phenomena so much that they cannot actually happen a lesson well learned in artificial intelligence). Like perfecting all the conditions for walking by removing all sources of impediment and friction, we end up actually being unable to walk because the impediments, the friction, are precisely what we need in order to walk. In both these senses, we need the goo. We need, as Wittgenstein put it, to get back to the rough ground.

While the ethological tradition has always taken goo seriously with the clear conviction that the key to making sense of behaviour lay in its function 'in the wild', developmental psychology, despite its avowed interest in the social, has largely gone down a different path (see Carpendale & Lewis 2004 for one recent attempt to change its direction). As someone who has been up to my neck in goo for approximately 20 years, as a participant observer of infants and mothers in everyday life, dealing with small samples and frustrating rare examples of phenomena (and coming up repeatedly against things of which infants are not 'supposed' to be capable), the case for prioritising real-life deception seems overwhelming. In this paper, I explore the emergence of deceptive communication in human infancy. In §§3 and 4, I report two studies presenting the empirical challenges to a 'clean' theory-driven approach to the emergence of verbal lies (Newton *et al.* 2000). In §5, I apply the Whiten and Byrne functional taxonomy of tactical deception (Whiten & Byrne 1988; Byrne & Whiten 1990, 1992) to data from studies on early, often non-verbal, communication, which—although not explicitly focused on deception (Dunn 1988; Reddy 1991, 1998)—show surprising results about its early manifestations. In §6, I discuss continuities and parallels between truthful and false informing, challenging the idea of an early inability to deceive. In §7, I attempt an affective and engagement-based explanation of the development of deceiving. But first, in §2, I explore why the practice of deception (rather than its theoretical logic) needs to be given primacy.

9.2 Taking deception seriously

Deception has been central to many studies in the study of social intelligence because it seemed to be the epitome of intelligent social action: the natural 'counter intelligence'. But having started from Robert Mitchell's beautiful descriptions of deceptive encounters between dogs and humans (Mitchell & Thompson 1986) and a spectacular corpus of reports of tactical deception in non-human primates (Whiten & Byrne 1988; Byrne & Whiten 1990), something strange happened to the study of deception. In developmental psychology, it became, one might say, hi-jacked by a very specific logical idea—false beliefs. Defined almost exclusively as an action directed at the creation of false beliefs in others, the study of deception became 'refined' to the point that its rather messy occurrences in actual social life were an embarrassment rather than an objective. Today, we have not anywhere near as comprehensive a corpus of data for deceptive acts in human infants and toddlers as we do for non-human primates. Real examples of deception, far from being the *object* of our inquiries, became secondary to the theory.

The following quote captures this primacy of theory and logic in the identification of deception particularly clearly:

> The *when* can a child lie question is answered by understanding the child's mind to determine whether or not the child has the capability to lie, and at what age he or she gains this ability. If a child *can't* lie, then the question whether he or she *will* lie becomes irrelevant. It is only at the age in which the child *can* engage in a particular kind of lie does the *will* he or she lie question become relevant.
>
> (Frank 1992, p. 135)

The 'when can' question has not, however, been answered with any confidence, and the notion of false beliefs has been regularly redefined. Such a position, of course, holds to a clean distinction between competence and performance, neglecting the situatedness of intelligence. Within this approach, when real life data are discrepant in terms of the theory it becomes easier to dismiss the data and combined with the tendency to redefine the phenomena of interest (such as what is a lie) in terms of the theory, we get 'pseudo-phenomena'. In the past hundred years, there has been quite a collection of these in developmental psychology ranging from pseudo-deception and pseudo-lies (Stern & Stern 1909, cited in Piaget 1932/1977; Perner 1991; Newton 1994) to pseudo-conversation (Kaye 1982), pseudo-repairs (Shatz & O'Reilly 1990), and so on (see Reddy & Morris 2004).

The criterion for pseudoness seems to derive not simply from a general mis-fit with theories, but from a specific assumption of dual process in intelligent action—the assumption that there is first an internal mental representational process followed by an external behavioural process (Ryle 1949; see Sharrock & Coulter 2004 for a discussion). Given this assumption, the 'real' criterion for intelligence necessarily shifts away from action: it is the internal process in which we become interested. However, the evidence for thinking of cognition as internal and necessarily detached and separable from action is as questionable as is the evidence for separating mental processes from the bodily (see also Barrett *et al.* 2007). The more we focus on the internal, the more blind we become to the availability of intelligence in action itself. Our touchstone becomes logical schemata rather than the *functioning* of intelligent action in real life. This must be a dysfunctional slippage, and certainly goes against the grain of the social living enquiry!

In §3, I will describe briefly the predictions about the occurrence of deception drawn from the idea of false beliefs and then describe a challenge to this idea from two studies conducted by my student Paul Newton (Newton *et al.* 2000) of deception in the home by pre-school children too young to pass false belief tasks.

9.3 Lies before false beliefs?

The theory of the theory of mind argued strongly for a fundamental cognitive transformation at around 4 years of age: 'after that, but not before, children grasp that people can entertain a counter-factual state of affairs, and mistakenly regard that as the actual state of affairs' (Sodian *et al.* 1991, p. 469), and it is only at this stage that 'tricks, secrets and lies become possible' (Olson 1988, p. 424). There were strong reasons for the claims: first, there was *a priori* logic (Flanagan 1992) and the fact that three year olds failed false belief tasks (Perner *et al.* 1987) even when administered by parents sceptical about the possibility of their failure at this task (V. Reddy 1989, personal observation); second, the finding that three year olds in experimental tasks of deception seemed *unable* to 'point out the wrong window' to an experimenter despite intense frustration at repeatedly losing the 'reward' of a chocolate trial after trial (Russell *et al.* 1991), although they were capable of physically sabotaging a competitor's success (Sodian 1991, 1994); and third, the remarkable set of findings that high functioning children with autism failed 'theory of mind' tasks (Baron-Cohen *et al.* 1985) and were reportedly unable to lie. In addition, three year olds did not seem able to understand lying in others (Coleman & Kay 1981[1]) and even parents (when asked to report in general and retrospectively) reported low frequencies of different forms of lying before 4 years of age (Stouthamer-Loeber 1991), although when asked to actually observe and report on their three year olds' *current* deceptions, they did label them deceptive (Newton 1994).

In the face of all this, the 'anecdotal' evidence of verbal lies told by children too young to understand false beliefs (Dunn 1988; LaFreniere 1988; Triplett 1900; Sullivan & Winner 1993) seemed questionable. Even experimental evidence of deception in two and three year olds (Chandler *et al.* 1989; Chandler & Hala 1991) seemed dismissible on procedural grounds.

More recently, however, it has become clear that even by 2½ years of age, and despite not passing false belief tasks, children engage in a range of intentional verbal falsifications of reality. In one study, we trained parents to observe their children's verbal lies and record these on dictaphone and in interviews over a six-month period and compared these with success on a battery of false belief tasks; in another, we observed in more detail the lies of one two and a half-year old over a six month period (Newton *et al.* 2000).

As can be seen in figure 9.1, the lies of 'passers' (those who passed all four tests) did not differ in the range of verbal falsehoods from the lies of 'failers' (those who failed all four). Neither, as seen in figure 9.2, did the prevalence of lying differ between 'developers' (those who failed all four at start but passed all four at the end of study) before and after they passed the test battery. Passing and failing the false belief test was irrelevant to the nature or complexity or variety of lies they told. These findings were supported by a further study (Wilson *et al.* 2003) of videotaped observations of family interactions involving two siblings and at least one parent. Even on brief two hour visits, lying was observable in the home in (two-thirds of the sample of) two and a half year olds far too young to pass false belief tasks. The range of motives in these early lies are broad and not dissimilar to those of adults (Lippard 1988) with the exception of lies to protect other people's feelings (or white lies, which do not appear to emerge until approximately 5 or 6 years of age; Saarni & von Salisch 1993).

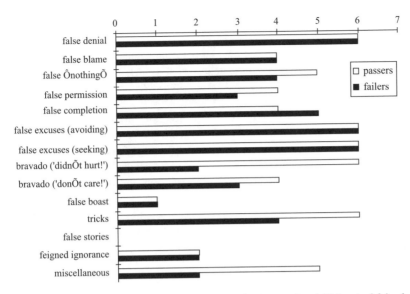

Fig. 9.1 The prevalence of different forms of deception in 'passers' and 'failers' of false-belief tasks (number of 'passers' and 'failers': $n = 6$ in each group; secondary and primary data combined.) Reprinted from Newton *et al.* (2000), *British Journal of Developmental Psychology* **18**, 297–317.

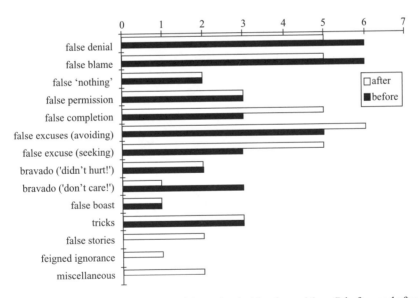

Fig. 9.2 The prevalence of different forms of deception in 'developers' ($n = 6$) before and after passing the false-belief task battery (secondary and primary data combined). Reprinted with permission from Newton *et al.* (2000), *British Journal of Developmental Psychology* **18**, 297–317.

9.4 Simplicity, rigidity and implausibility in early lies? The case of bravado

The intellectual significance of lies occurring before the understanding of false beliefs is usually challenged on three sorts of grounds: simple defensiveness and materialism of *motive*, implausibility and inappropriateness of *content*[2], rigidity[3] and simplicity[4] of *form*. I will consider one category of lies—bravado or face-saving lies—to counter these challenges. These lies, occurring even in some two and a half year olds, are interesting not only owing to their non-material motive, but because they are complex and creative, and because they cannot have been learned as simple formulae or rules, rigidly applied. In fact many categories of lies in three year olds are often elaborate, and go way beyond single-word formulaic denials. Bravado can involve a verbal falsification of desire (emotion about the future), pain (current emotional/feeling state), or shared reality (past factuality). A fascinating power play is evident in these instances, where the child is either denying the experience of the pain being intentionally inflicted on him or her by a parent, or denying the desire for something that he or she has no further hope of obtaining, or re-describing a reality which was detrimental to the child's ego and image of competence. In §5, some examples from a more substantial database of early lies (Newton 1994) are described in order to illustrate and bring to life the different types of bravado or face-saving lies.

Parents' descriptions of what might be called *'Doesn't hurt' bravado* were on occasion heart-rending. Take for instance the following:

> You can smack her legs until they're red raw, and if she's in one of her wilful moods she'll go: 'Didn't hurt!'. On a couple of occasions when she's been threatened with a good hiding for misbehaviour she's even dropped her trousers for you. The other day she did this and then said 'It dun't hurt!'.
>
> (Newton *et al.* 2000, Study 1)

Not all occurred in such emotionally charged situations. Some were in more minor conflicts such as the following:

> (He) had been playing on top of a table, despite having been warned that he would hurt himself, when he fell and appeared to cause himself pain. M reminded him, 'I told you you'd get hurt' to which he 'forced' a laugh and replied 'It didn't hurt!' M could tell that it had hurt because (he) had fallen with quite a force and was biting his lip.
>
> (Newton *et al.* 2000, Study 1)

In addition, there was also what might be called *'Don't care' bravado*. Here's a subtle one:

> (She) had recently been bought a toy spider, unfortunately she hated it and wouldn't go near it. Because (she) was being particularly naughty, F threatened her 'If you don't behave I'll get that spider out!' She replied 'I don't care, I've been playing with it all day'. M (who had been with her all day) noted that she had never played with the spider and had not been near it that day, let alone played with it all day.
>
> (Newton *et al.* 2000, Study 1)

The face-saving lies in the two and a half year old (Newton *et al.* 2000, Study 2), motivated by a desire to be seen to be right—showing what might be called *'I was right' bravado*—were even more subtle. Take this attempt to alter shared memory of past reality:

> It was early morning and S (sibling) had been staying overnight at a friend's. I was still in bed when R came in and asked me 'Shall we go and pick up S in a minute?' Contradicting him, I said 'No, no. Not in a minute. Later.' R exclaimed 'I said 'shall we go and pick up S later on', that's what I said. I said 'shall we go and pick up S later on'.' This incident struck me and after a few minutes I asked him again 'What did you say?' He answered 'I already said, 'shall we go and pick up S later', I said'.
>
> (Newton *et al.* 2000, Study 2)

That there was no question of confusion about reality in this child can be seen by the fact that this example was not isolated; there were others by the same child—uniquely different— but seeking the same ego-defence (Newton 1994). In some cases, the lie was even acknowledged with a laugh when it failed.

Bravado lies were neither rigid in form (often involving several words rather than simple 'yes'/ 'no'/'nothing' forms), nor formulaically learned (they were all unique examples), nor simply materialist in motive (involving in some cases, misrepresentation of feelings and desires). And, like other lies, they often extended over several conversational turns, adapting to disbelief and challenge, as in the following apparently pointless lie (from Study 1, Newton et al. 2000) in the face of an anxious father looking out for the postman: 'The postman's already been', 'No, he hasn't', 'I saw him go past', 'No, you didn't', 'I did, I did, he came when you were upstairs'. Just at the point when the parents were beginning to believe it, the child blew it at the last minute by adding 'He brought something for me'. Simplicity and rigidity of form was certainly not this child's problem! Although such elaborations do increase with age, an observational study by Wilson et al. (2003) showed that there was no difference between two and a half year olds and four year olds in their use of simple denials—in fact, these increased with age! Further, children's lies are not generally reinforced by success (Wilson et al. 2003), suggesting that learning formulae for tricking people cannot be as easy as all that!

Early lies do not even appear to be so implausible. Newton (1994) examined 'false blame' lies in detail for implausibility. While 9 of his 24 children did, at least once, blame a toy (implausibly) for a misdemeanour, only three children did this more than once, and except for one child, false blame was most frequently (and not implausibly) directed at siblings. The one exception was a child with no siblings, who on two occasions blamed an imaginary friend and a toy. Most interestingly, of these nine toy-blaming children, eight had passed at least two of the false belief tasks! Similarly, Wilson et al. (2003) found only two examples of implausible lies in their observational records: both were from the group of four year olds rather than from the two and a half year olds! One could argue that the real challenge to the claim that these are indeed lies should be inappropriateness (to the purpose) rather than implausibility. After all, plausibility depends on how much information you have about various aspects of the world rather than either your intent to deceive or the creativity of your lie. In Newton's corpus of lies which included a whole set of false excuses, most were reasonably appropriate. There was just one rather dubious one— a child trying to avoid going to bed by using the excuse 'I've got a sore throat' (similar to the now famous 'Can't go to bed because I am too tired' example from Perner 1991). Here is an example of a lie at 2 years and 5 months, completely implausible, but (potentially) perfectly 'appropriate'!

> I returned home with the children as their uncle and aunt arrived for the weekend. After a brief chat the aunt asked 'Where's your daddy?' R chattily volunteered (with no evidence) 'He's upstairs'. A little later his father's voice was heard coming from the backdoor (rather than from upstairs). R said immediately 'My *other* daddy's upstairs'. His aunt (who had forgotten his previous statement) looked puzzled. I started laughing, realizing the purpose of his statement (and there was indeed no one else upstairs!).
>
> (Newton et al. 2000, Study 2)

A preoccupation with the logic of false belief understanding has generally precluded an exploration of such everyday lying (but see Astington (2003) for a re-assessment). With the recent finding that even 15 month olds appear to pass a false belief task (Onishi & Baillargeon 2005; although see debate between Ruffman & Perner (2005) and Leslie (2005)) the possibility of genuine deception in everyday social life becomes important not only in pre-schoolers, but also in infants and toddlers.

9.5 Deception before lying: teasing, concealing, distracting and pretending

So what happens before two years of age? There is a distinct paucity of information. While there is an impressive corpus of data from the social lives of nonhuman primates, encompassing a range of deceptive encounters including what could be called teasing, pretending, concealing and distracting (Whiten & Byrne 1988; Byrne & Whiten 1990), there is no equivalent information for human infants and children. Whiten and Byrne's functional definition of tactical deception[5] allowed them to bypass the issue of knowledge of false beliefs and take a much broader look at non-human primate deception in real social situations than has happened in studies of young children (but see Dunn (1988) and Reddy (1991)).

I attempt below to adapt this functional taxonomy of tactical deception to human infants. I use data from two studies exploring teasing and interpersonal play in infants from 7 to 12 months (Reddy 1991) and from 8 to 24 months (Reddy 1998), other observations (Dunn 1988) as well as data from the explicit studies of deception discussed above (Newton *et al.* 2000). Compared to the non-human primates, there were differences in the prevalence of different kinds of deception, necessitating the addition of one new subcategory (*creating an image of self-competence*) and the adaptation of two others (*creating an affiliative image* and *creating a threatening image*) to the rather different kinds of examples in infants than typically found among other mature primates. In addition, I included a further subcategory: *passive hiding*. In general, however, many of the infant examples found ready parallels in the Whiten & Byrne corpus and I found it remarkably easy to apply the taxonomy to infant behaviour.

In their second round of classification, Byrne & Whiten (1990) report three aspects of an interaction for inclusion as tactical deception: 'an animal being made to misinterpret the situation', 'by an agent who benefits from the misinterpretation' 'using a behaviour deployed tactically—that is, not in the normal and expected way for the species'. The different worlds that human infants live in (safe, supportive and often well resourced), their relative lack of motor skills, mobility and power to act independently, as well as the much richer information available about their behaviour (reported in detail from the recipient's and partner's perspective and including fuller developmental histories than usually available in the non-human primates, with the exception of human-reared animals) necessitated an adaptation of these criteria.

I adapted the first criterion to include *potential* misinterpretations. A parent is unlikely to be fooled for long by infant deceptiveness in the same way as might one mature animal by another. Rather than attempt to include only successful deceptions (which would create its own paradox), I included those acts where the misinterpretation was brief or at least possible according to parental report. Most importantly, this criterion ensures that the act is not merely socially manipulative or involving of 'above board' bargaining or trading. The recipient must be deceived into enabling the reward rather than merely allowing the reward. In the case of human infants if, for example, an apparently tricky or deceptive act always leads to a certain reward or outcome, there would be good reason to argue that the act is not deceptive at all. If a mother regularly kissed her baby whenever he pointed to things, there would be no deception involved in pointing for a kiss unless the pointing actually 'meant' something else (in previous interactions).

The second criterion was non-problematic other than in the determination of 'benefit'. What counts as benefit for a human infant? While the sexual and food-related struggles of the mature non-human primates were irrelevant here, there were several others that were easy to identify: being allowed to do what they want to do; eating what they want to eat; getting parental attention when they want it; avoiding being interrupted when busy; getting the emotional reactions they want from others; feeling successful or amused, and so on. The difference lay in the extent to which these 'benefits' involved play and fun rather than simply serious rewards.

The third—and most important—criterion required a judgement about what is 'normal' for the infant rather than the species, and in this case included some additional checks. Playful acts which had become normal for the infant (even though they might in other circumstances be deceptive) were excluded—such as tricks which had become routines and were part of an established game. With infants (given the different nature of the information) it was often single acts which were more convincing than the repeated use of a tactic. When considering deception in other primates, Byrne (2003) sees the latter as necessary to confirm the tacticalness of an act. In addition, given the immaturity of the infants, I needed to ensure that the deceptive act (whether gesture or word or expression) was also present in its 'straight' form in the normal repertoire of the infants—otherwise its 'mis'-use would not be meaningful. This would exclude playfighting in animals, where the serious version of the act is probably absent from the animal's experience (suggesting that the act itself is above board—a thing in itself). It would also exclude simple provocation—pulling hair, jumping on someone, biting, and some of what Adang (1984) calls 'quasi-aggressive behaviour'.

Table 9.1 shows the data. I discuss in the sections below, examples from four categories—*concealment*, *distraction*, *attraction* and *creating an image*—where examples were available from early in human infancy. The wealth of human infant examples in *creating an image* made it initially the most difficult category to apply and highlights potential differences with the data from the non-human primates[6].

(a) Concealment

Passive hiding of forbidden activities was the earliest type of concealment. Eight month-old P, for example, had a passion for shutting the curtain in the living room. He usually waited for his mother to go into the kitchen before approaching the curtain:

> … if I just go into the kitchen to get something ….(he) makes a beeline for the curtain …you can see him looking over his shoulder to see if I'm watching him, and if I tell him from the kitchen 'no' he stops and looks at you and grins for a while… as soon as I've turned my back he makes another move for it.
>
> Mother of P, 8 months, in interview (Reddy 1991)

Whiten & Byrne (1988) may not have included this as tactical deception because it involved avoidance rather than deception (and in the data they had, could have resulted from the desire not to see others rather than not be seen). I do include this category, however, because the situation and the data seem different for infants: it involved forbidden activities, it involved a deliberateness in the waiting until someone was out of visual contact before rapidly engaging in the activity (potentially overlapping with the category of creating an image of neutrality), and because other evidence of simple visual perspective taking from experimental studies at this age suggests that the mother's report— that he looks to see if he is being watched even when she has indeed gone out of the room—suggests that he is seeking to avoid visual attention. And given other evidence from mothers about infants teasing—by doing forbidden things while making sure that they are being watched—this kind of deception, as an attempt to conceal an activity, is not surprising. More *active concealment*, however, such as using the body

Table 9.1. Byrne & Whiten's (1990) functional taxonomy of tactical deception adapted for human infants and toddlers.

Categories and subcategories (Byrne & Whiten 1990)	Categories for human infants and toddlers	Ages and examples from human infants and toddlers
concealment (of something from another)		
by silence[a]	*doing forbidden things quietly*	no clear data
by hiding	*passive hiding* from other's view: waiting until moment parent leaves room to engage in forbidden activity.	*8/9 months* waiting until other leaves room before rushing to forbidden activity: eating cheese plant, pulling curtains, etc. (Reddy 1991, 1998)
	active hiding from other's view: turning the back or using body to screen forbidden activity or object from other's view.	*16 months* turning back so that body screens forbidden object or activity from view (V. Reddy 1992, personal observation) *18 months* going behind the settee to engage in forbidden activity (pulling at stitches) (Dunn 1988)
by inhibiting interest in object[a]	*verbal denial* of misdemeanour or forbidden activity or object.	*2+ years* 'What have you got behind your back?' 'Nothing'; several examples (Newton et al. (2000))
by ignoring	*ignoring other's calls* with stiffened and still body	*9 months/11 months* pretending not to hear or pretending to be deaf when called (either because they are engrossed in a toy, or because doing something forbidden), but holding the body so still and not even turning to the sound, that it looks clearly motivated (Reddy 1991, 1998)
by hiding an object		*11 months* unexpectedly hiding the ball under own legs in a game when expected to roll it back, looking at mother and laughing: not a prior game (Reddy 1998)
distraction (of the other's attention away from a certain spatial locus thus attaining goal at that locus)		
by calling		*17.5 months* calling mother to look at dog in order to repeat playful throwing of gloves (Sully 1896 in Dunn 1988)
by looking[a]		
by threat[a]		
by leading[a]		
by close-range behaviour	*holding the other's eyes* while engaging in forbidden activity.	*11 months/13 months* staring the other out while performing the forbidden act in surreptitious manner; two examples (Reddy 1998)
by acquired signing[a]		
attraction (of the other to a certain spatial locus and thus attaining goal at that locus)		
by calling	*fake crying* (the spatial locus is the self)	*8 months/9 months* using cries to 'call' the other, with the cries themselves identifiable as 'fake' with non-distressed 'waiting for response'; several reports (Reddy 1991, 1998)

by looking[a]

by leading[a]

by close-range behaviour — *fake laughing* (the spatial locus is the self) — *6 months/7+ months* laughing in an 'artificial' manner when overhearing other laughing, in 'order to join in' with them, be part of a group; several reports (Reddy 1991, 1998; V. Reddy 1986, personal observation)

creating an image (which conceals the agent's intentions and facilitates attainment of goal: it may be):

neutral (to appear of little or no significance to other, e.g. suppressing aggression or 'smiles') — *feigning innocence/ignorance* — *11 months* when caught approaching forbidden soil in house plant, waving/scooping hand up, as if pretending not really going to touch it; repeated several times; single report (Reddy 1998) *30 months* 'What's happened to this? 'I don't know.' 'I don't know who messed it (the tidy room) up.'; several reports (Newton et al. 2000) *33 months* pretending to clean paint off the TV (to be allowed to remain there) (Dunn 1988)

affiliative (to appear to increase affiliation with other, e.g. offer of grooming or of hand before rapid change of action) — *feigning offer (playful)* of object, or of self before withdrawing rapidly — *9+ months* after evidence of successful offer and release skill, offering and rapid withdrawing of object; several examples around this age and later (Reddy 1991, 1998) *11 months* on request to 'come to me' putting hands out to go, then backing off laughing – a regular game, not shy, and not with new people only, also with mother, father, grandmother, 'just pretending'; single example at this age (Reddy, 1998)

threatening (to appear to show a threat to the other) — *feigning misdemeanour/non-compliance(playful/ attention seeking* — *9 months* pretending going to touch something, not actually wanting to touch it, flicking finger on hot tea cup, etc; several examples (Reddy 1998) *11 months* pretending to take bite out of cardboard box; pretending to bash TV; 'almost touching' plant in friend's house (Reddy 1998); pretending to touch cooker (V. Reddy 1992, personal observation) *3 years* 'I'm going to write on the floor ... only joking' (Newton et al. 2000)

feigning error (playful) — *11 months* calling mother 'daddy' (Reddy 1998) *2.5 years* 'I dun wee wee here on the wall.' 'It's (the bedroom) there, it's there!' (pointing to the bathroom and grinning); pointing to all the wrong drawers, asking where the pyjamas are, deliberately pretending not to know where they are, and avoiding the one mother was verbally indicating (Newton et al. 2000)

(continued)

Table 9.1. (*contd.*)

Categories and subcategories (Byrne & Whiten 1990)	Categories for human infants and toddlers	Ages and examples from human infants and toddlers
self competence	*'didn't hurt' bravado* denial of pain following smacking for misdemeanour or injury upon doing forbidden act	*2.5 years* 'That didn't real hurt!'; several examples (Newton *et al.* (2000))
	'don't care' bravado denial of desire for (desired) object; denial of fear for threatened (frightening) object	*2.5 years* 'I didn't want it anyway'; 'I don't care, I been playing with it all day' (Newton *et al.* (2000))
	false boasts claiming possession of object or skill which isn't true	*3 years* 'I got one of them too'; several examples (Newton *et al.* (2000))
	denial of error by pretending original action was different, by trying to alter current reality	*2.5 years* 'My other Daddy's upstairs'; 'I said we'll pick her up later that's what I said'; 'That were me making the noise (not the bowl)' (Newton *et al.* (2000))
	false blame	*2.5 years* 'Someone else, not me'; 'Carol did it'; several examples (Dunn 1988; Newton *et al.* (2000)) *3 years* false accusation of third person to justify self fantasy (Dunn 1988)
deflection (diverting a threat onto an innocent third-party: may include distraction but goes further to divert an attack, not just attention)		
using a social too (manipulating a third-party in order to deliberately influence the other)		
tool deceived[a]		
target deceived	*false promise* about future act with an object (a physical rather than social tool)	*2.5 years* 'No...I won't do it again (if you give it to me)' (Newton *et al.* (2000))
tool and target deceived	*false permission-assertion* (by another authority figure)	*2.5 years* 'Daddy said I could'; 'Dad said yes, but ask you as well'; 'Mum lets me walk here'; several examples (Newton *et al.* (2000))
counterdeception (reducing the success of the other's tactical deception; may or may not involve countering deception with deception)[a]	*'before she tricks me, I'm going to trick her'*	

[a] No evidence available in this category for infants and toddlers.

to screen a forbidden activity from the other's view, may not happen until the second year (some isolated reports at this age; Dunn 1988). Similarly, we know too little about acoustic concealment (doing forbidden things quietly) in infancy—thus far, there are no data to make a judgement on this category.

One interesting category of concealment was the inhibition of attentional response to bids for attention—the 'feigning deafness' or *'ignoring'* of social calls—especially when being called while they are doing something they are enjoying, or are doing something that they know they will be stopped from doing. In the presence of clearly audible calling, they can sit silently unreactive, with a stiffened back and rigidly held head belying the unreactiveness. In contrast to the confidence with which parents reported this type of ignoring, there are no reports, until at least the middle of the second year, of infants inhibiting attentional reactions to 'objects' which a competitor might desire. The reason for this difference might well arise from the more distal and triadic nature of acts in which attention to an object must be coordinated with the attention of another person, in contrast to the dyadic nature of ignoring another's bid. This difference is apparent also in the next category—distraction.

(b) Distraction

The category of distraction which Whiten and Byrne call *close-range behaviour* was used in a fascinatingly different way by human infants in the first year[7]. There are examples from only two infants in this category, at 11 and 13 months, but reported to have occurred on a number of occasions:

> If you give her toast and she doesn't want it … she … she's sneaky, she's very sneaky, she'll sit there looking at you and while she's got your eyes looking at her eyes, she picks it up and puts it under her arm like that [indicating with a surreptitious movement] and throws it behind her.. and she thinks you can't see it…
>
> Mother of AL, 11 months, interview (Reddy 1998)

> (These days he is still) continuing to undo the tapes on his nappy … Although now he is much more serious about it. He lies on his changing mat… and he wants to pull the tab off… he almost sort of stares you out … And really fixes his eye onto my eye and is exceedingly serious, as though he hopes that because he is looking at you and making you look straight at him, you would not note him undoing … his nappy tab. It is really rather funny actually, but he is so dead serious about it. Doesn't go on (at) every nappy change, but has certainly happened 7 or 8 times a week.
>
> Mother of JB, 13 months, Dictaphone (Reddy 1998)

In contrast to these examples of more proximal triangulation of attention between infant, person and object, there is to date only one example of more distal triangulation, shown in table 9.1 in the category distraction by calling. Sully (1896 and cited by Dunn 1988) reports an infant in the middle of the second year apparently distracting the mother by 'calling' her attention to a different location before gleefully throwing a glove once again out of the pram. Undoubtedly we have not yet got the full picture of the data, but the more distal triangulation of interests involved in this category, like that of concealment of interest in objects, may be causally linked to its late appearance.

(c) Attraction

In the first year, there were two kinds of apparently deceptive behaviour which might fit this category: attracting the other's attention to the self by fake crying (conceivably akin to fake 'lost calls' in the primates), and seeking to join in the other's activity/attracting attention to self by fake laughing (in a way, a sort of close-range behaviour, but only fitting this category very loosely). The control of affective expressions is known to be possible from around nine months of age (Izard & Malatesta 1987), confirming the parents' perceptions of the deliberateness of these expressions at this age. It is easy enough to detect the difference in sound between genuine and fake crying and the situations in which fake crying can occur are often a dead giveaway. One common situation is where the infant fakes upset at being told off:

> (She) definitely knows when she is doing something she shouldn't. She headed over towards the video, looked round to see if anyone is going to tell her off and then actually gone to touch it. When Paul [her father] told her off, she actually sat there and tried to make herself cry, but the tears just wouldn't come.
>
>   Mother of VT, 8 months, Dictaphone (Reddy 1998)

And another is where the infant wants attention and uses fake crying to get it.

> Surreptitiously watching eight month-old C in the middle of the night, her mother saw her 'shout, sort of as in crying, but no tears, for about thirty seconds and she'd stop and listen to see if she could hear me coming or moving…and she'd start again…. She just lay there and she'd shout and then she'd stop and listen and when she realized I wasn't there, she'd carry on screaming but no tears, not one single tear, and she carried on and on and on…
>
>   Mother of CS, 8 months, Interview (Reddy 1991)

Fake laughing, reported in the second half of the first year by many parents, often occurs in situations where the infant is near but not involved with two or more others. Parents report that 'fake' or artificial laughter has a distinct and identifiable quality to it. Reports of such laughter often cite situational contexts of social 'exclusion' in which the infant appears to want to 'join in' with the laughing others.

> he seems to have stopped that now actually [the artificial laugh] …he did have a sort of a…laugh that he would laugh almost because everyone else was laughing. But he seems to have stopped that at the moment, to be honest…I noticed it when the girls were laughing at something…and he would laugh…but now he's more mobile, he doesn't seem…so…I suppose because he doesn't have to sort of sit there and listen and watch them all the time, he can get off more on his own.
>
>   Mother of SS, 11 months, Interview (Reddy 1998)

Fake laughing in such a situation may not really merit the label deception: except very briefly, it does not really deceive anyone and does seem rather above board. However, it is interesting for two reasons: it illustrates that crying is not the only emotional expression that can be and is used by infants 'falsely'—that is, out of its normal expressive function, and it indicates a simple form of misuse of expression that occurs somewhat earlier than the misuse of crying.

(d) Creating an image

The category of creating an image seems to have been intended primarily for fairly sophisticated suppression of agonistic or pleasure expressions from a target animal in order to conceal an activity the agent is engaged in with a forbidden object or animal. Infant behaviour in the first year seems to differ from these non-human primate examples both motivationally (except in the more detailed reports of home-reared chimpanzees) and in sophistication. In addition to the three subcategories of creating a neutral, affiliative and threatening image, a fourth subcategory of creating an image of self-competence was added for human children, mostly, but not solely, including the bravado lies described earlier. This subcategory will, therefore, not be discussed further here.

(i) Of neutrality: ignorance/innocence

You can make yourself look innocent while actually doing something 'naughty' in a number of ways. The example below—the only one of its kind so far—may be better categorized as distraction (and if so, by something other than any of the subcategories that Byrne and Whiten propose). However, it seemed to fit equally here, with the perhaps simpler gloss of appearing to be doing something other than the actual activity.

> We were in (…) spare room tidying up and A started playing with the rubber plant, so I told him no, and he stopped. But he obviously still fancied playing with the soil so he went over to play with it again and I said no, and he sort of scooped his hand up as though he was saying oh I wasn't really going to touch the soil Mum, I was waving at you, and he kept on doing this. If I said no, he suddenly waved at me, pretending he wasn't really going for the rubber plant at all.
>
> Mother of AW, 11 months, Dictaphone (Reddy 1998)

There is no evidence for the intentional *suppression* of expressions (as in Whiten & Byrne's examples) in the first year. The only evidence we have is from two personal observations of the same infant at 18 and 20 months (see more detailed description in Reddy 2001) of embarrassed smile suppression in the face of unexpected attention from visitors. The 'motive' for this smile suppression was nothing like the self-protection of the ape examples and perhaps is better classified as creating an image of self-competence.

The most interesting examples of creating an image in human infants in the first year were the subcategories of creating images of affiliation and threat. All of them were playful, but were fascinating in their creativity and richness.

(ii) Of affiliation: offering and withdrawing/requesting and refusing

Pretending to offer something and then rapidly taking it away (with an anticipatory cheeky half smile broadening into a broader smile or laugh indicating some degree of prior planning) has been observed from around nine months (Reddy 1991) and in the second year (Chevalier-Skolnikoff 1986). As a form of deception, sometimes but not always, motivated by more malign inclinations, offering and then withdrawal of the offer is commonplace, often among siblings, and observable even among adults in more subtle forms. But there are many variations on this. Infants can also offer and withdraw the self, as in the following example:

> When you ask her to come to you, she puts her hands out to go, then backs off and laughs—a regular game. She's not shy, and doesn't do it with new people. Its with M, F, Gm. She's 'just pretending'
>
> Mother of VTu, 11 months, Interview (Reddy 1998)

> He requested juice while M was talking to the visitor, then refused it when she gave it to him, and repeated the request and refusal again a few times until M noticed that this was odd, and saw he was looking at her with a half smile
>
> Mother of JB, 11 months, observation (Reddy 1998)

While the example above of offering the 'self' and then pulling back is questionable because it was part of a game and its history was obscure, the second example of requesting and then refusing, or the more common examples of offering and withdrawing objects were often much more clearly identifiable as isolated incidents or as games 'begun' by the infant.

(iii) Of threat: feigning misdemeanour or error

There were, perhaps unsurprisingly, no examples of pretend threats in the human infants! The closest was pretend misdemeanours, involving either a playful pretence at doing something forbidden or a watchful approach to the forbidden activity, but stopping short of the actual act. The earliest such examples were from nine months on and were seen even when the activity is not actually desired: appearing to touch a hot cup of tea, or putting hands close to the fire. The infant's attention is, in all cases, focused on the reactions of the parent and the 'threat' itself not followed through. Sometimes the action itself is a giveaway, involving careful flicking movements, or slow approach movements, which stop a few inches away, not actually *doing* the forbidden act. Sometimes it is only the expression on the face and the knowledge that the infant really has no desire to do the act other than as a tease, which clarifies the intention. There were many such examples: pretending to take a bite out of the cardboard box; 'almost touching' the plant; almost touching the saucepan on the stove and so on. Parents were often fooled—at least the first time such an act occurred—into thinking that it was a serious intention and then learning that it was not.

Deliberate errors, too, can be sometimes done with a play of seriousness, which can deceive the other temporarily into thinking it to be a genuine mistake. Infants from around one year can feign errors (and sometimes fool others). The earliest example was of eleven month-old Anna, who had been confidently and correctly naming herself as 'Baby' and had already been correctly naming her mother as 'Mummy' and her father as 'Daddy'. One day she pointed to her arm, said 'Baby', then suddenly pointing to her mother said 'Daddy'. The mother's puzzled correction led only to an insistence on the 'error' until her 'cheeky look' with 'her head on her side' gave the game away.

In both the 'threat' and 'affiliation' examples, the benefit to the infant was the emotional reactions of the parent. Although some of the examples reported here involve play and teasing, many do not. It does not seem to be the case, as has been claimed, that playful motives are the only—and earliest—deceptive contexts in human infants (LaFreniere 1988). Looking at function in the sense of the 'ultimate' function of the act, it is clear that early deceptive acts *do not* only show up in play. The 'benefits' sought by the infant under one year in these acts are varied and sometimes very serious, ranging from obtaining attention, escape from a scolding, the opportunity to engage in forbidden acts, as well as 'surprised' reactions in play.

9.6 Early onset to deceptive acts. Continuities and parallels with truthful informing.

In terms of their function then, evidence of infant deceptive acts can be seen considerably earlier than we would expect from a cognitive structural analysis of deception. Not only do many of the functional categories appear to be present even by the end of the first year, but within several of the categories in Table 9.1, we can see continuities over time in the use of the categories, albeit with increasingly complex and increasingly verbal behaviour. What is striking is that these data come from studies which have not directly targeted deception nor asked parents about deception. To fill in what are very likely to be missing data from this table we need a systematic meta-study in the manner of Whiten & Byrne (1988) as well as more direct participant observations (that is, by training parents) of infants in their natural environments in the manner of Newton *et al.* (2000).

The simplicity and very early appearance of such (usually non-verbal) data of teasing, pretending, concealing and distracting thus far suggest that the verbal lies of the two and a half year old cannot only *not* be dismissed as pseudo-lies, but are already founded on a long tradition of non-verbal manipulation and misrepresentation of shared meanings. Like the verbal lies, these non-verbal deceptions too occur in more than just a single context and are motivated by more than a simple desire to escape punishment or seek rewards. The fact that they occur in play as well as seriousness suggests that the meanings they are misrepresenting are not confused with their misrepresentation. Additionally, the interpretation of their status as manipulations of information is validated by the finding that they do seem to happen more or less simultaneously with the earliest attempts to communicate anything at all. In other words, they can occur about as early as truthful information giving.

In contrast to the great difficulty in experimental studies of getting even three year old children to suppress current reality and lie (even though they appear to badly *want* to do so; Russell *et al.* 1991), the present findings suggest that even toddlers do not have a problem in communicating false realities to others. This conclusion challenges current beliefs in developmental psychology, where, even when there is no theoretical commitment to the significance of false beliefs, there is a strong conviction that counter factuality—or at least the ability to go against current reality in one's communication—is profoundly difficult. See, for example, the recent controversy about whether children's difficulty at three years lies in grasping any sort of belief at all, whether true or false (Riggs 2005), or whether it centres around the inability to *overcome current reality* in understanding false beliefs (Russell 2005). While the tricky infants and lying toddlers discussed here may not be following the criteria for belief creation, they certainly seem to be intentionally *violating current reality*—sometimes for a self-specific advantage, sometimes in play—and *presenting this information to others* around them. It also challenges biblical assumptions of childhood innocence!

Table 9.2 attempts to map what we know in early communication of true informing, expressing, naming, correcting, indicating and gesturing, with false informing, expressing, naming, correcting, indicating and gesturing. What we know about these continuities and parallels seems inadequate—the data are often missing and often not directly appropriate or equivalent. But from the little we do know, two things emerge: that deliberate false communication seems to appear as early as deliberate true communication, and that the two may develop in parallel.

The manipulation of emotional expressions for obtaining a separate goal (using existing expressions in 'false' circumstances) seems to emerge around nine months of age, but the suppressing of emotional expressions does not appear to emerge until around the middle of the second year (and suppressing or manipulating these for conventional or 'caring' reasons not until the early school years). The use of gesture in both true and false contexts (in particular the offering gesture, but possibly also 'requests' and 'refusals') seems also to be possible from around nine months of age. While it could be argued that the 'mis'-use of gestures is simply a 'new' use in a new game rather than a 'mis'-use, the fact that the same gesture continues to be used to indicate both genuine intentions and false intentions (without apparent confusion) is significant and it cannot easily be dismissed as a completely different kind of activity from the truthful use of the same act. The existence of feigned misdemeanours is similarly important, because it exists simultaneously with the ability to not misbehave in the same domain. While the feigning of misdemeanours logically follows after the ability to 'behave', both do seem to emerge at roughly the same sort of age. The giving of information to others, using a conservative definition of the intentional communication of information (Camaioni 1993; Liszkowski et al. 2004) and even specifically to ignorant others (Tomasello & Haberl 2003), is evident from at least the end of the first year. The earliest example available of *false* informing (false naming), is from 11 months, in which the infant is juxtaposing in the same incident, the

Table 9.2. Parallels and continuities in true and false informing, expressing and gesturing.

Age (months)	'True' informing, 'true' expressing and 'true' intentional gestures	'False' informing, 'false' expressing and 'false' intentional gestures (concealment or inhibition of 'information')
9–10	shaking head to refuse (Bates *et al.* 1976) offering objects and giving	'fake' expressions, gestures, passive hiding of actions
11–12	informative pointing (Liszkowski *et al.* 2006) giving novel object to surprised adult (Tomasello & Haberl 2003)	mis-naming, pretend misdemeanour (intentions), 'holding the eyes' to obscure actions, suppressing response
14	correcting communicative misunderstanding (Golinkoff 1983, 1986)	
16–20	distinguishing true and false statements (Pea, 1982; Hummer, Wimmer & Antes 1993) rejecting false informants (Baldwin & Moses 2001) selective informing about object existence and object features to ignorant others (Reddy & Simone 1995) correcting verbal contradictions about reality (Dunn 1988)	feigning injury, feigning dirty nappy, active hiding (turning body, going behind screen), smile suppression (in embarrassment)
30	selective giving of information about object location to ignorant others (O'Neill 1996)	false blame, false permission, false promise, ego-defensive false information, false information about reality
36	spontaneous informing when other has a false belief (Teerwogt *et al.* 1999)	

correct naming of self and pointing to her own arm, with incorrect naming of her mother (at a time when the names for her mother and father were already convincingly established). If pointing is genuine informing at 11 months of age, then intentional mispointing must also be misinforming—unless there is every reason to believe otherwise. If offering an object with the expectation and desire that it will be taken is a truthful intentional act, then (given other evidence that it is intended from the start to be withdrawn) offering it and rapidly withdrawing it is in those terms, a false intentional act. Similarly with the 11 month olds' feigned misdemeanours. This is not to argue that these infants are engaging in some kind of meta-representational acts, but merely to argue that *if* the serious versions of the acts are to be interpreted representationally (that is, as a result of the infant's representation of the other's representations), then there is evidence that the feigned versions of the acts should be too.

9.7 Towards an explanation of developing deception

So, if a picture of real social living is necessary not only for getting a functional picture of behaviour in its developmental (or evolutionary) contexts, but also for *explaining* its development (the 'why' question) what do these data tell us about why deception emerges at all? And how would current cognitive developmental theories explain them?

(a) Current cognitive-developmental explanations

The dominant 'theory–theory' can neither plausibly explain the range and consistency of these infant 'tactical deceptions', nor can it easily incorporate into itself recent findings that, given a suitably non-verbal habituation method, 15 month olds (Onishi & Baillargeon 2005) and possibly even 13 and 14 month olds (Song 2006; Surian *et al.*2006) can pass false-belief tasks. 'Theory-theorists' (e.g. see Ruffman & Perner 2005) argue that these (experimental) findings can be explained by the learning of complex triadic associations by the infants rather than by inference about 'hidden' concepts such as false beliefs, and therefore without invoking any need for a theory of mind. Whether or not we accept this challenge, there is indeed a problem with retaining the theory–theory version of the infants' actions in these experimental tasks and in the tactical deceptions in the present paper.

A simple assimilation of the findings by shifting of the age of acquisition from 4 years or so to early in the second year might seem possible (given the many other developments at this age such as naming, pretending, referencing, helping, and so on; Leslie 1987; Baldwin & Moses 2001; Warneken *et al.* 2006). However, it would take a seriously acontextual logic for any theory to survive such a mauling without damage to its conception of the nature and implications of the landmark skill. How can the concept, the thing that is supposedly understood, be the same or nearly the same, barring local conditions, at such diverse ages? Further, even a simple lowering of watershed age would not suffice. If these skills are indeed dependent on theoretical 'realizations' or conceptual 'discoveries' we would need to invoke a new realization or theory at different levels—at eight months (avoiding detection by seeking private situations), at 9–10 months (deceptive use of gesture to mean X when they intend it as Y), at 11 months (distracting or distorting others' view of reality by 'holding' the eyes), at 11–12 months (false misdemeanours or false naming for provoking a reaction), at 18 months (false claims to injury for obtaining sympathy or deflecting criticism), at 24 and 30 months (false statements about the self and about reality), and so on. It certainly does not seem very parsimonious to seek such a series of realizations to explain early deception and informing. Nor does it really deal with the question of why deceiving emerges, relying on an individualistic idea of 'it happens because it *can*'.

Leslie's (1987) version of the 'theory–theory' positing the ability at 18 months to de-couple 'primary' from 'meta' representations, more easily allows for the much earlier emergence of knowledge of others' mental states. It could be argued that Leslie's theory of mind mechanism (ToMM)—an innate language acquisition device (LAD)-like 'learning mechanism'—could explain not only 15 month olds passing false-belief tasks, but also the earlier tactical deceptions of the not-yet-one-year-old. Such a mechanism offers an age-free theory to explain any phenomena relevant to the domain of minds and to deceiving them. However, like Chomsky's LAD (Chomsky 1965), Leslie's ToMM too is an insistently nativist theory, in this case applying to the knowledge of minds and beliefs. Bruner's famous challenge to the LAD from the social and interactive language acquisition support system (LASS; Bruner 1983) applies to ToMM as it applies to any theory which posits pre-determined and pre-experiential knowledge. Although Leslie *et al.* (2004) argue intriguingly for ToMM as a *learning* mechanism, the role of engagement and dialogue in this mechanism seems secondary to its 'native' conceptual inclinations: engagement is a mere provider of information for the conceptual machinery. The similarity to Chomskian preconceptions is strong and the explanation does not really seem to *explain* the emergence of the skills.

(b) An affective/dialogic alternative: perceiving and experiencing deceivedness

I suggest an experience-based alternative to explaining the emergence of deceiving which seeks to avoid the dualist emphasis on conception (of false beliefs) at the expense of action (deceiving). The search for deception, which begins by looking for an awareness of false beliefs, necessarily goes down a meta-representational route. And meta-representation to explain these early phenomena must either come from an early theorizing of false beliefs or an innate module; in both, the process of its emergence and the 'why' question are left hanging unsatisfactorily. An alternative route is to look within infants' interactions with others, at its origins in dialogue[8] and the effective perception and experience of *deceivedness*.

Deceiving, like any other form of communication, *is* first of all, communication. And like any communication, it needs an intentional partner: to occur at all and to *mean* something. Unless the deception is morphological or a fixed pattern of response (which none of these infants' deceptions are), they cannot be done outside of the engagement with another person. And second, like any other communicative action, deceiving is born within the unscripted openness offered in dialogic engagement. Rather than be prescribed or planned alone as an insightful but individual act, deceiving must be drawn out in dialogue by the intentional partner—by their reactions, their invitations and their encouragement and tolerance. Whether the communication is informationally 'true' or 'false' depends, not only on the possibly separate motives affecting each partner, but also on the immediate demands and invitations in the other person's acts. Both truth and falsehood must not only be invited by the context and the partner's act, but be defined by them too. Deception is not a single head achievement.

What we know from the data presented in this paper is that long before infants can plausibly be said to infer and represent complex conceptual entities, they are engaging in subtle manipulations of their own and others' actions, which succeed in deceiving others at least temporarily. These acts are so varied that simple formula-based explanations become clumsy and unconvincing. The alternative I suggest is that the crucial feature explaining the emergence of deception is the *deceivedness* which is manifested in these engagements. Beginning from a motivation to engage and a reciprocal emotional responsiveness (both evolutionary givens for humans at least), infants get drawn into deceiving others within engagement. Engagement—or emotional dialogue—often involves acts which are unexpected by the other; dialogue which is totally predictable is hardly dialogue. The other's *deceivedness* is evident in emotional reactions, responsive actions and situational consequences. These, of course, need not only be inferred by the infant as casual relations between conceptual entities but can be *perceived* in actions, and much more importantly, *felt* by the infant in his or her own emotional responses to the other's reactions (such as delight that the other has been surprised or discomfited). Infants engage in deceiving owing to a motivation to engage with others in emotional dialogue. The infant's deceiving develops in complexity with age—a development which is evident in the content of the deceptive acts. It is the perceiving and experiencing of deceivedness, however, which provides the crucial explanation of the development of deception (see also Clayton *et al.* 2007).

Let me draw a parallel between explanations of the ability to deceive and explanations of the awareness of attention. As in the study of the emergence of deceiving, the emergence of the awareness of attention too has been bedevilled by attempts to pin it down to a point in time where the other's representation of the world (attention) can be represented by the infant. The onset of triangular attentional engagements involving spatially distal objects at 9 or 10 months, or joint attention, is the commonly identified point for the infant's discovery of attention (Bates *et al.*1976; Tomasello 1999). However, the infant's attentional engagements from the first few months of life show emotional responses to others' attention (initially only to the self; Trevarthen 1977; Adamson & Bakeman 1991) and initiatives to seek other's attention, which are similar in range and variety to those found at the middle or end of the first year (when the other's attention is perceived when directed to more complex and distal objects and events). Elsewhere (Reddy 2003, 2005), I have argued that these earlier attentional engagements do two things: they allow the infant to *feel* the other's attention in real engagements when it is directed to the self, to parts of the self's body, to the self's actions, to objects in the self's hand and so on (gradually expanding outwards), and they draw the infant into further and more complex attentional engagements. In the face of evidence that the same sorts of emotional responses and the same sorts of initiation of actions to obtain attention exist through the first year, developing primarily in relation to different 'objects' or 'topics' (Reddy 2003, 2005), positing a single and belated age for a representational awareness of attention is unhelpful (even obstructive).

In the same way, early deceptive engagements may achieve two things: first, they allow the infant to *feel* the other's deceivedness to the infant's acts (with the content of the infant's deceiving act becoming more complex and distal over time) and second, they draw the infant into developing more complex deceptive acts. The infant in actual deceptive engagements in the first year must *feel* an emotional reaction to the other's reactions of surprise, disruption, alarm, amusement, misaction, etc., especially when these reactions are in response to the infant's own acts and when they matter to the infant. And these early engagements involving affective expressions, gestures and information must inevitably draw the infant into further exploration of their violation and manipulation, and allow the expansion of deception. The evidence presented in this paper, showing a shift with age from more dyadic (or 'close-range' forms) to more distal 'triadic' forms (as in concealment of interest in object, distraction by calling to distal location, etc.) supports this conclusion and the parallel with developments in the awareness of attention. Deceivedness involves both a feeling and a misrepresentation of information. Deceiving others and understanding that they are deceived must begin with perceiving and feeling this feeling in others, in everyday engagements. And in the same way as with awareness of attention, the awareness of deceivedness cannot sensibly be pinned to a single and belated age of onset.

As in the case of attention (Reddy 2003), a prediction could be made here, that the development of the ability to deceive another person depends upon the ability to *feel* in the self, the process of true and false close-range communication with the other. Perhaps if the infant cannot deceive in a dyadic situation, more distal deceptions become impaired and, in some formulaic or other way, 'inappropriate'. Emotional engagement provides the fuel both for the emergence of deceiving and for the developing complexity of the objects or topics of deceiving. Such an explanation is distinctly nonlinear (see Suddendorf & Whiten (2001) for a subtle critique of linear developmental explanations in evolutionary as well as ontogenetic developmental domains), possibly avoiding, among other things, the 'developmental fallacy' (Costall 1994), where we treat infants and other animals as preparing to live social lives when they 'grow up', rather than already living such lives now. The social lives they do live hold the answer to the 'why' of social intelligence—an answer that stage models of one type or the other will not yield—whether dealing with infant development or the bigger evolutionary picture. The challenge that we face is that we cannot really understand social living without getting in there and living too, engaging both with the children we study and with the parents they engage with.

Funding for the studies reported in this paper was received from the ESRC (Grant No. R000235481) and the University of Portsmouth (Ph.D. studentship for Dr Paul Newton and support from Small Grant Fund, Department of Psychology). Many thanks are due to the incisive comments of Prof. Alan Costall.

Endnotes

1   Whereas adults, in judging a lie, were reported to take into account not only the factuality of the utter-
    ance, but also the speaker's belief in its factuality and the speaker's intention to deceive (Coleman &
    Kay 1981), three year olds don't appear to; they are either unsystematic in their responses or barely
    respond to questions in an experimental scenario about whether someone was telling a lie, the truth
    or something else (Strichartz & Burton 1990). However, there is a recent and replicated finding in
    (Lillard 2002; Mitchell & Neal 2005) that not until about 6 years of age do children answer similar
    questions about– and therefore understand–pretending in other people. There is no doubt amongst
    psychologists, however, that children do pretend from around 18 months of age. The understanding of
    the complex acts (of pretending, or in our case, of deceiving) in another person may be evident later
    than its intelligent use by the self.
2   'Cover stories are as likely to be ridiculous as plausible. The teddy bear may be accused of the act as
    often as the sibling' (Morton 1988, p. 36); also the oft cited 'I didn't break the lamp and I won't do it
    again' from Vasek (1986)
3   'It is exactly the rigidity with which these early 'lies'are used that reveals them as no more than previ-
    ously successful strategies for avoiding the undesirable, rather than genuine cases of deception
    designed to manipulate the other person's belief' (Perner 1991, p. 193).
4   'Four year olds' lies typically take the form of simple denial ('No') or misleading confirmation ('Yes')
    rather than the more sophisticated elaborations of older children and adults' lies' (Bussey 1992,
    p. 99).
5   'acts from the normal repertoire of the agent, deployed such that another individual is likely to misin-
    terpret what the acts signify, to the advantage of the agent' (Whiten & Byrne 1988)
6   Teasing: Two subcategories of Creating an Image (Affiliation and Threat) involve instances of playful
    teasing by human infants. Not all teasing involves deception: jumping on someone, biting them, pull-
    ing hair, trying to get any reaction, are all non-serious and in some sense, 'play' or 'quasi-aggressive'
    behaviour (Adang 1984), but involve deception only if there is some attempt to disguise the act or the
    acts leading up to it. The openly smiling 'silent scream' produced by a 12 month-old when told not to
    scream (JB, in Reddy 1998), was a sophisticated provocation but not deceptive. In contrast to such
    quasi-aggression or to playfighting where 'real' fighting may not yet be in the animal's repertoire,
    playful teasing may often have some false information, embedded in its sequence (see Chevalier-
    Skolnikoff 1986). Evidence of the false use of an action (as in deliberate misnaming, misdemeanours
    and non-compliance) can be obtained by establishing the presence of their 'proper' usage at the same
    point in time: evidence that they are not coincidental or accidental can be obtained through the shift
    or change in actions and demeanour and evidence that they are not a 'change of mind' can be obtained
    from facial expressions as well as from information allowing the discounting of the infant's desire for
    the forbidden object or activity. Teasing may not meet the 'self advantage' criterion of W&B other
    than in the sense of getting a reaction that you want through a feigned act. However, we would not use
    that criterion in adults or older children (or even in animals–e.g. see example 172 of teasing by C-S
    in Byrne & Whiten 1990 corpus).
7   Example 20 in *Cebus apella* by Collinge (1990, in the Byrne & Whiten 1990 corpus) (jumping on to
    shoulder and playing with hair for the first time ever 'in order to' pull out the stop watch newly hidden
    inside the jumper: this example is much more sophisticated than the distraction by 'holding the eyes',
    of the one year old human infants, involving a more complex set of deceptive behaviours and prior
    planning (see also Example 170 in gorillas, C-S) and probably a more complex understanding of
    the mechanics of vision (e.g., awareness of 'cannot see behind' may develop around 18 months in
    humans, Butterworth & Jarrett 1991).
8   Mitchell (2002) suggests that non-verbal deception in most of the higher apes and human children can
    be explained as 'script-violation' rather than in terms of complex meta-representational abilities.
    Script theory allows complex learning of social contingencies and routines and effects, and complex
    variations and violations on themes, without having to invoke meta-representation and meta-commu-
    nication. However, while, representation may be a bit of a red herring for understanding deception,
    script theory is not necessarily the answer. It still does not explain the why, the motive.

References

Adamson, L. & Bakeman, R. 1991 The development of shared attention during infancy. In *Annals of child development*, vol. 8 (ed. R. Vasta), pp. 1–41. London, UK: Jessica Kingsley.

Adang, O. 1984 Teasing in young chimpanzees. *Behaviour* **88**, 98–122.

Astington, J. W. 2003 Sometimes necessary, never sufficient: false-belief understanding and social competence. In *Individual differences in theory of mind: implications for typical and atypical development* (eds B. Repacholi & V. Slaughter), pp. 13–38. Macquarie Monographs in Cognitive Science Series. New York, NY: Psychology Press.

Baldwin, J. M. 1909 The influence of Darwin on theory of knowledge and philosophy. *Psychol. Rev.* **16**, 207–218.

Baldwin, D. & Moses, L. 2001 Links between understanding and early word learning: challenges to current accounts. *Soc. Dev.* **10**, 309–329. (doi:10.1111/1467-9507.00168)

Barrett, L., Hei, P. & Rendall, D. 2007 Social brains, simple minds: does social complexity really require cognitive complexity? *Phil. Trans. R. Soc. B* **362**, 561–575. (doi:10.1098/rstb.2006.1995)

Baron-Cohen, S., Leslie, A. M. & Frith, U. 1985 Does the autistic child have a 'theory of mind'? *Cognition* **27**, 37–46. (doi:10.1016/0010-0277(85)90022-8)

Bates, E., Camaioni, L. & Volterra, V. 1976 Sensorimotor performatives. In *Language and context: the acquisition of pragmatics* (ed. E. Bates), p. 49. New York, NY: Academic Press.

Bruner, J. S. 1983 *Child's talk: learning to use language.* Oxford, UK: Oxford University Press.

Bussey, K. 1992 Children's lying and truthfulness: implications for children's testimony. In *Cognitive and social factors in early deception* (eds S. J. Ceci, M. DeSimone Leichtman & M. Putnik), pp. 89–110. Hillsdale, NJ: LEA.

Butterworth, G. & Jarrett, N. 1991 What minds have in common is space: spatial mechanisms serving joint visual attention in infancy. *Br. J. Devel. Psychol.* **9**, 55–72.

Byrne, R. W. 2003 Tracing the evolutionary path of cognition. In *The social brain: evolution and pathology* (eds M. Bruene, H. Ribbert & W. Shiefenhoevel), pp. 43–60. London, UK: Wiley.

Byrne, R. W. & Whiten, A. 1990 Tactical deception in primates: the 1990 database. *Primate Rep.* **27**, 1–101.

Byrne, R. W. & Whiten, A. 1992 Cognitive evolution in primates: evidence from tactical deception. *Man* **27**, 609–627.

Camaioni, L. 1993 The development of intentional communication: a re-analysis. In *New perspectives in early communicative development* (eds J. Nadel & L. Camaioni), pp. 82–96. London, UK: Routledge.

Carpendale, J. & Lewis, C. 2004 Constructing an understanding of mind: the development of children's social understanding within social interaction. *Behav. Brain Sci.* **27**, 79–151.

Chandler, M., Fritz, A. S. & Hala, S. 1989 Small-scale deceit: deception as a marker of two-, three-, and four-year-olds' early theories of mind. *Child Dev.* **60**, 1263–1277. (doi:10.2307/1130919)

Chandler, M. & Hala, S. 1991 Trust and children's developing theories of mind. In *Children's interpersonal trust: sensitivity to lying, deception, and promise violations* (ed. K. J. Rotenberg), pp. 135–159. Berlin, Germany: Springer.

Chevalier-Skolnikoff, S. 1986 An exploration of the ontogeny of deception in human beings and nonhuman primates. In *Deception: perspectives on human and nonhuman deceit* (eds R. W. Mitchell & N. S. Thompson), pp. 205–220. Albany, NY: SUNY Press.

Chomsky, N. 1965 *Aspects of a theory of syntax.* Harvard, MA: MIT Press.

Clayton, N. S., Dally, J. M. & Emery, N. J. 2007 Social cognition by food-caching corvids. The western scrub-jay as a natural psychologist. *Phil. Trans. R. Soc. B* **362**, 507–522. (doi:10.1098/rstb.2006.1992)

Coleman, L. & Kay, P. 1981 Prototype semantics: the English word 'lie'. *Language* **57**, 26–44. (doi: 10.2307/414285)

Costall, A. 1994 On neonatal competence: sleepless nights for representational theorists? *Ann. Theor. Psychol.* **10**, 27–41.

Dewey, J. 1910 *The influence of Darwin on philosophy and other essays in contemporary thought.* Oxford, UK: Holt.

Dunn, J. 1988 *The beginnings of social understanding.* Oxford, UK: Basil Blackwell.

Flanagan, O. 1992 Other minds, obligation and honesty. In *Cognitive and social factors in early deception* (eds S. J. Ceci, M. DeSimone Leichtman & M. Putnik), pp. 111–126. Hillsdale, NJ: LEA.

Frank, M. G. 1992 Commentary: on the structure of lies and deception experiments. In *Cognitive and social factors in early deception* (eds S. J. Ceci, M. DeSimone Leichtman & M. Putnik), pp. 127–146. Hillsdale, NJ: LEA.

Golinkoff, R. M. 1983 When is communication a 'meeting of minds'? *J. Child Lang.* **20**, 199–207.

Golinkoff, R. M. 1986 'I beg your pardon? the preverbal negotiation of failed messages. *J. Child Lang.* **13**, 455–476.

Hummer, P., Wimmer, H. & Antes, G. 1993 On the origins of denial negation. *J. Child Lang.* **20**, 607–618.

Humphrey, N. 1976/1988 The social function of intellect. In *Machiavellian intelligence* (eds R. Byrne & A. Whiten), pp. 13–26. Oxford, UK: Clarendon Press.

Izard, C. & Malatesta, C. Z. 1987 Perspectives on emotional development 1: differential emotions theory of early emotional development. In *Handbook of infant development* (ed. J. Osofsky), pp. 494–554. Chichester, Sussex: Wiley.

Kaye, K. 1982 *The mental and social life of babies*. Chicago, IL: University of Chicago Press.

LaFreniere, P. 1988 The ontogeny of tactical deception in humans. In *Machiavellian intelligence: social expertise and the evolution of intellect in monkeys, apes and humans* (eds R. W. Byrne & A. Whiten), pp. 238–252. Oxford, UK: Oxford University Press.

Leslie, A. 1987 Pretense and representation: the origins of 'theory of mind'. *Psychol. Rev.* **94**, 412–426. (doi:10.1037/0033-295X.94.4.412)

Leslie, A. M., Friedman, O. & German, T. P. 2004 Core mechanisms in 'theory of mind'. *Trends Cogn. Sci.* **8**, 528–533.

Leslie, A. 2005 Developmental parallels in understanding minds and bodies. *Trends Cogn. Sci.* **9**, 459–460. (doi:10.1016/j.tics.2005.08.002)

Lillard, A. S. 2002 Just through the looking glass: children's understanding of pretence. In *Pretending and imagination in animals and children* (ed. R. W. Mitchell), pp. 102–114. Cambridge, UK: Cambridge University Press.

Lippard, P. V. 1988 'Ask me no questions, I'll tell you no lies': situational exigencies for interpersonal deception. *West. J. Speech Commun.* **52**, 91–103.

Liszkowski, U., Carpenter, M., Henning, A., Striano, T. & Tomasello, M. 2004 Twelve-month-olds point to share attention and interest. *Dev. Sci.* **7**, 297–307. (doi:10.1111/j.1467-7687.2004.00349.x)

Liszkowski, U., Carpenter, M., Striano, T. & Tomasello, M. 2006 12-and 18-month-olds point to provide information for others. *J. Cogn Dev.* **7**, 173–187.

Mead, G. H. 1934 *Mind, self and society*. Chicago, IL: University of Chicago Press.

Mitchell, R. W. 2002 *Pretending and imagination in animals and children*. Cambridge, UK: Cambridge University Press.

Mitchell, R. W. & Neal, M. 2005 Children's understanding of their own and other's mental states. Part A. Self-understanding precedes understanding of others in pretence. *Br. J. Dev. Psychol.* **23**, 175–200. (doi:10.1348/026151004X21107)

Mitchell, R. W. & Thompson, N. S. 1986 *Deception: perspectives on human and non-human deceit*. Albany, NY: SUNY Press.

Morton, J. 1988 When can lying start? *Issues Criminol. Legal Psychol.* **13**, 35–36.

Newton, P. 1994 An investigation into the cognitive prerequisites for deception. Unpublished Ph.D. thesis, University of Portsmouth.

Newton, P., Reddy, V. & Bull, R. 2000 Children's everyday deception and performance on false-belief tasks. *Br. J. Dev. Psychol.* **18**, 297–317. (doi:10.1348/026151000165706)

Olson, D. 1988 On the origins of beliefs and other intentional states in children. In *Developing theories of mind* (eds J. W. Astington, P. L. Harris & D. R. Olson), pp. 414–426. Cambridge, UK: Cambridge University Press.

O'Neill, D. 1996 Two-year-old children's sensitivity to a parent's knowledge state when making requests. *Child Dev.* **67**, 659–677. (doi:10.2307/1131839)

Onishi, K. & Baillargeon, R. 2005 Do 15-month-old infants understand false beliefs? *Science* **308**, 214–216. (doi:10.1126/science.1107621)

Pea, R. D. 1982 Origins of verbal logic: spontaneous denials by two-and three-year-olds. *J. Child Lang.* **9**, 597–626.

Perner, J. 1991 *Understanding the representational mind.* Cambridge, MA: MIT Press.

Perner, J., Leekam, S. & Wimmer, H. 1987 3-year-olds' difficulty with false belief: the case for conceptual deficit. *Br. J. Dev. Psychol.* **5**, 125–137.

Piaget, J. 1932/1977 *The moral judgement of the child.* Harmondsworth, UK: Penguin.

Reddy, V. 1991 Playing with others' expectations: teasing and mucking about in the first year. In *Natural theories of mind: evolution, development and simulation of everyday mindreading* (ed. A. Whiten), pp. 143–158. Oxford, UK: Blackwell.

Reddy, V. 1998 Person-directed play: humour and teasing in infants and young children. Report on Grant No. R000235481 received from the Economic and Social Research Council. Interview transcripts from this study.

Reddy, V. 2001 Positively shy! Developmental continuities in the expression of shyness, coyness and embarrassment. In *International handbook of social anxiety: concepts, research and interventions relating to the self and shyness* (eds W. R. Crozier & L. E. Alden), pp. 77–99. New York, NY: Wiley.

Reddy, V. 2003 On being an object of attention: implications for self-other-consciousness. *Trends Cogn. Sci.* **7**, 397–402. (doi:10.1016/S1364-6613(03)00191-8)

Reddy, V. 2005 Before the 'third element': understanding attention to self. In *Joint attention: communication and other minds: issues in philosophy and psychology* (eds N. Eilan, C. Howerl, T. McCormack & J. Roessler), pp. 85–109. New York, NY: Oxford University Press.

Reddy, V. & Morris, P. 2004 Participants don't need theories: knowing minds in engagement. *Theory Psychol.* **14**, 647–665. (doi:10.1177/0959354304046177)

Reddy, V. & Simone, L. 1995 Acting on attention: towards an understanding of knowing in infancy. Paper presented at the Annual Conference of the Developmental Section of the British Psychological Society, Strathclyde, September.

Riggs, K. 2005 Thinking harder about false belief. *Trends Cogn. Sci.* **9**, 410–411.

Ruffman, T. & Perner, J. 2005 Do infants really understand false belief? *Trends Cogn. Sci.* **9**, 462–463. (doi:10.1016/j.tics.2005.08.001)

Russell, J. 2005 Justifying all the fuss about false belief. *Trends Cogn. Sci.* **9**, 307–308. (doi:10.1016/j.tics.2005.05.002)

Russell, J., Mauthner, N., Sharpe, S. & Tidswell, T. 1991 The 'windows task' as a measure of strategic deception in preschoolers and autistic children. *Br. J. Dev. Psychol.* **9**, 331–350.

Ryle, G. 1949 *The concept of mind.* Harmondsworth, UK: Penguin.

Saarni, C. & von Salisch, M. 1993 The socialisation of emotional dissemblance. In *Lying and deception in everyday life* (eds M. Lewis & C. Saarni), pp. 106–125. New York, NY: Guildford.

Sharrock, W. & Coulter, J. 2004 ToM: a critical commentary. *Theory Psychol.* **14**, 579–600.

Shatz, M. & O'Reilly, A. 1990 Conversational or communicative skill? A reassessment of two-year-olds' behaviour in miscommunication episodes. *J. Child Lang.* **17**, 131–146.

Sodian, B. 1991 The development of deception in children. *Br. J. Dev. Psychol.* **9**, 173–188.

Sodian, B. 1994 Early deception and the conceptual continuity claim. In *Children's early understanding of mind: origins and development* (eds C. Lewis & P. Mitchell), pp. 385–401. Hove, UK: LEA.

Sodian, B., Taylor, C., Harris, P. L. & Perner, J. 1991 Early deception and the child's theory of mind: false trails and genuine markers. *Child Dev.* **62**, 468–483. (doi:10.2307/1131124)

Song, H.-J. 2006 Infants' reasoning about others' misperceptions and false beliefs. Paper presented at the XVth International Conference on Infant Studies, Kyoto, Japan.

Stern, C. & Stern, W. 1909 *Mongraphien uner die seelische Entwicklung das kindes 2. Band: Erinnerung, Aussage und luge in der ersten Kindheit.* Leipzig, Germany: Barth.

Stouthamer-Loeber, M. 1991 Young children's verbal misrepresentations of reality. In *Children's interpersonal trust: sensitivity to lying, deception, and promise violations* (ed. K. J. Rotenberg), pp. 20–42. Berlin, Germany: Springer.

Strichartz, A. F. & Burton, R. V. 1990 Lies and the truth: a study of the development of the concept. *Child Dev.* **61**, 211–220. (doi:10.2307/1131060)

Suddendorf, T. & Whiten, A. 2001 Mental evolution and development: evidence for secondary representation in children, great apes and other animals. *Psychol. Bull.* **127**, 629–650. (doi:10.1037/0033-2909.127.5.629)

Sullivan, K. & Winner, E. 1993 Three year-olds' understanding of mental states: the influence of trickery. *J. Exp. Psychol.* **56**, 135–148.

Sully, J. 1896 *Studies of Childhood*. New York, NY: D. Appleton and Co.

Surian, S., Caldi, S. & Sperber, D. 2006 Infants' ability to attribute mental states to agents. Paper presented at the XVth International Conference on Infant Studies, Kyoto, Japan.

Teerwogt, M. M., Rieffe, C., Tuijn, A. H., Harris, P. L. & Mant, I. 1999 Children's spontaneous correction of false beliefs in a conversation partner. *Int. J. Behav. Dev.* **23**, 113–124. (doi:10.1080/016502599384026)

Tomasello, M. 1999 Social cognition before the revolution. In *Early social cognition: understanding others in the first months of life* (ed. P. Rochat), pp. 155–188. Mahwah, NJ: Lawrence Erlbaum Associates.

Tomasello, M. & Haberl, K. 2003 Understanding attention: 12-and 18-month-olds know what is new for other persons. *Dev. Psychol.* **39**, 906–912. (doi:10.1037/0012-1649.39.5.906)

Trevarthen, C. 1977 Descriptive analyses of infant communicative behaviour. In *Studies in mother–infant interaction: the Loch Lomond symposium* (ed. H. R. Schaffer), pp. 227– 270. London, UK: Academic Press.

Triplett, N. 1900 The psychology of conjuring deceptions. *Am. J. Psychol.* **6**, 439–510. (doi:10.2307/1412365)

Vasek, M. E. 1986 Lying as a skill: the development of deception in children. In *Deception: perspectives on human and nonhuman deceit* (eds R. W. Mitchell & N. Thompson), pp. 271–292. Albany, NY: SUNY Press.

Warneken, F., Chen, F. & Tomasello, M. 2006 Altruistic helping in human infants and young chimpanzees. *Child Dev.* **77**, 640–663. (doi:10.1111/j.1467-8624.2006.00895.x)

Watts, A. W. 1965 The individual as man/world. In *The psychedelic reader* (eds G. M. Weil, R. Metzner & T. Leary), pp. 47–57. New York, NY: University Books.

Wilson, A. E., Smith, M. D. & Ross, H. S. 2003 The nature and effects of young children's lies. *Soc. Dev.* **12**, 21–45. (doi:10.1111/1467-9507.00220)

Whiten, A. & Byrne, R. 1988 Tactical deception in primates. *Behav. Brain Sci.* **11**, 233–273.

Wittgenstein, L. 1953 *Philosophical investigations*. Oxford, UK: Blackwell.

10

Cooperation and human cognition: the Vygotskian intelligence hypothesis

Henrike Moll and Michael Tomasello

Nicholas Humphrey's social intelligence hypothesis proposed that the major engine of primate cognitive evolution was social competition. Lev Vygotsky also emphasized the social dimension of intelligence, but he focused on human primates and cultural things such as collaboration, communication and teaching. A reasonable proposal is that primate cognition in general was driven mainly by social competition, but beyond that the unique aspects of human cognition were driven by, or even constituted by, social cooperation. In the present paper, we provide evidence for this Vygotskian intelligence hypothesis by comparing the social-cognitive skills of great apes with those of young human children in several domains of activity involving cooperation and communication with others. We argue, finally, that regular participation in cooperative, cultural interactions during ontogeny leads children to construct uniquely powerful forms of perspectival cognitive representation.

Keywords: communication; cooperation; human children; primate cognitive evolution; social intelligence; Vygotskian intelligence hypothesis

10.1 Introduction

Nicholas Humphrey's (1976) social intelligence hypothesis proposed that the major engine of primate cognitive evolution was social interaction. The competitive aspect of social interaction was emphasized later proposals espousing 'primate politics' (de Waal 1982) and Machiavellian intelligence (Byrne & Whiten 1988). In all of these proposals, the basic idea was a kind of arms race in which individuals who outsmarted others—who were also trying to outsmart them—were at a competitive advantage evolutionarily.

Interestingly, at about the same time as Humphrey's original proposal, Lev Vygotsky's (1978) general theory of culture first appeared in English translation. Vygotsky also emphasized the social dimension of intelligence, but he focused on cooperative things such as culture, collaboration, communication and teaching, and he was concerned more with ontogeny than with phylogeny. Vygotsky argued and presented evidence that the cognitive skills of human children are shaped by, or in some cases even created by, their interactions with others in the culture or with the artefacts and symbols that others have created for communal use. In all, it is difficult to find reference in any of Vygotsky's work to competition; the stress is almost exclusively on the crucial role of cooperative social interactions in the development of cognitive skills.

The resolution to this seeming conflict—an emphasis on competition versus cooperation in the formation of primate cognitive skills—is straightforward. Humphrey and his successors were talking mostly about nonhuman primates, whereas Vygotsky was talking mostly about humans. Among primates, humans are by far the most cooperative species, in just about any way this appellation is used, as humans live in social groups (a.k.a. cultures) constituted by all kinds of cooperative institutions and social practices with shared goals and differentiated roles (Richerson & Boyd 2005). A reasonable proposal is therefore that primate cognition in general was driven mainly by social competition, but beyond that the unique aspects of human cognition—the cognitive skills needed to create complex technologies, cultural institutions and systems of symbols, for example—were driven by, or even constituted by, social cooperation (Tomasello et al. 2005).

We call this the Vygotskian intelligence hypothesis. Our goal in this paper is to provide evidence for this hypothesis by comparing the social-cognitive skills of great apes, mainly chimpanzees, with those of young human children, mainly 1-year-olds, in several domains of activity involving cooperation with others. These comparisons illustrate especially human children's powerful skills and motivations for cooperative action and communication and other forms of shared intentionality. We argue, finally, that regular participation in cooperative, cultural interactions during ontogeny leads children to construct uniquely powerful forms of cognitive representation.

10.2 Great ape social cognition

A species' skills of social cognition are adapted for the specific kinds of social interactions in which its members typically participate. Thus, some non-social species may have very few social-cognitive skills, and even some social species may have no need to understand others as anything other than animate agents, since all they do socially is keep in spatial proximity to conspecifics and interact in very simple ways. However, for species that are more intensely social—that is, those whose social interactions with group mates are complex and characterized by various strategies of competition and cooperation—it would seem to be a great advantage to understand others more deeply in terms of their goals, perceptions and behavioural decision making, so that their behaviour might be predicted in novel circumstances. Non-human primates clearly do this, but recent experimental research suggests that they do it much more readily in competitive, as opposed to cooperative, circumstances.

Take, for example, the question of whether chimpanzees understand what others see. Although chimpanzees follow the gaze direction of others quite readily, even to locations behind barriers (Tomasello et al. 1999; Bräuer et al. 2005), this could be accomplished by a very simple co-orientation mechanism not requiring an understanding of seeing. This non-cognitive explanation was, at one time, supported by two lines of research. First, in a series of experiments, Povinelli & Eddy (1996) tested young chimpanzees' understanding of how humans must be bodily oriented for successful communication to take place (see also Povinelli et al. 1999; Reaux et al. 1999). They trained subjects to approach and choose which one of two humans to beg food from—where one human was in a position to see their gesture and the other was not. In this Gesture Choice experimental paradigm, subjects did not gesture differentially for a human who wore a blindfold over his eyes (as opposed to one who wore a blindfold over his mouth), or for one who wore a bucket over his head (as opposed to one who held a bucket on his shoulder), or for one whose back was turned and was looking away (as opposed to one whose back was turned but who looked over his shoulder to the subject). Povinelli and colleagues thus concluded that chimpanzees do not understand seeing.

The second experimental paradigm causing chimpanzees problems is the Object Choice paradigm. In a number of different experiments from a number of different laboratories, chimpanzees have shown a very inconsistent ability to use the gaze direction of others to help them locate the food hidden under one of several objects. For example, Call *et al.* (1998) presented chimpanzees with two opaque containers, only one of which contained food (and chimpanzees knew that they could choose only one). A human experimenter then looked continuously at the container with food inside. Not one of six chimpanzees used this cue to find the food. Tomasello *et al.* (1997*a*) and Call *et al.* (2000) provided chimpanzees with several other types of visual–gestural cues (including pointing) in this same paradigm and also found mostly negative results (see also Itakura *et al.* 1999; Povinelli *et al.* 1999).

But concluding from chimpanzees' failures in these two experimental paradigms that they do not understand seeing would be premature. In a more recent series of studies, Hare *et al.* (2000) have shown that in the right situation chimpanzees can use the gaze direction of others to make an effective foraging choice. They do this, however, not when that conspecific is attempting to be cooperative, as in the Gesture Choice and Object Choice paradigms, but rather when the conspecific is attempting to compete with them for food. The basic set-up was as follows. A subordinate and a dominant individual were placed in competition over food. The trick was that sometimes the subordinate could see a piece of food that the dominant could not see due to a physical barrier of some sort. The general finding was that subordinates took advantage of this situation in very flexible ways—by avoiding the food the dominant could see and instead pursuing the food she could not see (and even showing a knowledge that transparent barriers do not block visual access). In a second set of studies, Hare *et al.* (2001) found that subordinates even knew whether the dominant had just witnessed the hiding process a moment before (they knew whether she 'knew' its current location even though she could not see it now).

The findings of these studies thus suggest that chimpanzees know what conspecifics can and cannot see, and, further, that they use this knowledge to maximize their acquisition of food in competitive situations. (See also Melis *et al.* 2006*b*; Hare *et al.* 2006 for evidence of chimpanzees' ability to conceal their approach to food from the visual attention of a competitor.) The question is then why they cannot do something similar in the Object Choice and Gesture Choice paradigms. The key, in our opinion, is cooperative communication versus competition. The situation in which another individual is trying to inform them about the location of food, as in the Object Choice paradigm, is clearly not the one chimpanzees normally experience, since they spend their whole lives competing with group mates for food. And so the subject in the Object Choice paradigm does not take the gaze or point of the other as an informative cue because no individual would behave like that in the presence of food she could take for herself. Subjects in this experimental paradigm just do not know or care why the other is indicating one container and not another because such behaviour does not suggest the presence of obtainable food for them. In the Gesture Choice paradigm, subjects are choosing whom to communicate with, also a very unnatural situation. When experiments with the same logic are done—but without this element of choosing a communicative partner—chimpanzees perform much more impressively (Kaminski *et al.* 2004).

Human beings either have done well, or would very likely do well, in all of the experimental paradigms described above, both competitive and cooperative. It is not that human beings are not competitive—they most assuredly are—and they use their social-cognitive skills in competitive situations every day. But human beings can also coordinate well with others, and understand their intentional states, when cooperating or communicating with them. The difference

between humans and chimpanzees in this regard is perhaps best illustrated by directly comparing young human children to our nearest primate relatives in tasks requiring skills of cooperative interaction and communication.

10.3 Cooperative activities

Individuals of virtually all primate species engage in group activities on a daily basis. These
activities may be considered cooperative in a very broad sense of the term. However, we focus
here on forms of cooperation much more narrowly defined. As in previous theoretical work
(Tomasello *et al.* 2005), we use here a modified version of Bratman's (1992) definition of
'shared cooperative activities'. Joint or shared cooperative activities are mainly characterized
by three features. First, the participants in the cooperative activity share a joint goal, to which
they are jointly committed. Second, and relatedly, the participants take reciprocal or complementary roles in order to achieve this joint goal. And third, the participants are generally motivated and willing to help one another accomplish their role if needed (the criterion of 'mutual
support' in Bratman's account).

One well-known phenomenon that has been suggested as a demonstration of cooperation in
nonhuman primates is group hunting. Boesch and colleagues (Boesch & Boesch 1989; Boesch
& Boesch-Achermann 2000; Boesch 2005) have observed chimpanzees in the Taï forest
hunting in groups for arboreal prey, mainly monkeys. In the account of these researchers, the
animals take complementary roles in their hunting. One individual, called the *driver*, chases
the prey in a certain direction, while others, the so-called *blockers*, climb the trees and prevent
the prey from changing directions. An *ambusher* then silently moves in front of the prey, making an escape impossible. Of course, when the hunting event is described with this vocabulary
of complementary roles, then it appears to be a joint cooperative activity: complementary
roles already imply that there is a joint goal, shared by the role-takers. But the question really
is whether this vocabulary is appropriate at all. A more plausible characterization of the hunting event, from our perspective, is as follows: each animal fills whatever spatial position is
still available at any given time so that the encircling is accomplished in a stepwise fashion,
without any kind of prior plan or agreement to a shared goal or assignment of roles. Then,
without pursuing a joint goal or accomplishing a certain role within a higher order framework,
each individual chases the prey from its own position (see also Tomasello *et al.* 2005). This
event clearly is a group activity or group action, because, to use another one of Bratman's
terms, the chimpanzees are 'mutually responsive'as they coordinate their behaviours with
that of the others in space and time (see also Melis *et al.* 2006*a*). But what seems to be missing
is the 'togetherness' or 'jointness' that distinguishes shared cooperative activities from other
sorts of group actions. This interpretation is strongly supported by studies that have investigated chimpanzees' abilities to cooperate in experimental settings.

In one study, Warneken *et al.* (2006) tested three juvenile human-raised chimpanzees with
a set of four different cooperation tasks. In two of these tasks, a human tried to engage the
chimpanzee to cooperate in order to solve a problem (e.g. extracting a piece of food from an
apparatus). In the other two tasks, the human tried to engage the ape to play a social game. The
authors looked at two things: the chimpanzees' level of behavioural coordination and the
chimpanzees' behaviours in the so-called interruption periods in which the human suddenly
stopped participating in the activity. The results were very consistent: in the problem-solving
tasks, chimpanzees coordinated their behaviours quite well with that of the human, as shown

by the fact that they were mostly successful in bringing about the desired result, as, for instance, extracting the piece of food from the apparatus. However, they showed no interest in the social games, and so the level of coordination in these tasks was low or absent. Most important was what happened when the human suddenly interrupted the activity. In none of the tasks did a chimpanzee ever make a communicative attempt to re-engage the partner. Such attempts were missing even in the cases where they should have been highly motivated to obtain the desired result, as in the problem-solving task involving food. The absence of any efforts by the chimpanzees to re-engage their human partner is crucial: it shows that the chimpanzees did not cooperate in the true sense, since they had not formed a joint goal with the human. If they had been committed to a joint goal, then we would expect them, at least in some instances, to persist in trying to bring it about and in trying to keep the cooperation going.

For humans, the situation is different from very early on in ontogeny. Warneken *et al.* (2006) conducted an analogous study with 18-and 24-month-old human children. Unlike the chimpanzees, children cooperated quite successfully and enthusiastically not only in the problem-solving tasks, but also in the social games. For example, these infants enjoyed playing a 'trampoline' game together, in which both partners had to simultaneously lift up their sides of a small trampoline with their hands, such that a ball could bounce on it without falling off. Most importantly, when the adult stopped participating at a certain point during the activity, every child at least once produced a communicative attempt in order to re-engage him. In some cases, the children grabbed the adult by his arm and drew him to the apparatus. The older children of 24 months of age also often made linguistic attempts to tell the recalcitrant partner to continue. Unlike the chimpanzees, we thus find in human infants the ability to cooperate with joint commitment to a shared goal: the children 'reminded' the recalcitrant partner of their shared goal and expected him to continue in order to achieve it. There was even some evidence that the children already understood the normativity behind the social games and the way they 'ought to be played'. For example, in one of the games, they always used a can in order to catch a toy when it came falling out of one end of a tube after their partner had thrown it in from the other end. They could have also caught it with their hands, but they preferred to do it the way it had previously been demonstrated to them. This implies that they perceived the can as a constitutive element of the game, and they wanted to play the game the way it 'ought' to be played. The chimpanzees, on the other hand, never used the can in order to catch the toy—if they engaged in the game at all, they simply used their hands.

It thus seems that human infants by the age of 18 months, in contrast to apes, are able to jointly commit to a shared goal. The second criterion for cooperation, as we define it, is role-taking. True cooperation should involve that the partners perform reciprocal roles and also understand them, in the sense that they coordinate their actions and intentions with the possibility of reversing roles and even helping the other with his role if needed. This form of role-taking would suggest that each partner represents the entire collaboration, its shared goal and reciprocal roles, holistically from a 'bird's eye view' instead of just from within whatever role they happen to be taking at the moment. One study purporting to show role reversal in chimpanzees is that of Povinelli *et al.* (1992). In that study, chimpanzees were trained in one of two roles of a cooperative hiding game with a human. Some chimpanzees were trained in the role of a communicator, who indicated to the human where a piece of food was located. The other chimpanzees were trained in the complementary role of the 'operator', who extracted the food from the location indicated by the human. When the chimpanzees had learned their initial role to criterion, a role switch was initiated and the question was whether the chimpanzees would spontaneously reverse roles. One of the chimpanzees, whose initial role was that of the communicator, was immediately successful as operator after the switch. But the problem is that this individual most likely comprehended human indicating gestures *before* the study—as this animal had had extensive interactions with humans. The two individuals that switched to be a communicator also seemed to reverse roles effectively, as they were reported to provide the human with cues about the location of the food fairly quickly. However, the problem in this case is that it is not clear that the chimpanzees actually produced any communicative signals at all, but instead the humans simply interpreted their natural bodily orientation to the food.

A more well-controlled investigation of role reversal skills in chimpanzees was done by Tomasello & Carpenter (2005) with the same three young human-raised chimpanzees which participated in Warneken *et al.*'s (2006) study. In this study, a human demonstrated to the chimpanzee various actions with each of four pairs of objects. For each pair of objects, one functioned as a 'base' and the other as an 'actor'. The human then demonstrated to the chimpanzee how the two, the actor and the base, are put together. For instance, she put a 'Tigger' figure on a plate and 'Winnie the Pooh' figure in a little toy car. Then E gave the actor (e.g. Tigger) to the chimpanzee and held out the base (the plate) towards the chimpanzee, thus offering that the chimpanzee put the actor on the base to complete the act. If chimpanzees did not perform the role of putting the actor on the base spontaneously, E encouraged them to do so by vocalizing and, and if they still did not respond, by helping them put the actor on the base. To test for role reversal, E then handed the chimpanzee the base (the plate) and held out the actor to see whether she would spontaneously offer the base. Two of the three chimpanzees held out the base object at some point. But, crucially, none of these responses occurred spontaneously, and more importantly, in none of these responses was the holding out of the base accompanied by a look to E's face. A look to the partner's face while holding out the object is a key criterion of 'offering' used in all studies with human infants (Bates 1979; Camaioni 1993). Thus, in Tomasello & Carpenter's (2005) study, there was no indication that the chimpanzees offered the base to the human, and so there were no acts of role reversal.

An analogous study with human infants of 12 and 18 months of age was conducted by Carpenter *et al.* (2005). As in the study with the chimpanzees, situations were set up in which an adult did things like hold out a basket in which the infant was asked to place a toy. After the infant complied, in the test for role reversal, the adult placed the basket within the infant's reach and held up the toy herself. Impressively, even some of the 12-month-olds spontaneously held out the basket for the adult while at the same time looking to her face, presumably in anticipation of her placing the toy inside. Thus, the infant's handing behaviours, in contrast to those of the chimpanzees, were clearly acts of offering learned through role reversal.

It thus looks as though chimpanzees, in contrast to young human children, do not fulfil either of the first two criteria of cooperation: sharing a joint goal and understanding the roles of a joint activity in some general way. The third criterion is that, if needed, the partners of a joint cooperative activity help one another do their part successfully. In two recent studies, chimpanzees did not take an opportunity to 'help' another individual obtain food (Silk *et al.* 2005; Jensen *et al.* 2006). But food is a resource over which apes used to compete, and so maybe helping is better investigated in situations that do not revolve around food. Given our interest in helping as a constituent of cooperation, the most important form of helping is 'instrumental helping', in which one individual helps another instrumentally to achieve a behavioural goal. We know of only one study investigating instrumental helping in non-human primates. Warneken & Tomasello (2006) had three human-raised juvenile chimpanzees watch a human attempt, but failed to achieve different kinds of individual goals. Reasons for her failure were that her desired objects were out of reach, that she ran into physical obstacles or clumsily produced wrong results, or used ineffective means. The chimpanzees helped the human with some problems. However, the range of situations in which they helped was very limited: only when the adult effortfully reached and failed to grasp objects did the chimpanzees help her by fetching them for her.

An analogous study was conducted with 18 month old human infants, who also saw an adult fail to reach her goals for the same reasons (Warneken & Tomasello 2006). In this study, infants as young as 18 months of age helped the adult in various scenarios: for instance, they spontaneously removed physical obstacles that hindered the adult (e.g. they opened a cabinet so that the adult could place books inside) and showed him means that they knew were effective to bring about the intended result. It thus seems that, even though some helping behaviour can be found in non-human primates, only human infants display helping actions in a variety of situations, providing whatever help is needed in the given situation.

What we conclude from these experimental studies is that, despite their group hunting in the wild, chimpanzees do not have 'we-intentionality' (see Bratman 1992; Searle 1995; Tuomela 2002). They do not form a joint commitment to a shared goal and they do not perform reciprocal roles in the true sense as they do not generally understand both roles from a bird's eye view, in the same representational format.

Finally, they seem to be limited in their abilities to help another individual—which is a necessary prerequisite to engage in cooperative activities narrowly defined. Human infants and young children, in contrast, have this we-intentionality and act cooperatively from at least 14 to 18 months of age. They 'remind' their partner of the joint commitment to a shared goal, as they re-engage her when she suddenly interrupts the activity (Warneken et al. 2006; Warneken & Tomasello in press); they begin to reverse and understand roles as early as 12 months of age (Carpenter et al. 2005); and they help others in the fulfilment of their individual roles in various ways by at least 14–18 months (Warneken & Tomasello 2006, 2007).

10.4 Cooperative communication

A related domain, which also requires some form of cooperation is communication. As noted above, chimpanzees usually perform poorly in experiments that require some understanding of cooperative communication. Here, we address this issue in more detail by first looking at non-human primates' own production of communicative gestures, and then at their comprehension of such gestures produced by others.

Chimpanzees gesture to one another in different contexts. Some of these gestures are clearly intentional, in the sense that they are not just triggered by certain environmental conditions, but used flexibly to do such things as elicit play in the other (by an 'arm-raise') or to request nursing (by a 'touch-side'). That these gestures are indeed used flexibly is illustrated by a number of phenomena, for instance, the fact that visual gestures are only used in instances in which the recipient is visually oriented towards the sender (e.g. Tomasello et al. 1997b; Kaminski et al. 2004). One might think that if chimpanzees can gesture flexibly and understand some things about visual perception (see §2) they should also use gestures to direct another chimpanzee's attention to a certain event or object by pointing. There are certainly occasions in which it would be very helpful if one ape pointed for another ape to indicate the locus of some relevant event. It must therefore seem somewhat surprising that, in fact, there has not been a single reliable documentation of any scientist in any part of the world of one ape pointing for another. But captive apes which have had regular interactions with humans point for their human caretakers in some situations. Leavens & Hopkins (1998, 2005) conducted a study with chimpanzees in which a human experimenter placed a piece of food outside of the ape's reach and then left. When another human came in, the chimpanzees pointed to the food so that the human would get it for him (pointing was usually done with the whole hand, but some points were produced with just the index finger; see also Leavens *et al*. 2004). Human-raised chimpanzees have also been found to point to humans in order to obtain access to locations where there is food (Savage-Rumbaugh 1990), and some orangutans point for humans to the location where they can find a hidden tool, which they will then hopefully use to obtain food for the orangutans (Call & Tomasello 1994).

   We thus find that apes do sometimes point for humans—given that they have had some contact with humans in the past. Importantly though, they use this manual gesture imperatively only. That is, they point for humans either in order to obtain a desirable object from them directly, as in the studies by Leavens & Hopkins (1998, 2005), or indirectly by requesting from the human to provide the necessary conditions for them to get the object themselves, as in Savage-Rumbaugh's (1990) study. It thus seems that what the apes have learned from their experience with humans is that the human will help them, and that they can use the pointing gesture instrumentally in order to make him help them. They thus 'use' the human as a 'social tool' in order to get things they otherwise could not get, and they have learned that pointing gets this tool to work (the term social tool was first used by Bates *et al*. (1975)). However, no ape has ever been observed to point for another ape or for a human declaratively—that is, just for the sake of sharing attention to some outside entity, or to inform others of things cooperatively, as humans often do. Liszkowski *et al*. (2004, 2006) have shown in a series of experiments that even when they first begin to point at around 1 year of age, human infants do this with a full range of different motives—including the motive to share attention and interest. In one study (Liszkowski *et al*. 2004), an adult reacted differently towards infants' points, and the infant's response to the adult reaction was investigated. The main finding was that if the adult did not jointly attend to the event with the infant (by alternating gaze between infant and event and commenting on it)—but instead either (i) just 'registered' the event without sharing it with the infant or (ii) only looked and emoted positively to the infant while ignoring the event—the infants were dissatisfied and tried to correct the situation. In contrast, in the joint attention condition, infants appeared satisfied with the response. Using the same basic methodology, Liszkowski *et al*. (2006) found that beyond the classic distinction of imperative and declarative pointing, 12 month olds point for others also to inform them about things that are relevant for them. In that study, they directed an adult's attention to the location of an object for which that person was searching. What this suggests is that in human ontogeny, pointing is used from the very beginning not just in order to obtain certain objects via helpful adults as social tools, but with the motivation to help/inform others or to just jointly attend to things in the world with them.

   The question is thus why apes do not point to share interest and inform others as human infants do from very early in development (see also Tomasello 2006). They clearly have the necessary motor abilities to do so. And again, it would surely be useful if they spatially indicated important events for one another. So why do they not do it? To answer this question, one needs to look at apes' understanding of pointing. As mentioned earlier, one of the main paradigms that has been used to assess chimpanzees' comprehension of pointing is the Object Choice task. In the task designed by Tomasello *et al*. (1997a), one human, the hider, hides a piece of food for the ape in one of several containers. Then another human, the helper, shows the ape where it is by tilting the container so that she can look inside and see the food.

After this 'warm-up', the hider again places a piece of food in one of the containers, but now the helper indicates the location of the food for the ape by pointing at the baited container with his index finger (or by gazing at it). Variations of this method involve other kinds of communicative cues (Call & Tomasello 2005) and a trained chimpanzee instead of a human as the provider of the cue (Itakura *et al*. 1999). The results were the same in all these studies: the apes performed poorly, that is, they chose the correct container at chance level. They often followed the human's point (or gaze cue) to the container with their eyes, but they did not make any inferences from there about the location of food. That is, they cannot use or exploit the information that is conveyed to them via the pointing gesture—they do not know what it means. When following the human's point with their eyes, all they perceive is a useless bucket. To understand that the point is not directed at the bucket as such, but at the bucket qua location or qua container of a desired object, the apes would need to understand something about cooperation or communication. They would need to understand that the other is trying to communicate to them something that might be relevant for the achievement of their goal. In other words, an understanding of the meaning of the pointing gesture presupposes a more general understanding that others might want to help or inform us about things which they assume are relevant for our purposes. And this understanding obviously goes beyond the apes' social-cognitive skills.

The view that the challenge of the Object Choice task does indeed lie in its cooperative structure is supported by recent studies using a competitive version of the task. In one version, Hare & Tomasello (2004), instead of pointing to the baited container, reached unsuccessfully for it. Superficially, this reaching behaviour is very similar to the pointing gesture: the human's hand is oriented towards the container in which the food is hidden (the difference being that when pointing, only the index finger is stretched out, whereas in the case of reaching, all fingers point at the container). However, the chimpanzees' response in the reaching version was very different, as they successfully retrieved the food from the correct container. The reason for this must be that, even though the two tasks are superficially highly similar, their underlying structure is very different. Our interpretation is that in the case of reaching, the chimpanzees just need to perceive the goal-directedness of the human's reaching action and 'infer' that there must be something desirable in the container. This task can thus be solved with some understanding of the individual intentionality of the reaching action. In contrast, to understand pointing, the subject needs to understand more than the individual goal-directed behaviour. She needs to understand that by pointing towards a location, the other attempts to communicate to her where a desired object is located; that the other tries to inform her about something that is relevant for her. So the ape would need to understand something about this directedness towards itself ('this is for me!') and about the communicative intention behind the gesture in order to profit from it. Apparently, apes do not understand that the cue is 'for them'—used by the other in a helpful, informative and communicative way. Even though they are quite skilful in understanding intentional behaviour that is directed at objects in the world (see Tomasello *et al*. (2005) for a review), they do not understand communicative intentions, which are intentions that are not directed at things or behaviours but at another individual's intentional states (with the embedded structure: 'I intend for you to know that I intend for you x').

In order to explain why the apes fail to understand communicative intentions, one needs to broaden the perspective and focus on what we call the 'joint attentional frame'. The joint attentional frame or common ground (Clark & Brennan 1991) is what gives a pointing gesture its meaning—it is what 'grounds' the communication in the shared space of meaning. To illustrate the point, imagine you are walking down the aisle of a hardware store and all of a sudden a stranger looks at you and points to a bucket standing in one of the shelves. You see the bucket, but, with a quizzical look on your face, look back at the stranger, because you do not know what is going on. The reason why you do not know what is going on is that you lack a joint attentional frame with the stranger, which would give the point its meaning. The pointing as such, in this frameless scenario, does not mean anything. But if, instead, you are walking down the same aisle with a friend because you are looking for a bucket to use for cleaning purposes, and your friend points out the bucket to you, you would know immediately what he means: 'Here is one!' The presence of the joint attentional frame, which could be described by something like 'we are searching for a bucket', grounds the point in the ongoing activity and gives it its meaning. Another possible scenario could be that you and your friend are looking for anything that is made of a certain kind of plastic because you like it so much. In this case, your friend's point would have a different meaning, namely something like: 'Here is an item which is made of that plastic that you like so much!' The referent of the pointing gesture thus varies as a function of the joint attentional frame in which the pointing is anchored. One can imagine an endless number of joint attentional frames for the same basic scenario, with the referents of the pointing gesture being, for instance, 'item with texture of kind x', 'item which is similar to that other item we just saw' and so forth. The pointing gesture does not just indicate some spatial location, but instead it already contains a certain perspective from which the indicated object or location is to be viewed. And the perspective is carried by the joint attentional frame.

Humans can read pointing gestures based on joint attentional frames from as early as 14 months of age. Behne et al. (2005) found that 14 month olds choose thecorrect container in theObjectChoicetask significantly above chance, thus demonstrating that they understand the pointing gesture cooperatively. Infants also know that the 'functioning' of a joint attentional frame is specific to those people who share it. Liebal et al. (in preparation) had 18 month old infants clean up with an adult by picking up toys and putting them in a basket. At one point, the adult stopped and pointed to a ring toy, which infants then picked up and placed in the basket, presumably to help clean up. However, when the adult pointed to this same toy in this same way but in a different context, infants did not pick up the ring toy and put it in the basket; specifically, when the infant and adult were engaged in stacking ring toys on a post, children ignored the basket and brought the ring toy back to stack it on the post. The crucial point is that in both conditions the adult pointed to the same toy in the same way, but the infant extracted a different meaning in the two cases—based on the two different joint attentional frames involved, and the jointness is indeed a crucial component here. Thus, in a control condition, the infant and adult cleaned up exactly as in the shared clean-up condition, but then a second adult who had not shared this context entered the room and pointed towards the ring toy in exactly the same way as the first adult in the other two conditions. In this case, infants did not put the toy away into the basket, presumably because the second adult had not shared the cleaning context with them. Rather, because they had no shared frame with this adult, they seemed most often to interpret the new adult's point as a simple invitation to note and share attention to the toy.

We thus find that apes communicate individualistically, to get others to do things, and without joint attentional frames to ground the communicative intentions in a pre-existing space of shared meaning. Human infants, on the other hand, communicate cooperatively—to simply share interest in things and inform others of things—and they construct and participate in joint attentional frames, which give cooperative gestures their meaning, prelinguistically from as early as 14 months of age.

10.5 Joint attention and perspective

We thus find that human infants in their second year of life are much more skilled, and much more motivated, than are great apes at participating in collaborative problem solving and cooperative communication. Following Tomasello *et al.* (2005), our claim is that the reason for this difference is that human infants are biologically adapted for social interactions involving shared intentionality. Even at this tender age, human infants already have special skills for creating with other persons joint goals, joint intentions and joint attention, and special motivations for helping and sharing with others.

However, our claim goes further. Our Vygotskian intelligence hypothesis is that participation in interactions involving shared intentionality transforms human cognition in fundamental ways. First and most fundamentally, it creates the notion of perspective. Thus, consider how infants might come to understand that another person might see the same situation as they do, but from a different perspective. Just following someone else's gaze direction to another location is not enough. A difference in perspective can occur only when two people see the same thing, but differently (Perner *et al.* 2003). And so we would argue that young infants can come to appreciate that others see the same thing as they do, but from a different perspective only in situations in which they first appreciate the sharedness of attention, the joint attention on a single thing and then note differences (see also Barresi & Moore 1996).

Evidence that infants as young as 12–14 months of age are capable of something in this direction comes from a series of studies in which infants must determine what an adult is attending to (and knows) in a situation in which gaze direction is non-diagnostic. Tomasello & Haberl (2003) had 12- and 18 month old infants play with an adult with two toys in turn. Before a third toy was brought out by an assistant, the adult left the room. During her absence, the infant played with the third toy together with the assistant. Finally, all three toys were held in front of the infant, at which point the adult returned into the room and exclaimed excitement followed by an unspecified request for the infant to give her a toy (without indicating by gazing or pointing which specific toy she was attending to). Surprisingly, infants of both ages selected the toy the adult had not experienced (was new for her). In order to solve this task, infants had to understand (i) that people get excited about new, not familiar things and (ii) which of the toys was new for the adult and which she was already familiar with from previous experience.

In this study, infants knew what was familiar for the adult because they had participated with her in joint attention around two of the objects (but not the third). This suggests the possibility that infants attend to and register another person's experience most readily when they are jointly attending with that person, and so the difference of others' attention to the infants' own attention is mutually manifest—the foundation of perspective. And this is what was basically found in the two studies by Moll and colleagues (Moll & Tomasello 2007a; Moll *et al.* 2007b). Following the basic procedure of Tomasello & Haberl (2003), 14-and 18 month old infants either (i) became familiar with the first two objects in a joint attentional frame together with the adult or (ii) simply witnessed the adult become familiar with the known objects individually. In each case, infants themselves became equally familiar with all three objects, as in the original study. The result was that infants knew which of the three objects was new for the adult and thus captured her attention only when they had explored the known objects in a joint attentional format with her (they could not make this distinction when they had just witnessed her exploring them on her own, outside of any joint attentional frame). Ironically, noticing that another person's attention to, perhaps perspective on, a situation is different from our own is achieved most readily when we share attention to it at the outset.

   The notion of perspective—we are experiencing the same thing, but potentially differently—
is, we believe, unique to humans and of fundamental cognitive importance. As we have previously proposed (Tomasello 1999; Tomasello *et al.* 2005), young children's participation in
activities involving shared intentionality actually creates new forms of cognitive representation, specifically, perspectival or dialogic cognitive representations. In understanding and
internalizing an adult's intentional states, including those directed towards her, at the same
time she experiences her own psychological states towards the other, the child comes to con-
ceptualize the interaction simultaneously from both first and third persons'perspective (Barresi
& Moore 1996)—forming a bird's eye view' of the collaboration in which both commonalities
and differences are all comprehended with a single representational format. The cognitive
representations underlying truly cooperative activities must thus contain both some notion of
jointness and some notion of perspective. Such perspectival representations are necessary not
only for supporting cooperative interactions online, but also for the creation and use of certain
kinds of cultural artefacts, most importantly linguistic and other kinds of symbols, which are
socially constituted and bi-directional in the sense of containing simultaneously the perspective of speaker and of listener (since the speaker is a listener; Mead 1934).
   Perspectival cognitive representations pave the way for later uniquely human cognitive
achievements. Importantly, following Harris (1996), Tomasello & Rakoczy (2003) argued and
presented evidence that coming to understand false beliefs—the fact that someone else's perspective on things is different from what I know to be true from my perspective—depends on
children's participation over a several year period in perspective-shifting discourse. In linguistic discourse—including such things as misunderstandings and requests for clarification—
children experience regularly that what another person knows and attends to is often different
from what they know and attend to, and the understanding of false beliefs—which, in almost
every-one's account, is fundamental to mature human social cognition—is apparently unique
to humans (Call & Tomasello 1999).
   Perspectival cognitive representations and the understanding of beliefs also pave the way
for what may be called, very generally, collective intentionality (Searle 1995). That is, the
essentially social nature of perspectival cognitive representations enables children, later in the
preschool period, to construct the generalized social norms that make possible the creation of
social-institutional facts, such as money, marriage and government, whose reality is grounded
totally in the collective practices and beliefs of a social group conceived generally (Tomasello
& Rakoczy 2003). Importantly, when children internalize generalized collective conventions
and norms and use them to regulate their own behaviour, this provides for a new kind of social
rationality (morality) involving what Searle (1995) calls 'desire-independent reasons for action'.
At this point, children have become norm-following participants in institutional reality, that is
to say, fully functioning members of their cultural group.
   Our argument is thus that the species-unique aspects of human cognition reflect their cooperative roots in fundamental ways. The ability to take the perspective of others—which spawns
the understanding of false beliefs, perspectival cognitive representations and collective/
institutional reality—is only possible for organisms that can participate in social interactions
involving shared intentionality, especially interactions involving joint attention. Let us be very
clear on this point. Participation in these interactions is critical. A child raised on a desert
island would have all of the biological preparations for participation in interactions involving
shared intentionality, but because she did not actually participate in such interactions, she
would have nothing to internalize into perspectival cognitive representations. Ontogeny in this
case is critical.

10.6 Human evolution

The data reviewed here suggest that non-human primates and human infants share the ability to understand others as goal-directed, perceiving actors, and non-human primates display their skills most readily in competitive contexts. But human infants seem to display special skills and motivations in cooperative tasks involving shared intentionality—that is, those involving shared goals, joint attention, joint intentions and cooperative communication. Our proposal, the Vygotskian intelligence hypothesis, is thus that cooperation involving shared intentionality is a derived trait in human beings, emerging only after humans began down their own evolutionary pathway some 6 million years ago. This led to the emergence of cumulative cultural evolution as a process—involving various kinds of cultural learning and creation—and leading to the construction of all kinds of cultural artefacts, practices and institutions. It also led to the ability to create perspectival cognitive representations during ontogeny, which transformed human cognition from a mainly individual enterprise into a mainly collective cultural enterprise involving shared beliefs and practices, the foundation of cultural/institutional reality.

We do not have a detailed story of how skills and motivations of shared intentionality arose in human evolution. But, in general, to get from apes' skills of cooperation and social cognition to humans' skills of cooperation and social cognition evolutionarily, we think two key steps are needed. Three recent studies help to set the stage for this hypothesis.

— Melis *et al.* (2006*b*) tested chimpanzees in a simple collaboration task in which two individuals had to pull together to retrieve food. Whereas non-tolerant partners (asassessedinaninindependent test) cooperated very little, tolerant partners cooperated much better.

— Leavens et al. (e.g. Leavens & Hopkins 1998) documented that for a human, many captive chimpanzees point reliably to food they cannot reach, so that humans will retrieve it for them, even though they never point for conspecifics.

— Warneken & Tomasello (2006) found that young chimpanzees help human adults to retrieve out of reach objects—but not as often or in as many situations as 1 year old human infants.

These findings suggest that when they are interacting with especially tolerant and helpful partners—either conspecifics or humans—chimpanzees are able to behave in more cooperative ways. Hare & Tomasello (2004) thus proposed a two-stage theory of the evolution of human cooperation. First, some early humans had to become less aggressive/competitive and more tolerant/friendly with one another. One way to describe this process is a kind of self-domestication, in which the more aggressive and less cooperative members of the group were somehow ostracized or killed. In this case, the remaining humans were then free to engage in all kinds of group activities, including group foraging and feeding, with less competition and aggression. The research cited just above suggests that in this new cooperative environment, new cooperative behaviours would emerge without any additional cognitive evolution (e.g. imperative pointing). Second, under the assumption that the first stage put our hominids in a new adaptive space of many friendly group activities, a second stage of selection could then have selected for individuals with especially powerful social-cognitive and -motivational skills for sophisticated cooperative activities involving shared intentionality. This second step would involve, especially, social-cognitive skills for forming shared goals, intentions and attention with others; for communicating cooperatively with others during collaboration and for helping others as needed in collaborative activities as well.

Whereas many previous accounts of the evolution of human culture, including our own, have emphasized the non-genetic transmission of skills and information across generations—via imitation and other forms of social learning—just as important are the cooperative group activities and communication in which much of human social interaction occurs, and in which many new cognitive skills are generated. If cumulative cultural evolution of the human kind requires faithful transmission in a kind of cultural ratchet across generations, it also requires innovations, and perhaps many such acts of cultural creation emerge from collaborative activities in which groups of individuals accomplish things that no one individual could have accomplished on their own. And these activities are of course made possible, in our account, by the ability to participate in and internalize social interactions involving shared intentionality, resulting in collective norms, beliefs and institutions.

10.7 Conclusion

The central question in the evolution of human beings' cooperative and cultural capacities and motivations is whether these could have evolved only through processes of individual selection, or whether, in addition, some group-level selection was involved as well. In the modern context, multi-level selection theories stress that the so-called 'strong reciprocity' could be the basis of human cooperative interactions (see Fehr & Gächter (2002) for a review), and this in the context of the so-called cultural group selection (Richerson & Boyd 2005). The intuitive appeal of these theories is that human cooperation seems to be something very different, and so it would not be surprising to discover that a slightly different set of evolutionary processes was at work. In any case, the data we have presented here will constrain any such theories by being specific about precisely how humans and their nearest primate relatives are similar and how they are different in the ways they collaborate, communicate and learn from conspecifics.

References

Barresi, J. & Moore, C. 1996 Intentional relations and social understanding. *Behav. Brain Sci* **19**, 107–154.

Bates, E. 1979 *The emergence of symbols: cognition and communication in infancy.* New York, NY: Academic Press.

Bates, E., Camaioni, L. & Volterra, V. 1975 The acquisition of performatives prior to speech. *Merrill-Palmer Q.* **21**, 205–224.

Behne, T., Carpenter, M. & Tomasello, M. 2005 One-year-olds comprehend the communicative intentions behind gestures in a hiding game. *Dev. Sci.* **8**, 492–499. (doi:10. 1111/j.1467-7687.2005.00440.x)

Boesch, C. 2005 Joint co-operative hunting among wild chimpanzees: taking natural observations seriously. *Behav. Brain Sci.* **28**, 692–693. (doi:10.1017/S0140525X05230121)

Boesch, C. & Boesch, H. 1989 Hunting behavior of wild chimpanzees in the Taï-National-Park. *Am. J. Phys. Anthropol.* **78**, 547–573. (doi:10.1002/ajpa.1330780410)

Boesch, C. & Boesch-Achermann, H. 2000 *The chimpanzees of the Taï forest: behavioural ecology and evolution.* Oxford, UK: Oxford University Press.

Bratman, M. E. 1992 Shared co-operative activity. *Phil. Rev.* **101**, 327–341. (doi:10.2307/2185537)

Bräuer, J., Call, J. & Tomasello, M. 2005 All great ape species follow gaze to distant locations and around barriers. *J. Comp. Psychol.* **119**, 145–154. (doi:10.1037/0735-7036.119.2.145)

Byrne, R. & Whiten, A. (eds) 1998 *Machiavellian intelligence: social expertise and the evolution of intellect in monkeys, apes and humans.* Oxford, UK: Oxford University Press.

Call, J. & Tomasello, M. 1994 The production and comprehension of referential pointing by orangutans. *J. Comp. Psychol.* **108**, 307–317. (doi:10.1037/0735-7036.108.4.307)

Call, J. & Tomasello, M. 2005 What do chimpanzees know about seeing revisited: an explanation of the third kind. In *Issues in joint attention* (eds N. Eilan, C. Hoerl, T. McCormack & J. Roessler), pp. 45–64. Oxford, UK: Oxford University Press.

Call, J., Hare, B. A. & Tomasello, M. 1998 Chimpanzee gaze following in an object-choice task. *Anim. Cogn.* **1**, 89–99. (doi:10.1007/s100710050013)

Call, J., Agnetta, B. & Tomasello, M. 2000 Social cues that chimpanzees do and do not use to find hidden objects. *Anim. Cogn.* **3**, 23–34. (doi:10.1007/s100710050047)

Camaioni, L. 1993 The development of intentional communication: a re-analysis. In *New perspectives in early communicative development* (eds J. Nade & L. Camaioni), pp. 82–96. New York, NY: Routledge.

Carpenter, M., Tomasello, M. & Striano, T. 2005 Role reversal imitation and language in typically-developing infants and children with autism. *Infancy* **8**, 253–278. (doi:10.1207/s15327078in0803_4)

Clark, H. H. & Brennan, S. A. 1991 Grounding in communication. In *Perspectives on socially shared cognition* (eds L. B. Resnick, J. M. Levine & S. D. Teasley), pp. 127–149. Washington, DC: APA Books.

de Waal, F. 1982 *Chimpanzee politics*. New York, NY: Harper.

Fehr, E. & Gächter, S. 2002 Altruistic punishment in humans. *Nature* **415**, 137–140. (doi:10.1038/415137a)

Hare, B. & Tomasello, M. 2004 Chimpanzees are more skillful in competitive than in cooperative cognitive tasks. *Anim. Behav.* **68**, 571–581. (doi:10.1016/j.anbehav.2003.11.011)

Hare, B., Call, J., Agnetta, B. & Tomasello, M. 2000 Chimpanzees know what conspecifics do and do not see. *Anim.Behav.***59**, 771–785. (doi:10.1006/anbe.1999.1377)

Hare, B., Call, J. & Tomasello, M. 2001 Do chimpanzees know what conspecifics know? *Anim. Behav.* **61**, 139–151. (doi:10.1006/anbe.2000.1518)

Hare, B., Call, J. & Tomasello, M. 2006. Chimpanzees deceive a human by hiding. *Cognition* **101**, 495–514.

Harris, P. 1996 Desires, beliefs, and language. In *Theories of theories of mind* (eds P. Carruthers & P. Smith), pp. 200–222. Cambridge, UK: Cambridge University Press.

Humphrey, N. 1976 The social function of intellect. In *Growing points in ethology* (eds P. P. G. Bateson & R. A. Hinde), pp. 303–317. Cambridge, UK: Cambridge University Press.

Itakura, S., Agnetta, B., Hare, B. & Tomasello, M. 1999 Chimpanzees use human and conspecific social cues to locate hidden food. *Dev. Sci.* **2**, 448–456. (doi:10.1111/1467-7687.00089)

Jensen, K., Hare, B., Call, J. & Tomasello, M. 2006 Are chimpanzees spiteful or altruistic when sharing food? *Proc. R. Soc. B* **273**, 1013–1021. (doi:10.1098/rspb.2005.3417)

Kaminski, J., Call, J. & Tomasello, M. 2004 Body orientation and face orientation: two factors controlling apes' begging behavior from humans. *Anim. Cogn.* **7**, 216–223. (doi:10.1007/s10071-004-0214-2)

Leavens, D. & Hopkins, W. 1998 Intentional communication by chimpanzees: a cross-sectional study of the use of referential gestures. *Dev. Psychol.* **34**, 813–822. (doi:10.1037/0012-1649.34.5.813)

Leavens, D. & Hopkins, W. 2005 Multimodal concomitants of manual gesture by chimpanzees (*Pan troglodytes*). *Gesture* **5**, 73–88.

Leavens, D., Hostetter, A., Wesley, M. & Hopkins, W. 2004 Tactical use of a unimodal and bimodal communication by chimpanzees, *Pan troglodytes*. *Anim. Behav.* **67**, 467–476. (doi:10.1016/j.anbehav.2003.04.007)

Liebal, K., Behne, T. & Carpenter, M., Tomasello, M. In preparation. One-year-olds use common ground to interpret pointing gestures.

Liszkowski, U., Carpenter, M., Henning, A., Striano, T. & Tomasello, M. 2004 Twelve-month-olds point to share attention and interest. *Dev. Sci.* **7**, 297–307. (doi:10.1111/j.1467-7687.2004.00349.x)

Liszkowski, U., Carpenter, M., Henning, A., Striano, T. & Tomasello, M. 2006 Twelve-and 18-month-olds point to provide information for others. *J. Cogn. Dev.* **7**, 183–187.

Mead, G. H. 1934 *Mind, self, and society*. Chicago, IL: University of Chicago Press.

Melis, A. P., Hare, B. & Tomasello, M. 2006a Chimpanzees recruit the best collaborators. *Science* **311**, 1297–1300. (doi:10.1126/science.1123007)

Melis, A., Call, J. & Tomasello, M. 2006bChimpanzees conceal visual and auditory information from others. *J. Comp. Psychol.* **120**, 154–162.

Moll, H. & Tomasello, M. 2007a How 14- and 18-month-olds know what others have experienced (ie. How 14-and 18-month olds know what others have experienced). *Dev. Psychol.* **43**, 307–317.

Moll, H., Carpenter, M. & Tomasello, M. 2007b Fourteen-month-old infants know what others know only from joint engagement. *Dev. Sci.* doi: 10.111/j.1467-7687.2007.00615.

Perner, J., Brandl, J. & Garnham, A. 2003 What is a perspective problem? Developmental issues in understanding belief and dual identity. *Facta Phil.* **5**, 355–378.

Povinelli, D. J. & Eddy, T. J. 1996 What young chimpanzees know about seeing. *Monogr. Soc. Res. Child Dev.* **61**.

Povinelli, D. J., Nelson, K. E. & Boysen, S. T. 1992 Comprehension of role reversal in chimpanzees—evidence of empathy. *Anim. Behav.* **43**, 633–640. (doi:10.1016/ 0003-3472(92)90085-N)

Povinelli, D. J., Bierschwale, D. T. & Cech, C. G. 1999 Comprehension of seeing as a referential act in young children, but not juvenile chimpanzees. *Br. J. Dev. Psychol.* **17**, 37–60. (doi:10.1348/026151099165140)

Reaux, J. E., Theall, L. A. & Povinelli, D. J. 1999 A longitudinal investigation of chimpanzees' understanding of visual perception. *Child Dev.* **70**, 275–290. (doi:10.1111/1467-8624.00021)

Richerson, P. J. & Boyd, R. 2005 *Not by genes alone. How culture transformed human evolution.* Oxford, UK: Oxford University Press.

Savage-Rumbaugh, S. 1990 Language as a cause-effect communication system. *Phil. Psychol.* **3**, 55–76.

Searle, J. R. 1995 *The construction of social reality.* New York, NY: Free Press.

Silk, J. B., Brosnan, S. F., Vonk, J., Henrich, J., Povinelli, D. J., Richardson, A. S., Lambeth, S. P., Mascaro, J. & Schapiro, S. J. 2005 Chimpanzees are indifferent to the welfare of unrelated group members. *Nature* **437**, 1357–1359. (doi:10.1038/nature04243)

Tomasello, M. 1999 *The cultural origins of human cognition.* Cambridge, MA: Harvard University Press.

Tomasello, M. 2006 Why don't apes point? In *Roots of human sociality* (eds N. Enfield & S. Levinson), pp. 506–524. New York, NY: Wenner-Grenn.

Tomasello, M. & Carpenter, M. 2005 The emergence of social cognition in three young chimpanzees. *Monogr. Soc. Res. Child Dev.* **70**, 133–152. (doi:10.1111/j.1540-5834.2005.00333.x) (Serial No 279).

Tomasello, M. & Haberl, K. 2003 Understanding attention: 12-and 18-month-olds know what is new for other persons. *Dev. Psychol.* **39**, 906–912. (doi:10.1037/0012-1
649.39.5.906)

Tomasello, M. & Rakoczy, H. 2003 What makes human cognition unique? From individual to shared to collective intentionality. *Mind Lang.* **18**, 121–147.

Tomasello, M., Call, J. & Gluckman, A. 1997a Comprehension of novel communicative signs by apes and human children. *Child Dev.* **68**, 1067–1080. (doi:10.2307/1132292)

Tomasello, M., Call, J., Warren, J., Frost, T., Carpenter, M. & Nagell, K. 1997b The ontogeny of chimpanzee gestural signals: a comparison across groups and generations. *Evol. Commun.* **1**, 223–253.

Tomasello, M., Hare, B. & Agnetta, B. 1999 Chimpanzees follow gaze direction geometrically. *Anim. Behav.* **58**, 769–777. (doi:10.1006/anbe.1999.1192)

Tomasello, M., Carpenter, M., Call, J., Behne, T. & Moll, H. 2005 Understanding and sharing intentions: the ontogeny and phylogeny of cultural cognition. *Behav. Brain Sci.* **28**, 675–735. (doi:10.1017/ S0140525X05000129)

Tuomela, R. 2002 Collective goals and communicative action. *J. Phil. Res.* **27**, 29–64.

Vygotsky, L. S. 1978 *Mind in society: the development of higher psychological processes.* Cambridge, MA: Harvard University Press.

Warneken, F. & Tomasello, M. 2006 Altruistic helping in human infants and young chimpanzees. *Science* **3**, 1301–1303. (doi:10.1126/science.1121448)

Warneken, F. & Tomasello, M. 2007 Helping and Co-operation at 14-months of age. *Infancy.* **11**, 271–294.

Warneken, F., Chen, F. & Tomasello, M. 2006 Co-operative activities in young children and chimpanzees. *Child Dev.* **77**, 640–663.

11

Understanding primate brain evolution

R. I. M. Dunbar and Susanne Shultz

We present a detailed reanalysis of the comparative brain data for primates, and develop a model using path analysis that seeks to present the coevolution of primate brain (neocortex) and sociality within a broader ecological and life-history framework. We show that body size, basal metabolic rate and life history act as constraints on brain evolution and through this influence the coevolution of neocortex size and group size. However, they do not determine either of these variables, which appear to be locked in a tight coevolutionary system. We show that, within primates, this relationship is specific to the neocortex. Nonetheless, there are important constraints on brain evolution; we use path analysis to show that, in order to evolve a large neocortex, a species must first evolve a large brain to support that neocortex and this in turn requires adjustments in diet (to provide the energy needed) and life history (to allow sufficient time both for brain growth *and* for 'software' programming). We review a wider literature demonstrating a tight coevolutionary relationship between brain size and sociality in a range of mammalian taxa, but emphasize that the social brain hypothesis is not about the relationship between brain/neocortex size and group size *per se*; rather, it is about social complexity and we adduce evidence to support this. Finally, we consider the wider issue of how mammalian (and primate) brains evolve in order to localize the social effects.

Keywords: brain evolution; life history; neocortex; primate; social brain hypothesis

11.1 Introduction

The social brain hypothesis was originally proposed explicitly as an explanation for the fact that primates have unusually large brains for body size when compared with other vertebrates (including all other mammals; Byrne & Whiten 1988; Barton & Dunbar 1997; Dunbar 1998). Its main claim was that because they had an unusually complex social life, primates needed a comparably large brain to cope with the computations involved. Initially, it was assumed that the social brain hypothesis applied only to primates. However, a number of analyses subsequently suggested that the hypothesis might apply more widely to other mammalian groups (including whales, carnivores and at least some insectivores; Marino 1996; Dunbar & Bever 1998). However, these studies were limited in scope and focused only on possible correlations between sociality and brain size.

Two issues arise out of these findings. One fact is that, with the exception of Shultz & Dunbar (2006), the focus has been mainly on bivariate correlations between brain size and either sociality (usually indexed as social group size) or some ecological variable (e.g. range size, an index of frugivory); little attempt has been made to evaluate whether the relationship between group size and brain size is actually a confound of these ecological variables. In part, this reflected a methodological constraint; existing statistical tools made it difficult to evaluate dichotomous and quantitative variables in the same model. Statistical methods that have been developed recently now make it possible both to test a wider range of hypotheses simultaneously and, more importantly perhaps, to include dichotomous as well as continuous variables in the same analysis. They also allow the problem of phylogenetic inertia to be handled in a more sophisticated way than was previously the case. The second issue raised by these findings is the question as to just what it is about sociality that creates the cognitive load that is so demanding of neural computational power. There has been a tendency for the social brain hypothesis to be couched solely in terms of group size (the variable that most analyses have used as their assay of sociality). But, in fact, the hypothesis has quite explicitly always been about the *complexity* of social relationships (their *quality* rather than merely their *quantity*). Group size is certainly a correlate of social complexity (if only because the number of dyads and triads that have to be tracked and managed socially increases as a power function of the number of individuals in the group), but it is at best a crude proxy.

We address these two issues here. First, we present new analyses which incorporate a number of additional ecological and demographic variables. Our aims here are: (i) to confirm that the original findings hold up across a wider mammalian perspective when new more powerful statistical methods are used and (ii) to view brain evolution within a broader ecological and life-history perspective. Second, we consider in more detail the nature of the socio-cognitive demands that underpin the social brain effects and the way in which these relate to brain structure.

First, however, it is necessary to clarify one point that seems to have been repeatedly confused in the literature. The social brain hypothesis has sometimes been interpreted as though it was ecology-free and represented a contrast between ecology and sociality as the driving force of brain evolution. This is possibly because, in the original analyses (Dunbar 1992), sociality was pitted against a set of alternative ecological hypotheses. It is important to remember that the social brain hypothesis is itself an ecological hypothesis; the claim is that one or more ecological problems (survival, foraging, rearing offspring) are more effectively solved *socially* than by an individual's unaided efforts. The key issue here is whether an animal's solutions to the problems of successful survival and reproduction are social (either as an emergent property of group living or, perhaps, through social imitation) or are the product of individual problem solving. In other words, is the relationship between brain size and ecology direct (e.g. via trial-and-error learning or individual problem solving) or indirect (mediated via sociality)?

More importantly, a clear distinction can be drawn between two versions of the cognitive challenge that underpins the social intelligence hypothesis. These differ in terms of what they consider the critical factor selecting for differences in socio-cognitive abilities. One view (that encompassed in the original Machiavellian hypothesis of Byrne & Whiten (1988), and developed in more detail by Dunbar (1992, 1998)) focuses on social bonding of groups as the critical issue. The other assumes that feeding (and hence nutrient flow) is the critical constraint, and thus that social learning of efficient foraging strategies has been the principal selection pressure for the evolution of socio-cognitive skills (Reader & Laland 2002). Both the primate and the general vertebrate literatures have remained ambivalent as to which of these has been the more important force of natural selection, although the consensus is that predation risk has been the more important influence on primate social evolution (Dunbar 1988).

11.2 The social brain in mammalian perspective

The social brain hypothesis has been extensively tested on primates (Sawaguchi & Kudo 1990; Dunbar 1992, 1998; Barton 1993, 1996; Deaner *et al*. 2000) and the results seem, in general, to be robust with respect to statistical methodology. While there have been a number of analyses suggesting that the social brain hypothesis might also hold in, at least, some other non-primate mammals (Marino 1996, 2004; Dunbar & Bever 1998), there have been few detailed tests of the hypothesis for mammalian groups other than primates. However, such analyses have recently been published for both carnivores and ungulates. Perez-Barberia & Gordon (2005) and Shultz & Dunbar (2006) have independently shown that sociality correlates with both relative brain and relative neocortex size in ungulates (social species have bigger brains/neocortices). Group size and diet made no independent contribution, but there was a significant independent effect of preferred habitat type. In this case, habitat was considered as a trichotomy (open, closed and mixed) and species adapted to mixed habitats had larger brains than those that were open or closed habitat specialists.

More importantly, perhaps, Perez-Barberia et al. (in press) have shown, using Pagel's DISCRETE method, that for all three orders, there is very strong coevolution between relative brain (or neocortex) size and sociality in these two orders, as well as in primates; the two traits tend to change in synchrony rather than sequentially within each order's phylogenetic tree. This implies that the two traits are under tightly coupled selection; changes in one trait (sociality) are only possible if they are associated with changes in the other trait (brain size). This result lends support to the social brain hypothesis and weakens the alternative hypothesis that sociality is a by-product of having a large brain, when large brains have evolved for some other more conventional reason (e.g. to solve some ecological problem on a non-social basis).

Nonetheless, there was evidence in the Perez-Barberia et al. (in press) analyses for lagged evolution in all three orders (primates, ungulates and carnivores). In primates, there were back transitions from large-brain/ more-social to small-brain/more-social and forward transitions from large-brain/less-social to large-brain/more-social, but there were no consistent pathways whereby primates moved from small-brain/less-social to large-brain/more-social via intermediate steps. In ungulates, there seemed to have been a certain amount of switching back and forth between large-brain/social and, on one hand, small-brain/social and large-brain/ asocial, but again without any suggestion that these constituted intermediate steps in an evolutionary sequence. Carnivores exhibited much greater flexibility, with most transitional steps occurring more often than expected despite the fact that, overall, they showed the same strong correlated evolution. This suggests that in a limited number of cases (but especially in carnivores), it has been possible to develop a degree of sociality without large brains and we would predict that, in these cases, sociality is characterized by some 'looseness' (i.e. lack of group cohesion). We might interpret this finding as implying that sociality can more easily be decoupled from brain (or cognitive) constraints in carnivores than is possible in either ungulates or primates.

11.3 Primate brain evolution revisited

In the light of these new findings, we have undertaken new analyses of the primate data, in order to be able to evaluate in greater depth the relationships between primate brain size and species-specific behavioural, ecological and life-history characteristics. A number of recent studies have sought to evaluate the relative importance of ecology (Reader & Laland 2002), life history (Ross 1992; Joffe 1997; Deaner et al. 2003) and allometric scaling relationships (Finlay & Darlington 1995; Finlay et al. 2001; de Winter & Oxnard 2001; Barton & Harvey 2000) for primate brain evolution. Life-history characteristics can impose considerable constraint on the timing and flexibility of developmental processes and are crucial in determining the potential adaptive pathways available to a population. External mortality drives the onset of reproduction and constrains the investment individuals can make in non-reproductive age classes (Charnov 2001). Only long-lived individuals that experience low mortality rates can afford the growth and learning period necessary to develop large brains (Clutton-Brock & Harvey 1980). Similarly, ecological flexibility and complexity have previously been linked to cognitive capacity and brain size in primates (Reader & Laland 2002; Lefebvre *et al.* 2004), other mammals (Gittleman 1986) and birds (Lefebvre *et al.* 1997; Sol *et al.* 2002, 2005).

However, the associations that have been identified between these traits and brain size have not yet been placed into an overarching framework of brain evolution in primates. Nor has there been any serious attempt to assess how they might relate to the social brain hypothesis. To explore this in more detail, we carried out an evaluation of the ecological and social characteristics associated with primate brain size and social complexity using a three-step analysis. First, we use univariate analyses to determine how different behavioural and ecological traits are associated with measures of relative brain size. Second, we use general linear models to test between alternative models of how these characteristics relate to both brain size and social complexity. Third, we build and test a path model that integrates life history, ecology and social complexity as causes and consequences of brain size. Finally, in addition, we consider the question of the appropriate level of analysis for the brain by comparing analyses using different indices of brain volumetric change, including the brain as a whole, neocortex volume (adjusted in three different ways for scaling effects of body/brain size) and relative cerebellum size. We use cerebellum size as a way of testing whether the functional relationships we describe are generic to all brain components (i.e. simply reflect overall changes in brain volume) or are specific to certain brain units (specifically, the neocortex). Methodological details are given in full in Dunbar & Shultz, 2007.

(a) Univariate relationships

We initially explored the relationship between different estimates of relative brain or neocortex size and behavioural, life-history and ecological characteristics using simple univariate tests (either one-way ANOVAs or linear regression).

With the exception of dispersal, all of the indices of sociality were significantly related to indices of brain volume (table 11.1). However, for each of these behavioural indices, one of the measures of relative neocortex size explained more variation than either total brain size or relative cerebellum size. Indeed, relative cerebellum size was not consistently associated with the social indices. Life-history measures were also associated consistently with the various indices of brain volume. However, in contrast to the social variables, total brain size explained more of the variation than the neocortex size for two of the four life-history variables, basal metabolic rate (BMR) and longevity. Species with large brains have, on average, higher metabolic rates (when corrected for body size), larger bodies, longer life spans and longer juvenile periods. Note, however, that while total brain size is strongly correlated with residual BMR (when neocortex volume and all other variables are partialled out), neocortex volume itself is not correlated with residual BMR when total brain volume is partialled out (figure 11.1). This relationship implies that life-history traits can permit species to support larger brains (metabolically and developmentally), but the overall architecture of the brain is not itself tied to—or necessarily constrained by—life-history characteristics. Interestingly, the direction of the relationship (or slope) between relative cerebellum size and life history was opposite that of the relationships with brain and neocortex. Overall, the consistent relationship between

Table 11.1 Univiariate relationships between behavioural, ecological and life-history characteristics and relative brain size.

		brain-body	neo-rest	neo-brain	neo-med	cere-rest
behavioural	log group	$F_{1,41} = 35.86$	$F_{1,41} = 41.11$	$F_{1,41} = 33.40$	$F_{1,41} = 29.35$	$F_{1,41} = 20.80$
		$p < 0.001$	$p < 0.001$	$p < 0.001$	$p < 0.001$	$p < 0.001$
		$\beta = 0.23$	$\beta = 0.16$	$\beta = 0.06$	$\beta = 0.18$	$\beta = -0.091$
		$r_{adj} = 0.45$	$r_{adj} = 0.49$	$r_{adj} = 0.44$	$r_{adj} = 0.40$	$r_{adj} = 0.32$
	social system	$F_{3,39} = 4.83$	$F_{3,39} = 6.88$	$F_{3,39} = 10.06$	$F_{3,39} = 4.08$	$F_{3,39} = 2.12$
		$p = 0.006$	$p = 0.001$	$p < 0.001$	$p = 0.01$	$p = 0.11$
		$r_{adj} = 0.22$	$r_{adj} = 0.30$	$r_{adj} = 0.39$	$r_{adj} = 0.18$	$r_{adj} = 0.07$
	dispersal	$F_{2,29} = 1.65$	$F_{2,29} = 0.23$	$F_{2,29} = 0.24$	$F_{2,29} = 4.09$	$F_{2,29} = 0.60$
		$p = 0.21$	$p = 0.79$	$p = 0.79$	$p = 0.03$	$p = 0.94$
		$r_{adj} = 0.04$	$r_{adj} = 0.05$	$r_{adj} = 0.05$	$r_{adj} = 0.17$	$r_{adj} = 0.06$
	coalitions-harem, mm	$F_{1,22} = 17.59$	$F_{1,22} = 18.14$	$F_{1,22} = 22.95$	$F_{1,22} = 8.96$	$F_{1,22} = 24.62$
		$p < 0.001$	$p < 0.001$	$p < 0.001$	$p = 0.007$	$p < 0.001$
		$r_{adj} = 0.42$	$r_{adj} = 0.43$	$r_{adj} = 0.49$	$r_{adj} = 0.26$	$r_{adj} = 0.51$
life history	log body	$F_{1,41} = 6.16$	$F_{1,41} = 7.05$	$F_{1,41} = 4.19$	$F_{1,41} = 6.01$	$F_{1,41} = 1.04$
		$p = 0.02$	$p = 0.01$	$p = 0.05$	$p = 0.02$	$p = 0.31$
		$\beta = 0.085$	$\beta = 0.06$	$\beta = 0.018$	$\beta = 0.071$	$\beta = -0.017$
		$r_{adj} = 0.11$	$r_{adj} = 0.13$	$r_{adj} = 0.07$	$r_{adj} = 0.12$	$r_{adj} = 0.001$
	residual BMR	$F_{1,16} = 6.14$	$F_{1,16} = 5.03$	$F_{1,16} = 5.80$	$F_{1,16} = 4.09$	$F_{1,16} = 2.12$
		$p = 0.03$	$p = 0.04$	$p = 0.03$	$p = 0.06$	$p = 0.17$
		$\beta = 0.54$	$\beta = 0.52$	$\beta = 0.20$	$\beta = 0.40$	$\beta = -0.19$
		$r_{adj} = 0.23$	$r_{adj} = 0.19$	$r_{adj} = 0.22$	$r_{adj} = 0.15$	$r_{adj} = 0.06$
	longevity	$F_{1,30} = 26.82$	$F_{1,30} = 4.68$	$F_{1,30} = 2.06$	$F_{1,30} = 20.07$	$F_{1,30} = 0.56$
		$p < 0.001$	$p = 0.04$	$p = 0.16$	$p < 0.001$	$p = 0.46$
		$\beta = 0.01$	$\beta = 0.002$	$\beta = 0.001$	$\beta = 0.005$	$\beta = -0.001$
		$r_{adj} = 0.42$	$r_{adj} = 0.09$	$r_{adj} = 0.03$	$r_{adj} = 0.35$	$r_{adj} = 0.01$
	juvenile period	$F_{1,27} = 5.60$	$F_{1,27} = 5.52$	$F_{1,27} = 3.35$	$F_{1,27} = 5.83$	$F_{1,27} = 0.55$
		$p = 0.03$	$p = 0.03$	$p = 0.08$	$p = 0.02$	$p = 0.47$
		$\beta = 0.03$	$\beta = 0.03$	$\beta = 0.01$	$\beta = 0.03$	$\beta = -0.01$
		$r_{adj} = 0.14$	$r_{adj} = 0.14$	$r_{adj} = 0.08$	$r_{adj} = 0.15$	$r_{adj} = 0.02$
ecological	diet	$F_{3,39} = 4.32$	$F_{3,39} = 1.56$	$F_{3,39} = 1.49$	$F_{3,39} = 2.64$	$F_{3,39} = 3.68$
		$p = 0.01$	$p = 0.22$	$p = 0.23$	$p = 0.06$	$p = 0.02$
		$r_{adj} = 0.19$	$r_{adj} = 0.04$	$r_{adj} = 0.03$	$r_{adj} = 0.11$	$r_{adj} = 0.16$
	habitat	$F_{1,41} = 7.32$	$F_{1,41} = 9.58$	$F_{1,41} = 2.72$	$F_{1,41} = 4.51$	$F_{1,41} = 3.90$
		$p = 0.01$	$p = 0.004$	$p = 0.11$	$p = 0.04$	$p = 0.06$
		$r_{adj} = 0.13$	$r_{adj} = 0.17$	$r_{adj} = 0.04$	$r_{adj} = 0.08$	$r_{adj} = 0.06$
	strata	$F_{2,40} = 3.30$	$F_{2,40} = 3.71$	$F_{2,40} = 2.11$	$F_{2,40} = 3.48$	$F_{2,40} = 1.82$
		$p = 0.05$	$p = 0.03$	$p = 0.14$	$p = 0.04$	$p = 0.18$
		$r_{adj} = 0.10$	$r_{adj} = 0.11$	$r_{adj} = 0.05$	$r_{adj} = 0.11$	$r_{adj} = 0.04$
	home range	$F_{1,28} = 15.33$	$F_{1,28} = 19.67$	$F_{1,28} = 17.75$	$F_{1,28} = 20.03$	$F_{1,28} = 9.63$
		$p = 0.001$	$p < 0.001$	$p < 0.001$	$p < 0.001$	$p = 0.004$
		$\beta = 0.09$	$\beta = 0.07$	$\beta = 0.03$	$\beta = 0.08$	$\beta = -0.04$
		$r_{adj} = 0.33$	$r_{adj} = 0.39$	$r_{adj} = 0.37$	$r_{adj} = 0.40$	$r_{adj} = 0.23$
	day range	$F_{1,30} = 13.88$	$F_{1,30} = 13.27$	$F_{1,30} = 12.13$	$F_{1,30} = 10.24$	$F_{1,30} = 14.88$
		$p = 0.001$	$p = 0.001$	$p = 0.002$	$p = 0.003$	$P = 0.001$
		$\beta = 0.27$	$\beta = 0.20$	$\beta = 0.07$	$\beta = 0.20$	$\beta = -0.15$
		$r_{adj} = 0.29$	$r_{adj} = 0.28$	$r_{adj} = 0.26$	$r_{adj} = 0.24$	$r_{adj} = 0.31$
	activity	$F_{1,41} = 19.97$	$F_{1,41} = 30.23$	$F_{1,41} = 37.83$	$F_{1,41} = 15.40$	$F_{1,41} = 13.04$
		$p < 0.001$	$p < 0.001$	$p < 0.001$	$p < 0.001$	$p = 0.001$
		$r_{adj} = 0.31$	$r_{adj} = 0.41$	$r_{adj} = 0.48$	$r_{adj} = 0.26$	$r_{adj} = 0.22$

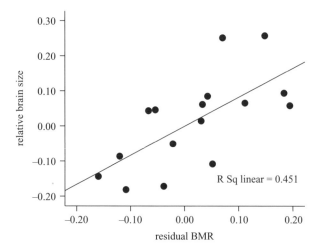

Fig. 11.1 Basal metabolic rate (BMR), controlling for body size (residuals from a linear regression of basal metabolic rate versus log-transformed body size), plotted against relative brain size. Species with higher metabolic rates than expected for their body size also have larger than expected brain size.

'slow' life-history characteristics and higher than predicted metabolic rates indicates that a suite of life-history characteristics are necessary to support the development of large brains. The importance of life history is given additional emphasis by an earlier finding by Joffe (1997) showing that, while total brain size correlates with the conventional gestation+lactation measure of parental investment, relative neocortex volume (at least when the primary visual area is excluded) correlates better with the length of the juvenile period (i.e. weaning to first reproduction), suggesting an important role for social learning of socio-cognitive skills. Thus, extended life histories may be necessary both to allow the laying down of large quantities of brain tissue and to allow that neural tissue to be tuned through social and other more conventional learning processes.

The ecological traits we considered are also consistently related to brain size. The fact that diet is associated with overall brain size, but not with the size of the neocortex relative to the rest of brain, indicates that diet may be a metabolic constraint rather than being cognitively demanding. If diet was cognitively challenging, we could expect that diet would be more strongly associated with executive brain components (e.g. neocortex) rather than total brain size. As with the life-history traits, the relationship between ecological traits and cerebellum size is in the opposite direction to those for total brain and neocortex size. However, the relationships between ecological variables and the various indices of brain size may be an artefact of the fact that both ecology and brain size are strongly associated with group size. Thus, in order to support the energetic needs of all group members, individuals must solve ecological problems in order to maintain large groups. Hence, the association between indices of brain size and ecological characteristics may be causally indirect; it is the behavioural flexibility required to feed group members that drives cognitive evolution rather than the ecological problem solving *per se*. Alternatively, direct causal relationships between group size and ecology may mean that ecology also covaries with brain size (assuming that brain size is simply a function of group size).

(b) Minimum adequate models

In order to tease apart the relationship between ecology, group size and brain size, we used forward and backward stepwise general linear models. We constructed a global model of how life history, ecology, brain size and sociality are interrelated using general linear models to identify which sets of characteristics are most strongly associated with brain size, group size and the ecological variables. For this set of analyses, we restrict our brain size estimates to two measurements: brain/body residuals and neocortex/rest-of-brain residuals. A minimum adequate model (MAM) approach was chosen over an information criterion one because the sample sizes for different parameters are not equal. We used a subset of species with data available for all parameters (see §3c below) to test whether there was significant phylogenetic autocorrelation in the modelled data by estimating Pagel's λ and comparing log-likelihoods of phylogenetic models with those of non-phylogenetic models (Freckleton *et al.* 2002).

The identified MAM's are summarized in table 11.2. Brain size was best explained by a combination of neocortex size and longevity; neocortex size was best explained by total brain size, group size and longevity; home range by body size, group size and day range; and day range by diet and home range. The least stable model was for group size: in this case, three

Table 11.2 Generalized linear matrix MAM results for relationships suggested by the path diagram shown in figure 11.2. (λ represents the optimized degree of phylogenetic autocorrelation (or contribution of the species relatedness covariance matrix to the overall model fit), where λ = 0 indicates no autocorrelation and λ = 1 means the degree of covariance between species conforms to the assumption of Brownian motion trait evolution. Parentheses represent whether the log-likelihood of the phylogenetic model varies significantly from a model that does not include phylogeny.)

factor	predictors included	model r^2_{adj}	d.f.	F	p	λ	factors excluded
relative brain size	max. lifespan	0.81	1,32	44.65	< 0.001	0	body size, group size, activity, home range size, day range length, habitat
	diet		2,32	5.83	0.003	(n.s.)	
	neocortex		1,32	47.05	< 0.001		
relative neo-cortex to rest of brain	group size	0.67		10.23	0.003	0	day range, home range, body size, diet, activity, habitat
	brain size			24.43	< 0.001	(n.s.)	
	max. lifespan			8.49	0.006		
group size	activity	0.60		12.08	0.001	0.13	diet, body size, lifespan, brain size, day range, habitat
	neocortex or home range activity or home range neocortex			10.36	0.003	(n.s.)	
home range	body size	0.76		11.84	0.002	0	diet, activity, brain size, neocortex size, lifespan, habitat
	group size			7.58	0.01	(n.s.)	
	day range			10.93	0.003		
day range	home range	0.49		12.94	0.002	0	body size, brain size, neocortex size, activity, lifespan, habitat
	diet			3.71	0.03	(n.s.)	

combinations of factors provided equal support (neocortex size and home range; home range and activity; and neocortex size and activity). These models were indistinguishable on the basis of their respective information criteria values. We interpret this as reflecting the complex interaction between ecological (i.e. time budget) and cognitive constraints on group size as previously proposed by Dunbar's (1996, 2002) linear programming model of primate group sizes.

We excluded BMR from these analyses, as the sample is too small to provide enough power for discrimination. However, we can use the reduced dataset to identify which factors are associated with BMR and residual BMR. Overall, BMR is most strongly associated with diet ($F_{3,15} = 14.85$, $p < 0.001$, $r^2_{adj} = 0.62$); in contrast, residual BMR (or BMR corrected for body size) is strongly associated with both total brain and neocortex size (table 11.1, figure 11.1). However, a stepwise regression indicates that residual brain size is the only factor that influences residual BMR (partial $r = 0.631$, $t_{15} = 3.15$, $p = 0.007$); relative neocortex size is dropped from the model (partial $r = 0.036$, $p = 0.896$). We interpret these results as implying two important conclusions. First, for a given body size, individuals can only invest extra available energy into evolving and maintaining expensive brain architecture if they can commandeer sufficient resources to exceed their basic metabolic requirements. Second, while BMR constrains total brain size, it does not have a strong influence on the way gross brain volume is allocated to different brain units (i.e. on brain architecture).

(c) Path analysis

We now evaluate how the suite of ecological, life-history and social characteristics can be integrated into a global model of primate brain evolution. The model we propose is premised on the following assumptions: (i) inherent life-history characteristics are necessary to allow species to support the development and maintenance of large brains, (ii) these characteristics and the high metabolic demands of large brains drive and/or constrain ecology, and (iii) social complexity (or group size) represents the functional benefit of maintaining large brains. Part of the purpose in building the model is to test of the validity of these assumptions by asking whether they provide us with a better understanding of primate brain evolution than do alternative explanations.

Using the MAM analyses, we integrated the various relationships between life history, sociality, brain size and ecology into a global model of brain evolution and group size (figure 11.2). We have also used evidence from previous studies to incorporate additional relationships into the path diagram in order to help infer causality. These include BMR correlating with brain size, longevity and life history (Armstrong 1985; Ross 1992; Allman et al. 1993), group size correlating with home range size, day range and predation (Grant et al.1992; Wrangham et al. 1993; Hill & Dunbar 1998; Hill & Lee 1998; Shultz et al. 2004) and, of course, brain size correlating with group size (Dunbar 1992; Barton 1996).

In order to determine whether our proposed model actually provides the best causal explanation for group size, we compared alternative 'causal' models, or pathways, for group size. Our test model (that shown in figure 11.2) was that the factors most closely associated with group size on the diagram (neocortex, activity and home range size) are better predictors than the factors that are more deeply embedded in the diagram. Although we could potentially test every permutation of factors to identify the 'best of all possible models', in the interests of parsimony we based our candidate alternative models on the MAMs identified in the previous section (table 11.2). More explicitly, we took group size as the dependent variable and tested

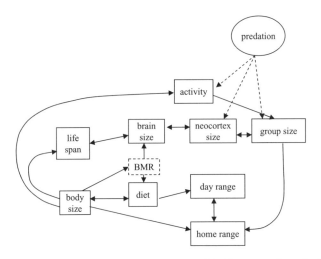

Fig. 11.2 Path diagram of predicted relationships between life history, ecology, brain size and group size in primates. Group size is pushed upwards by external factors such as predation, but is limited by ecological and cognitive constraints. Brain size is, in turn, limited by energetic and life-history constraints.

a subset of models that focused, in turn, on successive layers of independent variables in the path diagram. This allows us to ask whether our model (which assumes that the three most proximate factors in the path model are the best predictors) is better than a model that considers successively more remote sets of independent variables that, in the model shown in figure 11.2, only influence group size indirectly. We consider two successively remote layers in the model shown in figure 11.2: a set of variables that are one step removed from the core variables of our proposed model (e.g. day range, diet, brain size) and the most distal set (body size, diet and lifespan).

We used two methods to compare between alternative models on a complete subset of species with data available for all parameters: (i) change in Bayesian information criterion (BIC) values for small sample sizes (Schwartz 1978) and (ii) likelihood ratio test (LRT; Burnham & Anderson 2002) using the following formula:

$$LRT = -2(\log(L_1) - \log(L_2)),$$

which approximates a χ^2 -distribution.

The model proposed by the path diagram received strong support over other candidate models: not only does our main model have a lower BIC value than all alternatives, but also all alternative models are significantly less good at predicting group size (table 11.3). This suggests that, of the variables presented in the path diagram, the factors that are most strongly associated with group size are relative neocortex size, activity pattern and home range size. The ecological and life-history variables that are embedded in the diagram help to facilitate (or, alternatively, constrain) the maintenance of large brains and thus large group size, but are not directly causally related to the relationship between neocortex size and group size.

We interpret external factors such as predation as having a ratchet effect on the system, putting upward pressure on group size, and thus in turn brain size and, through that, ultimately life history. That predation risk is a critical factor influencing primate brain evolution is indicated by two different analyses. First, Shultz *et al.* (2004) showed that gross predation rate

Table 11.3 Information criteria model selection. (χ^2) log-likelihood (LL) and p values represent the χ^2 value for the change in log-likelihood values between the best model (1) and other candidate models.)

model	variables	n	BIC	ΔBIC	χ^2 LL	p
1	neocortex, home range, activity	24	18.6	0		
2	brain, home range, activity	24	20.63	2.03	4	0.05
3	brain, day range, activity	24	25.5	6.9	13.72	< 0.001
4	brain, diet, activity	24	28.93	10.33	20.58	< 0.001
5	body, diet, lifespan	24	31.3	12.7	29.54	< 0.001

(summed predation rates from all predators on an individual prey species) is a negative function of social group size. Second, Shultz & Dunbar (2007) have shown that predator bias (the rate with which a predator takes a prey species, relative to its abundance in the ecological community) is a negative function of brain size (relative to body size), and that this relationship is consistent across two different predators (chimpanzees and large felids) at six different sites on two continents. In other words, predation seems to be imposing both direct selection on brain size (acting through prey species' ability to evade predation attempts, whether this is done at an individual or a social level) *and* indirect selection via the buffering effect of large group size (with large group size in turn selecting for large brain size). The importance of predation, combined with the lack of any direct role for diet, leads us to conclude that the demands of foraging *per se* have not been the main driving force of primate cognitive/brain evolution, although foraging innovation may well have been a beneficial by-product of the cognitive sophistication required by social strategies designed to minimize predation risk.

The path diagram and analyses indicate that there are two pathways that limit maximum group size: one cognitive and one ecological. Because residual BMR explains much more of the variance in brain size than diet does, we can infer that a high energy diet is necessary to support a large brain, but that a large brain is not vital for managing a high quality diet. Large brained species *must* be able to support their brains metabolically, and this constrains the range of possible diets and energy use patterns to those that provide sufficient surplus calories. Operating from the other end, individuals in large groups have to be able to mitigate the heightened competition for resources between group members. For species with limiting resources, this means expanding home ranges or, in those with contestable resources, day range length (Isbell 1991). The intersection of these two limiting factors can be used to describe the maximum group size obtainable by any population (Dunbar 1996). Once group size is pushed past either the ecological or cognitive limits of the species, groups are expected to either fission or adopt a fission–fusion social structure (Dunbar 1996).

11.4 The nature of social complexity

Although the social brain hypothesis has often been formulated in terms of group size, it is more correct to think of it in terms of the complexity of social relationships. Several studies have now produced evidence to support this claim. Kudo & Dunbar (2001), for example, showed that the size of grooming cliques (interpreted as coalitions) correlated significantly with neocortex ratio (neocortex volume divided by the volume of the rest of the brain) across primates, while Byrne & Corp (2004) showed that frequencies of tactical deception (standardized for the frequencies with which species have been studied) also correlate with neocortex ratio.

The latter finding is of particular interest for the fact that it focuses on cognitively complex behaviour (tactical deception, whereby animals appear to deliberately mislead other individuals). Similarly, Pawlowski *et al.* (1998) showed that, when number of males in the group is partialled out, neocortex ratio negatively predicts the correlation between male dominance rank and mating success. In effect, low-ranking males in large-brained species do not simply accept a poor return in terms of mating rate, but rather exploit subtle social strategies like alliances or female choice to circumvent what would otherwise be the high-rank males' power-based monopoly over matings. Similarly, when we compared relative neocortex volume in species that habitually form coalitions with those that do not (as defined by Plavcan *et al.* 1995), we found that species in which coalitions are reported to be common have significantly larger neocortices, when all other variables including phylogeny are held constant (figure 11.3). Finally, Lewis (2000) has shown, for a small sample of primate species, that the proportion of all play that is social (as opposed to solitary or instrumental) is also positively correlated with neocortex ratio.

The latter finding highlights another frequently overlooked aspect of cognitive evolution, namely an important role for development and learning by experience in a social context. Having a large brain may not, of itself, be sufficient to allow an animal to engage in complex social behaviour; the brain wetware merely provides the capacity. The hardware needs the equivalent of software programming and this comes through the learning experiences of socialization. Social play offers one context in which that learning takes place. In support of this, Joffe (1997) showed that the volume of the neocortex frontal to the primary visual area is better predicted by the length of the period of socialization (the period between weaning and first reproduction). Growing up in a social environment may thus be at least as important as having a brain of the right size.

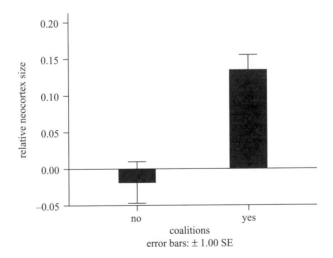

Fig. 11.3 Relative neocortex size (as measured by a linear regression of log-transformed neocortex volume over log-transformed volume of the rest of the brain) in species that do and do not form coalitions with other group members (solitary and monogamous species excluded from analysis). We use Plavcan *et al.*'s (1995) categorization of coalition-forming species.

It is worth noting here that these analyses do not all use the Stephan brain database. Several of the analyses reported in this section used neocortex ratios estimated from cranial volume because some of the species in an analysis did not occur in the Stephan database. Indeed, some of the analyses reported here have used databases obtained by different methods using different specimens (e.g. Fuster's prefrontal cortex dataset, Semedenferi's frontal lobe dataset and Rilling's magnetic resonance imaging-derived brain component volume dataset), with only partial overlap in the species contained in each database. Despite this, the results are robustly consistent. We make this point because over-reliance of the Stephan database has sometimes been raised as a criticism.

11.5 How to evolve a big brain

This leads us to the final issue, namely the question of how brain evolution has occurred. There has been considerable debate in the recent literature as to whether developmental constraints have forced a significant degree of uniformity on brain structure, i.e. species differences in the volume of particular brain units merely reflect species differences in total brain volume (Finlay & Darlington 1995; Finlay et al. 2001; de Winter & Oxnard 2001), or whether there has been mosaic evolution whereby some brain units have enlarged more rapidly than others (Barton & Harvey 2000). There can be no doubt about the fact that there must be both developmental (Martin 1981) and energetic (Aiello & Wheeler 1995) constraints on final brain size; indeed, we have demonstrated above that such constraints do exist. However, the real issue here is whether brain units enlarge proportionally as total brain volume enlarges (Finlay et al. 2001), or do so disproportionately as a function of specific selection pressures (Barton & Harvey 2000). There is currently no real agreement on this.

One reason why there may be proportional convergence in brain component volumes is that higher order representations of sensory systems within the brain seem to be organized on a direct functional basis: upstream systems seem to be volumetrically correlated with their input systems (Stevens 2001). Thus, increasing convergence in proportional volumes may reflect increasing integration of units from different functional groupings as a result of increased sharing of information. In support of this it is known that, in the primate brain, there are direct axonal links from subcortical areas like the amygdala and the cerebellum to the frontal lobe of the neocortex, whereas this is much less extensively the case in carnivores (Fuster 1988). Using a different approach, we were here able to confirm that the cerebellum, at least, is unrelated to social group size when total brain and neocortex volumes are partialled out. Interestingly, cerebellum volume correlates negatively with those life-history variables that correlate positively with neocortex volume, suggesting that not all brain units are under the same linked selection regime (see also Barton & Harvey 2000).

A more general issue of some importance concerns the overall pattern of brain evolution. Finlay & Darlington (1995) have pointed out that, although brain units scale very tightly with each other, the scaling coefficient is not always unity. Of particular significance in the present context is the fact that, across mammals, the scaling coefficient for neocortex volume relative to the brain as a whole is significantly higher than unity: in fact, the scaling relationship against the whole brain ranges from 1.103 for neocortex as a whole, to 1.115 for the frontal lobe (Semendeferi et al.1997), indicating that the neocortex in general, and the frontal lobe in particular, have increased disproportionately during the course of primate brain evolution.

Large-brained primates like apes and humans have disproportionately large frontal lobes—even though, as Semendeferi *et al.* (1997) pointed out, they do not deviate from the general primate allometric scaling relationship. This is significant because the frontal lobe is widely understood to be primarily responsible both for integration across sensory and association units and for those cognitive processes generally referred to as 'executive functions' (Kolb & Wishaw 1996).

One reason for the steep positive allometric scaling of the frontal lobe is the fact that the brain evolves (and, indeed, develops and myelinates; Gogtay *et al.* 2004) from back (the visual areas) to front (the executive areas). Thus, when brain evolution occurs, it mainly involves adding more frontal cortex rather than increasing all brain units proportionately. Given that visual acuity is limited only by retinal area and not by body size or total brain size, there is limited value in adding more visual cortex (located mainly in the occipital lobe at the back of the brain) than is minimally necessary to map the inputs from the retina. This effectively means that there is increasing frontal lobe volume available for executive-type functions. Dunbar (2003) showed that, in primates, the area of the primary visual cortex (commonly known as V1) is linearly (and tightly) related to the both volume of the visual pathway (lateral geniculate nucleus and the visual tract) and the volume of the orbit (the main factor determining retinal area). Figure 11.4 shows the consequences of this; the volume of the primary visual cortex (V1) quickly reaches an asymptotic value as a function of total brain volume, but the volume of the rest of the neocortex (non-V1 cortex) increases dramatically. Unfortunately, with Stephan's database, we are unable to partition the neocortex down into smaller units, but the volumetric analyses provided by Semendeferi *et al.* (1997) for frontal lobe and by Fuster (1988)

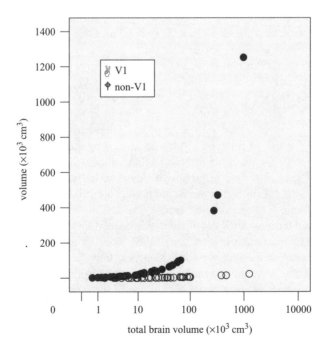

Fig. 11.4 Volumes of primary visual cortex (V1) and rest of neocortex (non-V1) plotted against total brain volume for primates. Source: data from Stephan *et al.* (1981).

for prefrontal cortex imply even steeper relationships for these more frontal units that are specifically involved in cognitive executive functions. Since it is these rather than the visual areas *per se* that are likely to be responsible for the social brain effect, it may be no accident that increasing brain size correlates with increasing social skills (and hence group size).

11.6 Conclusions

We have shown that brain volume (and in primates, specifically neocortex volume) correlates with sociality. In primates, this emerges as a strong relationship with social group size, but this belies a deeper relationship with behavioural indices of social complexity (including coalition formation, the use of tactical deception, the use of more subtle social strategies, and social play). More intriguingly, however, there is some evidence to suggest that there may be a phase shift in the form of the social brain between primates (where the social brain hypothesis has a quantitative form: a direct correlation with social group size) and non-primate mammals (where it has a qualitative form: a correlation with sociality, but not social group size). At present, we do not understand why this should be so, but it may suggest one reason why primates seem to be in a different social league to non-primates. We have yet to explore whether, within this general pattern, some non-primate taxa exhibit any kind of convergence in this respect (elephants and toothed whales are obvious candidates).

A further important issue is the fact that brain evolution involves a suite of traits (an adaptive complex): constraints or consequences arise in the context of life history, development, diet and other aspects of ecology as well as behaviour, and these have to be solved if a species is to be able to increase its brain (or neocortex) size. Since neocortex size constrains group size, major phase shifts in constraint variables may be necessary for a species to increase its group size in response to an ecological challenge.

It is important to remember that primates, in particular, may be under a dual constraint on group size. Not only may the cohesion of groups be limited by their cognitive abilities, but they may also be constrained by time budgeting issues that arise from ecology (Dunbar 1996; Lehmann *et al.* in press). Animals have to invest time in grooming in order to create social bonds of sufficient intensity to enable large groups of individuals to forage together as a cohesive social unit. If the size of foraging groups demanded by the ecology exceeds those with which the species can cope on either or both of these dimensions, it may not necessarily be impossible for the species to live in groups of this size, but there will be dramatic consequences for their social cohesiveness. We would predict a much looser form of sociality and a greater degree of fission–fusion in these cases.

We have identified the neocortex as critical in this context (at least within primates), and the evidence points to the particular importance of the more frontal units (especially the frontal lobe). However, at present we have very little idea as to how the brain produces these effects. We have suggested that, as brain size increases, a disproportionate amount of executive function computational power becomes available, allowing for increasingly sophisticated social behaviour. However, our understanding of the mechanisms involved in how the brain handles any kind of secondary information processing (i.e. anything above basic sensory processing) is very limited at present. Nor do we have much idea as to the genetic mechanisms involved, although recent studies have indicated the existence of genes that play an important role in the neurophysiology of brain activity, e.g. clearing neurons of the by-products of activity, so as to reduce their refractory times (Dorus *et al.* 2004).

REFERENCES

Aiello, L. C. & Wheeler, P. T. 1995 The expensive tissue hypothesis: the brain and the digestive system in human evolution. *Curr. Anthropol.* **36**, 199–221. (doi:10.1086/204350)

Allman, J., McLaughlin, T. & Hakeem, A. 1993 Brain-weight and life-span in primate species. *Proc. Natl Acad. Sci. USA* **90**, 118–122. (doi:10.1073/pnas.90.1.118)

Armstrong, E. 1985 Relative brain size in monkeys and prosimians. *Am. J. Phys. Anthropol.* **66**, 263–273. (doi:10.1002/ajpa.1330660303)

Barton, R. A. 1993 Independent contrasts analysis of neocortex size and socioecology in primates. *Behav. Brain Sci.* **16**, 694–695.

Barton, R. A. 1996 Neocortex size and behavioural ecology in primates. *Proc. R. Soc. B* **263**, 173–177. (doi:10.1098/rspb.1996.0028)

Barton, R. A. & Dunbar, R. I. M. 1997 Evolution of the social brain. In *Machiavellian intelligence II* (eds A. Whiten & R. W. Byrne), pp. 240–263. Cambridge, UK: Cambridge University Press.

Barton, R. A. & Harvey, P. H. 2000 Mosaic evolution of brain structure in mammals. *Nature* **405**, 1055–1058. (doi:10.1038/35016580)

Burnham, K. P. & Anderson, D. R. 2002 *Model selection and multi-model inference: a practical information-theoretic approach.* New York, NY: Springer.

Byrne, R. W. & Corp, N. 2004 Neocortex size predicts deception rate in primates. *Proc. R. Soc. B* **271**, 1693–1699. (doi:10.1098/rspb.2004.2780)

Byrne, R. W. & Whiten, A. 1988 *Machiavellian intelligence: social expertise and the evolution of intelligence in monkeys, apes and humans.* Oxford, UK: Oxford University Press.

Charnov, E. L. 2001 Evolution of mammal life histories. *Evol. Ecol. Res.* **3**, 521–535.

Clutton-Brock, T. H. & Harvey, P. H. 1980 Primates, brains and ecology. *J. Zool.* **190**, 309–323.

Deaner, R. O., Nunn, C. L. & van Schaik, C. P. 2000 Comparative tests of primate cognition: different scaling methods produce different results. *Brain Behav. Evol.* **55**, 44–52. (doi:10.1159/000006641)

Deaner, R. O., Barton, R. A. & van Schaik, C. P. 2003 Primate brains and life histories: renewing the connection. In *Primate life histories and socioecology* (eds P. M. Kappeler & M. E. Pereira), pp. 233–265. Cambridge, UK: Cambridge University Press.

Dorus, S., Vallender, E. J., Evans, P. D., Anderson, J. R., Gilbert, S. L., Mahowald, M., Wyckoff, G. J., Malcom, C. M. & Lahn, B. T. 2004 Accelerated evolution of nervous system genes in the origin of *Homo sapiens. Cell* **119**, 1027–1040. (doi:10.1016/j.cell.2004.11.040)

Dunbar, R. I. M. 1988 *Primate social systems.* London, UK: Chapman and Hall.

Dunbar, R. I. M. 1992 Neocortex size as a constraint on group-size in primates. *J. Hum. Evol.* **22**, 469–493. (doi:10.1016/0047-2484(92)90081-J)

Dunbar, R. I. M. 1996 Determinants of group size in primates: a general model. In *Evolution of culture and language in primates and humans* (eds J. Maynard Smith, G. Runciman & R. Dunbar), pp. 33–57. Oxford, UK: Oxford University Press.

Dunbar, R. I. M. 1998 The social brain hypothesis. *Evol. Anthropol.* **6**, 178–190. (doi:10.1002/(SICI) 1520-6505(1998)6:5 <178::AID-EVAN5>3.0.CO;2-8)

Dunbar, R. I. M. 2002 Modelling primate behavioural ecology. *Int. J. Primatol.* **23**, 785–819. (doi: 10.1023/A:1015576915296)

Dunbar, R. I. M. 2003 Why are apes so smart? In *Primate life histories and socioecology* (eds P. Kappeler & M. Pereira), pp. 285–298. Chicago, IL: Chicago University Press.

Dunbar, R. I. M. & Bever, J. 1998 Neocortex size predicts group size in carnivores and some insectivores. *Ethology* **104**, 695–708.

Dunbar, R. I. M. & Shultz, S. 2007 Understanding primate brain evaluation. *Phil. Trans. Roy. Soc. B.* **362**, 649–658.

Finlay, B. L. & Darlington, R. B. 1995 Linked regularities in the development and evolution of mammalian brains. *Science* **268**, 1578–1584. (doi:10.1126/science.7777856)

Finlay, B. L., Darlington, R. B. & Nicastro, N. 2001 Developmental structure in brain evolution. *Behav. Brain Sci.* **24**, 263–308. (doi:10.1017/S0140525X01003958)

Freckleton, R. P., Harvey, P. H. & Pagel, M. 2002 Phylogenetic analysis and comparative data: a test and review of evidence. *Am. Nat.* **160**, 712–726. (doi:10.1086/343873)

Fuster, J. M. 1988 *The prefrontal cortex: anatomy, physiology and neuropsychology of the frontal lobe.* New York, NY: Lippincott Williams & Wilkins.

Gittleman, J. L. 1986 Carnivore brain size, behavioral ecology, and phylogeny. *J. Mammal.* **67**, 23–36. (doi:10.2307/1380998)

Gogtay, N. *et al.* 2004 Dynamic mapping of human cortical development during childhood through early adulthood. *Proc. Natl Acad. Sci. USA* **101**, 8174–8179. (doi:10.1073/pnas.0402680101)

Grant, J. W. A., Chapman, C. A. & Richardson, K. S. 1992 Defended versus undefended home range size of carnivores, ungulates and primates. *Behav. Ecol. Sociobiol.* **31**, 149–161. (doi:10.1007/BF00168642)

Hill, R. A. & Dunbar, R. I. M. 1998 An evaluation of the roles of predation rate and predation risk as selective pressures on primate grouping behaviour. *Behaviour* **135**, 411–430.

Hill, R. A. & Lee, P. C. 1998 Predation risk as an influence on group size in cercopithecoid primates: implications for social structure. *J. Zool.* **245**, 447–456. (doi:10.1111/j.1469-7998.1998.tb00119.x)

Isbell, L. A. 1991 Contest and scramble competition: patterns of female aggression and ranging behaviour among primates. *Behav. Ecol.* **2**, 143–155.

Joffe, T. H. 1997 Social pressures have selected for an extended juvenile period in primates. *J. Hum. Evol.* **32**, 593–605. (doi:10.1006/jhev.1997.0140)

Kolb, B. & Wishaw, I. Q. 1996 *Fundamentals of human neuropsychology.* San Francisco, CA: Freeman.

Kudo, H. & Dunbar, R. I. M. 2001 Neocortex size and social network size in primates. *Anim. Behav.* **62**, 711–722. (doi:10.1006/anbe.2001.1808)

Lefebvre, L., Whittle, P., Lascaris, E. & Finkelstein, A. 1997 Feeding innovations and forebrain size in birds. *Anim. Behav.* **53**, 549–560. (doi:10.1006/anbe.1996.0330)

Lefebvre, L., Reader, S. M. & Sol, D. 2004 Brains, innovations and evolution in birds and primates. *Brain Behav. Evol.* **63**, 233–246. (doi:10.1159/000076784)

Lehmann, J., Korstjens, A. H. & Dunbar, R. I. M. In press. Group size, grooming and social cohesion in primates. *Anim. Behav.*

Lewis, K. P. 2000 A comparative study of primate play behaviour: implications for the study of cognition. *Folia Primatol.* **71**, 417–421. (doi:10.1159/000052740)

Marino, L. 1996 What can dolphins tell us about primate evolution? *Evol. Anthropol.* **5**, 81–86. (doi:10. 1002/(SICI)1520-6505(1996)5:3 < 81::AID-EVAN3 >3.0.CO;2-Z)

Marino, L. 2004 Cetacean brain evolution: multiplication generates complexity. *J. Comp. Psychol.* **17**, 1–16.

Martin, R. D. 1981 Relative brain size and basal metabolic-rate in terrestrial vertebrates. *Nature* **293**, 57–60. (doi:10.1038/293057a0)

Pawlowski, B., Lowen, C. B. & Dunbar, R. I. M. 1998 Neocortex size, social skills and mating success in primates. *Behaviour* **135**, 357–368.

Perez-Barberia, F. J. & Gordon, I. J. 2005 Gregariousness increases brain size in ungulates. *Oecologia* **145**, 41–52.

Perez-Barberia, F. J., Shultz, S. & Dunbar, R. I. M. In press. Evidence for intense coevolution of sociality and brain size in three orders of mammals. *Evolution*

Plavcan, J. M., van Schaik, C. P. & Kappeler, P. M. 1995 Competition, coalitions and canine size in primates. *J. Hum. Evol.* **28**, 245–276. (doi:10.1006/jhev.1995.1019)

Reader, S. M. & Laland, K. N. 2002 Social intelligence, innovation, and enhanced brain size in primates. *Proc. Natl Acad. Sci. USA* **99**, 4436–4441. (doi:10.1073/pnas.062041299)

Ross, C. 1992 Environmental correlates of the intrinsic rate of natural increase in primates. *Oecologia* **90**, 383–390. (doi:10.1007/BF00317695)

Sawaguchi, T. & Kudo, H. 1990 Neocortical development and social-structure in primates. *Primates* **31**, 283–289. (doi:10.1007/BF02380949)

Schwartz, G. 1978 Estimating the dimension of a model. *Ann. Statistics* **6**, 461–464.

Semendeferi, K., Damasio, H. & Frank, R. 1997 The evolution of the frontal lobes: a volumetric analysis based on three-dimensional reconstructions of magnetic resonance scans of human and ape brains. *J. Hum. Evol.* **32**, 375–388. (doi:10.1006/jhev.1996.0099)

Shultz, S. & Dunbar, R. I. M. 2006 Both social and ecological factors predict ungulate brain size. *Proc. R. Soc. B* **273**, 207–215. (doi:10.1098/rspb.2005.3283)

Shultz, S. & Dunbar, R. I. M. 2007 Chimpanzee and felid diet composition is influenced by prey brain size. *Biol. Lett.* **2**, 505–508. (doi:10.1098/rsbl.2006.0519)

Shultz, S., Noe, R., McGraw, W. S. & Dunbar, R. I. M. 2004 A community-level evaluation of the impact of prey behavioural and ecological characteristics on predator diet composition. *Proc. R. Soc. B* **271**, 725–732. (doi:10.1098/rspb.2003.2626)

Sol, D., Timmermans, S. & Lefebvre, L. 2002 Behavioural flexibility and invasion success in birds. *Anim. Behav.* **63**, 495–502. (doi:10.1006/anbe.2001.1953)

Sol, D., Duncan, R. P., Blackburn, T. M., Cassey, P. & Lefebvre, L. 2005 Big brains, enhanced cognition, and response of birds to novel environments. *Proc. Natl Acad. Sci. USA* **102**, 5460–5465. (doi:10.1073/pnas.0408145102)

Stephan, H., Frahm, H. & Baron, G. 1981 New and revised data on volumes of brain structures in insectivores and primates. *Folia Primatol.* **35**, 1–29.

Stevens, C. F. 2001 An evolutionary scaling law for the primate visual system and its basis in cortical function. *Nature* **411**, 193–195. (doi:10.1038/35075572)

de Winter, W. & Oxnard, C. E. 2001 Evolutionary radiations and convergences in the structural organisation of mammalian brains. *Nature* **409**, 710–714. (doi:10.1038/35055547)

Wrangham, R. W., Gittleman, J. L. & Chapman, C. A. 1993 Constraints on group-size in primates and carnivores—population-density and day-range as assays of exploitation competition. *Behav. Ecol. Sociobiol.* **32**, 199–209. (doi:10.1007/BF00173778)

12

Before and below 'theory of mind': embodied simulation and the neural correlates of social cognition

Vittorio Gallese

The automatic translation of folk psychology into newly formed brain modules specifically dedicated to mind-reading and other social cognitive abilities should be carefully scrutinized. Searching for the brain location of intentions, beliefs and desires—*as such*—might not be the best epistemic strategy to disclose what social cognition really is. The results of neurocognitive research suggest that in the brain of primates, mirror neurons, and more generally the premotor system, play a major role in several aspects of social cognition, from action and intention understanding to language processing. This evidence is presented and discussed within the theoretical frame of an embodied simulation account of social cognition. Embodied simulation and the mirror neuron system underpinning it provide the means to share communicative intentions, meaning and reference, thus granting the parity requirements of social communication.

Keywords: embodied simulation; folk psychology; mind-reading; mirror neurons; monkey; theory of mind

12.1 Introduction

The traditional view in the cognitive sciences holds that humans are able to understand the behaviour of others in terms of their mental states—intentions, beliefs and desires—by exploiting what is commonly designated as 'folk psychology'. According to a widely shared view, non-human primates, including apes, do not rely on mentally based accounts of each other's behaviour.

This view prefigures a sharp distinction between non-human species, confined to behaviour-reading, and our species, whose social cognition makes use of a different level of explanation, i.e. mind-reading. However, it is by no means obvious that behaviour-reading and mind-reading constitute two autonomous realms. In fact, during our social transactions, we seldom engage in explicit interpretative acts. Most of the time, our understanding of social situations is immediate, automatic and almost reflex-like. Therefore, it seems preposterous to claim that our capacity to reflect on the intentions, beliefs and desires determining the behaviour of others is *all there is* in social cognition. It is even less obvious that, while understanding the intentions of others, we employ a cognitive strategy totally unrelated to predicting the consequences of their observed behaviours. A growing sense of discomfort towards a blind faith in folk psychology to characterize social cognition is indeed surfacing within the field of philosophy of mind. It has recently been stressed that the use of folk psychology in social cognition of the belief–desire propositional attitudes is overstated (see Hutto 2004). As emphasized by Bruner (1990, p. 40), 'when things *are as they should be*, the narratives of folk psychology are unnecessary'.

Another problem for the mainstream view on social cognition is posed by the relationship between mind-reading and linguistic competence. Recent evidence shows that 15-month-old infants understand false beliefs (Onishi & Baillargeon 2005). These results suggest that typical aspects of mind-reading, like the attribution of false beliefs to others, can be explained on the basis of low-level mechanisms which develop well before full-blown linguistic competence.

The point I want to stress is that social cognition is not only 'social metacognition'; that is, *explicitly* thinking about the contents of someone else's mind by means of symbols or other representations in propositional format. We can certainly 'explain' the behaviour of others by using our complex and sophisticated mentalizing abilities. And we should add that the neural mechanism underpinning such complex mentalizing abilities are far from being fully understood. Most of the time, though, we do not need to do this. We have a much more direct access to the inner world of others. Direct understanding does not require explanation. This particular dimension of social cognition is embodied, in that it mediates between the multimodal experiential knowledge of our own lived body and the way we experience others.

I have presented elsewhere the accounts of how embodied simulation can underpin basic forms of social cognition like the capacity of empathizing with others' emotions and sensations (Gallese 2001, 2003a,b, 2005a,b). The main goal of the present article is more ambitious. It is to show that embodied simulation can play an explanatory role not only on low-level mechanisms of social cognition—like those involved in empathy—but also on its more sophisticated aspects—like the attribution of mental states to others, and language. For this purpose, I briefly summarize the functional properties of the mirror neuron system in monkeys and humans. I show that this system is involved in different aspects of social cognition like action and intention understanding and social communication. I also show that the premotor system is at the basis of different aspects of the faculty of language. I conclude by introducing that the 'neural exploitation hypothesis', according to which a single functional mechanism, embodied simulation, is probably at the basis of various and important aspects of social cognition.

12.2 The mirror neuron system for actions in monkeys and humans

More than a decade ago, a new class of motor neurons, mirror neurons, was discovered in area F5 within the ventral premotor cortex of the macaque monkey. These neurons discharge not only when the monkey executes goal-related hand and/or mouth acts like grasping objects, but also when observing other individuals (monkeys or humans) executing similar actions (di Pellegrino *et al.* 1992; Gallese *et al.* 1996; Rizzolatti *et al.* 1996; Ferrari *et al.* 2003). Neurons with similar mirroring properties, matching action observation and execution, have also been discovered in a sector of the posterior parietal cortex reciprocally connected with area F5 (see Rizzolatti *et al.* 2001; Gallese *et al.* 2002; Fogassi *et al.* 2005). It has been proposed that this 'direct matching' may underpin a direct form of action understanding (Gallese *et al.* 1996; Rizzolatti *et al.* 1996, 2001; Gallese *et al.* 2004; Rizzolatti & Craighero 2004) by exploiting embodied simulation, a specific mechanism by means of which the brain/body system models its interactions with the world (Gallese 2001, 2003a,b, 2005a,b, 2006).

In order to test the hypothesis that mirror neurons underpin action understanding via embodied simulation, we assessed their activation in conditions in which the monkey understands the meaning of the occurring action, but has no access to the visual features that activate mirror neurons. If mirror neurons really underpin action understanding, their activity should reflect the meaning of the observed action rather than its visual features. Experiments by

Umiltà *et al.* (2001) showed that F5 mirror neurons become active also during the observation of partially hidden actions, when the monkey can predict the action outcome, even in the absence of the complete visual information about it (Umiltà *et al.* 2001). Macaque monkey's mirror neurons therefore map actions made by others not just on the basis of their visual description, but also on the basis of the anticipation of the final goal of the action, by means of the activation of its motor representation in the observer's premotor cortex.

In another series of experiments, we showed that a particular class of F5 mirror neurons ('audio–visual mirror neurons') respond not only when the monkey executes and observes a given hand action, but also when it just hears the sound typically produced by the action (Kohler *et al.* 2002). These neurons respond to the sound of actions and discriminate between the sounds of different actions, but do not respond to other similarly interesting sounds. In sum, the different modes of presentation of events intrinsically different, as sounds, images or willed motor acts, are nevertheless bound together within a simpler level of semantic reference, underpinned by the same network of audio–visual mirror neurons. The presence of such a neural mechanism within a non-linguistic species can be interpreted as the neural correlate of the dawning of a conceptualization mechanism (Gallese 2003*c*; Gallese & Lakoff 2005).

Different experimental methodologies and techniques have also demonstrated in the human brain the existence of a mirror neuron system matching action perception and execution. During action observation, there is a strong activation of premotor and parietal areas, the probable human homologue of the monkey areas in which mirror neurons were originally described (for review, see Rizzolatti *et al.* 2001; Gallese 2003*a*,*b*, 2006; Gallese *et al.* 2004; Rizzolatti & Craighero 2004). The mirror neuron system in humans is somatotopically organized, with distinct cortical regions within the premotor and posterior parietal cortices being activated by the observation/execution of mouth-, hand- and foot-related actions (Buccino *et al.* 2001). More recently, it has been shown that the mirror neuron system in humans is directly involved in the imitation of simple finger movements (Iacoboni *et al.* 1999), as well as in learning previously never-practised complex motor acts (Buccino *et al.* 2004*b*).

A recent study by Buxbaum *et al.* (2005) on posterior parietal neurological patients with 'ideomotor apraxia' has shown that they were not only disproportionately impaired in the imitation of transitive gestures, when compared with intransitive gestures, but also showed a strong correlation between imitation deficits and the incapacity of recognizing observed goal-related meaningful hand actions. These results further corroborate the notion that the same action representations underpin both action production and action understanding.

12.3 The mirror neuron system for communicative actions in monkeys and humans

The macaque monkey premotor area F5 also contains neurons related to mouth actions. In the most lateral part of area F5, we described a population of mirror neurons mostly related to the execution/observation of mouth-related actions (Ferrari *et al.* 2003). The majority of these neurons discharge when the monkey executes and observes transitive object-related ingestive actions, such as grasping, biting or licking. However, a small percentage of mouth-related mirror neurons discharge during the observation of communicative facial actions performed by the experimenter in front of the monkey ('communicative mirror neurons'; Ferrari *et al.* 2003). These actions are affiliative gestures like lip-smacking and lips or tongue protrusion. A behavioural study showed that the observing monkeys correctly decoded these and other communicative gestures performed by the experimenter in front of them, because they elicited congruent expressive reactions (Ferrari *et al.* 2003). Communicative mirror neurons could be an evolutionary precursor of social communication mediated by facial gestures.

A recent brain-imaging study, in which human participants observed mouth actions performed by humans, monkeys and dogs (Buccino *et al.* 2004*a*), corroborates this hypothesis. The observed mouth actions could be either object-directed, like a human, monkey or dog biting a piece of food, or communicative, like human silent speech, monkey lip-smacking and dog barking. The results showed that the observation of all biting actions led to the activation of the mirror neuron system, encompassing the posterior parietal and ventral premotor cortices (Buccino *et al.* 2004*a*). Interestingly, the observation of communicative mouth actions led to the activation of different cortical foci according to the different observed species. The observation of human silent speech activated the pars opercularis of the left inferior frontal gyrus, the premotor sector of Broca's region. The observation of monkey lip-smacking activated a smaller part of the same region bilaterally. Finally, the observation of the barking dog activated only extra-striate visual areas.

Actions belonging to the motor repertoire of the observer (e.g. biting and speech-reading) or very closely related to it (e.g. monkey's lip-smacking) are mapped on the observer's motor system. Actions that do not belong to this repertoire (e.g. barking) are mapped and, henceforth, categorized on the basis of their visual properties. These results show two things. First, the activation of the mirror neuron system is proportionate to the degree of congruence between the observed actions and the observer's motor repertoire (see also Calvo-Merino *et al.* 2005). Second, embodied simulation is not the only mechanism mediating action understanding. What I take to be crucially different between the understanding mediated by embodied simulation and that mediated by the cognitive interpretation of a visual scene (as in the case of the observed barking dog) is the quality of the experience coupled with the understanding. Only the embodied simulation mediated by the activation of the mirror neuron system enables the capacity of knowing 'how it feels' to perform a given action. Only this mechanism enables intentional attunement with the observed agent (Gallese 2006).

The involvement of the motor system during observation of communicative mouth actions is also testified by the results of a transcranial magnetic simulation (TMS) study by Watkins *et al.* (2003), in which they showed that the observation of silent speech-related lip movements enhanced the size of the motor-evoked potential in lip muscles. This effect was lateralized to the left hemisphere. Consistent with the brain-imaging data of Buccino *et al.* (2004*a*), the results of Watkins *et al.* (2003) show that the observation of communicative, speech-related mouth actions facilitates the excitability of the motor system involved in the production of the same actions.

12.4 The mirror neuron system for actions and the understanding of intentions

What does the presence of mirror neurons in different species of primates such as macaques and humans tell us about the evolution of social cognition? The evidence collected so far seems to suggest that the mirror neuron system for actions is sophisticated enough to enable its exploitation for social purposes. This matching mechanism indeed supports social facilitation in monkeys. It has recently been shown that the observation and hearing of noisy eating actions facilitates eating behaviour in pigtailed macaque monkeys (Ferrari *et al.* 2005).

Another recently published study shows that the pigtailed macaque monkeys recognize when they are imitated by a human experimenter (Paukner *et al.* 2005). The pigtailed macaques preferentially look at an experimenter imitating the monkeys' object-directed actions when compared with an experimenter manipulating an identical object, but not imitating their actions. Since both experimenters acted in synchrony with the monkeys, the monkeys based their gaze preference not on temporal contingency, but evidently took into account the structural components of the experimenters' actions.

Even if it is true, as repeatedly stated, that macaque monkeys are not capable of *motor* imitation—though recent evidence by Subiaul *et al.* (2004) shows that they are capable of *cognitive* imitation—the study by Paukner *et al.* (2005) nevertheless shows that macaque monkeys do entertain the capacity to discriminate between very similar goal-related actions on the basis of their degree of similarity with the goal-related actions the monkeys themselves have just executed. This capacity appears to be cognitively sophisticated, because it implies a certain degree of metacognition in the domain of purposeful actions.

But monkeys do not entertain the full-blown mentalization typical of humans. Thus, since both species do have mirror neurons, what makes humans different? The easiest answer is, of course, the presence of language. This answer, though, is at least partly question-begging, because it only transposes the human cognitive endowment to be explained. Furthermore, it implies a perfect overlap between language and our mentalizing abilities. A discussion of this debated issue is beyond the scope and space limits of this article, but I will come back to the issues of language and the evolution of social cognition in the final sections.

At present, we can only make hypotheses about the relevant and still poorly understood neural mechanisms underpinning the mentalizing abilities of humans. In particular, we do not have a clear neuroscientific model of how humans understand the intentions promoting the actions of others they observe. When an individual starts a movement aimed to attain a goal, such as picking up a pen, he/she has clearly in mind what he/she is going to do, for example writing a note on a piece of paper. In this simple sequence of motor acts, the final goal of the whole action is present in the agents' mind and is somehow reflected in each motor act of the sequence. The action *intention*, therefore, is set before the beginning of the movements. This also means that when we are going to execute a given action, we can also predict its consequences.

However, in social contexts, a given act can be originated by very different intentions. Suppose, one sees someone else grasping a cup. Mirror neurons for grasping will most probably be activated in the observer's brain. A simple motor equivalence between the observed act and its motor representation in the observer's brain, though, can only tell us *what* the act is (it is a grasp) and not *why* it occurred. This has led us to argue against the relevance of mirror neurons for social cognition and, in particular, for determining the intentions of others (see Jacob & Jeannerod 2005).

We should ask ourselves the following question: what does it mean to determine the intention of the action of someone else? I propose a deflationary answer. Determining *why* a given act (e.g. grasping a cup) was executed can be equivalent to detecting the goal of the still not executed and impending subsequent act (e.g. bringing the cup to the mouth).

These issues were experimentally addressed with a functional magnetic resonance imaging (fMRI) study (Iacoboni *et al.* 2005). Volunteers watched three kinds of stimuli: hand grasping acts without a context; context only (a scene containing objects); and hand grasping acts embedded in contexts. In the latter condition, the context suggested the intention associated with the grasping (either drinking or cleaning up). The observation of motor acts embedded in contexts, compared with the other two conditions, yielded a significant signal increase in the posterior part of the inferior frontal gyrus and the adjacent sector of the ventral premotor cortex, where hand actions are represented. Thus, premotor mirror areas—areas active during the execution and the observation of action—previously thought to be involved only in action recognition—are actually also involved in understanding the 'why' of action, i.e. the intention promoting it. These results suggest that for simple actions such as those employed in this study, the ascription of intentions occurs by default and it is underpinned by the mandatory activation of an embodied simulation mechanism (Gallese 2006; see also Gallese & Goldman 1998).

The neurophysiological mechanism at the basis of the relationship between intention detection and action prediction was recently clarified. Fogassi *et al.* (2005) described a class of parietal mirror neurons whose discharge during the observation of an act (e.g. grasping an object) is conditioned by the type of not-yet-observed subsequent act (e.g. bringing the object to the mouth), specifying the overall action intention. This study shows that parietal mirror neurons discharge in association with the execution/observation of motor acts (grasping) only when they are embedded in a specific action aimed at a more specific distal goal. It must be emphasized that the neurons discharge before the monkey itself executes, or observes the experimenter starting, the second motor act (bringing the object to the mouth or placing it into the cup). Single motor acts are dependent on each other, as they participate in the overarching distal goal of an action, thus forming pre-wired intentional chains, in which each subsequent motor act is facilitated by the previously executed one.

This suggests that in addition to recognizing the goal of the observed motor act, mirror neurons allow the observing monkey to predict the agent's next act, henceforth the action overall intention. This mechanism can also be interpreted as the precursor of more sophisticated intention understanding abilities, such as those characterizing our species.

The mechanism of intention understanding just described appears to be rather simple, i.e. depending on which motor chain is activated, the observer is going to activate the motor schema of what, most probably, the agent is going to do. How can such a mechanism be formed? The statistical frequency of act sequences, as they are habitually performed or observed in the social environment, could constrain preferential paths of act inferences/predictions. This could be accomplished by chaining together different motor schemata. At the neural level, this would be equivalent to the chaining of different populations of mirror neurons coding not only the observed motor act, but also those that would normally follow in a given context.

Ascribing intentions would therefore consist in predicting a forthcoming new goal. According to this perspective, action prediction and the ascription of intentions are related phenomena, underpinned by the same functional mechanism, i.e. embodied simulation. In contrast with what mainstream cognitive science would maintain, action prediction and the ascription of intentions—at least of simple intentions—do not appear to belong to different cognitive realms, but are both related to embodied simulation mechanisms underpinned by the activation of chains of logically related mirror neurons.

The neuroscientific evidence presented so far shows that our brains, as well as those of macaques, have developed a basic functional mechanism, embodied simulation, which can provide a direct access to the meaning of the actions and intentions of others. This evidence suggests that many aspects of social cognition are tractable at the neural level of description. Let us now examine to what extent the embodied simulation account of social cognition can also be applied to the most distinctive aspect of human social cognition, i.e. language.

12.5 Social cognition and language

Any account of human social cognition cannot get away from language. Language is the most specific hallmark of what it means to be human. The search for where and how language evolved and the study of the functional mechanisms at the basis of the language capacity become toolkits to explore human nature. In spite of a very long history of studies and speculations, the intimate nature of language and the evolutionary process producing it still remain somewhat elusive. One reason for such elusiveness stems from the complexity and multidimensional nature of language. What do we refer to when we investigate the language faculty and its evolution? Is language the outcome of a dedicated system, or does it include more general cognitive abilities?

What can a neuroscientific perspective add to such a controversial debate, and how can it help in clarifying social cognition? A possible starting point is to consider the fact that human language for most of its history has been just spoken language. This may suggest that language most probably evolved in order to provide individuals with a more powerful and flexible social cognitive tool to share, communicate and exchange knowledge (Tomasello *et al.* 2005). According to this perspective, the social dimension of language becomes crucial for its understanding.

In §§6–8, I will address the issue of the relation among the faculty of language, action and embodied simulation. I will show that when processing language, humans show activation of the motor system. This activation occurs at different levels. The first level can be defined as 'motor simulation at the vehicle level', and pertains to the phono-articulatory aspects of language. The second level can be defined as 'motor simulation at the content level', and concerns the semantic content of a word, verb or proposition. Finally, I will briefly touch upon the topic of syntax.

12.6 Embodied simulation and language: motor simulation at the vehicle level

Broca's region, traditionally considered as an exclusive speech production area, contains representations of orofacial gestures and hand actions, and it is known to be part of the mirror neuron system (for review, see Bookheimer 2002; Rizzolatti & Craighero 2004; Nishitani *et al.* 2005). In a TMS experiment, Fadiga *et al.* (2002) showed that listening to phonemes induces an increase of motor-evoked potentials (MEPs) amplitude recorded from the tongue muscles involved in their execution. This result was interpreted as an acoustically related resonance mechanism at the phonological level. These results have been complemented by a TMS study of Watkins *et al.* (2003), who showed that listening to and viewing speech gestures enhanced the amplitude of MEPs recorded from the lip muscles. An activation of motor areas devoted to speech production during passive listening to phonemes has recently also been demonstrated in an fMRI study (Wilson *et al.* 2004). Finally, Watkins & Paus (2004) showed that during auditory speech perception, the increased size of the MEPs obtained by TMS over the face area of the primary motor cortex correlated with cerebral blood flow increase in Broca's area.

It is worth noting that not only speech perception, but also covert speech activates phono-articulatory simulation within the motor system. McGuigan & Dollins (1989) showed with electromyography that the tongue and lip muscles are activated in covert speech in the same way as during overt speech. An fMRI study by Wildgruber *et al.* (1996) showed primary motor cortex activation during covert speech. A recent study by Aziz-Zadeh *et al.* (2005) showed covert speech arrest after transient inactivation with repetitive transcranial magnetic simulation (rTMS) over the left primary motor cortex and left BA44.

The above-mentioned presence in Broca's region of both hand and mouth motor representations is crucial not only for the evolution of language (Rizzolatti & Arbib 1998; Corballis 2002, 2004; Arbib 2005; Gentilucci & Corballis 2006), but also for its ontogeny. Developmental psychologists have shown the existence of a close relationship between the development of manual and oral motor skills. Goldin-Meadow (1999) proposed that speech production and speech-related hand gestures could be considered as outputs of the same process. Canonical babbling in children aged 6–8 months is accompanied by rhythmic hand movements (Masataka 2001). Hearing babies born to deaf parents display hand actions with a babbling-like rhythm. Manual gestures pre-date early development of speech in children, and predict later success even up to the two-word level (Iverson & Goldin-Meadow 2005).

It must be emphasized that the same intimate relationship between manual and oral language-related gestures persists in adulthood. Several pioneering works by Gentilucci and colleagues (Gentilucci 2003; Gentilucci *et al.* 2001, 2004*a,b*) have demonstrated a close relationship between speech production and the execution/observation of arm and hand gestures. In one of these studies (Gentilucci *et al.* 2004*a*), participants were required either to grasp and bring to the mouth fruits of different size like a cherry or an apple, or to observe the same actions performed by someone else, while simultaneously uttering the syllable 'ba'. The results showed that the second formant of the vowel 'a' (related to tongue position) increased when they executed or observed the act of bringing the apple (the larger object) to the mouth, or its pantomime, with respect to when they did the same with the cherry (the smaller object).

The execution/observation of the action of bringing an object to the mouth activates a mouth articulation posture probably related to food manipulation, which selectively influences speech production. This suggests that the system involved in speech production shares (and may derive from) the neural premotor circuit involved in the control of hand/arm actions.

In another related study (Gentilucci *et al.* 2004*b*), both adults and 6-year-old children were required to observe grasping and bringing to the mouth actions performed by others while uttering the syllable 'ba'. The results showed that the different observed actions influenced lip-shaping kinematics and voice formants. The observation of grasping influenced the first formant (which is related to mouth opening), while the observation of bringing to the mouth, as in the previous experiment, influenced the second formant of the voice spectrum, related to tongue position. It must be stressed that the effects on speech were greater in children. This study indicates that action observation induces the activation of the normally subsequent motor act in the observer; that is, mouth grasping when observing hand grasping and chewing when observing bringing to the mouth. This in turn affects speech production. As proposed by the authors of this study, this mechanism may have enabled the transfer from a primitive arm gesture communication system to speech. Given the stronger effects displayed by the children when compared with the adults, the same mechanism could be useful during speech learning in infancy.

In a very recent paper, Bernardis & Gentilucci (2006) asked participants to pronounce words (e.g. bye-bye, stop), to execute communicative arm gestures with the same meaning or to emit the two communication signals simultaneously. The results showed that the voice spectra of spoken words were reinforced by the simultaneous execution of the corresponding-in-meaning gesture when compared with those of word pronunciation alone. This was not observed when the gesture was meaningless. Conversely, pronouncing words tended to inhibit the simultaneous execution of the gesture, as shown by the slowing down of the arm kinematics parameters. Comparable effects were not observed when pseudo-words were pronounced.

The results therefore showed that the word and the corresponding-in-meaning communicative gesture influenced each other when they were emitted simultaneously. The second formant in the voice spectra was higher when the word was pronounced together with the gesture. No modification in the second formant was observed when executing a meaningless arm movement, which nevertheless involved the same joints as the three meaningful gestures. Conversely, the second formant of a pseudo-word was not affected by the meaningful gestures.

Next, it was tested whether observing word pronunciation during gesture execution affected verbal responses in the same way as emitting the two signals. The voice spectra of words pronounced in response to simultaneously listening to and observing the speaker making the corresponding-in-meaning gesture were reinforced, just as they were by the simultaneous emission of the two communication signals.

The results of this elegant study seem to suggest that spoken words and symbolic communicative gestures are coded as a single signal by a unique communication system within the premotor cortex. The involvement of Broca's area in translating the representations of communicative arm gestures into mouth articulation gestures was recently confirmed by transient inactivation of BA44 with rTMS (Gentilucci *et al.* 2006). Since this brain region contains mirror neurons, it is most probable that through embodied simulation the communicative meaning of gestures is fused with the articulation of sounds required to express them in words.

12.7 Embodied simulation and language: motor simulation at the content level

The meaning of a sentence, regardless of its content, has been classically considered to be understood by relying on symbolic, amodal mental representations (Pylyshyn 1984; Fodor 1998). An alternative hypothesis, now more than 30 years old, assumes that the understanding of language relies on 'embodiment' (Lakoff & Johnson 1980, 1999; Lakoff 1987; Glenberg 1997; Barsalou 1999; Glenberg & Robertson 2000; Pulvermüeller 1999, 2002, 2005; Gallese 2003c; Feldman & Naranayan 2004; Gallese & Lakoff 2005; Gentilucci & Corballis 2006).

According to the embodiment theory, for action-related sentences, the neural structures presiding over action execution should also play a role in understanding the semantic content of the same actions when verbally described. Empirical evidence shows this to be the case. Glenberg & Kaschak (2002) asked participants to judge if a read sentence was sensible or nonsense by moving their hand to a button, requiring movement away from the body (in one condition) or towards the body (in the other condition). Half of the sensible sentences described action towards the reader and half away. Readers responded faster to sentences describing actions whose direction was congruent with the required response movement. This clearly shows that action contributes to sentence comprehension.

The most surprising result of this study, though, was that the same interaction between sentence movement direction and response direction was also found with abstract sentences describing transfer of information from one person to another, such as 'Liz told you the story' versus 'you told Liz the story'. These latter results extend the role of action simulation to the understanding of sentences describing abstract situations. Similar results were recently published by other authors (Borghi *et al.* 2004; Matlock 2004).

A prediction of the embodiment theory of language understanding is that when individuals listen to action-related sentences, their mirror neuron system should be modulated. The effect of this modulation should influence the excitability of the primary motor cortex, henceforth the production of the movements it controls. To test this hypothesis, we carried out two experiments (Buccino *et al.* 2005). In the first experiment, by means of single-pulse TMS, either the hand or the foot/leg motor areas in the left hemisphere were stimulated in distinct experimental sessions, while participants were listening to sentences expressing hand and foot actions. Listening to abstract content sentences served as a control. MEPs were recorded from hand and foot muscles. Results showed that MEPs recorded from hand muscles were specifically modulated by listening to hand action-related sentences, as were MEPs recorded from foot muscles by listening to foot action-related sentences.

In the second behavioural experiment, participants had to respond with the hand or the foot while listening to sentences expressing hand and foot actions when compared with abstract sentences. Coherently, with the results obtained with TMS, reaction times of the two effectors were specifically modulated by the effector-congruent heard sentences. These data show that processing sentences describing actions activates different sectors of the motor system, depending on the effector used in the listened action.

Several brain-imaging studies have shown that processing linguistic material in order to retrieve its meaning activates regions of the motor system congruent with the processed semantic content. Hauk *et al.* (2004) showed in an event-related fMRI study that silent reading of words referring to face, arm or leg actions led to the activation of different sectors of the premotor–motor areas that were congruent with the referential meaning of the read action words. Tettamanti *et al.* (2005) showed that listening to sentences expressing actions performed with the mouth, the hand and the foot produces activation of different sectors of the premotor cortex, depending on the effector used in the listened action-related sentence. These activated sectors correspond, albeit only coarsely, with those active during the observation of hand, mouth and foot actions (Buccino *et al.* 2001).

These data support the notion that the mirror neuron system is involved not only in understanding visually presented actions, but also in mapping acoustically or visually presented action-related sentences. The precise functional relevance of the involvement of action embodied simulation for language understanding remains unclear. One could speculate that such an involvement is purely parasitic, or, at best, reflects motor imagery induced by the upstream understanding process. The study of the spatio-temporal dynamic of language processing becomes crucial in settling this issue. Evoked readiness potential (ERP) experiments on silent reading of face-, arm- and leg-related words showed category-specific differential activations approximately 200 ms after word onset. Distributed source localization performed on stimulus-triggered ERPs showed different somatotopically arranged activation sources, with a strongest inferior frontal source for face-related words and a maximal superior central source for leg-related words (Pulvermüeller *et al.* 2000).

This dissociation in brain activity patterns supports the idea of stimulus-triggered early lexico-semantic processes taking place within the premotor cortex. In order to control for a putative role of motor preparation processes in determining that effect, the same group of researchers carried out experiments in which the same response—a button press with the left index finger—was required for all words (Hauk & Pulvermüeller 2004). The results showed a persistence of the early activation difference between face- and leg-related words, thus ruling out the motor preparation hypothesis. Pulvermüeller *et al.* (2003) used magnetoencephalography to investigate the time course of cortical activation underlying the magnetic mismatch negativity elicited by hearing a spoken action-related word. The results showed that auditory areas of the left superior temporal lobe became active 136 ms after the information in the acoustic input was sufficient for identifying the word, and activation of the left inferior frontal cortex followed after an additional delay of 22 ms.

In sum, although these results are far from being conclusive on the effective relevance of the embodied simulation of action for language understanding, they show that simulation is specific, automatic and has a temporal dynamic compatible with such a function. More inactivation studies will be required to validate what at present is a little more than a plausible hypothesis.

12.8 Embodied simulation, action and syntax

I have reviewed in the previous sections empirical evidence demonstrating a consistent involvement of action and motor cortical circuits in various aspects of social cognition, including the processing of language. We should now frame what we have discussed so far about action, social cognition and language within an evolutionary perspective, and in doing so, introduce syntax.

Hauser *et al.* (2002) proposed to differentiate two domains within the language faculty: a 'narrow language faculty' (LFN), encompassing aspects that are specific to language, and a 'broad language faculty', supposedly inclusive of more general cognitive functions, not unique to humans, but shared with non-human animals. According to the same proposal, at the core of LFN is 'recursion', a specifically human computational mechanism at the basis of language grammar, which, nevertheless, might have evolved for functions other than language. The merit of this proposal in my opinion lies in its greater evolutionary plausibility in comparison with alternative discontinuist views, like those positing a linguistic 'big-bang' out of which full-blown human language supposedly emerged (Bickerton 1995). It should be emphasized that even critics of the 'recursion-only hypothesis' applauded the merit of abandoning a monolithic view of language (see Pinker & Jackendoff 2005).

If embodied simulation is crucial in social cognition, language being the most distinctively human component of social cognition, syntax appears to be a crucial domain in which the relevance of embodied simulation for human social cognition can be tested. Syntax is a basic ingredient of the LFN, as defined by Hauser *et al.* (2002). According to the modular approach to syntax, syntactic processing is typically operated by a serial parsing encapsulated system, in which the initial phase of processing has access only to information about syntax. According to Fodor (1983, p. 77), '… to show that [the syntactic] system is penetrable (hence informationally unencapsulated), you would have to show that its processes have access to information that is not specified at any of the levels of representation that the language input system computes'.

Recent behavioural studies, though, show that the syntactic system *is* penetrable. Syntactic ambiguities are evaluated using non-linguistic constraints like real-world properties of referential context. Empirical research shows that humans continuously define linguistically relevant referential domains by evaluating sentence information against the situation-specific affordances. These affordances are not encoded as part of the linguistic representation of a word or phrase. Listeners use predicate-based information, like action goals, to anticipate upcoming referents. For example, a recent study by Chambers *et al.* (2004) shows that syntactic decisions about ambiguous sentences are affected by the number of referential candidates that can afford the action evoked by the verb in the unfolding sentence. These results suggest that even a key component of the supposed LFN is intimately intertwined with action and its embodied simulation.

A further evidence of the involvement of goal-related action with syntax comes from the fMRI studies, showing a clear relationship between the premotor system and the mapping of sequential events. Schubotz & von Cramon (2004) contrasted the observation of biological hand actions with that of abstract motion (movements of geometric shapes). In both conditions, 50% of the stimuli failed to attain the normally predictable end-state. The task of participants was to indicate whether the actions were performed in a goal-directed manner or not, and whether the abstract motions were performed regularly or not. Results showed that both conditions elicited significant activation within the ventral premotor cortex. In addition, the prediction of biological actions also activated BA44/45, which is part of the mirror neuron system. Schubotz & von Cramon (2004) concluded that their findings point to a basic premotor contribution to the representation or processing of sequentially structured events. This contribution appears to be even more specifically related to language, as the fMRI studies have shown selective activation of premotor BA44 during the acquisition of artificial linguistic grammars characterized by long-distance, non-local syntactic dependencies (Tettamanti *et al.* 2002; Musso *et al.* 2003; see also Friederici 2004).

We said that the human language faculty is grounded in the unique ability to process hierarchically structured recursive sequences, configured as a phrase structure grammar (PSG). The human species is capable of mastering PSG, while other non-human primate species are confined to the use of much simpler finite state grammars (FSGs; see Hauser *et al.* 2002; Hauser & Fitch 2004). A recent fMRI study by Friederici *et al.* (2006) shows that the premotor sector of the inferior frontal gyrus, part of the mirror neuron system, is specifically activated during the processing of an artificial grammar bearing the PSG structure.

On the basis of all these results, it can be hypothesized that PSG is the computational output of a cortical premotor network originally evolved to control/represent the hierarchical structure of goal-related action. When in evolution, selective pressure led to the emergence of language, the same neural circuits doing computations to control the hierarchy of goal-related actions were 'exploited' to serve the newly acquired function of language syntax. A similar functional overlap between action and language acquisition is indeed evident during children's development, i.e. children parallel their capacity to master hierarchical complexity both in the domain of language and goal-related action (Greenfield 1991). My hypothesis can be easily tested with brain-imaging experiments. The prediction is that the opercular region of the inferior frontal gyrus should be activated by tasks involving the processing of complex, PSG-like hierarchical structures, both in the domain of action and language.

12.9 Cognitive continuity in primates' social cognition: the neural exploitation hypothesis

We are now in the position to better specify the wider implications of embodied simulation for social cognition, by formulating the neural exploitation hypothesis. The main claim is that key aspects of human social cognition are underpinned by neural exploitation; that is, the adaptation of sensory-motor-integrating brain mechanisms to serve new roles in thought and language, while retaining their original functions as well (see Gallese 2003c; Gallese & Lakoff 2005).

The execution of any complex coordinated action must make use of *at least* two brain sectors—the premotor and motor cortices, which are linked by reciprocal neural connections. The motor cortex controls individual synergies—relatively simple movements like extending and flexing the fingers, turning the wrist, flexing and extending the elbow, etc. The role of the premotor cortex is—not surprisingly—motor control, i.e. structuring such simple behaviours into coordinated motor acts, with the simple synergies performed at the right time, moving in the right direction, with the right force, for the right duration. This implies that the premotor cortex must provide a phase structure to actions and specify the right parameter values in the right phases. This information must be conveyed from the premotor to the motor cortex by neural connections activating specific regions of the motor cortex. In addition, as epitomized by the mirror neuron system, the same premotor circuitry that governs motor control for action execution must govern the embodied simulation of the observed actions of others.

There is therefore a 'structuring' computational circuit within the premotor system that can function in two modes of operation. In the first mode, the circuit can structure action execution and/or action perception and imagination, with neural connections to motor effectors and/or other sensory cortical areas. In the second mode of operation, the same system is decoupled from its action execution/perception functions and can offer its structuring computations to non-sensory-motor parts of the brain (see Lakoff & Johnson 1999; Gallese & Lakoff 2005). As a result, the computational structure of the premotor system is applied, on the one hand, to master the hierarchical structure of language and, on the other hand, to 'abstract' domains, yielding 'abstract inferences'. According to this hypothesis, the same circuitry that controls how to move our body and enables our understanding of the action of others can, in principle, also structure language and abstract thought.

How can we reconcile the undisputable discontinuity among primate species in the capacity of processing complex recursive structures with the idea of cognitive continuity in primates' evolution of social cognition? My suggestion is that one important difference between humans and non-human primates could be the higher level of recursivity attained in our species—among many other neural systems—by the premotor cortex, of which the mirror neuron system is part. In fact, considering the impressive amount of evidence reviewed above, the premotor system is probably one of the most important brain regions where this evolutionary process might have taken place. The hypothesis I put forward is that the quantitative difference in computational power and degree of recursivity attained by the human brain—and, in particular, by the mirror neuron system—with respect to the brains of non-human primates could produce a qualitative leap forward in social cognition.

However, the computational divide between humans and other primates is probably not the only explanation. A second consideration must be added. The evolution of social cognition should not be conceived like a monotonic function, with a strict correlation between the chronological position a species occupies in phylogeny and its level of social 'cognitive smartness'. Hare & Tomasello (2005) show that dogs exhibit social communicative skills in tasks where apes fail, like finding food on the basis of human communicative gestures like pointing or gaze cues. These authors suggest that the remarkable social communicative skills displayed by dogs could be the outcome of their domestication process. This would represent a case of convergent evolution with humans, in which the initial selection of strictly speaking 'non-cognitive', emotional traits like tameness could have played a crucial bootstrapping role. If Hare & Tomasello (2005) are right, then one could argue that the specific social cognitive endowments of our species are the evolutionary outcome of the selection of mechanisms that are not intrinsically cognitive or, at the very least, certainly not mind-reading specific.

The appeal of the present hypothesis consists in its parsimony. Embodied simulation and its neural underpinnings may well fall short of providing a thorough account of what is implied in our sophisticated social cognitive skills. However, I believe that the evidence presented here indicates that embodied mechanisms involving the activation of the premotor system, of which the mirror neuron system is a part, do play a major role in social cognition.

12.10 Conclusions

Our sophisticated mind-reading abilities probably involve the activation of large regions of our brain, certainly larger than a putative and domain-specific theory of mind module. My point is that these brain sectors do encompass the premotor system and, in particular, the mirror neuron system. The social use of language is one of the most powerful cognitive tools to understand others' minds. Embodied simulation mechanisms are involved in language processing, and might also be crucial in the course of the long learning process children require to become fully competent in how to use folk psychology. This learning process greatly benefits from the repetitive exposure to the narration of stories about the actions of various characters (for a putative role of narrative practices in the development of a competent use of folk psychology, see Hutto 2004).

As suggested by Arciero (2006), to imbue words with meaning requires a fusion between the articulated sound of words and the shared meaning of action. Embodied simulation does exactly that. Furthermore, and most importantly, embodied simulation and the mirror neuron system underpinning it provide the means to share communicative intentions, meaning and reference, thus granting the parity requirements of social communication (Tomasello et al. 2005).

As I have argued elsewhere (Gallese 2006; Gallese & Umiltà 2006), the automatic translation of the folk-psychology-inspired 'flow charts' into encapsulated brain modules, specifically adapted to mind-reading abilities, should be carefully scrutinized. Language can typically play ontological tricks by means of its 'constitutiveness'; that is, its capacity to give an apparent ontological status to the concepts words embody (Bruner 1986, p. 64). Space can provide an illuminating example of how our language-based definitions do not necessarily translate into real entities in the brain. Space, although unitary when examined introspectively, is not represented in the brain as a single multipurpose map. There is no central processing unit for space in our brain to support the unitary idea of it that humans entertain. On the contrary, in the brain there are numerous spatial maps (see Rizzolatti et al. 1997). The same might be true for our language-mediated definition of what it means to mind-read, namely the employment of the cognitive tools of folk psychology. We can do better than merely looking for the brain location of intentions, beliefs and desires *as such*. A more promising and potentially fruitful strategy lies in the comparative study of the role played in social cognition by the premotor system of primate brains.

This work was supported by MIUR (Ministero Italiano dell'Istruzione, dell'Università e della Ricerca), and also this work, being a part of the European Science Foundation EUROCORES Programme OMLL, was supported by the funds to V.G. from the Italian C.N.R.

References

Arbib, M. A. 2005 From monkey-like action recognition to human language: an evolutionary framework for neurolinguistics. *Behav. Brain Sci.* **28**, 105–168. (doi:10.1017/ S0140525X05000038)

Arciero, G. 2006 *Sulle tracce disé*. Milano, Italy: Bollati-Boringhieri.

Aziz-Zadeh, L., Cattaneo, L., Rochat, M. & Rizzolatti, G. 2005 Covert speech arrest induced by rTMS over both motor and nonmotor left hemisphere frontal sites. *J. Cogn. Neurosci.* **17**, 928–938. (doi:10.1162/0898929054021157)

Barsalou, L. W. 1999 Perceptual symbol systems. *Behav. Brain Sci.* **22**, 577–609. (doi:10.1017/S0140525X99002149)

Bernardis, P. & Gentilucci, M. 2006 Speech and gesture share the same communication system. *Neuropsychologia* **44**, 178–190. (doi:10.1016/j.neuropsychologia.2005.05.007)

Bickerton, D. 1995 *Language and human behavior*. Seattle, WA: University of Washington Press.

Bookheimer, S. 2002 Functional MRI of language: new approaches to understanding the cortical organization of semantic processing. *Annu. Rev. Neurosci.* **25**, 151–188. (doi:10.1146/annurev.neuro.25.112701.142946)

Borghi, A. M., Glenberg, A. M. & Kaschak, M. P. 2004 Putting words in perspective. *Mem. Cognit.* **32**, 863–873.

Bruner, J. 1986 *Actual minds, possible worlds*. Cambridge, MA: Harvard University Press.

Bruner, J. 1990 *Acts of meaning*. Cambridge, MA: Harvard University Press.

Buccino, G. *et al.* 2001 Action observation activates premotor and parietal areas in a somatotopic manner: an fMRI study. *Eur. J. Neurosci.* **13**, 400–404. (doi:10.1046/j.1460-9568.2001.01385.x)

Buccino, G., Lui, F., Canessa, N., Patteri, I., Lagravinese, G., Benuzzi, F., Porro, C. A. & Rizzolatti, G. 2004*a* Neural circuits involved in the recognition of actions performed by nonconspecifics: an fMRI study. *J. Cogn. Neurosci.* **16**, 114–126. (doi:10.1162/089892904322755601)

Buccino, G., Vogt, S., Ritzl, A., Fink, G. R., Zilles, K., Freund, H.-J. & Rizzolatti, G. 2004*b* Neural circuits underlying imitation learning of hand actions: an event-related fMRI study. *Neuron* **42**, 323–334. (doi:10.1016/S0896-6273(04)00181-3)

Buccino, G., Riggio, L., Melli, G., Binkofski, F., Gallese, V. & Rizzolatti, G. 2005 Listening to action-related sentences modulates the activity of the motor system: a combined TMS and behavioral study. *Cogn. Brain Res.* **24**, 355–363. (doi:10.1016/j.cogbrainres.2005.02.020)

Buxbaum, L. J., Kyle, K. M. & Menon, R. 2005 On beyond mirror neurons: internal representations subserving imitation and recognition of skilled object-related actions in humans. *Cogn. Brain Res.* **25**, 226–239. (doi:10.1016/j.cogbrainres.2005.05.014)

Calvo-Merino, B., Glaser, D. E., Grezes, J., Passingham, R. E. & Haggard, P. 2005 Action observation and acquired motor skills: an FMRI study with expert dancers. *Cerebral Cortex* **15**, 1243–1249. (doi:10.1093/cercor/bhi007)

Chambers, C. G., Tanenhaus, M. K. & Magnuson, J. S. 2004 Actions and affordances in syntactic ambiguity resolution. *J. Mem. Lang.* **30**, 687–696.

Corballis, M. C. 2002 *From hand to mouth: the origins of language*. Princeton, NJ: Princeton University Press.

Corballis, M. C. 2004 FOXP2 and the mirror system. *Trends Cogn. Sci.* **8**, 95–96. (doi:10.1016/j.tics.2004.01.007)

di Pellegrino, G., Fadiga, L., Fogassi, L., Gallese, V. & Rizzolatti, G. 1992 Understanding motor events: a neurophysiological study. *Exp. Brain Res.* **91**, 176–180. (doi:10.1007/BF00230027)

Fadiga, L., Craighero, L., Buccino, G. & Rizzolatti, G. 2002 Speech listening specifically modulates the excitability of tongue muscles: a TMS study. *Eur. J. Neurosci.* **15**, 399–402. (doi:10.1046/j.0953-816x.2001.01874.x)

Feldman, J. & Narayanan, S. 2004 Embodied meaning in a neural theory of language. *Brain Lang.* **89**, 385–392. (doi:10.1016/S0093-934X(03)00355-9)

Ferrari, P. F., Gallese, V., Rizzolatti, G. & Fogassi, L. 2003 Mirror neurons responding to the observation of ingestive and communicative mouth actions in the monkey ventral premotor cortex. *Eur. J. Neurosci.* **17**, 1703–1714. (doi:10.1046/j.1460-9568.2003.02601.x)

Ferrari, P. F., Maiolini, C., Addessi, E., Fogassi, L. & Visalberghi, E. 2005 The observation and hearing of eating actions activates motor programs related to eating in macaque monkeys. *Behav. Brain Res.* **161**, 95–101. (doi:10.1016/j.bbr.2005.01.009)

Fodor, J. 1983 *The modularity of mind*. Cambridge, MA: MIT Press.

Fodor, J. 1998 *Concepts*. Oxford, UK: Oxford University Press.

Fogassi, L., Ferrari, P. F., Gesierich, B., Rozzi, S., Chersi, F. & Rizzolatti, G. 2005 Parietal lobe: from action organization to intention understanding. *Science* **302**, 662–667. (doi:10.1126/science.1106138)

Friederici, A. D. 2004 Processing local transitions versus long-distance syntactic hierarchies. *Trends Cogn. Sci.* **8**, 245–247. (doi:10.1016/j.tics.2004.04.013)

Friederici, A. D., Bahlmann, J., Heim, S., Schubotz, R. I. & Anwander, A. 2006 The brain differentiates human and non-human grammars: functional localization and structural connectivity. *Proc. Natl Acad. Sci. USA* **103**, 2458–2463. (doi:10.1073/pnas.0509389103)

Gallese, V. 2001 The "shared manifold" hypothesis: from mirror neurons to empathy. *J. Conscious. Stud.* **8**, 33–50.

Gallese, V. 2003*a* The manifold nature of interpersonal relations: the quest for a common mechanism. *Phil. Trans. R. Soc. B* **358**, 517–528. (doi:10.1098/rstb.2002.1234)

Gallese, V. 2003*b* The roots of empathy: the shared manifold hypothesis and the neural basis of intersubjectivity. *Psychopathology* **36**, 171–180. (doi:10.1159/000072786)

Gallese, V. 2003*c* A neuroscientific grasp of concepts: from control to representation. *Phil. Trans. R. Soc. B* **358**, 1231–1240. (doi:10.1098/rstb.2003.1315)

Gallese, V. 2005*a* Embodied simulation: from neurons to phenomenal experience. *Phenomenol. Cogn. Sci.* **4**, 23–48. (doi:10.1007/s11097-005-4737-z)

Gallese, V. 2005 "Being like me": self-other identity, mirror neurons and empathy. In *Perspectives on imitation: from cognitive neuroscience to social science*, vol. 1 (eds S. Hurley & N. Chater), pp.101–118. Cambridge, MA: MIT Press.

Gallese, V. 2006 Intentional attunement: a neurophysiological perspective on social cognition and its disruption in autism. *Cogn. Brain Res.* **1079**, 15–24.

Gallese, V. & Goldman, A. 1998 Mirror neurons and the simulation theory of mind-reading. *Trends Cogn. Sci.* **12**, 493–501. (doi:10.1016/S1364-6613(98)01262-5)

Gallese, V. & Lakoff, G. 2005 The brain's concepts: the role of the sensory-motor system in reason and language. *Cogn. Neuropsychol.* **22**, 455–479.

Gallese, V. & Umiltà, M. A. 2006 Cognitive continuity in primate social cognition. *Biol. Theory* **1**, 25–30. (doi:10.1162/biot.2006.1.1.25)

Gallese, V., Fadiga, L., Fogassi, L. & Rizzolatti, G. 1996 Action recognition in the premotor cortex. *Brain* **119**, 593–609. (doi:10.1093/brain/119.2.593)

Gallese, V., Fogassi, L., Fadiga, L. & Rizzolatti, G. 2002 Action representation and the inferior parietal lobule. In *Attention and performance XIX* (eds W. Prinz & B. Hommel), pp. 247–266. Oxford, UK: Oxford University Press.

Gallese, V., Keysers, C. & Rizzolatti, G. 2004 A unifying view of the basis of social cognition. *Trends Cogn. Sci.* **8**, 396–403. (doi:10.1016/j.tics.2004.07.002)

Gentilucci, M. 2003 Grasp observation influences speech production. *Eur. J. Neurosci.* **17**, 179–184. (doi:10.1046/ j.1460-9568.2003.02438.x)

Gentilucci, M. & Corballis, M. C. 2006 From manual gesture to speech: a gradual transition. *Neurosci. Biobehav. Rev.* **30**, 949–960. (doi:10.1016/j.neubiorev.2006.02.004)

Gentilucci, M., Benuzzi, F., Gangitano, M. & Grimaldi, S. 2001 Grasp with hand and mouth: a kinematic study on healthy subjects. *J. Neurophysiol.* **86**, 1685–1699.

Gentilucci, M., Santunione, P., Roy, A. C. & Stefanini, S. 2004*a* Execution and observation of bringing a fruit to the mouth affect syllable pronunciation. *Eur. J. Neurosci.* **19**, 190–202. (doi:10.1111/ j.1460-9568.2004.03104.x)

Gentilucci, M., Stefanini, S., Roy, A. C. & Santunione, P. 2004*b* Action observation and speech production: study on children and adults. *Neuropsychologia* **42**, 1554–1567. (doi:10.1016/ j.neuropsychologia.2004.03.002)

Gentilucci, M., Bernardis, P., Crisi, G. & Volta, R. D. 2006 Repetitive transcranial magnetic stimulation of Broca's area affects verbal responses to gesture observation. *J. Cogn. Neurosci.* **18**, 1059–1074. (doi:10.1162/jocn.2006.18.7.1059)

Glenberg, A. M. 1997 What memory is for. *Behav. Brain Sci.* **20**, 1–19. (doi:10.1017/S0140525X97000010)

Glenberg, A. M. & Kaschak, M. P. 2002 Grounding language in action. *Psychon. Bull. Rev.* **9**, 558–565.

Glenberg, A. M. & Robertson, D. A. 2000 Symbol grounding and meaning: a comparison of high-dimensional and embodied theories of meaning. *J. Mem. Lang.* **43**, 379–401. (doi:10.1006/jmla.2000.2714)

Goldin-Meadow, S. 1999 The role of gesture in communication and thinking. *Trends Cogn. Sci.* **3**, 419–429. (doi:10.1016/S1364-6613(99)01397-2)

Greenfield, P. M. 1991 Language, tools, and brain: the ontogeny and phylogeny of hierarchically organized sequential behavior. *Behav. Brain Sci.* **14**, 531–550.

Hare, B. & Tomasello, M. 2005 Human-like social skills in dogs? *Trends Cogn. Sci.* **9**, 439–444. (doi:10.1016/j.tics. 2005.08.010)

Hauk, O. & Pulvermüller, F. 2004 Neurophysiological distinction of action words in the fronto-central cortex. *Hum. Brain Mapp.* **21**,191–201. (doi:10.1002/hbm.10157)

Hauk, O., Johnsrude, I. & Pulvermüller, F. 2004 Somatotopic representation of action words in human motor and premotor cortex. *Neuron* **41**, 301–307. (doi:10.1016/S0896-6273(03)00838-9)

Hauser, M. D. & Fitch, W. T. 2004 Computational constraints on syntactic processing in a non-human primate. *Science* **303**, 377–380. (doi:10.1126/science.1089401)

Hauser, M. D., Chomsky, N. & Fitch, W. T. 2002 The faculty of language: what is it, who has it, and how did it evolve? *Science* **298**, 1569–1579. (doi:10.1126/science.298.5598.1569)

Hutto, D. H. 2004 The limits of spectatorial folk psychology. *Mind Lang.* **19**, 548–573.

Iacoboni, M., Woods, R. P., Brass, M., Bekkering, H., Mazziotta, J. C. & Rizzolatti, G. 1999 Cortical mechanisms of human imitation. *Science* **286**, 2526–2528. (doi:10.1126/science.286.5449.2526)

Iacoboni, M., Molnar-Szakacs, I., Gallese, V., Buccino, G., Mazziotta, J. & Rizzolatti, G. 2005 Grasping the intentions of others with one's owns mirror neuron system. *PLoS Biol.* **3**, 529–535. (doi:10.1371/journal.pbio.0030079)

Iverson, J. M. & Goldin-Meadow, S. 2005 Gesture paves the way for language development. *Psychol. Sci.* **16**, 367–371. (doi:10.1111/j.0956-7976.2005.01542.x)

Jacob, P. & Jeannerod, M. 2005 The motor theory of social cognition: a critique. *Trends Cogn. Neurosci.* **9**, 21–25. (doi:10.1016/j.tics.2004.11.003)

Kohler, E., Keysers, C., Umiltà, M. A., Fogassi, L., Gallese, V. & Rizzolatti, G. 2002 Hearing sounds, understanding actions: action representation in mirror neurons. *Science* **297**, 846–848. (doi:10.1126/science.1070311)

Lakoff, G. 1987 *Women, fire, and dangerous things: what categories reveal about the mind*. Chicago, IL; London, UK: University of Chicago Press.

Lakoff, G. & Johnson, M. 1980 *Metaphors we live by*. Chicago, IL; London, UK: University of Chicago Press.

Lakoff, G. & Johnson, M. 1999 *Philosophy in the flesh*. New York, NY: Basic Books.

Masataka, N. 2001 Why early linguistic milestones are delayed in children with Williams syndrome: late onset of hand banging as a possible rate-limiting constraint on the emergence of canonical babbling. *Devel. Sci.* **4**, 158–164. (doi:10.1111/1467-7687.00161)

Matlock, T. 2004 Fictive motion as cognitive simulation. *Mem. Cognit.* **32**, 1389–1400.

McGuigan, F. J. & Dollins, A. B. 1989 Patterns of covert speech behavior and phonetic coding. *Pavlovian J. Biol. Sci.* **24**, 19–26.

Musso, M., Moro, A., Glauche, V., Rijntjes, M., Reichenbach, J., Buchel, C. & Weillir, C. 2003 Broca's area and the language instinct. *Nat. Neurosci.* **6**, 774–781. (doi:10.1038/nn1077)

Nishitani, N., Schurmann, M., Amunts, K. & Hari, R. 2005 Broca's region: from action to language. *Physiology* **20**, 60–69. (doi:10.1152/physiol.00043.2004)

Onishi, K. H. & Baillargeon, R. 2005 Do 15 months-old understand false beliefs? *Science* **308**, 255–258. (doi:10.1126/science.1107621)

Paukner, A., Anderson, J. R., Borelli, E., Visalberghi, E. & Ferrari, P. F. 2005 Macaques (*Macaca nemestrina*) recognize when they are being imitated. *Biol. Lett.* **1**, 219–222. (doi:10.1098/rsbl.2004.0291)

Pinker, S. & Jackendoff, R. 2005 The faculty of language: what's special about it? *Cognition* **95**, 201–236. (doi:10.1016/j.cognition.2004.08.004)

Pulvermüeller, F. 1999 Word in the brain's language. *Behav. Brain Sci.* **22**, 253–336. (doi:10.1017/S0140525X9900182X)

Pulvermüeller, F. 2002 *The neuroscience of language.* Cambridge, UK: Cambridge University Press.

Pulvermüeller, F. 2005 Brain mechanisms linking language and action. *Nat. Rev. Neurosci.* **6**, 576–582. (doi:10.1038/nrn1706)

Pulvermüller, F., Härle, M. & Hummel, F. 2000 Neurophysiological distinction of verb categories. *Neuroreport* **11**, 2789–2793.

Pulvermüeller, F., Shtyrov, Y. & Ilmoniemi, R. J. 2003 Spatio-temporal patterns of neural language processing: an MEG study using minimum-norm current estimates. *Neuroimage* **20**, 1020–1025. (doi:10.1016/S1053-8119(03)00356-2)

Pylyshyn, Z. W. 1984 *Computation and cognition: toward a foundation for cognitive science.* Cambridge, MA: MIT Press.

Rizzolatti, G. & Arbib, M. A. 1998 Language within our grasp. *Trends Neurosci.* **21**, 188–194. (doi:10.1016/S0166-2236(98)01260-0)

Rizzolatti, G. & Craighero, L. 2004 The mirror neuron system. *Annu. Rev. Neurosci.* **27**, 169–192. (doi:10.1146/annurev.neuro.27.070203.144230)

Rizzolatti, G., Fadiga, L., Gallese, V. & Fogassi, L. 1996 Premotor cortex and the recognition of motor actions. *Cogn. Brain Res.* **3**, 131–141. (doi:10.1016/0926-6410 (95)00038-0)

Rizzolatti, G., Fadiga, L., Fogassi, L. & Gallese, V. 1997 The space around us. *Science* **277**, 190–191. (doi:10.1126/ science.277.5323.190)

Rizzolatti, G., Fogassi, L. & Gallese, V. 2001 Neurophysiological mechanisms underlying the understanding and imitation of action. *Nat. Neurosci. Rev.* **2**, 661–670. (doi:10.1038/35090060)

Schubotz, R. I. & von Cramon, D. Y. 2004 Sequences of abstract non-biological stimuli share ventral premotor cortex with action observation and imagery. *J. Neurosci.* **24**, 5467–5474. (doi:10.1523/JNEUROSCI.1169-04.2004)

Subiaul, F., Cantlon, J. F., Holloway, R. L. & Terrace, H. S. 2004 Cognitive imitation in rhesus macaque. *Science* **305**, 407–410. (doi:10.1126/science.1099136)

Tettamanti, M., Alkadhi, H., Moro, A., Perani, D., Kollias, S. & Weniger, D. 2002 Neural correlates for the acquisition of natural language syntax. *Neuroimage* **17**, 700–709. (doi:10.1016/S1053-8119(02)91201-2)

Tettamanti, M. et al. 2005 Listening to action-related sentences activates fronto-parietal motor circuits. *J. Cogn. Neurosci.* **17**, 273–281. (doi:10.1162/08989290 53124965)

Tomasello, M., Carpenter, M., Call, J., Behne, T. & Moll, H. 2005 Understanding and sharing intentions: the origins of cultural cognition. *Behav. Brain Sci.* **28**, 675–691. (doi:10.017/S0140525X05000129)

Umiltà, M. A., Kohler, E., Gallese, V., Fogassi, L., Fadiga, L., Keysers, C. & Rizzolatti, G. 2001 "I know what you are doing": a neurophysiological study. *Neuron* **32**, 91–101.

Watkins, K. E. & Paus, T. 2004 Modulation of motor excitability during speech perception: the role of Broca's area. *J. Cogn. Neurosci.* **16**, 978–987. (doi:10.1162/0898929041502616)

Watkins, K. E., Strafella, A. P. & Paus, T. 2003 Seeing and hearing speech excites the motor system involved in speech production. *Neuropsychologia* **41**, 989–994. (doi:10.1016/S0028-3932(02)00316-0)

Wildgruber, D., Ackermann, H., Klose, U., Kardatzki, B. & Grodd, W. 1996 Functional lateralization of speech production at primary motor cortex: a fMRI study. *NeuroReport* **7**, 2791–2795. (doi:10.1097/00001756-199611040-00077)

Wilson, S. M., Saygin, A. P., Sereno, M. I. & Iacoboni, M. 2004 Listening to speech activates motor areas involved in speech production. *Nat. Neurosci.* **7**, 701–702. (doi:10.1038/nn1263)

13

The social brain?

Chris D. Frith

The notion that there is a 'social brain' in humans specialized for social interactions has received considerable support from brain imaging and, to a lesser extent, from lesion studies. Specific roles for the various components of the social brain are beginning to emerge. For example, the amygdala attaches emotional value to faces, enabling us to recognize expressions such as fear and trustworthiness, while the posterior superior temporal sulcus predicts the end point of the complex trajectories created when agents act upon the world. It has proved more difficult to assign a role to medial prefrontal cortex, which is consistently activated when people think about mental states. I suggest that this region may have a special role in the second-order representations needed for communicative acts when we have to represent someone else's representation of our own mental state. These cognitive processes are not specifically social, since they can be applied in other domains. However, these cognitive processes have been driven to ever higher levels of sophistication by the complexities of social interaction.

Keywords: social brain; perspective taking; second-order representations

13.1 The social brain

In her seminal review, Brothers (1990) proposed that there was a circumscribed set of brain regions that were dedicated to social cognition. She called this set of regions the social brain and listed amygdala, orbital frontal cortex and temporal cortex as its major components. The evidence for her proposal came largely from studies of monkeys. After lesions to the amygdala, monkeys become socially isolated (Kling & Brothers 1992) and lesions to orbital frontal cortex can also alter social behaviour (Raleigh & Steklis 1981). Neurons in the superior temporal sulcus respond to aspects of faces such as expression and gaze direction (Perrett *et al.* 1992). With the advent of brain imaging, it has become possible to study social brain in human volunteers. Brothers' conjecture has stood up well to this barrage of new evidence (e.g. Adolphs 2003). However, there have been two major additions to the list of social brain regions. First, the medial prefrontal cortex and the adjacent paracingulate cortex have been consistently implicated in studies where participants have to think about mental states (Amodio & Frith 2006). Second, a 'mirror' system has been found in the brain of monkeys and humans, which allows us, to some extent, to share the experiences of others (Rizzolatti & Craighero 2004). In this essay, I shall briefly review the evidence concerning the mirror system and the four specific brain regions considered to have a role in social cognition: (i) the posterior superior temporal sulcus (pSTS) and the adjacent temporo-parietal junction (TPJ), (ii) the amygdala, (iii) the temporal poles, and (iv) the medial prefrontal cortex (MPFC) and the adjacent anterior cingulated cortex (ACC). I will speculate on the precise roles of these various systems and consider to what extent their functions are specifically social.

(a) What is the social brain for?

But first, I must consider what the social brain is for. It is the social brain that allows us to interact with other people. As with all our interactions with the world, we can do much better if we can predict what is going to happen next. The better we can predict what someone is going to do next, the more successful our interactions with that person will be. I shall argue that the function of the social brain is to enable us to make predictions during social interactions. These predictions need not be conscious and deliberated. For example, classical Pavlovian conditioning allows us to anticipate what will happen after a conditioned stimulus. Such basic conditioning has social relevance if the conditioned stimulus is a face with a certain expression.

(b) Prediction in social interactions

Perhaps the most important attribute of the social brain is that it allows us to make predictions about people's actions on the basis of their mental states. This assumption that behaviour is caused by mental states has been called taking an 'intentional stance' (Dennett 1987) or 'having a theory of mind' (Premack & Woodruff 1978). The largely automatic process by which we 'read' the mental states of others is called mentalizing.

There are many different types of mental states that can affect our behaviour. There are long-term dispositions: one person may be trustworthy while another is unreliable. There are short-term emotional states like fear and anger. There are desires like thirst which lead to specific goal-directed behaviours. There are the beliefs that we have about the world which determine our behaviour even when they are false. For example, I will look in my bookcase for a book that is not there if someone has borrowed it without telling me. Finally, there is the rather special intention to communicate with others, and the associated ability to recognize that certain behaviours are communicative.

13.2 The role of the amygdala

One of the unexpected results from early brain imaging studies was the fragmentation of emotion. There is no single brain system dedicated to emotion. Rather, each emotion has its own specific system. For example, fear is associated with activity in the amygdala (Morris *et al.* 1998), while disgust is associated with activity in the insular (Phillips *et al.* 1997). In these examples, the activity was elicited, not by the emotion directly, but by observing the expression of the emotion in a face. Thus, through its role in recognizing expressions such as fear, the amygdala has a role in social interactions.

(a) Prejudice

But this is not its only role. The amygdala is also activated by presentation of faces rated as untrustworthy (Winston *et al.* 2002). This is an example of prejudice since the faces were of people unknown to the participants in the experiment. Race prejudice has been studied in a number of imaging paradigms and amygdala activation has been consistently found in association with the unconscious fear that is elicited by viewing the face of someone from another race. When white Americans were shown the faces of unknown black Americans, activity was observed in the amygdala (Phelps *et al.* 2000). The magnitude of the activity in the amygdala correlated with implicit measures of race prejudice. However, amygdala damage does not remove race prejudice (Phelps *et al.* 2003), and amygdala response magnitude does not correlate with explicit measures of race prejudice. Our consciously held attitudes about race are often at variance with our implicit prejudices and there is evidence that we try to suppress these rapid automatic responses. The amygdala response to black faces was reduced when the faces were presented for 525 ms rather than 30 ms and, associated with this reduction, there was increased activity in areas of frontal cortex concerned with control and regulation (Cunningham *et al.* 2004).

(b) Prejudice and conditioning

Race prejudice is an example of stereotyping: associating mental attributes with a group of people and then applying this prejudice to individual members of that group. The amygdala is involved in this process owing to its role in fear conditioning. Extensive research with animals has shown that the amygdala is part of a system that learns to associate value with stimuli (Dolan 2002), whether or not these stimuli are social (LeDoux 2000). This system operates on both positive and negative values. For example, the amygdala responds to objects that elicit fear owing to their association with punishment (negative value), but the amygdala also responds to objects associated with food and sex (positive value).

In the experiments on race prejudice, the amygdala is responding to black faces in the same way as it responds to any object that has acquired a conditioned fear response (Buchel *et al.* 1998). The role of the amygdala in recognizing expressions of fear most probably has the same origin. A fearful expression is a signal (the conditioned stimulus) that there is something fearful near at hand (the unconditioned stimulus), so that a fearful face will eventually elicit a fear response. The amygdala is involved in social cognition owing to its role in associating the value (positive or negative) with individual objects and classes of object. This system applies to people just as it does to objects. Our long-term prejudices about individuals and groups are built up through a conditioning process involving the amygdala, but this process is not specifically social.

13.3 Temporal poles

(a) Social scripts

Through experience, we build up a rich store of knowledge about the world (Schank & Abelson 1977) that is important for our ability to mentalize. We learn facts about specific people: what they look like, where they live, whether they are trustworthy and so on. We also learn facts about social situations: the moment-to-moment changes in behaviour appropriate to the situations in which people frequently find themselves and also how feelings and dispositions affect the behaviour of people in these situations. Damage to the temporal poles can impair the ability to use this knowledge (Funnell 2001). This observation is consistent with the suggestion that the temporal poles are convergence zones, where simpler features from different modalities are brought together to define, by their conjunction, unique individuals and situations (Damasio *et al.* 2004). Through this convergence of information, our understanding of an object can be modified by the context in which it appears (Ganis & Kutas 2003). These processes instantiated in the temporal poles are important for mentalizing. They allow us to apply our general knowledge about social situations to the situation that currently confronts us. They specify the kinds of thoughts and feelings most likely to occur in a particular context, e.g. the pride or embarrassment that we have felt or observed in similar situations in the past. But, of course, situations are never exactly repeated. There is much to be learned by observing the moment-to-moment changes in expression and behaviour in the person we are interacting with. This is the role for the brain's mirror system.

13.4 The brain's mirror system

(a) A Bayesian approach to mentalizing

Our social brain has two problems to solve. First, it must read the mental state of the person we are interacting with. Second, it must make predictions about future behaviour on the basis of that mental state. From a Bayesian perspective, these two problems are not independent. The error in my prediction of future behaviour indicates how good my reading of the mental state was and enables me to make a better estimate of that mental state. In principle, the same mechanism can be used for reading mental states as for reading hidden states of the world outside the social domain. For example, when I reach for a coffee pot, I have to estimate how heavy it is. On the basis of this estimate, I can initiate the appropriate grasping behaviour and predict the consequences of my action. If my estimation of the hidden state of the coffee pot is wrong, my prediction will be incorrect. For example, if the pot is lighter than I expected, then my hand will move up faster than I expected. This error tells me that the coffee pot is lighter. Wolpert *et al.* (2003) have outlined how such an action system could provide the basis for reading the hidden intentions of others during action observation (see also Wilson & Knoblich 2005).

One problem for the Bayesian mechanism I have outlined is for it to get started. Where does the initial estimate of mental state come from? I suggest that this problem can be solved by the brain's mirror system. Since Gallese (2007) will be discussing this system in detail in his contribution to this issue, my comments will be brief and will emphasize my particular view.

(b) Mirroring emotions and actions

The idea that there is a mirror system in the brain arises from the observation that the same brain areas are activated when we observe another person experiencing an emotion as when we experience the same emotion ourselves (e.g. Wicker *et al.* 2003). The brain's mirror system is engaged by actions as well as emotions and, indeed, it was this aspect of the system that was first identified (for a recent review, see Rizzolatti & Craighero 2004). Motor areas of the brain become active when we observe others moving, and also we tend to imitate the movements of others automatically (Chartrand & Bargh 1999), even when this interferes with our own actions (Kilner *et al.* 2003). The mirror system also operates for touch and for pain. Somatosensory brain regions are activated when we see someone else being touched (Keysers *et al.* 2004; Blakemore *et al.* 2005). Pain areas in the brain become active when we see someone receiving a painful stimulus (Morrison *et al.* 2004; Jackson *et al.* 2005) or even when a symbolic cue tells us that someone is receiving pain (Singer *et al.* 2004). These mirror effects can occur for auditory as well as visual cues (Kohler *et al.* 2002).

The brain's mirror system is not tied to any particular brain region. The location of the activation will depend upon what is being observed. Underpinning the mirror system, there must be some rather general mechanism by which sensory or symbolic cues can be converted into covert actions. One possibility is that the brain represents actions in the same way, whether perceiving them or planning them (the common coding principle; Prinz 1997). Such a representation does not specify who is performing the action and would be accessed when both perceiving and performing an action.

(c) Contagion: a first step in mentalizing

Whatever the mechanism, the result is that actions are contagious. When we see someone smiling, we will automatically imitate that smile and feel happier ourselves. Through this mechanism, we can experience the emotional states of another person. I believe this phenomenon supplies the first step in mentalizing, i.e. the initial estimate of the mental state of the person we are interacting with. However, experiencing the same emotion as another is only the first step. It will not necessarily reveal the cause of the emotion. If we know that someone is afraid, we might predict that they will run, but we cannot predict where they will run unless we know what they are afraid of. Likewise, covertly performing the same movement as another is not sufficient to infer the goals and intentions behind that movement. Furthermore, as Mitchell *et al.* (2006) point out, while the mirror system is ideally suited for tracking the continually changing states of emotion and intention of the other, it can tell us nothing about the stable attitudes and predilections of the other, which are also important determinants of behaviour.

13.5 The role of posterior superior temporal sulcus/temporo-parietal junction

Through the resonance of our brain's mirror system, we might know that someone is afraid because we are sharing their experience. But how do we know what they are afraid of? One way to discover the cause of their fear is to observe where they are looking. The region of the brain at the pSTS and the adjacent TPJ is a prime candidate for this process.

(a) Predicting movement trajectories

This region is activated when participants observe someone moving their eyes (e.g. Pelphrey *et al.* 2005) and this activity is modulated by the context in which the eye movement occurs. For example, more activity is elicited in pSTS if the actor moves her eyes away from, rather than towards, a flashing target (Pelphrey *et al.* 2004a,b). Similar effects are found when participants observe someone making reaching movements (Pelphrey *et al.* 2004a,b). One possibility is that pSTS is concerned with predicting the trajectory of movements and that greater activity is associated with prediction errors, i.e. when the movement is unexpected. For example, Saxe *et al.* (2004) showed participants a video in which an actor walked across a room. On some trials, the actor was hidden behind a bookcase. When the actor paused behind the bookcase, so that he emerged later than expected, greater activity was seen in pSTS.

But is this prediction system dedicated solely to the prediction of biological movements? Observing two balls that move in mathematically defined trajectories with no specifically biological appearance will elicit activity in pSTS as long as they appear to be interacting (Schultz *et al.* 2004, 2005). There is evidence that pSTS is involved in predicting complex movement trajectories of any kind (reviewed in Kawawaki *et al.* 2006). Perhaps the trajectory to be predicted needs to be complex, but not specifically biological to elicit activity in pSTS.

(b) Perspective taking

By looking at someone's eyes, we can discover where they are looking, but how do we know what they can see? At the simplest level (level I perspective taking), we know that someone cannot see what we can see, as their line of sight is blocked by an obstacle. At a more complex level (level II perspective taking), we know that people looking at the same scene from different angles will arrive at different descriptions of the scene. From my point of view, the pole might be in front of the block, while from your point of view, the pole might be to the left of the block (see Aichhorn *et al.* (2005) for a useful review of perspective taking). There have been few imaging studies of this kind of spatial perspective taking, with somewhat equivocal results. Zacks *et al.* (2003) and Aichhorn *et al.* (2005) observed activity in the TPJ when participants had to describe a scene from another viewer's perspective. However, such activity was not observed in the study of Vogeley *et al.* (2004), possibly because this study involved level I rather than level II perspective taking.

Knowing where a fearful person is looking and what they can see, given their vantage point, enables us to know what they are looking at and thus identify the cause of their fear. This ability to see the world from another's perspective enables us to realize that other people can have different knowledge from us and may have false beliefs about the world, e.g. 'he thinks he is safe because he can't see the bear coming up behind him'. There is evidence that the TPJ has a critical and more general role in the performance of tasks that depend upon understanding that a person has a false belief about the world from both imaging (Saxe & Kanwisher 2003) and lesion studies (Apperly *et al.* 2004).

Recently, the TPJ (63,−37,20) has been shown to have a critical role in how we perceive our own body in space. Abnormal electrical activity in this area in patients can create out-of-the-body experiences, in which patients experience looking down at their own body from above. Furthermore, disruption of activity in this region with transcranial magnetic stimulation in healthy volunteers can impair performance of a task which requires the imagination of one's own body as if seen from outside (Blanke *et al.* 2005). Perspective taking has an important role in social cognition, but has a role in other domains also. The ability to imagine one's body in another position in space is important for spatial memory (e.g. Nardini *et al.* 2005) as well as for social cognition.

13.6 The role of medial prefrontal cortex

Activity in MPFC was observed in the earliest studies of mentalizing (Fletcher *et al.* 1995; Goel *et al.* 1995). These observations were subsequently confirmed with a very wide range of tasks, which required participants to think about mental states (reviewed in Amodio & Frith 2006).

(a) Is the MPFC really necessary for mentalizing?

There are, however, some unresolved problems for the interpretation of these results. First, it is not clear whether this region needs to be intact for successful performance of mentalizing tasks. On one hand, several group studies have shown that patients with damage to prefrontal cortex perform badly on mentalizing tasks and that this impairment is independent of problems with traditional executive tasks (Rowe *et al.* 2001; Stuss *et al.* 2001; Gregory *et al.* 2002). On the other hand, there is a report of a patient with damage restricted to MPFC who was not impaired on performance of mentalizing tasks (Bird *et al.* 2004). Second, there is an observation that activation of MPFC is often observed during rest or low demand tasks in comparison to high demand tasks. As a result, while activity may be seen in MPFC when mentalizing is compared with a control task (such as reasoning about physical causality), this is not always the case when mentalizing is contrasted with rest. One possible explanation for this phenomenon is that during 'rest' or low demand tasks, participants frequently indulge in mentalizing, thinking, for example, about why they volunteered to take part in the study or what might be the real motives of the experimenter (see Amodio & Frith (2006) for a discussion of this problem).

(b) Which kinds of task activate MPFC?

At least, three categories of task elicit activity in MPFC and they are as follows: (i) *Mentalizing* tasks in which participants have to understand the behaviour of characters in terms of their mental states. These tasks typically involve false beliefs and can be presented as stories or cartoons (e.g. Gallagher *et al.* 2000). However, MPFC is also active when participants engage in real-time social interactions (e.g. McCabe *et al.* 2001) or even when they simply observe social interactions (Iacoboni *et al.* 2004). These tasks presumably involve predicting people's behaviour in terms of their current beliefs and intentions. (ii) *Person perception* tasks in which participants answer questions about long-term dispositions and attitudes. These can be general (e.g. Can people be dependable?—Mitchell *et al.* 2002) or specific (e.g. Is your mother talkative?—Schmitz *et al.* 2004) and need not apply only to people (e.g. Can dogs be dependable?—Mitchell *et al.* 2005). (iii) *Self-perception* tasks in which participants answer questions about their own long-term dispositions (e.g. Are you talkative?—Kelley *et al.* 2002) or about their current feelings (Does this photo make you feel pleasant?—Ochsner *et al.* 2004). These three kinds of task have in common the need to think about mental states. These can be short-term or long-term mental states and can be of the self or another.

(c) Location of the mentalizing region within MPFC

There is little evidence for any systematic differences in the location of the activity associated with these three kinds of task. The activity is located in a diffuse region (paracingulate cortex) on the border of anterior cingulate cortex (BA 32) and medial prefrontal cortex proper (BA 10). This region has been labelled the 'emotional' region of MPFC and is more anterior and inferior to the region labelled 'cognitive' (Steele & Lawrie 2004). In anatomical terms, it can be labelled anterior rostral MPFC (Amodio & Frith 2006). A meta-analysis of studies where activity has been observed in area 10 (Gilbert *et al.* 2006) shows that activity associated with mentalizing tasks is medial rather than lateral and is posterior to the activity associated with multi-task coordination, which is observed at the frontal pole.

(d) A role for anterior rostral MPFC?

There is, however, strong evidence for a different role for anterior rostral MPFC in comparison to the adjacent regions of medial prefrontal cortex. For example, in the study of Mitchell *et al.* (2006), participants were told about two target individuals who were described as having liberal or conservative views. They were then asked to predict the feelings and attitudes of these two individuals in various situations (e.g. 'would he enjoy having a roommate from a different country?'). The results show a different pattern when thinking about a similar or a dissimilar other. Thinking about similar others was associated with activity in ventral mPFC (18,57,9: in the region labelled anterior rostral MFC in Amodio & Frith 2006), while thinking about a dissimilar other was associated with activity in a more dorsal region of mPFC (−9,45,42: posterior rostral MFC).

Previous studies had also observed distinctions between anterior and posterior rostral MPFC. Walter *et al.* (2004) asked participants to make inferences about private intentions (changing a broken light bulb in order to read a book) in contrast to communicative intentions (showing someone a map in order to ask the way). Thinking about communicative intentions activated a more ventral region (−3,54,15: arMPFC) than thinking about private intentions. Grezes *et al.* (2004*a*) asked participants to infer whether the movements associated with the lifting of a box were intended to be deceptive since the actor was pretending that the box was heavier than it really was. Movements thought to be deceptive activated arMPFC (−8,42,20). In another experiment (Grezes *et al.* 2004*b*), the participants observed movements, which sometimes included unexpected adjustments, because the box being picked up was lighter than the actor expected. Observing these unexpected adjustments was associated with activity in prMPFC (2,26,52).

These results suggest that arMPFC has a special role in handling communicative intentions. This is a more complex process than simply thinking about intentions, since we have to recognize that the communicator is also thinking about our mental state. This involves a second-order representation of mental state. We have to represent the communicator's representation of our mental state. This is a form of triadic social interaction, such as joint attention, that Saxe (2006) also associates with dorsal MPFC. In relation to the observations of Mitchell *et al.* (2006), when we think about the mental states of people with similar attitudes to ourselves, perhaps we automatically think in terms of our shared view of the world.

Such second-order representations are not necessary when thinking about another person's private intentions or their beliefs about the weight of a box. In these examples, we are simply predicting the outcomes of actions. Several studies have investigated the prediction and monitoring processes associated with the selection of action. Walton *et al.* (2004) observed activity in the prMFC when participants monitored the outcome of actions that were self-selected. Knutson *et al.* (2005) reported that the activity in the prMPFC was correlated with trial-by-trial variations in the anticipated probability of monetary gain. In research by Coricelli *et al.* (2005), a similar region of prMPFC activity was associated with regret, i.e. discovering that an unselected action would have led to a better outcome. Finally, Brown & Braver (2001) reported that prMFC activation was associated with prediction of the probability of error.

These results all suggest that this region is concerned with predicting the probable value of actions of the self. However, the results of EEG studies show that this region is also involved when we observe the actions of others. A negative event-related potential component arising from the MPFC is seen not only when we make an error, but also when we receive delayed error feedback (Gehring & Willoughby 2002; Luu *et al.* 2003) or observe someone else making an error (van Schie *et al.* 2004; Bates *et al.* 2005).

Inferior to the arMPFC is the orbital region. This region seems to be concerned with feelings rather than actions, particularly feelings relating to anticipated rewards and punishments. In monkeys, Padoa-Schioppa & Assad (2006) have shown that the value of offered goods is represented in orbital frontal cortex. In humans, Coricelli *et al.* (2005) found that activity in this region (−10,40,−24) was associated with anticipated regret. Again, this monitoring of feelings seems to apply to others as well as the self. Hynes *et al.* (2006) asked participants to make inferences about what other people were thinking (cognitive perspective taking) or what they were feeling (emotional perspective taking). Thinking about people's feelings was associated with activity in medial orbital cortex (18,63,−7), while perspective taking in general was associated with activity in more dorsal regions (2,59,15; −4,60,30).

13.7 The function of intellect

I have speculated about the role of various components of the social brain, but in most cases, I believe that these processes are not specifically social. The exception is the brain's mirror system.

(a) Accessing the mirror system: the role of social variables

Activation of the mirror system seems to be a largely automatic process that is not under conscious control. But we do not mirror everything that moves and not everyone receives our empathy. Watching a moving human arm will interfere with our own movements, but this interference does not happen when we watch a moving robot arm (Kilner et al. 2003). This tuning of the mirror system to purposeful agents rather than machines is observed in brain activity as well as behaviour in monkeys and humans (for a review, see Tai et al. 2004). These results suggest that signals from an 'agent detector' or perhaps a 'conspecific detector' are needed to turn on the action mirror system.

In the case of empathy, or mirroring of emotions, the situation is more complex. How much empathy we show to conspecifics is modified by our social relationship with the object of our empathy. We feel less empathy, in terms of subjective report and brain activity, if someone who has just treated us unfairly receives pain, especially if we are male (Singer et al. 2006). We also show more empathy with the pain of another if we are in eye contact with them at the moment they receive the pain (Bavelas et al. 1986). Showing one's emotion is, in part, a communicative act (Parkinson 2005) facilitated by the presence of others. It is not yet known whether the neural correlates of empathy are also modified by communicative contact, but, in any case, the functioning of our brain's mirror system is clearly subject to exquisite modulation by social variables.

(b) Cognition in the service of social interaction

The amygdala is concerned with conditioning, enabling emotional valence to be associated with an object. This object may often be a face, but the process also applies to objects, such as snakes, with no social connotations. The role of the temporal poles is less well understood, but here again, while the high-level concepts and the scripts for different circumstances instantiated here are of great importance for social cognition, these forms of knowledge are important for interacting with the physical as well as the mental world.

I have already suggested that the role of pSTS in processing biological motion might be a consequence of a more general role in predicting complex movement trajectories. While such trajectories are often created by biological agents, they can have other sources. Likewise, if the role of the TPJ is, as I suggest, to compute different spatial perspectives, then while this is very useful for social interactions, the process has much more general applications.

Most speculative and least well specified of all the suggestions in this essay is the role of anterior rostral MPFC. In terms of anatomy, there is some evidence that this region has shown disproportionate expansion in recent evolution (Semendeferi *et al.* 2001). The evidence for phylogenetic expansion of the social brain is discussed in some detail by Dunbar in this issue (Dunbar & Shultz 2007). In cognitive terms, this region of medial prefrontal cortex seems to be activated in scenarios involving communicative intent. Such scenarios involve second-order representations of mental states, since, to understand your attempt to communicate with me, I have to represent your representation of my mental state. This example concerns a high-level social interaction, but such second-order representations need not have social content. For example, second-order representations may have something in common with the higher-order thoughts that may be necessary for conscious experience (Rosenthal 2005). However, these are essentially general purpose operations that can be applied to any domain.

(c) The needs of social interaction drive cognition

However, although these mechanisms are not specifically social, they have been strongly influenced by the needs of social interactions. Humans are not only much more sophisticated in their social interactions than other animals; they are also much cleverer and more inventive in many domains that are not social, for example in the use of materials for making novel objects. This is the critical point that Nick Humphrey (1976) made in his paper: these cognitive functions have evolved to their high level because they have been driven by the complexities of social living. In order to avoid untrustworthy faces, we need a visual system that can process the subtle visual features which reveal personality. To discover what someone is interested in, we need to be able to compute what someone on the other side of the room can see. We need to acquire and store the complex scripts that enable us to behave appropriately at discussion meetings. And, above all, we need to be able to represent what other people think about us so that we can use such venues to enhance all our reputations.

I am grateful to Uta Frith for discussion and comments. This work was supported by the Wellcome Trust.

References

Adolphs, R. 2003 Cognitive neuroscience of human social behaviour. *Nat. Rev. Neurosci.* **4**, 165–178. (doi:10.1038/nrn1056)

Aichhorn, M., Perner, J., Kronbichler, M., Staffen, W. & Ladurner, G. 2005 Do visual perspective tasks need theory of mind? *Neuroimage* **30**, 1059–1068. (doi:10.1016/j.neuroimage.2005.10.026)

Amodio, D. M. & Frith, C. D. 2006 Meeting of minds: the medial frontal cortex and social cognition. *Nat. Rev. Neurosci.* **7**, 268–277. (doi:10.1038/nrn1884)

Apperly, I. A., Samson, D., Chiavarino, C. & Humphreys, G. W. 2004 Frontal and temporo-parietal lobe contributions to theory of mind: neuropsychological evidence from a false-belief task with reduced language and executive demands. *J. Cogn. Neurosci.* **16**, 1773–1784. (doi:10.1162/0898929042947928)

Bates, A. T., Patel, T. P. & Liddle, P. F. 2005 External behavior monitoring mirrors internal behavior monitoring: error-related negativity for observed errors. *J. Psychol.* **19**, 281–288.

Bavelas, J. B., Black, A., Lemery, C. R. & Mullett, J. 1986 I show how you feel—motor mimicry as a communicative act. *J. Pers. Soc. Psychol.* **50**, 322–329. (doi:10.1037/0022-3514.50.2.322)

Bird, C. M., Castelli, F., Malik, O., Frith, U. & Husain, M. 2004 The impact of extensive medial frontal lobe damage on 'Theory of Mind' and cognition. *Brain* **127**, 914–928. (doi:10.1093/brain/awh108)

Blakemore, S. J., Bristow, D., Bird, G., Frith, C. & Ward, J. 2005 Somatosensory activations during the observation of touch and a case of vision-touch synaesthesia. *Brain* **128**, 1571–1583. (doi:10.1093/brain/awh500)

Blanke, O., Mohr, C., Michel, C. M., Pascual-Leone, A., Brugger, P., Seeck, M., Landis, T. & Thut, G. 2005 Linking out-of-body experience and self processing to mental own-body imagery at the temporoparietal junction. *J. Neurosci.* **25**, 550–557. (doi:10.1523/JNEUROSCI.2612-04.2005)

Brothers, L. 1990 The social brain: a project for integrating primate behavior and neurophysiology in a new domain. *Concepts Neurosci.* **1**, 27–51.

Brown, J. W. & Braver, T. S. 2005 Learned predictions of error likelihood in the anterior cingulate cortex. *Science* **307**, 1118–1121. (doi:10.1126/science.1105783)

Buchel, C., Morris, J., Dolan, R. J. & Friston, K. J. 1998 Brain systems mediating aversive conditioning: an event-related fMRI study. *Neuron* **20**, 947–957. (doi:10.1016/S0896-6273(00)80476-6)

Chartrand, T. L. & Bargh, J. A. 1999 The chameleon effect: the perception-behavior link and social interaction. *J. Pers. Soc. Psychol.* **76**, 893–910. (doi:10.1037/0022-3514.76.6.893)

Coricelli, G., Critchley, H. D., Joffily, M., O'Doherty, J. P., Sirigu, A. & Dolan, R. J. 2005 Regret and its avoidance: a neuroimaging study of choice behavior. *Nat. Neurosci.* **8**, 1255–1262. (doi:10.1038/nn1514)

Cunningham, W. A., Johnson, M. K., Raye, C. L., Gatenby, J. C., Gore, J. C. & Banaji, M. R. 2004 Separable neural components in the processing of black and white faces. *Psychol. Sci.* **15**, 806–813. (doi:10.1111/j.0956-7976.2004.00760.x)

Damasio, H., Tranel, D., Grabowski, T., Adolphs, R. & Damasio, A. 2004 Neural systems behind word and concept retrieval. *Cognition* **92**, 179–229. (doi:10.1016/j.cognition.2002.07.001)

Dennett, D. C. 1987 *The intentional stance.* Cambridge, MA: The MIT Press.

Dolan, R. J. 2002 Emotion, cognition, and behavior. *Science* **298**, 1191–1194. (doi:10.1126/science.1076358)

Dunbar, R. I. M. & Schultz, S. 2007 Understanding primate brain evolution. *Phil. Trans. R. Soc. B* **362**, 649–658. (doi:10.1098/rstb.2006.2001)

Fletcher, P. C., Happe, F., Frith, U., Baker, S. C., Dolan, R. J., Frackowiak, R. S. & Frith, C. D. 1995 Other minds in the brain: a functional imaging study of 'theory of mind' in story comprehension. *Cognition* **57**, 109–128. (doi:10.1016/0010-0277(95)00692-R)

Funnell, E. 2001 Evidence for scripts in semantic dementia. Implications for theories of semantic memory. *Cogn. Neuropsychol.* **18**, 323–341. (doi:10.1080/02643290042000134)

Gallagher, H. L., Happe, F., Brunswick, N., Fletcher, P. C., Frith, U. & Frith, C. D. 2000 Reading the mind in cartoons and stories: an fMRI study of 'theory of mind' in verbal and nonverbal tasks. *Neuropsychologia* **38**, 11–21. (doi:10.1016/S0028-3932(99)00053-6)

Gallese, V. 2007 Before and below 'theory of mind': embodied simulation and the neural correlates of social cognition. *Phil. Trans. R. Soc. B* **362**, 659–669. (doi:10. 1098/rstb.2006.2002)

Ganis, G. & Kutas, M. 2003 An electrophysiological study of scene effects on object identification. *Cogn. Brain Res.* **16**, 123–144. (doi:10.1016/S0926-6410(02)00244-6)

Gehring, W. J. & Willoughby, A. R. 2002 The medial frontal cortex and the rapid processing of monetary gains and losses. *Science* **295**, 2279–2282. (doi:10.1126/science.1066893)

Gilbert, S. J., Spengler, S., Simons, J. S., Steele, J. D., Lawrie, S. M., Frith, C. D. & Burgess, P. W. 2006 Functional specialization within rostral prefrontal cortex (area 10): a meta-analysis. *J. Cogn. Neurosci.* **18**, 932–948.

Goel, V., Grafman, J., Sadato, N. & Hallett, M. 1995 Modeling other minds. *Neuroreport* **6**, 1741–1746. (doi:10.1097/00001756-199509000-00009)

Gregory, C., Lough, S., Stone, V., Erzinclioglu, S., Martin, L., Baron-Cohen, S. & Hodges, J. R. 2002 Theory of mind in patients with frontal variant frontotemporal dementia and Alzheimer's disease: theoretical and practical implications. *Brain* **125**, 752–764. (doi:10.1093/brain/awf079)

Grezes, J., Frith, C. & Passingham, R. E. 2004a Brain mechanisms for inferring deceit in the actions of others. *J. Neurosci.* **24**, 5500–5505. (doi:10.1523/JNEUROSCI.0219-04.2004)

Grezes, J., Frith, C. D. & Passingham, R. E. 2004b Inferring false beliefs from the actions of oneself and others: an fMRI study. *Neuroimage* **21**, 744–750. (doi:10.1016/S1053-8119(03)00665-7)

Humphrey, N. K. 1976 The social function of intellect. In *Growing points in ethology* (eds P. P. G. Bateson & R. A. Hinde), pp. 303–317. Cambridge, UK: Cambridge University Press.

Hynes, C. A., Baird, A. A. & Grafton, S. T. 2006 Differential role of the orbital frontal lobe in emotional versus cognitive perspective-taking. *Neuropsychologia* **44**, 374–383. (doi:10.1016/j.neuropsychologia. 2005.06.011)

Iacoboni, M., Lieberman, M. D., Knowlton, B. J., Molnar-Szakacs, I., Moritz, M., Throop, C. J. & Fiske, A. P. 2004 Watching social interactions produces dorsomedial prefrontal and medial parietal BOLD fMRI signal increases compared to a resting baseline. *Neuroimage* **21**, 1167–1173. (doi:10.1016/j.neuroimage.2003.11.013)

Jackson, P. L., Meltzoff, A. N. & Decety, J. 2005 How do we perceive the pain of others? A window into the neural processes involved in empathy. *Neuroimage* **24**, 771–779. (doi:10.1016/j.neuroimage. 2004.09.006)

Kawawaki, D., Shibata, T., Goda, N., Doya, K. & Kawato, M. 2006 Anterior and superior lateral occipito-temporal cortex responsible for target motion prediction during overt and covert visual pursuit. *Neurosci. Res.* **54**, 112–123. (doi:10.1016/j.neures.2005.10.015)

Kelley, W. M., Macrae, C. N., Wyland, C. L., Caglar, S., Inati, S. & Heatherton, T. F. 2002 Finding the self? An event-related fMRI study. *J. Cogn. Neurosci.* **14**, 785–794. (doi:10.1162/089892902601 38672)

Keysers, C., Wicker, B., Gazzola, V., Anton, J. L., Fogassi, L. & Gallese, V. 2004 A touching sight: SII/PV activation during the observation and experience of touch. *Neuron* **42**, 335–346. (doi:10.1016/ S0896-6273(04)00156-4)

Kilner, J. M., Paulignan, Y. & Blakemore, S. J. 2003 An interference effect of observed biological movement on action. *Curr. Biol.* **13**, 522–525. (doi:10.1016/S0960-9822(03)00165-9)

Kling, A. S. & Brothers, L. 1992 The amygdala and social behaviour. In *The amygdala: neurobiological aspects of emotion, memory, and mental dysfunction* (ed. J. P. Aggleton), pp. 353–377. New York, NY: Wiley-Liss.

Knutson, B., Taylor, J., Kaufman, M., Peterson, R. & Glover, G. 2005 Distributed neural representation of expected value. *J. Neurosci.* **25**, 4806–4812. (doi:10.1523/JNEUR-OSCI.0642-05.2005)

Kohler, E., Keysers, C., Umilta, M. A., Fogassi, L., Gallese, V. & Rizzolatti, G. 2002 Hearing sounds, understanding actions: action representation in mirror neurons. *Science* **297**, 846–848. (doi:10.1126/science.1070311)

LeDoux, J. E. 2000 Emotion circuits in the brain. *Annu. Rev. Neurosci.* **23**, 155–184. (doi:10.1146/annurev. neuro. 23.1.155)

Luu, P., Tucker, D. M., Derryberry, D., Reed, M. & Poulsen, C. 2003 Electrophysiological responses to errors and feedback in the process of action regulation. *Psychol. Sci.* **14**, 47–53. (doi:10.1111/ 1467-9280.01417)

McCabe, K., Houser, D., Ryan, L., Smith, V. & Trouard, T. 2001 A functional imaging study of cooperation in two-person reciprocal exchange. *Proc. Natl Acad. Sci. USA* **98**, 11 832–11 835. (doi:10.1073/ pnas.211415698)

Mitchell, J. P., Heatherton, T. F. & Macrae, C. N. 2002 Distinct neural systems subserve person and object knowledge. *Proc. Natl Acad. Sci. USA* **99**, 15 238–15 243. (doi:10.1073/pnas.232395699)

Mitchell, J. P., Banaji, M. R. & Macrae, C. N. 2005 General and specific contributions of the medial prefrontal cortex to knowledge about mental states. *Neuroimage* **28**, 757–762. (doi:10.1016/ j.neuroimage.2005.03.011)

Morris, J. S., Friston, K. J., Buchel, C., Frith, C. D., Young, A. W., Calder, A. J. & Dolan, R. J. 1998 A neuromodulatory role for the human amygdala in processing emotional facial expressions. *Brain* **121**, 47–57. (doi:10.1093/brain/121.1.47)

Morrison, I., Lloyd, D., di Pellegrino, G. & Roberts, N. 2004 Vicarious responses to pain in anterior cingulate cortex: is empathy a multisensory issue? *Cogn. Affect. Behav. Neurosci.* **4**, 270–278.

Nardini, M., Burgess, N., Breckenridge, K. & Atkinson, J. 2005 Differential developmental trajectories for egocentric, environmental and intrinsic frames of reference in spatial memory. *Cognition* **101**, 153–172. (doi:10.1016/j.cognition.2005.09.005)

Ochsner, K. N., Knierim, K., Ludlow, D. H., Hanelin, J., Ramachandran, T., Glover, G. & Mackey, S. C. 2004 Reflecting upon feelings: an fMRI study of neural systems supporting the attribution of emotion to self and other. *J. Cogn. Neurosci.* **16**, 1746–1772. (doi:10.1162/0898929042947829)

Padoa-Schioppa, C. & Assad, J.A. 2006 Neurons in the orbitofrontal cortex encode economic value. *Nature* **441**, 223–226. (doi:10.1038/nature04676)

Parkinson, B. 2005 Do facial movements express emotions or communicate motives? *Pers. Soc. Psychol. Rev.* **9**, 278–311. (doi:10.1207/s15327957pspr0904_1)

Pelphrey, K. A., Morris, J. P. & McCarthy, G. 2004a Grasping the intentions of others: the perceived intentionality of an action influences activity in the superior temporal sulcus during social perception. *J. Cogn. Neurosci.* **16**, 1706–1716. (doi:10.1162/0898929042947900)

Pelphrey, K. A., Viola, R. J. & McCarthy, G. 2004b When strangers pass: processing of mutual and averted social gaze in the superior temporal sulcus. *Psychol. Sci.* **15**, 598–603. (doi:10.1111/j.0956-7976.2004.00726.x)

Pelphrey, K. A., Morris, J. P., Michelich, C. R., Allison, T. & McCarthy, G. 2005 Functional anatomy of biological motion perception in posterior temporal cortex: an FMRI study of eye, mouth and hand movements. *Cereb. Cortex* **15**, 1866–1876. (doi:10.1093/cercor/bhi064)

Perrett, D. I., Hietanen, J. K., Oram, M. W. & Benson, P. J. 1992 Organization and functions of cells responsive to faces in the temporal cortex. *Phil. Trans. R. Soc. B* **335**, 23–30. (doi:10.1098/rstb.1992.0003)

Phelps, E. A., O'Connor, K. J., Cunningham, W. A., Funayama, E. S., Gatenby, J. C., Gore, J. C. & Banaji, M. R. 2000 Performance on indirect measures of race evaluation predicts amygdala activation. *J. Cogn. Neurosci.* **12**, 729–738. (doi:10.1162/089892900562552)

Phelps, E. A., Cannistraci, C. J. & Cunningham, W. A. 2003 Intact performance on an indirect measure of race bias following amygdala damage. *Neuropsychologia* **41**, 203–208. (doi:10.1016/S0028-3932(02)00150-1)

Phillips, M. L. *et al.* 1997 A specific neural substrate for perceiving facial expressions of disgust. *Nature* **389**, 495–498. (doi:10.1038/39051)

Premack, D. & Woodruff, G. 1978 Does the chimpanzee have a theory of mind? *Behav. Brain Sci.* **1**, 515–526.

Prinz, W. 1997 Perception and action planning. *Eur. J. Cogn. Psychol.* **9**, 129–154.

Raleigh, M. J. & Steklis, H. D. 1981 Effect of orbitofrontal and temporal neocortical lesions on the affiliative behavior of vervet monkeys (*Cercopithecus aethiops sabaeus*). *Exp. Neurol.* **73**, 378–389. (doi:10.1016/0014-4886(81)90273-9)

Rizzolatti, G. & Craighero, L. 2004 The mirror-neuron system. *Annu. Rev. Neurosci.* **27**, 169–192. (doi:10.1146/annurev.neuro.27.070203.144230)

Rosenthal, R. 2005 *Consciousness and mind*. Oxford, UK: Clarendon Press.

Rowe, A. D., Bullock, P. R., Polkey, C. E. & Morris, R. G. 2001 'Theory of mind' impairments and their relationship to executive functioning following frontal lobe excisions. *Brain* **124**, 600–616. (doi:10.1093/brain/124.3.600)

Saxe, R. 2006 Uniquely human social cognition. *Curr. Opin. Neurobiol.* **16**, 235–239. (doi:10.1016/j.conb.2006.03.001)

Saxe, R. & Kanwisher, N. 2003 People thinking about thinking people. The role of the temporo-parietal junction in 'theory of mind'. *Neuroimage* **19**, 1835–1842. (doi:10.1016/S1053-8119(03)00230-1)

Saxe, R., Xiao, D. K., Kovacs, G., Perrett, D. I. & Kanwisher, N. 2004 A region of right posterior superior temporal sulcus responds to observed intentional actions. *Neuropsychologia* **42**, 1435–1446. (doi:10.1016/j.neuropsychologia.2004.04.015)

Schank, R. C. & Abelson, R. P. 1977 *Scripts, plans, goals and understanding: an inquiry into human knowledge structures*. Hillsdale, NJ: L. Erlbaum.

Schmitz, T. W., Kawahara-Baccus, T. N. & Johnson, S. C. 2004 Metacognitive evaluation, self-relevance, and the right prefrontal cortex. *Neuroimage* **22**, 941–947. (doi:10.1016/j.neuroimage.2004.02.018)

Schultz, J., Imamizu, H., Kawato, M. & Frith, C. D. 2004 Activation of the human superior temporal gyrus during observation of goal attribution by intentional objects. *J. Cogn. Neurosci.* **16**, 1695–1705. (doi:10.1162/0898929042947874)

Schultz, J., Friston, K. J., O'Doherty, J., Wolpert, D. M. & Frith, C. D. 2005 Activation in posterior superior temporal sulcus parallels parameter inducing the percept of animacy. *Neuron* **45**, 625–635. (doi:10.1016/j.neuron.2004.12.052)

Semendeferi, K., Armstrong, E., Schleicher, A., Zilles, K. & Van Hoesen, G. W. 2001 Prefrontal cortex in humans and apes: a comparative study of area 10. *Am. J. Phys. Anthropol.* **114**, 224–241. (doi:10.1002/1096-8644(200103)114:3<224::AID-AJPA1022>3.0.CO;2-I)

Singer, T., Seymour, B., O'Doherty, J., Kaube, H., Dolan, R. J. & Frith, C. D. 2004 Empathy for pain involves the affective but not sensory components of pain. *Science* **303**, 1157–1162. (doi:10.1126/science.1093535)

Singer, T., Seymour, B., Doherty, J., Stephan, K. E., Dolan, R. J. & Frith, C. D. 2006 Empathic neural responses are modulated by the perceived fairness of others. *Nature* **439**, 466–469. (doi:10.1038/nature04271)

Steele, J. D. & Lawrie, S. M. 2004 Segregation of cognitive and emotional function in the prefrontal cortex: a stereotactic meta-analysis. *Neuroimage* **21**, 868–875. (doi:10.1016/j.neuroimage.2003.09.066)

Stuss, D. T., Gallup Jr, G. G. & Alexander, M. P. 2001 The frontal lobes are necessary for 'theory of mind'. *Brain* **124**, 279–286. (doi:10.1093/brain/124.2.279)

Tai, Y. F., Scherfler, C., Brooks, D. J., Sawamoto, N. & Castiello, U. 2004 The human premotor cortex is 'mirror' only for biological actions. *Curr. Biol.* **14**, 117–120. (doi:10.1016/j.cub.2004.01.005)

van Schie, H. T., Mars, R. B., Coles, M. G. & Bekkering, H. 2004 Modulation of activity in medial frontal and motor cortices during error observation. *Nat. Neurosci.* **7**, 549–554. (doi:10.1038/nn1239)

Vogeley, K., May, M., Ritzl, A., Falkai, P., Zilles, K. & Fink, G. R. 2004 Neural correlates of first-person perspective as one constituent of human self-consciousness. *J. Cogn. Neurosci.* **16**, 817–827. (doi:10.1162/089892904970799)

Walter, H., Adenzato, M., Ciaramidaro, A., Enrici, I., Pia, L. & Bara, B. G. 2004 Understanding intentions in social interaction: the role of the anterior paracingulate cortex. *J. Cogn. Neurosci.* **16**, 1854–1863. (doi:10.1162/0898929042947838)

Walton, M. E., Devlin, J. T. & Rushworth, M. F. 2004 Interactions between decision making and performance monitoring within prefrontal cortex. *Nat. Neurosci.* **7**, 1259–1265. (doi:10.1038/nn1339)

Wicker, B., Keysers, C., Plailly, J., Royet, J. P., Gallese, V. & Rizzolatti, G. 2003 Both of us disgusted in My insula: the common neural basis of seeing and feeling disgust. *Neuron* **40**, 655–664. (doi:10.1016/S0896-6273(03)00679-2)

Wilson, M. & Knoblich, G. 2005 The case for motor involvement in perceiving conspecifics. *Psychol. Bull.* **131**, 460–473. (doi:10.1037/0033-2909.131.3.460)

Winston, J. S., Strange, B. A., O'Doherty, J. & Dolan, R. J. 2002 Automatic and intentional brain responses during evaluation of trustworthiness of faces. *Nat. Neurosci.* **5**, 277–283. (doi:10.1038/nn816)

Wolpert, D. M., Doya, K. & Kawato, M. 2003 A unifying computational framework for motor control and social interaction. *Phil. Trans. R. Soc. B* **358**, 593–602. (doi:10.1098/rstb.2002.1238)

Zacks, J. M., Vettel, J. M. & Michelon, P. 2003 Imagined viewer and object rotations dissociated with event-related FMRI. *J. Cogn. Neurosci.* **15**, 1002–1018. (doi:10.1162/089892903770007399)

Broader Perspectives

14

Socially intelligent robots: dimensions of human–robot interaction

Kerstin Dautenhahn

Social intelligence in robots has a quite recent history in artificial intelligence and robotics. However, it has become increasingly apparent that social and interactive skills are necessary requirements in many application areas and contexts where robots need to interact and collaborate with other robots or humans. Research on human–robot interaction (HRI) poses many challenges regarding the nature of interactivity and 'social behaviour' in robot and humans. The first part of this paper addresses dimensions of HRI, discussing requirements on social skills for robots and introducing the conceptual space of HRI studies. In order to illustrate these concepts, two examples of HRI research are presented. First, research is surveyed which investigates the development of a cognitive robot companion. The aim of this work is to develop social rules for robot behaviour (a 'robotiquette') that is comfortable and acceptable to humans. Second, robots are discussed as possible educational or therapeutic toys for children with autism. The concept of interactive emergence in human–child interactions is highlighted. Different types of play among children are discussed in the light of their potential investigation in human–robot experiments. The paper concludes by examining different paradigms regarding 'social relationships' of robots and people interacting with them.

Keywords: social robots; human–robot interaction; robotiquette; robot companion

14.1 Introduction: the nature of artificial (social) intelligence

Humans seem to have a particular curiosity about understanding and simulating nature in general, and, specifically, human beings. This desire has found its manifestations in a variety of 'simulacra', including moving and 'speaking' statues in Egypt *ca* 2000 years ago. Hero of Alexandria's work is an outstanding example of building highly sophisticated devices using the scientific knowledge available at that time, i.e. exploiting physics, e.g. water or vapour powering movable parts connected via ropes and levers in order to impress people by opening doors of temples, moving statues seemingly autonomously (Richter 1989). Other impressive examples of simulations of humans include the 'androids' built in the sixteenth, seventeenth and eighteenth centuries in Europe, where a variety of machines were constructed simulating human activities, such as writing, dancing or, as shown in figure 14.1, trumpet playing, based on delicate and sophisticated clockwork mechanisms available at that time. The design of these androids focused on humanlike realistic appearance and the simulation of a few human activities, different from later research on artificial intelligence (AI), which was similarly aiming at simulating human activities, but focused on the 'mind'. Thus, instead of a realistic replication of one or very few human activities, replicating the flexibility and adaptability of human intelligence became a big challenge.

Since its origin, which can be dated back to 1956, AI research has been strongly inspired and motivated by human intelligence; human thinking and problem-solving dominated until the late 1980s, whereby chess-playing, theorem-proving, planning and similar 'cognitive' skills were considered to exemplify human intelligence and were proposed as benchmarks for

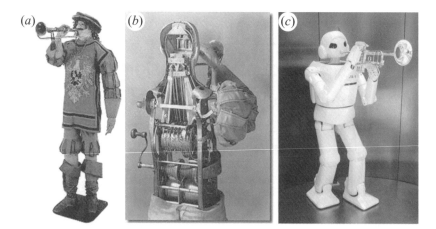

Fig. 14.1 People have long been interested in machines that simulate natural processes, in particular machines that simulate human behaviour and/or appearance. (*a, b*) The famous trumpet player designed by Friedrich Kaufmann in Dresden, Germany, (source: http://www.deutsches-museum.de/ausstell/meister/ e_tromp.htm; copyright Deutches Museum, Munich). A variety of other androids were created trying to simulate appearance and behaviour of humans (and other animals), based on clockwork technology available at the time. Pierre Jaquet-Droz and Jacques de Vaucanson are among the famous designers of early androids in the eighteenth century. (*c*) A recent example, using the latest twenty-first century robotics technology, to simulate aspects of human behaviour: the Toyota robot at the Toyota Kaikan in Toyota City (This Wikipedia and Wikimedia commons image is from the user Chris 73 and is freely available at http://commons.wikimedia.org/wiki/Image: Toyota_Robot_at_Toyota_Kaikan.jpg under the creative commons cc-bu-sa 2.5 license.)

designing systems that should either simulate human intelligence (weak AI) or become intelligent (strong AI). In this human-centred viewpoint, any creatures other than adult human beings, e.g. elephants, dolphins, non-human primates as well as three-month-old children, were not considered to be relevant subjects for the study or modelling of 'intelligence'. While progress has been made in the domains of what is considered now 'classical AI', e.g. chess-playing programs are able to beat expert human chess players, and AI technology is widely used, e.g. in e-commerce and other applications involving software agents, from the perspective of trying to understand or create human intelligence, it has become apparent that such skills are not necessarily those that 'make us human'. Also, attempts to put 'AI' on wheels, i.e. to design AI robots, illuminated a fundamental problem with the view of intelligence as 'disembodied' and 'symbolic', i.e. getting a robot to do even very 'simple things', e.g. wandering around in an office environment and not to bump into obstacles, turned out to be very surprisingly difficult. Other simple things that humans do with 'little thinking', e.g. recognizing a cup placed on a table behind a vase, grasping and carrying the cup filled with coffee to the dining room without spilling the coffee, turned out to be big scientific challenges. More fundamentally, skills involving sensing and acting and close couplings between these in order to deal with the dynamics and unpredictability of the 'real world' have become the new big challenges. Rather than focusing on the 'problem-solving mind', the 'mind in the body', placed in and part of a surrounding environment, became a focus of attention.

More recently, sensorimotor skills emphasizing the embodied nature of human intelligence (including locomotion, object manipulation, etc.) are considered to be the more fundamental but certainly more biologically and developmentally plausible milestones that researchers are aiming at, highlighting the close relationships between mind, body and environment, work that has been pioneered by Brooks and others since the 1980s (see collection of articles by Steels (1994), Brooks (1999) and Pfeifer & Scheier (1999)). In such a 'nouvelle AI' viewpoint, a robot is more than a 'computer on wheels', as it had been considered in AI for decades. A nouvelle AI robot is embodied, situated, surrounded by, responding to and interacting with its environment. A nouvelle AI robot takes its inspirations not necessarily from humans, i.e. insects, slugs or salamanders can be equally worthwhile behavioural or cognitive models depending on the particular skills or behaviours that are under investigation. This paradigm shift in AI had important consequences for the type of robotics experiments that researchers conducted in the field of nouvelle AI, i.e. an ecological balance between the complexity of 'body', 'mind' and 'environment' was considered highly important. The complexity of a robot's sensor system and the amount of sensory information to be processed need to be balanced and find a correspondence in a creature's ability to interact with and respond to the environment, given its particular internal goals and/or tasks imposed by its designers/experimenters. According to this approach, it is, for example, not advisable to put high-resolution sensor systems on a robot that possesses only two degrees of freedom (i.e. is able to move around on the floor). Most robotic platforms available in the 1990s, either self-built using, for example, Lego construction kits, or commercially available robots such as Kheperas, Koalas (K-Team) or Pioneers (Active Media Robotics), were restricted in their sensorimotor abilities to wander in a purpose-built arena, avoid certain obstacles and sometimes respond to certain gradients in the environments (e.g. light) via specific sensors (figure 14.2). The simplicity of the sensor and actuator systems made many researchers focus on 'internal operations' of the robot, i.e. its control system (whether designed by the experimenter or evolved using evolutionary algorithms). A typical behaviour set of a 1990s nouvelle AI robot consists of {Wander, Avoid-Obstacle, Positive or Negative Phototaxis}. Such robotic test beds have been widely used to investigate the development of machine learning techniques applied to robot controllers, whereby the robot learns to avoid obstacles or 'find' a light source (which was often modelled as a 'food source'). Other more biologically inspired scenarios included robots in a simulated 'ecosystem' where they had to operate self-sufficiently, including recharging their batteries,

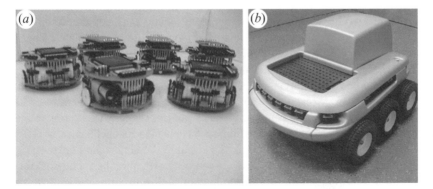

Fig. 14.2 Experimental platforms that have been used widely in 'nouvelle AI' research: (*a*) Khepera and (*b*) Koala, both from K-Team (http://www.k-team.com). Both robots have two degrees of freedom that allow wandering in the environment. Optionally, grippers can be fitted to pick up objects.

or experiments inspired by swarm intelligence in social insects (e.g. Bonabeau *et al.* 1999). The kind of intelligence that these robots could demonstrate was clearly far from any behaviour considered human-like: behaviours such as wandering around in the environment and being able to respond to certain stimuli in the environment are exhibited even by bacteria. Insects, far from simple as biological complex systems, but nevertheless showing behaviour as individuals closer in magnitude to the limited scope of behaviour that can be simulated with machines available in the 1990s, became popular models for 'behaviour-based AI', the branch of nouvelle AI concerned with developing behaviour control systems for robots.

By the mid-1990s, new research initiatives took off, following, in principle, the nouvelle AI paradigm, but aiming at robots with human-like bodies and humanlike minds, most famously the Massachusetts Institute of Technology robot 'Cog', an upper torso humanoid robot, later accompanied in the same laboratory by 'Kismet', a robot that consisted of an articulated face and expressed 'emotions'. Cog, in particular, was aimed at modelling, if not synthesizing, human-like intelligence, a goal too ambitious to reach within a few years. However, this initiative by Rodney A. Brooks revived an interest in studying human-like intelligence in machines (Brooks *et al.* 1999).

Despite impressive examples of sensorimotor skills in the present-day robots and some examples of social interactions of robots with other robots or people, reaching human-like intelligence remains a big challenge and the cognitive abilities of present-day robots are still limited, while research dominantly focuses on how to instantiate human-like intelligence in machines that can intelligently interact with the environment and solve tasks.

An alternative viewpoint towards AI, for which the author has been arguing since 1994 (Dautenhahn 1994, 1995, 1998, 1999*a*, 2004*a*), is to propose that one particular aspect of human intelligence, namely *social intelligence*, might bring us closer to the goal of making robots smarter (in the sense of more human-like and believable in behaviour); the social environment cannot be subsumed under 'general environmental factors', i.e. humans interact differently with each other than with a chair or a stone. This approach is inspired by the social intelligence hypothesis (also called social brain hypothesis; Dunbar 1993, 1996, 1998, 2003), which suggests that primate intelligence primarily evolved in adaptation to social complexity, i.e. in order to interpret, predict and manipulate conspecifics (e.g. Byrne & Whiten 1988; Byrne 1995, 1997; Whiten & Byrne 1997). The social intelligence hypothesis originated in the studies of nonhuman primates: the seminal work of Alison Jolly, who studied lemur intelligence and noted that while they lack the intelligence to learn about and manipulate objects, different from monkeys, they show similarly good social skills, led her to conclude that, 'primate society, thus, could develop without the object-learning capacity or manipulative ingenuity of monkeys. This manipulative, object cleverness, however, evolved only in the context of primate social life. Therefore, I would argue that some social life preceded, and determined the nature of, primate intelligence' (Jolly 1966, p. 506).

Thus, there may be two important aspects to human sociality: it served as an evolutionary constraint that led to an increase of brain size in primates, which in turn led to an increased capacity to further develop social complexity. The argument suggests that during the evolution of human intelligence, a transfer took place from social to non-social intelligence, so that hominid primates could transfer their expertise from the social to the non-social domain (Gigerenzer 1997). Note that for the present paper, it is not important whether the social domain was the primary factor in the evolution of primate and human intelligence, it is sufficient to know and accept that it did play an important role, possibly in conjunction with or secondary to other factors, e.g. ecological or social learning capacities (Reader & Laland 2002).

AI since its early days has tried to simulate or replicate human intelligence in computers or robots. Given what has been suggested about the phylogeny of human intelligence, whereby the importance of the social environment also becomes apparent in ontogeny, making robots social might bring us a step further towards our goal of human-style AI.

However, despite a change in viewpoint from the so-called 'classical' to the 'nouvelle' direction of AI, social intelligence has not yet been fully recognized as a key ingredient of AI, although it has been widely investigated in fields where researchers study animal and human minds. Acknowledging the social nature of human intelligence and its implications for AI is an exciting challenge that requires truly interdisciplinary viewpoints. Such viewpoints can be found in the field of *human–robot interaction* (*HRI*), where researchers are typically addressing robots in a particular service robotics task/application scenario, e.g. robots as assistants, and where social interaction with people is necessarily part of the research agenda. However, it is still not generally accepted that a robot's social skills are more than a necessary 'add-on' to human–robot interfaces in order to make the robot more 'attractive' to people interacting with it, but form an important part of a robot's cognitive skills and the degree to which it exhibits intelligence.

Applying the 'social intelligence hypothesis' to AI implies that social intelligence is a key ingredient of human intelligence and, as such, a candidate prerequisite for any artificially intelligent robot. Research on intelligent robots usually focuses first on making robots cognitive by equipping them with planning, reasoning, navigation, manipulation and other related skills necessary to interact with and operate in the non-social environment, and then later adding 'social skills' and other aspects of social cognition. Alternatively, inspired by findings from research into social intelligence in humans and other social animals, social intelligence should be viewed as a fundamental ingredient of intelligent and social robots. To phrase it differently, developing an intelligent robot means developing a socially intelligent robot. Particularly promising to reach the goal of (social) intelligence in robots is the research direction of 'developmental robotics' (Lungarella *et al.* 2004). Figure 14.3 shows a robotic platform used for the study of interaction games between robots and humans, work carried out within a European project in developmental robotics called Robotcub (http://www.robotcub.org).

In the rest of this paper, we shall illustrate work on robots that have the beginnings of rudimentary social skills and interact with people, research that is carried out in the field of HRI.

First, we discuss the dimensions of HRI, investigating requirements on social skills for robots and introducing the conceptual space of HRI studies. Definitions of 'social robots' are discussed. In order to illustrate these concepts, two examples of research in two current projects will be presented. First, research into the design of robot companions, work conducted within the Cogniron project, will be surveyed. A robot companion in a home environment needs to 'do the right things', i.e. it has to be useful and perform tasks around the house, but it also has to 'do the things right', i.e. in a manner that is believable and acceptable to humans. Second, HRIs in the context of the Aurora project, which investigates the possible use of robots as therapeutic or educational toys for children with autism, will be discussed. The emergent nature of interactions between the children and a simple mobile robot will be discussed, emphasizing that the behaviour that might appear 'social' from an observer's point of view does not necessarily involve specific internal modelling of interaction or 'social intelligence'. The paper concludes by examining different paradigms regarding 'social relationships' of robots and people interacting with them.

14.2 What social skills does a robot need?

Investigating social skills in robots can be a worthwhile endeavour for the study of mechanisms of social intelligence, or other aspects regarding the nature of social cognition in animals and artefacts. While here the inspiration is drawn from basic research questions, in robotics and

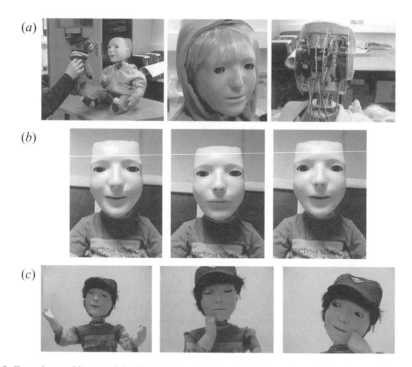

Fig. 14.3 Experimental humanoid robot platform for the study of synchronization, turn-taking and inter-action games inspired by child development. Kaspar, a child-sized humanoid robot developed by the Adaptive Systems Research Group at the University of Hertfordshire. (*a*) Kaspar has a minimally expressive head with eight degrees of freedom in the neck, eyes, eyelids and mouth. The face is a silicon rubber mask, which is supported on an aluminium frame. It has two degrees of freedom in the eyes fitted with video cameras and a mouth capable of opening and smiling. It has six degrees of freedom in the arms and hand and is thus able to show a variety of different expressions. (*b*) Kaspar's expressions: happy; neutral; and surprised (Blow *et al.* 2006). (*c*) Some of Kaspar's expressions using movements in the head and arms.

computer science, many research projects aim at developing interactive robots that are suitable for certain application domains. The classification and evaluation of HRIs with respect to the application area is an active area of research (e.g. Yanco & Drury 2002, 2004; Scholtz 2003; Steinfeld *et al.* 2006).

However, given the variety of different application domains envisaged or already occupied by robots, why should such robots, where their usefulness and functionality are a primary concern, possess social skills, given that the development of social skills for robots is costly and thus needs to provide an 'added value'? The answer to this question depends on the specific requirements of a particular application domain (see Dautenhahn 2003). Figure 14.4 shows a list of different application domains, where increasing social skills are required. At one end of the spectrum, we find that robots, e.g. when operating in space, do not need to be social, unless they need to cooperate with other robots. In contrast, a robot delivering the mail in an office environment has regular encounters with customers, so within this well-defined domain, social skills contribute to making the interactions with the robot more convenient for people. At the other end of the spectrum, a robot that serves as a companion in the home for the elderly or *spectrum of requirements for robot social skills:*

- remote controlled/spatially–temporally separated
  (surveillance, space robots)
- agriculture, cleaning, firefighting
- tour guides, office/hotel assistants
- entertainment
- robots in nursing care, rehabilitation, therapy, e.g. autism therapy
- robot companion in the home

Fig. 14.4 Increasing requirements for social skills in different robot application domains.

assists people with disabilities needs to possess a wide range of social skills which will make it acceptable for humans. Without these skills, such robots might not be 'used' and thus fail in their role as an assistant.

In order to decide which social skills are required, the application domain and the nature and frequency of contact with humans need to be analysed in great detail, according to a set of evaluation criteria (Dautenhahn 2003), each representing a spectrum (figure 14.5).

14.3 Human–robot interaction: the conceptual space of HRI approaches

The field of HRI is still relatively young. The annual IEEE RO-MAN conference series that originated in 1992 in Japan and has since then travelled across the world reflects this emerging new field. HRI is a highly interdisciplinary area, at the intersection of robotics, engineering,

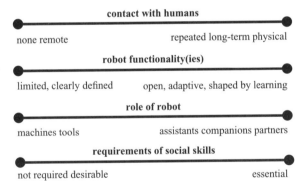

Fig. 14.5 Evaluation criteria to identify requirements on social skills for robots in different application domains. Contact with humans ranges from none, remote contact (e.g. for robots operating in deep-sea environments) to long-term, repeated contact potentially involving physical contact, as is the case, for example, in assistive robotics. The functionality of robots ranges from limited, clearly defined functionalities (e.g. as vacuum cleaning robots) to open, adaptive functions that might require robot learning skills (e.g. applications such as robot partners, companions or assistants). Depending on the application, domain requirements for social skills vary from not required (e.g. robots designed to operate in areas spatially or temporally separated from humans, e.g. on Mars or patrolling warehouses at night) to possibly desirable (even vacuum cleaning robots need interfaces for human operation) to essential for performance/acceptance (service or assistive robotics applications).

computer science, psychology, linguistics, ethology and other disciplines, investigating social behaviour, communication and intelligence in natural and artificial systems. Different from traditional engineering and robotics, *interaction with people* is a defining core ingredient of HRI. Such interaction can comprise verbal and/or non-verbal interactions.

(a) Approaches to social interactions with robots

HRI research can be categorized into three, not mutually exclusive, directions, which are as follows.

— *Robot-centred HRI* emphasizes the view of a robot as a *creature*, i.e. an *autonomous entity* that is pursuing its own goals based on its motivations, drives and emotions, whereby interaction with people serves to fulfil some of its 'needs' (as identified by the robot designer and modelled by the internal control architecture), e.g. *social needs* are fulfilled in the interaction, even if the interaction does not involve any particular task. Skills that enable the robot to 'survive in the environment' or otherwise 'fulfil internal needs' (motivations, drives, emotions, etc.) are a primary concern in this approach. Research questions involve, for example, the development of sensorimotor control and models and architectures of emotion and motivation that regulate interactions with the (social) environment.

— *Human-centred HRI* is primarily concerned with how a robot can fulfil its task specification in a manner that is *acceptable and comfortable to humans*. Here, research studies how people react to and interpret a robot's appearance and/or behaviour, regardless of its behavioural robot architecture and the cognitive processes that might happen inside the robot. Challenges include the following: finding a balanced and consistent design of robot behaviour and appearance; designing socially acceptable behaviour; developing new methods and methodologies for HRI studies and evaluation of HRIs; identifying the needs of individuals and groups of subjects to which a robot could adapt and respond; or avoiding the so-called 'uncanny valley' (Mori 1970; Dautenhahn 2002; MacDorman & Ishiguro 2006), where more and more human-like robots might appear 'unnatural' and evoke feelings of repulsion in humans. The perception of machines is influenced by anthropomorphism and the tendency of people to treat machines socially: see studies by Reeves & Nass (1996), which showed that humans tend to treat computers (and media in general) in certain ways as people, applying social rules and heuristics from the domain of people to the domain of machines. This 'media equation' they proposed (media equals real life) is particularly relevant for robotics research with the 'human in the loop', namely where people interact with robots in the role of designers, users, observers, assistants, collaborators, competitors, customers, patients or friends.

— *Robot cognition-centred HRI* emphasizes the robot as an *intelligent* system (in a traditional AI sense, see §1), i.e. a machine that makes decisions on its own and solves problems it faces as part of the tasks it needs to perform in a particular application domain. Specific research questions in this domain include the development of cognitive robot architectures, machine learning and problem solving.

Often we find an approach of decomposition of responsibilities for aspects of HRI research investigated in single disciplines and only at a later stage brought together, e.g. development of the robot's body separately from the development of the robot's 'behaviour' as it appears to humans and its 'mind'. This bears the risk of arriving at an unbalanced robot design, a 'patchwork' system with no overall integration. A synthetic approach requires collaboration during the whole life cycle of the robot (specification, design, implementation, etc.), which remains a big challenge considering traditional boundaries between disciplines and funding structures.

However, only a truly interdisciplinary perspective, encompassing a *synthesis* of robot-centred, human-centred and robot cognition-centred HRIs, is likely to fulfil the forecast that more and more robots will in the future inhabit our living environments.

Defining socially acceptable behaviour, implemented, for example, as social rules guiding a robot's behaviour in its interactions with people, as well as taking into account the individual nature of humans, could lead to machines that are able to adapt to a user's preferences, likes and dislikes, i.e. an individualized, personalized robot companion. Such a robot would be able to treat people as individuals, not as machines (Dautenhahn 1998, 2004*b*). In §4, this notion of a robot companion is elaborated in more detail.

(b) What are social robots?

Various definitions of social robots or related concepts have been used in the literature, including the ones that are as follows.

  (i) *Socially evocative.* Robots that rely on the human tendency to anthropomorphize and capitalize on feelings evoked, when humans nurture, care or involve with their 'creation' (Breazeal 2002, 2003).
 (ii) *Socially situated.* Robots that are surrounded by a social environment which they perceive and react to. Socially situated robots are able to distinguish between other social agents and various objects in the environment (Fong *et al.* 2003).
(iii) *Sociable.* Robots that proactively engage with humans in order to satisfy internal social aims (drives, emotions, etc.). These robots require deep models of social cognition (Breazeal 2002, 2003).
 (iv) *Socially intelligent.* Robots that show aspects of human-style social intelligence, based on possibly deep models of human cognition and social competence (Dautenhahn 1998).

Fong *et al.* (2003) propose the term 'socially interactive robot', which they define as follows.

  (v) *Socially interactive robots.* Robots for which social interaction plays a key role in peer-to-peer HRI, different from other robots that involve 'conventional' HRI, such as those used in teleoperation scenarios.

Socially interactive robots exhibit the following characteristics: express and/or perceive emotions; communicate with high-level dialogue; learn models of or recognize other agents; establish and/or maintain social relationships; use natural cues (gaze, gestures, etc.); exhibit distinctive personality and character; and may learn and/or develop social competencies.

As can be seen from the above lists, the notion of social robots and the associated degree of robot social intelligence is diverse and depends on the particular research emphasis.

(c) Relationships between HRI approaches

Let us consider the range from a robot cognition viewpoint that stresses the particular cognitive and social skills a robot possesses, to the human-centred perspective on how people experience interaction and view the robot and its behaviour from an observer's perspective. Here, socially evocative robots are placed at one extreme end of the spectrum where they are defined by the responses they elicit in humans. In this sense, it would not matter much how the robot looked or behaved (like a cockroach, human or toaster), as long as it were to elicit certain human responses. At the other end of the spectrum, we find socially interactive robots that possesses a variety of skills to interact and communicate, guided by an appropriate robot control and/or cognitive architecture. For socially interactive robots, while internal motivations and how people respond to them are important, the main emphasis lies on the robot's ability to engage in interactions. Towards the robot-centred view, we find sociable machines, the robot-as-creature view, where a robot engages in interactions for the purpose of fulfilling its own internal needs, while cognitive skills and responses of humans towards it will be determined by the robot's needs and goals (see Breazeal 2004). Sociable robots are similar to socially intelligent robots in terms of requiring possibly deep models of cognition; however, the *emphasis* here is on the robot engaging in interactions in order to satisfy its internal needs. Socially situated robots are similarly related to the viewpoint of a robot-as-creature, but less so. Here, robots are able to interact with their social environment and distinguish between people and other agents (not as a symbolic distinction, but, for example, based on sensor information able to distinguish between humans and objects). A socially situated robot does not need to possess any model of 'social intelligence', 'social interactions' emerge from the robot being situated in and responding to its environment. Socially situated robots do not need to have human appearance or behaviour. Section 5 gives an example of a socially situated robot and the emergence of HRI games involving a robot that is not using any explicit 'social rules'. Finally, socially intelligent robots possess explicit models of social cognition and interaction and communication competence inspired by humans. Such a robot is simulating, if not instantiating, human social intelligence. It behaves similarly to a human, shows similar communicative and interactive competences, and thus is likely also to match human appearance to some degree, in order to keep behaviour and appearance consistent. The way in which humans perceive and respond to a socially intelligent robot is similarly important, since its interactions with humans model human–human interactions. Consequently, for a socially intelligent robot, robot-centred, human-centred and robot cognition-centred HRI is required. Figure 14.6 shows the three different views on HRI discussed in this section, highlighting the emphasis used in different approaches

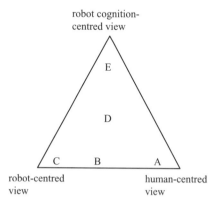

Fig. 14.6 The conceptual space of HRI approaches. A, socially evocative; B, socially situated; C, sociable; D, socially intelligent; E, socially interactive (see text for explanations). Note: any robotic approach that can possibly be located in this framework also involves a more or less strong robotics component, i.e. the robot needs to be able to perform behaviours and tasks which can involve substantial challenges in the cases of a robot that possesses a variety of skills, as required, for example, for robots in service applications. This is less so in the cases where, for example, HRI research can be carried out with simple toy-like robots, such as Lego robots.

using different definitions of robot social behaviour and forming a conceptual space of HRI approaches where certain definitions are appropriate, as indicated.

14.4 A case study of human–robot interaction: robot companions

Service robots are estimated to become increasingly prevalent in our lives. Typical tasks developed for domestic robots include vacuum cleaning, lawn-mowing and window cleaning. In robotics research, community service robotics, where robots perform tasks for people and/or in interaction with people, has become an interesting challenge: see Thrun (2004) for a discussion of past- and present-day robotics in the context of HRI.

As part of the European project Cogniron (cognitive robot companion), we investigate the scenario of a robot companion in the home, i.e. in a domestic environment shared with people. In this context, we define a robot companion as follows:

> A robot companion is a robot that (i) makes itself 'useful', i.e. is able to carry out a variety of tasks in order to assist humans, e.g. in a domestic home environment, and (ii) behaves socially, i.e. possesses social skills in order to be able to interact with people in a socially acceptable manner.

The concept of a robot companion comprises both the 'human-centred view' (it needs to perform these tasks that are believable, comfortable and acceptable to the humans it is sharing the environment with) and the robot cognition point of view: a variety of tasks need to be performed in a flexible and adaptive manner; the robot needs to adapt to and learn new and dynamically changing environments; and the overall behaviour of the robot needs to be 'consistent' (figure 14.7). The robot-as-creature viewpoint, e.g. how the robot can satisfy its needs, only plays a minor role.

A truly *personalized robot companion* takes into consideration an individual human's likes, dislikes and preferences and adapts its behaviour accordingly (Dautenhahn 2004*b*). Also, different people might have different preferences in terms of what tasks the robot should perform or what its appearance should be like. A variety of products are on the market, which differ in

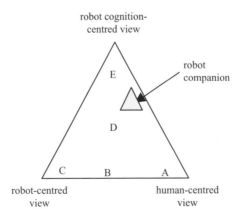

Fig. 14.7 Challenges for a robot companion at the intersection of human-centred and robot cognition-centred views. The right balance needs to be found between how the robot performs its tasks as far as they are perceived by humans (human point of view) and its cognitive abilities that will determine, e.g. decision-making and learning (robot cognition view).

appearance, usability and range of features, even for devices where the functionality seems clearly defined, e.g. cars or mobile phones. However, there is no 'one car for all drivers' and similarly we hypothesize that 'one robot for all' will not exist, i.e. will not be accepted by consumers.

What social skills does a robot companion need? Using the evaluation criteria proposed in §2, we arrive at the following characterization.

— *Contact with humans* is repeated and long term, possibly 'lifelong'. The concept of a robot companion is a machine that will share our homes with us over an extended period of time. The owner should be able to tailor certain aspects of the robot's appearance and behaviour, and likewise the robot should become personalized, recognizing and adapting to its owner's preferences. The attitude towards and opinion of such a machine will be biased by 'first impressions', but will change during long-term experiences.

— *A robot's functionality* can be limited, e.g. vacuuming or window cleaning; however, different from such single-purpose machines, a robot companion will possess a variety of skills, e.g. in addition to performing typical household tasks it will be able to communicate and interact with its users to negotiate tasks and preferences, or even to provide 'companionship'. Ideally, the machine is able to adapt, learn and expand its skills, e.g. by being taught new skills by its 'owner', and, possibly, occasional software updates. Thus, its functionality will be open, adaptive and shaped by learning.

— *The role of a companion* is less machine-like and more human-like in terms of its interaction capabilities. Rather than a machine that, if broken, is replaced, people living in the household might develop a relationship with the robot, i.e. view the companion robot as part of the household, possibly, similarly to pets.

— *Social skills* are essential for a robot companion. Without these, it will not be accepted on a long-term basis. For example, a robot that says in the morning 'good morning, would you like me to prepare breakfast for you' is interesting, but would we want this robot to say the same phrase *every* morning? Likewise, a robot that approaches and says 'would you like me to bring a cup of tea' is appealing, but would we want the robot to ask this question while we are watching our favourite television programme? Thus, social skills, the development of a robotic etiquette (Ogden & Dautenhahn 2000), or robotiquette, as a set of heuristics and guidelines on how a robot should behave and communicate in its owner's home are not only desirable, but also essential for the acceptance of a robot companion.

Within work in Cogniron on social behaviour and embodiment, the University of Hertfordshire team adopts a human-centred perspective and investigates robot behaviour that is acceptable to humans in a series of user studies, i.e. experiments where human subjects are exposed to and/or interact with a robot. The studies take place in simulated or real living rooms; experiments include laboratory studies in simulated living rooms (transformed lecture or meeting rooms) or in a more naturalistic environment, the University of Hertfordshire Robot House (a more naturalistic and ecologically valid environment, which has been found to be more suitable in order to make subjects comfortable and feel less 'assessed' and 'monitored' during the experiments). The studies were exploratory since no comparative data or theories were available which could be applied directly to our experiments. Other research groups are typically studying different scenarios and tasks, using different robot platforms with different kinds of HRI, and their results can thus not be compared directly (e.g. Thrun 1998; Nakauchi & Simmons 2000; Goetz & Kiesler 2002; Severinson-Eklundh *et al.*2003; Kanda *et al.* 2004; Robins *et al.* 2004*a*; Kahn *et al.* 2006).

Within Cogniron, we have performed a series of HRI studies since the start of the project in January 2004. In this paper, we focus on a particular HRI study carried out in summer 2004. The robots used in the study are commercially available, human-scaled, PeopleBot robots (Activ Media Robotics). Details of the experimental set-up are described elsewhere (e.g. Walters *et al.* 2005*a*, 2006). Here, we briefly outline the main rationale for this work and briefly summarize the results.

In our first study in a simulated living room, we investigated two scenarios involving different tasks: a negotiated space task (NST) and an assistance task (AT). In both scenarios, a single subject and the robot shared the living room. The NST involved a robot and a human moving in the same area, which resulted in 'spatial encounters', e.g. when the robot and human were on collision course. The AT involved the subject sitting at a table being assisted by the robot, which notices that a pen is missing and fetches it (figure 14.8). Figure 14.9 shows the layout of the simulated living room. The dashed lines indicate the movement directions of the subjects and the robot. The study included 28 subjects balanced for age-, gender- and technology-related background. The robot's behaviour was partially autonomous and partially remote controlled (Wizard-of-Oz, WoZ technique; see Gould *et al.* 1983; Dahlback *et al.* 1993; Maulsby *et al.* 1993), whereby the illusion is given to the subjects during the experiment that the robot operates fully autonomously.

Each subject performed both tasks twice. The behaviour of the robot was either 'socially interactive' or 'socially ignorant'. These two robot behaviour styles were designed by an interdisciplinary research team. The selection and classification of behaviours into these two categories was done, for the purposes of this experiment, purely on the basis of what changes the robot would make to its behaviour if no human were present. If the robot performed in an 'optimal way' (from a robotics perspective, e.g. taking the shortest path between two locations), and made little or no change to its behaviour in the presence of a human, then the behaviour was classified as *socially ignorant*. If the robot took account of the human's presence, by modifying its optimum behaviour in some way, this was classified as *socially interactive* behaviour. As little was known about how the robot should actually behave in order to be seen to be socially interactive or socially ignorant, this assumption was chosen as it was in accord with what would be seen as social behaviour by the robot from a robotics perspective.

The following behaviours were classified as *socially ignorant*.

(i) When moving in the same area as the human, the robot always took the direct path. If a human was in the way, the robot simply stopped and said 'excuse me' until the obstacle was removed.

Fig. 14.8 (*a*) Negotiated space task and (*b*) assistance task.

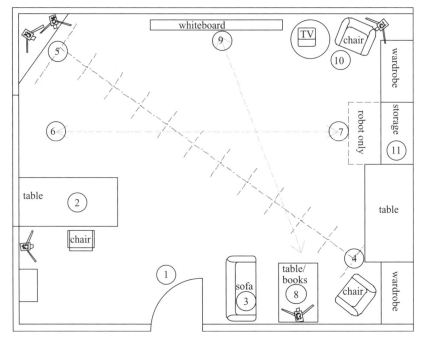

Fig. 14.9 Layout of the experimental room for the negotiated space and assistance tasks. The room was provided with a whiteboard (9) and two tables. One table was furnished with a number of domestic items— coffee cups, tray, water bottle, kettle, etc. The other table (2) was placed by the window to act as a desk for the subject to work at while performing the assistance task, a vase with flowers, a desk light, and a bottle and glass of water were placed on the table. The room also included a relaxing area, with a sofa (3), a small chair and a low rectangular coffee table. Directly opposite, next to the whiteboard, was another low round coffee table, with a television placed on it. A second small chair stood in the corner. Five network video cameras were mounted on the walls in the positions indicated, recording multiple views of the experiment.

(ii) The robot did not take an interest in what the human was doing. If the human was working at a task, the robot interrupted at any point and fetched what was required, but did not give any indication that it was actively involved, or was taking any initiative to complete the task.

(iii) The robot did not move its camera, and hence its apparent 'gaze', while moving or stationary unless it was necessary to accomplish the immediate task.

These behaviours were classified as *socially interactive*, which are as follows.

(iv) When moving in the same area as a human, the robot always modified its path to avoid getting very close to the human. Especially, if the human's back was turned, the robot moved slowly when closer than 2 m to the human and took a circuitous route.

(v) The robot took an interest in what the human was doing. It gave the appearance of look-ing actively at the human and the task being performed. It kept a close eye on the human and anticipated, by interpreting the human's movements, if it could help by fetching items. If it talked, it waited for an opportune moment to interrupt.

(vi) When either moving or stationary, the robot moved its camera in a meaningful way to indi-cate by its gaze that it was looking around in order to participate or anticipate what was happening in the living room area.

During the trials, the subjects used a comfort level device, a hand-held device that was developed specifically for this experiment and used to assess their subjective discomfort in the vicinity of the robot. Comfort level data were later matched with video observations of subjects' and robot's behaviour during the experiments. Also, a variety of questionnaires were used before the experiment, after the experiment and between the sessions, with distinct robot behaviour styles, i.e. socially ignorant and socially interactive. These included questionnaires on subjects' and robot's personality as well as general questions about attitudes towards robots and potential applications. In the same experiment, other issues were investigated, including human-to-robot and robot-to-human approach distances, documented elsewhere (Walters *et al.* 2005*b*, 2006).

In this exploratory study, we addressed a number of specific research questions. These concerned the relationship between subjects' personality characteristics and their attribution of personality characteristics to the robot, including the effect of gender, age, occupation and educational background. We also investigated whether subjects were able to recognize differences in robots' behaviour styles (socially ignorant and socially interactive) as different 'robot personalities'. In the NST we were interested in which robot behaviours made subjects most uncomfortable and how robot and subjects dynamically negotiated space. In the AT we investigated which approach (robot behaviour style) subjects found most suitable. Moreover, we assessed which robot tasks and roles people would envisage for a robot companion.

The following provides a summary of some of the main results.

— *Subject and robot personality.* For individual personality traits, subjects perceived themselves as having stronger personality characteristics compared to robots with both socially ignorant and socially interactive behaviour, regarding positive as well as negative traits. Overall, subjects did not view their own personality as similar to that of the robot's, whereby factors such as subject gender, age and level of technological experience were important in the extent to how subjects viewed their personality as being dissimilar/similar to the robot personality. Overall, subjects did not distinguish between the two different robot behaviour styles (socially ignorant and socially interactive) in terms of individual personality traits (for further details, see Woods *et al.* 2005).

— *Negotiated space task.* Results show that the majority of the subjects disliked the robot moving behind them, blocking their path or on collision path towards them, especially when the robot was within 3 m proximity. The majority of subjects experienced discomfort when the robot was closer than 3 m, within the social zone reserved for human–human face-to-face conversation between strangers, while they were performing a task. The majority of subjects were uncomfortable when the robot approached them when they were writing on the whiteboard (i.e. robot was moving behind them) or trying to move across the experimental area between the whiteboard and the desk, where the books were located (figure 9; for further details, see Koay *et al.* (2005, 2006)). Note that the results from this study need to be interpreted in the context of this particular task. In other studies where the robot approached a person or a person approached a robot, most people were comfortable with approach distances characteristic of social interaction involving friends (Walters *et al.* 2005*b*, 2006). In these situations, the subjects were not interrupted by the robot and thus were probably more tolerant of closer approach distances. This issue highlights the problem of generalizing results from HRI studies to different scenarios, robots, tasks, robot users and application areas.

— *Attitudes towards robots.* The questionnaire data showed that 40% of participants in the current study were in favour of the idea of having a robot companion in the home, compared to 80% who stated that they liked having computer technology in the home. Most subjects saw the potential role of a robot companion in the home as being an assistant, machine or servant. Few were open to the idea of having a robot as a friend or mate. Ninety per cent stated that it would be useful for the robot to do the vacuuming, compared to only 10% who would want the robot to assist with childcare duties. Subjects wanted a future robot companion to be predictable, controllable, considerate and polite. Human-like communication was desired for a robot companion. Human-like behaviour and appearance were less important (for details, see Dautenhahn *et al.* (2005)).

As can be seen from the brief description of the experiments here, the tasks for the subjects and the robot's behaviour, and the overall approach, were highly exploratory but can lay the foundation for 'robotiquette', i.e. a set of rules or heuristics guiding the robot's behaviour. However, do (aspects of) social intelligence necessarily need to be implemented in terms of specific social rules for a robot? How much of the social aspects of the behaviour are emergent and only become social in the eyes of a human observer without any corresponding, dedicated mechanisms located inside the robot?

In order to illustrate these issues, §5 investigates the case of a socially situated robot, a 'social robot without any (social) rules', whereby social behaviour emerges from simple sensorimotor rules situated in a human–robot play context.

14.5 Emerging social interaction games

In order to highlight the point that social behaviour can emerge without necessarily any specific 'social' processes being involved in creating that behaviour, we describe in the following how turn-taking behaviour was achieved in trials where a mobile robot interacted with children, in this particular case children with autism, as part of the Aurora project (described fully in §6). The principle of interactive emergence can also be found in other robotics works, including Grey Walter's biologically inspired famous robots, the 'tortoises', built in the late 1940s (Walter 1950, 1951). The robots called Elsie and Elmer could 'dance' with each other due to phototaxis, leading to mutual attraction with a light source attached to each robot, without any specific perception of 'the other robot' and with no special social rules implemented. More recent examples of emerging social behaviour between robots include, for example, experiments using simple robot–robot following behaviour that resulted from sensorimotor coordination and gave rise to imitation learning (Billard & Dautenhahn 1998). A similar principle of 'social behaviour without (social) rule' is embodied in Simon Penny's robot 'Petit Mal', built 45 years after the tortoises, with the specific purpose to interact with museum visitors as an artistic installation (Penny 2000).

Figure 14.10 shows the mobile robot used in this research. Describing the robot's control architecture goes beyond the scope of this paper, but for the purpose of this paper, it is relevant to note that the robot's behaviour was guided by the following two basic implemented behaviours:

— *obstacle avoidance*: using its infrared sensors, it causes the robot to avoid the object and move away and
— *approaching heat source*: using input from its heat sensor about directions of heat sources, it causes the robot to turn and move towards the heat source.

Both behaviours are active at the same time and triggered by their respective sensor systems. The robot's behaviour was purely reactive, without any internal representations of the environment.

Fig. 14.10 The Labo-1 robot used in the trials on playful interaction games with children with autism. The robot is 38×28 cm large, 21 cm high, mass 6.5 kg and has four wheels. Its four-wheel differential drive allows smooth turning. The robot has eight active infrared sensors positioned at the front (four sensors), rear (two) and one sensor on each side. A pyroelectric heat sensor was mounted on the front end of the robot and enabled it to detect head sources. This sensor was used to detect children. A voice generation device was used optionally to create speech phrases such as 'hello there', 'where are you', 'can't see you', depending on its sensory input (e.g. whether a child was detected or not). The speech was used purely to add variety to the robot's behaviour.

At the beginning of the trials with children, the robot is placed in the centre of the room with some open space. Thus, with no obstacles or heat sources within the robot's range, it will remain motionless until it perceives either an obstacle or a heat source. Note that the heat sensor could similarly respond to a warm radiator, since nowhere within the robot's control system were the children 'recognized'. The child could interact with the robot in any position they liked, e.g. standing or kneeling in front of the robot or lying on the floor. As long as the child was within the robot's sensor range, interaction games could emerge (Figure 14.11).

Since a child, from the perspective of the robot, is perceived as an obstacle and at the same time as a heat source, these two simultaneously active processes gave rise to a variety of situations. Once the robot perceives a heat source, it will turn towards it and approach as closely as possible. While it approaches closely, the infrared sensors activate the obstacle-avoidance behaviour, so that the robot will move away from the heat source. From a distance, it can again detect the heat source and approach. This interplay of two behaviours resulted in the following situations.

(i)   If the child remains stationary and immobile, the robot will approach and then remain at a certain distance from the child, the particular distance being determined by internal variables set in the computer program as well as properties of the robot's sensorimotor system. From an interaction perspective, the observed behaviour can be called 'approach'.

(ii) If the child moves around the room without paying attention to the robot, the robot will approach and seemingly 'try to keep a certain distance' from the child. As long as the child stays within the robot's sensor range, this will result in a 'following' behaviour. From an interaction perspective, the behaviour can be called 'keeping contact'.

(iii) If the child moves around the room but pays attention to the robot in a 'playful' manner, the child might run away from the robot, waiting for it to approach again, upon approach running away again. Here, the child can be said to 'play' with the robot a game where he is being chased.

(iv) If the child approaches the robot, the robot will move away. If done repeatedly, this can cause the robot to be 'chased across the room' or even 'cornered'. While being 'chased away', the robot will remain 'focused' on the child, due to its heat sensors that cause it to turn towards the child. Here, the child plays a chasing game with the robot, whereby roles are reversed compared to (iii).

(v) Alternating phases of (iii) and (iv) can lead to the emergence of interaction games involving turn-taking (see example in figure 14.11*b* showing a child lying on the floor in front of the robot). The child stretches his arm out towards the robot and moves his hand towards the robot's front (where the infrared sensors are located), which causes the robot to back-up (i.e. triggering obstacle-avoidance behaviour). The robot then moves backwards, but only up to a certain distance where it again starts to approach the child (guided by its heat sensor). It approaches the child up to a point where the infrared sensors (triggered by the child's body or stretched-out hand held at the same height as the infrared sensor) cause obstacle avoidance once again. As far as approach and avoidance behaviours are concerned, we observe turn-taking in the interaction (figure 14.12). In this situation, the child very quickly 'discovered' how to make the robot back-up and the interaction continued for approximately 20 min until the child had to leave and go back to class.

The interactive situations (iii)–(v) described above are robust in the sense that any movements of the child that bring parts of his body closer to the robot can trigger the heat or infrared

Fig. 14.11 (*a*) A child with autism playing a chasing game. The boy went down on his knees, which gives him a better position facing the robot. (*b*) Another child decided to lie down on the floor and let the robot approach, resulting in turn-taking games. (*c*) A third child playing chasing games with a different mobile robot (Pekee, produced by Wany Robotics).

Fig. 14.12 Playing turn-taking games with the robot. See text for a detailed description of this game.

sensors: the system does not depend on the precise perception of the child's body position, location and movements. However, this robustness requires the interactive context of a child playing with the robot, or, in other words, the robot's environment must provide salient stimuli in the 'appropriate' order and with appropriate timing to which the robot can respond appropriately (according to its design). The lack of this context and the corresponding stimuli can result in 'non-social' behaviour, e.g. if the robot were placed in front of a radiator, it would approach up to a certain distance, stop and remain immobile. Also, for example, in situation (ii) described above, if the child moves around in the room too quickly so that the robot loses contact, then the robot will stop unless any other obstacles or heat sources are perceived. Exactly the same two behaviours are responsible for these non-social as well as the other socially interactive behaviours.

Situations (iii)–(v) above exemplify interactive games played between the child and the robot, representing a case of interactive emergence, defined by Hendriks-Jansen (1996), whereby 'patterns of activity whose high-level structure cannot be reduced to specific sequences of movements may emerge from the interactions between simple reflexes and the particular environment to which they are adapted'. The adaptation of the robot to the 'interactive environment', i.e. the tuning of its sensorimotor behaviour, was done by the robot's programmer. All the situations described above depend on a variety of parameters (e.g. the robot's speed) that had to be determined in preliminary experiments. Thus, the robot's behaviour has been carefully tuned to afford playful interactions when placed in a context involving children. The robot's reflex-like programming based on the two behaviours controlling approach and avoidance was complemented by the child discovering how to interact with the robot via its two sensor systems (heat and infrared sensors) located at its front. The patterns of turn-taking and/or chasing emerged without an explicit representation in the robot's control program, no internal or external clock drove the turns and no internal goal or representation of the environment was used. The timing of the turns and chasing games emerged from the embodied sensorimotor coupling of the two interaction partners, i.e. the child and the robot in the environment. This aspect of mutual activity in interaction is reflected in Ogden et al.'s (2002) definition of interaction as a reciprocal activity in which the actions of each agent influence the actions of the other agents engaged in the same activities resulting in a mutually constructed pattern of complementary behaviour.

Note that turn-taking is a widely studied phenomenon in psychology as well as computer science and robotics, whereby various research questions are studied, such as the evolution of turn-taking (e.g. Iizuka & Ikegami 2004), or the design of a psychologically and neurobiologically plausible control architecture for a robot that can give rise to turn-taking and imitative behaviour (e.g. Nadel et al. 2004). In the above example, the robot's control program is non-adaptive; it does not learn but simply responds reactively to certain environmental stimuli. However, the very simple example above shows that very few (in this case two) carefully designed behaviours for a simple robot (simple compared to the state of the art in robotics in 2006) can result in interesting and (from the point of view of the children) enjoyable interaction games played with children. Such a bottom-up perspective on socially interactive behaviour demonstrates that for the study of certain kind of social behaviour, assumptions about the robot's required level of social intelligence need to be considered carefully. Rather than modelling the social environment explicitly in the robot's control program, placing the robot in such an environment where it is equipped with simple behaviours responding to this particular environment serves its purpose ('the social world is its own best model'). From an observer's point of view, the robot played interaction games with the children, without any explicit knowledge about turn-taking or the 'meaning' of interactions. However, as long as the robot is involved in interactions with a child, numerous hypotheses might be created about the robot's (social) intelligence. Only when taken out of the interactive context which it had been designed for and adapted to (e.g. when placed in front of a radiator) can different hypotheses be tested, in this case illuminating the basic processes driving the robot's behaviour that do not entail any social dimension.

Now, let us extrapolate this work, assuming a sophisticated robot that has been carefully designed to afford a variety of interactions. With a large number of sensors and actuators, a simple parallel execution of behaviour will not be adequate, so more sophisticated behaviour-arbitration mechanisms need to be used (e.g. as described by Arkin (1998)), and internal states may regulate its interactions with the environment. The robot's movements, timing of behaviours, etc. have been carefully designed for the specific purpose of interacting with people. Thus, it can not only approach and avoid, but also interact verbally and non-verbally in a variety of ways inspired by human behaviour (body language, speech, gestures, etc., its interaction kinesics mimicking humans). Now, let us assume that the robot is indistinguishable in its appearance from humans, it is an android (MacDorman & Ishiguro 2006). We observe the robot in different situations where it meets and interacts with people. How can we find out about the robot's level of social intelligence, whether it is 'purely a clever collection of stimulus-response behaviours' or whether it has an internal representation of 'social behaviour'? Similar to putting our small mobile robot in front of a radiator, we might test the android by exposing it to various types of social situation, attempting to see it failing, so that the nature of the failure might illuminate its (lack of) assumptions and knowledge about the world. We might design a rigorous experimental schedule, but for such a sophisticated robot, we might spend a lifetime going through all possible (combinations of) social situations. But if we are lucky, then we might see the robot failing, i.e. behaving inappropriately in a social situation. It might fail disastrously, e.g. getting stuck in front of a radiator. However, it might fail similarly to how humans might fail in certain social situations, e.g. showing signs of 'claustrophobia' on a packed underground train or expressing anxiety when being monitored and assessed in experiments. If it fails in a human-like manner, we probably consider it as a candidate machine with human-like social intelligence, or even consider that these failures or flaws might merit it to be treated as human. But we will still not know exactly what mechanisms are driving its social behaviour. However, does it matter?

14.6 Playing with robots: the Aurora project

The interactions described in §5 were observed as part of research carried out in the Aurora project, which investigates the usage of robotic playmates in autism therapy. The aspect of play is a core part of the project.

Play therapy can play an important part in increasing quality of life, learning skills and social inclusion.[1] According to the National Autistic Society (NAS; http://www.nas.org.uk), the following argument can be put forward in favour of teaching children with autism to play. Play allows children to learn and practise new skills in safe and supportive environments (Boucher 1999), providing a medium through which they develop skills, experiment with roles and interact with others (Restal & Magill-Evans 1994). Children with autism are disadvantaged in their use of play for these purposes. Play also matters for children with autism, because playing is the norm in early childhood, and a lack of play skills can aggravate children's social isolation and underline their difference from other children (Boucher 1999). Boucher emphasizes that play should be fun. Improving the play skills of children with autism gives them a sense of mastery and increases their pleasure and their motivation to play (that is a justifiable aim in itself). Play gives children with autism, who may have difficulty in expressing feelings and thoughts in words, chances to express themselves, and offers opportunities to engage within mutually satisfying social play, which can be used as a vehicle for developing the social skills that they so often lack. These opportunities are created by a shared understanding of pleasure experienced in play episodes (Sherratt & Peter 2002). It also prevents secondary disabilities by enabling participation in social and cultural events (Jordan & Libby 1997). Sherratt & Peter (2002) suggest that teaching children with autism to play may increase a fluidity of thought and reduce conceptual fragmentation. In particular, if play is taught to young children, it may assist them in reducing repetitive and rigid behavioural patterns and encourage communication development. Wolfberg's (1999) review of the intervention literature discovered that play (particularly with peers) has had a relatively small role in the education and treatment of children with autism.

The Aurora project investigates the use of robots in autism therapy, trying to engage children in therapeutically relevant playful interactions with a robot (involving turn-taking, imitation, joint attention and proactive behaviour), as well as using robotic toys as mediators to the social environment.

In Dautenhahn & Werry (2004), the basic motivation, starting points, related work, as well as the psychological background of this work are discussed in detail. Here, we can only provide a brief summary of the main rationale underlying the project. Literature suggests that people with autism enjoy interacting with computers (e.g. Powell 1996; Murray 1997; Moore 1998), which provides a starting point for our investigations. Robots are different from computers, since interacting with them is embodied and situated in the real world, and requires the child to involve their body in a more extensive way (compared to just operating a mouse or keyboard). Thus, the starting point of our work is the assumption that autistic children enjoy *playing* with robots. The enjoyment of the children is an important element in our work, based on our belief that interaction itself could be rewarding to the child. Typically developing children can experience social interaction as rewarding and enjoyable. Consequently, they are not just responding to other people, but they actively seek contact. It is unclear to what extent robots can teach autistic children the 'fun' of play and interaction, but it seems that a playful context is a good starting point for our investigations, similar to an approach put forward by Ferrara and Hill for language therapy:

> … A more appropriate starting place for therapeutic intervention with autistic children might be to focus on their development of social play. Social objects with low intensity should first be presented in a game that has a highly predictive and repetitive sequence of activities. Complexity of social stimuli and game activities should gradually increase in intensity. When the child begins to show pleasure in these games and to initiate them, the introduction of language and cognitive tasks matching the complexity of the game would be appropriate.
>
> (Ferrara & Hill 1980, p. 56)

Robots have been proposed to be used for the study of child development (Michaud & Caron 2002; Michaud *et al.* 2005) or rehabilitation (Plaisant *et al.* 2000), autism therapy (Weir & Emanuel 1976; Dautenhahn 1999*b*; Werry & Dautenhahn 1999; Kozima 2002; Michaud & Théberge-Turmel 2002; Davis *et al.* 2005; Kozima *et al.* 2005) and autism diagnosis (Scassellati 2005). For a critical discussion of using robots in autism therapy, see Robins *et al.*(2005*a*).

The use of robots in autism therapy poses many challenges. Potentially different solutions might prove suitable for different groups of children with different abilities and personal interests.

The particular therapeutic issues that should be addressed are also likely to influence the choice of robotic designs used.

So far, we have been using two types of robots: a small humanoid robotic doll and mobile robots (figures 14.13 and 14.14). The robots are small and safe for children to use. Our initial trials confirmed that autistic children generally take great interest in the robots and seem to enjoy playing with them. Many children smiled, laughed or showed other signs of enjoyment during the interactions with the robot. We also observed vocalizations and verbalizations addressed to the robots. We use this playful scenario as a context where the children can be engaged in therapeutically or educationally useful behaviour. Encouraging proactiveness of behaviour in autistic children is one of the major goals of the Aurora project. Addressing deficits in turn-taking and imitation skills are additional goals. Importantly, our motivation is not to develop the robot as a replacement for teachers, other caretakers or people in general. The Aurora viewpoint is that robots should mediate between the (from an autistic child's perspective) widely unpredictable world of 'people' and the much more predictable world of machines. However, due to their situatedness and embodiment, the robots never behave completely predictably. This is an important issue, since otherwise the robots would only perpetuate repetitive or stereotypical behaviour. The purpose of our robots is to help autistic children to better understand and interact with other people. So far, no clinical trials have been carried out regarding the therapeutic impact of interaction with the robot. However, results are encouraging, in particular those gained in a longitudinal study, which exposed children with autism to the robot repeatedly over several months.

We study robots with different appearances and capabilities in order to facilitate, investigate and compare different types of interactions. We adopted an approach where the children can freely interact with the mobile robots, e.g. while playing with the robot, the children can sit on the floor, move around the robot, touch the robot or simply stand in a corner of the room and watch the robot. Figure 14.15 shows that children thus use their whole body in interactions with the robot.

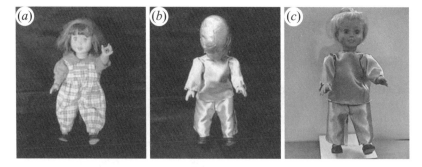

Fig. 14.13 (*a*) The Robota robot and (*b*, *c*) its modified appearances used in the trials with children with autism. The robot's main body contains the electronic boards and the motors that drive the arms, legs and head (Billard 2003). A pilot study showed the use of the robot's sensing abilities and autonomous behaviour was not suitable for our trials, thus the robot has since then been used as a remote-controlled puppet (controlled by the experimenter). A summary of the use of this robot in autism therapy and developmental psychology is provided by Billard *et al.* (2006). Experiments describing how children with autism react to different robot appearances are reported by Robins *et al.*(2004*b,d*).

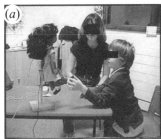  

Fig. 14.14 Children with autism playing with a robot. (*a*) The picture shows a child interacting with Robota, the humanoid robot doll, playing an imitation game, whereby the robot can imitate arm movements when the child is sitting opposite the robot facing it and moving its arms in explicit ways that can be recognized by the robot (Dautenhahn & Billard 2002). Shown are the robot, the child and a carer providing encouragement. This was the first trial using Robota for playing with children with autism. Owing to the constrained nature of the set-up, required by the limitations of current robotic technology, we decided not to use this robot any longer as an autonomously operating machine, and later only used the robot remotely controlled by the experimenter (out of the children's sight). In one of the experiments, we varied the appearance of the robot and found that the children's initial response towards a 'plain-looking' robot is more interactive than towards the robot with its doll face (Robins *et al.* 2004*b*; figure 14.13). (*b*) The picture shows a child with autism playing imitation games with the robot. Note the completely unconstrained nature of the interactions, i.e. the child himself had decided to move towards and face the robot, on his own terms, after he had become familiar with the robot (as part of a longitudinal study; Robins *et al.* 2004*c*, 2005*b*). (*c*) The picture shows an autistic child playing with a mobile robot (Pekee, produced by Wany Robotics). The advantage of small mobile robots is that it allows the children to move around freely and adopt different positions, e.g. lying on the floor, kneeling, walking, even stepping over the robot, etc., exploring the three-dimensional space of potential interactions. In experiments with typically developing children, we developed a technique that can classify interactions of the children with the robot, using clustering techniques on the robot's sensor data. We were able to identify different play patterns that could be linked to some general activity profiles of the children (e.g. bold, shy, etc.; Salter *et al.* 2004). We will use this technique in the future to allow the robot to adapt to the child during the interactions (Salter *et al.* 2006; François *et al.* 2007). In principle, this technique might also be used to assess the children's play levels or, possibly, for diagnostic purposes.

The mobile robots we have been using are *Labo-1* (donated by Takashi Gomi from Applied AI Systems) and *Pekee* (produced by Wany Robotics). The mobile robots are programmed so that the children can play simple interaction games with them, such as chasing, following and other simple turn-taking games. In a comparative study involving children with autism playing with Labo-1 as well as a non-robotic passive toy of the same size (figure 14.16), we found that children with autism pay significantly more attention to the robot and direct more eye gaze at the robot (Werry & Dautenhahn, 2007).

The small humanoid robot Robota (Billard 2003) is a doll shaped versatile robot that can move its arms, legs and head, in addition to having facilities for vision, speech and for producing music. However, interactions with Robota, e.g. whereby the robot can imitate children's arm movements, are more constrained, i.e. they require the children to sit at a table and face the robot (Dautenhahn & Billard 2002). Consequently, we performed a series of trials using the robot as a puppet controlled by an experimenter. This approach turned out to be very successful and resulted in a series of trials where children demonstrated interactive and communicative competencies, using the robot as *mediator* in order to interact with the experimenter

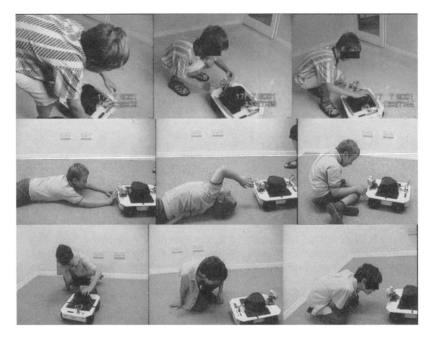

Fig. 14.15 Varieties of interactions in playful encounters of children with autism and a mobile robot. Note the embodied nature of the interactions: children are using a variety of different postures and movements in order to play with the robot.

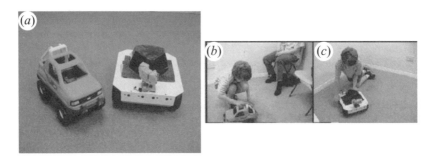

Fig. 14.16 (*a*) Toy truck on the left and Labo-1 robot on the right. (*b*) Child interacting with the toy truck and (*c*) the robot. This comparative study involved 17 children with autism between 6 and 9 years old. Trials lasted approximately 10 min, i.e. the children interacted with the robot for 4 min. Next, both toy truck and robot were present for 2 min (robot switched off). Then, children played with the toy truck for 4 min. The order of presenting the toy truck and the robot was randomized. The toy truck (robot) was hidden during interactions with the robot (toy truck). Owing to the nature of our approach, we stopped a trial when a child seemed to become bored, distressed or wanted to leave the room. Interactions with the toy truck involved a lot of repetitive behaviour, e.g. spinning the wheels, pushing it against a wall; all children very quickly lost interest. Interactions with the robot were much more 'lively', the children were more engaged and played with the robot longer than with the toy truck. Note that any statements we make about the engagement of the children have been confirmed by teachers, carers and autism experts watching the videos with us. Differences were confirmed in behavioural coding of attention and eye gaze in both conditions. Details of this work are reported by Werry (2003) and Werry & Dautenhahn (2007).

or other children (Werry *et al.*2001; Dautenhahn 2003; Robins *et al.* 2004*a*, 2005*c*), as shown in figure 14.17. Generally, the experimenter played an important part in these trials, very different from other experimental set-ups, which try to remove the experimenter as much as possible. Instead, the experimenter, who in our case is an experienced therapist as well as computer scientist, played a crucial part in how he remotely controlled the robot, being sensitive to the children's behaviour and the overall context (Robins & Dautenhahn 2006; figure 14.17, top row).

Our general set-up of the trials is very playful; the children are not required to solve any tasks other than playing, and the only purpose of the robot is to engage children with autism in therapeutically relevant behaviours, such as turn-taking and imitation. A key issue is that the children proactively initiate interactions rather than merely respond to particular stimuli. Additionally, the chosen set-up is social, i.e. it involves not only the robot and the autistic child present, but also can include other children, the teacher or other adults. This social scenario is used by some

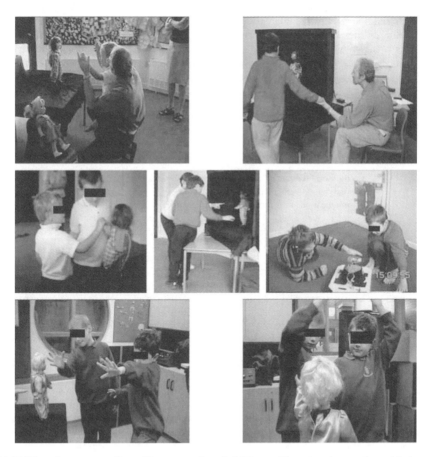

Fig. 14.17 The robot as a mediator. Top: examples of children with autism interacting with the experimenter, with the robot acting as a mediator (Robins *et al.* 2005*b*). Middle and bottom: the robot as a mediator facilitating interactions between children with autism. These examples emphasize the ultimate goal of the Aurora project, namely to help children with autism to connect to the social world of humans, and not necessarily to bond with robots.

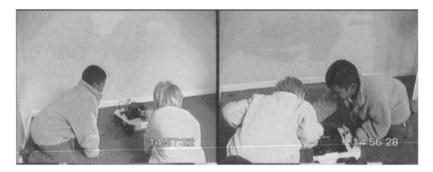

Fig. 14.18 A pair of children with autism simultaneously playing with the Labo-1 robot.

Table 14.1 Summary of trials where pairs of children played with the robot (see details in Werry *et al.*
(2001)). (The children were paired up by the teachers according to mutual familiarity and social/
communication abilities. Although only three pairs were studied, interesting differences in how the
children are playing with each other and the robot can be identified. This case study clearly shows how
a robot can mediate play and interactions among children with autism. Further studies need to
investigate whether the robot can improve children's social play skills. The table is modified from
Dautenhahn (2003).)

social abilities in social interactions with people	level of interest in robot	play style	child behaviours directed at robot
highest (interacting with people)	high interest in robot—a very strong focus of attention and curiosity; good verbal and communication skills used to interact with adults (robot-centred communication, e.g. asking questions about what robot can do)	social play: children were playing and communicating with each other, the robot, and the adults present; social learning/teaching: in one instance, the experimenter instructed one child how to chase the robot, the child then instructed the other child	exploratory and interactive play with robot (touching, operating, etc.), interest in chasing, following a robot's speech, questioning experimenters about robot's skills, great interest in 'what robot should do', etc.
medium (few interactions with people)	varied interest in the robot; examples: one child was more interested in the car park visible through the room's window than in the robot, and another child interacted with the robot, but treated other people present in the room as an 'audience'	non-social play: children were playing with robot simultaneously, but not playing with each other, 'accidental' interaction when both competed for robot's 'attention', the teacher occasionally had to give guidance/calm children down when children grew bored	interest in robot's destructive skills, cornering robot, shouting at robot to get it to move, operating robot (touching, manipulating)
lowest (withdrawn, very little interaction with people)	both children showed great interest in playing with the robot	non-social play: one child dominates the interaction, an open competition for robot emerges, occasional use of communication skills in trying to obstruct the other child, e.g. 'leave him alone'	giving vocal commands and directions to robot, operating robot

children in a very constructive manner, demonstrating their communicative competence, i.e. they use the robot as a focus of attention in order to interact and/or communicate with other people in the room. Trials with a mobile robot included pair-trials, where pairs of children were simultaneously exposed to the robot (Werry *et al.* 2001; figure 14.18). Table 14.1 presents different play styles that could be observed, ranging from social to non-social and competitive play. Similarly, trials involving the small robot doll and pairs of children elicited a variety of interactions among the children (Robins *et al.* 2005c).

An important part of our work is the development of appropriate scenarios and techniques in order to evaluate details of robot–child interactions. We developed a technique that can be used to quantitatively evaluate video data on robot–child interactions. The technique is based on micro-behaviours (Tardiff *et al.* 1995), including eye gaze and attention. We used this technique in the comparative study mentioned above, where we studied how autistic children interact with a mobile robot as opposed to a non-robotic toy (Werry 2003; Werry & Dautenhahn, in press). The same technique has also been used in analysing interactions of children with autism with the small robotic doll (e.g. Robins *et al.* 2004c, 2005b). A range of different qualitative as well as quantitative evaluation techniques are likely to be needed in order to reveal not only statistical regularities and patterns, but also meaningful events of behaviour in context. An application of conversation analysis has revealed interesting aspects of how the robot can elicit communication and interaction competencies of children with autism (Dautenhahn *et al.* 2002; Robins *et al.* 2004a). Thus, using robots in autism therapy and education poses many challenges. Our work, grounded in assistive technology and computer science, is highly exploratory in nature: new robot designs, novel experimental set-ups and scenarios and new experimental paradigms are investigated; also, various evaluation techniques, known from ethology and psychology, need to be adapted to the specific context of this work. Aurora is a long-term project the author has been pursuing since 1998. Results do not come easily, but the work remains challenging and rewarding; the enjoyment of the children is the best reward.

From a conceptual viewpoint, which types of play could any type of robot encourage with children with autism? Studies of play and social participation lead to conceptual distinctions suggested by Parten (1932; table 14.2). With respect to these categories, in the context of using robots as assistive technology, what type of social participation can occur and/or can be encouraged? Table 14.2 provides suggestions on possible studies involving robots and children. The range of possible play scenarios involving robots and children is potentially huge. For children with autism, as well as other children, robots are fun to play with. Thus, robots seem a promising tool to teach children with autism how to play in a way that might integrate them better in groups of typically developing and autistic children.

The Aurora project is an example of HRI research, where human–robot as well as human–human relationships matter. Possible relationships between robots and people are discussed in more detail in §7.

14.7 Different paradigms regarding human–robot relationships in HRI research

In this section, two paradigms regarding the relationships between humans and robots in HRI research are distinguished as follows:

— the caretaker paradigm and
— the assistant /companion paradigm

Table 14.2 Types of play and social participation according to Parten (1932) and applied to robot–child play.

types of play and social participation	characterizations for activities in children	possible studies involving robots and children with autism
unoccupied behaviour	child is apparently not playing, observing any activities that might be exciting, otherwise moves their body around or glances around the room	will be observed if a child is not interested in the robotic set-up at all and/or when other stimuli present are stronger and more attractive to the child; we can expect their will look at the experimenters or other adults/children present, out of the window, etc; in one of the trials where pairs of children played with the Labo-1 robot (see table 14.1 and figure 14.18), we observed this behaviour with an autistic boy who loved cars, in a situation where the experimental room had a window facing the car park; instead of playing with the robot, let alone the other child, he decided to watch the car park during the trials, despite encouragement from the teacher present to investigate the robot
onlooker	child watches other children play from close distance; often talks to the children who are playing, but does not enter the game	if a situation involves a robot and two or more children, this situation might arise when one or more children play with the robot and another child or other children are 'onlookers'; depending on the interest of the children, the robot might be used as a motivational object to 'join in'.
solitary independent play	child plays alone and independently with toys different from those used by other children who can be in the vicinity, child pursues their own activity independently of what others are doing	this is the typical situation in a scenario involving one child and the robot, unless the set-up facilitates 'mediation', i.e. allowing contact to be made to the experimenter or other children, as discussed above; it might also happen in a set-up involving one robot and two children; in this case one child withdraws (or is made to withdraw by the other child; see table 14.1, which mentions an instance of competitive play) and the other child is left alone playing with the robot; note: in trials with pairs of children described above (Werry *et al.* 2001), we also identified non-social, competitive play, i.e. children competed with each other for access to the (robotic) toy; this can be expected, in particular, for autistic children with low social skills
parallel activity	child plays independently but with similar toys as children in the vicinity use, plays beside other children, no attempt to influence or modify the other children's behaviour, does not try to engage with them	let us assume a hypothetical experimental set-up involving two robots and two children; here, both children might then play 'on their own' with the robot, manipulating objects, etc., beside the other child, without any connection between their play; let us now consider a modified scenario involving one mobile robot whereby parts of the robot can be controlled independently by two children, e.g. one child can control the robot's movements on the ground and the other can control the robot's arm that can pick up objects; we might observe parallel play; however, the situation might afford coordination of the children's activities and thus lead to cooperative play; see below

Table 14.2 (*cont.*)

types of play and social participation	characterizations for activities in children	possible studies involving robots and children with autism
associative play	child plays with other children, borrowing and loaning material, but no coordination or organization of activities around 'goals' or materials, each child acts as they like; all children in a group will be engaged in very similar or identical activity, which is the focus of the conversation	in the case of two children playing with two robots, the children might coordinate to play the same game with the robot, e.g. a chasing game as the common goal, but each child is playing it on his own
cooperative or organized supplementary play	child plays in group organized for some purpose: achieving some competitive goal, making a product, playing a formal game, etc; strong sense of belonging to the group; one or two members direct activities of others, roles are assigned, division of labour so that children's activities complement each other to achieve a common goal	children play truly 'together', e.g. assign roles to each other, divide the labour into different jobs, try to achieve the goal together; based on the scenario involving a robot controlled by two children, in this situation, the children might pay attention to what the other is doing, thus coordinating the robot's movements on the ground and its arm movements; a common goal could be, for example, to arrange objects and build structures together, etc; through coordination, they could achieve results that none of them could achieve alone: e.g. picking up objects and building a tower, or collecting objects in the play area and arranging them into a pile; if competition is considered to be useful, a game could be introduced, e.g. in the case of robots that can manipulate objects building a tower as high as possible; in the case of a mobile robot, 'herding' the robot together could be common goal; investigating how the robot responds or 'plays' with each child could be another goal the children could explore

(a) The caretaker paradigm in human–robot interaction

This paradigm considers humans as caretakers of robots: the role of the human is to identify and respond to the robot's emotional and social 'needs'. The human needs to keep the robot 'happy' which implies showing behaviours towards the robot characteristic of behaviour towards infants or baby animals.

In this approach, humans interacting with the robot are expected to adopt the role of a 'care-taker' for the robot, which is considered an 'artificial creature'. In this robot-centred view, the human needs to identify and respond to the robot's internal needs, e.g. by satisfying its 'social drives'. This approach is clearly demonstrated in Breazeal's (2002) work on Kismet, a robotic head with facial features. The robot is treated as a 'baby infant' or 'puppy robot' with characteristic specific and exaggerated child-like features satisfying the 'Kindchenschema' (baby pattern, baby scheme, *schéma <<bébé>>*). The Kindchenschema is a combination of features that are characteristic of infants, babies or baby animals, which appeals to the nurturing instinct in people (and many other mammals) and trigger respective behaviours. The concept of the Kindchenschema goes back to the ethologist Lorenz (1971), who claimed that when confronted with a child, certain social behaviour patterns involved when 'caring for the young' are released by an innate response to certain cues typically characterizing babies. These cues include, for example, a proportionally large head with a protruding forehead, large ears and eyes below the midline of the head, small nose, and, generally, a rounded body shape. Such a set of characteristics has been exploited widely in the toy market, for comics, and also recently for computer animated characters. The young ones of many animals, most notably mammals, and even the adults of certain species (e.g. bear, squirrel, dolphin) show certain of these features that make them more attractive to people than other animals that do not show these features.

Note that eliciting social responses towards artefacts does not necessarily require implementation of features of the Kindchenschema. Braitenberg (1984) discussed in a series of thought experiments that people would attribute goals, intentions and even emotions to his vehicles, whose behaviour was guided by simple sensorimotor couplings, e.g. a robot that would go towards a light source whenever it could perceive it might be interpreted as 'liking' the light source, a different robot avoiding the light source and driving away at high speed might be said to 'be afraid' of it. Seminal experiments by Heider & Simmel (1944) had already demonstrated the tendency of subjects to interpret the behaviour of moving geometric shapes on a screen in terms of intentionality. With regard to computers, Reeves & Nass (1996) provided a powerful argument for what they labelled the media equation: media = real life—'People treat new media like real people …. People confuse media and real life …. People's responses to media are fundamentally social and natural …. Media are full participants in our social and natural world'. Indeed, experiments show that computers even elicit cultural and gender stereotypes; they evoke emotional and other responses as part of our natural social pattern of interaction (see a fuller discussion of these issues by (Dautenhahn 2004*a*)).

However, similarly to a child who might pretend that the wooden stick in his hand is a sword but clearly knows that the object is not a real sword, we *know* that computers are not people: we easily dispose of them, we clearly do not treat them as family members or friends, etc. Work by Kahn *et al.* (2006) has shown that while children treat an AIBO robot in many ways like a real dog and interact with it socially, they do not perceive it exactly like a real dog, e.g. do not attribute moral standing to it. Thus, while we are building (some kind of) social relationship with technological devices, including computers and robots, do we *really* want to *bond* with computers?

According to Dunbar and the social brain hypothesis (Dunbar 1993, 1996, 1998, 2003), one important factor in the evolution of primate brains and primate intelligence was the need to deal with increasingly complex social dynamics (primate politics), which justifies the 'expensive' nature of large brains, i.e. approximately 20% of our resting energy being used to keep the brain operational. Also, Dunbar argues that human language has evolved as an efficient means of social bonding (2.8 times more efficient than physical grooming used by non-human primates as a bonding mechanism). However, humans need to be selective regarding how many 'friends' they have: according to Dunbar there is an evolutionary constraint, a cognitive limit of 150 on the number of members of our social networks (individualized relationships, not counting 'anonymous' contacts we could potentially build, e.g. via email with strangers). Thus, as I have argued in more detail elsewhere (Dautenhahn 2004*a*), robots (or virtual 'pets') trying to be our friends, and requiring us to treat them like friends, might overload our cognitive capacities.

Moreover, maintaining good relationships with family and friends does not come 'for free', it involves certain efforts, which include the following:

— *Emotional investment* in our children, other family members and friends (implies not only fun in interaction, but also entails expectations, commitments, concerns, disappointments, etc.).

— *Psychological investment.* Although for most people applying a theory of mind, perceiving and expressing empathy, paying close attention to others' needs, reading others' behaviour and identifying subtle cues that might be important in regulating interactions, listening and interpreting language, coordinating turns in interaction, managing cooperation, handling arguments and discussions in dyadic and group situations, memorizing interaction histories, etc., seem to come 'naturally', many of these skills require (modification by) learning during early socialization and development; thus they come at a psychological 'cost'. For example, how much empathy can we express in one day? A 'mechanical', psychologically/emotionally detached response could be given easily. However, empathizing in the sense of re-experiencing and relating to own and other's experiences requires far more effort. Medical staff can adopt a 'professional attitude', but with the real danger of looking at the 'patient', rather than the 'person'; they have been criticized for this lack of empathy. Recently, state-of-the-art virtual environment technology has been used to foster empathy with patients, allowing medical doctors to see and experience the world through their patients' eyes and body, continuing other activities which have been ongoing for several decades aimed at fostering empathy using interpersonal communication, and also empathy training for medical students and doctors (Kramer *et al.* 1989; Evans *et al.* 1991). The need for such types of training highlights the problem of empathizing with strangers very frequently, even after short-term contact, and on a daily basis. If empathy came for free, it would not be considered demanding or exhausting to communicate in an 'empathic' way with dozens of patients each day.

— *Physiological investment.* Communication and interaction are energy consuming, and speaking, gesturing, an extended period of firm concentration, etc., are physical activities. Giving a keynote speech can be as exhausting as chasing behind a bus.

Elaborating the above points in great detail would go beyond the scope of this paper. The main purpose is to indicate that social interaction involves emotional, physical and physiological activities that have a cost. What do we get in return from interactions with humans or other social animals (e.g. dogs)? The answer is that usually we gain *a lot*, e.g. emotional support from family, friendship, love and companionship, apart from the fact that cooperation is a core ingredient of, and makes possible, human culture. However, humans, dogs and other biological organisms, which we might consider our friends are sensitive beings, i.e. we 'invest' in them and the return is 'real' (as far as one can tell that emotions, love and friendship really exist).

How about possible investments towards robots? Social interaction and communication with robots are costly too. If humans are expected to interact with robots similarly to human friends or children, then these costs will also occur in HRI. Do we want to make the same investments in robots that we make, for example, in our friends or children? Do we want to worry about how to fulfil our robots' emotional and social needs? Do we get the same 'reward' from an infant robot smiling at us compared to a child (assuming that for the time being, we are still able to clearly distinguish between robots and humans in face-to-face interaction; cf. discussion of robot/human indistinguishability by Dautenhahn (2004*a*) and MacDorman & Ishiguro (2006)). Is a robot really 'happy' when it smiles, or are robot emotions simulated or real? Can mechanical interactions be as rewarding as those with biological organisms? Do we get the same pay-off from HRI as from human–human interaction in terms of emotional support, friendship and love? Answers to these questions are likely to be culturally dependent, as well as specific to certain application areas (e.g. medical benefits might outweigh other concerns). Is it ethically justifiable to aim to create robots that people bond with, e.g. in the case of elderly people or people with special needs?

(b) The companion paradigm in human–robot interaction

> This paradigm considers robots as caretakers or assistants of humans: the role of the robot is to identify and respond to the human's needs, primarily in the sense of assisting in certain tasks. The robot needs to ensure the human is satisfied and happy (with its behaviour), which implies showing behaviours towards the human that are comfortable and socially acceptable considering a particular user.

In §4 the concept of a robot companion was discussed in more detail. The companion paradigm emphasizes the assistant role of a robot, i.e. a useful machine, able to recognize and respond to a human's needs, trying to be useful. A companion robot assisting a person in everyday environments and tasks adopts a role similar to that of personal assistants or butlers, consistent with our results reported in §4. Important characteristics for such a robot are to be considerate, proactive and non-intrusive, to work towards a relationship of trust and confidentiality with the human, to possess 'smooth' communicative skills, to be flexible, willing to learn and adapt, and be competent.

Note that this is different from a 'master–slave' metaphor of human–robot relationships. Relationships with robots were also an issue in Karel Čapek's famous play RUR (Rossum's Universal Robots), which premiered in 1921 and introduced the word 'robot'. Here, robots were 'artificial people', machines that could be mistaken for humans (thus more closely related to present-day work on androids; MacDorman & Ishiguro 2006). The play introduces a robot factory that sells these human-like robots as a cheap labour force, while later the robots revolt against their human masters, a favourite scenario in the science fiction literature and movies, but a highly unlikely scenario from a robotics point of view.

The notion of a 'robot companion' emphasizes primarily its usefulness for people, as well as the robot's 'benign' behaviour. In this way, the approach pursued in the Cogniron (§4) and Aurora projects (§6) is consistent with a companion approach.

14.8 Conclusion

This paper provides an introduction to HRI research in the context of human and robot social intelligence, developing a conceptual framework and using two concrete HRI projects as case studies in order to illustrate the framework. Different definitions of social robots and viewpoints have been discussed, emphasizing different aspects of robot cognition and human responses and attitudes towards robots. The discussion highlighted that HRI studies and experiments on social robots address fundamental issues on the nature of social behaviour and people's (experimenters' as well as users') view of robots. Any particular project in the area of HRI could identify its fundamental research goals and aims in the context of this framework.

Two examples of HRI studies have been presented. Research into a robot companion, meant to become a service robot in the home, aims at developing explicit social rules (a robotiquette) which should allow people to interact with robots comfortably. This approach is different from developing robots as therapeutic 'playmates' for children with autism. Here, the concept of interactive emergence has been highlighted, whereby turn-taking games emerge in play between the children and a simple robot that only possesses very basic behavioural 'rules', but appears social when situated in a play context. In the latter case, the social rules are implicit, emerging from the interactions, while based on the careful design of the robot's sensory and behavioural repertoire.

HRI is a growing but still young research field. The future will tell whether it can develop into a scientific field that will have its long-lasting place in the scientific landscape. Several challenges need to be faced, most prominently, those that follow.

(i) Future research in HRI needs to build a foundation of theories, models, methods, tools and methodologies which can advance our understanding of HRI and allow experiments to be replicated by other research groups. At present, results are difficult to compare across experiments due to the impact of a robot's behaviour, appearance and task, as well as the interaction scenarios studied, as mentioned in §4. Any particular HRI study can only investigate a small fraction in the huge design space of possible HRI experiments. But without a scientific culture of being able to replicate and confirm or refute other researchers' findings, results will remain on the level of case studies.

(ii) New methodological approaches are needed. Many useful inspirations can be derived from the study of animal–animal or human–human interactions in ethology, psychology and social sciences. Similarly, the field of human–computer interaction can provide starting points for the design and analysis of HRI experiments. However, *robots are not people*. In interactions with machines, humans use heuristics derived from human–human interaction (Reeves & Nass 1996), which gives us interesting insights into the 'social heritage' of our intelligence. However, people do not treat machines identically to human beings (e.g. we do not hesitate to replace our broken or insufficient laptop with a new one). Thus, care needs to be taken when adopting methodologies, for example from social sciences, and apply them unchanged to HRI studies. Also, *robots are not computers*, either. Interacting with physically embodied and socially situated machines is different from interaction via computer interfaces. Other fields can provide important input to HRI methodologies, but a range of novel methodologies are necessary in order to advance the field, and researchers in HRI have indeed started to take the first steps (e.g. Robins *et al.* 2004*d* or Woods *et al.* 2006*a,b*).

HRI is a highly challenging area that requires interdisciplinary collaboration between AI researchers, computer scientists, engineers, psychologists and others, where new methods and methodologies need to be created in order to develop, study and evaluate interactions with a social robot. While it promises to result in social robots that can behave adequately in a human-inhabited (social) environment, it also raises many fundamental issues on the nature of social intelligence in humans and robots.

Humphrey (1988), in a famous paper (originally published in 1976), which discusses primate intelligence, argues for the necessity of developing a laboratory test of 'social skill'. His suggestion is as follows. 'The essential feature of such a test would be that it places the subject in a transactional situation where he can achieve a desired goal only by adapting his strategy to conditions which are continually changing as a consequence partly, but not wholly of his own behaviour. The 'social partner' in the test need not be animate (though my guess is that the subject would regard it in an 'animistic' way); possibly it could be a kind of 'social robot', a mechanical device which is programmed on-line from a computer to behave in a pseudo-social way'.

Now, 30 years after the original publication of Humphrey's idea, it is within our grasp to have robots, humanoid or non-humanoid, taking the role of a social partner in such a social intelligence test. However, 40 years after Alison Jolly's original article indicating that it is the social domain that defines us as human primates, it is still open as to what social intelligence for robots could or should mean from the perspective of humans. Despite the potential usefulness of social robots as scientific tools for understanding the nature of social intelligence on the one hand, and for the design of robotic assistants, companions or playmates that will have their places in society on the other hand, it is unclear whether the 'social–emotional' dimension in human–human interaction can be fulfilled by robots, i.e. whether the inherently 'mechanical nature' of HRIs can be replaced by truly meaningful social exchanges. While I doubt that robots can overcome their 'robotic heritage', viewing them as part of a social environment where meaning in interactions is provided by the richness and depth of human experiences might be a more realistic and more 'humane' vision for social robots than viewing them as 'selfish' machines.

Part of the survey on the Aurora project in this article formed the basis of Ben Robins's and IainWerry's Ph.D. theses. I acknowledge their contribution to the work and the photo material. The particular work summarized in the context of the Cogniron project was carried out by the following researchers: Michael L. Walters, Kheng Lee Koay, Sarah Woods and Christina Kaouri. We are grateful to Takashi Gomi who donated the Labo-1 robot, and Aude Billard who designed the humanoid doll Robota and made it available to our studies. I would like to thank Gernot Kronreif for discussions on robotic toys for children. The work described in this paper was partially conducted within two EU Integrated Projects: COGNIRON (The Cognitive Robot Companion) funded by the European Commission Division FP6-IST Future and Emerging Technologies under Contract FP6-002020, and RobotCub (Robotic Open-architecture Technology for Cognition, Understanding, and Behaviours) funded by the European Commission through Unit E5 (Cognition) of FP6-IST under Contract FP6-004370.

Endnote

1. According to the PTUK organization (Play Therapy in UK, http://www.playtherapy.org.uk), studies indicate that 20% of children have some form of psychological problem and that 70% of these can be helped through therapies, including play therapy.

References

Arkin, R. C. 1998 *Behavior-based robotics*. Cambridge, MA: MIT Press.

Billard, A. 2003 Robota: clever toy and educational tool. *Robot. Auton. Syst.* **42**, 259–269. (doi:10.1016/S0921-8890(02)00380-9)

Billard, A., Robins, B., Dautenhahn, K. & Nadel, J. 2007 Building Robota, a mini-humanoid robot for the rehabilitation of children with autism. *RESNA Assistive Technol. J.* **19**, 37–49.

Billard, A. & Dautenhahn, K. 1998 Grounding communication in autonomous robots: an experimental study. *Robot. Auton. Syst.* **24**, 71–79. (doi:10.1016/S0921-8890 (98)00023-2)

Blow, M. P., Dautenhahn, K., Appleby, A., Nehaniv, C. L. & Lee, D. 2006 Perception of robot smiles and dimensions for human–robot interaction design. In *Proc. 15th IEEE Int. Symp. on Robot and Human Interactive Communication (RO-MAN06), Hatfield, UK, 6–8 September 2006*, pp. 469–474.

Bonabeau, E., Dorigo, M. & Theraulaz, G. 1999 *Swarm intelligence–from natural to artificial systems*. Oxford, UK: Oxford University Press.

Boucher, J. 1999 Editorial: interventions with children with autism methods based on play. *Child Lang. Teaching Therapy* **15**.

Braitenberg, V. 1984 *Vehicles—experiments in synthetic psychology*. Cambridge, MA: MIT Press.

Breazeal, C. 2002 *Designing sociable robots*. Cambridge, MA: MIT Press.

Breazeal, C. 2003 Towards sociable robots. *Robot. Auton. Syst.* **42**, 167–175. (doi:10.1016/S0921-8890(02)00373-1)

Breazeal, C. 2004 Social interaction in HRI: the robot view. *IEEE Trans. Syst. Man Cyber.: Part C* **34**, 181–186. (doi:10.1109/TSMCC.2004.826268)

Brooks, R. A. 1999 *Cambrian intelligence*. Cambridge, MA: MIT Press.

Brooks, R. A., Breazeal, C., Marjanovic´, M., Scassellati, B. & Williamson, M. M. 1999 The Cog project: building a humanoid robot. In *Computation for metaphors, analogy, and agents* (ed. C. L. Nehaniv) Springer Lecture Notes in Artificial Intelligence, no. 1562, pp. 52–87. New York, NY: Springer.

Byrne, R. W. 1995 *The thinking ape*. Oxford: Oxford University Press.

Byrne, R. W. 1997 Machiavellian intelligence. *Evol. Anthro-pol.* **5**, 172–180. (doi:10.1002/(SICI)1520-6505(1996)5: 5 < 172::AID-EVAN6 > 3.0.CO;2-H)

Byrne, R. W. & Whiten, A. (eds) 1988 *Machiavellian intelligence: social expertise and the evolution of intellect in monkeys, apes and humans*. Oxford, UK: Oxford University Press.

Dahlback, A., Jonsson, L. & Ahrenberg. 1993 Wizard of Oz studies—why and how. In *Proc. First Int. Conf. on Intelligent User Interfaces, Orlando, Florida*, USA, pp. 193–200.

Dautenhahn, K. 1994 Trying to imitate—a step towards releasing robots from social isolation. In *Proc. 'From Perception to Action' Conference, Lausanne, Switzerland, 7–9 September 1994* (eds P. Gaussier & J.-D. Nicoud), pp. 290–301. Los Alamitos, CA: IEEE Computer Society Press.

Dautenhahn, K. 1995 Getting to know each other—artificial social intelligence for autonomous robots. *Robot. Auton. Syst.* **16**, 333–356. (doi:10.1016/0921-8890(95)00054-2)

Dautenhahn, K. 1998 The art of designing socially intelligent agents—science, fiction, and the human in the loop. *Appl. Artif. Intell.* **12**, 573–617. (doi:10.1080/088395198117550)

Dautenhahn, K. 1999a Embodiment and interaction in socially intelligent life-like agents. In *Computation for metaphors, analogy and agents* (ed. C. L. Nehaniv). Springer Lecture Notes in Artificial Intelligence, no. 1562, pp. 102–142. New York, NY: Springer.

Dautenhahn, K. 1999b Robots as social actors: Aurora and the case of autism. In *Proc. CT99, The Third International Cognitive Technology Conference, August, San-Francisco*, pp. 359–374. East Lansing, MI: Michigan State University.

Dautenhahn, K. 2002 Design spaces and niche spaces of believable social robots. In *Proc. IEEE Int. Workshop on Robot and Human Interactive Communication (RO-MAN 2002), 25–27 September, Berlin, Germany*, pp. 192–197. Piscataway, NJ: IEEE Press.

Dautenhahn, K. 2003 Roles and functions of robots in human society: implications from research in autism therapy. *Robotica* **21**, 443–452. (doi:10.1017/S0263574703004922)

Dautenhahn, K. 2004a Socially intelligent agents in human primate culture. In *Agent culture: human–agent interaction in a multicultural world* (eds R. Trappl & S. Payr), pp. 45–71. New Jersey, NJ: Lawrence Erlbaum Associates.

Dautenhahn, K. 2004b Robots we like to live with?!—A developmental perspective on a personalized, life-long robot companion. In Proc. *3rd IEEE Int. Workshop on Robot and Human Interactive Communication (RO-MAN 2004), 20–22 September 2004, Kurashiki, Japan*, pp. 17–22. Piscataway, NJ: IEEE Press.

Dautenhahn, K. & Billard, A. 2002 Games children with autism can play with Robota, a humanoid robotic doll. In *Universal access and assistive technology* (eds S. Keates, P. M. Langdon, P. J. Clarkson & P. Robinson), pp. 179–190. London, UK: Springer.

Dautenhahn, K. & Werry, I. 2004 Towards interactive robots in autism therapy: background, motivation and challenges. *Pragmatics Cogn.* **12**, 1–35.

Dautenhahn, K., Werry, I., Rae, J., Dickerson, P., Stribling, P. & Ogden, B. 2002 Robotic playmates: analysing interactive competencies of children with autism playing with a mobile robot. In *Socially intelligent agents—creating relationships with computers and robots* (eds K. Dautenhahn, A. Bond, L. Cañamero & B. Edmonds), pp. 117–124. Dordrecht, The Netherlands: Kluwer Academic.

Dautenhahn, K., Woods, S., Kaouri, C., Walters, M., Koay, K. L. & Werry, I. 2005 What is a robot companion—friend, assistant or butler? In *Proc. IEEE IRS/RSJ Int. Conf. on Intelligent Robots and Systems (IROS 2005), 2–6 August 2005, Edmonton, Alberta, Canada*, pp. 1488–1493. Piscataway, NJ: IEEE Press.

Davis, M., Robins, B., Dautenhahn, K., Nehaniv, C. L. & Powell, S. 2005 A comparison of interactive and robotic systems in therapy and education for children with autism. In *Proc. 'Assistive Technology from Virtuality to Reality', 8th European Conference for the Advancement of Assistive Technology in*

Europe (AAATE '05), Lille, France, 6–9 September 2005, pp. 353–357. Amsterdam, The Netherlands: IOS Press.

Dunbar, R. I. M. 1993 Coevolution of neocortical size, group size and language in humans. *Behav. Brain Sci.* **16**, 681–735.

Dunbar, R. I. M. 1996 *Grooming, gossip and the evolution of language*. Cambridge, MA: Faber and Harvard University Press.

Dunbar, R. I. M. 1998 The social brain hypothesis. *Evol. Anthropol.* **6**, 178–190. (doi:10.1002/(SICI)1520-6505(1998)6:5<178::AID-EVAN5>3.0.CO;2-8)

Dunbar, R. I. M. 2003 The social brain: mind, language and society in evolutionary perspective. *Annu. Rev. Anthropol.* **32**, 163–181. (doi:10.1146/annurev.anthro.32.061002.093158)

Evans, B. J., Stanley, R. O., Mestrovic, R. & Rose, L. 1991 Effects of communication skills training on students' diagnostic efficiency. *Med. Educ.* **25**, 517–526.

Ferrara, C. & Hill, S. D. 1980 The responsiveness of autistic children to the predictability of social and non-social toys. *J. Autism Dev. Disorders* **10**, 51–57. (doi:10.1007/BF02408432)

Fong, T., Nourbakhsh, I. & Dautenhahn, K. 2003 A survey of socially interactive robots. *Robot. Auton. Syst.* **42**, 143–166. (doi:10.1016/S0921-8890(02)00372-X)

François, D., Polani, D. & Dautenhahn, K. 2007 Online behaviour classification and adaption to human–robot interaction styles. In *Proc. Second ACM/IEEE Int. Conf. on Human Robot Interaction (HRI07)*, pp. 295–302. *Washington DC, USA*.

Gigerenzer, G. 1997 The modularity of social intelligence. In *Machiavellian intelligence II: extensions and evaluations* (eds A. Whiten & R. W. Byrne), pp. 264–288. Cambridge, UK: Cambridge University Press.

Goetz, J. & Kiesler, S. 2002 Cooperation with a robotic assistant. In *Proc. SIGCHI '02 Conf. on Human Factors in Computing Systems, Minneapolis, MN, 20–25 April 2002*. New York, NY: ACM Press.

Gould, J. D., Conti, J. & Hovanyecz, T. 1983 Composing letters with a simulated listening typewriter. *Commun. ACM.* **26**, 295–308. (doi:10.1145/2163.358100)

Heider, F. & Simmel, H. 1944 An experimental study of apparent behavior. *Am. J. Psychol.* **57**, 243–259. (doi:10. 2307/1416950)

Hendriks-Jansen, H. 1996 *Catching ourselves in the act: situated activity, interactive emergence, evolution and human thought*. Cambridge, MA: MIT Press.

Humphrey, N. K. 1988 The social function of intellect. In *Machiavellian intelligence: social expertise and the evolution of intellect in monkeys, apes and humans* (eds R. W. Byrne & A. Whiten), pp. 13–26. Oxford, UK: Clarendon Press.

Iizuka, H. & Ikegami, T. 2004 Adaptability and diversity in simulated turn-taking behavior source. *Artif. Life* **10**, 361–378. (doi:10.1162/1064546041766442)

Jolly, A. 1966 Lemur social behavior and primate intelligence. *Science* **153**, 501–506. (doi:10.1126/science.153.3735.501)

Jordan, R. & Libby, S. 1997 Developing and using play in the curriculum. In *Autism and learning: a guide to good practice* (eds S. Powell & R. Jordan), London, UK: David Fulton.

Kahn Jr, P. H., Friedman, B., Perez-Granados, D. R. & Freier, N. G. 2006 Robotic pets in the lives of pre-school children. *Interact. Studies.* **7**, 405–436.

Kanda, T., Hirano, T. & Eaton, D. 2004 Interactive robots as social partners and peer tutors for children: a field trial. *Human Comp. Interact.* **19**, 61–84. (doi:10.1207/s15327051hci1901&2_4)

Koay, K. L., Walters, M. L. & Dautenhahn, K. 2005 Methodological issues using a comfort level device in human–robot interactions. In *Proc. IEEE Workshop on Robots and Human Interactive Communication (RO-MAN 2005), Nashville, Tennessee, 13–15 August 2005*, pp. 359–364. Piscataway, NJ: IEEE Press.

Koay, K. L., Dautenhahn, K., Woods, S. N. & Walters, M. L. 2006 Empirical results from using a comfort level device in human–robot interaction studies. In *Proc. 1st Int. Conf. on Human Robot Interaction (HRI '06), Salt Lake City, Utah, 2–3 March 2006*, pp. 194–201. New York, NY: ACM Press.

Kozima, H. 2002 Infanoid: a babybot that explores the social environment. In *Socially intelligent agents: creating relationships with computers and robots* (eds K. Dautenhahn, A. H. Bond, L. Cañamero & B. Edmonds), pp. 157–164. Amsterdam, The Netherlands: Kluwer Academic.

Kozima, H., Nakagawa, C. & Yasuda, Y. 2005 Interactive robots for communication-care: A case-study in autism therapy. In *Proc. IEEE Workshop on Robots and Human Interactive Communication (RO-MAN 2005), Nashville, Tennessee, 13–15 August 2005*, pp. 341–346. Piscataway, NJ: IEEE Press.

Kramer, D., Ber, R. & Moores, M. 1989 Increasing empathy among medical students. *Med. Educ.* **23**, 168–173.

Lorenz, K. 1971 Part and parcel in animal and human societies. *Studies in animal and human behavior*, pp. 115–195. Cambridge, MA: Harvard University Press (originally published 1950).

Lungarella, M., Metta, G., Pfeifer, R. & Sandini, G. 2004 Developmental robotics: a survey. *Connect. Sci.* **15**, 151–190. (doi:10.1080/0954009031000165511 0)

MacDorman, K. & Ishiguro, H. 2006 The uncanny advantage of using androids in cognitive and social science research. *Interact. Studies.* **7**, 297–337.

Maulsby, D., Greenberg, S. & Mander, R. 1993 Prototyping an intelligent agent through Wizard of Oz. In *Proc. ACM SIGCHI Conf. on Human Factors in Computing Systems*, pp. 277–284. Amsterdam, The Netherlands: ACM Press.

Michaud, F. & Caron, S. 2002 Roball, the rolling robot. *Auton. Robots* **12**, 211–222. (doi:10.1023/A:1014005728519)

Michaud, F. & Théberge-Turmel, C. 2002 Mobile robotic toys and autism. In *Socially intelligent agents— creating relationships with computers and robots* (eds K. Dautenhahn, A. Bond, L. Cañamero & B. Edmonds), pp. 125–132. Dordrecht, The Netherlands: Kluwer Academic.

Michaud, F., Laplante, J.-F., Larouche, H., Duquette, A., Caron, S. & Masson, P. 2005 Autonomous spherical mobile robot to study child development. *IEEE Trans. Syst. Man Cybern.* **35**, 471–480. (doi:10.1109/TSMCA.2005.850596)

Moore, D. 1998 Computers and people with autism. *Communications* Summer, pp. 20–21.

Mori, M. 1970 Bukimi no tani [the uncanny valley]. *Energy* **7**, 33–35.

Murray, D. 1997 Autism and information technology: therapy with computers. In *Autism and learning: a guide to good practice* (eds S. Powell & R. Jordan), pp. 100–117. London, UK: David Fulton.

Nadel, J., Revel, A., Andry, P. & Gaussier, P. 2004 Toward communication: first imitations in infants, low-functioning children with autism and robots. *Interact. Studies* **5**, 45–74.

Nakauchi, Y. & Simmons, R. 2000 A social robot that stands in line. In *Proc. IEEE/RSJ Int. Conf. on Intelligent Robots and Systems (IROS 2000), Takamatsu, Japan, 31 October–5 November 2000*, pp. 357–364. Piscataway, NJ: IEEE Press.

Ogden, B. & Dautenhahn, K. 2000 Robotic etiquette: Structured interaction in humans and robots. In *Proc. 8th Symp. on Intelligent Robotic Systems (SIRS 2000), The University of Reading, England, 18–20 July 2000*.

Ogden, B., Dautenhahn, K. Stribling, P. 2002 Interactional structure applied to the identification and generation of visual interactive behaviour: Robots that (usually) follow the rules. In: *Gesture and sign languages in human–computer interaction* (eds I. Wachsmuth, & T. Sowa), Springer Lecture Notes LNAI 2298, pp. 254–267. Berlin, Germany: Springer.

Parten, M. B. 1932 Social participation among pre-school children. *J. Abnormal. Social Psychol.* **27**, 243–268. (doi:10.1037/h0074524)

Penny, S. 2000 Agents as artworks and agent design as artistic practice. In *Human cognition and social agent technology* (ed. K. Dautenhahn), pp. 395–414. Amsterdam, The Netherlands: John Benjamins.

Pfeifer, R. & Scheier, C. 1999 *Understanding intelligence*. Cambridge, MA: Bradford Books.

Plaisant, C., Druin, A., Lathan, C., Dakhane, K., Edwards, K., Vice, J. M. & Montemayor, J. 2000 A storytelling robot for pediatric rehabilitation. In *Proc. ASSETS'00, Washington, Nov. 2000*, pp. 50–55. New York, NY: ACM Press.

Powell, S. 1996 The use of computers in teaching people with autism. *Autism on the agenda: papers from the National Autistic Society conference*. London, UK: National Autistic Society.

Reader, S. M. & Laland, K. N. 2002 Social intelligence, innovation, and enhanced brain size in primates. *Proc. Natl Acad. Sci. USA* **99**, 4436–4441. (doi:10.1073/pnas.062041299)

Reeves, B. & Nass, C. 1996 *The media equation—how people treat computers, television, and new media like real people and places*. Cambridge, UK: Cambridge University Press.

Restall, G. & Magill-Evans, J. 1994 Play and preschool children with autism. *Am. J. Occup. Therapy.* **48**, 113–120.

Richter, S. 1989 *Wunderbares Menschenwerk: Aus der Geschichte der mechanischen Automaten.* Leipzig, Germany: Edition Leipzig.

Robins, B. & Dautenhahn, K. 2006 The role of the experimenter in HRI research—a case study evaluation of children with autism interacting with a robotic toy. In *Proc. 15th IEEE Int. Symp. on Robot and Human Interactive Communication (RO-MAN06), Hatfield, UK, 6–8 September 2006*, pp. 646–651. New York, NY: IEEE Press.

Robins, B., Dickerson, P., Stribling, P. & Dautenhahn, K. 2004a Robot-mediated joint attention in children with autism: A case study in a robot–human interaction. *Interact. Studies* **5**, 161–198.

Robins, B., Dautenhahn, K., te Boelhorst, R., Billard, A. 2004b Robots as assistive technology—does appearance matter? In *Proc. 13th IEEE Int. Workshop on Robot and Human Interactive Communication (RO-MAN 2004), 20–22 September, Kurashiki, Japan*, pp. 277–282. IEEE Press.

Robins, B., Dautenhahn, K., te Boekhorst, R. & Billard, A. 2004c Effects of repeated exposure of a humanoid robot on children with autism. In *Designing a more inclusive world* (eds S. Keates, J. Clarkson, P. Langdon & P. Robinson), pp. 225–236. London, UK: Springer.

Robins, B., Dautenhahn, K. & Dubowski, J. 2004d Investigating autistic children's attitudes towards strangers with the theatrical robot—a new experimental paradigm in human–robot interaction studies? In *Proc. 13th IEEE Int. Workshop on Robot and Human Interactive Communication (RO-MAN 2004), Kurashiki, Japan, 20–22 September 2004*. Piscataway, NJ: IEEE Press.

Robins, B., Dautenhahn, K. & Dubowski, J. 2005a Robots as isolators or mediators for children with autism? A cautionary tale. In *Proc. AISB'05 Symp. Robot Companions Hard Problems and Open Challenges in Human–Robot Interaction, 14–15 April 2005, University of Hertfordshire, UK*, pp. 82–88. Hatfield, UK: SSAISB. See http://www. aisb.org.uk/publications/proceedings.html.

Robins, B., Dautenhahn, K., te Boekhorst, R. & Billard, A. 2005b *Robotic assistants in therapy and education of children with autism: can a small humanoid robot help encourage social interaction skills? Universal Access in the Information Society (UAIS).* New York, NY: Springer.

Robins, B., Dickerson, P. & Dautenhahn, K. 2005c Robots as embodied beings—interactionally sensitive body movements in interactions among autistic children and a robot. In *Proc. 14th IEEE Int. Workshop on Robot and Human Interactive Communication (RO-MAN 2005), Nashville, Tennessee, USA, 13–15 August 2005*, pp. 54–59. Piscataway, NJ: IEEE Press.

Salter, T., te Boekhorst, R. & Dautenhahn, K. 2004 Detecting and analysing children's play styles with autonomous mobile robots: a case study comparing observational data with sensor readings. In *Proc. 8th Conf. on Intelligent Autonomous Systems (IAS-8), 10–13 March 2004*, p. 61. Amsterdam, The Netherlands: IOS Press.

Salter, T., Dautenhahn, K. & te Boekhorst, R. 2006 Learning about natural human–robot interaction. *Robot. Auton. Syst.* **54**, 127–134. (doi:10.1016/j.robot.2005.09.022)

Scassellati, B. 2005 Quantitative metrics of social response for autism diagnosis. In *Proc. IEEE Workshop on Robots and Human Interactive Communication (RO-MAN 2005, Nashville, Tennessee)*, pp. 585–590. Piscataway, NJ: IEEE Press.

Scholtz, J. 2003 Theory and evaluation of human robot interactions. In *Proc. Hawaii Int. Conf. on System Science 36, Jan 2003*.

Severinson-Eklundh, K., Green, A. & Hüttenrauch, H. 2003 Social and collaborative aspects of interaction with a service robot. *Robot. Auton. Syst.* **42**, 223–234. (doi:10.1016/S0921-8890(02)00377-9)

Sherratt, D. & Peter, M. 2002 *Developing play and drama in children with autistic spectrum disorders.* London, UK: David Fulton.

Steels, L. 1994 The artificial life roots of artificial intelligence. *Artif. Life* **1**, 89–125.

Steinfeld, A. M., Fong, T. W., Kaber, D., Lewis, M., Scholtz, J., Schultz, A. & Goodrich, M. 2006 Common metrics for human–robot interaction. In *Proc. 2006 Human–Robot Interaction Conference (HRI 2006), March 2006*, pp. 33–40. New York, NY: ACM Press.

Tardiff, C., Plumet, M. H., Beaudichon, J., Waller, D., Bouvard, M. & Leboyer, M. 1995 Micro-analysis of social interactions between autistic children and normal adults in semi-structured play situations. *Int. J. Behav. Dev.* **18**, 727–747.

Thrun, S. 1998 When robots meet people. *IEEE Intell. Syst.* **27**, 29.

Thrun, S. 2004 Towards a framework of human–robot interaction. *Human Comput. Interact.* **19**, 9–24. (doi:10.1207/s15327051hci1901&2_2)

Walter, W. G. 1950 An imitation of life. *Sci. Am.* **182**, 42–45.

Walter, W. G. 1951 A machine that learns. *Sci. Am.* **185**, 60–63.

Walters, M. L., Woods, S. N., Koay, K. L. & Dautenhahn, K. 2005a Practical and methodological challenges in designing and conducting interaction studies with human subjects. In *Robot companions: hard problems and open challenges in human–robot interaction, Symposium at AISB'05, University of Hertfordshire, UK*, pp. 110–119. Hatfield, UK: SSAISB.

Walters, M. L., Dautenhahn, K., Koay, K. L., Kaouri, C., te Boekhorst, R., Nehaniv, C. L., Werry, I. & Lee, D. 2005b Close encounters: Spatial distances between people and a robot of mechanistic appearance. In *Proc. IEEERAS Int. Conf. on Humanoid Robots (Humanoids2005), December 5–7, Tsukuba, Japan*, pp. 450–455. New York, NY: IEEE Press.

Walters, M. L., Dautenhahn, K., Woods, S. N., Koay, K. L., te Boekhorst, R. & Lee, D. 2006 Exploratory studies on social spaces between humans and a mechanical-looking robot. *Connect. Sci.* **18**, 429–442.

Weir, S. & Emanuel, R. 1976 *Using Logo to catalyse communication in an autistic child*. DAI research report No. 15, University of Edinburgh.

Werry, I. 2003 *Development and evaluation of a mobile robotic platform as a therapy device for children with autism*. Unpublished Ph.D. thesis, University of Reading, UK.

Werry, I. & Dautenhahn, K. 2007 Human–robot interaction: An experimental study with children with autism. In: *Modeling Biology: Structures, Behaviors, Evolution* (eds. M. Laubichler & G. B. Müller), Vienna Series in Theoretical Biology. Cambridge, MA: MIT Press.

Werry, I. & Dautenhahn, K. 1999 Applying robot technology to the rehabilitation of autistic children. In *Proc. 7th Int. Symp. on Intelligent Robotic Systems (SIRS99)*, pp. 265–272.

Werry, I., Dautenhahn, K., Ogden, B. & Harwin, W. 2001 Can social interaction skills be taught by a social agent? The role of a robotic mediator in autism therapy. In *Proc. Fourth Int. Conf. on Cognitive Technology: Instruments of Mind* (eds M. Beynon, C. L. Nehaniv, & K. Dautenhahn), pp. 57–74. LNAI 2117. Cambridge, UK: Springer.

Whiten, A. & Byrne, R. W. (eds) 1997 *Machiavellian intelligence II: extensions and evaluations*, Cambridge, UK: Cambridge University Press.

Wolfberg, P. J. 1999 *Play and imagination in children with autism*. New York, NY: Teachers College Press.

Woods, S., Dautenhahn, K., Kaouri, C., te Boekhorst, R. & Koay, K. L. 2005 Is this robot like me? Links between human and robot personality traits. In *Proc. IEEE-RAS International Conference on Humanoid Robots (Humanoids2005), December 5–7, Tsukuba International Congress Center, Tsukuba, Japan*, pp. 375–380. New York, NY: IEEE Press.

Woods, S. N., Walters, M. L., Koay, K. L. & Dautenhahn, K. 2006a Comparing human robot interaction scenarios using live and video based methods: towards a novel methodological approach. In *Proc. 9th IEEE Int. Workshop on Advanced Motion Control (AMC'06), March 27–29, Istanbul, Turkey*, pp. 750–755. New York, NY: IEEE Press.

Woods, S. N., Walters, M. L., Koay, K. L. & Dautenhahn, K. 2006b Methodological issues in HRI: A comparison of live and video-based methods in robot to human approach direction trials. In *Proc. 15th IEEE Int. Symp. on Robot and Human Interactive Communication (RO-MAN06), Hatfield, UK, September 6–8, 2006*, pp. 51–58. New York, NY: IEEE Press.

Yanco, H. A. & Drury, J. 2002 A taxonomy for human–robot interaction. In *Proc. AAAI Fall Symp. on Human–Robot Interaction, Falmouth, Massachusetts, November 2002*, AAAI Technical Report FS-02-03, pp. 111–119. AAAI Press.

Yanco, H. A. & Drury, J. 2004 Classifying human–robot interaction: an updated taxonomy. In *Proc. IEEE Conf. on Systems, Man and Cybernetics, The Hague, The Netherlands*, vol. 3, pp. 2841–2846. New York, NY: IEEE Press.

15

Did farming arise from a misapplication of social intelligence?

Steven Mithen

The origins of farming is the defining event of human history—the one turning point that has resulted in modern humans having a quite different type of lifestyle and cognition to all other animals and past types of humans. With the economic basis provided by farming, human individuals and societies have developed types of material culture that greatly augment powers of memory and computation, extending the human mental capacity far beyond that which the brain alone can provide. Archaeologists have long debated and discussed why people began living in settled communities and became dependent on cultivated plants and animals, which soon evolved into domesticated forms. One of the most intriguing explanations was proposed more than 20 years ago not by an archaeologist but by a psychologist: Nicholas Humphrey suggested that farming arose from the 'misapplication of social intelligence'. I explore this idea in relation to recent discoveries and archaeological interpretations in the Near East, arguing that social intelligence has indeed played a key role in the origin of farming and hence the emergence of the modern world.

Keywords: agriculture; archaeology; farming; human mind; material culture; social intelligence

15.1 Introduction

(a) The cognitive impact of farming

This contribution concerns the role of sociality and social intelligence in the key development of humankind, that which has made modern humans a particularly intelligent type of primate. This development has nothing to do with *Homo habilis* or handaxes, bipedalism or brain size. It is the origin of farming at, or soon after, 10 000 years ago. It is only with the economic basis that farming provides that writing, mathematics and digital technology could be invented and it is these that effectively define the nature of our cognition today. The brain is important, of course, but it now plays a mere supporting role to a cognitive system that is primarily located in materials entirely outside of the body—books, computers, paintings, digital stores of data and so forth. There are, of course, our capacities for empathy, mind reading and social interaction that no digital computer is ever likely to replace. But I doubt if these today are very different to those of our early human ancestors living several million years ago (Mithen 1996). Indeed, if anything, I suspect they have deteriorated through lack of use as we have become dependent on material items as the source of social information.

To appreciate the significance of farming, compare our cultural achievements over the last 10 000 years with those of the Neanderthals throughout the entire 250 000 years of their existence—remembering that the two species have equivalent sized brains but that the Neanderthals always remained as hunter-gatherers (for a review of Neanderthal anatomy and lifestyles see Stringer & Gamble 1993; Mellars 1996). We have gone from living in small, relatively isolated Neolithic communities to a globalized society, with a scientifically based understanding for the origin of the cosmos and life on Earth, with the works of Shakespeare and Bach, with space probes visiting the stars, nanotechnology and the manipulation of DNA. The Neanderthals became extinct doing much the same as they had been doing throughout the entirety of their existence—hunting, gathering, making stone artefacts, sitting in caves, probably feeling rather cold and hungry—even though they may have had third, fourth and possibly even fifth orders of intentionality (Dunbar 2004).

I do not want to denigrate that Neanderthals. I have no doubt that they lived in socially complex communities; their stone tools were extraordinarily difficult to make and to have survived in the ice age of Europe they must have had a profound understanding of the natural world (Mithen 1996). There is also substantial evidence that they had a sophisticated system of aural communication, which some might wish to describe as language. I have recently proposed that their communication would have been highly musical in character making use of variations in pitch, melody and rhythm (Mithen 2005). They were, I believe, highly emotional and sensitive beings, probably far more so than we are today as our abilities have become compromised by a dependency on material culture.

The fact of the matter is, however, that the Neanderthals appear to have been very constrained in their range of behaviours and showed very limited, if any, signs of a creative intelligence: no visual art; no architecture; no body ornaments. Their world was one of cultural stasis. And be sure that they were not living in some Garden of Eden—if any human community could have benefited from the invention of a spear thrower, a bow and arrow or a sewing needle it was surely that of the Neanderthals in light of their demographic profile which suggests they were a marginally viable population (Trinkaus 1995). Moreover, they lived through a wide range of climatic conditions—glacial and interglacial periods—and hence one cannot invoke environmental constraints for their lack of innovation and cultural change. The only explanation I have been able to find for why the Neanderthals can be so like us in some regards and yet so different in others is that their minds had a degree of compartmentalism that we lack today, a domain-specific mentality (figure 1). I proposed this a decade ago in my 1996 book *The prehistory of the mind* and have found no reason to alter my interpretation of the fossil and archaeological record.

The minds of modern humans appear to be quite different: ways of thinking and stores of knowledge about the social, natural and technical worlds flow unconstrained into each other, enabling us to live within a world of metaphors and analogies (figure 2; Mithen 1996). This is a cognitively fluid mind which arises, I believe, from the evolution of compositional language and the role of inner speech (see also Carruthers 2002). It is one in which natural objects, plants and animals can become understood in social terms as members of one's kin, such as the polar bear by the Inuit (Saladin D'Angulure 1990). We see this in all traditional societies, whether in terms of specific understandings of particular animals or general attitudes to the natural world which are frequently—perhaps universally—imbued with a sense of will and purpose. 'The forest as parent' is a powerful metaphor found among many forest-dwelling groups (Bird-David 1990).

While we see here the imposition of a social way of thinking onto the natural world and physical objects, we must also note that an equally important characteristic of humans is to treat other persons as non-social objects. In this regard, people use ways of thinking appropriate to physical objects to manipulate other people without recourse to their feelings and relationships—the most extreme form of this being racism. Indeed, the capacity of modern humans to act without recourse to empathy, mind reading or any other feature of social intelligence is a key defining feature of the modern mind. All too often we have acted as the most socially non-intelligent species on the planet.

The roots of cognitive fluidity can be traced back to the Middle Stone Age of Africa, as in the shell beads and decorated ochre recovered from Blombos Cave dating to *ca* 74 000 years ago (Henshilwood *et al.* 2002; D'Errico *et al.* 2005), but the evidence becomes most striking after 50 000 years ago with the advent of the Upper Palaeolithic in Europe (figure 3; Mithen 1996, 1998). Stone flakes are no longer mere tools for killing or butchering animals—they are invested with social significance and become symbols and emblems, they embody memories and become social currency; the cave paintings tell us that animals are no longer just for eating—they are kindred spirits within an ice age world, seemingly able to transform themselves into human form. While we may have no direct evidence, we certainly should not doubt that the ice age landscape itself—the hills, rivers, woodlands and so forth—was enthused with symbolic meanings, with a will and a purpose of its own; nature was a metaphor for social life.

Nevertheless, even with such cognitively fluid minds, modern humans remained living as hunter-gatherers from their emergence at *ca* 200 000 years ago until less than 10 000 years ago—and for many communities a great deal more recently than that. Those modern human hunter-gatherer communities certainly had cultural achievements that we admire today, but they remained technologically and socially constrained prior to the origin of farming—no metal work, monumental architecture, writing, state-organization and so forth. We must be

Fig. 15.1 The domain-specific intelligence of the Neanderthal mind (Mithen 1996).

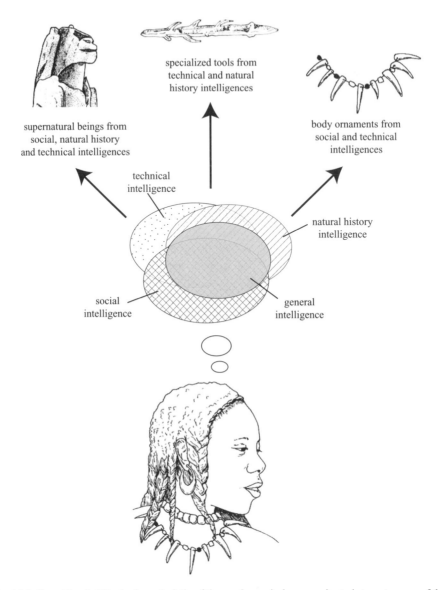

Fig. 15.2 Cognitive fluidity is characteristic of the modern mind–a capacity to integrate ways of thinking and stores of knowledge to generate creative ideas and which underlies the pervasive use of metaphor and analogy in human thought (Mithen 1996). This figure illustrates how cognitive fluidity gave rise to the art, ideology and technology of the Upper Palaeolithic.

cautious, however, as late Pleistocene and early Holocene hunter-gatherers were certainly more technologically diverse than was once believed. The invention of pottery, for instance, was once thought to be associated with farming (e.g. Childe 1958) but this is now recognized as a Eurocentric view as ceramics were invented by hunter-gatherers in many parts of the world including tropical south America, the Eastern Sahara, and throughout East Asia where the earliest examples reach back to at least 12 500 years ago (Imamura 1996; Rice 1999; Kuzman 2006).

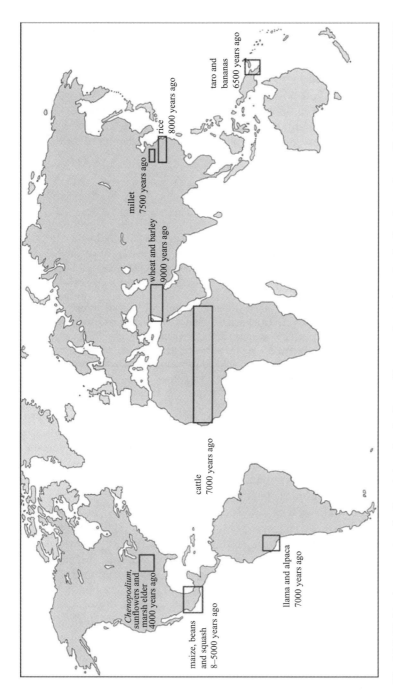

Fig. 15.3 Eight primary centres for the origins of agriculture with approximate dates for the first domesticates (Smith 1995; Mithen 2003).

Here, I should stress that I view the modern mind and intelligence as being as much constituted by items of material culture as by the brain—broadly following arguments for 'active externalism' by Clark (1997, 2003) and Clark & Chalmers (1998). The clever trick that modern humans learned was to use material culture such as rock art and shell beads, and most recently written texts and mathematical notation, to extract more out of their brains than nature had intended (Mithen 1998). A similar idea was developed by Renfrew (2001), who drew on Donald's (1991) idea of 'external symbolic storage' when discussing the Neolithic Revolution. He was arguing that symbols had to come before concepts, whereas my proposition is less philosophical in nature: it is simply that the economic basis provided by farming enabled a massive expansion in the diversity and quantity of material culture, which had a profound impact on the nature of human cognition, epitomized by the invention of writing within the early civilizations.

(b) The origin of farming

So it is to the origin of farming that we must look to understand the source and nature of human intelligence today. What was the role of sociality and social intelligence in causing this turning point of human history? The idea that social intelligence may have played a role in the origins of farming can be attributed to Nicholas Humphrey. The following quote is taken from his 1984 book, *Consciousness Regained*:

> The care which a gardener gives to his plants (watering, fertilising, hoeing, pruning etc) is attuned to the plants' emerging properties … True, plants will not respond to ordinary social pressures (though men do talk to them), but the way in which they give to and receive from a gardener bears, I suggest, a close structural similarity to a simple social relationship. If … [we] … can speak of a conversation between a mother and her two month old baby, so too might we speak of a conversation between a gardener and his roses or a farmer and his corn.
>
> (Humphrey 1984, pp. 26–27)

In this quote, Humphrey was suggesting that the 'fortunate misapplication of social intelligence' may have played a key role in the origin of agriculture. So archaeologists should ask whether there is any evidence that this was indeed the case. I will do so below, drawing on evidence from one of my own excavations in the Near East and making what, I will readily admit, are some rather speculative interpretations of that evidence. First however, let me provide a very brief background to the origins of agriculture.

There were multiple centres of animal and plant domestication throughout the Old and New Worlds in the Early and Middle Holocene (Mithen 2003). Smith (1995) highlighted seven— Near East, Central Mexico, South China, North China, South Eastern Andes, Eastern United States, Sub-Saharan Africa (figure 3)—but it is now evident that there are numerous others, including localities in India and the Eastern Sahara. Its earliest occurrence was in the Near East and based on the domestication of wheat, barley and legumes, followed by sheep, goat and cattle (Bar-Yosef & Meadow 1995); in China, rice may have been domesticated at a similar time (Zhao 1998), while in the Andes, the earliest domesticates were rather later and were animals, llama and alpaca (Rick 1980), although potato and quinua may have been domesticated at a contemporary or even earlier date. Cattle were independently domesticated in the Eastern Sahara (Blench & MacDonald 2000), while in Highland New Guinea the first domesticates were crops such as taro and banana (Denham *et al.* 2003).

Archaeologists have been discussing and debating the origins of farming ever since the discipline began. Just like in the debates about modern human origins, archaeologists now have ever increasing amounts of evidence about modern day genetic diversity which is providing an improved chronology for the domestication of plants and animals. At present, it seems most likely that there were quite different processes leading to farming in each region of the world, and there may have even been localized variation within regions such as the Near East. The only common factors appear to be farming that arose by the activities of *Homo sapiens* during the early Holocene.

Theories for the origins of farming have been diverse (e.g. see reviews and articles in Smith 1995; Harris 1996; Mithen 2003). Population pressure on wild resources, arising from either increasing numbers of people or climatically imposed environmental degradation, has been a popular idea (e.g. Binford 1968; Cohen 1977) but has always struggled to find strong support. The basic problem with this and several other theories is that the mobile hunter-gatherer life-style always looks far more attractive than sedentism, which creates problems of refuse disposal, hygiene and social conflict within one's neighbours—hunter-gatherers solve these by simply moving away, whether from their rubbish or other people. That is no longer an option after one has invested in field clearance, irrigation ditches, stock fences and so forth.

Social explanations for the origins of farming have also been prominent (e.g. Bender 1978; Hayden 1990) and in some cases are persuasive. In central Mexico, the first domesticates were plants such as squash, maize and beans (Smith 1995, 1997). The evidence comes from desiccated plant remains from sites such as Guilá Naquitz in the Oaxaca Valley, a site famous for having taking six weeks to excavate and then more then 20 years to analyse (figure 4; Flannery 1986). It is unlikely that these foods were staples of the diet and we know that they were domesticated while people remained as mobile hunter-gatherers. They may have been grown as prestige or luxury foods, for use in feasts to impress visitors and perhaps for exchange in a context where groups and individuals were in social competition with each other (for a speculative scenario, see Mithen 2003, pp. 281–284). For instance, the cultivation of teosinte that led to maize may have been for its sugary pith rather than its grain, to then use in alcohol production (Smalley & Balke 2003).

Fig. 15.4 Guilá Naquitz, Oaxaca Valley, Mexico, undergoing excavation in 1966 (© Kent Flannery).

(c) Sociality and the origin of farming in the Levant

The most studied region of the world for the origin of farming is the Near East, or to be more specific the Levant (Southeast Turkey, Lebanon, Syria, Isreal, Palestine and Jordan), where the earliest domesticated form of wheat (emmer & einkorn) and barley have been found at *ca* 10 000 years ago (Bar-Yosef & Meadow 1995). In this region, we have a succession of cultural entities that broadly relate to the changing climatic conditions of the late glacial and early Holocene (figure 5; Bar-Yosef & Belfer-Cohen 1989). At 15 000 years ago, the archaeological evidence indicates mobile hunter-gatherers in a cold and dry landscape, who left scatters of chipped stone artefacts referred to as the Kebaran industry. During the late glacial interstadial between 14 700 and 12 800 years ago, a period of increased rainfall and warmer temperatures, substantial settlements consisting of circular stone dwellings appeared, along with major technological developments, the creation of cemeteries and art objects. This is referred to as the Natufian culture which some archaeologists interpret as sedentary hunter-gatherers, exploiting the rich plant and animal resources that arose from the spread of mixed oak woodland (Bar-Yosef 1998; Mithen 2003). Whether such settlements reflect sedentary or mobile hunter-gatherers, they did not survive during the Younger Dryas, 12 800–11 600 years ago, although several elements of the Natufian culture continued.

The dramatic global warming at *ca* 11 600 years ago which marks the start of the Holocene sees the return of settlements with circular stone structures along with the introduction of new artefact types which denote the Pre-Pottery Neolithic A (PPNA; Kuijt & Goring-Morris 2002). This culture was first discovered in the lowest levels of Tell el-Sultan, Jericho (figure 6), when being excavated by Kathleen Kenyon in 1958, and is now represented by numerous sites throughout the Levant. It is followed by the Pre-Pottery Neolithic B culture constituted by settlements with rectangular buildings (e.g. figure 7), often densely packed together and having two storeys, associated with the remains of domesticated cereals, sheep and goat (Kuijt & Goring-Morris 2002). These were farming villages and hence the transition from hunter-gathering to farming occurs within the PPNA period, one that lasts for just 1000 years at most,

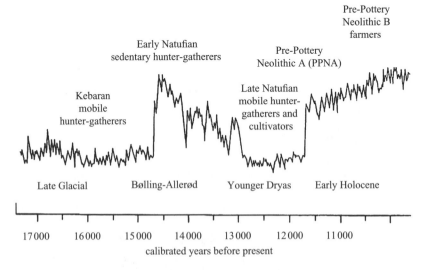

Fig. 15.5 The environmental and cultural sequence of the southern Levant during the Late Pleistocene and Early Holocene. The line is based on oxygen isotope ratios used as a proxy for global temperature.

Fig. 15.6 Tell el-Sultan, surrounded by the modern settlement of Jericho in Palestine (September 1999 (© Steven Mithen)).

and possibly no more than a few centuries. It was during the PPNA that hunter-gatherers chose to adopt sedentary lifestyles and began to cultivate cereals and legumes in such a manner that domesticated forms arose.

The reasons for doing so must be related in some manner to the climate changes associated with the start of the Holocene. Invoking the changing climate and environment does not, in

Fig. 15.7 The Pre-Pottery Neolithic B site of Ghuwyer 1, Wadi Faynan, southern Jordan. This shows the typical architecture for the Middle PPNB period with rectangular structures densely packed together (© Alan Simmons).

itself, provide an explanation for this dramatic change in lifestyles which laid the foundations for the early civilizations of Mesopotamia and Egypt.

Following Kenyon's excavations at Jericho, further PPNA sites were discovered and excavated throughout the Levant, but principally in the region of today's West Bank (figure 8). The best preserved and the most informative is Netiv Hagdud at which a variety of structures built with either stone or mud brick were discovered with typical below floor burials and ground stone artefacts such as pestles and mortars (Bar-Yosef & Gopher 1997). Wild barley had been cultivated, but it had not yet evolved into a domesticated form; meat principally game from the hunting of gazelle.

We need to look at the two sites that were discovered in the 1990s and which are both still undergoing study. The first is the most remarkable—the site of Göbekli Tepe in southern Turkey (figure 9). The discovery of this site in 1995 astounded archaeologists because it appears to be a Neolithic hill top sanctuary, the like of which had never been seen before.

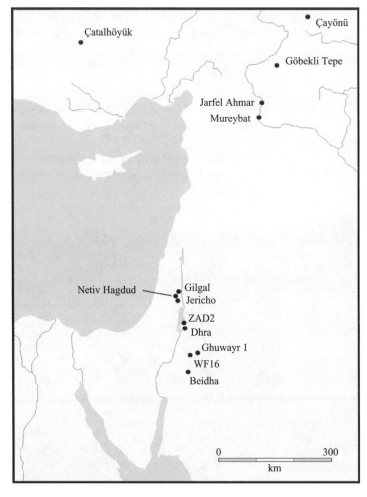

Fig. 15.8 The Levant showing the location of key Pre-Pottery Neolithic A sites, and the Pre-Pottery Neolithic B sites of Çayönü and Çatalhöyük.

Fig. 15.9 Göbekli Tepe, southern Turkey, undergoing excavation by Klaus Schmidt in October 2003 (© Steven Mithen).

Göbekli Tepe is still under excavation by Klaus Schmidt (2001) and any interpretation must be preliminary. At around 11 500 years ago, large semi-subterranean circular structures were constructed in the side of a hill and massive pillars of stone erected in their interior. These were decorated with images of wild animals—foxes, wild boar, water birds, snakes, spiders and aurochs (figure 10; Schmidt 1998, 1999). The imagery itself is familiar from the PPNA site of Jerf el Ahmar in Syria (Stordeur *et al.* 1997) and the rather later Çatalhöyük in Turkey (Mellaart 1967; Hodder 2006). But never had such monumental structures been seen in the early Neolithic. The site looks and feels like an amalgamation of Lascaux Cave and Stonehenge.

The investment in time and labour to have created this site must have been vast. When visiting, one's feet literally crunch across stone flakes littering the ground because these pillars of stone were quarried dressed and then decorated with no more than flint flakes. The largest standing stones are estimated to weigh 7 tons; at the quarry site, one pillar remains still partly embedded in the rock and is twice the size of any successfully removed.

The meaning of the images is lost to us. It is striking that just at the moment in history when domesticated animals and plants are about to cause an economic, social and cultural revolution, there should be such an investment in representing the wild and dangerous. It does not seem outlandish to suggest that these wild animals may have been totems, animals that formed ancestors for particular social groups. As such, we have here a classic example of cognitive fluidity, the imposition of social intelligence, a way of thinking that had evolved for interacting with other human beings, onto the non-human world.

Whatever the social and symbolic role of these animal images, they must have formed part of a remarkably strong ideology that motivated people to create the structures at Göbekli Tepe.

Fig. 15.10 Stone pillar incised with image of a fox at Göbekli Tepe (© Steven Mithen).

We must assume that this locality was one where people aggregated from the surrounding region, most likely for public ritual, feasting, exchange and status competition. What makes Göbekli Tepe of even greater interest is that it is no more than 30 km from the Karacadağ hills (figure 11). That is where geneticists have suggested domesticated einkorn wheat originated (Heun *et al.* 1997)—although questions have been raised about their methodology (Allaby & Brown 2003) and a more likely scenario is for multiple sources of domestication of wheat and barley in the northern and southern Levant. Nevertheless, the possibility remains that such plants originated owing to the intensive exploitation of wild plants in the vicinity of sites such as Göbekli Tepe to feed the large numbers of people who formed aggregations for whatever ideological purpose such sites served—perhaps a celebration of the wild (Mithen 2003). As such, there would have been no intention to domesticate wild cereals, no climatic cause and the population pressure would have been a highly localized phenomenon. But if to feed the residents and visitors to Göbekli Tepe and similar sites, the wild cereals and legumes were frequently weeded, transplanted, had their insect pests removed, had their seed collected and then planted, watered and so forth the transition to domesticated forms would have arisen. So sociality—in this case group size—may have played a key role in the transition to agriculture. But the ultimate cause would have been the ideological need that caused such aggregations to occur, represented to us today by the astonishing pillars of Göbekli Tepe.

Fig. 15.11 View looking eastwards from the summit of Göbekli Tepe towards the Karacadağ hills where geneticists have pinpointed the earliest strains of domesticated wheat (© Steven Mithen).

While this may be a further example of sociality playing a role in the most important cultural transition of humankind, it cannot be characterized as a misapplication of social intelligence. For a potential example of this, we can look at another PPNA site, one located in the southern Levantin Wadi Faynan (figure 12). This is the site of WF16, one that I discovered in 1996 and where I have undertaken some small excavations with my colleague Bill Finlay-son (Mithen *et al.* 2000; Finlayson & Mithen, 2007), prior to what we hope will be a major open-area excavation in the near future. That will be to excavate large structures that we have detected by geophysics and which most likely contain well preserved and stratified deposits.

WF16 is a Neolithic village with typical structures and material culture of the PPNA: circular 'dwellings' with stone walls; grinding stones embedded in floors (figure 13); chipped stone artefacts forming a bladelet industry with El-Khiam points and many other pointed artefacts; diverse range of ground stone artefacts; beads made from shell and stone. As with other sites of this period, it has human burials below house floors, some of which appear to have had bones repeatedly added to and removed (figure 14). These burials are literally the imposition of the social, i.e. persons, into the natural, i.e. the ground, providing a dramatic material representation of what I suspect was a cognitively fluid understanding of the world.

The art objects at WF16 and at PPNA sites in the southern Levant in general lack the wild animal imagery of the northern Levant and consist of geometric designs and rather schematic figurines (figure 15). Figurines are also found in northern regions and at some later sites, notably Çatalhöyük in Turkey, where they have traditionally been interpreted as Goddesses, images of Mother Earth or symbols of fertility (e.g. Mellaart 1967; Gimbutas 1974; Cauvin 2000). Such interpretations have no scientific basis and are most likely inaccurate. My interest is with

Fig. 15.12 Wadi Faynan, southern Jordan. The Pre-Pottery Neolithic site of WF16 covers the two knolls in the foreground. The white Landrover is adjacent to Trench 2 (see figure 14), while the circular dwellings found in Trench 3 (see figure 13) are located on the knoll in the immediate foreground (© Steven Mithen).

Fig. 15.13 Circular stone structures within Trench 3 at WF16. Structures of this type are typical of the Pre-Pottery Neolithic A period. They are likely to have been the base of dwellings with walls made from timber, reeds and hides (© Steven Mithen).

Fig. 15.14 Human secondary burial, initially placed within a plaster floor of a small circular structure within Trench 2 at WF16. The burial was adjacent to a large grinding stone also embedded within the floor. During the use life of the structure, which may have been a period of several hundred years, the burial was periodically opened and bone either inserted or removed (© Steven Mithen).

the apparently more mundane coarse stone artefacts from WF16, artefacts that were used to process plant materials—mortars, grinding stones (figure 16), pestles (figure 17) and processors (figure 18; Shaffrey 2007)—and are normally kept quite separate from any discussions about prehistoric ideology.

By their very nature, pestles and processors are phallic in form and the manner of their use, insertion into the deep cup-hole mortars typical of the PPNA, lends itself to a sexual metaphor. During excavation at WF16, a stone phallus was recovered (figure 15, SF1005), along with another item that may be either an unfinished phallus or simply an unfinished pestle (figure 19). With the evidence from these two objects, the idea that other artefacts initially classified as no more than utilitarian tools may in fact be phallic representations, or far more likely artefacts of both a utilitarian and a symbolic nature, deliberately ambiguous, becomes more plausible (such as figure 17 SF2012, SF2105; figure 18 SF283 and SF2034; Mithen *et al.* 2005). Indeed, I have become persuaded that the processing of plant foods at WF16, and possibly throughout the PPNA, was imbued with a sexual metaphor—what one might describe as the misapplication of social intelligence.

This cannot, of course, be more than interpretation based on scarce and ambiguous evidence, and at present it is little more than a proposal which I intend to explore in my forthcoming research. However, it is worthwhile noting that plant-processing equipment, procedures

SF1005

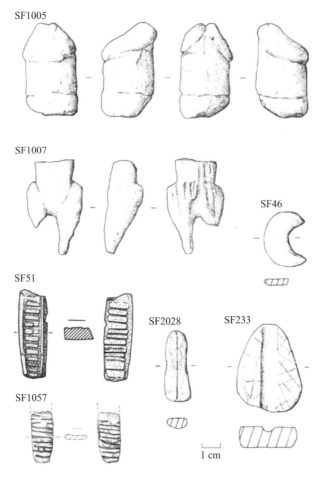

Fig. 15.15 'Non-utilitarian' ground stone items from WF16. Objects with geometric designs and figurines are typical of the Pre-Pottery Neolithic A from the southern Levant.

and products have been frequently associated with sexual symbolism throughout human history. Explicit sexual imagery is found on stone artefacts and bowls from the Northwest of America from 5000 years ago to the nineteenth century (Marshall 2000). In the Old Testament, Job (31:9–10) uses a mortar and pestle grinding grain as a metaphor for sex. Among the Shona people of Zimbabwe, domestic artefacts are imbued with sexual meanings on the basis of their shape; Shona men were believed to become impotent if they sat upon a mortar (Jacobsen-Widding 1992). In modern day Jordan, the language of cultivation is replete with sexual associations; the name for the stole of the ard being the same as that for penis, and the relationship between the ard and the land being seen as similar to that between men and women (Palmer 1998). With regard to food itself, Camporesi's (1993, p. 16) study of nineteenth century Italian peasant society described bread as the 'most grandiose sexual metaphor ever invented'. While further examples could be given, these can do no more than to lend plausibility to the interpretation of the PPNA plant-processing equipment at WF16 that I have proposed, and the need is to find further sources of direct evidence.

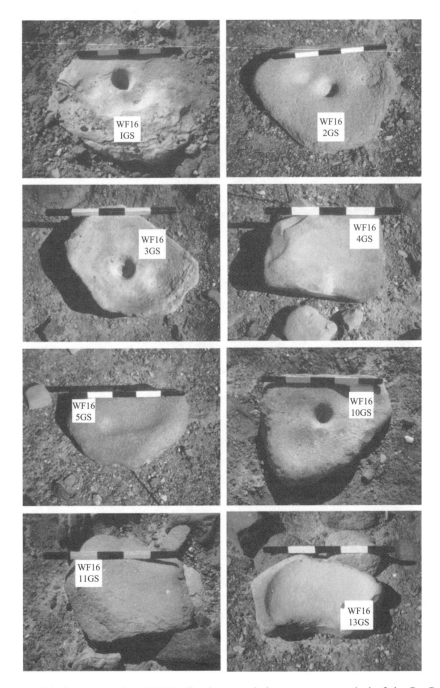

Fig. 15.16 Grinding stones from WF16. The deep cop-hole mortars are typical of the Pre-Pottery Neolithic A period.

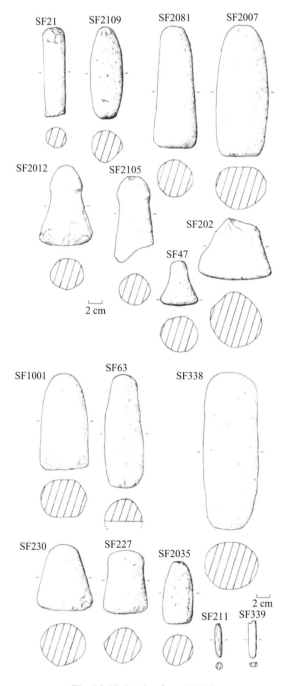

Fig. 15.17 Pestles from WF16.

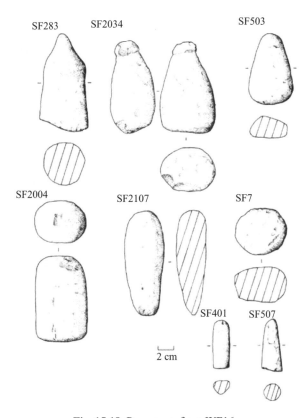

Fig. 15.18　Processors from WF16.

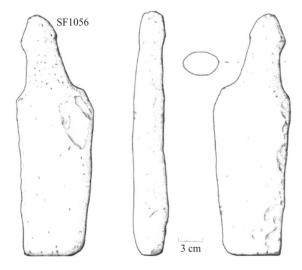

Fig. 15.19　Ground stone item from WF16. This appears to be either an unfinished pestle, a phallus or an object which has deliberately ambiguous associations.

15.2 Summary

I intend to do that, but I must now conclude by returning to the core of my argument. In 1984, Nicholas Humphrey asked if the origin of farming may have arisen from the misapplication of social intelligence. More generally, we can ask what role sociality played in causing this fundamental change in human economy and culture. Although debates will continue, it can be argued that processes of social competition influenced the development of cultivated and then domesticated forms of squash, maize and beans in Mexico; these were not grown for basic sustenance but as a means of acquiring prestige, and the similar processes of social competition may have also been significant elsewhere in the world. In Southeast Turkey, it may have been the large aggregation of people at sites such as Göbekli Tepe and the consequent intensive exploitation of wild plants that led to the accidental emergence of domesticated forms.

In addition to these factors of social competition and group size, the evidence at Göbekli Tepe and WF16—the burials, the art, the plant processing equipment—suggest that both the natural world and the material culture were perceived with a manner of thought that would have originated for thinking about human relationships—the misapplication of social intelligence. As such, the origin of farming may indeed be a consequence of the cognitive fluidity that is characteristic of modern humans, while it was the domain-specific mentality of the Neanderthals that left them as hunter-gatherers for the entirety of their existence. And once farming had originated, the pathway to towns, cities and civilization appears to have been almost inevitable, as does that to writing, mathematics and a massive expansion of human knowledge, a fundamental change in the nature of cognition, if not intelligence itself.

I am grateful to Nathan Emery and an anonymous referee for comments on an earlier draft of this paper. I would also like to thank the organizers of the 'Social intelligence: from brain to culture' Discussion Meeting for having invited me to participate.

References

Allaby, R. & Brown, T. 2003 AFLP data and the origins of domesticated crops. *Genome* **46**, 448–453. (doi:10.1139/g03-025)

Bar-Yosef, O. 1998 The Natufian culture in the Levant, threshold to the origins of agriculture. *Evol. Anthropol.* **6**, 159–177. (doi:10.1002/(SICI)1520-6505(1998)6:5<159::AID-EVAN4>3.0.CO;2-7)

Bar-Yosef, O. & Belfer-Cohen, A. 1989 The origins of sedentism and farming communities in the Levant. *J. World Prehistory* **3**, 477–498.

Bar-Yosef, O. & Gopher, A. (eds) 1997 *An Early Neolithic village in the Jordan Valley part 1: the archaeology of Netiv Hagdud.* Cambridge, MA: Harvard University Press.

Bar-Yosef, O. & Meadow, R. H. 1995 The origins of agriculture in the Near East. In *Last hunters–first farmers: new perspectives on the transition to agriculture* (eds T. D. Price & A. B. Gebauer), pp. 39–94. Santa Fe, New Mexico: School of American Research Press.

Bender, B. 1978 Gatherer-hunter to farmer: a social perspective. *World Archaeol.* **10**, 204–222.

Binford, L. 1968 Post-Pleistocene adaptations. In *New perspectives in archaeology* (eds S. Binford & L. Binford), pp. 313–342. Chicago, IL: Aldine.

Bird-David, N. 1990 The 'giving environment': another perspective on the economic system of gatherer-hunters. *Curr. Anthropol.* **31**, 189–196. (doi:10.1086/203825)

Blench, R. M. & MacDonald, K. C. 2000 *The origins and development of African livestock. Archaeology, Genetics, linguistics and ethnography.* London, UK: UCL Press.

Camporesi, P. 1993 *The magic harvest: food, folklore and society.* Cambridge, UK: Polity Press.

Carruthers, P. 2002 The cognitive functions of language. *Brain Behav. Sci.* **25**, 657–726. (doi:10.1017/S0140525X02000122)

Cauvin, J. 2000 *The birth of the gods and the origins of agriculture*. Cambridge, UK: Cambridge University Press.

Childe, V. 1958 *The prehistory of European society*. London, UK: Penguin.

Clark, A. 1997 *Being there: putting brain, body and world together again*. Cambridge, MA: MIT Press.

Clark, A. 2003 *Natural born cybords: minds, technologies, and the future of human intelligence*. Oxford, UK: Oxford University Press.

Clark, A. & Chalmers, D. 1998 The extended mind. *Analysis* **58**(10-23), 1998.

Cohen, M. 1977 *The food crisis in prehistory*. New Haven, CT: Yale University Press.

D'Errico, F., Henshilwood, C., Vanhaeren, M. & van Niekerk, K. 2005 *Nassarius kraussianus* shell beads from Blombos Cave: evidence for symbolic behaviour in the Middle Stone Age. *J. Hum. Evol.* **48**, 3–24. (doi:10.1016/j.jhevol.2004.09.002)

Denham, T. P., Haberle, S. G., Lentfer, C., Fullagar, R., Field, J., Therin, M., Porch, B. & Winsborough, B. 2003 Origins of agriculture at Kuk Swamp in the highlands of New Guinea. *Science* **5630**, 189–193. (doi:10.1126/science.1085255)

Donald, M. 1991 *Origins of the modern mind*. Cambridge, MA: Harvard University Press.

Dunbar, R. 2004 *The human story*. London, UK: Faber & Faber.

Finlayson, B. & Mithen, S. J. (eds) 2007 The Early Prehistory of Wadi Faynan, Southern Jordan: evaluation of the Pre-Pottery Neolithic A site of WF16 and archaeological survey of Wadis Faynan, Ghuwayr and al Bustan. London, UK: CBRL Monographs.

Flannery, K. 1986 *Guilá Naquitz*. New York, NY: Academic Press.

Gimbutas, M. 1974 *The goddesses and gods of old Europe*. London, UK: Thames & Hudson.

Harris, D. R. 1996 Domesticatory relationships of people, plants and animals. In *Redefining nature: ecology, culture and domestication* (eds R. Ellen & K. Fukui), pp. 437–463. Oxford, UK: Berg.

Hayden, B. 1990 Nimrods, piscators, pluckers and planters: the emergence of food production. *J. Anthropol. Archaeol.* **9**, 31–69. (doi:10.1016/0278-4165(90)90005-X)

Henshilwood, C. S. *et al.* 2002 Emergence of modern behaviour: Middle Stone Age engravings from South Africa. *Science* **295**, 1278–1279. (doi:10.1126/science.1067575)

Heun, M., Schafer-Pregl, R., Klawan, D., Castagna, R., Accerbi, M., Borghi, B. & Salamini, F. 1997 Site of einkorn wheat domestication identified by DNA fingerprinting. *Science* **278**, 1312–1314. (doi:10.1126/science.278.5341.1312)

Hodder, I. 2006 *Çatalhöyük: the Leopard's Tale*. London, UK: Thames & Hudson.

Humphrey, N. 1984 *Consciousness regained*. (12. The colour currency of nature, pp. 146–152). Oxford, UK: Oxford University Press.

Imamura, K. 1996 *Prehistoric Japan: new perspectives on insular East Asia*. Honolulu, HI: University of Hawai'i Press.

Jacobsen-Widding, A. 1992 Pits, pots and snakes—an anthropological approach to ancient African symbols. *Nordic J. Afr. Stud.* **1**, 5–25.

Kuijt, I. & Goring-Morris, A. 2002 Foraging, farming, and social complexity in the Pre-Pottery Neolithic of of the southern Levant: a review and synthesis. *J. World Prehistory* **16**, 361–440. (doi:10.1023/A:1022973114090)

Kuzman, Y. V. 2006 Chronology of the earliest pottery in East Asia: progress and pitfalls. *Antiquity* **80**, 362–371.

Marshall, Y. 2000 Reading images stone b.c. *World Archaeol.* **32**, 222–235. (doi:10.1080/00438240050131207)

Mellaart, J. 1967 *Çatal Höyük: a Neolithic Town in Turkey in Anatolia*. London, UK: Thames & Hudson.

Mellars, P. 1996 *The Neanderthal legacy*. Princeton, NJ: Princeton University Press.

Mithen, S. J. 1996 *The prehistory of the mind: a search for the origins of art, science and religion*. London, UK: Thames & Hudson.

Mithen, S. J. 1998 A creative explosion: theory of mind, language and the disembodied mind of the Upper Palaeolithic. In *Creativity in human evolution and prehistory* (ed. S. Mithen), pp. 165–192. London, UK: Routledge.

Mithen, S. J. 2003 *After the Ice: a global human history 20,000–5000 BC*. London, UK: Weidenfeld & Nicolson.

Mithen, S. J. 2005 *The singing Neanderthals*. London, UK: Weidenfeld & Nicolson.

Mithen, S. J., Finlayson, B., Pirie, A., Carruthers, D. & Kennedy, A. 2000 WF16: new evidence for economic and technological diversity in the PPNA. *Curr. Anthropol.* **41**, 655–662. (doi:10.1086/317393)

Mithen, S., Finlayson, B. & Shaffrey, R. 2005 Sexual symbolism in the Early Neolithic of the Southern Levant: pestles and mortars from WF16. *Documenta Praehistorica* **XXXII**, 103–110.

Palmer, C. 1998 "Following the Plough": the agricultural environment of northern Jordan. *Levant* **XXX**, 129–165.

Renfrew, C. 2001 Symbol before concept: material engagements and the early development of society. In *Archaeological theory today* (ed. I. Hodder), pp. 122–140. Cambridge, UK: Cambridge University Press.

Rice, P. 1999 On the origins of pottery. *J. Archaeol. Method Theory* **6**, 1–54. (doi:10.1023/A: 1022924709609)

Rick, J. W. 1980 *Prehistoric hunters of the high Andes*. New York, NY: Academic Press.

Saladin D'Anglure, B. 1990 Nanook, super-male: the polar bear in the imaginary space and social time of the Inuit of the Canadian Arctic. In *Signifying animals: human meaning in the natural world* (ed. R. G. Willis), pp. 173–195. London, UK: Unwin Hyman.

Schmidt, K. 1998 Beyond daily bread: evidence of Early Neolithic ritual from Göbekli Tepe. *Neo-lithics* **2/98**, 1–5.

Schmidt, K. 1999 Boars, ducks and foxes—the Urfa-Project 99. *Neo-lithics* **3/99**, 12–15.

Schmidt, K. 2001 Göbekli Tepe. Southeastern Turkey. A preliminary report on the 1995–1999 excavations. *Paléorient* **26**, 45–54.

Shaffrey, R. 2007 The ground stone. In *The early prehistory of Wadi Faynan, Southern Jordan: evaluation of the Pre-Pottery Neolithic A site of WF16 and archaeological survey of Wadis Faynan, Ghuwayr and al Bustan* (eds B. Finlayson & S. Mithen), pp. 323–355. London, UK: CBRL Monographs.

Smalley, J. & Balke, M. 2003 Sweet beginnings: stalk sugar and the domestication of maize. *Curr. Anthropol.* **44**, 675–703. (doi:10.1086/377664)

Smith, B. D. 1995 *The emergence of agriculture*. New York, NY: Scientific American Library.

Smith, B. D. 1997 The initial domestication of *Cucurbita pepo* in the Americas 10,000 years ago. *Science* **276**, 932–934. (doi:10.1126/science.276.5314.932)

Stordeur, D., Helmer, D. & Willcox, G. 1997 Jerf el-Ahmar, un nouveau site de l'horizon PPNA sur le moyen Euphrate Syrien. *Bulletin de la Société Préhistorique Française* **94**, 282–285.

Stringer, C. B. & Gamble, C. 1993 *In search of the Neanderthals*. London, UK: Thames & Hudson.

Trinkaus, E. 1995 Neanderthal mortality patterns. *J. Archaeol. Sci.* **22**, 121–142. (doi:10.1016/S0305-4403(95)80170-7)

Zhao, Z. 1998 The middle Yangtze region in China is one place where rice was domesticated: phytolith evidence from the Diaotonghuan Cave, northern Jiangxi. *Antiquity* **72**, 885–897.

16

Social intelligence, human intelligence and niche construction

Kim Sterelny

This paper is about the evolution of hominin intelligence. I agree with defenders of the social intelligence hypothesis in thinking that externalist models of hominin intelligence are not plausible: such models cannot explain the unique cognition and cooperation explosion in our lineage, for changes in the external environment (e.g. increasing environmental unpredictability) affect many lineages. Both the social intelligence hypothesis and the social intelligence–ecological complexity hybrid I outline here are niche construction models. Hominin evolution is hominin response to selective environments that earlier hominins have made. In contrast to social intelligence models, I argue that hominins have both created and responded to a unique foraging mode; a mode that is both social in itself and which has further effects on hominin social environments. In contrast to some social intelligence models, on this view, hominin encounters with their ecological environments continue to have profound selective effects. However, though the ecological environment selects, it does not select on its own. Accidents and their consequences, differential success and failure, result from the combination of the ecological environment an agent faces and the social features that enhance some opportunities and suppress others and that exacerbate some dangers and lessen others. Individuals do not face the ecological filters on their environment alone, but with others, and with the technology, information and misinformation that their social world provides.

Keywords: evolution of cooperation; niche construction; social intelligence; division of labour; strong reciprocity

16.1 The explanatory target

Our australopithecine ancestors had approximately chimp-sized brains and a technological toolkit that was not much more complex than that of contemporary chimps. Nor is there reason to suppose that their social lives were more complex than those of surviving great apes. Over the next 4.5 Myr, a lot happened. The geographical and ecological range of these primates expanded greatly and diets changed. Hominins depended increasingly on meat and high-value plant foods, and processing food after its acquisition became increasingly important. In particular, cooking detoxified much plant food, reduced the physical stresses of chewing and released more nutrients (Wrangham *et al.* 1999; Wrangham 2001). Hominin technology increased greatly in complexity and variety. Hominin social life became obligatorily cooperative, as the acquisition of crucial resources came to depend on a division of labour. Beginning with *Homo ergaster*, expansion into new habitats began. As this expansion continued, it co-occurred with, and sometimes depended on, an expansion of expertise and cooperation. The deserts and tundras into which early sapiens and its immediate ancestors expanded were not otherwise survivable. Our ancestors of 4 Myr ago lived in a world as they found it. We have transformed our physical, biological, social and informational environments. Humans of one generation bequeath an engineered world to the next generation, who often alter it further before transmitting it to their successors (Odling-Smee *et al.* 2003; Sterelny 2003). With these ecological, economic and cognitive changes, a transformation occurred in hominin morphology and life history. Humans are less sexual dimorphic than australopithecines, but we are larger, with relatively larger brains. Our cortical regions, especially, have expanded, despite the expense of these tissues and the life-history price they carry with them. We live longer and are dependent on adult provisioning longer. We have become a singleton. Through most of hominin evolution, there were a number of hominin species extant at any one time, but not now. There is certainly something to explain. All species are unique, but some, including ours, are more unique than others (for a recent overview of hominin evolution, see the five linked entries on hominid evolution in Pagel 2002).

The social intelligence hypothesis is one candidate explanation of this extraordinary transformation. This idea has been pressed into service to explain the distinctive features of primate, great ape and human intelligence; its service in this final role will be my concern. The social intelligence hypothesis dates to papers by Jolly and by Humphrey (Jolly 1966; Humphrey 1976); it became central to theories of cognitive evolution as a result of two very salient collections edited by Byrne & Whiten (Byrne and by Whiten 1988; Whiten & Byrne 1997). The crucial idea is that the sophistication of primate (ape, human) intelligence is an adapted response to the complexity of the social environment in which primates (apes, humans) act. Different versions of the social intelligence hypothesis focus on different dimensions of this complexity. Robin Dunbar, for instance, emphasizes the pressure social stress management imposes on an animal's time budget as group size increases (Dunbar 1996, 2003). Humphrey's original paper emphasizes competitive manoeuvring: the anticipation and counter-anticipation of social chess as agents compete for scarce resources in generationally complex environments. Jolly's much earlier paper centres on socially mediated learning rather than Machiavellian manoeuvring.

The plausibility of these models of hominin evolution depends on two linked thoughts: on intuitions about the sheer complexity of human social worlds, and the idea that there is a feedback loop between human cultural and cognitive complexity that drives the elaboration of each. Human sociality is spectacularly elaborate, and of profound biological importance. Our social groups are characterized by extensive cooperation and division of labour, with different individuals specializing in different tasks. There is cooperation within the family: males invest in their (presumptive) children, and there is often extensive cooperation, resource sharing and division of labour between sexual partners. There is intergenerational cooperation, too, when adults provision children and when middle age women forgo reproduction to invest instead in their younger children and their grandchildren. These economic and sexual forms of human sociality are interwoven with our complex systems of communication and affiliation. We are ultrasocial.[1]

There is much plausibility in the suggestion that human social worlds are extremely complex, and McShea has shown how to make this idea precise (McShea 1996; Anderson & Franks 2001; Anderson & McShea 2001; Anderson et al. 2001). In McShea's framework, we measure complexity in two dimensions. Social groups are hierarchically structured: individuals are embedded in families, extended families, sometimes in clans or villages as well as tribes and in tribal alliances. Hence, one dimension ('vertical complexity') measures the depth of the hierarchical organization an agent experiences. Another dimension 'horizontal complexity' measures size and differentiation at a level. As Dunbar has emphasized, numbers matter, in part because the number of relationships in a group grows much faster than group size itself (very much faster, if every member of a group interacts significantly with every other member). But differentiation matters too. The more the individual agents differ from one another, the more complex the agent's social world. These differences may be in expertise, economic role, physical capital, dispositions to cooperate or not and mate choice and life-history strategies. Vertical complexity measures structure between the level of individuals and that of the group as a whole. In a vertically simple environment, the social world consists of just individuals and the group as a whole. Add kin groups, clans and totem groups, economic/ecological teams—for instance, the cooperative whale-hunting groups studied by Alvard (Alvard 2002; Alvard & Nolin 2002)— and the social environment becomes vertically complex. For an agent's prospects will depend in part on his interactions with these proto-institutions. Thus, the complexity of an agent's social environment depends both on its horizontal and vertical complexity.

Given this framework, it is evident that there has been a massive expansion of the social complexity of hominin life. It is one thing to construct a mental map of an australopithecine band of 20, or so, individuals, with fairly homogenous technical and foraging skills but with (say) differing sexual politics (keep an eye on that just-subadult male). It is another to do the same for 150 individuals with quite varied technical and foraging expertise, and divided into kin groups and totem alliances. Recent hominin social worlds are not just large great ape worlds. They are more vertically complex, and they are far more differentiated.

The second feature of the social intelligence hypothesis is its identification of a putative feedback loop: an increase in social intelligence selects for yet further increases by increasing the complexity of the social environment. This feedback loop depends on a fundamental problem in human society: that of enjoying the benefits of cooperation without being exploited by others. Cooperation can be very profitable, because a group acting jointly can generate a higher return than the sum of each of them acting individually. Brian Skyrms' *The Stag Hunt* is a game-theoretic exploration of such synergies. Two hunters acting together can capture a stag, whereas each hunting individually can take only a hare apiece. Cooperation is favoured because a stag is worth more than twice a hare (Skyrms 2003). Collective defence, likewise, will typically be far more effective than individual defence. So there is a potential benefit to cooperation, but only if the costs of defection can be contained. For cooperative actions are not free, and the benefits of cooperation often do not fully depend on every agent paying the full cooperation cost. Collective defence can still be successful even if one defender lurks in the rear. These circumstances generate a temptation to avoid the costs of cooperation while collecting the benefits. For cooperation to be stable, the costs of defection need to be contained. Machiavellian versions of the social intelligence hypothesis focus on the cognitive challenge of managing cooperation in an environment in which defection is a threat. The feedback loop between individual capacity and social complexity makes the social intelligence hypothesis a niche construction hypothesis: the evolution of hominin cognition depends on features of the environment that hominins have created themselves.

In such an environment, the socially adept agent must calculate and police reciprocal bargains, scrutinize signals for their honesty, decide on her own disclosure principles, negotiate alliances and calculate whether it is worth defecting herself. These challenges lead to a feedback loop between individual cognitive capacity and social complexity. A crucial element of this model is that an increase in individual cognitive sophistication generates further social complexity. That link is well-motivated in Machiavellian versions of the social intelligence hypothesis. For increases in cognitive sophistication bring improved strategies of deception, counter-deception and cabal formation. This is the *Machiavellian loop* through which social chess generates social complexity. This mechanism was clearly identified by Humphrey, who wrote of the feedback loop as a ratchet, a 'self-winding watch to increase the general intellectual standing of the species' (Humphrey 1976, p. 311). For a recent version of this view, see Flinn *et al.* (2005). The link is less well motivated if social worlds are mostly cooperative.

For in that case, the challenges of social life mostly consist of coordination problems, and increases in intelligence can make coordination easier. Signals become less ambiguous, plans more explicit and coordination can be organized by negotiating norms and customs. The social environment can thus become more informationally transparent, and selection for further intelligence would be self-limiting.

Contemporary social life can make the Machiavellian loop seem more central to human cognitive evolution than it really is. For the problems of deception and defection are far more serious in contemporary mass societies than in the social worlds in which the cooperative framework of human life evolved. Mass societies are anonymous. Many interactions are one-off, with strangers. Communication is often disembodied and decontextualized, via arms-length media. Perhaps, most important of all, agents are highly mobile, making a defect-shift strategy available. The attraction of that strategy has been boosted by the invention of money. Money may not be the root of all evil, but it facilitates the defect-shift strategy by making resources extremely portable, and by making immense gains from a single interaction possible. These are all novel facets of human worlds. We cannot project our institutional policing mechanisms back in time to explain the stability of hominin ultrasociality in the face of defection. But nor can we project the contemporary risk back in time as a threat to that sociality. Hominin ultrasociality was assembled in smaller and far from anonymous social worlds; and social worlds in which shifting between groups was not a routinely available, low-cost option.

Even on these more intimate scales, defection is a serious threat, and containing its costs takes cognitive investment. But I shall argue that the Machiavellian loop rests on a misconceived view of the evolution of cooperation in hominin life. Cooperation did not survive and expand in hominin worlds as a result of individuals vigilantly policing reciprocal exchanges of cooperative benefit. It did not evolve as a result of each individual efficiently scrutinizing their rate of return from cooperative exchanges in iterated prisoner's dilemmas, using the threat of withdrawing cooperation to keep others honest. Human cooperation has been seen too much through the lens of reciprocal altruism modelled as an iterated prisoner's dilemma. As with the social intelligence hypothesis, I shall suggest a model of human evolution in which niche construction plays a central role. In altering their social, biological and technological environment, we transformed the selective forces acting on our lineage. But I shall suggest that crucial early forms of cooperation were hunting and defence coalitions. These do raise defection problems, and hence generate a commitment problem. An agent should join a defence coalition only if he is sure others will join too. But since the benefits of cooperation, if achieved, are delivered immediately and since participation in a cooperative alliance, when it happens, is typically unambiguous, the cognitive demands on partner choice and partner assessment are contained. Moreover, traditional forager societies have been organized (and probably adapted) in ways that minimize the cognitive price of policing while still reducing temptations to defect. There is public information about the agents in these worlds, and that makes the problem of partner choice more tractable. Norms regulate cooperation: they reduce the calculative load on honest cooperators, and make defection, when it occurs, unambiguous. They thus make these small-scale social worlds more informationally transparent. Human psychology has evolved in conformity to that social organization. Most humans are *default* rather than *calculating reciprocators*: they enter social relations with the intention of cooperating if they expect other agents to do the same (Fehr & Fischbacher 2003, 2004). The cognitive cost of policing is not trivial. But social worlds in which there are cheap heuristics for detecting likely defectors, and in which most agents are default cooperators and which are organized to reduce temptations to defect, are not dominated by a deception/counter-deception arms race. Or so I argue in §2.

I shall argue, instead, that the cognitive expansion of the later hominins was driven by positive feedback loops between social and ecological competence. As a consequence, the distinction between social and foraging domains has been undermined. For the great apes and, I assume, early hominins, that distinction is valid: the cognitive demands ecology imposes on great ape intelligence can vary independently of the demands imposed by sociality. Indeed, the great apes vary very considerably in their social lives: gorillas live in extended family groups; orang-utans live fairly solitary lives (though probably they are more social than was once supposed); and the two chimp species live in complex fission–fusion social worlds. But Byrne has argued that they face a similar kind of ecological challenge: they all depend on defended or elusive resources. As a result, they are all skilled foragers. Gorillas and orang-utans, for example, harvest plant foods that defend themselves with spines, thorns or stings. Eating them safely takes skill and dexterity: anyone who doubts this can try their hand at preparing stinging-nettle salad. In particular, Byrne argues that processing highly defended plant foods requires the mastery of an appropriate behavioural programme incorporating precision handling with bimanual role differentiation, a regular, sequential and arguably hierarchically organized task structure (Byrne 1997, 2003, 2004). In short, the great apes have expertise, and they have expertise as a result of ecological selection. Though social and ecological innovative capacities tend to covary with one another (Reader & Laland 2002), social and technological competence are more decoupled among the great apes than in our lineage.

We cannot draw this distinction for the later hominins, for they have evolved into cooperative technological foragers, and the social and ecological domains have fused. Our distinctive intelligence is not due to the complexities of our social lives, though those lives are complex. Nor is it due to the fact that our lifeways have long depended on information and technology-intensive resource harvesting. It is due to the fact that our working lives have become our social lives. Cooperative social environments can evolve if agents can solve two problems: those of the generation and distribution of benefit. To generate benefit, agents need to solve coordination and differentiation problems. For cooperation to be stable, the profit of cooperation has to be distributed in ways that maintain incentives to cooperate. In the evolution of cooperation literature, there has been an inordinate focus on the distribution of benefit. I shall argue, in §3, that the generation of cooperative benefit drove hominin cognitive evolution.

16.2 A Machiavellian loop?

The evolution of cooperation has typically been explained as a form of reciprocal altruism and modelled in the framework of an iterated prisoner's dilemma. This framework makes Machiavellian versions of the social intelligence hypothesis plausible: cooperation seems both valuable and risky. In the right circumstances, cooperation can be very rewarding, and an agent who missed out on these rewards would be in real trouble, for example in many forager environments, hunting failures are frequent,[2] and cooperating hunters can insure one another against these failures. It makes sense for an agent who catches a pig to share, if he can be confident that his favour will be returned. For a pig is a large food package, but one that (in traditional societies) cannot be stored. The marginal value to the hunter of his remaining pig parts will decline as he and his family eat generously; so the last half of the pig will be much more valuable to those still hungry than to the successful hunter. In an environment in which one's own success is unpredictable, and not synchronized with the success of others, and in which one is likely to have a long history of interaction, cooperative food sharing is highly beneficial. So if families interact with one another regularly and if they are able to monitor one another's continued cooperation, the threat of withdrawing cooperation is likely to be important enough to make defection irrational.

On this model, cooperation is sustained (and occasionally fails) by the calculation of self-interest in a community of self-interested maximizers. Mutual scrutiny and the shadow of the future keep us honest. But we are always under selection to evade the scrutiny of others, thus gaining the rewards of cooperation without paying its full cost. Even more, we are under selection to ensure that others do not evade our scrutiny. And effective scrutiny is cognitively demanding (Stevens & Hauser 2004). Reciprocation obviously relies on identifying agents and representing their past actions, and these demands on memory become significant in multi-player interactions. Moreover, the cooperating agent needs to be able to judge his own investment and an expected return on it from his partner. This task of assessing return on investment is made more difficult by the need to discount future benefits. The cooperating agent needs to be able to represent the temporal gap between investment and payback, and to apply an appropriate discount rate.

If this is the right model of cooperation and its evolution, it would be true that the increasing complexity of human social worlds, and the increasing cognitive complexity of other agents, would ramp up the cognitive costs of cooperation. But in the past few years, an alternative to this calculative model of human cooperation has been developed. This model consists of three elements: (i) humans are (mostly) *strong reciprocators*: they enter social situations disposed to cooperate if they expect others to cooperate in return, without this disposition being dependent on their expectation that cooperation is economically optimizing for them. Humans are typically default rather than calculative cooperators. Moreover, they respond to defection with punishment, not just withdrawal (Fehr *et al.* 2002; Fehr & Fischbacher 2003). (ii) Humans live in 'symbolically marked' groups: groups which have common and distinctive customs, norms and values. This population structure makes cooperation more stable by making defecting more expensive. Shifting between symbolically marked groups is often impossible and is never routine. Some symbolically marked groups are now large enough for agents to try a defect-shift strategy within such a group, but this is a recent phenomenon. (iii) Norms help solve coordination problems: it is easier to anticipate what others will do and what they expect of you. But they also help solve problems that arise through the distribution of benefit, for cooperation is often channelled through norms and customs. Norm-regulated cooperation, and especially of norm-regulated distribution of benefit, reduces the calculative burden of strong reciprocation. In regulated interaction, no one has to try to calculate the fair return of cooperative investment in a joint product, taking into account temporal discounts, differential contributions to success and the like. Even in a community of honest cooperators, a fair negotiation of every joint product would be difficult, time consuming and conflict generating. Norms disambiguate a social environment: in norm-governed interactions, what is expected of an agent is public knowledge. This helps a strong reciprocator: he or she knows what to do and what expectations he or she should have of others. And it makes defection more obvious. Someone who fails to conform to a norm is defecting: the violation of expectations cannot be explained as an honest difference in view as to the fair contribution to or from a joint effort. Norms make the social environment more transparent.

Thus, Bowles, Ginits, Fehr and their collaborators have argued that *strong reciprocation* is the distinctive form of human cooperation. In strategic interactions, strong reciprocators cooperate if they expect other agents to cooperate too, even though they could gain by defecting. Their cooperation is not conditional on the expectation that their cooperation has the highest economic reward of their available options. Strong reciprocators enter a social situation disposed to begin by cooperating; they respond to cooperation by further, perhaps even enhanced, cooperation. They also punish failures to cooperate. They respond to defection not only by not cooperating in return, but also by punishment, even when punishment comes at a price and with no expectation of future benefit (Bowles & Gintis 2001; Fehr et al. 2002; Bowles & Gintis 2003, 2004; Fehr & Fischbacher 2003).

Experimental economists have revealed this behavioural syndrome by studying interactions in strategic games, where the experimental subjects had real gains and losses to make. It is striking that in these interactions, humans do not act like calculating cooperators: they do not cooperate if and only if they expect it to pay (for an overview, see Bowles & Gintis 2003), for example in a 'public goods game', N players simultaneously decide their contribution to a joint pool from an endowment. That joint pool grows (modelling the synergy of cooperation) and is then divided into N equal shares. Each agent keeps their non-donated contribution plus an equal share of the joint product. A calculating reciprocator would contribute nothing. A typical player contributes 50% of their stake in a one-shot game. But if the game is iterated, the donation declines to nothing over time. For the typical response is not universal, some defect. So agents reciprocate expected cooperation and only expected cooperation. The situation changes if communication and especially punishment are added to the game. In this form of the game, at the end of a round, agents can invest in punishment that reduces the take of defectors. If punishment is effective and not too expensive, agents punish, even when they will not interact with the punished player again, and that increases and stabilizes cooperation. Very strikingly, if subjects are allowed to choose between participating in a public goods games with punishment and one without (after experience), they almost all end up choosing a punishment game and cooperating maximally. When agents choose a game which allows punishment of defection, they contribute more of their stake to the common pool. They take the choice to enter such a regime to be an honest signal of willingness to contribute and to punish, and hence they ramp up their own contributions (Fehr & Rockenbach 2004).

This pattern is not an artefact of this particular game. Ultimatum and dictator games show a similar picture of our strategic dispositions. In the ultimatum game, player A proposes a division of a fixed resource to B, who can accept the proposal or decline it. If B declines the offer, both get nothing. If the interaction is one-off and anonymous, if both A and B were calculating cooperators, A would offer B the minimum possible fraction of the resource and B would accept the offer. In fact, most offers are between 0.3 and 0.5; about 50% of offers under 0.25 are rejected. A's knowledge that unfair offers are likely to be rejected constrains his strategy, but that is not the whole story (there is extensive cross-cultural research on this game; see Henrich et al. 2004). The dictator game is like the ultimatum game except B has no power to veto the decision. Even here, A typically offers B something. There is a lot of variation, but the average offer is about 0.25 of the stake. In the third-party punishment game, A and B play a dictator game. C observes and can punish A, at some cost, if she so chooses. Again, if everyone were calculating cooperators, A would give B nothing, and C would never punish A. In fact, the less A gives B, the more the C punishes A. Agents respond to perceived unfairness by punishing it, so long as it is effective and not too expensive (Fehr & Fischbacher 2004). There is good reason to believe that human agents are typically strong reciprocators.

Strong reciprocation, Bowles, Gintis and Fehr all argue, itself depends on prosocial emotion. Agents are disposed to cooperate with other cooperators through some combination of affiliative and empathetic emotions. We cooperate because we can identify with our partners in cooperation. And we cooperate through a sense of fairness and justice. Prosocial emotions induce an agent to act prosocially and to motivate punishment when others fail to act prosocially. They induce some mix of guilt/regret and shame when the agent himself/herself fails to act prosocially. The victim of defection might punish through anger and resentment. But third-party punishment must be based on judgements of unfairness, and be motivated by anger (and even disgust) at violations of norms of unfairness.

Human ultrasociality depends on the fact that most humans are default cooperators, but not only on that: cooperation is supported by demographic structure. Throughout most of the species lifespan, humans have lived in relatively small, 'symbolically marked' populations. The signature of modern human ecology—extensive, regionally varied toolkits, the capacity to invade most habitats and spread geographically, a broad foraging niche—emerged in rough synchrony with archaeological signs of symbolic group marking, i.e. of groups identifying themselves and being identified by others by their distinctive norms and customs. An archaeo-logical signature of ideology is inevitably much more ambiguous than that of ecology, but there is such a signature. Camp sites begin to show the use of ochre. We find stylistic variation in, and decoration of, tools. Totem-like objects appear in the record. The dead are buried, sometimes with grave goods. Later, there is clear evidence of cave paintings and the like. Collectively, this foraging and ideational complex is known as behavioural modernity, and it seems to have emerged gradually and roughly synchronically (though there is considerable debate about the extent to which it is a true linked package; Henshilwood & Marean 2003) in Africa between 200 000 and 50 000 years BP (McBrearty & Brooks 2000; Foley & Lahr 2003; Henshilwood & Marean 2003).

Norms often directly support prosocial action (Fehr & Fischbacher 2004). Human motiva-tional mechanisms do not seem to have kept pace with our increased lifespan and capacities to plan. Even by our own lights, we too readily trade future harms against current pleasure. Norms incentivate our own preference functions: violating a norm against (say) drunkenly groping your superior's partner will have immediate and hence motivationally salient costs, not just distant disutility. But norms can also stabilize behaviour by making the informational environment of strong reciprocation transparent. Norms make explicit the requirements of reciprocity. In doing so, norms reduce the cost of calculation among strong reciprocators, and by making the expectations of others unambiguous and explicit, they make failures to cooperate both salient and negatively marked.[3] So norms can support adaptive action by cog-nitively limited agents (Boyd & Richerson 2001). Alvard's portrait of the Lamalera is a lovely example of norm-regulated division which solves coordination and division problems of this kind. When a whale is caught, it is divided into shares (anatomical parts) which then go to particular stakeholders, for example whole shares go to the crew, and there are further norms about how the crew's share is divided among harpooner, his assistant, the helmsman, the bail-ers and the rest of the crew. Likewise, craftsmen also receive shares as of right: these go to the smith, the sailmaker, the carpenter and the boat manger, in addition to any entitlement they may have qua crewmember (Alvard & Nolin 2002). Having norms of division of this kind is not unusual, for example in group hunts by Efe Pygmies, shares depend on specific roles in the hunt: the hunter who shoots the first arrow gets about 35% of the prey, the hunter who shoots second about 10% and the owner of the dog gets 20% (Gurven 2004, p. 557). Importantly, these divisions of the hunt often involve rewards to invisible members: to the Lamalera crafts-men and to those Ache who cut trails, carry game and provision the hunting party rather than foraging directly (Gurven 2004, p. 558).

Moreover norms, together with customs and other forms of social life that are distinctive of particular groups, can play an indirect role in stabilizing cooperation. For the result of symbolic marking in a human population is divided into groups which tend to be internally homogenous while varying one from another. Furthermore, movement between such groups is restricted. These are conditions which make cultural group selection effective, and cultural group selection, presumably, will favour groups which police norms promoting effective coordination and cooperation (Sober & Wilson 1998; Boehm 1999). Moreover, individual level selection in favour of defecting from norms of cooperation will be weak. There will be no selection in favour of disobeying norms like those which regulate the division of a jointly caught whale. For violating these norms would incur punishment. If there is a temptation to defect, it will be defecting from paying the costs of punishing norm violation. But for those, the costs of punishment are likely to be low; perhaps very low. In a world that is already cooperative, some punishments cost little while effectively penalizing their target. Withdrawing social esteem and prestige are cheap punishments that impose a serious cost. Moreover, most of the population are strong reciprocators, so the cost of punishment is shared. Finally, punishment is rarely necessary because the threat of it is effective (Boyd & Richerson 1992). The individual cost of cooperation may well be very low; group selection in favour of cooperation will not be countered by strong individual selection in favour of defection. Thus, this demographic structure—populations divided into smallish groups, each group with a distinctive set of norms and customs—favours the evolutionary stability of cooperation.

Both iterated prisoner's dilemma and strong reciprocation models of cooperation share a common core: their paradigm of cooperation is the sequential exchange of favours over time. I share some of my pig with you today; in two weeks I receive a chunk of armadillo from you. An alternative paradigm for the evolution of cooperation is collective action (Alvard & Nolin 2002). Agents generate a joint benefit acting together in hunting large game, in the coordinated harvesting of large amounts of small game, in collective defence and, perhaps, in coalitional enforcement of egalitarian social orders against would-be alpha males. Hunting coalitions, collective defence and (perhaps) enforcement coalitions are plausible early forms of hominin cooperation. These are examples of mutualistic interaction. And they sidestep the cognitive costs of policing reciprocation. If joint action is successful, the profit is shared jointly and simultaneously (and shared automatically, in the case of successful collective defence). Dividing the spoils after a successful buffalo hunt is not difficult. It is not delayed in time. The buffalo can be dismembered on the spot in circumstances in which each is monitored by all.

These are not pure coordination games in the sense of Schelling's *The Strategy of Conflict*; there is a temptation to cheat. The cooperation problem with a buffalo hunt is to manage coordination and wholehearted participation in the hunt itself. As with reciprocation over time, there is a defection threat to joint action, for it is very important to avoid the sucker's pay-off. You do not want to be the only agent standing your ground against the charging buffalo or the attacking predator. Frank (1988) has written impressively on the role of the emotions in solving this class of coordination problems; in signalling trust and trustworthiness. These emotions and their signals are difficult to fake, especially between agents who have interacted regularly (Frank 1988). Moreover, some emotional signalling problems are ancient and predate the establishment of highly cooperative social worlds, for example establishing that threats are credible. This helps make collective action a plausible model for an early form of cooperation. One set of prosocial emotions that are not typically discussed in the evolution of cooperation literature, but which are important in this context, are those manifest in contemporary team sports. We find successful joint action intrinsically rewarding: perhaps especially when it is a high-energy, high-stress, high-arousal activity. Such collective activities both depend on and fuel affiliative bonds between the players; the more dangerous the activity, the more intense this affiliation cycle. Virtually, every memoir of infantry service centres on this affiliation circle and the role it plays in motivating action in combat (e.g. Graves 1929; Sassoon 1930; Fraser 2001).

If this is an important model of early hominin cooperation, two implications follow. First, vertical complexity is a key aspect of social complexity. Teams—coordinated work groups, often with specialist roles—generate important benefits, which flow preferentially to members of the team. Gurven and his colleagues note that in near-contemporary forager societies, the first division of spoils from big game hunting typically goes to members of the hunting partnership, though there may be a secondary flow from those hunters to others. Teams and their formation are important. In turn, this implies that partner choice models rather than partner control models are crucial in explaining the initial growth of cooperation in hominin life. Iterated prisoners dilemma models and their relatives are *partner control* models of cooperation. Agents improve their net benefit from cooperation by inducing favourable changes in partner behaviour; conditional willingness to cooperate and/or punishing defection induces partner cooperation. But as Ronald Noë has pointed out, these models are not biologically plausible: in real biological interactions, agents do not act simultaneously, each in ignorance of the other's act. So Noë argues that it is important to develop accounts of cooperation structured around *partner choice* models (Noë 2006). Forming hunting teams and enforcement coalitions is a partner choice problem, not a partner control problem. This changes our model of the cognitive demands of cooperation. The task becomes that of identifying the honest cooperators in your social world—if there are any to choose—and pursuing your joint endeavours with them, rather than monitoring reciprocation and its failure. If such partners can be identified and recruited, the intractable tasks of micro-managing and micro-accounting interactions disappear. In intimate social worlds in which there is mutual knowledge of the behavioural and emotional profiles of others, partner assessment is not cognitively intractable.

16.3 The generation and distribution of benefit

The evolutionary biology of the evolution of cooperation has generated a massive literature on the distribution of benefit. But there is much less on the generation of benefit; for an exception, see Alvard & Nolin (2002); for the importance to evolutionary theory of this neglect, see Calcott (2006). Yet, this too can require major cognitive investment. Synergies of cooperation sometimes depend just on joint action: a pack of African wild dogs hunting together can kill a wildebeest without role specialization by swamping that animal's defence. Very often though, the generation of benefit involves both specialization and coordination. Anderson & Franks (2001) review team-work—collective activity with role differentiation—in animal social life; hominins have gone a long way down this road. Behaviourally modern human foraging depends on coordination and specialization. In turn, coordination, specialization, technology and the skills to use it require an investment in cognitive resources. Teams must act in unison, in coordinated fashion, often while being aware of, and adjusting to, the acts of others. Collective action itself can be cognitively challenging. Moreover, human foraging is technologically enhanced, for example Inuit foraging would simply be impossible without kayaks and umiaks, harpoons, sewn clothing and footwear, and sleds. Technological dependence adds invisible partners to the hunt: those that provide the technology and informational tools without which the hunt would be impossible. Behaviourally modern foragers need a major investment to assemble the skill base on which coordinated technologically enhanced action rests.

Boyd, Richerson and their students have made this point strikingly and in detail (though for some of the problems we face in testing such evolutionary models of cooperation, see Rosenberg & Linquist 2005). They show that traditional societies depend on the skills, technologies and information that have been accumulated over many generations and which are transmitted, as critical cognitive capital, to the next generation (Henrich & McElreath 2003; Richerson & Boyd 2005). As this culturally transmitted skill base becomes more important, selection for the capacity to acquire and transmit such information intensifies; humans alter our environment in ways that transform the selective forces acting on us.

This investment in cooperative technological foraging collapses the distinction between social and ecological expertise, and generates feedback loops selecting for the further development of expertise. For coordinated foraging, and especially coordinated hunting, requires a fusion of social and ecological skills. The regular exploitation of large game like Cape Buffalo is often taken to be one signature of the appearance of behaviourally modern humans, for such large and potentially dangerous animals can be harvested only with appropriate ecological information, technology and coordinated action. Hunting requires foraging expertise: hunters need to be aware of the animal, its capacities, and its likely responses to threat. They need a precise understanding of their technology, its limits and their power to use it. But joint hunting is also an intensely social activity: hunters must have mutual knowledge of one another. Each hunter must know what others are doing and are likely to do; they must understand both their intentions and their capacities. Moreover, each must be aware of what others expect of him. Effective safe action depends on the smooth integration of social and ecological expertise (Laland & Hoppitt 2003). Plants, shellfish, animals down burrows and under rocks do not impose such heavy demands on fast-response decision making, though while trees do not fight back or run away, they can fall on you. But even harvesting these resources requires communication, planning and coordination. For one synergistic benefit of cooperation is *efficient search*. A group will forage more effectively, if they divide both targets and territory and if foragers ensure that every likely spot is searched, but that the same spot is not picked over twice. The social skills of communication and negotiation need to be allied with knowledge of natural history and local geography. The sexual division of labour typical in foraging societies is adaptive for this reason. Each gender specializes in the role for which it has a comparative advantage, though it is not clear whether traditional foraging societies routinely benefit in other ways as well from these search synergies. For foraging for plants and small items of animal food tends to be more individualistic, both in the search itself and in sharing the product (Boehm 1999).

A similar fusion is evident in the acquisition of foraging skills. Traditional lifeways depend on the accurate intergenerational transfer of foraging expertise: of information about the local geography, with its resources and dangers; natural history information; and information about the technology needed to acquire and process the resources on which those lifeways depend. Human minds and social worlds are adapted to enhance the reliability of inter-generational information transfer (e.g. Tomasello 1999*a,b*; Alvard 2003). Imitation, language and theory of mind all play key roles in this intergenerational transfer of information. Language, for example has many utilities, but learning and teaching is surely one. It is a crucial medium for pure cultural learning: in conversation, information is pumped from one mind to another. But much human learning is hybrid learning. The trial-and-error learning of the one generation is structured by its parental generation, making exploration safer and more productive. Apprentice craftsmen, hunters, foragers get advice and instruction as they practice. Moreover, they often get this advice and instruction from the most expert members of the previous generation (though they often have to pay a price in deference and respect to these experts (Henrich & Gil-White 2001)). Many traditional societies are organized so that information flows collectively from one generation to the next; many members of the upstream generation contribute to the cognitive capital of each member of the downstream generation. Language plays an important role in structuring and supporting exploration learning. It is well suited to encoding forager expertise, incorporating rich natural history and technical vocabularies (as ethnobiologists have shown; Atran 1990; Berlin 1992). It enables agents to describe environmental features qualitatively, quantitatively and probabilistically. Moreover, language allows the parental generation to substitute social signals for those from the world itself. As warnings ('no, that one is poisonous') substitute for error, the cost of exploration falls (Castro & Toro 2004; Castro *et al.* 2004).

Imitation, likewise, plays its most central role in hybrid learning. In contrast to young apes, human children are early and incorrigible imitators (Tomasello 1999*a,b*). Even so, few life skills are learned by imitation alone. Rather, adult demonstration is combined with practice, trial-and-error exploration and instruction in skill acquisition. Language and imitation show that human minds are extensively adapted for cultural learning. But they also show that the tools for cultural learning are not used just for learning *about* culture. Our adaptations for cultural learning allow us to use others' mind as sources of information about the non-human world. The same is true of human theory of mind capacities. Machiavellian versions of the social intelligence hypothesis emphasize the role of mind-reading in social chess; mind-reading allows one agent to anticipate what others are likely to do and say. But it also allows one agent to use another as a source of information about the world, and it adds to the efficiency of other adaptations for cultural learning. For a theory of mind makes teaching more efficient (Brockway 2003). Teaching is more effective if a teacher recognizes a student's existing capacities and understands what they find easy and what they find difficult, and when they are highly motivated and when they are beginning to lose motivation. But the effective transfer of craft and natural history skills is also promoted by a reflective understanding of the task domain itself. It is hard to pass on a skill that has become obligatorily automatized. To effectively teach a behavioural programme, that programme needs to be articulated. A performance needs to be slowed down; crucial subroutines need to be exaggerated or repeated; the programme as a whole needs to be decomposed into elements which can be taught and practiced independently, and hence demonstrated and described independently. Being able to disarticulate a skill is not an automatic consequence of having it. An effective teacher of a skill has to understand his or her own skill. Perhaps this reflective understanding is not an introspective theory of mind, but it is some form of cognitive self-awareness. It is also important that a student understands the teacher's demonstrations as demonstrations: she understands that a particular element of a skill is slowed down and exaggerated, and why, and also understands the crucial element of the total behavioural suite to which she should attend. Critical cognitive tools of human culture exist (I hypothesize) owing to selection for their use in the acquisition and deployment of ecological skills. In the lives of ancient humans, selection pressures generated by ecological complexity do not act independently of those derived from social complexity.[4]

This fusion of the social and the ecological has an important informational effect. The more coordinated action becomes part of the life of a group, the more agents know about each other. Joint foraging generates social information as a side effect. When individuals are engaged in a collective activity, they broadcast information about their personality, emotional states, skills and capacities, and reliability as an informant. The longer the association, the more often it is repeated, the greater the variety of circumstances in which joint activity is pursued, the more agents advertise themselves. Time-pressured, stressful or dangerous activities are especially revealing (for in those circumstances, inhibition is less effective). Agents disclose their personalities, because information leaks through cues rather than signals; through actions whose primary purpose is ecological rather than communicative. Agents reveal their patience or its absence, their temperament in a crisis and their capacity to function when wet, tired and hungry. Interactions with an unforgiving and indifferent world are natural signs of the psychological dispositions of an agent. Extended joint activity gives every agent extensive exposure to a large repertoire of such natural signs. A workplace—and a Pleistocene foraging band was a workplace—is simultaneously a social and an ecological domain. Team formation leads to better team formation: good partners are able to recognize one another increasingly well over time. As collective foraging is established, it will become increasingly difficult to seem like a good partner without being a good partner. If, therefore, it is important to be chosen, selection will favour the psychology of strong reciprocation.

Section 2 developed a sceptical view of the Machiavellian positive feedback loop, of the idea that cognitive sophistication breeds social complexity which breeds further cognitive sophistication, as managing reciprocal cooperation becomes ever more necessary and ever more demanding, as hominin social worlds become ever more complex. However, hominin cognitive complexity does depend on feedback loops, and that social complexity is part of that loop. However, the loop involves ecological as well as social complexity. It is the combination of the increasing information requirements of hominin resource extraction and the increasing social complexity of hominin worlds that drives the evolution of late hominin intelligence. One positive feedback loop is between ecological innovation, social complexity and cultural transmission. One major shift among the hominin is a change in the pattern and the magnitude of cultural learning. Among most animals, social learning typically takes place between members of the same generation, the information that flows has a short shelf-life, and it flows as a side effect of agents' ordinary ecological lives. Among the later hominin, there is extensive intergenerational flow of information with a long shelf-life (Reader & Laland 2002; Laland & Hoppitt 2003). This rich form of cultural transmission, characteristic of behaviourally modern humans, depends on the extension of human childhood, the invention of adolescence and the concomitant extension of human lifespans. Those changes in human life history, in turn, depend on ecological innovation. Cross-generational information flow both depends on and helps sustain the cross-generational flow of physical resources. The extension of human lifespan and the investment in a long childhood depended on controlling extrinsic causes of mortality: reducing threats of death through predation or accident and reducing the risk of starvation when ill, injured or unlucky (Hill & Kaplan 1999). For these human life-history patterns depend on within-family and between-generation resource transfers, on the fact that adults (and especially adult males) generate far more resources than they consume themselves. For human populations to be viable, the adults of generation $N+1$ must survive long enough to pump resources to generation $N+2$ equivalent to those they received from generation N. So, human life-history characteristics coevolve with technological competence and cultural learning. The technological and informational bases of cooperative technological foraging typically require deep educations. Foragers do not peak in their resource acquisition powers until they are about 30; they do not begin to produce more than they consume until about 18. The resource debt that individuals acquire as children and adolescents is not paid off until around 50. Extensive, apprentice-style cultural transmission supports the development of technological foraging skills that generate very rich returns;

the life history that makes such cultural transmission possible is paid for by those same skills (Robson & Kaplan 2003; Kaplan *et al.* 2005).

In addition to this feedback relationship between human life-history patterns, cultural transmission of information and information-intensive foraging, there is also a feedback loop between innovation and group structure, especially group size. Technology and foraging competence impact on group size. Group size, in turn, impacts on vertical complexity and the division of labour. Many adaptations are zero-sum: they change the distribution of traits within a population without affecting the size of that population at equilibrium. A mutation that makes an individual resistant to malaria can spread through a group exposed to that disease without changing population size at all. The adaptations that made technological cooperative foraging possible were not zero-sum adaptations. When technology and cooperation are combined, their profit drives population growth. Cooperative technological foraging gives a group access to resources that were previously unavailable, and allows more efficient harvesting of previous targets. The same adaptive complex gives better protection against predators. As a consequence, groups in which this complex establishes are less tied to specific habitats, for example good anti-predator defences might mean that grasslands—areas without natural refuges—can be exploited, and lesser predators can be driven from their kills (for the importance in hominin evolution of this habitat, see Potts 1996). The resource envelope increases; predation causes less mortality: the population expands. This population growth allows specialization. A band of 20 or so probably cannot afford a knapping specialist or a specialist fire-maker. The specialist will not have enough customers to support his/her skill; a band of twice that size may well do so (Ofek 2001). Size improves access to the enormous benefits of the division of cognitive labour. Moreover, larger groups maintain their cognitive resources more reliably. It is much safer to have a few old heads that know where water is to be found in dry times than have that knowledge restricted to one, vulnerable, old head (Henrich 2004). Much more speculatively, an expanding energy budget fuelled by the marriage of technology and cooperation might explain how hominin afforded their expensive brains (Aiello & Wheeler 1995).

As group size increases, the selective environment favours a further expansion of cognitive resources. Expansion can never be unchecked. At some stage, population expansion will put pressure on the existing resource base. For there is likely to be a population overshoot rather than a new equilibrium: the invention of a new technology (say, a first fish trap) is likely to lead to resources being harvested faster than the rate at which they are replenished. That pressure will select for a more intense exploitation of currently used resources. It also selects for adding resources: for geographical and/or ecological expansion. As resources are added, and exploited intensely, further specialization becomes economically viable. If wildfowl are eaten only occasionally as lucky windfalls, it will not pay to develop the specialist skills and tools needed to take them most efficiently. If they are regularly exploited, these special skills and technologies pay their way. Finally, expansion must eventually lead to more frequent and/or more intense intergroup conflict. Thus, geographical expansion, increasing resource breadth and more severe intergroup conflict all select for social or technological improvements in foraging and defence. Both the growth phase triggered by innovation and the constraint phase that follows it select for further innovation. Selection need not be efficacious: appropriate variations may not appear. Stasis and extinction are both possible. But if appropriate innovations are found and established, the cycle will iterate. Technological innovation will tend to cause populations to expand in numbers and area. Such expansion, in turn, tends to select for further innovation.

16.4 Conclusion

Richard Potts has argued that hominin evolution is a response to an increasingly challenging because increasingly variable physical and biological environment (Potts 1996). This might be the correct view of early hominin evolution, but there is a rough consensus that later hominin evolution is not explained in an externalist, adaptationist mode, as a lineage's adaptive response to an externally caused change in the environment. Both the social intelligence hypothesis and the social intelligence–ecological complexity hybrid I have proposed are niche construction models. Hominin evolution is hominin response to selective environments that earlier hominin have made. In contrast to social intelligence models, I have argued that hominins have both created and responded to a unique foraging mode, a mode that is both social in itself and which has further effects on hominin social environments. In contrast to the social intelligence model recently defended by Flinn *et al.* (2005), on this view, hominin encounters with their ecological environment continue to have profound selective effects. Flinn and his allies doubt this: they argue that the ecological dominance of humans results in humanity being 'its own principal hostile force of nature' (Flinn *et al.* 2005, p. 14). Selection on humans is the result of action by other humans. This is a mistake. For one thing, the fossil record of Neanderthals suggests that even technological and cooperative hunting is physically stressful and accident prone (Klein 1999, pp. 474–475). Even though Neanderthal rates of trauma reflect the extremely hostile nature of their environment, foraging is not safe. It results in significant mortality and morbidity. But even if that were not true, differential success (of both individuals and groups) in interaction with the nonhuman environment has selective consequences. However, though the ecological environment selects, it does not select on its own. Accidents and their consequences, differential success and failure, result from the combination of the ecological environment an agent faces and the social features that enhance some opportunities and suppress others; that exacerbate some dangers and lessen others.[5] Individuals did not face the ecological filters on their environment alone, but with others, and with the technology, information and misinformation that their social world provides. Ecological and social complexity became fused, as the ecological problem of extracting resources as individuals from a world we did not make became the economic problem of extracting resources collectively from and in a human world.

Thanks to Nick Shea, Kevin Laland and audiences at Victoria University of Wellington, the Royal Society Discussion Meeting and the ANU for feedback on earlier versions of this paper.

Endnotes

1. Indeed, Foster & Ratnieks (2005) have suggested (perhaps not wholly seriously) that humans are a second eusocial mammal.
2. Kaplan *et al.* (2005) note that Ache hunters return empty-handed 40% of the time; Hazda, hunters of large game, return with meat on only 3% of their hunting days.
3. In discussing the Ache and reporting on the !Kung, Kaplan, Gurven and their colleagues note that reservation life, based on cultivation, made the issue of sharing and cooperation among the Ache much more fraught. Even in a culture with strong traditions of sharing and reciprocation, it is hard to hammer out a consensus conception of what counts as being fair, what counts as being cooperative, but not a sucker (Kaplan *et al.* 2005, Part III).
4. It is important here to recall that the social intelligence hypothesis is a view of the selective environment of hominin evolution, not cognitive architecture. In particular, the social intelligence hypothesis does

not share the controversial assumptions of the 'massive modularity hypothesis'. According to this hypothesis, the distinctive features of human intelligence depend on an ensemble of special purpose cognitive subsystems rather than enhanced domain general learning and problem solving capacities (Barkow *et al.* 1992; Pinker 1997; Sperber & Hirschfeld in press). On one view of this cognitive architecture, we have a 'mind-reading' module: an innately based specialist subsystem that enables us to anticipate the actions of others by representing their cognitive and affective states. These nativist theories of cognitive architecture are committed to the idea that the informational bases of adaptive action in a particular domain are stable over evolutionary time. Neither social intelligence hypothesis nor this idea about the ecological–social feedback loop has any such commitment. We may well have enhanced general purpose problem solving capacities as a result of selection favouring enhanced capacity to solve the problems posed by our social environments.

5. Social facts, for example, profoundly affect the pathogens to which a population is exposed (Ewald 1994).

References

Aiello, L. C. & Wheeler, P. 1995 The expensive-tissue hypothesis: the brain and the digestive system in human and primate evolution. *Curr. Anthropol.* **36**, 199–221. (doi:10.1086/204350)

Alvard, M. 2002 Carcass ownership and meat distribution by big-game cooperative hunters. *Soc. Dimensions Econ. Process* **21**, 99–131.

Alvard, M. 2003 The adaptive nature of culture. *Evol. Anthropol.* **12**, 136–149. (doi:10.1002/evan. 10109)

Alvard, M. & Nolin, D. 2002 Rousseau's whale hunt? Coordination among big game hunters. *Curr. Anthropol.* **43**, 533–559. (doi:10.1086/341653)

Anderson, C. & Franks, N. 2001 Teams in animal societies. *Behav. Ecol.* **12**, 534–540. (doi:10.1093/beheco/12.5.534)

Anderson, C. & McShea, D. W. 2001 Individual versus social complexity with particular reference to ant colonies. *Biol. Rev.* **76**, 211–237. (doi:10.1017/S1464793101005656)

Anderson, C., Franks, N. R. & McShea, D. W. 2001 The complexity and hierarchical structure of tasks in insect societies. *Anim. Behav.* **62**, 643–651. (doi:10.1006/anbe.2001.1795)

Atran, S. 1990 *Cognitive foundations of natural history*. Cambridge, UK: Cambridge University Press.

Barkow, J. H., Cosmides, L. & Tooby, J. 1992 *The adapted mind: evolutionary psychology and the generation of culture*. Oxford, UK: Oxford University Press.

Berlin, B. 1992 Ethnobiological classification: principles of categorization of plants and animals in traditional societies. Princeton, NJ: Princeton University Press.

Boehm, C. 1999 *Hierarchy in the forest*. Cambridge, MA: Harvard University Press. Bowles, S. & Gintis, H. 2001 *Prosocial emotions. Working paper*. Santa Fe, NM: Santa Fe Institute.

Bowles, S. & Gintis, H. 2003 Origins of human cooperation. In *Genetic and cultural evolution of cooperation* (ed. P. Hammerstein), pp. 429–443. Cambridge, MA: MIT Press.

Bowles, S. & Gintis, H. 2004 *The evolutionary basis of collective action. Santa Fe working papers*, pp. 1–20. Santa Fe, NM: Santa Fe Institute.

Boyd, R. & Richerson, P. 1992 Punishment allows the evolution of cooperation (or anything else) in sizable groups. *Ethol. Sociobiol.* **13**, 171–195.

Boyd, R. & Richerson, P. 2001 Norms and bounded rationality. In *Bounded rationality: the adaptive toolbox* (eds G. Gigerenzer & R. Selten), pp. 281–296. Cambridge, MA: MIT Press.

Brockway, R. 2003 Evolving to be mentalists: the 'mindreading mums' hypothesis. In *From mating to mentality: evaluating evolutionary psychology* (eds J. Fitness & K. Sterelny), pp. 95–124. Hove, UK: Psychology Press.

Byrne, R. W. 1997 The technical intelligence hypothesis: an additional evolutionary stimulus to intelligence? In *Machiavellian intelligence II: extensions and evaluations* (eds R. Byrne & A. Whiten), pp. 289–311. Cambridge, UK: Cambridge University Press.

Byrne, R. 2003 Imitation as behaviour parsing. *Phil. Trans. R. Soc. B* **358**, 529–536. (doi:10.1098/rstb.2002.1219)

Byrne, R. 2004 The manual skills and cognition that lie behind hominid tool use. In *Evolutionary origins of great ape intelligence* (eds A. Russon & D. R. Begun), pp. 31–44. Cambridge, UK: Cambridge University Press.

Byrne, R. & Whiten, A. 1988 *Machiavellian intelligence: social expertise and the evolution of intellect in monkeys, apes and humans.* Oxford, UK: Oxford University Press.

Calcott, B. 2006 Transitions in biological complexity. Ph.D Thesis. Canberra: Australian National University.

Castro, L. & Toro, M. 2004 The evolution of culture: from primate social learning to human culture. *Proc. Natl Acad. Sci. USA* **101**, 10 235–10 240. (doi:10.1073/pnas.0400156101)

Castro, L., Medina, A. & Toro, M. 2004 Hominid cultural transmission and the evolution of language. *Biol.Philos.***19**, 721–737. (doi:10.1007/s10539-005-5567-7)

Dunbar, R. 1996 *Grooming, gossip and the evolution of language.* London, UK: Faber and Faber.

Dunbar, R. 2003 The social brain: mind, language and society in evolutionary perspective. *Annu. Rev. Anthropol.* **32**, 163–181. (doi:10.1146/annurev.anthro.32.061002.093158)

Ewald, P. W. 1994 *Evolution of infectious disease.* Oxford, UK: Oxford University Press.

Fehr, E. & Fischbacher, U. 2003 The nature of human altruism. *Nature* **425**, 785–791. (doi:10.1038/nature02043)

Fehr, E. & Fischbacher, U. 2004 Social norms and human cooperation. *Trends Cogn. Sci.* **8**, 185–189. (doi:10.1016/j.tics.2004.02.007)

Fehr, E. & Rockenbach, B. 2004 Human altruism: economic, neural and evolutionary perspectives. *Curr. Opin. Neurobiol.* **14**, 784–790. (doi:10.1016/j.conb.2004.10.007)

Fehr, E., Fischbacher, U. & Gächter, S. 2002 Strong reciprocity, human cooperation and the enforcement of social norms. *Hum. Nat.* **13**, 1–25.

Flinn, M., Geary, D. C. & Ward, C. V. 2005 Ecological dominance, social competition, and coevolutionary arms races: why humans evolved extraordinary intelligence. *Evol. Hum. Behav.* **26**, 10–46. (doi:10.1016/j.evolhumbe-hav.2004.08.005)

Foley, R. & Lahr, M. M. 2003 On stony ground: lithic technology, human evolution and the emergence of culture. *Evol. Anthropol.* **12**, 109–122. (doi:10.1002/evan.10108)

Foster, K. & Ratnieks, F. 2005 A new eusocial vertebrate? *Trends Ecol. Evol.* **20**, 363–364. (doi:10.1016/j.tree.2005.05.005)

Frank, R. 1988 *Passion within reason: the strategic role of the emotions.* New York, NY: WW Norton.

Fraser, G. M. 2001 *Quartered safe out here: are collection of the war in Burma.* London, UK: Akadine Press.

Graves, R. 1929 *Goodbye to all that.* London, UK: Jonathan Cape.

Gurven, M. 2004 To give and to give not: the behavioral ecology of human food transfers. *Behav. Brain Sci.* **27**, 543–583.

Henrich, J. 2004 Demography and cultural evolution: why adaptive cultural processes produced maladaptive losses in Tasmania. *Am. Antiq.* **69**, 197–221.

Henrich, J. & Gil-White, F. 2001 The evolution of prestige: freely conferred deference as a mechanism for enhancing the benefits of cultural transmission. *Evol. Hum. Behav.* **22**, 165–196. (doi:10.1016/S1090-5138(00)00071-4)

Henrich, J. & McElreath, R. 2003 The evolution of cultural evolution. *Evol. Anthropol.* **12**, 123–135. (doi:10.1002/evan.10110)

Henrich, J., Boyd, R., Bowles, S., Camerer, C., Fehr, E. & Gintis, H. 2004 *Foundations of human sociality.* Oxford, UK: Oxford University Press.

Henshilwood, C. & Marean, C. 2003 The origin of modern behavior. *Curr. Anthropol.* **44**, 627–651. (doi:10.1086/377665)

Hill, K. & Kaplan, H. 1999 Life history traits in humans: theory and empirical studies. *Annu. Rev. Anthropol.* **28**, 397–430. (doi:10.1146/annurev.anthro.28.1.397)

Humphrey, N. 1976 The social function of intellect. In *Growing points in ethology* (eds P. P. G. Bateson & R. A. Hinde), pp. 303–317. Cambridge, UK: Cambridge University Press.

Jolly, A. 1966 Lemur social behaviour and primate intelligence. *Science* **153**, 501–506. (doi:10.1126/science.153.3735.501)

Kaplan, H., Gurven, M., Hill, K. & Hurtado, A. M. 2005 The natural history of human food sharing and cooperation: a review and a new multi-individual approach to the negotiation of norms. In *Strong reciprocity: modeling the roots of cooperative exchange. The moral sentiments and material interests: the foundations of cooperation in economic life* (eds S. Bowles, R. Boyd, E. Fehr & H. Gintis). Cambridge, MA: MIT Press.

Klein, R. G. 1999 *The human career: human biological and cultural origins*. Chicago, IL: University of Chicago Press.

Laland, K. & Hoppitt, W. 2003 Do animals have culture? *Evol. Anthropol.* **12**, 150–159. (doi:10.1002/evan.10111)

McBrearty, S. & Brooks, A. 2000 The revolution that wasn't: a new interpretation of the origin of modern human behavior. *J. Hum. Evol.* **39**, 453–563. (doi:10.1006/jhev.2000.0435)

McShea, D. W. 1996 Metazoan complexity and evolution: is there a trend? *Evolution* **50**, 477–492. (doi:10.2307/2410824)

Noë, R. 2006 Cooperation experiments: coordination through communication versus acting apart together. *Anim. Behav.* **71**, 1–18. (doi:10.1016/j.anbehav.2005.03.037)

Odling-Smee, F. J., Laland, K. N. & Feldman, M. W. 2003 *Niche construction: the neglected process in evolution*. Princeton, NJ: Princeton University Press.

Ofek, H. 2001 *Second nature: economic origins of human evolution*. Cambridge, UK: Cambridge University Press.

Pagel, M. (ed.) 2002 *Encyclopedia of evolution*. Oxford, UK: Oxford University Press.

Pinker, S. 1997 *How the mind works*. New York, NY: W. W. Norton.

Potts, R. 1996 *Humanity's descent: the consequences of ecological in stability*. New York, NY: Avon.

Reader, S. & Laland, K. 2002 Social intelligence, innovation and enhanced brain size in primates. *Proc. Natl Acad. Sci. USA* **99**, 4436–4441. (doi:10.1073/pnas.062041299)

Richerson, P. J. & Boyd, R. 2005 *Not by genes alone: how culture transformed human evolution*. Chicago, IL: University of Chicago Press.

Robson, A. & Kaplan, H. 2003 The evolution of human life expectancy and intelligence in hunter–gatherer economies. *Am. Econ. Rev.* **93**, 150–169. (doi:10.1257/000282803321455205)

Rosenberg, A. & Linquist, S. 2005 On the original contract: evolutionary game theory and human evolution. *Anal. Kritik* **27**, 136–157.

Sassoon, S. 1930 *Memoirs of an infantry officer*. London, UK: Faber and Faber.

Skyrms, B. 2003 *The stag hunt and the evolution of social structure*. Cambridge, UK: Cambridge University Press.

Sober, E. & Wilson, D. S. 1998 *Unto others: the evolution and psychology of unselfish behavior*. Cambridge, MA: Harvard University Press.

Sperber, D. & Hirschfeld, L. In press. Culture and modularity. In *The innate mind: culture and cognition* (eds T. Simpson, P. Carruthers & S. Stich). Oxford, UK: Oxford University Press.

Sterelny, K. 2003 *Thought in a hostile world*. New York, NY: Blackwell.

Stevens, J. & Hauser, M. 2004 Why be nice? Psychological constraints on the evolution of cooperation. *Trends Cogn. Sci.* **8**, 60–65. (doi:10.1016/j.tics.2003.12.003)

Tomasello, M. 1999a *The cultural origins of human cognition*. Cambridge, MA: Harvard University Press.

Tomasello, M. 1999b The human adaptation for culture. *Annu. Rev. Anthropol.* **28**, 509–529. (doi:10.1146/annurev.anthro.28.1.509)

Whiten, A. & Byrne, R. W. (eds) 1997 *Machiavellian intelligence II: extensions and evaluations*. Cambridge, UK: Cambridge University Press.

Wrangham, R. W. 2001 Out of the Pan, into the fire: how our ancestors' evolution depended on what they ate. In *Tree of life* (ed. F. B. M. de Waal), pp. 121–143. Cambridge, MA: Harvard University Press.

Wrangham, R. W., Holland Jones, J., Laden, G., Pilbeam, D. & Conklin-Brittain, N. L. 1999 The raw and the stolen: cooking and the ecology of human origins. *Curr. Anthropol.* **40**, 567–594. (doi:10.1086/300083)

17

On the lack of evidence that non-human animals possess anything remotely resembling a 'theory of mind'

Derek C. Penn and Daniel J. Povinelli

After decades of effort by some of our brightest human and non-human minds, there is still little consensus on whether or not non-human animals understand anything about the unobservable mental states of other animals or even what it would mean for a non-verbal animal to understand the concept of a 'mental state'. In the present paper, we confront four related and contentious questions head-on: (i) What exactly would it mean for a non-verbal organism to have an 'understanding' or a 'representation' of another animal's mental state? (ii) What should (and should not) count as compelling empirical evidence that a non-verbal cognitive agent has a system for understanding or forming representations about mental states in a functionally adaptive manner? (iii) Why have the kind of experimental protocols that are currently in vogue failed to produce compelling evidence that non-human animals possess anything even remotely resembling a theory of mind? (iv) What kind of experiments could, at least in principle, provide compelling evidence for such a system in a non-verbal organism?

Keywords: theory of mind; folk psychology; mental state attribution; parsimony; chimpanzees; corvids

17.1 Introduction

Are humans alone in their capacity to reason about unobservable mental states, such as perceptions, intentions, emotions, desires and beliefs? Over a quarter-century ago, Premack & Woodruff (1978) launched a multinational industry dedicated to answering this question and coined the term, 'theory of mind' (hereafter, ToM) to refer to this distinctive capacity: 'a system of inferences of this kind', they observed, 'may properly be regarded as a theory because such [mental] states are not directly observable, and the system can be used to make predictions about the behavior of others' (p. 515).

Unfortunately, after decades of effort by some of our brightest human and non-human minds, there is still little consensus on whether or not non-human animals understand anything about unobservable mental states or even what it would mean for a non-verbal animal to understand the concept of a 'mental state'. Nearly 10 years ago, Heyes (1998) observed that there had been 'no substantial progress' (p. 101) on Premack & Woodruff's (1978) original question for many years. It is debatable whether there has been any more agreement on the matter since then (for the latest version of these ongoing and seemingly intractable debates, see Povinelli & Vonk 2003, 2004; Tomasello *et al.* 2003*a*,*b*; Tomasello & Call 2006).

Povinelli & Vonk (2004) pointed out one glaring reason for the impasse, namely comparative researchers have never specified 'the unique causal work' that representations about mental states do above and beyond the work that can be done by representations of the observable features of other agents' past and occurrent behaviours. As a result, almost all of the experimental protocols that have been used to test the ToM capabilities of non-human animals over the past quarter-century, including those that are currently in vogue today, are incapable, even in principle, of validating or falsifying the hypotheses being tested. One does not need to hold a Popperian view of science to acknowledge that arguments among unfalsifiable hypotheses are likely to be of little or no value to practicing scientists.

There seems to be a dire need, then, to focus more attention on the basic definitional and evidential issues confronting comparative researchers and spend less time arguing over ambiguous experimental results. In this paper, we will confront four related and contentious questions head-on:

(i) What exactly would it mean for a non-verbal organism to have an 'understanding' or a 'representation' of another animal's mental state?

(ii) What should (and should not) count as compelling empirical evidence that a non-verbal cognitive agent has a system for understanding or forming representations about mental states in a functionally adaptive manner?

(iii) Why have the kind of experimental protocols that are currently in vogue failed to produce compelling evidence that non-human animals possess anything even remotely resembling a theory of mind?

(iv) What kind of experiments could, at least in principle, provide compelling evidence for such a system in a non-verbal organism?

Only after we have addressed these fundamental issues in a formal, principled fashion will we be in a position to attempt to answer the fascinating question that Premack & Woodruff (1978) first posed so many years ago.

Theory of mind, *sensu* Premack & Woodruff (1978), entails the capacity to make lawful inferences about the behaviour of other agents on the basis of abstract, theory-like representations of the causal relation between unobservable mental states and observable states of affairs. This is certainly not the only way to construe the capacity in question (for an overview of the possibilities, see Davies & Stone 1995*a,b*; Carruthers & Smith 1996). Many researchers have argued, for example, that the ability to take the causal role of mental states into account does not involve theory-like inferences at all, but is grounded in practical, sensorimotor, simulative abilities (e.g. Gordon 1986, 1996; Goldman 1993).

For the purposes of the present essay, we wish to remain rigorously agnostic as to *how* the capacity to take other agents' mental states into account is implemented. We will henceforth use the acronym ToM, to refer to *any* cognitive system, whether theory-like or not, that predicts or explains the behaviour of another agent by postulating that unobservable inner states particular to the cognitive perspective of that agent causally modulate that agent's behaviour. We believe this construal of ToM *sensu lato* is about as broad and minimalist as possible without losing the distinctive character of the capacity in question.

In our opinion, the major impediment that has stood in the way of understanding whether or not other species employ a ToM has been our species' inveterate intuitions about how our own ToM works. Appeals to folk psychological assumptions and reasoning by analogy to introspective intuitions have played an inordinate role in comparative researchers' claims over the last quarter-century (see Povinelli & Giambrone 1999; Povinelli *et al*. 2000; Povinelli & Vonk 2003, 2004). Thus, to undermine the insidious role that introspective intuitions and folk psychology play in the comparative debate, we propose to treat the ToM explanandum here in more formalistic terms than is typical among comparative researchers. Our approach is as follows:

(i) present a simple formalism to clarify exactly what is (and is not) at stake with respect to the comparative ToM explanandum,

(ii) use the formalism in (i) to specify what should (and should not) count as evidence for a ToM system in a non-verbal organism,

(iii) take a prominent experimental result with chimpanzees as a case study for exposing why the kind of protocols currently in vogue do not satisfy the conditions set out in (ii),

(iv) show why the analysis in (iii) applies, mutatis mutandis, to the protocols currently being employed with corvids as well, and

(v) propose two sample experimental protocols that could, at least in principle, provide compelling positive evidence for a ToM system in a nonhuman species.

17.2 A simple formalism

To begin, let us agree without too much argument that cognitive agents—biological or otherwise—can learn from their past experience, in part because they have dynamic internal states that are decoupled from any immediate physical connection to the external world. Some of these internal states carry information about what the agent has learned about the world that is distinct from the information immediately available to the system's perceptual inputs. And some of these internal states describe goal states against which actual states of the organism can be compared so that the organism's behaviours can be dynamically adjusted in order to close the gap. Let us denote all these internal goals states by the variable, g, and all the informational states that affect and/or mediate the goal-directed behaviour of a cognitive agent by the variable, r.

Our rough-and-ready definition of r- and g-states is meant to be as ecumenical as possible. For example, we are entirely agnostic (for our present purposes anyway) about whether an organism's r- and g-states are modal or amodal, discrete or distributed, symbolic or connectionist or even about how they come to have their representational or informational qualities to begin with. And we make no judgment about whether r- and g-states as we have defined them here bear any resemblance to the mental state concepts putatively posited by our commonsense folk psychology. We do not pretend that this definition of g- and r-states puts to rest the entire (or even a small part of the) controversy over what counts as goal-directed behaviour or internal mental representations (see Markman & Dietrich 2000 for a better start); but it is good enough for our present purposes.

Of course, there are innumerable other factors that also contribute to shaping a biological organism's behaviour, including information from sensory inputs, feedback from perception–action loops, autonomic– visceral states, the physical structure and capabilities of the organism's body and all the other many variables that influence the actions of situated, embodied, biological agents in the wild. But for our present purpose, these many multifarious influences can be reduced to two additional variables and an ellipsis. We will use the variable, p, to denote any dynamic, occurrent information obtained through perceptual inputs (including autonomic and proprioceptive channels); and we will use the variable, q, to denote feedback from the organism's sensorimotor loops (including online and offline emulators). Using this notation, any cognitive behaviour, b, can be described formally (albeit simplistically) as follows:

$$b = f(g, r, p, q, \ ). \tag{17.2.1}$$

In other words, any cognitive behaviour is some function of the system's g- and r-states plus any occurrent information from perceptual inputs and sensorimotor emulators at the time the function is computed—plus any other cognitive variables not incorporated in the present model. The reason we are unconcerned with unpacking such broad variables as g, r, p and q, or with what falls under the ellipsis, is because we are only concerned, herein, with the question of whether or not a given cognitive agent possesses a ToM. And the question of whether or not a given cognitive agent possesses a ToM boils down to the question of whether or not that agent is able to treat other agents as if their behaviour is a function of the kind of variables described in equation (17.2.1). The only condition that must be met in order to qualify as a ToM, by our minimalist standards, is that the system must be able to produce and employ a particular class of information, namely information about the state of these cognitive variables from the perspective of that agent *as distinct from the perspective of the system itself*. We will refer to this special class of information by the variable, *ms*.

What exactly does it mean for one cognitive information state to be 'about' some other state of affairs? Much greater minds than ours have tried to answer this question (for example, Dretske 1988); and the complexities of taking this question seriously would take us far beyond the scope of the present essay. So here is a simple stop-gap answer that will suffice for our present purposes: let us agree that an *ms* variable carries information about some other cognitive state if the state of the *ms* variable covaries with the state of the other cognitive state in a generally reliable manner such that, *ceteris paribus*, variations in the *ms* variable can be used by the consuming cognitive system to infer corresponding variations in the other cognitive state.

In a genuine mind-reader, the function describing the informational relation between one agent's *ms* variables and another agent's cognitive state variables might be something like the following:

$$ms = f_{mr}(g^*, r^*, p^*, \ ), \tag{17.2.2}$$

where * denotes the state of the corresponding variable for the other agent and f_{mr} denotes a cognitive function capable of intuiting the state of these unobservable variables directly, for example, telepathically.

Of course, there are no genuine mind-readers on this planet and all the relevant cognitive variables are, strictly speaking, unobservable from the point of view of the aspiring mind-reader. Hence, any purported mind-reading being performed on this planet is, in fact, a trick. A very good trick, to be sure, but a trick nevertheless. The trick is to be able to infer the state of the unobservable cognitive variables that will influence the behaviour of another agent using information observed from the perspective of the system itself:

$$ms = f_{ToM}(r, p, \ ), \tag{17.2.3}$$

where f_{ToM} denotes a special function that computes an *ms* variable based on the inputs available to sentient, situated, embodied but non-telepathic organisms.

There is a burgeoning debate over how f_{ToM} might be implemented (for examples of the debate, see Davies & Stone 1995a,b; Carruthers & Smith 1996; Hurley & Chater 2005). Traditionally, f_{ToM} has been construed as a kind of inferential function that uses a database of law-like generalizations to make logical inferences about other agents' g- and r-states in a theory-like manner. This is certainly the kind of f_{ToM} that Premack & Woodruff (1978) had in mind when they coined the term that started the debate. But, as we noted previously, there are many alternative hypotheses at play today, some of which propose that f_{ToM} is implemented via offline simulation capabilities that encode *ms* variables about other subjects' internal states using the same mechanisms that are used to encode *ms* variables about the subject's own internal states. Still other researchers advocate hybrid functions between theory and simulation (e.g. Nichols & Stich 2003; Meltzoff 2007). For our present purposes, we are agnostic as to how the f_{ToM} is implemented; we simply note that a cognizer that has a ToM system of any kind must have an f_{ToM} of some kind. And any f_{ToM} must take information from the system's own inputs and produce (or enact) a special class of information, i.e. information that is postulated to be from the cognitive perspective of another agent and relevant to predicting the behaviour of that agent.

The simple formalism we have proposed here leaps over innumerable details and complex, unresolved issues; but it nevertheless helps to keep track of what is and what is not at stake with respect to the question of whether or not chimpanzees or any other nonhuman animal have a ToM. Our definition of an f_{ToM} does not require the agent to have any insight into the subjective phenomenological experience of others. Nor does our definition require *ms* variables to have an isomorphic relationship with the content or structure of the mental state that is being represented. Metarepresentations are one way of implementing *ms* variables. But they are certainly not the only way. Some theorists, for example, have argued that apes' representations of mental states might simply involve 'intervening variables' (aka 'secondary representations') rather than explicitly structured metarepresentations (Whiten 1996, 1997, 2000; Suddendorf & Whiten 2001; Whiten & Suddendorf 2001). We believe Whiten and Suddendorf are right in this sense: being able to recode perceptually disparate behavioural patterns resulting from the same underlying cognitive state as instances of the same abstract equivalence class is a bona fide example of postulating an *ms* variable in the sense defined hereinabove (we differ from Whiten & Suddendorf, however, in that we do not see any compelling evidence of this ability in non-human animals; see discussion below).

We particularly want to point out that the debate concerning whether or not non-human animals possess an f_{ToM} should not be concerned with whether or not they are cognitive creatures capable of reasoning about general classes of past and occurrent behaviours (e.g. <threat posture>, <eye or face direction>, <body position> or <eye-direction-in-relation-to-objects-in-the-world >). Indeed, they *must* be able to do so if they are potential candidates for a ToM at all. The theory of mind debate among comparative researchers should turn only around the question of whether, in addition to the representational abilities that any cognitive agent possesses as defined in equation (17.2.1), some particular cognitive system in the agent in question also produces information that is specific to the cognitive perspective of another agent and uses this information to predict the behaviour of that agent.

17.3 What should count as evidence of f_{ToM}?

We hope that our simplistic formalism will also help define more clearly what should and should not count as compelling evidence for an f_{ToM}. The subtle confounding problem, from an experimentalist's point of view, is that all organisms with the potential to have an f_{ToM} are also, necessarily, cognitive agents in the sense defined by equation (17.2.1) above.[1] The unavoidable null hypothesis is that any agent capable of possessing an f_{ToM} must already be employing the information provided by g, r, p and q in their cognitive behaviours. Thus, in order to produce experimental evidence for an f_{ToM} one must first falsify the null hypothesis that the agents in question are simply using their normal, first-person cognitive state variables as defined by equation (17.2.1). One must, in other words, create experimental protocols that provide compelling evidence for the cognitive (i.e. causal) necessity of an f_{ToM} *in addition to* and *distinct from* the cognitive work that could have been performed without such a function.

The last qualification is crucial. Imagine an organism, **A**, that always manifests some determinate set of observable cues, C_1, whenever it is in a given r-state, **r-state$_1$**, such that $P(\textbf{r-state}_1|C_1) = 1$ and $P(\textbf{r-state}_1|\sim C_1) = 0^2$. And suppose that **r-state$_1$** causes **A** to emit behaviour b_1. A second cognitive agent having perceptual access to organism A and its observable traits, C_1, would have no need to infer the presence of **r-state$_1$** in order to predict the occurrence of b_1; simply observing C_1 suffices. Thus, a researcher observing that a given experimental subject is able to reliably predict the occurrence of b_1 in **A** after observing 1 would have no basis for concluding that the subject possesses an f_{ToM} dedicated to inferring **r-state$_1$** (even though she, herself, may know that **r-state$_1$** causes b_1) unless she can also show that possessing information directly about **r-state$_1$** does some special causal work for **A** in addition to predicting b_1. Although this is rarely noted by experimentalists, we believe this point to be indisputable (see Povinelli & Vonk 2003, 2004). Curiously, though, it is nevertheless often disputed, or completely ignored (see Tomasello *et al.* 2003a,b; Tomasello & Call 2006).

When framed in formalistic terms, the point appears obvious. But a simple real-life example will illustrate how easy it is to be duped by commonsense. A chimpanzee (the subject) observes a second chimpanzee turn her head and look off in the distance. In response, the subject turns his head in the same direction. From a folk psychological point of view (i.e. from the point of view of any normal adult human observer), it is tempting to conclude that the subject's act of turning his head is mediated by an internal representation of the second chimpanzee's belief that there is something interesting to look at and an implicit understanding that 'seeing' leads to a change in the internal, epistemic state of the looker. In other words, our commonsense intuitions assume that the subject's behaviour was mediated by an *ms* variable (i.e. the subject had some understanding of the second chimpanzee's *g*- and *r*-states). Indeed, many comparative researchers have been tempted to attribute *ms* variables to their subjects under similar experimental circumstances (Call *et al.*1998; Tomasello *et al.* 1999; Bugnyar & Heinrich 2005; Flombaum & Santos 2005; Santos *et al.* 2006; Tomasello & Call 2006).

What commonsense intuition overlooks, however, is that it is also possible for the same behaviour to be produced without an f_{ToM} of any kind. The set of perceptual cues available to the subject (i.e. 'eye or face direction', 'body position', 'eye-direction-in-relation-to-objects-in-the-world', etc.) are sufficient to explain the subject's behaviour. Any socially intelligent subject like a chimpanzee must possess a rich database of *r*-states based on what he has learned about perceptually similar situations in the past and the conditional dependencies that tend to hold between these observable cues and other animals' subsequent behaviour. Thus, the subject may have turned his head in the direction of the other chimp's head simply because it learned from past experience (or was born with the propensity to learn) that the given pattern of perceptual cues is a reliable indicator of something worth looking at in the direction inferred by the other agent's eyes and head. There is no need for the subject to reason in terms of an *ms* state variable, and positing an *ms* state variable does no additional explanatory work in the given situation.

The evidential case for an *ms* variable is no better simply because the second chimpanzee looks behind a barrier and the subject adjusts his position to see behind the barrier as well (e.g. Povinelli & Eddy 1996b). Barriers are, of course, visible entities. Subjects who have learned (or are born knowing) that they must alter their own position in order to see behind a barrier if a conspecific's eyes are directed towards a location behind a barrier do not necessarily need, *in addition*, to form representations postulating the hypothetical content of the conspecific's perceptual field or to understand that 'seeing' leads to any change at all in the looker's r-states (see also Povinelli *et al.* 2002).

And the evidential case is still no better just because the subject 'checks back' with the looker if he does not find anything interesting behind the barrier. Chimpanzees check back with moving objects all the time in order to update their internal representation of the object's location and projected trajectory without thereby postulating that all moving objects have mental states.

Following the gaze of a conspecific, checking behind barriers and checking back with the looker when nothing is found certainly *seem* to be compelling evidence for reasoning in terms of unobservable mental states when interpreted from a commonsense point of view. And it is easy to understand why normal adult human beings reflexively make this assumption when they interpret the behaviour of animals (Dennett 1987). From a scientific stance, however, we are only warranted in attributing an *ms* variable to the subject if we can specify why an f_{ToM} of some kind is computationally necessary in order to perform the given behaviour and why the information provided by the resulting *ms* variable is not redundant with the information provided by the r, p, g and q variables which we have already posited to exist. The role of an experimentalist (as opposed to the folk observer) is to construct situations or protocols in which the unique cognitive work performed by the *ms* variables can be distinguished from the work that could be performed by r, p, g and q inputs alone.

Here is the crux of the matter then, and possibly the most important point we will make in this essay: in almost all experimental procedures reported to date, purported *ms* variables appear to be causally superfluous re-descriptions of the other observable inputs and representations that are logically required by the experimental design. No special f_{ToM} is required. The problem with existing protocols is that they fail to create situations in which the information purportedly carried by the *ms* variables is not causally redundant with the information already carried by the r, p, g and q variables.

Now, we are ready to evaluate the evidence with respect to the formalism we have outlined.

17.4 An experimental protocol that cannot, even in principle, provide evidence for f_{ToM}

This is not the forum for an exhaustive examination of all claims for theory of mind in chimpanzees (let alone other species). Our strategy, therefore, will be to examine what has come to be seen as the 'strongest' case for the existence of theory of mind in chimpanzees: the work of Hare *et al.* (2000, 2001). To be perfectly clear, we do not believe these studies have any bearing whatsoever, positive or negative, on the question of whether chimpanzees reason about mental states. However, because many other scholars believe they do, we shall use this protocol as a case study to expose the conceptual confusion that dominates this area of research.

We will take the 'most significant' experiment reported by Hare *et al.* (2001) as our example, but it must be noted that our analysis applies with equal force to all the experiments in this series (see also Povinelli & Vonk 2004). Two chimpanzees, one subordinate to the other, were kept in separate chambers on either side of a middle area. Two cloth bags in the middle chamber served as hiding places for small food items. Opaque doors on each side chamber prevented the respective chimpanzees from entering the middle chamber and retrieving the food until the doors were raised. On each trial, the subordinate's door was partially raised while the food was being hidden, allowing the subordinate to peek out and see where the food items were placed and whether or not the dominant was present and looking. On each trial, the dominant's door was either partially raised or completely closed while the food items were placed in one of the two containers. Once the food had been placed, the dominant's door was closed and the subordinate was released into the middle chamber and given a slight headstart before the dominant was released as well.

Hare et al. (2001) reported a number of experimental conditions based on this protocol. In only one of these experiments, however, was the critical metric statistically significant[3]. In the uninformed condition of experiment 1, the dominant's door was kept closed while the food was hidden and the subordinate could see that the dominant's door was closed; in the control condition, the dominant could see where the reward was hidden and the subordinate could see that the dominant was watching. The subordinate 'approached' the hidden food more often in the uninformed condition than in the control condition. On the basis of this result, Hare et al. (2001) concluded that 'chimpanzees know what individual groupmates do and do not know' (p. 148). Reversing their previous opinion on the matter (see Tomasello & Call 1997; Visalberghi & Tomasello 1998), Tomasello et al. (2003a) cite these experiments as 'breakthrough' (p. 154) evidence that chimpanzees 'understand some psychological states in others' (p. 156). Tomasello et al. are hardly alone. The Hare et al. (2000, 2001) results are now widely cited as supporting evidence for the idea that chimpanzees possess some kind of f_{ToM}.

Unfortunately, as our research group has pointed out (see Karin-D'Arcy & Povinelli 2002; Povinelli & Vonk 2003, 2004), the protocol employed by Hare et al. (2001) lacks the power, even in principle, to distinguish between responses by the subordinate that could have been produced simply by employing observable information and representations of past behavioural patterns (i.e. p- and r-states) from responses that must have required computations involving information about the dominant's unobservable mental states (i.e. ms states). For example, Povinelli & Vonk (2003) point out that the behaviour of the subordinates might result from a simple strategy glossed by 'Don't go after food if a dominant who is present has oriented towards it'. The additional claim that the chimpanzees adopted this strategy because they understood that 'The dominant knows where the food is located' is intuitively appealing but causally superfluous.

Let us re-examine the problem with Hare et al.'s protocol using the formalism we developed above. Imagine an organism, $\mathbf{A}$, that manifests some determinate set of observable cues, $\mathbf{C_1}$, when it is in a given r-state, $\mathbf{r\text{-}state_1}$, where $\mathbf{C_1}$ = ('eyes of A oriented towards food', 'uninterrupted visual access between A and placement of food', 'food is placed in location X',) and $\mathbf{r\text{-}state_1}$ = ('A knows that food is in location X'). And suppose further that $\mathbf{r\text{-}state_1}$ causes $\mathbf{A}$ to emit behaviour $\mathbf{b_1}$, where $\mathbf{b_1}$ = ('A tries to retrieve food in location X'). A second cognitive agent having perceptual access to organism A and its observable traits, $\mathbf{C_1}$, would have no need to infer the presence of $\mathbf{r\text{-}state_1}$ in order to predict the occurrence of $\mathbf{b_1}$; simply observing $\mathbf{C_1}$ suffices. Thus, a researcher observing that a given experimental subject is able to reliably predict the occurrence of $\mathbf{b_1}$ in $\mathbf{A}$ after observing $\mathbf{C_1}$ would have no basis for concluding that the subject possesses an f_{ToM} dedicated to inferring $\mathbf{r\text{-}state_1}$ (even if she herself knows that $\mathbf{r\text{-}state_1}$ causes $\mathbf{b_1}$), unless she can also show that possessing information directly about $\mathbf{r\text{-}state_1}$ does some special causal work in addition to predicting $\boldsymbol{b_1}$. Once again, we believe this point to be indisputable— though, as in the case of Hare et al. (2001), persistently (and inexplicably) disputed (see Tomasello et al. 2003a,b; Tomasello & Call 2006).

17.5 What about corvids?

Chimpanzees, of course, are not the only non-human species which might be potential candidates for an f_{ToM}. And, indeed, some of the most well-controlled results and provocative claims in recent years have not come from experiments with primate subjects at all, but from experiments with corvids (for general reviews of the literature, see Clayton *et al.* 2001; Emery 2004; Emery & Clayton 2004, 2005; Clayton & Emery 2005; see also Clayton *et al.* 2007). Corvids are quite adept at pilfering the food caches of other birds and will adjust their own caching strategies in response to the potential risk of pilfering by others. Indeed, not only do they remember which food caches were observed by competitors, but also they appear to remember the specific individuals who were present when specific caches were made and modify their re-caching behaviour accordingly (Dally *et al.* 2006). Corvids' cognitive prowess is not limited to caching and pilfering. In many tool-use tasks, their cognitive abilities also seem to be superior to those of nonhuman primates in certain respects (for example, Hunt 1996, 2004; Seed *et al.* 2006; Tebbich *et al.* in press). What is at issue here, however, is not whether or not corvids are cognitively sophisticated creatures, but whether or not, *in addition*, any of their sophisticated cognitive abilities require the possession of an f_{ToM}.

Many comparative researchers clearly feel the answer to this question is yes. For example, Emery & Clayton (2001, 2004, 2005) suggest that corvids discriminate between competitors who possess knowledge of cache sites from those that do not by attributing specific, contentful *r*-states to knowledgeable competitors. Moreover, Emery and Clayton suggest that corvids may be able to understand the internal mental experience of their conspecifics by analogy to their own first-hand experience (see also Emery 2004). Similarly, Bugnyar & Heinrich (2006) showed that ravens delay pilfering from cache sites when confronted by the individuals who made those caches and suggest that this is consistent with the hypothesis that corvids possess a sophisticated understanding of others' visual perception as well as the ability to tactically manipulate competitors' mental states (see also Bugnyar & Heinrich 2005).

While we certainly agree with these researchers that it is *possible* that corvids are capable of reasoning in terms of the *r*-states of their competitors, we nevertheless must point out that none of the evidence to date provides convincing evidence for this hypothesis. One of the defining characteristics of *ms* variables, as defined above, is that they are construed from the cognitive perspective of the other agent as distinct from the cognitive perspective of the subject itself. Unfortunately, none of the reported experiments with corvids require the subjects to infer or encode any information that is unique to the cognitive perspective of the competitor. For example, none of the reported experiments require the subjects to reason in terms of the *counterfactual* content of their competitors' *r*-states. As Dennett (1987) pointed out a long time ago, without evidence that a subject is able to reason in terms of counterfactual as well as factual *r*-states in another agent, it is very difficult, if not impossible, to provide evidence that they are cognizing the other agent's *r*-states qua *r*-states at all.

In all of the experiments with corvids cited above, it suffices for the birds to associate specific competitors with specific cache sites and to reason in terms of the information they have observed from their own cognitive perspective: e.g. 'Re-cache food if a competitor has oriented towards it in the past', 'Attempt to pilfer food if the competitor who cached it is not present', 'Try to re-cache food in a site different from the one where it was cached when the competitor was present', etc.[4] The additional claim that the birds adopt these strategies because they understand that 'The competitor knows where the food is located' does no additional explanatory or cognitive work.

The case for 'experience projection' is no stronger than the case for 'knowledge attribution'. Emery & Clayton (2001) showed that scrub jays who had had previous experience pilfering food from others were more likely to re-cache food that had been observed by competitors than birds who had had no previous experience pilfering from others. 'This result raises the exciting possibility,' Emery (2004, p. 21) writes, 'that birds with pilfering experience can project their own experience of being a thief onto the observing bird, and so counter what they would predict a thief would do in relation to their hidden food' (see also Emery & Clayton 2004).

The fact that only birds with previous pilfering experience re-cache observed food sites is an interesting result but sheds no light on the internal mental representations or cognitive processes being employed by the birds in question. This experimental result certainly does not demonstrate that ex-pilferers understand anything about the internal, subjective experience of their potential competitors. Monkeys, after all, often initiate aggressive acts against innocent third parties after they themselves have been attacked but this hardly means that they are projecting their own subjective experience of being attacked onto the potential victims. There are any number of much lower-level explanations for this redirected aggression (see Silk (2002) for a review)—as there are for the connection between pilfering and re-caching in corvids.

To be sure, many researchers explicitly acknowledge that an explanation based on reasoning about observed cues alone is sufficient to account for the existing data. Dally *et al.* (2006), for example, acknowledge, that scrub jays' ability to keep track of which competitors have observed which cache sites 'need not require a humanlike 'theory of mind' in terms of unobservable mental states, but [ ] may result from behavioral predispositions in combination with specific learning algorithms or from reasoning about future risk'. Similarly, Bugnyar & Heinrich (2006) acknowledge that a representation of 'states in the physical world' would be sufficient for explaining the available evidence concerning the manipulative behaviours of ravens. Notwithstanding the foregoing, these researchers continue to hold out the 'possibility' that the birds' behaviour could be consistent with a more generous, mentalistic interpretation and suggest that more generous interpretations might be more 'parsimonious' (see also Tomasello & Call 2006).

Admittedly, explanations in terms of folk psychological abilities do appear more 'parsimonious' at first blush. But the fact that such explanations are 'simpler for us' to understand does not mean, as Heyes (1998) pointed out, that they are 'simpler for them' to implement (see also Dennett 1987). The cognitive mechanisms that would be required to actually implement these purported f_{ToM} abilities at a subpersonal, causal level are hardly simple at all— they only seem simple because folk psychological explanations gloss over all the devilish details. Comparing the simplicity of a folk psychological explanation, e.g. 'chimpanzees understand seeing', 'corvids know what others do and do not know', to the complexity of a subpersonal cognitive explanation is like comparing a marketing description of Microsoft Word, e.g. 'prints, saves and edits complex documents', to a detailed functional specification of the underlying application architecture. The fact that the detailed functional specification of Microsoft Word runs to thousands of pages, and the marketing pitch takes one sentence is not a reasonable metric for comparing the merits of the two descriptions. Likewise, while folk psychological descriptions may be invaluable heuristics for ethologists in the field (Dennett 1987), they should not be confused or compared with cognitive hypotheses framed at a subpersonal, functional level of explanation.

Our position is that chimpanzees and corvids (like many other non-human animals) possess representational architectures of enormous sophistication and flexibility. We also believe that they employ both inferential and simulative mechanisms for forming abstractions about classes of behaviours and environmental conditions that are relevant to their goal-directed actions. Furthermore, we believe that non-human animals are able to generalize the lessons learned from these abstractions to novel scenarios.

Thus, unlike the motley collection of learning experiences that might be required in an associationist model, our hypothesis is that non-human animals are able to respond intelligently to novel situations based on general, abstract representations (i.e. r-states) they have formed about similar situations in the past and specific, concrete representations they have formed about the events leading up to the present moment (including, at least in the case of corvids, the 'what', 'when' and 'where' information associated with those events).

Our principal disagreement with those who explain non-human behaviours in terms of an f_{ToM} is not about the inferential or learning abilities that non-human animals possess (at least for our present purposes; but see Penn & Povinelli 2007). Our principle disagreement is about the kind of representations over which these inferential and learning processes operate. The available evidence suggests that chimpanzees, corvids and all other non-human animals only form representations and reason about *observable* features, relations and states of affairs from their own cognitive perspective. We know of no evidence that non-human animals are capable of representing or reasoning about *unobservable* features, relations, causes or states of affairs or of construing information from the cognitive perspective of another agent. Thus, positing an f_{ToM}, even in the case of corvids, is simply unwarranted by the available evidence.

17.6 Two experimental protocols that could, in principle, provide evidence for f_{ToM}

In response to the kind of critiques that our research group has levelled, some scholars have claimed that the distinctions we are proposing are experimentally intractable and/or empirically vacuous. For example, Andrews (2005) worries that 'any success in a predictive paradigm can be explained as the result of a behavioristic psychological system that relies on behavioral, rather than mental, intervening variables' (p. 528 and see also Leavens *et al.* 2004; Hurley & Nudds 2006). Tomasello *et al.* (2003b) worry that our extreme stinginess in attributing mentalistic abilities to chimpanzees is an example of 'derived behaviourism' and will only lead to 'despair' (p. 239).

To forestall any worry that a theoretically rigorous stance towards the interpretation of comparative experimental results will lead only to despair, we will now propose two separate experimental protocols that could, in fact, provide principled evidence for an f_{ToM} in chimpanzees or corvids and could be easily adapted for other non-verbal cognitive organisms as well. The first tests a non-verbal subject's ability to reason from first-to third-person mental states. The second tests a subject's ability to use *ms* variables to solve prediction problems that would be computationally unsolvable otherwise. We hope these two proposals will demonstrate that our stringent criteria for attributing an f_{ToM} to a non-human animal are neither empirically vacuous nor experimentally intractable.

(a) The opaque visor experiment

Building on previous suggestions, Povinelli & Vonk (2003, 2004) highlighted (in a version appropriate for chimpanzees) one protocol that could provide principled positive evidence for

f_{ToM} in a non-verbal organism. Since this proposal has now been critiqued, we briefly summarize its logic, and show why the critiques are invalid.

During an initial training session, subjects are given first-hand experience wearing two mirrored visors. One of the visors is see-through; the other is not. The visors themselves are of markedly different colours (and/or shape). During the subsequent test session, the subjects are given the opportunity to use their species-typical begging gesture to request food from one of the two experimenters, one wearing the see-through visor and the other wearing the opaque visor. Subjects who beg significantly more often from an experimenter wearing the see-through visor have manifested evidence of possessing an f_{ToM} in the sense defined herein.

This protocol has been tested on highly human-enculturated chimpanzees (Vonk *et al.* 2005, unpublished work; manuscript available on request), who failed. A functionally equivalent variation of the protocol (using trick blindfolds) has been tested on 18-month-old human infants (Meltzoff 2007), who passed. These results would seem to provide positive confirmatory evidence that even very young human infants possess some sort of f_{ToM} whereas even highly enculturated adult chimpanzees do not.

There have been several criticisms of the experimental protocol, ranging from the claim that it is formally inadequate (Andrews 2005; Hurley & Nudds 2006) to the claim that it has 'very low ecological validity' (Tomasello *et al.* 2003*b*). We will first defend why the proposed experiment does, in fact, provide principled evidence for an f_{ToM} and, secondly, why the charge of 'low ecological validity' is misplaced.

Both Hurley & Nudds (2006) and Andrews (2005) argue that a subject could pass the proposed experiment simply by reasoning about the analogy between first-person manifest physical behaviours and third-person manifest behaviours. As Andrews (2005) puts it:

> the chimp might make the behavioral connection between wearing the opaque bucket and *not being able to do things* [emphasis in the original]. From whom should he beg? Certainly not the person who isn't able to do things (p. 530).

It is certainly true that reasoning from first-to third-person behaviours forms a crucial part of the human cognitive tool-kit (for example, Meltzoff & Moore 1997; Meltzoff 2007). And there is substantial evidence that neural systems, such as 'mirror neurons', in both human and non-human animals register correspondences between first-and third-person behaviours (for reviews of the literature, see Hurley & Chater 2005). Thus, it is possible (though certainly not proven) that the capacity to find behavioural equivalences between self and other is, as Hurley & Nudds (2006) argue, developmentally and phylogenetically prior to the capacity to find mentalistic equivalences between self and other.

However, the ability to form first-to third-person equivalences in terms of manifest physical behaviours is not sufficient to solve the protocol proposed by Povinelli & Vonk. The reason the bucket protocol works as a test of mental state reasoning is because there is, in fact, no way (i.e. no computationally tractable way) to draw the necessary correspondences based purely on representations of observable information and manifest behaviours.

In this context, let us examine more closely the data available to a subject lacking an f_{ToM}. Such a subject would be limited to *r*-states about his own manifest behaviour while wearing the opaque visor (e.g. 'I stumbled around while wearing the red visor') and occurrent *p*-states about the experimenter (e.g. 'she is wearing a red visor'). However, a subject lacking an f_{ToM} would not have access to *r*-states about his own internal cognitive states while wearing the visors (e.g. 'I was unable to see while wearing the red visor'). Nor would such a subject have any information concerning his own propensity to respond to begging gestures while wearing the opaque visor, since he never attempted to respond to begging gestures while wearing the visor.

Thus, a subject capable of cognizing analogies between first- to third-person physical behaviours, but incapable of cognizing analogies between unobservable mental states, might be able to infer that the experimenter will stumble around and bump into things while wearing the red visor; but there would be no basis for this subject to infer that wearing the red visor will necessarily preclude the experimenter from *physically* producing the actions necessary to respond to begging gestures. Indeed, the subject would have every reason to believe that wearing the red visor will have no effect at all on the experimenter's ability to respond to begging gestures.

In the proposed protocol, the only manifest physical actions required for the experimenter to respond to begging gestures are the ability to sit still, move her arm and keep her eyes open and directed straight ahead. The subject has first-hand experience that he is perfectly capable of sitting still, of freely moving his arms and of keeping his eyes open while wearing the red visor. Thus, based on the manifest behavioural evidence, a subject without an f_{ToM} would have no reason to suspect any limitation on the experimenter's ability to perform the physical acts required to respond to begging gestures. In order to infer that the experimenter is not likely to respond to begging gestures while wearing the red visor, the subject must realize that responding to begging gestures requires more than a set of manifest physical actions and observable conditions. To be precise, the subject must realize (by logical inference or embodied simulation, or some combination of the two) the following:

(i) wearing the opaque visor results in an inability to 'see-what-is-going-on' (i.e. a general epistemic condition applicable to any subsequent behaviour not just a particular manifest physical effect of bumping-into-things),

(ii) this general epistemic condition will be experienced, analogously, by the other subject when she wears the red visor but not the blue visor, and

(iii) a subject who experiences this general epistemic condition will not respond to begging gestures.

The preceding three steps are a paradigmatic example of encoding an *ms* variable about a first-person internal state (i.e. the general epistemic condition of not-being-able-to-see) that results from a given manifest contingency (i.e. wearing the red visor) and then using these representations to predict the behaviour of another cognitive agent to a novel situation (i.e. responding to begging gestures). We contend that without the *ms* variable, the subject could not immediately solve the problem presented.

Some (e.g. Andrews 2005) might still object that during the initial, first-person familiarization phase, the chimpanzee could form a general aversion to red visors or might make the blanket inference that since 'I can't do anything with the red visor on', others will not be able to do anything either.

We should first point out that no such generalized aversion to the opaque bucket was observed in the familiarization phase of this experiment with chimpanzees (Vonk *et al.* 2005, unpublished work; manuscript available on request). More importantly, the protocol calls for the subjects to learn that they can do many things while wearing the opaque visors: they run about, reach out, feel objects and their body, and they themselves engage in acts that look very much like begging gestures (Vonk *et al.* 2005, unpublished work; manuscript available on request). Thus, it is simply false that the subjects learn that 'I can't do anything with the red visor on'.[5]

We now turn to Tomasello *et al.*'s (2003*b*) objection that the visor test lacks 'ecological validity' because it involves a 'cooperative-communicative' rather than a 'competitive' paradigm (Hare 2001) and because it involves strange artefacts like visors.

Several things need to be noted about this objection. First, it is simply false to claim that chimpanzees are more likely to reveal their true cognitive potential under 'competitive' situations rather than 'cooperative/communicative' ones (Hare 2001). Certainly, they may exhibit different cognitive abilities in competitive versus cooperative/communicative situations, but there is no empirical or theoretical basis for claiming that the abilities revealed under competitive paradigms are either more fundamental or more sophisticated than those revealed under cooperative ones.

For example, consider the chimpanzees' natural food-begging gesture (Goodall 1986), a gesture that has been observed in all captive and free-ranging populations of chimpanzees. In a simple experimental setting, if a chimpanzee is confronted with two caretakers who could potentially give them food, but one is facing towards them and the other is facing away, the chimpanzee will immediately (from trial one forward) gesture to the one facing them (Povinelli & Eddy 1996a–c). Chimpanzees are even capable of selectively employing auditory rather than visual behaviours as a function of specific perceptual/behavioural cues exhibited by the caretaker from whom they are begging (Hostetter et al. 2001; Leavens et al. 2004). It is only when more subtle experimental manipulations are employed, that chimpanzees display their lack of understanding of the specific causal relation between the disposition of the eyes or face of the caretaker and the caretaker's mental state (see Povinelli (2003) chapter 3 for a review).[6] Of course, this cooperative– communicative act—gesturing to the front (as opposed to the back) of a communication partner—is part of the natural social behaviour of chimpanzees (see Tomasello et al. 1994), as is competition over food resources (Karin-D'Arcy & Povinelli 2002). In other cooperative experimental settings, where a chimpanzee needs help in obtaining a just-out-of-reach food item, chimpanzees will robustly modulate their gestures to fit the locations to where their cooperative partner is looking (Povinelli & Vonk 2004). Thus, we are just as impressed by the sophistication of chimpanzee social cognition in cooperative–communicative situations as we are by their sophistication in competitive ones.

Claiming that visors are ecologically 'unnatural' (Hare 2001, p. 276) is a disingenuous argument. When chimpanzees pass tests involving ecologically bizarre artefacts, such as blindfolds, locked boxes, transparent tubes and mirrors, the same experimenters are quick to claim victory. When chimpanzees fail, the visors are to blame.

In any case, the point of the proposed protocol is not the visors. The point of the proposed protocol is the functional, informational challenge it poses. There are certainly many species for whom having a visor covering their eyes is not a species-typical experience. It suffices to find an alternative implementation of the experiment that retains the same informational and functional challenge in a more species-acceptable form. Meltzoff (2007) provides an exemplary case study: he cleverly adapted the proposed protocol for human infants using blindfolds and recorded whether or not infants were more likely to track the gaze of an adult wearing an opaque blindfold than one wearing a see-through blindfold. Notably, although tracking the gaze of blindfolded adults has pretty low ecological validity for human children as well, the 18-month-old children, nevertheless, passed.

To be sure, it is true that failure on any experimental test of this sort is not demonstrative evidence of a lack of f_{ToM}: false negatives are a fact of life in comparative research as they are in ToM research in general (see Birch & Bloom 2004). *Ceteris paribus*, ecological validity is often (but not always) a desirable feature of comparative experimentation. But the more critical issue is to isolate experimental procedures that are capable, at least in principle, of providing positive (or negative) evidence for the specific cognitive skills. Unfortunately, most of the 'ecologically valid' protocols currently in vogue cannot provide principled evidence for or against the presence of f_{ToM}. The proposed visor protocol is simply one example of an experiment that can.

For those who nonetheless insist that only competitive paradigms will reveal the true nature of chimpanzee cognition, we propose a second experimental protocol below that retains the purported 'ecological validity' of Hare *et al.*'s (2001) competitive paradigm while, nevertheless, proffering the possibility of positive evidence for an f_{ToM}.

(b) A systematic version of Hare et al.'s competitive food protocol

As in Hare *et al.*'s (2001) experiment described above (see §4), a subordinate and a dominant chimp are kept in separate compartments on opposite sides of a middle chamber and each side chamber is separated from the middle chamber by an opaque shuttle door (see figure 17.1). The doors are raised and lowered and the two subjects released into the middle chamber. Unlike Hare et al.'s set-up, however, the middle chamber has *n* stalls (e.g. 5) spaced evenly across the width of the compartment, divided from each other by Plexiglas walls. There are five buckets on the floor at the centre of each stall in full view of the subjects. The contents of the bucket, however, are not directly visible to the subjects. On each trial, the experimenter places two different amounts of food into two different buckets: a larger amount of food is placed in one bucket and a visibly smaller amount of food is placed in another. The order in which the amounts are placed is randomized (i.e. on one-half of the trials, the larger amount is placed first).

The experiment is carried out in a series of incrementally more challenging steps. In the step 1, subjects are exposed to a series of non-competitive trials. There is no rival present during these trials and both rewards are placed in full view of the subject. When the subject is released, it is only allowed to approach and retain the contents of one bucket. Trials continue until the subject learns to reliably approach and retain the more desirable reward.

In step 2, chimpanzees are paired in dominant/subordinate dyads. In each dyad, both chimpanzees have full visual access to the placement of both rewards. Only dyads in which subordinates learn to retrieve the less desirable reward and dominants retrieve the more desirable reward in a reliable fashion are allowed to continue to the third and final session.

In the step 3, the following conditions are randomly presented (Note that in all conditions, the subordinate has complete visual access to the activities of the experimenter. Only the dominant's visual access is manipulated as described.):

— Informed control. Both chimpanzees have full visual access to the placement of both food rewards.

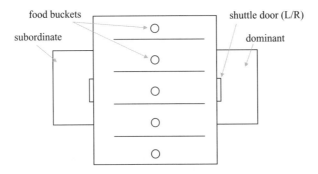

Fig. 17.1 General experimental set-up for five-bucket protocol (see §6*b* for details).

— *Partially uninformed*. One reward is placed while the dominant chimp is looking and the other reward is placed while the dominant's door is down. Whether or not the dominant's door is down during the initial placement or the subsequent placement is randomized.

— *Removed informed*. Both rewards are placed while the dominant subject is looking. Then, one of the rewards is removed from the middle chamber and replaced with an empty bucket while the dominant is looking.

— *Removed uninformed*. Both rewards are placed while the dominant subject is looking. Then, one of the rewards is removed from the middle chamber and replaced with an empty bucket while the dominant's door is down.

— *Moved*. The dominant's door is down during the initial placement of two rewards; then the dominant's door is open and both rewards are moved to new locations while the dominant is watching.

— *Replaced*. The dominant witnesses the placement of one of the two rewards and then the dominant's door is closed while that reward is moved to a new location and the amount not witnessed is placed in the previously occupied bucket.

— *Misinformed*. Both rewards are placed while the dominant is looking; then, while the dominant's door is down, one of the buckets (which may or may not have food in it) is moved to the location occupied by one of the rewards, that bucket and its reward are moved to a new location and the bucket at that location is put back in the stall originally occupied by the first bucket.

— *Swapped*. Both rewards are placed while the dominant is looking, then the locations of the two buckets are swapped while the dominant's door is down.

— *Other variations*. Note that the conditions described above only represent a subset of the systematic variations which could be employed.

The initial two steps can be mastered using simple heuristics based on observable contingencies. However, if the subject learns to pass the initial sessions using only observable contingencies, and does not have access to an f_{ToM}, the final test session presents an intractable mess.

For example, the response rule 'Don't go after food if the dominant has oriented towards it in its present location' (Povinelli & Vonk 2003), which worked perfectly in the original protocol proposed by Hare *et al.* (2001), no longer suffices. The relational rule 'always retrieve the less desirable of two rewards when there's a dominant present' only works consistently under the *informed control* and *moved* conditions. Even the higher-order relational strategy, 'Go after the less desirable reward unless the dominant has previously oriented towards it in its current location' fails any condition in which it would be optimal for the subordinate to retrieve the larger food item (e.g. the *swapped* condition). Based purely on patterns of observable cues, each condition requires a different response rule; and there is no way to systematically generalize from familiar to novel conditions.

For the purposes of testing whether or not a subject possesses an f_{ToM}, the critical conditions are those which require the subject to formulate an *ms* variable that keeps track of where the dominant believes the food rewards are located as distinct from where they are actually located, e.g. the *removed uninformed*, *replaced*, *misinformed* and *swapped* conditions. In the context of the present protocol, i.e. randomly interspersed among the other conditions, there is no way for a subject to reliably pass these critical conditions without the ability to keep track of the counterfactual state of affairs from the dominant's cognitive perspective while simultaneously keeping track of the occurrent state of affairs from the subject's own perspective. The subject must not only understand that the competitor was present and oriented; he must also cognize the specific content of the competitor's counterfactual r-states and relate these counterfactual r-states to the competitor's subsequent behaviour. Success on these conditions is thus functionally (though not necessarily psychologically) equivalent to reasoning in terms of a competitor's 'false beliefs' and would provide compelling evidence for an f_{ToM}.

Failure, however, is no less instructive than success. A subject who has passed the first two training steps has clearly understood the procedural aspects of the task, and the protocol retains the competitive food paradigm advocated so vigorously by Hare (2001) and others. Thus, unlike previous nonverbal 'false belief' tests (e.g. Call & Tomasello 1999) or even the protocol proposed by Hare et al. (2001), failure on this one cannot be blamed on interspecific misunderstandings, ecological implausibility or the subjects' inability to understand the procedural aspects of the task.

Indeed, it is the *pattern* of successes and failures on different conditions in our protocol that is likely to provide the most interesting evidence concerning the cognitive strategy being employed by a given nonhuman subject. For example, a subject who employs a 'Don't go after a food reward if the dominant has oriented towards it' strategy will pass a different set of conditions than a subject employing a 'Always retrieve the less desirable of the two food amounts' strategy. Similarly, a subject who passes the *removed informed* condition but not the *removed uninformed* condition (or vice versa) has revealed something significant about the characteristics and the limitations of the cognitive strategy he is employing.

It might be objected that the complexity of the conditions in our version of Hare et al.'s protocol is too great for chimpanzees or corvids to handle and that the processing capacity limitations of these subjects are orthogonal to the question of whether or not they possess an f_{ToM}. The conditions in our five-bucket protocol do, indeed, pose a significant degree of 'relational complexity' (Halford et al. 1998), but we disagree with the claim that this invalidates the protocol as a test of a subject's ability to reason about what their conspecifics do and do not know.

While our five-bucket protocol poses an intractable computational challenge to a subject without an f_{ToM} of any kind, our protocol would be much less daunting to a subject who is able to encode the appropriate *ms* state variables. As Whiten and Suddendorf pointed out, one function of an f_{ToM} is to reduce the complexity of social interactions by positing abstract hidden variables that encode abstract, relational similarities between perceptually disparate behavioural patterns (Whiten 1996, 1997, 2000; Suddendorf & Whiten 2001; Whiten & Suddendorf 2001). For example, a subject endowed with the appropriate simulative abilities should be able to significantly reduce the relational complexity of the task by first simulating what they would do from the perspective of the dominant competitor. (Indeed, we suspect that many readers did exactly this while reading the description of each condition.)

Furthermore, we would argue that the ability to perceive relational similarities between perceptually disparate behavioural patterns (i.e. to form 'abstract equivalence classes'; in Whiten's (1996) terms) and to postulate the existence of unobservable causes like mental states are paradigmatic examples of higher-order relational reasoning (see Gentner et al. 2001 for an overview of the current literature; see Penn & Povinelli (2007) for a relational analysis of non-human causal cognition). Consistent with this hypothesis, Andrews et al. (2003) have shown that children's ability to reason relationally and their ability to reason about unobservable mental states is closely linked, both computationally and ontogenetically (see also Halford et al. 1998; Zelazo et al. 2002). Thus, the ability to encode *ms* variables via an f_{ToM} is probably inseparable, both computationally and phylogenetically, from the ability to reason about the relational similarity between complex behavioural patterns and higher-order causal relations.

(c) Take-home lessons from the proposed experimental protocols

The key point to be taken from the two protocols proposed herein is not that they constitute an acid test for an f_{ToM} in a chimpanzee or corvid, or that failure on these tests would be demonstrative evidence of an absence of an f_{ToM}. Rather, they are a direct response to the concern that success in any predictive paradigm can be explained as the result of a behaviouristic psychological system rather than mental, intervening variables (e.g. Andrews 2005). If this concern were true, then the entire project of testing non-human animals' ability to use an f_{ToM} to predict the behaviour of their conspecifics would be experimentally intractable and otiose. While this concern applies to virtually all other experimental protocols to date, the present proposals are existence proofs that experimental protocols can be constructed that could provide positive, principled evidence for the predictive function of an f_{ToM} in nonverbal organisms.

We hope our proposed protocols also put to rest the worry that an f_{ToM} has no functional, adaptive value or, worse, may by a figment of our folk psychological imagination. Regardless of our doubts concerning the ontological status of the hypothetical entities posited by our folk psychology, it is clear to us that the ability to cognize the world from the cognitive perspective of another agent would provide an animal with enormous advantages over and above the ability to reason in terms of observable first-person relations alone. Our proposed experiments set forth two artificial examples of how the value of such an f_{ToM} might manifest itself. Hundreds of experimental studies with young children have shown that they are able to solve the kind of tasks that require an f_{ToM} in the sense defined herein (e.g. Meltzoff (2007); and see Wellman *et al.* (2001) for a review and meta-analysis). And there are good reasons for believing that the traditional hallmarks of human cognition, language and culture, are intimately dependent on f_{ToM} systems of various kinds (for example, Bloom 2000, 2002; Tomasello *et al.* 2005). The problem is not that a ToM system has no value or is experimentally intractable; the problem is that there is still no evidence that non-human animals possess anything remotely resembling one.

The theoretical work developed in this essay was generously supported by a James S. McDonnell Foundation Centennial Fellowship to DJP.

Endnotes

1. Of course, not all comparative researchers believe that non-human animals are cognitive agents in the sense defined by equation (17.2.1). But all comparative researchers who believe that non-human animals are potentially capable of possessing an f_{ToM} must necessarily believe that these same animals are cognitive agents in the sense defined by equation (17.2.1) above.
2. NB: it is not necessary for there to be a deterministic relation between the observable and the unobservable variables. Our argument holds, mutatis mutandis, whenever $P(\mathbf{b}_1 \mid \mathbf{C}_1) > P(\mathbf{b}_1 \mid \sim \mathbf{C}_1)$ or, indeed, anytime a probabilistic model (e.g. Bayesian) can predict $\mathbf{b}_1$ on the basis of observable cues and past conditional dependencies without taking the value of $\mathbf{r\text{-state}}_1$ into account.
3. Hare *et al.* used two metrics, 'retrieve' and 'approach', to measure the animals' performance on these tests. The first recorded the percentage of food items actually retained by the subordinate. The second recorded the percentage of trials on which the subordinate left its own chamber and crossed into the middle chamber prior to the dominant being released. As Karin-D'Arcy & Povinelli (2002) note, given the fact that the dominant chimp often did not know where the food was located and given the fact that the subordinate was given a sizeable headstart, it is hardly meaningful that the subordinate retrieved more food. As an important and overlooked point of scholarship, it should be noted that the approach metric was not statistically significant in the Misinformed condition of experiment 1, or in any of the other experiments reported in Hare *et al.* (2001).

4. These glosses are not meant to suggest that corvids are constrained to simple conditional rules. We believe that corvids, like many other nonhuman animals, are perfectly capable of reasoning about the world in a flexible manner, albeit only with respect to observable first-person relations.

5. Andrews' (2005) objection nevertheless suggests an interesting modification to the visor protocol. First, train the chimpanzees to (i) make a begging gesture in front of experimenters who can see them and (ii) to produce an auditory cue (e.g. stomping) in front of any experimenter who cannot see them (using the kind of seeing/not-seeing conditions developed by Povinelli & Eddy (1996*b*), such as bucket-over-head, blindfold on and back turned). In the transfer session, present the subject with a single experimenter wearing either the opaque or see-through visor and test whether or not the subject stomps or begs in front of that experimenter. Chimpanzees who have simply learned to stomp in response to an arbitrary set of perceptual cues (e.g. bucket-over-head, blindfold on, back turned), without any understanding of the underlying epistemic states involved will stomp regardless of the kind of bucket being worn. Chimpanzees who have cognized the physical conditions that result in 'seeing' and physical conditions that result in 'not-seeing' will beg from the experimenter with the see-through visor, but stomp in front of the experimenter with the opaque visor.

6. One might ask why, given that chimpanzees do preferentially gesture to someone facing them as opposed to someone facing away, this is not *prima facie* evidence for an understanding of the perceptual state of seeing. The point to be clarified by the formalism of this paper is that immediate knowledge of how to respond to a social context is completely orthogonal to the question of whether the chimpanzee's underlying representation of the situation is comprised of r, p and ms variables, or r and p variables alone.

References

Andrews, K. 2005 Chimpanzee theory of mind: looking in all the wrong places? *Mind Lang.* **20**, 521–536.

Andrews, G., Halford, G. S., Bunch, K. M., Bowden, D. & Jones, T. 2003 Theory of mind and relational complexity. *Child Dev.* **74**, 1476–1499. (doi:10.1111/1467-8624.00618)

Birch, S. A. J. & Bloom, P. 2004 Understanding children's and adults' limitations in mental state reasoning. *Trends Cogn. Sci.* **8**, 255–260. (doi:10.1016/j.tics.2004.04.011)

Bloom, P. 2000 *How children learn the meaning of words.* Cambridge, MA: MIT Press.

Bloom, P. 2002 Mindreading, communication and the learning of names for things. *Mind Lang.* **17**, 37–54.

Bugnyar, T. & Heinrich, B. 2005 Ravens, *Corvus corax*, differentiate between knowledgeable and ignorant competitors. *Proc. R. Soc. B* **272**, 1641–1646. (doi:10.1098/rspb.2005.3144)

Bugnyar, T. & Heinrich, B. 2006 Pilfering ravens, *Corvus corax*, adjust their behaviour to social context and identity of competitors. *Anim. Cogn.* **9**, 369–376. (doi:10.1007/s10071-006-0035-6)

Call, J. & Tomasello, M. 1999 A nonverbal false belief task: the performance of children and great apes. *Child Dev.* **70**, 381–395. (doi:10.1111/1467-8624.00028)

Call, J., Hare, B. & Tomasello, M. 1998 Chimpanzee gaze following in an object-choice task. *Anim. Cogn.* **3**, 23–34. (doi:10.1007/s100710050047)

Carruthers, P. & Smith, P. K. (eds) 1996 *Theories of theory of mind.* New York, NY: Cambridge University Press.

Clayton, N. S. & Emery, N. J. 2005 Corvid cognition. *Curr. Biol.* **15**, R80–R81. (doi:10.1016/j.cub.2005.01.020)

Clayton, N. S., Griffiths, D. P., Emery, N. J. & Dickinson, A. 2001 Elements of episodic-like memory in animals. *Phil. Trans. R. Soc. B* **356**, 1483–1491. (doi:10.1098/rstb.2001.0947)

Clayton, N. S., Dally, J. M. & Emery, N. J. 2007 Social cognition by food-caching corvids. The western scrub-jay as a natural psychologist. *Phil. Trans. R. Soc. B* **362**, 507–522. (doi:10.1098/rstb.2006.1992)

Dally, J. M., Emery, N. J. & Clayton, N. S. 2006 Food-caching western scrub-jays keep track of who was watching when. *Science* **312**, 1662–1665. (doi:10.1126/science.1126539)

Davies, M. & Stone, T. (eds) 1995*a* *Folk psychology.* Oxford, UK: Blackwell Publishers.

Davies, M. & Stone, T. (eds) 1995*b* *Mental simulation*. Oxford, UK: Blackwell.

Dennett, D. C. 1987 *The intentional stance*. Cambridge, MA: MIT Press.

Dretske, F. I. 1988 *Explaining behavior*. Cambridge, MA: MIT Press.

Emery, N. J. 2004 Are corvids 'feathered apes'? Cognitive evolution in crows, jays, rooks and jackdaws. In *Comparative analysis of minds* (ed. S. Watanabe). Tokyo, Japan: Keio University Press.

Emery, N. J. & Clayton, N. S. 2001 Effects of experience and social context on prospective caching strategies by scrub jays. *Nature* **414**, 443–446. (doi:10.1038/35106560)

Emery, N. J. & Clayton, N. S. 2004 The mentality of crows: convergent evolution of intelligence in corvids and apes. *Science* **306**, 1903–1907. (doi:10.1126/science.1098410)

Emery, N. J. & Clayton, N. S. 2005 Evolution of the avian brain and intelligence. *Curr. Biol.* **15**, R946–R950. (doi:10.1016/j.cub.2005.11.029)

Flombaum, J. I. & Santos, L. R. 2005 Rhesus monkeys attribute perceptions to others. *Curr. Biol.* **15**, 447–452. (doi:10.1016/j.cub.2004.12.076)

Gentner, D., Holyoak, K. J. & Kokinov, B. K. (eds) 2001 *The analogical mind: perspectives from cognitive science*. Cambridge, MA: MIT Press.

Goldman, A. 1993 The psychology of folk psychology. *Behav. Brain Sci.* **16**, 15–28.

Goodall, J. 1986 The chimpanzees of Gombe; patterns of behavior. Cambridge, MA: Belknap, Harvard University Press.

Gordon, R. 1986 Folk psychology as simulation. *Mind Lang.* **1**, 158–171.

Gordon, R. 1996 'Radical' simulationism. In *Theories of theories of mind* (eds P. Carruthers & P. K. Smith), pp. 11–21. Cambridge, UK: Cambridge University Press.

Halford, G. S., Wilson, W. H. & Phillips, S. 1998 Processing capacity defined by relational complexity: implications for comparative, developmental, and cognitive psychology. *Behav. Brain Sci.* **21**, 803–864. (doi:10.1017/S0140525X98001769)

Hare, B. 2001 Can competitive paradigms increase the validity of experiments on primate social cognition? *Anim. Cogn.* **4**, 269–280. (doi:10.1007/s100710100084)

Hare, B., Call, J., Agnetta, B. & Tomasello, M. 2000 Chimpanzees know what conspecifics do and do not see. *Anim. Behav.* **59**, 771–785. (doi:10.1006/anbe.1999.1377)

Hare, B., Call, J. & Tomasello, M. 2001 Do chimpanzees know what conspecifics know? *Anim. Behav.* **61**, 771–785. (doi:10.1006/anbe.2000.1518)

Heyes, C. M. 1998 Theory of mind in nonhuman primates. *Behav. Brain Sci.* **21**, 101–148. (doi:10.1017/S0140525X98000703)

Hostetter, A. B., Cantero, M. & Hopkins, W. D. 2001 Differential use of vocal and gestural communication by chimpanzees (*Pan troglodytes*) in response to the attentional status of a human (*Homo sapiens*). *J. Comp. Psychol.* **115**, 337–343.

Hunt, G. R. 1996 Manufacture and use of hook-tools by New Caledonian crows. *Nature* **379**, 249–251. (doi:10.1038/379249a0)

Hunt, G. R. 2004 The crafting of hook tools by wild New Caledonian crows. *Proc. R. Soc. B* **271** (Suppl. 3), S88–S90. (doi:10.1098/rsbl.2003.0085)

Hurley, S. & Nudds, M. 2006 The questions of animal rationality: theory and evidence. In *Rational animals?* (eds M. Nudds & S. Hurley), pp. 1–83. Oxford, UK: Oxford University Press.

Hurley, S. & Chater, N. (eds) 2005 *Perspectives on imitation: from neuroscience to social science*. Cambridge, MA: MIT Press.

Karin-D'Arcy, M. R. & Povinelli, D. J. 2002 Do chimpanzees know what each other see? A closer look. *Int. J. Comp. Psychol.* **15**, 21–54.

Leavens, D.A., Hostetter, A.B., Wesley, M.J.& Hopkins, W.D. 2004 Tactical use of unimodal and bimodal communication by chimpanzees, *Pan troglodytes*. *Anim. Behav.* **67**, 467–476. (doi:10.1016/j.anbehav.2003.04.007)

Markman, A. B. & Dietrich, E. 2000 In defense of representation. *Cogn. Psychol.* **40**, 138–171. (doi:10.1006/cogp.1999.0727)

Meltzoff, A. 2007 'Like me': a foundation for social cognition. *Dev. Sci.* **10**, 126–134. (doi:10.1111/j.1467-7687.2007.00574.x)

Meltzoff, A. & Moore, M. K. 1997 Explaining facial imitation: a theoretical model. *Early Dev. Parenting* **6**, 179–192. (doi:10.1002/(SICI)1099-0917(199709/12)6:3/ 4<179::AID-EDP157>3.0.CO;2-R)

Nichols, S. & Stich, S. P. 2003 *Mindreading: an integrated account of pretence, self-awareness and understanding other minds.* Oxford, UK: Oxford University Press.

Penn, D. & Povinelli, D. J. 2007 Causal cognition in human and nonhuman animals: a comparative, critical review. *Annu. Rev. Psychol.* **58**, 97–118. (doi:10.1146/annurev.psych.58.110405.085555)

Povinelli, D. J. 2003 *Folk physics for apes.* Oxford, UK: Oxford University Press.

Povinelli, D. J. & Eddy, T. J. 1996a Chimpanzees: joint visual attention. *Psychol. Sci.* **7**, 129–135. (doi:10.1111/j.1467- 9280.1996.tb00345.x)

Povinelli, D. J. & Eddy, T. J. 1996b Factors influencing young chimpanzees' (*Pan troglodytes*) recognition of attention. *J. Comp. Psychol.* **110**, 336–345. (doi:10.1037/0735-7036.110.4.336)

Povinelli, D. J. & Eddy, T. J. 1996c What young chimpanzees know about seeing. *Monogr. Soc. Res. Child Dev.* **61**, i–vi. (doi:10.2307/1166159) 1–191.

Povinelli, D. J. & Giambrone, S. 1999 Inferring other minds: flaws in the argument by analogy. *Phil. Top.* **27**, 167–201.

Povinelli, D. J. & Vonk, J. 2003 Chimpanzee minds: suspiciously human? *Trends Cogn. Sci.* **7**, 157–160. (doi:10.1016/S1364-6613(03)00053-6)

Povinelli, D. J. & Vonk, J. 2004 We don't need a microscope to explore the chimpanzee's mind. *Mind Lang.* **19**, 1–28.

Povinelli, D. J., Bering, J. M. & Giambrone, S. 2000 Toward a science of other minds: escaping the argument by analogy. *Cogn. Sci.* **24**, 509–541. (doi:10.1016/S0364-0213(00)00023-9)

Povinelli, D. J., Dunphy-Lelii, S., Reauxa, J. E. & Mazza, M. P. 2002 Psychological diversity in chimpanzees and humans: new longitudinal assessments of chimpanzees' understanding of attention. *Brain Behav. Evol.* **59**, 33–53. (doi:10.1159/000063732)

Premack, D. & Woodruff, G. 1978 Does the chimpanzee have a theory of mind? *Behav. Brain Sci.* **4**, 515–526.

Santos, L. R., Nissen, A. G. & Ferrugia, J. 2006 Rhesus monkeys, *Macaca mulatta*, know what others can and cannot hear. *Anim. Behav.* **71**, 1175–1181. (doi:10.1016/j.anbehav.2005.10.007)

Seed, A. M., Tebbich, S., Emery, N. J. & Clayton, N. S. 2006 Investigating physical cognition in rooks (*Corvus frugilegus*). *Curr. Biol.* **16**, 697–701. (doi:10.1016/j.cub.2006.02.066)

Silk, J. B. 2002 The form and function of reconciliation in primates. *Annu. Rev. Anthropol.* **31**, 21–44. (doi:10.1146/annurev.anthro.31.032902.101743)

Suddendorf, T. & Whiten, A. 2001 Mental evolution and development: evidence for secondary representation in children, great apes and other animals. *Psychol. Bull.* **127**, 629–650. (doi:10.1037/ 0033-2909.127.5.629)

Tebbich, S., Seed, A. M., Emery, N. J. & Clayton, N. S. In press. Non-tool-using rooks (*Corvus frugilegus*) solve the trap-tube task. *Anim. Cogn.*

Tomasello, M. & Call, J. 1997 *Primate cognition.* New York, NY: Oxford University Press.

Tomasello, M. & Call, J. 2006 Do chimpanzees know what others see—or only what they are looking at? In *Rational animals?* (eds S Hurley & M. Nudds), pp. 371–384. Oxford, UK: Oxford University Press.

Tomasello, M., Call, J., Nagell, K., Olguin, R. & Carpenter, M. 1994 The learning and use of gestural signals by young chimpanzees: a trans-generational study. *Primates* **35**, 137–154. (doi:10.1007/ BF02382050)

Tomasello, M., Hare, B. & Agnetta, B. 1999 Chimpanzees, *Pan troglodytes*, follow gaze direction geometrically. *Anim. Behav.* **58**, 769–777. (doi:10.1006/anbe.1999.1192)

Tomasello, M., Call, J. & Hare, B. 2003a Chimpanzees understand psychological states—the question is which ones and to what extent. *Trends Cogn. Sci.* **7**, 153–156. (doi:10.1016/S1364-6613(03)00035-4)

Tomasello, M., Call, J. & Hare, B. 2003b Chimpanzees versus humans: it's not that simple. *Trends Cogn. Sci.* **7**, 239–240. (doi:10.1016/S1364-6613(03)00107-4)

Tomasello, M., Carpenter, M., Call, J., Behne, T. & Moll, H. 2005 Understanding and sharing intentions: the origins of cultural cognition. *Behav. Brain Sci.* **28**, 675–691. (doi:10.1017/S0140525X05000129)

Visalberghi, E. & Tomasello, M. 1998 Primate causal understanding in the physical and psychological domains. *Behav. Processes* **42**, 189–203. (doi:10.1016/S0376-6357(97)00076-4)

Wellman, H. M., Cross, D. & Watsonl, J. 2001 Meta-analysis of theory-of-mind development: the truth about false belief. *Child Dev.* **72**, 655–684. (doi:10.1111/1467-8624.*00304)*

Whiten, A. 1996 When does behaviour-reading become mind-reading. In *Theories of theory of mind* (eds P. Carruthers & P. K. Smith), pp. 277–292. New York, NY: Cambridge University Press.

Whiten, A. 1997 The Machiavellian mindreader. In *Machiavellian intelligence II: extensions and evaluations* (eds A. Whiten & R. W. Byrne), pp. 144–173. Cambridge, UK; New York, NY: Cambridge University Press.

Whiten, A. 2000 Chimpanzees and mental re-representation. In *Metarepresentations: a multidisciplinary perspective* (ed. D. Sperber), pp. 139–167. New York, NY: Oxford University Press.

Whiten, A. & Suddendorf, T. 2001 Meta-representation and secondary representation. *Trends Cogn. Sci.* **5**, 378. (doi:10.1016/S1364-6613(00)01734-4)

Zelazo, P. D., Jacques, S., Burack, J. & Frye, D. 2002 The relation between theory of mind and rule use: evidence from persons with autism-spectrum disorders. *Infant Child Dev.* **11**, 171–195. (doi:10.1002/icd.304)

18

The society of selves

Nicholas Humphrey

Human beings are not only the most sociable animals on Earth, but also the only animals that have to ponder the separateness that comes with having a conscious self. The philosophical problem of 'other minds' nags away at people's sense of who—and why—they are. But the privacy of conscious-ness has an evolutionary history—and maybe even an evolutionary function. While recognizing the importance to humans of mind-reading and psychic transparency, we should consider the consequences and possible benefits of being—ultimately—psychically opaque.

Keywords: consciousness; other minds; social intelligence; self-concept

The word *ujamaa* in Swahili has no simple translation into English. But its meaning is made plain in the *ujamaa* carvings created by the Makonde craftsmen of Tanzania. In these carvings, often called 'trees of life', human figures, of all sorts and ages, are intertwined in a rising column of ebony (figure 18.1, Humphrey 1972). Everyone is busy doing their own work: one cooks; another hammers; a third sews; and a fourth nurses her baby. The figures tumble up against each other so closely that their spaces and forms are defined by the bodies of their neighbours. Yet all the time they retain their separate identities and personalities. *Ujamaa*, it is clear, refers to nothing less than the capacity of human beings, despite their differences, to work together as a community—something that humans are better able to do than any other animal on Earth.

What gives humans this unparalleled capacity to get along together? What special talent do they have for doing 'natural psychology'? The answer that I and others have converged on is that there has evolved in the human line, maybe just within the last few million years, a talent and a desire for *deep intersubjectivity*: a special capacity for *mind-reading*, underpinned by *empathy* (the sharing of feelings) and *sympathy* (the sharing of goals). That is the message of several of the papers in this volume. *Humans alone know what it is like to be in someone else's place* and *humans alone care*.That is the message I began to spell out in my 1976 paper on the 'social function of intellect' (Humphrey 1976)and developed in Consciousness Regained (1983) and The Inner Eye (1986).

I am not going to tell you that I have changed my mind. However, I do want to use this occa-sion to pull back a bit, or at any rate to pull in another direction. For I am going to argue here that, in stressing shared consciousness and intersubjectivity, we may be missing something crucial. There is no great truth, it has been said, of which the opposite is not also a great truth. I want to suggest that, when it comes to it, human beings are not only exceptionally sociable, but also exceptionally *lonely*. And loneliness plays a key part in shaping human life and culture.

But I shall not start with this. For I have a debt, left over from the 1976 paper, that I want to settle first. In the 1880s, long before I or anyone else in evolutionary psychology came on the scene, the philosopher Friedrich Nietzsche was already speculating about the very same issues that have engaged the contributors to this volume, about the evolution of consciousness and its relation to social life. I am ashamed to say that I had not read Nietzsche when I wrote my first

Fig. 18.1 Makonde *tree of life ca* 1970.

paper on social intelligence or the papers that soon followed about theory of mind and consciousness. More shameful still, I confess that as an experimental psychologist educated at Cambridge, it never occurred to me that I ought to have read Nietzsche. So, it was not until much too late that I found out how closely Nietzsche's arguments anticipated mine. I suspect what was news to me may still be news to you.

Here is what Nietzsche wrote in The Gay Science (1887/1974):

The problem of consciousness... confronts us only when we begin to comprehend how we could dispense with it... For we could think, feel, will, and remember, and we could 'act' in every sense of that word, and yet none of all of this would have to 'enter consciousness'... The whole of life would be possible without, as it were, seeing itself in a mirror... *For what purpose*, then, any consciousness at all when it is in the main *superfluous*? I may now proceed to the surmise that... consciousness is really only a net of communication between human beings; a solitary human being who lived like a beast of prey would not have needed it. That our actions, thoughts, feelings and movements enter our own consciousness—at least a part of them—that is the result of a 'must' that for a terribly long time lorded it over man. As the most endangered animal, he *needed* help and protection, he needed his peers, he had to learn to express his distress and to make himself understood; and for all of this he needed 'consciousness' first of all, he needed to 'know' himself what distressed him, he needed to 'know' how he felt, he needed to 'know' what he thought... My idea is, as you see, that consciousness does not really belong to man's individual existence but rather to his social or herd nature.

Nietzsche not only highlighted this role for consciousness, but also had a proposal for precisely how the net of communication is created. Here is what he wrote in Daybreak (1881/1997):

Empathy—To understand another person, that *is to imitate his feelings in ourselves*,we... produce the feeling in ourselves after the *effects* it exerts and displays on the other person by imitating with our own body the expression of his eyes, his voice, his walk, his bearing. Then a similar feeling arises in us in consequence of an ancient association between movement and sensation. We have brought our skill in understanding the feelings of others to a high state of perfection and in the presence of another person we are always almost involuntarily practising this skill.

Nietzsche, in short, was ahead of me—and you—in all these ways. First, he formulated the social intelligence hypothesis, realizing that human beings have to be natural psychologists in order to survive. Second, he saw how this would have led to the evolution of a capacity for reflexive consciousness, as the basis for a theory of mind. Third, he recognized how empathy arises from simulation, mediated by imitation of action and expression.

These ideas have come into their own at last. They are being developed at the frontiers of ethology, psychology and neuroscience, as so well illustrated by other papers in this volume, and I have no need to remind you of the buzz that now surrounds them. Of course, the one thing Nietzsche did not anticipate (and nor, I may say, did I) was the existence of mirror neurons. But if anything was needed to give a fillip to the field, Gallese and Rizzolatti's discovery has certainly provided it. Ramachandran (2000) has said 'I predict that mirror neurons will do for psychology what DNA did for biology'. In a recent article, Gallese *et al.* (2004) bill mirror neurons as providing 'a unifying view of the basis of social cognition'. A headline in the New York Times calls these neurons 'cells that read minds' (Blakeslee 2006); and in the article that follows, Marc Iacoboni is quoted as claiming: 'you automatically have empathy for me. You know how I feel because you literally feel what I am feeling'.

Indeed, neuroscience itself is beginning to be wonderfully *in touch*. In 2005, the Dalai Lama was cheered to the rooftops at the Society for Neuroscience in Washington, when he explained the relevance of Buddhist ideas about the connectedness of everything. Typical of this new trend, a recent conference in Bologna addressed 'primordial questions about consciousness', centred on the question 'do you have a pragmatic proposal to make first-person experience intersubjectively shareable?' (ASIA 2006). It seems that the ideas about flow and connectedness are fast becoming not just politically but scientifically correct. If I do not feel your pain— or at any rate have a pragmatic proposal for feeling it—then I had better not let on!

Now, do not get me wrong. I would be the first to agree that the field of consciousness studies has entered an exceptionally exciting phase. Yet with the social brain and mirror neurons all the rage, I do think there is a danger that in the rush to emphasize empathy as a human birthright, we may be failing to recognize— perhaps even wilfully failing to recognize—the extent to which consciousness creates *barriers* between people, even as it unites them.

In both my early books, I used paintings by Paul Gauguin to illustrate what it means for us to look into and read another person's mind. Gauguin, writing of his 13-year-old wife, had said 'I strive to see and think through this child'. And the stated aim of many of his paintings was to understand the mystery of things and people by going inside them to reveal the deep structures that make them what they are. Likewise, I suggested, ordinary human beings are continually doing something similar to this in their daily social life. 'We all, every day of our lives, imagine more than we can see... And we do it most impressively and most importantly when—almost without noticing it—we make imaginative guesses about the hidden contents of the human mind. We have only so much as to glance at another human being and we at once begin to read beneath the surface. We see there another conscious person, like ourselves. We see someone with human feelings, memories, desires. A mind potentially like ours' (Humphrey 1986, p. 30).

But I should have looked more carefully, for now I think that my choice of Gauguin to illustrate the case of mind-reading was a perverse one. Gauguin as a painter was indeed a genius at going 'behind appearances' to reveal hidden meanings. But what he revealed about human society is actually very far from that legendary net of communication between human beings.

Within a year of arriving in Tahiti in 1891, Gauguin had made a carving with an uncanny resemblance to a Makonde tree of life (figure 18.2; Gauguin 1893*a*). It seems probable that he

Fig. 18.2 Paul Gauguin, ironwood carving 1893.

had in fact seen a Makonde carving, when he visited the Colonial Exhibition in Paris in 1889, where many works of African art were on display. In Gauguin's carving, as in the Makonde model, the figures line up next to each other, sharing the same bit of wood. However, that is where the resemblance ends. For Gauguin has done nothing to convey the spirit of *ujamaa*. The figures in his carving, rather than communicating, are more like straphangers in a crowded tube train, physically close but mentally shut off.

The *absence* of human communion is in fact one of the most striking features of Gauguin's representation of people in his Tahitian paintings (figure 18.3; Gauguin 1896). In the paintings, individuals never touch, nor hardly even look at each other. In stark contrast to a tree of life, each occupies his or her own mental world, private and separate. What Gauguin seems to want to stress is the psychological distance between people, the extent to which everyone remains an enigma to everyone else. Indeed, as if to underscore this, he gives titles to the paintings in the form of uncomprehending questions about what is going on: 'Why are you angry?'; 'What, are you jealous?'; and 'When will you marry?'.

These are paintings, I would *now* say, about the 'otherness of other people'. This phrase is one I have borrowed from John Banville (2005), in his novel, *The Sea*. Speaking of the girl he was obsessed with, the narrator writes, 'In her [Chloe], I had my first experience of the absolute otherness of other people. It is not too much to say—well it is, but I shall say it anyway— that in Chloe the world was first manifest for me as an objective entity... I never knew where I was with her, or what sort of treatment to expect at her hands'.

Fig. 18.3 Paul Gauguin, *Why are you angry?* 1896. (Reproduced with permission from the Art Institute of Chicago, Chicago, IL).

Let us note—it is important—that Chloe in this novel is no *stranger* to the narrator, no more than the people in Gauguin's paintings are strangers to each other. In fact, it seems to be part of the point being made by both novelist and painter that it is precisely when people get closest to others, and have come to know them well as familiar *objective entities*, that their psychological otherness becomes most obvious—and most alarming.

Sexual intimacy, in particular, can provide a worrying test. As Gauguin revealed in his letters and diaries, sex was never far from his thoughts. While rooming with Van Gogh in the Yellow House in Arles, he made provision in their joint budget for regular outings to

Fig. 18.4 Paul Gauguin, illustration to *Noa Noa*. (Reproduced with permission from Musée du Louvre, Paris, France; photograph © Hervé Lewandowski).

prostitutes for what he called 'hygienic excursions' to satisfy his insistent manhood. He did it, it seems, primarily for health reasons, and perhaps this was just as much true after he moved to Tahiti. Gauguin made only one picture of the act of sex. But it is a revealing one. The woman looks up and away, her mind quite clearly somewhere else (figure 18.4; Gauguin 1893*b*). In several paintings of his young wife in Tahiti, he shows her lying on her bed, post-coitus, the very picture of solitariness.

Possibly, Gauguin was unusually cavalier in his attitude to making love. Even so, the fact is that for all too many couples, sexual intercourse is actually a lesson in mental separateness, carnal knowledge a lesson in spiritual agnosia. Dryden (1684), in a translation of a poem by Lucretius, spelt out this stark reality:

They gripe, they squeeze, their humid tongues they dart,
As each would force their way to t'others heart:
In vain they only cruze about the coast,
For bodies cannot pierce, nor be in bodies lost...
All ways they try, successless all they prove,
To cure the secret sore of lingring love.

The poet W. B. Yeats called these lines 'the finest description of sexual intercourse ever written'—precisely because they illustrate just how impossible it is for two to become a unity. 'The tragedy of sexual intercourse', Yeats said, 'is the perpetual virginity of the soul' (Yeats 1949).

By the end of 1897, Gauguin had had enough. His hopes of discovering the essence of being human—through love, through friendship, through history—seemed to have come to nothing. He was disillusioned and depressed, and wanted to die. Still, in a last effort to make a grand statement of his ethical discoveries, he completed in a fever of work the biggest of all his paintings, and wrote on it—he said it was his signature—*D'où Venons Nous, Que Sommes Nous, Où Allons Nous* (figure 18.5; Gauguin 1897). Then, on New Year's Eve, he climbed the hill behind his house with a box of arsenic in his pocket, with the intent of killing himself. In this event, he took too much of the poison and vomited it up. After lying out a few hours, he dragged himself disconsolately home.

Fig. 18.5 Paul Gauguin, *Where do we come from? What are we? Where are we going?* 1897. (Reproduced with permission from the Museum of Fine Arts, Boston, MA).

Gauguin's attempt at suicide failed. But his attempt at revealing in this last picture something profound about *what it's like to be a human being* certainly succeeded. There have been a thousand interpretations of this painting. But I have no hesitation in telling you my own. What the puzzled, isolated figures of the painting speak to is the essential loneliness of the human condition.

Que sommes nous? What are we? The bottom line is that we are *not* a we. *We* are a set of *I*'s... individuals who due to the very nature of conscious selfhood are in principle unable to get through to one another and share the most central facts of our psychical existence. Nietzsche was wrong. When it comes to consciousness, we are on our own: 'soul', 'solo'. Etymologically, according to the Oxford English Dictionary, there is no connection between *soul* as a noun and *sole* as a predicate (though I may say I wonder). But psychologically and even logically, the connection is all too clear. There are no doors between one consciousness and another. Everyone knows directly only of his or her own consciousness and not anyone else's.

It is all so horribly obvious, when you think about it. And we *do* think about it. Since we were children, we have all played with the riddles of otherness that flow from the essential inaccessibility of other minds. To take John Locke's famous example of seeing colours: how do I know that my colour sensation when I see a violet is not like yours when you see a marigold. The answer, which it has never required a great philosopher to prove to us, is simply that I do not—because, as Locke said, 'one man's mind cannot pass into another man's body' (Locke 1690/1975). Of course, probably we long ago ceased to find this conclusion novel. Yet there is no denying how strange and upsetting it was—and is—at first discovery: not simply an interesting tease but a gaping hole at the centre of our need for communion.

If I cannot even tell what seeing red is like for you, what can I tell! Imagine. We are walking together in the woods after the rain, dappled sunshine filters through the dripping leaves, a blackbird sings and the scent of honeysuckle permeates the rich air. It may be that shared moments like these are needed to give meaning to our lives—shared moments of consciousness. What then if we should realize how little we are truly sharing: that if truth be told each of us is merely colouring in the other's consciousness as if it were his or her own?

I suggest that what Gauguin was showing in that last great painting is just how hard it is to come to terms with this result. To have to face the fact of being oneself—*one* self, *this* self and none other, this secret packet of phenomena, this singular bubble of consciousness. Press up against each other as we may, and the bubbles remain essentially inviolate. Share the same body even, be joined like Siamese twins, and there still remain two quite separate consciousnesses (figure 18.6, Beloit 2006). Perhaps, the tragedy of *being human* is the perpetual virginity of the soul.

But how funny all this is. I mean funny-peculiar. Nothing else in the world is *private* in quite the same, disturbing, way that conscious experience is. Everything else in the world joins up in the four-dimensional space–time manifold that basic physics says is sufficient to describe the universe. But consciousness it seems is essentially different. Indeed, each individual's consciousness would seem to be as much a world apart, on its own plane of existence, as is each separate universe in the 'multiverse' that cosmologists sometimes fantasize about. Let alone are there open doors between one conscious self and another; it seems there is not even the possibility of tunnelling though a wormhole.

It is hardly surprising that many ordinary people find this situation puzzling, even paradoxical. This puzzlement is not because they are missing something—not because they are making a category error, or because they do not know how to talk properly (though some philosophers persist in saying so). Consciousness really is deeply, fascinatingly, peculiarly private. And the

Fig. 18.6 Siamese twins, woodcut from the Nuremberg Chronicle, 1493.

meaning and explanation of this privacy continues to pose a major challenge to cognitive science and philosophy of mind.

My own approach as a scientist (Humphrey 1992, 2000, 2006) has been to look for an explanation for the privacy of consciousness in its deep evolutionary history. That is to say, I have tried to explain how consciousness could have evolved, little by little, always under natural selection, to be *so constructed as* to be private. In fact, I have argued that it has evolved to be private on two quite different levels. Consciousness has become private—*necessarily* private—on the *phenomenal level*: meaning that one person cannot in principle have access to another person's subjective awareness of *what it is like* to be conscious, to be sensing red, for example. But then consciousness has also become private—*contingently* private—on the *propositional* level: meaning that one person usually does not have access even to the objective fact *that* another person is sensing red.

This is not the place to go into this theory of consciousness in any great depth. But, still, if I may move to a more analytic kind of discussion for a moment, I shall try to summarize what I think the story is. And I will begin with an analogy.

When a person, let us say it is me, performs a *bodily action*, when I wiggle my right big toe, for example, there are two respects in which this action is something that uniquely belongs to me and/or that *I* have a unique take on. First, it is *I* only who am doing it, I am its *author*—and, of course, no one else does or logically could stand in this first-person subjective relation to the action of wiggling *my* toe. Thus, the doing of it is necessarily private. I cannot give away my action or share it even if I want to. True, you might perform a similar action with your body. You might even perform it at the very same time as I do. But, still, you would not be wiggling *my* toe, you would be wiggling *yours*.

Second, it is my *body* that is involved, the body to which I have a special spatio-temporal relationship—and so I can hardly miss the fact that the wiggle is occurring. True, I am not the only one who could, in principle, make this observation as an objective fact. If I am acting in public, it is logically possible you too could observe *that* I am wiggling my toe. But suppose I perform the action covertly, inside my boot, say. Then everyone else except me will be out of the observational loop. Thus, many of the observations I am able to make about my actions will be contingently private. I could, in principle, share the objective information with you, but in many cases I will not have to and will not choose to.

Now, how does this tie in with consciousness? What could my unique take on my bodily actions have to do with my unique take on my conscious sensations? What can the private nature of wiggling my toe have to do with the private nature of seeing red, or smelling a rose, or feeling pain? According to the theory I have developed, it can have everything to do with it: because sensations actually *are* a kind of bodily action—or, at any rate, they *were*. Sensations are not things that happen *to us*, they are indeed things *we do*.

When I look at a red screen, for example, I respond to what is happening at my eyes with a pattern of bodily activity that originated far back in evolutionary history as an instinctive evaluative response to the stimulus. In the beginning, such responses were indeed public behaviour—bodily expressions of liking or disgust, wriggles of acceptance or rejection. They would have been there for anyone to see. However, what happened in the course of evolution was that these responses became 'privatized': they began to get short-circuited before they reached the body surface, so that the motor signals instead of reaching all the way out to the site of stimulation now reached only to points closer and closer in on the incoming sensory nerve, until eventually the whole process became closed off from the outside world. In fact, the efferent signals now project only as far as sensory cortex, where they interact with the incoming signals from the sense organs to create, momentarily, a self-entangling, recursive loop (figure 18.7).

The upshot is that when looking at the screen, I am still responding to the stimulation with something like the ancient action pattern handed down from my ancestors. The action still retains vestiges of its original evaluative function, its intentionality and hedonic tone. But now it has become a 'virtual action pattern'—an *as-if response* directed to an *as-if body*, hidden inside my head.

So, now, for me to be *phenomenally conscious* of having the sensation, for there to be *something it is like* to be doing this, is nothing more or less than for me to be actively engaged in generating this as-if response—as extended, by the recursion, into the 'thick moment' of the conscious present. Meanwhile, for me to have the *propositional part of the experience*, to observe *that* I am having a red sensation, is simply for me to monitor the fact that I am so engaged.

Whence, then, the privacy of consciousness? Think back to the analogy of my wiggling my toe. If the theory is right, the necessary privacy of the phenomenal experience is guaranteed by the fact that the sensation is *my doing*. When I generate sensations, I experience the subjective qualia from a perspective which as a matter of principle is not available to any one else. This would be so even if the sensory responses had not been internalized. But they have been. So, the contingent privacy of the propositional part of the experience is guaranteed by the fact

local response   response becomes   response becomes
occurs at site of   targeted on incoming   'privatized' within
stimulation   sensory pathway   the brain

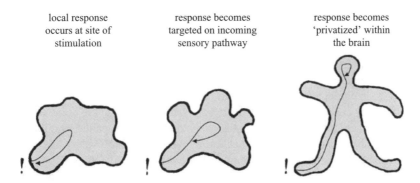

Fig. 18.7 The 'privatization' of sensation (from Humphery 2006, p. 95)

that my sensory responses are no longer public. Only I can observe that I am having a particular sensation because only I can observe what I am creating inside my head.

The point is not that you *could not* know that I am doing it, merely that in most circumstances you *will not* know—unless perhaps you can infer it from some external cue. If you do infer it, this could indeed lead to your mirroring the sensory response in your own brain. But note that this will not give you access to my phenomenal experience. Through mirroring the sensory response, you may indeed learn *that* I am sensing red, you may *sense red yourself*, but it will be you sensing *your* red.

So, has anyone got a pragmatic proposal to make first-person experience intersubjectively shareable? In the light of this analysis, you will see why I do not hold out much hope that any scientist or philosopher will ever be able to give the Buddhists the answer they want. 'I feel your pain'? No, when you are in pain, I may or may not recognize *that* you are feeling pain, I may indeed feel my own mirror version; but your pain remains strictly inalienable.

Consider again the case of Siamese twins. It is a matter of record—I mean the twins will tell anyone who asks—that their conscious minds are as private as the next person's. Does one conjoined twin know *what it is like* for the other twin to have a headache? No, yes, maybe, can't be sure…no more than you or I do. Oftentimes, one twin will not even know *that* the other has a headache. I confess, despite all my theorizing, I still find this fact astonishing.

So, let me return to society and trees of life. The fact is ordinary people have never needed any of this analysis to know the score. They have had a lifetime to check it out first hand. How was it for you? I presume that the honest answer will always have been 'virginal'—because there is simply no other way for it to be.

Yet, if the virginity of the soul is a reality, is it necessarily such a tragedy? I would say there are evolutionary grounds for thinking that it cannot be *too much* of a tragedy. For, if it were, then natural selection would never have allowed things to develop in the way they have done. To the contrary, the fact that natural selection has allowed it, even arranged for it, would suggest that the inaccessibility of consciousness may even be in some respects positively advantageous. However, in that case, there will be two separate questions to address: one, the advantage of the contingent privacy of propositional consciousness; the other, the advantage of the absolute privacy of phenomenal consciousness. And the first is much easier to deal with than the second.

As to the first, I expect many readers will already have run ahead of me. For it must be obvious enough to anyone steeped in sociobiology why a social animal such as a human being would be better off if it were to have at least the possibility of keeping the existence of its thoughts and feelings to itself. The capacity for mind-reading and for being mind-read is all very well. But human individuals even in the closest knit cooperative groups are still usually to some degree in competition. So there must certainly be times when individuals do not want to be a completely open book to others. Paul Valéry, the poet, made the point as succinctly as any of us might want to: 'credit requires that walls of coffers be opaque, and the interchange of human things between men requires that brains be impenetrable' (Valéry 1983). The advantages of tactical deception, as other chapters in this volume testify, are obvious even in apes and crows. If consciousness does provide a net of communication, nonetheless there is clearly much to be said for *facultative* privacy—for having the option of being able to logout and go off-line.

But now for the second question, about the absolute privacy of phenomenal consciousness. Could there be anything to be said for consciousness being so structured that individuals cannot share key aspects of their experience *even if they want to*? Let me explain just what it is I am asking here, for I expect most readers will in this case think the answer must be No. Could the fact that, for example, I must for ever be unsure whether what I experience as the sensation of red is the same as what you experience conceivably change my life in a positive way? Could it make any difference at all?

It is worth noting what John Locke (1690/1975) had to say. The passage in his *Essay* where he sets up the thought experiment about one man's marigold being another man's violet is quite well known.

> [Suppose] the idea that a violet produced in one man's mind by his eyes were the same that a yellow marigold produced in another man's, and vice versa. This could never be known: because one man's mind could not pass into another man's body, to perceive what appearances were produced.

But the passage that immediately follows this is hardly known at all. Surprisingly, Locke goes on to *deny* that colour inversion is a possibility worth taking seriously.

> I am nevertheless very apt to think that the sensible ideas produced by any object in different men's minds, are [in fact] indiscernibly alike. For which opinion there might be many reasons offered: but being besides my present business, I shall not trouble my reader with them: but only mind him that the contrary supposition, if it could be proved, is of little use, either for the improvement of our knowledge, or convenience of life.

Shades of the mathematician Fermat here ('I have a truly marvellous proof of this proposition which this margin is too narrow to contain'). But I think the fact is Locke has simply lost his philosophical nerve. And he is wrong to have done so. For in truth, neither he nor anyone else has ever been able to offer the reasons he alludes to why colour sensations *have to be* alike. Even Ludwig Wittgenstein would later concede in the *Philosophical Investigations* (1958):

> The essential thing about private experience is really not that each person possesses his own exemplar, but that nobody knows whether other people also have *this* or something else. The assumption would thus be possible—though unverifiable—that one section of mankind has one sensation of red and another section another.

However, central to *my* present business, I think Locke was wrong on another score, as well: namely, in saying that it is all of little consequence—'of little use for the convenience of life'. To the contrary, I believe the realization that other people may possibly experience the world differently is potentially life transforming.

How can that be? It is true of course that a difference between people, that is, as Wittgenstein says 'unverifiable', has to be *a difference that makes no difference*. Yet, this does not mean that the possibility of such a difference can make no difference. For why should it not be that what makes the difference is precisely *what someone makes of this possibility*?

Consider the following analogy. Imagine two men, A and B, each of whom has a private box with a clock in it, which he can use to tell the time. Their clocks are identical except for one peculiar feature: namely, that while the hands on A's clock turn in a clockwise way, the hands of B's turn in an anticlockwise way. When A and B read their clocks, they agree about what time it is, about the rate time is passing and so on. So it would seem that the direction of rotation is just such a difference that makes no difference. But, wait for it. Suppose A were to think: 'I wonder what it is like to be B watching his clock'—only to realize that he has no way of knowing whether B's clock rotates like his own or in the opposite direction. 'That's weird, B could be clockwise like me or anticlockwise, and I wouldn't know!' Now, suppose A were to find this situation challenging. Suppose A were to be *upset* that he does not know about B, or perhaps *pleased as Punch* that B does not know about him. Then here we would have a difference that makes no difference—but which makes a difference precisely because A realizes it makes no difference.

My point is that this is very much how it is with sensations. Conscious human beings find themselves landed in a situation where the realization that they cannot know what phenomenal consciousness is like for other people may itself have a significant impact on what they think and what they do. The absolute privacy of consciousness may strike them as provocative, tantalizing, alarming, awe-inspiring, all of the above—but one way or another it will *matter* to them, and so in large or small ways it may change their attitude to other people, to themselves and to the world.

I would suggest that there are two possible human responses to this situation that are of particular interest to an evolutionist. One is that people find it unacceptable, something to be denied or resisted. The other is that they find it wonderful, something to be celebrated.

So far, I have stressed only how unhappy it may make people to realize how solitary the soul is. Gauguin tried to kill himself. The poet John Clare, sadly complaining 'I am; but what I am none knows or cares', went quietly mad. Others, finding the whole thing too bewildering or too depressing to think about, push it aside or pretend they do not care. Clearly, no advantage comes from such responses. But there is another way of dealing with the problem—and that is to fight it, to struggle to get through to each other all the same.

I said there are no wormholes between conscious minds. Really there are not. But this does not stop people avidly searching for them. Indeed, the attempt to defeat the reality and find just such holes—or even open doors—underlies many of the most heroic efforts of human culture. Religious beliefs and practices pointedly stress spiritual communion, especially in a life to come. Group rituals and entertainments bring people together in the here and now: dancing together; singing together; and worshiping together. As bodies move in synchrony, minds may indeed get as close as they ever can to being united. Thanks to the existence of mirror neurons, it *kind of* works. Even if these communal activities bring people less close than they would hope—even if 'kind of working' is never quite enough—the quest will often prove beneficial, doing good things for social cohesion on other levels.

But the second way of responding to the situation is just the opposite, and potentially of even greater evolutionary significance. Instead of either running from the problem or trying to mend it, why not make the most of it? Just look *what we've got here*! If I myself have this astonishing phenomenon, known only to me, at the centre of my existence, and if (it is, of course, a big if) I can assume that you do too, then what does this say about the kind of people that we are? It is not just me. Each of us is a creative hub of consciousness, each has a soul, no one has more than one. All men have been endowed by the creator with an inalienable and inviolable mind-space of their own.

We are a society of selves. The idea that everyone is equally special in this way is extraordinarily potent—psychologically, ethically and politically. And I dare say it would be and is highly adaptive. I believe it is likely to have arisen within the human community as a direct response to reflecting on the remarkable properties of the conscious mind. And from the beginning, it will have transformed human relationships, encouraging new levels of mutual respect, and greatly increasing the value each person puts on their own and others' lives. Indeed, I would go so far as to suggest that it marked a watershed in the evolution of our species—the beginning of humanity's interest in the human project, a concern with humanity's past and humanity's future.

There is another Swahili word, *ubuntu*, that complements *ujamaa*. Desmond Tutu, the brave champion of human rights, gives this explanation (Tutu 2006): '[it] is the idea that you cannot be human in isolation... You are human precisely owing to relationships: you are a relational being or you are nothing.' But this is in no way contrary to what I am saying here. Human beings need relationships. But the deepest and best relationships are going to be those between people who recognize the existence in others of a conscious self that is as strange and precious—and private—as their own.

Can we say when historically this may have come about? Not yet. But I think that the archaeological record could still provide clues.In the village of Villafamés, in the Valencia region of Spain, there are some rock paintings in a cave just below the castle, dating to *ca* 15 000 years ago. When I visited the cave in 2006, I was taken aback to see the resemblance between one of the images (figure 18.8 UNESCO, 1998) and a drawing I made some years ago to illustrate the privatization of sensation (figure 18.9). Was this rock painting an early Neolithic representation—and celebration—of what it means to have a self?

Fig. 18.8 Rock painting, Villamés, Valencia, Spain.

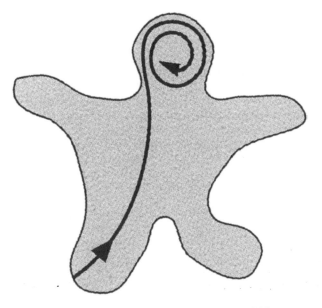

Fig. 18.9 Figure from Humphrey (2000, p. 249).

References

ASIA 2006 *Primordial questions about consciousness: a dialogue among science, philosophy and religion.* Centro studi ASIA, Bologna, June 25–July 1st 2006. http://www.associazio-neasia.it/csa/index.html.

Banville, J. 2005 *The sea*, pp. 167–168. London, UK: Picador.

Beloit 2006 Woodcuts from the Nuremberg Chronicle, CCXVIIr, 1493. Morse Library, Beloit College, http://www.beloit.edu/~nurember/book/images/Miscellaneous/ index.htm.

Blakeslee, S. 2006 Cells that read minds. *New York Times*, January 10.

Dryden, J. 1684 Translation of book IV of Lucretius. Quoted in Christopher Ricks, 1976. *Keats and embarrassment.* Oxford, UK: Oxford University Press p. 64

Gallese, V., Keysers, C. & Rizzolatti, G. 2004 A unifying view of the basis of social cognition. *Trends Cogn. Sci.* **8**, 396–403. (doi:10.1016/j.tics.2004.07.002)

Gauguin, P. 1893a *Idol with a shell. Ironwood, mother of pearl, bone. Private collection, France. Illustrated in Nicholas Wadley, 1985, Noa Noa: Gauguin's Tahiti*, p. 111. London, UK: Phaidon.

Gauguin, P. 1893b Lovers. From *Noa-Noa*, p. 75. Louvre ms. © Musée du Louvre.

Gauguin, P. 1896 *Why are You Angry?* (*No Te Aha Oe Riri*). Oil on canvas. Mr. and Mrs. Martin A. Ryerson Collection. 1933.119. The Art Institute of Chicago. © The Art Institute of Chicago.

Gauguin, P, 1897 *Where have we come from, What are we, Where are we going?* (*D'où Venons Nous, Que Sommes Nous, Où Allons Nous?*). Oil on canvas. Tompkins Collection. Museum of Fine Arts, Boston. © Museum of Fine Arts, Boston.

Humphrey, N. 1972 "Tree of Life", ebony, height 27 cm, Makonde tribe, purchased Nairobi 1972, collection of the author.

Humphrey, N. 1976 The social function of intellect. In *Growing points in ethology* (eds P. P. G. Bateson & R. A. Hinde), pp. 303–317. Cambridge, UK: Cambridge University Press.

Humphrey, N. 1983 *Consciousness regained: chapters in the development of mind.* Oxford, UK: Oxford University Press.

Humphrey, N. 1986 *The inner eye.* London, UK: Faber & Faber.

Humphrey, N. 1992 *A history of the mind.* London, UK: Chatto & Windus.

Humphrey, N. 2000 The privatization of sensation. In *The evolution of cognition* (eds L. Huber & C. Heyes), pp. 241–252. Cambridge, MA: MIT Press.

Humphrey, N. 2006 *Seeing red: a study in consciousness.* Cambridge, MA: Harvard University Press.

Locke, J. 1690/1975 *An essay concerning human understanding* (ed. P. Nidditch), Bk.II, Ch. XXXII, sect. 15. Oxford, UK: Clarendon Press.

Nietzsche, F. 1887/1974 *The gay science* (transl. W. Kaufmann), **354**, pp. 297–300. New York, NY: Vintage Books.

Nietzsche, F. 1881/1997 Daybreak (transl. R. J. Hollingdale), Book II, **142**, p. 89. Cambridge, UK: Cambridge University Press.

Ramachandran, V. S. 2000 Mirror neurons and imitation learning as the driving force behind "the great leap forward" in human evolution. *EDGE.* http://www.edge.org.

Tutu, D 2006 Reflections on the divine. *New Scientist*, 29 April.

UNESCO 1998 Rock painting, listed (but not illustrated) as Unesco World Heritage Site 874-359, http://whc.unesco.org/en/list/874. The image here was traced by the author from a photograph. Height 25 cm.

Valéry, P. 1983 Quoted by P. Johnson-Laird, Pictures of Ourselves, *London review of books*, 22 December, p. 20.

Wittgenstein, L. 1958 *Philosophical investigations* (transl. G. E. M. Anscombe), Part I, **272**, Oxford, UK: Blackwell.

Yeats, W. B. 1949 Quoted in Christopher Ricks, 1976. *Keats and embarrassment*, p. 64. Oxford, UK: Oxford University Press.

Index